PSYCHOTHERAPY AND THE
PSYCHOLOGY OF BEHAVIOR CHANGE

Arnold P. Goldstein and Sanford J. Dean

The investigation of psychotherapy: commentaries and readings, John Wiley and Sons, 1966

Arnold P. Goldstein

Therapist-patient expectancies in psychotherapy, Pergamon Press, 1962

Eugene J. Webb, Donald T. Campbell, Richard Schwartz, and Lee B. Sechrest

Unobtrusive measures: nonreactive research in the social sciences, Rand McNally, 1966

PSYCHOTHERAPY
AND THE PSYCHOLOGY
OF BEHAVIOR CHANGE

Arnold P. Goldstein
Syracuse University

Kenneth Heller
Indiana University

Lee B. Sechrest
Northwestern University

John Wiley & Sons, Inc.
New York · London · Sydney

Library of Congress Catalog Card Number: 66-17636
Printed in the United States of America

To Our Children —

Susan and Cindy

Carolyn and Daniel

Sara, Stuart, and Steven

ACKNOWLEDGMENTS

A number of persons have contributed in important ways to this book, and we wish here to indicate our grateful appreciation for these contributions. We have had the opportunity of using material from this book in graduate student seminars at our respective universities. Our students have consistently responded in a penetrating, insightful manner to our presentations. Their reactions have clarified much of the material that follows, and we feel ourselves strongly in their debt.

Several colleagues have read and incisively responded to one or more chapters of this book. Thus to Sanford Dean of Syracuse University, Donald Ford of Penn State, Leon H. Levy of Indiana University, Judson Mills of the University of Missouri, Douglas McNair of Boston University, and George Psathas of Washington University we wish to express our marked appreciation.

The psychology departments of Syracuse University, Indiana University, and Northwestern University have consistently provided us with the encouragement, time, materials, and general wherewithal to keep this manuscript moving toward completion, a contribution that we wish to acknowledge with gratitude.

The following publishers have generously granted their permission to quote from materials published by them: Addison-Wesley, Alfred A. Knopf, American Psychological Association, Basic Books, Columbia University Press, Educational Psychological Measurement, Grune and Stratton, Harper and Row, Holt, Rinehart and Winston, Houghton Mifflin, International Universities Press, John Wiley and Sons, Journal of Counseling Psychology, McGraw-Hill, National Association for Mental Health, New York Academy of Sciences, New York University Press, Pergamon Press, Prentice-Hall, Ronald Press, The Journal Press, University of Alabama Press, University of Chicago Press, William Alanson White Psychiatric Foundation, and Yale University Press.

A. P. G.

K. H.

L. B. S.

CONTENTS

I

INTRODUCTION

1

INTRODUCTION

Psychotherapy research, in a formal, controlled sense, has been a significant focus of behavioral scientists for more than a decade. During this period relevant measuring devices and experimental designs have been greatly improved. Therapist, patient, and situational variables under study have grown rapidly in number as the means for operationalizing them have been developed. Admirable ingenuity and creativity have been in evidence. Systematic research programs have been instituted and diverse research orientations, varying from naturalistic-observational to laboratory-based paradigms, have come into operation. Yet research findings have barely begun to find meaningful expression in more effective ways of changing patient behavior.

Concurrent with the growth of research examination of psychotherapy has been a greatly increased public acceptance of this general approach as one of the major treatments of choice for a wide range of mental health disorders. The demand for such services has been outdistancing the available supply of psychotherapists at an ever-increasing rate, and the consequent discrepancy gives little indication of narrowing in the foreseeable future. Thus society in general, as well as the overburdened therapist and his research-oriented counterpart, have a major stake in efforts aimed at either increasing the efficiency of contemporary psychotherapeutic practices or the development of new approaches and techniques for altering patient behavior. There are many potential ways in which such increased efficiency may be brought about. Perhaps therapists and patients can be more optimally paired to maximize the probability of a satisfactory relationship and therapeutic outcome. Therapists can become more aware of their unplanned and often nonverbal communications to patients, communications frequently having an adverse effect on therapeutic progress.

3

Interpretations made to patients can be made more effective and can have a more immediate and lasting influence on patient behavioral change. New techniques for enhancing active therapeutic participation by resistive patients can be developed, and procedures can be attempted between formal therapy sessions which augment the benefits accruing to patients during such sessions. Much the same might be said for the need to increase the proportion of satisfactory outcomes resulting from group psychotherapy. Better understanding and management of the composition, leadership, and cohesiveness of such groups are but a few of the broad avenues along which improved therapeutic efficiency might proceed.

These proposals are clearly only a minute sampling of the very large number that might be offered as potential means of increasing contemporary understanding and effectiveness of the psychotherapeutic process. However, are these not basically research questions? What personality characteristics under what therapeutic conditions contribute to an optimal therapist-patient pairing? What cues transmit unplanned communications or messages sent by the therapist, and which types of patients are characteristically most receptive to and influenced by such information? How can the therapist alter his presentation of an interpretation to enhance the likelihood that the patient will accept it and act on it? One may ask how the therapy group is to be constituted to maximize the subsequent rate of verbal interaction among its members. Under what circumstances and at what point in a course of group psychotherapy does a group-centered versus a leader-centered therapist orientation become more useful in producing a high level of group cohesiveness, and how is the shift in therapist orientation accomplished most readily?

Thus the research questions that might be posed are many, varied, and complex. Although initial answers to many such questions have become available in recent years, what remains to be learned about psychotherapy—what *must* be learned about psychotherapy—if it is to become a procedure of wider and more effective usefulness, far outweighs these glimmerings of understanding. It is our basic contention, central to all the chapters that follow, that increased understanding and efficiency, as well as the development of new techniques for altering patient behavior, may most rapidly and effectively be brought about by having major recourse to research findings from investigations initially oriented toward the psychology of behavior change. This assertion finds expression in this book by our frequent and repeated use of extrapolation; that is, we construct and present several series of research hypotheses, relevant to a variety of major psychotherapeutic variables, using primarily nonpsychotherapy research findings as our extrapolatory source. Wherever possible, the framing of these hypotheses and our suggestions for their implementation are oriented toward both formal and clinical research examination. Hopefully, such a presentation will lay many of the hypotheses open to test by the researcher using formal research techniques and the clinician in his daily practice.

Although our effort to achieve a relatively complete and integrated background picture for each hypothesis we develop requires that both psychotherapy and nonpsychotherapy research findings be drawn on, we place heaviest emphasis on extrapolating from findings in research domains characteristically viewed as "nonclinical" in nature. Thus, in drawing on what may be broadly termed the psychology of behavior change, our proposals for research aimed at a better understanding and management of the psychotherapeutic relationship will grow from findings in investigations dealing with interpersonal attraction and interpersonal influence, as well as cognitive dissonance research. Studies of persuasability, attitude change, and message structure contribute heavily to our hypotheses relevant to resistance in psychotherapy. Learning research dealing with transfer of training is examined in depth for purposes of proposing means for maximizing the chances that patient learning occurring within the therapy hour will carry over to extratherapy functioning. We consider group psychotherapy at some length and do so by extrapolating primarily from small-group and problem-solving-group research dealing with group composition, leadership, and cohesiveness. In like manner we deal with a series of additional variables of apparent major consequence in the psychotherapeutic transaction.

Because so much of what follows has its source in nonpsychotherapy or nonclinical research, a further word seems in order concerning the general appropriateness of our recourse to such materials. First, it is to be noted that others interested in the advance of psychotherapy have commented on the potential value of turning toward "outside" research findings. Frank (1961) asserts:

> . . . all research that deals with the dynamics of any one-to-one interpersonal relationship, such as with hypnosis, nonclinical studies of attitude change, etc., are relevant for an understanding of psychotherapy. One can reason that all these are but special instances of the dyadic relationship, therefore the phenomena pertinent to one should be pertinent to the others (pp. 89-90).

Similarly, Shoben (1953) notes:

. . . for all their important contributions, the various types of psycho-analysts and the client-centered group have, in the main, worked apart from their experimental confreres. What this means is that the "applied" science of psychotherapy has been essentially divorced from the "pure" science that presumably should most nourishingly feed it, general psychology . . . this seems most unfortunate. Certainly medicine would not have made the striking advances it has were it not for underlying developments in physiology and biochemistry, nor would engineering be capable of its dramatic accomplishments were it not for the growth of physics (p. 121).

A somewhat closer examination of this viewpoint as it has been propounded by others, however, reveals an important difference of opinion regarding the most appropriate sources for this extrapolation-generalization process. From the perspective of what broad classes of research evidence is it appropriate to consider psychotherapy? May (1953) argues:

. . . the crucial prerequisite for a method (of studying psychotherapy) is that the irreducible unit for study be taken as the individual human being in a real-life situation. The term "real" here means a situation in which the given human being is confronted with some decision . . . which involves in greater or lesser degree his own happiness and welfare and for which, therefore, he has some inescapable responsibility . . . . This is why confronting an individual with a conflict situation for experimental purposes in a laboratory does not produce a "real" situation (p. 36).

In marked contrast, Pascal (1959) comments:

The crucial question has been, and remains—can we extrapolate from laboratory findings to so-called "real life" behavior as it is manifested in clinical subjects? The psychologic laboratory is not a "real life" situation, but it is a place in which certain conditions affecting behavior can be controlled. . . . We have asserted that behavioral change, although confined for the most part to segmented and well defined responses, is something about which a good deal is known in the psychologic laboratory. We have cited experiments showing that behavior bearing a certain similarity to that found in clinic subjects can be produced in the laboratory and that this latter obeys the same principles and procedures found to hold true for the other, more simple behavior. The data are such that extrapolation from laboratory methodology to clinical procedures seems reasonable (p. 4).

These, then, are the two extremes of a "generalizability to psychotherapy" dimension. May prefers "real life" behavior as his source of light on the therapeutic darkness; Pascal leans toward the less direct, more rigorous evidence of the laboratory. Where do we stand? Although our own inclination is clearly in the direction of Pascal's viewpoint, we take essentially an acategorical position on this issue. The practice and rationale of psychotherapeutic processes are examined in the light of research from many sources and of many types: laboratory and "real-life"; clinical and nonclinical; naturalistic and manipulative; and so forth. We demand only that such research have a sound methodological basis and be of apparent relevance for psychotherapy. We base this extrapolatory catholicism on the general obscurity of much of contemporary psychotherapy, the clear and major need for new and different psychotherapeutic approaches, and the fact that such extrapolation is offered solely in a tentative manner. We strongly concur with Festinger's (1953) admonition:

> It should be stressed again that the problem of application of the results of . . . laboratory experiments to the real life situation is not solved by a simple extension of the results. Such application requires additional experimentation and study. It is undoubtedly important that the results of laboratory experiments be tested out in real life situations (p. 141).

Thus the ultimate incorporation or rejection of a given extrapolated research finding or series of findings by the researcher into psychotherapeutic theory or by the clinician into psychotherapeutic practice must not be a function of offerings such as this book. Hopefully, such incorporation or rejection will be a function of later formal or clinical research which will attempt the work that this book suggests.

Although the chapters that follow offer a large number of psychotherapy-relevant hypotheses, we could not and have not attempted to be exhaustive in our coverage. The hypotheses presented may be viewed as illustrations of an approach to hypothesis development that we hope will be adopted more widely by others interested in the advance of psychotherapy. Our own philosophy toward psychotherapy research leads us to urge that others becoming involved in such extrapolatory forays attempt to be bold and imaginative in their efforts to develop ideas unfettered by overconventionalized approaches to psychotherapy and the development of associated research proposals. As an example of our basis for this encouragement of innovation and boldness, a statement by Krasner (1962) is of interest:

> Many investigators imply that the process of psychotherapy, as now practiced, is the royal and only road to changing peoples' behavior. The yardstick for the acceptability of research then becomes "how close is this to the real psychotherapy process?" I feel strongly that we are losing sight of the purpose

of psychotherapy, which is to change peoples' behavior. The purpose of psychotherapy is *not* "to do" psychotherapy, as such. . . . The apologetic tone in papers which experimentally investigate behavior is uncalled for. . . . I am less and less inclined to call them "experimental analogues" of psychotherapy. Rather, I see them as part of a broader psychology of behavior control which is oriented toward devising techniques for the deliberate control, manipulation and change of behavior (p. 103).

Thus it is our intent to indicate, via our hypotheses, that it is patient behavior change and not minor elaboration of standard psychotherapeutic techniques in which we are interested. Any attempted innovation in therapeutic practice or any completely new therapeutic procedure, if not contraindicated by ethical considerations, is, according to our view, appropriate for research purposes if there exists sound research evidence suggesting that this innovation may foster constructive patient change.

Most of the research hypotheses we offer and develop in the chapters that follow are not only marked departures from current psychotherapeutic practices but almost all of these proposals put forth procedures that are highly manipulative in nature. As such, ethical questions regarding the appropriateness of behavior control, influence, or manipulation in psychotherapy may legitimately be raised. We respond to these questions at several points throughout this book, in the specific contexts in which they most appropriately arise. At this point in our discussion, however, it is important that our general position be made explicit. We view *all* psychotherapies as manipulative and cite evidence to this effect at a number of points in our later discussions. Thus the "criticism" that the procedures we have to suggest— if they survive the prerequisite experimental verification and are incorporated in psychotherapeutic practice—would lead to a highly manipulative psychotherapy, whereas psychotherapy as practiced today is generally nonmanipulative, is simply an untrue comparative assertion.

Manipulative approaches may be attacked on the grounds that they dehumanize, treat the patient as a machine or object or, more generally, that they reflect a nonhumanitarian orientation to sick or unhappy people. Our position, quite the contrary, is that *current* psychotherapeutic approaches are deficient on a humanitarianism continuum largely because they do *not* incorporate or reflect research findings regarding the most effective means of altering an individual's behavior—the raison d'etre of psychotherapy. To know that solid research dealing with attitude change, learning, and a score of other research domains offering other manipulative means of altering an individual's behavior exists, and to deny in an a priori manner the potential relevance of such research to the psychotherapy patient is to perform a disservice to both the advance of psychotherapy and to one's psychotherapy patients.

Obviously there will be limits that society will impose on its psychological practitioners. But to imply that these limits can be imposed without evidence, without research on behavior control, is to deny the experimental foundation on which science rests. We have an obligation to society and to our psychotherapy patients, and this obligation demands that we publicize and use the best possible scientific findings in our field. To do less than this, we hold, is a failure to meet our ethical responsibilities.

The chapter that follows examines a series of methodological issues of relevance to research in psychotherapy. We hope that it will serve to underscore a number of considerations relevant to experimental design which must be dealt with in any attempts to put our hypotheses to experimental test. The major portion of its substance, and the experimental design recommendations we offer therefrom, grow from methodological findings initially established by behavior-change research in fields *other than psychotherapy*. Thus we propose that the extrapolation-to-psychotherapy process will be profitably conducted not only with nonclinical research findings but with nonclinical research methodologies as well.

REFERENCES

Festinger, L. Laboratory experiments. In L. Festinger & D. Katz (Eds.), *Research methods in the behavioral sciences*. New York: Dryden Press, 1953. Pp. 136–172.

Frank, G. H. On the history of the objective investigation of the process of psychotherapy. *J. Psychol.,* 1961, 51, 89–95.

Krasner, L. Therapists' contribution. In H. H. Strupp & L. Luborsky (Eds.), *Research in psychotherapy*. Washington: American Psychological Association, 1962. Pp. 102–114.

May, R. Historical and philosophical presuppositions for understanding therapy. In O. H. Mowrer (Ed.), *Psychotherapy, theory and research*. New York: Ronald Press, 1953. Pp. 9–43.

Pascal, G. R. *Behavioral change in the clinic*. New York: Grune & Stratton, 1959.

Shoben, E. J. Some observations on psychotherapy and the learning process. In O. H. Mowrer (Ed.), *Psychotherapy, theory and research*. New York: Ronald Press, 1953. Pp. 120–139.

2

RESEARCH METHODS IN
PSYCHOTHERAPY

At the very outset we should like to make it clear that we do not regard research on psychotherapy as being so special or as involving such problems that it is unique as a research field. We believe that sound principles of research design and inference from research findings will lead inexorably to the untangling of the skein of confusion that represents our current level of understanding of the field of psychotherapy.

We should also like to state our conviction that the first order of business in psychotherapy research is the demonstration of the phenomenon (cf. Underwood, 1957); that is, there is such a thing as psycho*therapy* to do research on. Research efforts should be directed toward the study of the outcome(s) of psychotherapy. However, in line with our over-all bias about the field of psychotherapy we prefer to say that research should be directed toward the discovery or invention of ways of changing behavior and we need not speculate whether those ways are really "psychotherapy." Only after we have been able to demonstrate that we can consistently produce a particular change in behavior as a result of a particular manipulation does it seem advisable to expend effort in studying the "process" involved in the manipulation. We suggest that research be done on the changing of behavior. For those who insist that they want to do research on "psychotherapy" we suggest the applicability of Astin's (1961) thoughts concerning the functional autonomy of psychotherapy practice. Psychotherapy *research* may, too, come to be valued for its own sake.

Although we began this chapter with a disclaimer that there are research problems unique to psychotherapy, we do not deny that there are problems which seem particularly important to psychotherapy research and which complicate or even impede research efforts. Some of the frequently described problems, however, seem to us to have little substance and need not provide an impediment to research at all. As an example of this kind of problem we point to the frequent and sad apologies for the lack of certain control groups in psychotherapy research on the ground that ethical considerations prohibit the withholding of "treatment" from patients (e.g., Reznikoff & Toomey, 1959, p. 35). Because it is precisely the fact at point that the "treatment" has never been satisfactorily demonstrated, there would seem to be not much of an ethical problem involved. As others have pointed out, good ethical practice in medicine has not necessitated the indiscriminate administration of some procedure or other on the ground that some patients might be unfairly deprived of a potentially therapeutic agent. The better ethical position requires a perspective which considers the long-term benefits to humanity from a well-founded therapy rather than the only possible benefits to a particular patient. However, as we indicate later, the impreciseness of the definition of "no treatment" probably necessitates an alternative research strategy which largely if not completely obviates the objections of the ethically sensitive.

A second frequent lament about psychotherapy is that it is so much more complex than other problems that it is quite different in nature as a research field. To be sure, there are certainly many factors that can influence the outcome of efforts to change behavior, and to do really incisive research on such a problem is a considerable challenge. However, complex problems simply call for complex research strategies. The complexities of behavioral change probably can be unraveled by a combination of approaches which oversimplify on the one hand, for example, in single variable research, and admit complexity by way of multivariate analysis on the other. There probably are simpler problems in psychology, but those persons who deliberately choose a complex field in which to study should not feel sorry for themselves.

A real and more difficult problem for the researcher who chooses to tackle research in behavioral change, and one that is unquestionably of great importance in the study of psychotherapy, is that many variables admit of only the most tenuous control by the researcher. Certainly in most situations in which behavioral change in adult humans is concerned, the patient, that is, the person whose behavior is to be changed, has a will of his own, and it may be very difficult to carry out desirable experimental manipulations. A good example is provided by research in which it would be desirable, from the standpoint of the investigator, to have a randomly assigned group of patients receiving absolutely no treatment whatsoever. However, in practice it seems to be impossible to keep a patient from seeking any help at all from outside sources if he wishes to do so. To take another example, one might wish to study the effects on a group of patients who spend ten interviews talking about a given topic; it might be difficult to achieve the desired manipulation without introducing other very important factors. Moreover, it is not only the object of manipulation who is capable of independent action well outside the control of the researcher. In many instances, particularly in psychotherapy, it is necessary to have an agent (i.e., therapist) operating for the researcher, but this agent may also act to foil the plans of the investigator. The psychotherapist participating in a research project may for a variety of reasons fail to carry on his treatment as specified by the research plans, and to the extent that he fails, the researcher is frustrated in his major aim. Some behaviors may lie outside the capability of the psychotherapist, (e.g., to behave in an unemotional, detached manner) and others may be outside the role he is willing to assume (e.g., counterhostility). Again we should like to point out that the problem discussed here is not unique to psychotherapy research. Every rat-runner has encountered rats that simply will not run in the maze, and thus frustrate the intent of the experimenter, and every experienced employer of research assistants knows that there are occasionally those who either will not or cannot follow the behaviors prescribed for them. Yet it is considerably more likely that personal factors will limit experimental manipulations for humans than for lower organisms and for behavioral change research than for many other categories. There are, unfortunately, no research designs which can completely compensate for the limitations of both patient and therapist, but we discuss below some of the possibilities for the utilization of data marred in various ways.

Although by now it should be painfully evident that the evaluation of an attempt at behavioral change is by no means an easy task, one can still encounter instances of the putative successes and failures of psychotherapeutic efforts which may have stemmed from the particular measures of behavioral change employed (e.g., see Rogers & Dymond, 1954; Heller & Goldstein, 1961; Snyder & Sechrest, 1959). Once more, the problem of selecting the appropriate response measure is not peculiar to research on therapeutic change. The literature on animal learning is replete with discrepant findings for diverse measures of response strength such as latency and probability. Still, the problem is one that seems especially likely to plague the researcher interested in studying the ways in which human behavior can be altered in the direction of greater "desirability." It is from this concept of "desirable" change that many of the problems arise, for what might seem desirable to one individual (the psychotherapist) might not seem desirable to another (the patient). At an abstract level, however, the solution to the problem is remarkably simple—to discover what manipulations lead to what changes and what the relationships among various behaviors are. It is incumbent on the researcher to know what leads to what, but he need not himself decide on the value of the possible outcomes of manipulations. This is not to say that the researcher is likely to be ethically neutral in all phases of his work. He will probably not even try to produce some of the changes that he could imagine occurring, at least with human subjects. But aside from those behaviors for which there is a substantial social consensus concerning their undesirability (e.g., behaviors threatening the existence and physical welfare of other innocent persons) the researcher may well attempt no more than to show that particular behaviors can be consistently produced under a particular set of conditions and that the behaviors produced are either compatible or incompatible with other behaviors that might be regarded as important.

One aspect of the therapeutic change situation which distinguishes it somewhat from other research settings is that the participants in the process of change are by no means neutral to the outcome in the sense that a research assistant and a subject may be "neutral" to whether or not the subject's verbal responses are actually conditioned. In fact, both the therapist and the patient have a good deal at stake in the process in which they are involved and can scarcely be expected to be casual about its outcome. The involvement of both may limit the capacity of the researcher for intervention in order to achieve his own ends.

There are, for example, many rather doctrinaire assertions about the practice of psychotherapy which could and ought to be tested, but proposals for testing them often meet emphatic resistance from psychotherapists on the ground that the research would interfere with the goals of therapy. One of the writers has long had doubts about the rather dogmatic statements that are made concerning the traumatic effects on therapy of appointments missed or canceled by the therapist. However, it has proved impossible to persuade therapists to miss appointments deliberately in order to study the effect of this occurrence.* It would certainly not be correspondingly difficult to persuade the researcher on learning to attempt some manipulation that might lead to a decrement in learning. However, to show that the problem is not unique to psychotherapy research it is necessary only to point to research on educational practices in which there are also serious objections to some procedures that need to be studied. The problem arises not only because of the definition in ethical terms of the goal to be attained in a situation, but also because of premature convictions about the ways in which the goal may be attained. We do not argue that there are not some propositions that make such good sense, both common and theoretical, that one should be cautious in countering them, but the vagaries of human behavior suggest rather narrow limits within which untested propositions or assertions backed by no more than the force of opinion should be accepted. We plead for the freedom, even the responsibility, of the researcher to test hypotheses not well supported by empirical data, even though they may run counter to opinion, public or otherwise.

We have suggested that the object of our manipulations in therapeutic change research also has goals or expectations that may interfere with the procedures the researcher deems desirable. Ordinarily the patient expects to be changed for the better, and the definition of better is in his own terms. If the change he regards as desirable does not occur or he changes in ways he regards as threatening to himself, he may resist the treatment procedure and even discontinue his cooperation. However, we should like to point out that by no means all the possible "patients" we might study have particular goals, at least not in the sense in which the individual, voluntary psychotherapy patient has the goal of coming to "feel better." It may be quite possible to achieve some sort of therapeutic intervention with groups such as prisoners or schizophrenics who are not especially motivated to change, at least not in the way proposed by the experimenter-therapist [e.g., see Snyder and Sechrest (1959) for a report of work with mentally defective delinquents].

A final problem in behavioral change research, particularly in psychotherapy research, is making a distinction between the system

---

* It has come to our attention that Exner (1965) has done a group-therapy study much along these lines. In an experimental condition therapists attended only 50 per cent of the group sessions and did not explain their absences. The experimental groups showed greater progress than either groups with 100 per cent therapist attendance or groups without a therapist.

that the researcher thinks he is studying or intends to study and the actual practices he *is* studying. We might consider this as the distinction between the ideal and the real. Again, we do not believe that this is a problem limited to the area we are discussing; it pervades psychological research and probably research of most other varieties. The animal learning experimenter describes a procedure according to which animals were treated, but only the very naïve would suppose that things were ever quite so precise as often suggested by the experimental report. However, the departures from standard procedure are probably of small magnitude in most instances and they have no great impact on the outcome of the experiment. But in research on psychotherapy there is certainly the likelihood of important discrepancies between the behavior prescribed for a therapist and the behavior he actually produces (Luborsky, 1959). Research bearing on the variable of experience of the therapist (Ashby et al., 1957; Fiedler, 1950; Cartwright & Vogel, 1960) indicates the strong possibility that some therapists are unable to carry out the role assigned to them and that such failures can have an important effect on the outcome of research. In fact, the problem of accomplishing prescribed therapeutic techniques is such a serious one that it is even doubtful whether really meaningful psychotherapy research of the classical type can be carried on in many settings, except perhaps insofar as such research demontrates the actual state of psychotherapeutic practice.

All of the foregoing problems plus additional considerations spelled out in various places in this book lead us to the conclusion that there are great advantages in what we call "extrapolated" research, or the generalization of research findings from diverse areas to the problem of producing behavioral change. Somewhat the same considerations come into play as those undertaken in accomplishing physiological research or research involving punishment. Much of this research is simply not feasible with normal human Ss; therefore it is done on animals or abnormal human cases. We doubt that anyone anticipates that research will ever be done in which school children are subjected to serious punishment in order to discover its effects on their learning ability, but laboratory research and even animal research on punishment has been freely generalized to school and other learning situations. We believe a case can be made for the extrapolation of diverse research findings to the psychotherapeutic research situation.

Another strategy, and one that has a good bit to recommend it, is the development of an analogue for therapy or a therapy "in miniature" which could provide a testing ground for various propositions about psychotherapy. An interesting "miniature" therapy situation was developed by Keet (1948) and the initial report looked very promising, but subsequent failures to replicate his basic procedures (Grummon & Butler, 1953; Merrill, 1952) have cast serious doubts on the usefulness of the situation he developed. Undoubtedly more successful have been the developments of various analogues for therapy by Heller (1963), Heller, Myers, and Kline (1963), Krasner (1962), Martin, Lundy, and Lewin (1960), Matarazzo (1962), and others.

As an example of a "miniature" area in which psychotherapy (or other) research could profitably be carried on we suggest the concept of "test anxiety." Among the advantages of test anxiety as a problem on which therapy research might be done are (1) the existence of a good measure of the concept (Mandler & Sarason, 1952), (2) the ease with which behavioral referents might be specified, (3) the circumscribed nature of the problem, (4) the "real" motivation of the subject to change, (5) the repeated and extensive opportunities for observation of relevant behavior, and (6) the ease of specifying meaningful criteria for improvement. All that remains to be devised is a miniature therapy to go along with this miniature problem. Spielberger (Spielberger, Weitz, & Denny, 1962; Spielberger & Weitz, 1964) has focused on the alleviation of general anxiety in college freshmen and by using a variety of counseling procedures found that it was possible to bring about a definite improvement in grades, especially for subjects who were faithful in their attendance at therapy sessions. Perhaps some of the same procedures could be exploited in dealing with the more specific problem of test anxiety.

Another excellent miniature therapy paradigm has been developed by Paul (1964), who found that anxieties about making speeches in public were strong and fairly common among a large group of students enrolled in classes in public speaking. Moreover, he found that a variety of measures of anxiety could be employed with his subjects, including actual behavior measures during a speech. Thus he was able to test the efficacy of brief insight therapy, desensitization, and a placebo treatment with appropriate control groups. Paul's results, incidentally, showed a rather substantial superiority for the desensitization therapy. All of this indicated that the utilization of limited but meaningful problems in psychotherapy research has much to offer.

THE INTERNAL VALIDITY OF RESEARCH

We believe that Campbell and Stanley (1963) have made an important distinction between factors contributing to the *internal* and *external validity* of research and that Sidman (1960) has made a similar distinction which he refers to as *reliability* and *generality*. Internal validity refers to the confidence that the conclusions we draw from the research are correct ones, whereas external validity refers to the confidence we have that the conclusions we draw will apply to any groups or situations other than the ones on which the research was accomplished.

There are numerous factors that can affect the internal validity of research and we cannot consider all of them here. However, we should like to point to some that are particularly relevant to or plaguing for research in changing behavior, especially in psychotherapy. For critical research on the outcome of efforts to change behavior there are two possible conclusions at which we can arrive on the basis of research evidence: (1) the manipulation (e.g., psychotherapy) made a difference, and (2) the manipulation did not make a difference. The possibilities are so disarmingly simple that it seems difficult to be led astray. We suspect, however, that it is entirely possible.

Obviously the first requisite for drawing any sort of conclusion is that we have had the opportunity to observe the effects of both a manipulation and a nonmanipulation condition. This does not necessarily mean that two groups are needed, but at least two observations are. For example, we can draw no conclusion from the observation that 100 per cent of twenty-five patients who have undergone psychoanalysis are happy. However, as soon as we have the additional observation that all twenty-five were unhappy before undergoing psychoanalysis, we have all that is needed to state the conclusion that psychoanalysis has made these unhappy people happy.

We take the position that *all* conclusions about the outcomes of research are only tentative to the extent that they depart from the sheer repetition of the research findings. For example, the conclusion that twenty-five people are "happier" after undergoing psychoanalysis than they were before is only a repetition of a research finding and can be stated with whatever confidence is engendered by the measures and statistical tests used. On the other hand, the conclusion that psychoanalysis *caused* the increase in happiness must be a tentative conclusion, for it goes well beyond the bare research findings. Conclusions based on research are hypotheses that are only more or less likely than other hypotheses to escape disconfirmation by additional research. For any one research finding there are numerous explanations (i.e., conclusions) that must compete with one another for acceptance.

On an a priori basis there is no particular reason that one explanation should be accepted more than another, although the principle of parsimony has come to have rather firm status as a way of determining the a priori acceptability of one of a pair or more of explanations, but even it has come under some fire as an a priori principle (Battig, 1962). However, there has come to be in psychology, or at least in many parts of it, an a priori *preference* for "skeptical" explanations. Thus, if we rather naïvely drew the conclusions from the data given that psycho-analysis made the people happier, someone would surely object that the results were probably attributable to "normal self-curative pro-cesses" (or to repetition of the measurement or some other extraneous factor), as, indeed, they could be. But "self-cure" is only an alternative hypothesis to "psychoanalysis," and both hypotheses have to be evalu-ated for their probability. Whatever the conclusion drawn by the experimenter, there are always alternatives, and the responsibility for eliminating a competing hypothesis is about proportional to the likelihood of that hypothesis in comparison to the one held. Al-though we hope that few *experimenters* would be so casual, in the example we have been using we doubt that "self-cure" is any more parsimonious or otherwise likely than the psychoanalysis hypothesis and has no greater claim to respect. It is just as incumbent on the skeptic who suggests the "self-cure" hypothesis independently to demonstrate its plausibility as it is on the original experimenter to eliminate it from consideration. However, we, like most researchers in psychology, are of a somewhat conservative bent and would like to be able to anticipate as many skeptics as possible by eliminating as many competing hypotheses as possible through the careful design of our research. However, we would like to express our belief that weak re-search is not worthless research, some of our colleagues' opinions to the contrary (Underwood, 1957). A series of individually faulty researches with no consistent methodological weakness may add up to a fairly convincing conclusion. We do not condone research that is not so good as it could be, and researchers should be honest with themselves and potential consumers of their research. However, it should be recognized that considerations of utility enter into almost all research (cf. Frank, 1959) and that ultimately the price of precision is too high, a fact that tends to limit the size of experimental groups in even the best research. Many persons work in situations in which there are built-in limitations on their capacity to control certain variables or to provide for the elimination of competing hypotheses, but we should prefer to have their contributions, even with limitations, than to lose the small increments that their efforts might be able to provide. What we would do is caution that when decisions are made on the basis of weak research they be made with an appreciation of the weakness and with a view to subsequent revision. We also note, however, that the consequences of weak research to subsequent *researchers* are not likely to be serious in the long run; weaknesses are revealed and errors corrected in science. It is rather those who intend to use research to make important decisions or to bolster their convictions who must be especially cautious.

All of the preceding discussion is propadeutic to the topic of the internal validity of experiments, for it is the elimination of competing hypotheses that is at issue in considering internal validity. An admirable discussion of research designs which are of varying degrees of sophistication and which eliminate various and varying numbers of competing hypotheses is contained in a presentation by Campbell and Stanley (1963) prepared for use in educational situations but equally applicable to psychotherapy research. Our discussion draws heavily on this contribution.

We believe that it is in the spirit of our presentation to make extensive use of material prepared for another very different discipline, for one of our purposes is to show the advantages which may accrue from a wider and more imaginative attention to research in psychology. Obviously, the same considerations apply to research methodology.

The task of the experimenter is to design research in such a way that the maximum number of *plausible rival hypotheses* is eliminated. We agree with Campbell and Stanley that, strictly speaking, hypotheses may never be confirmed; they can only escape disconfirmation. On the other hand, hypotheses can probably never be absolutely *disconfirmed* either. It is probably nearly always possible to imagine a set of conditions under which any empirical findings could be made consistent with any hypothesis. However, the intellectual contortions which are necessary in order to justify some hypotheses make them so implausible that we can disregard them. Without any question research designs differ markedly in the number of rival hypotheses which they can disconfirm, but the elimination of even a single plausible rival hypothesis constitutes information of value to our science.

When we find a difference associated with an experimental manipulation, what are the plausible alternatives to the hypothesis that it was the manipulation that produced the difference? Or, to make the question specific to psychotherapy, when certain changes in psychotherapy patients are found, what are the alternatives to the conclusion that psychotherapy produced the changes? Campbell and Stanley list seven "threats to the internal validity of experiments." We will consider each of these in turn for its implications for psychotherapy research.

The first plausible rival hypothesis is *history*, by which is meant that events other than the experimental manipulations may have occurred in such a way as to give rise to the findings. In the preceding example, with only a single group of patients showing a change in happiness over time, it is impossible to counter the skeptic's argument satisfactorily that many other things occurring during that time might have accounted for the change (e.g., improvement in world situation, change in attitudes of relatives and friends, and assistance rendered by ministers or priests). "Time" per se is not an especially plausible rival hypothesis, but all the things that can occur during time are. Of course, an indefinite number of rival hypotheses, more or less plausible, are subsumed under the rubric of "history," and various research efforts may eliminate one or more of the possible alternatives without ensuring complete equivalence of history. Obviously, a powerful design that completely eliminates certain particularly likely rival hypotheses is worth doing.

The second threat to the internal validity of experiments is what Campbell and Stanley call *maturation,* by which is meant the naturally occurring processes within the individual which would lead to a change in status over time. For example, adolescents are often described as sensitive, lacking in self-confidence and so forth, but presumably as they approach adulthood there is an over-all improvement in such feelings. Therefore, any psychotherapy proposed for late adolescents would have to compete with the attractive rival hypothesis of maturation. Or, to take another example, it is not a far-fetched analogy to suppose that there are psychological processes similar to the physiological processes which lead to the curing of wounds and illnesses even without any treatment. The hypothesis that psychotherapy leads to improvement in various personality factors must, then, compete with the hypothesis that improvement comes about "naturally." Again reverting to our example, we could not argue well against the contention that the patients would have become happier without any therapeutic intervention because of self-curing tendencies.

Another threat to internal validity is provided by the effects of *testing*, that is, changes expected with the repeated administration of the same measure. An individual taking a test for the second time cannot be considered equivalent to an individual taking it for the first time, although tests undoubtedly differ widely in this respect. Campbell and Stanley use the term *reactivity* to refer to the changes in a measure which occur simply as a result of its prior administration. For example, consider two men who visit their physician and have their blood pressure measured. One is told that his blood pressure is fine, just right for his age, and the other is told that his blood pressure is suspiciously high. Would a subsequent blood pressure measurement for the two men be equivalent to the initial situation? Would it be surprising to find that the "abnormal" man has even higher blood pressure? Just what the effects of repeated administration of various measures are, is not well known at present, but the possibility exists for a great many measures that systematic changes will occur. Nor need it be supposed that improvement will always result. Some measures might yield changes for the worse and tend to obscure the effects of therapeutic efforts. Problems with reactive measures may be solved in part by appropriate experimental designs, (e.g., involving groups retested without the experimental treatment), but there are also reasons to prefer using nonreactive measures, a possibility that is examined later.

A fourth factor involved in the internal validity of experiments is called *instrumentation,* or as Campbell (1957) referred to it earlier, "instrument decay." In using observers or raters, one may find that the standards for rating change from one occasion to the next, that is, as observers become more expert, aware of the hypotheses of the experiment, or bored. Such changes are probably more likely for observers than for many other instruments, but even a casual examination of testing materials which have been used repeatedly will show evidences of change which might well affect experimental outcomes.

A fifth, and particularly plaguing factor affecting the internal validity of experiments is *statistical regression*. There is no substitute for a careful study of the presentation by Campbell and Stanley (1963) of the ways, often very subtle, in which statistical regression may operate to affect experimental results. To take an obvious example, our previous discussion of patients showing improvement in happiness during psychoanalytic treatment might well reflect nothing more than statistical regression. People are probably particularly likely to enter psychoanalysis (or any other form of treatment) at a point at which they feel especially bad or unhappy. However, even entering psychoanalysis is to some extent a fallible measure, and people who enter psychoanalysis at a low point are at that point in part because of temporary fortuitous circumstances that would not likely be obtained on some subsequent (or previous) occasion. Therefore, when they are remeasured at some later time, it is almost a foregone conclusion that some "improvement" will have occurred. We can take it as a general principle that whenever people are selected *because* of a particularly low performance, subsequent measurements will show evidence of improvement, and a control group is absolutely necessary to protect the inferences from the experiment. An example of an experiment possibly contaminated by regression effects is the study of self-ideal Q-sort discrepancies described in Rogers and Dymond (1954). At the beginning of therapy the correlation between self and ideal Q-sorts was only —.01, but at the end of therapy it was .34. The possibility of a regression effect is strongly suggested by the fact that the same correlation was .58 for a group of "normal" controls. Obviously the treated group was deviantly low in self-ideal correlation, and "improvement" might well have occurred without any treatment and for purely statistical reasons.

A sixth threat to the legitimacy of interpretations of experimental findings is the possibility of *differential mortality* in experimental and control groups. In psychotherapy evaluations mortality during the course of an experiment may be a serious problem and may operate either to enhance or detract from estimates of the effectiveness of the treatment. Mortality may occur because some patients get worse and have to be institutionalized, because they get better and lose their motivation for treatment, because treatment itself is disturbing to them, and probably for many other reasons; for example, in Paul's (1964) study subjects dropped out of the no-treatment control group because their anxiety was so high that they dropped the speech course in which they were enrolled. If the analysis of the data utilizes only those patients who stay in therapy, some groups in the experiment may be seriously biased. Differential mortality is likely to be a particular problem in efforts to compare therapies of different lengths, of differing intensities, or even those that proceed at different paces (Cartwright, 1955; Frank et al., 1957; Imber et al., 1957; Lorr et al., 1962; Taylor, 1956).

The final threat to internal validity of experiments comes from biases in the *selection* of Ss for experimental groups. For example, if administrative pressures are irresistible and certain very serious cases must be given therapy, then in comparison with a control group the experimental therapy group will consist of the more serious cases, a possibility which could, though it need not, operate against the efficacy of treatment. One reason the snap conclusion that such a bias would operate against the effectiveness of treatment should be avoided is that the "serious" cases might in fact consist of the more acute cases, leaving the control group relatively loaded with chronic and more difficult cases. Probably selection is the most obvious of experimental biases, and it is constantly inveighed against. However, most readers of the literature may conclude that selection bias is not uncommon; for example, in one very important investigation (Rogers & Dymond, 1954) there was a explicit admission that certain factors led to deviations from random assignment.

Campbell and Stanley discuss an eighth threat to the internal validity of experiments that consists of an interaction between two of the other factors, namely, selection and maturation. An interaction between selection and maturation occurs when the manner of selecting subjects for experimental groups results in groups with a different rate of maturation or "autonomous change." With respect to personality and psychopathological variables, differences in rate of "autonomous change" could be expected for comparisons of younger versus older persons, acute versus chronic patients, well educated versus poorly educated individuals, and volunteer versus nonvolunteer patients. Any experimental procedure that would produce differences between experimental groups in proportions of cases falling into different categories would constitute an example of a selection-maturation interaction. In such a blatant form the selection-maturation interaction is, we hope, uncommon. But there may be instances of the interaction that are far more subtle but damaging to the experiment nonetheless.

REDUCING THREATS TO INTERNAL VALIDITY

"Own-control" Designs

We have noted that the minimum requirement for a conclusion is the observation of manipulation and no-manipulation conditions. An obvious and useful research procedure is to make both observations on the same individuals at different points in time, thus conserving on subjects and eliminating the difficult and often costly process of forming a control group. This research technique is sometimes called the "own control" design; that is, because each subject experiences both the control and experimental conditions he can serve as his own obviously well-matched control (e.g., Cartwright & Vogel, 1960). However, the own-control or single-group design has serious weaknesses, particularly when, as with no-psychotherapy and psychotherapy conditions, there is only one order in which the conditions can occur. The possibility is high that factors other than the treatment can account for the findings, whatever they are. For example, a change in international tensions may have a desirable or an undesirable effect on the subjects. The inherent weaknesses of the design can be exaggerated by a misunderstanding of the precepts of experimental rigor. Consider the following arrangements: early in May 50 male psychotherapy patients, all 21 years of age, are tested and begin therapy. Then in November, six months after the beginning of therapy, they are retested and considerable improvement is shown. The spuriousness of the "rigor" in the experiment is revealed by the unnecessary susceptibility of the findings to very plausible rival hypotheses. For example, perhaps many of the subjects graduated from college in June, which gave them a new perspective and new opportunities in life; or a change in the economic situation in the country may have enhanced their prospects for the future, or perhaps all 21-year-old males underwent a considerable improvement in outlook during that year. With respect to a wide variety of events, most or all of the subjects have the same history.

Actually, a number of possible competing hypotheses may be eliminated by a judicious research design. The over-all strategy to be followed is to keep irrelevant factors as heterogeneous rather than as standard as possible. By using patients of varying ages, it is possible to eliminate the hypothesis that the findings are attributable to the passing of a particular "life crisis." By varying the time of day, month, and year that initial and final observations are gathered on individual subjects, one can decrease if not eliminate the possibility that the findings are attributable to such outside events as changes in international tensions, weather conditions, fatigue and the like. In passing we would note that physiological changes have been correlated with barometric pressure and humidity (Watson et al., 1957), and mental hospital admissions with radiological disturbances (Friedman et al., 1963, 1965). Of course no one experiment can achieve more than a modest degree of heterogeneity, and the remainder needed must come in an accumulative manner from a series of researches.

Additional increments of confidence in the effectiveness of psychotherapy can be provided by converting the simple one-group design into a time-series design (Campbell, 1963; Campbell & Stanley, 1963) by taking multiple measurements during the period prior to psychotherapy. Depending on the pattern shown by the successive measurements, one may be inclined either to implicate or to absolve psychotherapy in relation to the change. For example, consider Figure 1 in which two of the many possible outcomes of a series of measurements are plotted. It is the difference between the before- and after-therapy points that is crucial. Assuming that the occasions for measurement are really heterogeneous with respect to irrelevant variables, we would probably conclude that therapy had an effect for *A*, but not for *B*. There are, however, problems inherent in analysis of repeated meas-

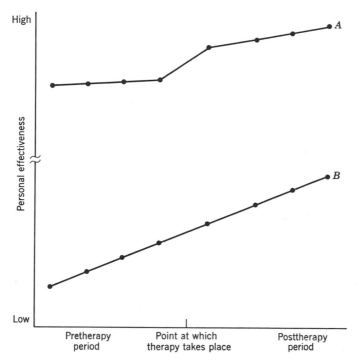

Figure 1. Two possible outcomes of a time-series study of psycho-therapy.

urements of the same individual, for example, change in response to the testing situation, that can complicate some time-series experiments (see Anderson, 1963; Holtzman, 1962). Probably the closest approxima-tion to a time-series experiment in the area of psychotherapy would be one in which patients waiting to undergo psychotherapy were shown to change only with the beginning of therapy. Such an experi-ment would be strengthened if the waiting period varied in length for different patients. Many experiments are not sufficiently well de-scribed to make it possible to tell whether the arrangements were really heterogeneous with respect to potential sources of extraneous variation. The discussion here of time-series investigations is only meant to be heuristic. The reader will benefit from a more complete presentation (e.g., Campbell, 1963).

Thus we see that the initially critically weak comparison of a single group's performance on two occasions can be made into something considerably more than a sow's ear, if not a silken purse. It gradually becomes easier to believe that psychotherapy produced the effect than to believe that, for otherwise unexplained reasons, a heterogeneous lot of individuals examined at different times just happened to become happy at a time which coincided with the beginning of psychotherapy. To be sure, the skeptic will not be satisfied, but it begins to become more his responsibility to substantiate rival hypotheses than for the experimenter to rule them out. Although, again, we definitely favor experiments that are as good as possible to begin with, as a general principle the responsibility for confirming a hypothesis is inversely proportional to its likelihood as judged by the fate of similar hypotheses, the rule of parsimony and similar considerations. The main weakness of the time-series experiment in psychotherapy is the necessity for repeated measurements of the same subjects and the attendant possibilities for both sensitization of the subjects to the measurement process and instrument decay. This problem is discussed more completely later.

We shall also point out later the arguments in favor of comparing two or more different treatments rather than making treatment–no treatment comparisons. It is frequently difficult to compare alternative treatments for the same subjects, but it is probably possible more often than might be thought. To be sure, if we think of a pathological condition that is cured or removed by treatment, only one order of conditions is possible, namely, no treatment followed by treatment. An analogy here would be with the treatment of cancer. If, however, we are faced with a chronic, recurring condition, for example, more analogous to arthritis, it is entirely possible to try different treatments in different orders. Perhaps many conditions faced by psychotherapists are recurrent and would lend themselves to comparisons of the efficacies of different treatments for the same subjects (for examples see Heckel, Wiggins, & Salzburg, 1963; Shapiro, Marks, & Fox, 1963).

Control Group Designs

A second approach to the observation of both manipulation and no-manipulation conditions is to observe the two conditions in separate groups, the no-manipulation condition usually being referred to as a control group. The principal problem is to ensure that the manipulation and no-manipulation groups are really equivalent in all respects other than the occurrence of the critical variable. Ideally, one would have a large pool of experimental subjects who would be assigned randomly to the two (or more) experimental conditions. However, it is immediately apparent that such conditions are difficult to meet in fact in most psychotherapy settings, and although various expedients have been resorted to, unfortunately all have flaws that are probably quite serious from a standpoint of providing answers about the exact outcome to be expected from psychotherapy. Some patients can be promised treatment at a later date, but the promise may be therapeutic or the delay may be taken as a rejection (Frank, 1959). Moreover, there are often pressures to take "urgent" cases (obviously a manifestation of the assumption that psychotherapy really works and remains only to be proved). The experimental group then comes to differ from the control group in unknown and largely unspecified ways. Or "normal" groups may be used for comparative purposes. Although the use of a normal group tested at two different times can be satisfactory in order to show that changes with repeated testing are larger in the experimental group than in the normal group (Rogers & Dymond, 1954), not much is actually gained in the way of experimental "convincingness." In any case, the tactic is marred by serious possibilities of regression errors (Campbell & Stanley, 1963) stemming from the fact that the experimental group will test low on the first occasion, and a subsequent testing will likely show "improvement." The regression error is just as posible even if there is no initial "testing" in the formal sense, for the diagnosis of self-admission of personal distress precedent to entering treatment is itself a "test."

Matching is a procedure which is often resorted to in an attempt to obtain equivalent groups, but there are two kinds of matching, and they are by no means equally to be recommended. There is a procedure followed for statistical reasons of "matching" pairs (or groups) of Ss on some presumably relevant variable(s), and then *randomly* assigning one of the pair (or group) to each of the experimental conditions. This kind of experimental matching accomplishes to some degree the same purpose as the "own-control" design, namely, reducing the within-groups error. It is particularly useful when the number of Ss available is small since it ensures comparability of groups to the extent that the variable(s) on which the matching is done is relevant. We choose to call this type of matching *within sample matching*. It is also known as "blocking" (Lindquist, 1953).

The other variety of matching is less to be recommended and

may even produce misleading results. In what we call *between sample matching* the idea is to equate previously selected samples on some relevant variable by matching pairs of Ss from the different samples who have the same score on the matching variable. For example, suppose we have a group of college student patients entering psychotherapy who have scored, on the average, at -1.5 σ on some measure of adjustment. Suppose we also have available the scores of a large group of individuals, say the entire freshman class, who have not asked for and therefore are not receiving psychotherapy. It would be the most natural thing if it occurred to the experimenter to "construct" an untreated control group consisting of those untreated students with equally low scores on the adjustment measure. Then after a period of treatment, if all subjects could be retested, the results should indicate the effectiveness of psychotherapy. Unfortunately for the experimenter he will have constructed a control group that has a built-in probability of change that is greater than that of the treated group because of the differential probabilities of statistical regression toward the mean, that is, improvement resulting from the fact that the control group has almost certainly been less reliably measured. The psychotherapy group has been measured in two ways: they have requested psychotherapy, presumably an indication of poor adjustment, and they have substantiated that diagnosis by a poor performance on a test. The control group, on the other hand, has been measured only once, and certainly in a group averaging -1.5 σ below the mean there must be a number of individuals with erroneously low scores, obtained perhaps because of carelessness, transient pessimism, or something of the sort. And when they are retested the control group is almost certain to show improvement. In the example just given the dice were loaded against psychotherapy, but it could just as well be the other way around. The problem is that in *between samples matching* it is difficult to establish that the subjects being matched are from equivalent parts of the distributions in their respective samples, and therefore possibilities for statistical regression are substantial. Also, the greater the discrepancy in adequacy of measurement in the two samples, the greater the possibilities for error.

Obviously, it is very difficult to construct, even roughly, demonstrably comparable groups of experimental and untreated subjects in the typical setting in which psychotherapy is conducted. A host of problems will beset the researcher who attempts to devise groups of patients comparable in every way except that some are getting treatment and some are not. However, one strategy which has been proposed (Campbell & Stanley, 1963) and which deserves further study and trial is *invited remedial treatment*. The procedure proposed is that in some way a sample of potential candidates for treatment be identified. The sample could then be divided randomly into treatment and no-treatment groups, the first receiving an invitation to participate in treatment (treatment by invitation is not unknown in the literature: see e.g., Paul, 1964; Spielberger, Weitz, & Denny, 1962; Spielberger & Weitz, 1964). Unlike most research on psychotherapy, the proposed technique does not require refusal or delay of treatment for any subjects. The no-treatment group would not necessarily know that it was a part of any experiment at all. Ultimately the procedures suggested would presumably result in three groups: (1) invited-accepted patients, (2) invited-refused subjects, and (3) uninvited control subjects. It is possible, of course, that the invitation itself with its associated implications of need for treatment would produce some change, but it should not prove impossible to develop a control; for example, invitation followed by a delay and remeasurement. Similar possibilities exist in situations in which researchers have substantial control over the fates of their potential subjects (e.g., in prisons and where subjects can be *enlisted* in treatment groups). Snyder and Sechrest (1959) were able to design an experiment on group psychotherapy in an institution for defective delinquent males in which a control group of untreated subjects had no knowledge of the fact that they were in any way involved in a research project. Gendlin (1962) has reported similar procedures used with schizophrenic patients. A feasible and useful strategy would involve comparisons of two or more treatments administered either to invited or enlisted subjects who could be randomly assigned to treatment groups.

Among the factors which seem quite capable of contributing to erroneous conclusions about experimental findings is the prior expectation of the subject about his treatment and the research in which he is playing a part (Frank, 1961; Goldstein, 1962). Lack of knowledge about the effects on the experiment of the prior expectations of subjects could lead to erroneous conclusions either about the existence (or nonexistence) of an experimental effect or about its source. There is a growing body of evidence concerning the powerful effects on experimental subjects of the very fact of being a participant in scientific research (e.g., Orne, 1962), and appropriate measures should be taken to isolate such effects in psychotherapy research. It should be noted that the effects being discussed by no means always operate in the favor of the experimenter, one possibility being that the fact of being an "experimental subject" might produce some degree of "improvement" in a patient's condition, thus decreasing the obtained difference between an experimental and an untreated control group. One of the advantages of the invited and enlisted treatment strategies discussed previously is that a control group is produced which has no expectations aroused by perceiving itself as a part of an experiment.

Multiple Control Groups

There are more powerful designs than single group designs for studying any phenomenon, and because of their power they are to be preferred and should generally be used wherever possible. However, there are exceptions to this rule.

First, the mere repetition of a measure may result in some changes in response; for example, the total impact of the initial measure may make the subject sensitive to what is being measured. The appropriate control for such effects is the administration of the measure on two occasions, not necessarily separated by the same period of time as the pre- and postexperimental measures. (If only the control for readministration of the same measure is required, there is no particular reason that the time interval need be greater than for the dissipation of "fatigue" or other momentary effects. It should be clear that the effects of readministration and of "time" are conceptually distinct. A single control group retested over the same interval as the experimental group represents a confounding of the effects of readministration of the same measure and of changes over time but may be sufficient for many purposes.) Or consider the experimental design which has come to be known as the Solomon four-group design (Solomon, 1949). This design came about because of concern about the effect of reactions of subjects to an experimental manipulation of the pretesting of the subjects; that is, suppose the pretesting sensitizes the subjects in some way to the experimental conditions. (See the discussion below.) The ordinary two groups, pretested experimental and control design, could not answer questions concerning effect of pretesting. Therefore Solomon proposed the addition of two control groups, one receiving the experimental treatment without the pretest and one receiving only the posttest. The four groups suggested would be scheduled as follows:

| Group I | Pretest | Treatment | Posttest |
| Group II | Pretest | | Posttest |

Group III	Treatment	Posttest
Group IV		Posttest

This precise design provides information about both the effect of pre-testing and the interaction of the pretesting with the experimental treatment, but, it will be noted, at a considerable cost. Twice as many subjects are needed as in a conventional experiment. Now, note the design numbered 6 in the Campbell and Stanley scheme:

Group I	Treatment	Posttest
Group II		Posttest

This simple design quite successfully eliminated the effects of pretest-ing. It is inferior to the Solomon four-group design only in not *measuring* the effects of pretesting. If we are not interested in the effects of pretesting in their own right, much of the precision and elegance of the four-group design is wasted. As Campbell and Stanley note, there is perhaps likely to be some reluctance to give up the pretest on the ground that it establishes that the experimental and control groups were really equivalent. However, it is random assignment of patients to groups that produces equivalent groups, not pretesting. Moreover, there may be substitute measures that can be used to check on the equivalence of the groups; for example, school grades instead of intelligence tests or ratings by others instead of self-ratings.

Of particular interest to psychotherapy researchers is the discussion by Campbell and Stanley (1963) of what they call "quasi-experimental" designs, designs that do not constitute a true experiment involving randomly assigned subjects to experimental groups, but that do provide for the elimination of some of the threats to internal validity. Over a series of experiments one hopes to achieve a set of experimental results with compensating strengths. For example, the time-series design may not ensure that the results are not explainable on the basis of extraneous history, but it does ensure that subjects could not have been selected in such a way as to be biased with respect to maturational factors. On the other hand, by using an untreated control group, even if it is not exactly equivalent to the experimental group, there is certainly the possibility that one group may exceed the other in, say, maturational factors, but the history will be controlled. If the same results are obtained with both designs, it might be more parsimonious to accept the hypothesis that the experimental manipulation produced the results than to have to assume the existence of two separate rival hypotheses.

THE EXTERNAL VALIDITY OF
PSYCHOTHERAPY RESEARCH

Limitations on the external validity of an experiment are limitations on the generalization of findings to conditions, persons, and the like, other than those involved in the experiment. There is nothing paradoxical about the fact that a perfectly good experiment from the standpoint of design and execution may have little if any external validity, for, by and large, questions of research design involve those issues that make it possible to have confidence in the conclusions drawn from the experiment but not necessarily with the application of those conclusions to new situations. The validity of applications of experimental findings to new situations, new groups of persons, and new procedures will depend on the degree to which the original experiment was representative of the new situations.

The first step in applying experimental findings is to examine the original experiment and the setting in which it is to be applied and then to determine whether the experimental arrangements were drawn from the same universe of arrangements as the "applied" situation (which, incidentally, may be a new experiment). Let us take an example of a problem which is involved in attempting to apply the results of experimentation.

Sensitization by Pretesting

A potentially important problem in psychotherapy research involves the arousal of expectations in the experimental setting which stems from the possible sensitization of subjects to the experimental treatment. This problem, which has been discussed thoroughly in other places (e.g., Campbell & Stanley, 1963; French, 1953; Underwood, 1957), arises from the fact that common research designs involve pretesting of subjects on issues which are directly relevant to the treatment they are to undergo. The administration of the pretest might well sensitize the subject to the subsequent experimental manipulation (i.e., psychotherapy) and make him more susceptible than he might otherwise have been (or conceivably less susceptible). To put the problem in another way, the pretreatment measurement may interact with the treatment itself and produce differences in its effectiveness. Solomon (1949) and Canter (1951) have both shown evidence for such effects in areas other than psychotherapy. To take an example from psychotherapy research, it is quite within the realm of possibility that the administration prior to therapy of self-ideal Q-sorts could sensitize an individual to certain aspects of the treatment bearing on the discrepancy between the two sortings. Note that we are not suggesting that a pretest will actually enhance the over-all effectiveness of psychotherapy; it may, however, enhance the possibility of subsequent change on the specific instrument used.

The limitation on generalization or external validity posed by a testing-treatment interaction is that the results are generalizable only to persons who have been pretested. Whatever the findings, they would not be applicable to persons who had not undergone the initial sensitization.

One research design solution to the problem of pretreatment sensitization is to include a control group for the sensitization effect consisting of nonpretested but treated subjects. Analysis of the differences between the posttreatment measures of pretested, nonpretested, and untreated subjects will indicate the magnitude of the experimental effect and how much of it was attributable to the pretesting of the subjects. Another solution, which is more of a planning than a design solution, is to employ premeasures that do not require the awareness of the subject. Such measures as frequency of disciplinary violations (Snyder & Sechrest, 1959), the Discomfort-Relief Quotient (Dollard & Mowrer, 1947), and the patient's manner of dress (Kane, 1958, 1959, 1962) cannot sensitize the subject to the experimental manipulations. Either design or planning solutions are reasonable, but ordinarily it is cheaper to avoid sensitizing subjects by the judicious selection of measures because the necessity of an extra treated-control group is avoided.

Reactive Experimental Arrangements

A similar threat to external validity of experiments is *reactivity of experimental arrangements*. An accumulating body of evidence (Orne, 1962) suggests that the mere fact of being in "an experiment" is of considerable importance for most people and that their reactions to being an experimental subject are often rather special and not representative of their ordinary performance. To the extent that either patients *or therapists* are aware that they are participating in a research project, their behavior may be rendered untypical, and therefore experimental findings would not necessarily hold true for more ordinary, nonresearch settings.

Obviously some experimental arrangements are far more reactive than others, and reactivity is likely to be greater for some kinds of problems than others. Experimental procedures which necessitate special apparatus, such as GSR recorders, unusual settings, wearing of special clothing, and the like, are certain to heighten the awareness of the subject that he is "in an experiment." On the other hand, many experimental procedures require little if any obvious intrusion into whatever is the normal pattern of events in which the patient is participating. It is more difficult to achieve nonreactive arrangements for a therapist (i.e., in which the therapist does not realize that he is part of an experiment). As will be made clear below (see p. 51 ff), our preference is for the use, wherever possible, of procedures and measurements involving as little reactivity as possible, especially in the final stages of psychotherapy research where the results are meant to be as directly applicable to practice as possible.

Our argument for the use of nonreactive procedures and measures should not be taken as a plea for "naturalistic" therapy research. In fact, we urge exactly the opposite: researchers should break out of the very confining bonds imposed by the stereotyped, usual way of going about psychotherapy. We ask for deliberate and extensive interventions in what might seem the right or natural way of doing things. Such interventions do not, however, necessitate the use of procedures and measures any more obvious or reactive than for "naturalistic" research.

Selection-treatment Interaction

A third factor that can limit external validity and one that is of great importance in psychotherapy research is interaction between selection processes and the experimental treatment. This interaction is such an obvious problem that one would suppose it could never be ignored, but it very often is. For example, the settings in which psychotherapy research is done almost always impose at least moderate and often stringent limitations on the kinds of patients who are available for the research. If only "neurotic" patients are available for research, and if neurotic patients respond differently than do psychotics, the research findings will be limited in applicability to neurotics. Such interactions of selection and response to treatment are probably not rare, and wherever they occur, the generality of the experiment is limited.

Sampling Considerations

At first blush much of the problem of external validity seems a straightforward one, a notion that is strongly reinforced by its treatment in most texts on research design. One simply defines the universe to which conclusions are to be made and then draws a representative sample from that universe by some standard means: random, representative, stratified, etc. (e.g., see Group for the Advancement of Psychiatry, 1959; Kish, 1953). Depending on the adequacy of the sample, the conclusions one wishes to generalize are more or less legitimate (or likely to be so). The issues, in fact, are scarcely so simple. One can only agree wholeheartedly with the assertion that sampling *must* occur; the issue is how it will be done (Group for the Advancement of Psychiatry, 1959).

In the first place let us consider what we have in mind as a "population" to which we wish to generalize. At the outset we can see that unless we have some very circumscribed interest (e.g., in living graduates of the Harvard class of 1939 or ants resident in a particular colony at a particular time) we will find it extremely difficult to draw anything like a random sample. In fact, because we are almost always interested in generalizing the results of experiments through time as well as space, it is impossible to draw a random or any other kind of sample from the population in which we are interested. Consider the possibility that we have developed a new counseling technique which we wish to validate for use with college freshmen, and being perfectly realistic we are willing to restrict our conclusions further to the freshmen in our own state university. Could we not conceivably obtain a list of all freshmen and draw a sample of some kind from that list? Yes, but then the conclusions would logically be restricted in applicability to the freshmen on the list on the day on which we drew our sample. Of course, we are really interested in an abstract population of "state university freshmen," none of whom are even enrolled in the university at the time we draw our sample (i.e., next year's and subsequent classes). Manifestly, we cannot sample from populations that do not yet exist, yet it is precisely to those populations to which we wish to generalize. One cannot sample randomly in future (or past) time. Strictly speaking, then, *any* conclusions we draw on the basis of an experiment are time-bound if bound in no other way.

Actually Patterson (1960) has made a very interesting point with respect to the question of generalizing from random samples. He suggests that, strictly speaking, an experimental finding that has been obtained for a random sample is generalizable *only* to other random samples. For example, if we demonstrated the efficacy of a particular treatment for a random sample from the universe of psychotherapy patients, that finding would not necessarily hold for any particular subset of patients (e.g., obsessive-compulsive college students). Patterson, of course, is quite correct, although his point is not well taken as an argument against attempts to obtain *representative* samples. The implication of his point is that if we wish to make specific generalizations of research findings we are on safest grounds if we have established the findings on a sample from the same population to which we wish to generalize, but—and the caveat is all important—it must be a *random* sample from that population. To be consistent with the point of view we are espousing, it should be a sample representative of the population in which we are interested. Patterson's point, then, is a plea for research of a more specific, pointed nature.

Sampling Relevant Universes

There is a second major problem involved in our attempts at sampling, again one that is not often treated adequately but must be dealt with in any attempt at generalization of experimental findings. Essentially the problem is that sampling efforts must be multidimensional if they are to be meaningful. Brunswick (1956) seems to have been one of the first persons to point to the necessity for "ecological sampling," and this issue has been discussed further by Hammond (1954). In psychotherapy research sampling efforts are usually directed toward obtaining a reasonably adequate sample of patients, if there are any sampling efforts at all, but several other universes ought to be sampled if generalizations of any breadth are to be drawn. Therapists, for example, are quite an important universe, yet one that is scarcely ever accorded any attention. Again, strictly speaking, a particular psychotherapy research finding cannot logically be generalized to therapists other than those involved in the experiment unless the therapists employed are a representative sample of the universe of therapists (Patterson, 1960). No matter how adequately patients are sampled, conclusions may be limited by the failure to employ a good sample of therapists. A particularly good example is afforded by the group therapy experiment of Snyder and Sechrest (1959), which, without regard to its adequacy in other respects, is strictly limited by the fact that all therapy was done by one person.

Moreover, patients and therapists are not the only variables that ought to be sampled. There is a universe of therapy procedures, a universe of therapeutic outcomes, a universe of situations in which therapy might take place, and so on. Failure to sample from some of these universes may not prove an obstacle to the generalizations we make if we are careful to restrict ourselves appropriately. We might not care to try to sample the universe of procedures, and we might be content to say that the particular procedures we use produce specifiable effects, and this is quite legitimate. However, there is unquestionably a tendency for other persons to make generalizations that may be doubtful (e.g., to generalize from findings on nondirective psychotherapy to the practice of psychotherapy of other types). Similar precautions must be exercised with respect to outcomes (e.g., in generalizing from improvement in self-ideal Q-sorts to the "goodness" of psychotherapy).

There is, in fact an apparent paradox stemming from considerations about the problem of generalizing from a particular set of experimental findings to some new situation(s), and that is that a little bit of "sloppiness" or, to use a somewhat more acceptable term, a moderate degree of standardization is desirable in an experiment. We have alluded to this point before (see the discussion on p. 18) but will remind the reader that if an experiment is extremely well standardized the results will have validity only for other similarly standard situations. Thus, from the standpoint of generalizing to the kind of psychotherapy *ordinarily practiced,* it may be better if not too much control is exercised over many aspects of therapy in the experimental situation.

Of course, innumerable facets to the practice of psychotherapy are never sampled in any way: for example, the time of day or the altitude above sea level at which therapy occurs or the color of the room in which it takes place. Most of these factors are probably of absolutely no importance and very few are of more than negligible importance, but it is highly desirable that the possible contribution of any of these factors be eliminated. The best recommendation that can be made to experimenters concerning trivial, seemingly irrelevant factors is that they be made as heterogeneous as possible so that they are never a constant value in any experiment. Campbell and Stanley (1963) refer to this as "heterogeneity of irrelevancies." For example, psychotherapy sessions should take place throughout the day, in different rooms, with therapists clothed in different ways. Ideally, the values represented by any one variable should represent a random sample of the values likely to be found in the universe to which one wishes to generalize. Deviant values need not be included unless they are to be studied in their own right. Therapists clad in overalls need not be included, for presumably few if any therapists practice in overalls.

Inductive Bases for Generalization

Having stated the obvious fact that random samples from universes of any meaning are impossible, it will be thought that the social scientist is left with a dilemma, and he is. Fortunately, it is a dilemma that can be resolved in the same way as those in other fields. The answer to the dilemma lies in the inductive process. If our observations over a period of time have led us to conclude that with respect to relevant variables one freshman class is about like another, we may anticipate that future classes will be like past ones and conclude that a counseling procedure which works on this year's freshman class will work on next year's and the following year's until such time as, for whatever reasons, the nature of freshmen has changed substantially. It should be noted that our generalizations hold if the classes are alike on *relevant* variables, whatever they may be. For example, a decision to begin admitting more 17-year-old freshmen would not necessarily invalidate our conclusions; we might have similar inductive bases for supposing that 17-year-olds are about like 18-year-olds.

It is on the basis of our inductive experiences with various factors that we are able to transcend the specific conditions under which any experiment is conducted. Experiments are conducted under conditions of spatial, temporal, and other limitations, but we have had ample opportunity to note (or even verify) that students in one school behave much like students in another school with respect to certain variables; that people in one state are about like those in another; that things happen in about the same way in a frame house as a brick house; and so on. Things do not have to be the same everywhere, at all times, under every condition. They need only be the same with respect to variables in which we are interested. Any generalizations we make may be quite erroneous if subtle changes occur in relevant variables and yet may hold well under seemingly drastic changes in other variables. For example, a particular research finding might hold for patients and therapists of different sexes and ages and yet not hold if a therapist has an accent suggestive of a particular geographic origin.

Our faith in the generalizations we make from research findings is and must of necessity be an inductive faith. Without prior experience, we are limited to the conditions specifically represented in the experiment.

Reactivity of the Environment

There is one further limitation on the generalizations made from experiments, no matter how well planned, and that is imposed by the fact that we as researchers live in an active world, not a world passively waiting to be operated on. Among other things to which the world may react are the experiments conducted by scientists. Social and behavioral scientists are particularly vulnerable to the possibility that the very performance (and publication) of an experiment may change things in such a way that the same results would no longer be obtained. For example, even supposing it should be shown that people are susceptible to subliminal advertising, is it likely that they would long remain so if they became aware that it was being employed on them? (Bevan, 1964; McConnell, Cutler, & McNeil, 1958.) Is it not likely that some therapeutic effects may be produced by novel treatments, effects that will not prove replicable over a period of time? There is already evidence to suggest that novelty is a powerful factor in dealing with psychiatric disorders and thus that effects will be attenuated over time (Shapiro, 1960). The problem of the reactive environment of social science has other facets relevant to the generalization of research on psychotherapy which stem from the fact that research on psychotherapy is published and is then available to subsequent populations of both therapists and patients, particularly the former. As an example of what *could* happen, let us suppose that research on the "placebo" effect in psychotherapy should be published and popularized, as has been done for aspirin. Would the placebo effect continue to exist? Perhaps not; probably not for those persons who read about it. For how long, then, would generalizations about placebo effects hold? It appears that any science operating in a reactive environment requires a continuing check on the status of its generalizations.

CONTROL GROUPS IN PSYCHOTHERAPY RESEARCH

One of the first principles of research design absorbed by every neophyte is that "you've got to have a control group." In fact the writers have had the disconcerting experience of hearing correlational studies criticized because there was "no control group." However, there are simple rules for the employment of control groups; it is pointless merely to specify that they must exist. The very adjective "control" is the crux of the problem, for it is a transitive verb used as an adjective and implies an object. Control of what? In research on the outcomes of psychotherapy there are a number of different factors for which one might like to have a control group, and no experiment can be considered "complete" which has only one control group. Let us consider some of the possible control groups which might be desirable in psychotherapy research. (See also Frank, 1959; Group for the Advancement of Psychiatry, 1959).

We have already mentioned the necessity for controlling research for the effects of repeated testing. We have also mentioned history as a factor that must be allowed for in assessing the effects of treatment procedures. It is unnecessarily naïve to suppose that time itself is likely to have any particular effect. What is important is the way in which time is filled; that is, what happens during the time elapsed from the initial to the final measurement, on the basis of which we are to assess the effectiveness of a treatment. To a considerable extent the appropriate "control" activity is dependent on the question we wish to ask about the effectiveness of psychotherapy.

The most obvious question about any treatment and probably the most fundamental question is whether it is better than no treatment at all. The question is, however, purely hypothetical in the case of psychotherapy, for, as pointed out elsewhere (Goldstein, 1960) "no treatment" is not "*no* treatment" but simply the absence of any specific or systematic treatment. Thus we can answer only the question whether psychotherapy is more effective than the kinds of treatments that an individual might seek or might be offered to him in the absence of provision for formal psychotherapy. Therefore an initial standard against which to judge the effectiveness of psychotherapy would be the changes over the same period of time in persons who a nonspecific treatment control group would produce results representing a confounding of the quasi-therapy they were able to find with all other events or processes that might take place during the same time, such as maturation, forgetting, or changes in international tensions. As suggested earlier, by keeping age of subjects, the time of year, or even the length of therapy rather heterogeneous at least some of the confounded effects could probably be eliminated. Because the aim of science is to achieve as complete an understanding as possible, it is highly recommended that confounded factors be unraveled. Various designs discussed by Campbell and Stanley (1963) offer interesting possibilities to the psychotherapy researcher for coming to a more differentiated view of the effects operating in both treated and untreated groups.

"Patched-Up" Designs

One recommendation we would make, which comes directly from the work of Campbell and Stanley (1963), is for the use of what they call "patched up" designs in psychotherapy research. Unquestionably, it is very rare that the psychotherapy researcher has an opportunity to make things come out his way, that is, to achieve the optimum experimental design, such as the Solomon four-group design, for the question he has in mind. What is almost certain to be the case is that administrative considerations, lack of subjects, insufficient cooperation from other staff members, and similar factors will make an elegant experimental design impossible. In such cases Campbell and Stanley recommend the use of patched up designs achieved by opportunistic use of whatever situations are available to achieve separate control over variables rendering rival hypotheses tenable. For example, even a normal group retested over the same period of time as the therapy group would make possible the disconfirmation of testing as a *main effect* although not as a factor possibly interacting with selection, that is, with type of subjects. Still other groups available at little cost and with minimum of administrative dislocation might be used to eliminate such hypotheses as history (e.g., nonpsychiatric patients hospitalized during the same time) and maturation (nonpsychiatric subjects of the same age). Even the "waiting list" control group may be looked on as a quasi-control group, making possible the weakening of only certain rival hypotheses. An accumulation of "control" groups for specific rival hypotheses can contribute substantially to the strength of an otherwise borderline research project.

Reactive Control Groups

We should like again to insist on the importance of the distinction between what we choose to call reactive and unreactive control groups. There really is more to the question whether psychotherapy is better than no psychotherapy than is immediately apparent. One question is whether the introduction of psychotherapy into a community in which it has been unavailable will result in an improvement in the mental health of the people in that community. A somewhat different question is whether in a community in which psychotherapy is available those persons receiving it are better off than a comparable group for whom it is unavailable. For the first question a control group which does not know that it is going "untreated" is clearly called for. We think of such a group as being "unreactive" to the procedures of the scientific experiment, and it is represented only by subjects who do not know what they are missing. In the second situation, and in many experimental procedures actually employed, the untreated subjects may have various feelings about their state of "untreatment" which can affect the outcome of the experiment. For example, if they feel deprived and rejected, they may show less response to nonspecific treatments than otherwise or they might become all the more persistent in seeking and finding outside help. If, on the other hand, untreated subjects believe that they are being deprived of treatment because their cases are not so serious, they may receive a great, if temporary, boost in spirits. We are of the firm conviction that unreactive control groups are essential in coming to a full appreciation of the effects, or lack of effects, of psychotherapy. To be sure, it is often difficult to obtain such groups, but we have already described the advantages of invited or enlisted treatment studies in providing for these controls. Another possibility for broader, larger projects is the use of communities matched for relevant variables and in which treatment facilities are differentially available. Such a research design has been used effectively in the study of the effects of television on a variety of behaviors (Schramm et al., 1961). Investigators alert for the opening of new treatment facilities in distinct, identifiable communities might be able to provide a good bit of information about the over-all impact of psychotherapy, if not the individual results.

Patient and Therapist Expectations

An additional important question about the effects of a therapy is whether they are a result of the specific properties of the therapy or whether they result from expectations induced in either the patient or therapist or both about the changes that should take place. Frank (1961), Goldstein (1962), and others have discussed and documented the importance of patient expectations for the outcome of psycho-- therapy, and Goldstein in particular has dealt with the importance of therapist expectations. Especially in the context of pharmacological research, patient expectations have been referred to as the "placebo" effect, that is, the therapeutic effect consequent to the patient's belief in the efficacy of the treatment. There has been a feeling for some time that psychotherapy research should incorporate the placebo effect into its designs, but this is not a particularly easy task. Unquestionably the principal obstacle is the difficulty in imagining a proper placebo for psychotherapy. Chemically speaking, a placebo is inert or at least has no pharmacological effects which are specifically efficacious for the condition being treated. But if, as many suggest, it is the warmth and understanding, the relationship, which is important for the psychotherapeutic effect, how could one devise a convincing substitute for psychotherapy in which the relationship variable has a zero value? Snyder and Sechrest (1959) attempted to devise a placebo treatment for group psychotherapy and employed the technique of bringing groups together merely with the explanation that it was for their own good, but without direction by the therapist. Although the procedure used did offer a control for the effects of staff interest and group meetings, it is not certain that the expectations aroused in the subjects were the same for both groups. Paul (1964) devised an ingenious "suggestion placebo" for anxiety about public speaking which involved an inert pill plus a task designed to convince the subject that his anxiety had actually been reduced. Thus it may be quite possible to develop placebos for certain aspects of psychotherapy.

An even more difficult problem arises when one realizes the obvious relevance of the therapist's expectations, and attempts to control for them. Very early in psychopharmacological research it became evident that the "blind" study in which patients did not know what drug they were getting was inadequate if the clinical and research staff did know (Shapiro, 1960). So the "double-blind" design was invented (Gold, 1946; 1954), a conceptually simple matter involving the manufacture of placebo and therapeutic agents identical in appearance but stamped with a code to be recorded and deciphered later. However, it is not a simple matter to keep a psychotherapist from knowing whether he is doing psychotherapy, and his expectations and confidence cannot be prevented from influencing the therapeutic outcome (if, in fact, they do). At our present stage of sophistication in psychotherapy research design we are not prepared to untangle the specific effects of a psychotherapeutic procedure from the expectations the therapist has about the therapeutic outcome. But this does not mean that it does not matter.

In order to complete the record, there is still one more sophistication offered by the advanced research designs available and employed in psychopharmacological research (Levitt, 1959). It was noted that some drugs in which investigators were interested produced rather salient side effects, such as tingling skin feelings and elevated temperature, which seemed incidental to their specific value and were missing in totally inert placebos. Thus there would be a discriminable difference between experimental and placebo groups, noticeable both to patients and to staff, yet unrelated to the primary effect of the drug. Such possibilities led to the search for and development of the "positive placebo," a drug that mimics the side effects of therapeutic agents (Levitt, 1959). At present we are in no position to say just what a "side effect" of psychotherapy is, but at some point the distinction between the positive and negative placebo may become relevant.

Comparisons with Less Expensive Therapies

Another question that might be asked of any therapeutic procedure is particularly relevant to psychotherapeutic research. In fact, by the careful phrasing of our question many design problems in psychotherapeutic research are obviated. The solution we should like to recommend, and one in line with suggestions of Frank (1959), is that rather than asking whether a particular psychotherapy is better than no treatment or whether it is better than an inert treatment, we ask *whether any particular therapy is more effective than some clearly defined, reasonable, but less expensive procedure.* As suggested by Campbell and Stanley (1963), the problem of evaluating relative efficacy of treatments is far simpler than the problem of evaluating "absolute" efficacy. For example, a good control for individual psychotherapy may be group psychotherapy; no patient need be denied treatment, his expectations for effectiveness may be aroused, and we need not concern ourselves that the intended placebo is not inert. We may even be able to keep therapists somewhat "blind" about the conduct of the experiment. Of course, it will be argued that the essence of psychotherapy is in group psychotherapy too. Well and good, but if so, and if it seems to be present in an amount that makes group psychotherapy indistinguishable in effect from individual psychotherapy, the case for expensive individual treatment is vitiated, and something important will have been discovered. We believe that the question whether psychotherapy is better than *no treatment at all* is insufficiently demanding with respect to the supposed impact of psychotherapy. A treatment should prove itself to be better than less expensive alternatives. If individual psychotherapy proves to be no more effective than group psychotherapy, we are left with the suspicion that neither may be more effective than no treatment. We can approach the answer to this question by evaluating group psychotherapy against still less expensive alternatives. Because we cannot achieve "no therapy" as an absolute, let us take calculus as our model and see what happens as we approach zero.

It will depend on the imagination of the researcher what less expensive alternatives to psychotherapy are investigated, but it should not be difficult to develop reasonable quasi-therapies. For example, with insecure, anxious adolescents one might test psychotherapy against special tutoring in athletic skills or against "charm" courses, both probably available at a cost lower than the going rate for psychiatrists. In an inpatient treatment center the efficacy of psychotherapy might be tested against an equal amount of time spent in occupational therapy. By using matched patients from different wards one could even preclude the patient's knowing that he was getting one treatment *instead* of another. Nor would the therapists necessarily need to know that their patients were experimental subjects. In this manner we believe that important increments in knowledge about the effectiveness and process of psychotherapy would ensue. We are not especially confident that the results of investigations pitting psychotherapy against the quasi-therapies we have been discussing would be comforting for those blindly committed to the practice of psychotherapy right or wrong, but they could be invaluable to those persons committed to a scientific appreciation of psychotherapy and the development of better ways of dealing with behavior disorders. It is pointless to pretend that psychotherapy and research on it is somehow or other "pure" and beyond considerations of utility. The only justification for the existence of psychotherapy is a utilitarian one, and the proper evaluation of psychotherapy is in a utilitarian context.

CORRELATIONAL METHODS IN PSYCHOTHERAPY RESEARCH

It is by now well known that "correlation does not equal causation," and therefore that the implications of correlation research for questions of causation are limited. Nonetheless, there are occasions on which correlational research seems to be the only way of getting information which is desired and in which conclusions are strongly presumptive if not certain. We must, however, be exceptionally cautious in interpreting results. To take one example, consider findings that have been reported of a differential effectiveness for experienced and inexperienced therapists (Cartwright & Vogel, 1960). Initially, one may be inclined to suppose that level of experience is a genuine experimental variable; it certainly resembles many experimental manipulations. However, it is clear that level of experience is not actually manipulated. Rather, groups of therapists are selected who have more or less of it. Results may then be expressed as a correlation between outcome and amount of experience of the therapist. But the crux of the matter becomes evident when one asks *why* some therapists are more experienced than others. Is it because the experimenters found a population of potential therapists and gave some of them three years experience? Probably not. Some therapists are more experienced than others because (perhaps) they are older, better motivated, brighter, better supervised and trained generally, have fewer other duties, are more self-confident of their abilities, and are more stable themselves. Is not experience only a variable that it occurred to the researchers to study? Would the results have been the same had older and younger therapists been compared? Now we should not care to argue about the likelihood of each of these "explanations," particularly in the light of their expected effect on therapeutic outcome, although for some of the variables mentioned the effect should not be negligible. We should simply like to suggest that what seems at first to be a rather straightforward finding with obvious implications is in fact only tentatively acceptable. On the other hand, experience of thera-pists is going to be somewhat difficult to manipulate, and most of our conclusions about experience must come from correlational studies similar to those that have been done. We can, however, improve on analyses that have been done by using correlations within subclasses of therapists homogeneous for other variables or by using partial correlations to hold constant such variables as age.

We should not be misled into supposing that any result expressed as a correlation is inappropriate as a basis for a causal assumption. Nearly any experimental result can be expressed in correlational terms, and the implications are not changed whether a correlation or an F-ratio is used to summarize the result of the experiment. For example, we might wish to dètermine whether patients seen one, two, three, . . . twelve times per month differ on some measure of therapeutic out-come. We could certainly assign incoming patients randomly to a treatment schedule, and, assuming no differential mortality in the various groups, we could claim to have manipulated the amount of treatment and to be able to make a legitimate causal comparison; for example, that more frequent treatment produces a better outcome. (However, see Lorr et al., 1962, for actual and contradictory evidence on this point.) Yet we could express the experimental finding either in terms of a correlation between amount (or frequency) of treatment and score(s) on some outcome measure or of an F-ratio from a standard one-way classification analysis of variance.

The distinction which is often made is between Response-Response and Stimulus-Response research (Spence, 1944). In R-R research two responses from the same individual are related, and the most that can be said is that they are related. That one response caused another is always open to question, although in some instances it might seem highly likely. In S-R research, if properly done, we can be more confident that the manipulation, that is, the stimulus, will produce the outcome in question. Now, however, we must revert to the research already discussed on the amount of therapist experience as it affects outcome so that we may understand clearly what it is that prevents us from drawing the conclusion that experienced therapists produce more favorable outcomes than inexperienced therapists. Certainly the investigations cited are apparently of the S-R variety, involving as they do the experience of the therapist and the improvement of the patient. We have already indicated that a severe limitation on the conclusion results from the possible confounding of level of experience with other variables such as age. We can only conclude that the therapist (as a gross manipulation) makes a difference in therapeutic outcome. Unfortunately, there is even a sense in which the research is R-R research and which places a further limitation on the conclusion that can legitimately be drawn. It is not necessary to consider the patient at all in the research. We could view the research exclusively as research on therapists, and improvement in patients could be regarded as an index of therapeutic competence on the ground that it is a manifestation of the therapist response. A therapist who makes good and appropriate responses in therapy will achieve a high index of competence, and a therapist who makes poor responses will achieve a low index. We have, then, two indices, experience and competence, on the same persons and can correlate them. But does experience "cause" competence or is it the other way around? Even if it were possible to say that therapists were homogeneous in age, intelligence, etc., we still could not be confident that experience results in therapeutic competence. Both might be attributable to some third factor; for example, some ineffable personality structure, that produces therapeutic competence and also the likelihood of greater experience.

We do not wish to be blatantly guilty of the "doubting Thomas" syndrome we described earlier and would not want to aver too vigorously that research on therapist competence of the kind discussed is uninterpretable. The ineffable personality factor hypothesis, the age hypothesis, or the motivation hypothesis all must be considered along with the experience hypothesis for their relative probabilities of veridicality. There is no sound logical reason to think that age is a more likely explanation of the results than experience, and the rule of parsimony would tend to leave us disappointed in the postulation of any ineffable personality traits. Thus we are inclined to suppose that level of experience has something to do with the outcome of psychotherapy. However, the research cited is instructive concerning possible pitfalls in the interpretation of even the simplest of research findings. No experimental manipulation is persuasive if the manipulated variable is confounded with other variables. We must be careful in interpreting even S-R research, when both stimulus and response come from persons interacting in such a way that the response of one person is actually a function of the response of the other person, thus making it reasonable to interpret the research as the R-R variety.

We are not persuaded that R-R research is meaningless, but we do believe that more evidence is necessary in order to make even a minimally convincing case for the truth of any causal generalization. To paraphrase the clever Chinese, one good experiment is worth a multitude of correlations. However, human nature being what it is, and subscribing as we do to the broad ethical traditions in which most of us are reared, some of the ultimate experiments are quite unlikely, if not impossible. For example, no matter how much we might like to study the effects of premarital sex experience on marital happiness, the possibilities of doing so in an experimental design seem limited. Probably we are also limited in the possibilities of studying some aspects of psychotherapy by experimental techniques. We should prefer to know the correlations between therapy outcome and such variables as therapist experience, patient's prior expectations, number of missed appointments, etc., than not to know them, even admitting that we should be hesitant to assume that they are indicative of causal factors. We reiterate our conviction that weak data are better than no data, if the weakness is recognized and appreciated.

MEASURING THE OUTCOME OF PSYCHOTHERAPY

Obviously it is going to be difficult to assess the outcome of such a complex experience as psychotherapy, probably not the least for the reason that psychotherapy takes place under high levels of anxiety about the outcome—on the part of everyone concerned. However, the major obstacles to measurement are two: (1) not knowing what to measure, and (2) not knowing how to measure it.

Perhaps it is more surprising than it should be that there is still little agreement on the outcome(s) to be expected from psychotherapy. Yet proponents of different forms of therapy have rather different ideas about appropriate measures of their efforts. Thus some groups have depended heavily on such self-report measures as Q-sorts; others have tended to employ projective measures such as the Rorschach; others have suggested "practical" criteria such as ability to hold a job; and others have opted for the alleviation of rather specific symptoms. A great deal of energy and a lot of polemic ink have been expended in arguing the legitimacy of various intended outcomes, nearly all of which have been labeled "trivial," "superficial," "vague," or some other equally pejorative term.

It is apparent to us that no one measure nor any single technique can suffice to substantiate or seriously weaken the case for psychotherapy. What is badly needed in every psychotherapy research program is a research plan which incorporates several different outcome measures, preferably methodologically, if not conceptually, independent. An extensive review (Harris, 1963) of problems in measuring change points in the same direction. As Campbell and Stanley (1963) have stated, the usual understanding of multivariate research has been research with multiple independent variables. It can and should, however, refer also to multiple dependent measures. By using two or more measures in a research project, information is gained both about the limitations of the therapy being practiced and the relationship among the measures that will allow a better understanding of other research. For example, suppose that by desensitization therapy a very fearful person is relieved of his phobic reaction. Would there also be a decrease in the discrepancy between his self and ideal Q-sorts; would the decrease be of the same magnitude as that achieved by other methods of therapy; or would there be an "improvement" in his Rorschach responses? We do not believe that the commitment to any particular form of therapy rules out any kind of measurement, even though it may seem more appropriate for a different form of therapy. One of the real strengths of the research reported by Rogers and Dymond (1954) was the use of different measures of therapy outcome, namely, Q-sorts, peer ratings, self-ratings, and TAT.

Unfortunately, the technology of measurement is not up to the demands that might be made on it by psychotherapy researchers. Unquestionably, there are outcomes of therapy that may be of considerable importance but cannot yet be measured with any great precision. On the other hand, it also seems to be true that some of the "outcomes" expected by some therapists cannot be defined in a way that suggests very clearly any behavioral referents or distinguishes them from other concepts. At the present time the researcher can only take a rather straightforward operationalist's position and adopt some likely measures for the concepts he has in mind. To be sure, someone else may deny that his operations really capture the "essence" of the concept, but it is the critic's responsibility to specify a better set of operations. A science cannot advance on the basis of availables that defy observation, but science has always advanced by successive approximations of ideal measurement operations, and psychotherapy can do likewise. If we lack the best measurements imaginable, that does not excuse the neglect of measurement altogether. We must use the best measurements now available and at the same time strive for better ones. A part of the solution to the measurement problem, we are convinced, lies in multiple and diverse measurements both within single projects and across several projects. If most of the ways of assessing therapy outcome have flaws (Berg, 1952), they do not have the same flaws—or the same strengths. A combination of measurements may prove effective if strengths and flaws are compensatory.

In evaluating psychotherapy, the most common procedure has been to obtain some measurement immediately following the termination of therapy, although follow-up measurements over a period of six months or so are becoming more common (Rogers & Dymond, 1954; Schlein, Mosak, & Dreikurs, 1962; Snyder & Sechrest, 1959). Although long-term effects of treatment are not absolutely necessary to justify it, it is certainly important to know over what period of time any demonstrated superiority of a treated group can be expected to exist, and there is an urgent need for followup of both treated and untreated (or differently treated) patients over long periods of time. Probably the well-known Cambridge-Somerville Youth Study (Powers & Witmer, 1951) with its ten-year period of study is the longest-term study extant. That its results were discouraging should not deter investigators. One methodological problem that is very nearly inherent in long-term studies is the high probability of differential mortality in the experimental groups. For example, there may be a variety of reasons why a treated group would remain accessible over a longer period of time than an untreated group, and the subjects lost from either group would probably not be a random sample of the total group.

Another methodological problem in long-term followup studies is that instrument decay is almost certain to occur. For example, if we were dealing with 18-year-old subjects, test items dealing with attitudes toward parents would be appropriate, and we would expect psychotherapy to produce some change in responses to such items. However, the items might not mean the same thing to the subjects ten years later, and the differences between treated and untreated groups might be altered in quite uncertain ways. Similar changes in instruments are likely to occur for a wide variety of measurement procedures. We would have to decide whether to risk a planned change in instruments supposedly reflecting changes in criterion behavior over the period of the study (e.g., ratings on variables appropriate for 18-year-olds and corresponding ratings on a different set for variables appropriate for 28-year-olds).

A somewhat separate issue from the question of persistence of psychotherapeutic effects is whether they might be delayed; that is, is it possible that one might find *greater* differences between treated and untreated groups after a period of time than at the termination of therapy? Such a question can probably be answered only if the measurement operations are the same at both times. If the instrument(s) were changed in any way, the question of relative magnitude of effects would be meaningless. To this point we know of no persuasive evidence for delayed effects of psychotherapy. Studies such as those reported by Rogers and Dymond (1954) indicate that the effects of therapy are at a maximum immediately on termination of therapy (or perhaps earlier).

Nonreactive Measures

Many of the issues and arguments discussed in this chapter point in a specific direction: we badly need measures of psychotherapeutic outcome which are nonreactive, that is, which can be repeatedly obtained without biasing subsequent results and do not interact with the experimental procedures being employed. The reader might find the review of cooperation-free, nonreactive measures by Webb et al. (1966) especially helpful. We believe that there are many reasons for caution in the use of standard "tests" and ratings in evaluating the effects of psychotherapy. Such measures are all too prone to be reactive; the Rorschach, at least by clinical opinion, is a notable example. Moreover, the "phoniness" of the procedures that must be followed to get many measures, for example, GSR, vitiates in part against their usefulness because of the possibility that they may interact with the therapy. If only a single measurement is needed, the posttest-only design is satisfactory. Otherwise different approaches to measurement are needed.

We should like to propose that researchers devote a part of their creative efforts to the task of measurement and that they attempt to develop nonreactive measures, preferably naturally occurring events, but at least measurements that can be obtained without the knowledge of the subject. Let us give a few examples of possible measurements that would seem to have some promise. The Discomfort-Relief Quotient (DRQ) was originally developed by Dollard and Mowrer (1947) to reflect the relative amounts of tension or discomfort in samples of writing or speech. It has been employed in evaluating psychotherapy and seems to change systematically over the course of therapy (Mowrer, 1953). It can be obtained without the knowledge of the patient and conceivably even without the knowledge of the therapist, yet it should be maximally useful in time-series studies. Probably its major weakness is that it would be difficult to obtain comparable samples of writing or discourse from both treated and untreated samples.

Peters and Jones (1951) studied changes in performance on two motor tasks, Porteus Mazes and Mirror-tracing, in treated and un-treated schizophrenic patients. There was significant improvement on both tests for the treated group but not for the controls. Hybl and Stagner (1952) found some improvement in "frustration tolerance" on simple motor tasks after therapy. Such measures are likely to be limited in usefulness to rather seriously impaired patients, but the task and procedures can easily be divorced from the treatment and the subjects need not see any connection, thus preventing the inter-action of the testing with treatment. Probably a fairly lengthy series of measures could be obtained without differential prejudice to sub-sequent measures. It should be pointed out that when any measures are obtained it is necessary that they be administered by a person equally well known to experimental and control subjects, thus ruling out the therapist as tester.

A variable that is presumably much affected by personality dif-ficulties and should be amenable to the influence of psychotherapy is "social distance." For example, schizophrenic subjects are supposedly inclined to maintain a high level of social distance, which ought to decrease with treatment. Recent experiments by Sommer (1962) and Leipold (1963) have shown remarkable success in operationalizing social distance in terms of linear distance. It would be quite simple and very meaningful to observe treated and untreated subjects with any frequency desirable in situations in which they were face to face with other people and measure the distance between the patient and the object person. Use of hidden cameras might simplify things, but it would not be necessary. The subject would not have to know that anything at all was being measured, and the situation could be com-pletely divorced from the treatment arrangements.

Kane (1958, 1959, 1962) has noted patterns of dress worn to inter-views by outpatients that should be related to progress in psycho-therapy. Of course, observations of habits in clothing and grooming could be done entirely without the knowledge of the patients, making reactivity zero (if the therapist did not comment on the clothing worn). If, as Kane says, dark, dull colors are associated with depression, one would expect differences between treated and untreated depressed patients.

In many situations in which treatment is carried on there are recurring observations or measurements which are a natural part of the situation and have no obvious, specific connection with treatment. Such things as school grades or scores on examinations, disciplinary offenses, nursing notes, requests for medication (e.g., sedatives), attendance at optional social affairs (e.g., parties), and ward ratings are all examples of recurring observations which could be taken advantage of. When observations are routine, they have the advantage of being minimally reactive and of not interacting with treatment (although caution would have to be exercised in using nursing notes or ward ratings when the persons making them are sophisticated about treatment arrangements). We may just list a number of other measures that might be exploited in evaluating psychotherapy and that seem to offer the dual advantages of being nonreactive and of not being a direct function of the treatment process: number of dancing partners at hospital parties, participation in voluntary activities, number of days absent from job, amount of time spent in bed, amount of time spent alone, number of cigarettes smoked, amount of alcohol consumed, amount of household work accomplished, proportion of dark areas in pictures painted, number of laughs during comedy show divided by number of laughs during drama (appropriateness of affect), amount of information about current events, number of hours sleep per night, eyeblink rate (Kanfer, 1960), and ability to forego an immediate, small reward in favor of a delayed, larger one (Mischel, 1961). Obviously a psychotherapist might with justice deny the importance of any of these events, and we would agree that any one of them is limited in meaning and importance. However, in aggregate, a number of these measures come to be quite meaningful; at least as meaningful as self-ideal Q-sorts and TAT stories. We do not wish to deny the importance of many other measures that might be used; we only wish to point to the possible advantages of expanding the measurement operations used to assess psychotherapy outcomes.

Individualized Measurements

When we consider the great variety of complaints expressed by patients and their relatives, of symptoms displayed, and the inclination of clinicians toward treatment of "individuals," it is rather surprising that psychotherapy researchers have not given more thought to the possibility of individualized measures of therapy outcome. Certainly it is easier to apply a single uniform instrument to all the patients in an experiment, but it would not be at all impossible to develop genuinely individual criteria. The idea of "target symptoms" (Levitt, 1959) toward which treatment procedures are particularly oriented is a step in the direction of individualized criterion measures. Rather than establishing a common criterion of successful psychotherapy for all patients, might it not be more reasonable and better to establish individual criteria suited to the particular case? To take but one example, is it true that successful psychotherapy for all patients would consist of a decrease in self-ideal Q-sort discrepancy; might there not be some patients for whom an increase in the discrepancy would be suggestive of improvement? (Block & Thomas, 1955; Loevinger & Ossorio, 1959). And might improvement for some patients consist of a change in the self-sort and for others a change in the ideal? A representative example of what might be done is provided by an unpublished study by Matkom (personal communication) of the Rorschach as a measure for success in therapy. Instead of specifying the differences which would be expected on the average between Rorschachs of successful and unsuccessful cases, Matkom made individual specifications for each patient. For example, an improvement for one patient might be represented by an increase in $W\%$ and by a decrease for another patient. Matkom's study was only a pilot effort and was methodologically deficient in certain respects, but for the 18 cases he studied there was a fairly high correspondence between "improvements" in the Rorschach record and improvements in work records as judged by a supervisor. Certainly the idea is a promising one.

An example of research on target symptoms is provided by Pascal and Zax (1956; Pascal, 1959), who take a firm stand for the ultimate necessity of measurement of *behavioral* outcomes in psychotherapy. Their procedure consisted of searching case files for successive sets of ten cases in which a fairly definite behavioral complaint was stated and which seemed to have had adequate therapy in terms of the original goals of the case. Although we might question the fact that the authors themselves noted the outcome of the cases and judged whether or not improvement had occurred, the results are nonetheless impressive: in 28 of the 30 cases there had been improvement. Hoehn-Saric et al. (1964), also employed target symptoms and found improvement with psychotherapy. It will seem unnecessarily crude in future studies to employ a single criterion for all patients unless they have been selected for similarity of initial complaints.

For investigations employing an experimental design the development of individual criteria for therapy outcomes would require only that pairs of patients with the same criteria be assigned to treatment and no treatment (or alternate treatment) groups, or that assignments be made at random from a large pool of patients. The design problems are probably of little consequence beside the problems of developing meaningful individual measurements. It should be pointed out, however, that the use of individual criteria of therapeutic success enables the study of heterogeneous groups of patients—patients under treatment for anorexia (hence weight gain) and patients under treatment for weight loss.

Perhaps we might inject one more comment here about the use of nonequivalent control groups, particularly "normal" control groups in psychotherapy research. If a control group is to have any meaning at all, the opportunities for change must be equal in both treated and untreated groups. Specifically, there must not be any artificial ceiling (or floor) effects limiting the changes that can be found in one group or the other. For example, consider a research project in which the criterion measure is adequacy of performance on arithmetic tests and a group of poorly performing students is given some remedial treatment and tested before and after treatment. It is apparent that some control for history and retesting is desirable, but suppose that only a group of superior students is available for a control group. It might be thought that their results, too, would show the effects of history, that is, changes in emphasis on arithmetic in the school, and retesting, but if the test has too low a ceiling the opportunities for improvement in the two groups would not be equal and the experiment could be quite misleading. Such an example is blatantly obvious, but consider some more subtle but still possible examples. With respect to achievement, it is easier to ensure underachievement than overachievement. Is the likelihood of change in achievement level for normal and underachieving students really equal, aside from regression effects? Or, when the self-ideal Q-sort correlation is already .58 in normal subjects (Rogers & Dymond, 1954), how much additional change is likely? It must be demonstrated that there are groups with a markedly higher self-ideal correlation before the failure of the normal group to show change can be evaluated. The solution is to show that on any measure for which one proposes to use normal controls there are superior groups with considerably higher scores. Otherwise we may suspect that the normal group is near the maximum level likely on the measure in question and therefore that improvement in their scores is not to be expected.

THE EVALUATION OF RESEARCH

Most of this chapter has centered on the problems of evaluating research on psychotherapy. However, in this section we would like to note a number of issues that have not been covered elsewhere. We believe that these issues are important both to the planning and accomplishing of research and to the intelligent reading of research reports.

Principle of Symmetry

As an initial approach to the evaluation of research, we present the *principle of symmetry in research evaluation*. The principle is a simple one, but it deserves attention and emphasis because of the frequency with which it is violated. It has two aspects that may be distinguished. First, any standard of relevance of research to a theoretical problem is equally applicable to research on both sides of the question. This aspect of the principle refers to the tendency of partisans of any position to apply different standards of relevance to research that supports their position than to research contrary to their position. Thus it is not uncommon for clinically-minded researchers to reject animal studies in general as being irrelevant to the behavior of human beings, yet to cite favorably those animal studies that support some position they wish to take. Now, animal studies may or may not be relevant to the behavior of humans, but we simply cannot pick and choose, accepting only those we like. To take another example, studies of accuracy of clinical prediction are sometimes rejected in general because of their artificiality and the fact that they do not involve "real" clinical prediction. However, when a published study shows positive results, it is likely to be cited triumphantly by the same persons who previously rejected all such artificial studies. To take but one further example, if laboratory studies of verbal conditioning are irrelevant to the field of psychotherapy, those that show one result should be as irrelevant as those that show another. Bandura and Walters (1963), for example, note the tendency of psychoanalytic theorists to reject negative findings of experiments based on translations of psychoanalytic theory into learning terms on the basis of the inadequacy of the translation, yet they embrace positive findings with the net result of an increase in entrenchment of psychoanalytic theory. We plead, then, for the consumer of research to set reasonable standards of relevance for evaluating research and to apply those standards conscientiously, whether the research in question favors his position or not.

The second aspect of the *principle of symmetry* is that methodological flaws which disqualify research on one side of an issue also disqualify research on the other side of that issue. If a study showing positive results for psychotherapy is rejected on the ground that the experimental and control groups were not equivalent, studies showing negative results must also be rejected if a similar inequality prevails. *N*s that are too small on one side of an issue are too small on the the other side of that issue. If failure of subjects to improve on self-ideal Q-sorts is rejected on the grounds of the superficiality of the criterion measure, positive results for self-ideal Q-sorts are equally superficial.

Taken together, the two aspects of the *principle of symmetry in research evaluation* represent a plea for reason and fair play. A perusal of writings in the area of psychotherapy will, we believe, reveal that the principle is an important one that deserves to be respected. It has been suggested, for example, that Eysenck's (1952) pessimistic conclusions about the efficacy of psychotherapy resulted from bias in interpretation of research and that the data presented by him do not justify either a favorable or an unfavorable opinion about psychotherapy (De Charms, Levy, & Wertheimer, 1954). We would, of course, point to equally apparent biases on the part of some who have criticized Eysenck (Reznikoff & Toomey, 1959; Rosenzweig, 1954).

Multiple Statistical Tests

A second caution that must be exercised in evaluating research is to take into account the number of statistical tests or analyses which were done or probably done to produce a particular set of significant findings. Obviously, if enough statistical tests are done, some significant findings will emerge. The problem of interpreting multiple statistical tests becomes even more complicated when they are not independent of each other; for example, if they are all done on the same set of subjects. If the data are not independent, presumably errors will be correlated and the result will be something of a statistical morass. Fortunately, Block (1960) has shown that for test items multiple statistical tests are likely to be a conservative estimate of the number of true findings. Whether Block's findings would hold true for other kinds of nonindependent tests is open to question.

Still, the problem of evaluating research is relatively simple if all analyses done are reported. However, it is a certainty that for one reason or another not all the analyses done, perhaps only a few of them, are reported in research write-ups. Probably in many cases the analyses are casual and informal, and the researcher himself may never recognize that an analysis has been performed. For example, in pondering how to make sense out of his data the researcher will probably examine a number of different aspects of the data, perhaps only by visual inspection. Anything which looks interesting will be checked by a more formal analysis, and anything which looks really promising will be subjected to a statistical test. Note, however, that many tentative schemes for "slicing the pie" were discarded precisely because they did not look promising, that is, because they did not seem likely to be significant at all. Those were statistical tests whether the formal test was done or not, and the one "significant" finding that emerged has to be evaluated in the context of the number of casual tests that were done and will not be reported because it will not occur to the researcher that they are of any importance. A very important principle is for the researcher to report the total number of alternative analyses which were done, even if they did not involve formal tests of statistical significance (see also Cronbach, 1949).

A variant on the theme of multiple analyses that must be guarded against is the *post hoc* analysis, that is, a supplementary analysis of data carried on to elucidate a main analysis. Let us take one example. Suppose that an experimenter has done a study of the effectiveness of some form of psychotherapy and has found no difference between treated and untreated subjects. At that point he wonders whether the outcome of his experiment might be explainable in terms of some other variable that he had not previously considered, and he begins to look at the characteristics of the treated subjects who improved and those who did not. He makes a list of two subgroups and begins to check various things about them. He finds (1) no difference in sex, (2) the ages are approximately the same, (3) the diagnoses do not seem to matter, (4) differences in education are not marked, but (5) the improved group proves to have been treated by the more experienced therapists. The analysis may well stop here, and the research reports only the one very intriguing finding. We must remain suspicious of analyses conducted to explain the main experimental findings unless we are assured in some manner about the total number of analyses of any sort from which the significant one was selected. Even then, when the criterion for stopping the analyses is the occurrence of a significant result, *post hoc* analyses lose much of any meaning they might have. Researchers will need to acquire the discipline and courage to note and report *all* the analyses they do and in just what order they are accomplished.

Verification of Data and Hypotheses

Finally, we should like to mention an important requirement for research that involves the testing of some hypothesis, particularly a new hypothesis, not precisely derived from prior theoretical structure. Let us suppose that a clinician notes that patients high on some Rorschach Factor X seem to do better in therapy than patients low on Factor X. The clinician thinks about his observation and decides that Trait Y, which is measured by Factor X, is probably important to progress in psychotherapy. He then plans a research project to test the hypothesis that patients high on Trait Y do better in psychotherapy than patients low on this trait, and his research involves measuring the response to psychotherapy of patients high and low on Factor X, an operational measure of Trait Y. However, no matter what his results, he will not legitimately be able to claim that he has verified his hypothesis. He will be entitled only to the claim of having verified his previous observation of a relationship between Factor X and the outcome of psychotherapy. A *hypothesis* can be said to have been supported only to the extent that there is methodological independence between the observations leading to the formation of the hypothesis and the observations leading to its verification. There is a distinction between verification of data and verification of hypotheses. Data are verified when a repetition of an "experiment," whether formal or not, produces the same results. Hypotheses are verified (more properly, they gain in credence) when *new* lines of evidence support them. A theoretical hypothesis cannot be confirmed by replication of the experiment on which it was originally formed; a replication of an experiment confirms the empirical outcome, not the theory. If our researcher had developed the hypothesis that Trait Y is relevant to the outcome of psychotherapy and had decided to use Factor X as an operational measure of Y, the research would have been a proper basis on which to conclude that the hypothesis had been confirmed (or rather had escaped disconfirmation). We would emphasize that, as in the case of multiple statistical tests, we are not impugning the integrity of scientists. We mean only to suggest that in certain instances greater respect needs to be paid to the logical basis of science.

OPTIMAL AND REAL EXPERIMENTS

There are two quite distinct questions which should be asked about the efficacy of psychotherapy, questions necessitated by the fact that the development of the practice of psychotherapy rapidly and by far outstripped the development of its research bases. It will take two rather different experiments to answer the questions. One is whether psychotherapy works; the other is whether psychotherapy *as it is currently practiced* works. The second is more easily answered and we now have the most evidence for it, evidence that is not extraordinarily encouraging. On the first question we maintain that there is almost no evidence and that what there is is only presumptive. We have argued before that psychotherapy is by definition a practical field in which considerations of utility are of paramount importance. Therefore it is critical that we have evidence concerning the effectiveness of psychotherapy as it is done by persons who are doing it today. No matter what the theories are, no matter how well experts might do, no matter how things might turn out under ideal circumstances, the practice of psychotherapy is not justified if it does not work under the conditions in which it is being used and by the practitioners devoted to it.

On the other hand, no matter how poor the outcome of psychotherapy under current conditions or in the hands of current practitioners, it still remains entirely possible that experts operating under good or even ideal conditions might achieve rather remarkable effects. If experts operating under ideal conditions do *not* achieve fairly impressive results, we may as well abandon the field as it is now conceived and begin again. Therefore what is needed is an approximation of what we choose to call the optimal experiment. The requirements for the optimal experiment are well established by the criticisms frequently made of "real" experiments. First and foremost, a sample of really expert psychotherapists should be identified. How they might be identified is probably not a critical issue, but the clinical community must acknowledge their superior competence. Second, these therapists must be allowed to select the patients with whom they will work. There is no reason to suppose that psychotherapy will work with every patient, and different therapists may have special areas of competence. All that would be necessary would be the identification of *pairs* of carefully matched patients, one of whom randomly chosen would be examined in some way and either accepted or rejected for treatment by the therapist. Whenever a patient is selected, his matched pair goes into a control group. The control group might be of the delayed treatment variety, or an invited or enlisted treatment design could be used. Third, the conditions for treatment should be established by the therapist to conform to his best judgment about such matters as the decor of his office, the schedule of visits, and the length of treatment. Finally, each therapist should be permitted to state the results he intended to produce by his ministrations and appropriate measures should be chosen or developed. In addition, it would probably be desirable to have an independent panel state for each patient just what outcomes would be considered evidence of successful therapy. After such efforts in design and planning, we would demand a clear-cut difference between the psychotherapeutically treated patients and their controls.

We would, to a certain extent, eschew the idea of the "crucial experiment" as have many experts in scientific methodology and experimental design (e.g., Campbell & Stanley, 1963). It is difficult to imagine any experimental arrangements that would satisfy *all* proponents of a particular position and provide conclusive evidence for the truth or falsity of some hypothesis. However, in the experiment just described, we believe that negative results would be fairly conclusive for the practice of psychotherapy *as it is currently conceived*. If experts operating under the best circumstances we can arrange cannot produce good results, it is asking too much to expect that ordinary therapists operating under the usual exigencies of clinical practice will be any better. On the other hand, positive results would not be similarly conclusive for clinical practice; they would only suggest what might be possible.

We have not been able to locate the optimal experiment in psychotherapy, although, within the limits of the problem involved and the techniques studied, that of Paul (1964) is a good approximation. All the other experiments known to us to this point are seriously flawed in one way or another, and perhaps that is why the results have not been more convincing of the final worth of psychotherapy. Better approximations to ultimate experiments have been done in the area of the clinical use of tests. A notable example is the well-planned experiment by Little and Schneidman (1958) employing apparently expert clinicians operating under favorable conditions and predicting to a realistic criterion. That the results of their experiment were discouraging is most unfortunate, for it is difficult to rationalize them away. Such experiments are badly needed in the field of psychotherapy.

On the other hand it is consonant with the purposes underlying this entire book to suggest that even negative results in the ultimate experiment we have described would not sound the death knell for psychotherapy. It is our firm thesis that psychotherapy can be improved, that even the "foremost experts" of today have not reached the maximum level of effectiveness in psychotherapy. We believe that by a more careful examination of the bases for the practice of psychotherapy and by greater attention to fundamental research in psychology the practice of psychotherapy may be greatly changed for the better. We believe that an objective examination of research to date and reflection on the probable outcome of "ultimate" experiments can only lead to the conclusion that the practice of psychotherapy can stand drastic improvement.

STANDARDS FOR RIGOR IN PSYCHOTHERAPY RESEARCH

We do not believe that is is possible to establish absolute standards for rigor in any research field except the absolute standard that research should always be as rigorous as is consistent with the aims of the experimenter and the circumstances under which is he is working. We suggest, however, that there are three separate aspects of experimentation to which considerations of rigor are relevant and that recommendations for each of them will be somewhat different. Those we wish to discuss are design, mensuration, and execution.

We believe that there is never an excuse for doing a weak experiment when a better one can be done, but we also believe that the purposes of the experiment may lead to the choice of a design that is less than maximally informative. A case in point is our previous recommendation of the posttest only design instead of the Solomon four-group design in which the experimenter has no special interest in the effects of pretesting but wants only to ensure that pretesting will not bias the experimental findings. We do not view the choice of a less informative but cheaper experiment as a sacrifice of rigor. There is a genuine sacrifice of rigor whenever an experimenter deliberately or carelessly permits an otherwise avoidable threat to the internal or external validity of his experiment. In that respect an experiment should always be the best possible under the circumstances.

It is impossible to set any absolute standard of rigor with respect to mensuration. It is unjustified to take standards of rigor from one field or discipline and apply them unthinkingly to another field, discipline, or area of research. A physicist's standards for measurement of time are inappropriate in most areas of psychology. In psychology it is always at least theoretically possible to increase the reliability of measurement (e.g., by lengthening a test), and the units of measurement could almost always be more precise (e.g., 6-inch squares in an "open field" test instead of 12-inch squares). Why not strive for greater and greater precision? Simply because the j.n.ds of precision ultimately become too expensive and inconsistent with the goals of the experimenter, the remainder of the experiment, or both. Ultimately the quest for precision becomes as meaningless as carrying out all calculations to eight decimal places. We suspect that researchers may often settle for less precision than is desirable in measurement, and overly precise measurement is probably rare, but it is unrealistic to suggest that precision is an absolute goal.

Finally, execution of the experimental plan is an important aspect of the total process and is certainly an aspect to which "rigor" is applicable. Here we can say that rigor should not be needlessly sacrificed, and that the level of rigor that is critical to the interpretation of the experiment should be adhered to. For example, if the experimental design calls for the random assignment of subjects to groups, they should be assigned randomly. We suspect that most instances in which randomness of assignment is violated are unnecessary abandonments of an achievable level of rigor. On the other hand, even the most ardent defenders of rigor in psychological research know that a "23-hour deprivation schedule" does not mean precisely that. Why not? Clearly, an experimenter who arranged things so that his rats would be set down in the runway at 23 hours plus or minus one second would be regarded as unbelievably compulsive and even trivial. Such precision is not worth it. As an alternative, however, we recommend that the level of precision achieved in the execution of an experiment be described. If 23 hours does not mean 23 hours *exactly,* it is probably not important, but it is important to know what the distribution of achieved deprivation scores is. Rather than strive for exceptional degrees of adherence to experimental plan, we suggest a reasonable standard plus a description of the degree of deviation from the plan.

There are many criticisms of "precision" in psychotherapy research (e.g., Group for the Advancement of Psychiatry, 1959; Reznikoff & Toomey, 1959; Strupp, 1960), usually on the ground that precision or rigor is incompatible with the meaningfulness of the research. Strupp, for example, says that "clinical penetration and scientific rigor have varied inversely" (1960, p. 63). It is difficult to see in what manner scientific rigor must imperil clinical research. We do not believe that the utilization of appropriate control groups can in any way lessen the meaningfulness of research, nor can good sampling procedures and random assignment to treatments. Neither can we grant the possibility that fidelity to an experimental plan might decrease the meaning of research for clinicians. As we have already noted, good experimental design and execution do not demand absolute uniformity within experimental conditions. Finally, we do not agree that precision or rigor in measurement is productive of sterility in research. Lack of imagination is what produces this sterility. The way to improve the usefulness of research to clinicians does not lie in experimental laxity but in inventiveness. We need imagination in planning research, not wishful thinking about the results.

REFERENCES

Anderson, T. W.   The use of factor analysis in the statistical analysis of multiple time series. *Psychometrika*, 1963, 28, 1–25.

Ashby, J. D., Ford, D. H., Guerney, B. G., Jr., & Guerney, L. F.   Effects on clients of a reflective and a leading type of psychotherapy. *Psychol. Monogr.*, 1957, 71, No. 7.

Astin, A. W.   The functional autonomy of psychotherapy. *Amer. Psychologist*, 1961, 16, 75–78.

Bandura, A., & Walters, R. H.   *Social learning and personality development.* New York: Holt, Rinehart & Winston, 1963.

Battig, W. F.   Parsimony in psychology. *Psychol. Repts.*, 1962, 11, 555–572.

Berg, I.   Measures before and after therapy. *J. clin. Psychol.*, 1952, 1, 46–50.

Bevan, W.   Subliminal stimulation: A pervasive problem for psychology. *Psychol. Bull.*, 1964, 61, 81–99.

Block, J.   On the number of significant findings to be expected by chance. *Psychometrika*, 1960, 4, 369–380.

Block, J., & Thomas, H.   Is satisfaction with self a measure of adjustment? *J. abnorm. soc. Psychol.*, 1955, 51, 254-259.

Brunswik, E.   *Perception and the representative design of psychological experiments.* Berkeley: Univer. of California Press, 1956.

Campbell, D. T.   Factors relevant to the validity of experiments in social settings. *Psychol. Bull.*, 1957, 54, 297–312.

Campbell, D. T.   From description to experimentation: Interpreting trends in quasi-experiments. In C. W. Harris (Ed.), *Problems in measuring change.* Madison: Univer. of Wisconsin Press, 1963.

Campbell, D. T., & Stanley, J. C.   Experimental designs for research on teaching. In N. L. Gage (Ed.), *Handbook of research on teaching*. Chicago: Rand McNally, 1963. Pp. 171–246.

Canter, R. R.   The use of extended control-group designs in human relations studies. *Psychol. Bull.*, 1951, **48**, 340–347.

Cartwright, D. S.   Effectiveness of psychotherapy: A critique of the spontaneous remission argument. *J. counsel. Psychol.*, 1955, **2**, 290–296.

Cartwright, R. D., & Vogel, J. L.   A comparison of changes in psychoneurotic patients during matched periods of therapy and no therapy. *J. consult. Psychol.*, 1960, **24**, 121–127.

Cronbach, L. J.   Statistical methods applied to Rorschach scores. *Psychol. Bull.*, 1949, **46**, 393–429.

De Charms, R., Levy, J., & Wertheimer, M.   A note on attempted evaluations of psychotherapy. *J. clin. Psychol.*, 1954, **10**, 233–235.

Dollard, J., & Mowrer, O. H.   A method of measuring tension in written documents. *J. abnorm. soc. Psychol.*, 1947, **42**, 3–32.

Exner, J. E.   Therapist attendance as a variable in group psychotherapy. Presented at Midwestern Psychological Assoc., Chicago, 1965.

Eysenck, H. J.   The effects of psychotherapy: An evaluation. *J. consult. Psychol.*, 1952, **16**, 319–324.

Fiedler, F.   A comparison of therapeutic relationships in psychoanalytic, nondirective and Adlerian therapy. *J. consult. Psychol.*, 1950, **14**, 436–445.

Frank, J. D.   Problems of controls in psychotherapy as exemplified by the psychotherapy research project of the Phipps Psychiatric Clinic. In E. A. Rubenstein & M. B. Parloff (Eds.), *Research in psychotherapy*. Washington: Amer. Psychological Assoc., 1959. Pp. 10–26.

Frank, J. D.   *Persuasion and healing*. Baltimore: Johns Hopkins Univer. Press, 1961.

Frank, J. D., Gliedman, L. H., Imber, S. D., Nash, E. H., Jr., & Stone, A. R.   Why patients leave psychotherapy. *Arch. neurol. & Psychiat.*, 1957, **77**, 283–299.

French, J. R. P., Jr.   Experiments in field settings. In L. Festinger & D. Katz (Eds.), *Research methods in the behavioral sciences*. New York: Dryden Press, 1953. Pp. 98–135.

Friedman, H., Becker, R. O., & Bachman, C. H.   Geomagnetic parameters and psychiatric hospital admissions. *Nature*, 1963, **200**, 626–628.

Friedman, H., Becker, R. O., & Bachman, C. H.   Psychiatric ward behavior and geophysical parameters. *Nature*, 1965, **205**, 1050–1052.

Gendlin, E. T.   Client-centered developments and work with schizophrenics. *J. counsel. Psychol.*, 1962, **3**, 205–212.

Gold, H.   Cornell Conference on Therapy. *N.Y.S. J. Med.*, 1946, **46**, 1718.

Gold, H.   Cornell Conference on Therapy. *Amer. J. Med.*, 1954, **17**, 722.

Goldstein, A. P.   Patient's expectancies and nonspecific therapy as a basis for (un)spontaneous remission. *J. clin. Psychol.*, 1960, **16**, 399–403.

Goldstein, A. P. *Therapist-patient expectancies in psychotherapy*. New York: Pergamon Press, 1962.

Group for the Advancement of Psychiatry. *Some observations on controls in psychiatric research*. Report No. 42. New York, 1959.

Grummon, D. L., & Butler, J. M. Another failure to replicate Keet's study, "Two verbal techniques in a miniature counseling situation." *J. abnorm. soc. Psychol.*, 1953, **48**, 597.

Hammond, K. R. Representative vs. systematic design in clinical psychology. *Psychol. Bull.*, 1954, **51**, 150–159.

Harris, C. W. (Ed.) *Problems in measuring change*. Madison: Univer. of Wisconsin Press, 1963.

Heckel, R. V., Wiggins, S. L., & Salzberg, H. C. Joining, encouraging, and intervention as means of extinguishing a delusional system. *J. clin. Psychol.*, 1963, **19**, 344–346.

Heller, K. Experimental analogues of psychotherapy: The clinical relevance of laboratory findings of social influence. *J. ner. ment. Dis.*, 1963, **137**, 420–426.

Heller, K., & Goldstein, A. P. Client dependency and therapist expectancy as relationship maintaining variables in psychotherapy. *J. consult. Psychol.*, 1961, **25**, 371–375.

Heller, K., Myers, R. A., & Kline, L. V. Interviewer behavior as a function of standardized client roles. *J. consult. Psychol.*, 1963, **27**, 117–122.

Hoehn-Saric, R., Frank, J. D., Imber, S. D., Nash, E. H., Stone, A. R., & Battle, C. C. Systematic preparation of patients for psychotherapy. I. Effects on therapy behavior and outcome. *J. psychiat. Res.*, 1964, **2**, 267–281.

Holtzman, W. H. Methodological issues in *P* technique. *Psychol. Bull.*, 1962, **59**, 248–256.

Hybl, A. R., & Stagner, R. Frustration tolerance in relation to diagnosis and therapy. *J. consult. Psychol.*, 1952, **16**, 163–170.

Imber, S. D., Frank, J. D., Nash, E. H., Stone, A. R., & Gliedman, L. H. Improvement and amount of therapeutic contact: An alternative to the use of no-treatment controls in psychotherapy. *J. consult. Psychol.*, 1957, **21**, 309–315.

Kane, F. Clothing worn by outpatients to interviews. *Psychiatric Communications*, 1958, **1**, No. 2.

Kane, F. Clothing worn by an outpatient: A case study. *Psychiatric Communications*, 1959, **2**, No. 2.

Kane, F. The meaning of the form of clothing. *Psychiatric Communications*, 1962, **5**, No. 1.

Kanfer, F. H. Verbal rate, eyeblink, and content in structured psychiatric interviews. *J. abnorm. soc. Psychol.*, 1960, **61**, 341–347.

Keet, C. D. Two verbal techniques in a miniature counseling situation. *Psychol. Monogr.*, 1948, **62**, No. 294.

Kish, L. Selection of the sample. In L. Festinger & D. Katz (Eds.), *Research methods in the behavioral sciences.* New York: Holt, Rinehart & Winston, 1953. Pp. 175–239.

Krasner, L.   The therapist as a social reinforcement machine. In H. H. Strupp & L. Luborsky (Eds.), *Research in psychotherapy.* Washington: Amer. Psychological Assoc., 1962. Pp. 61–94.

Leipold, W. D.   Psychological distance in a dyadic interview as a function of introversion-extroversion, anxiety, social desirability and stress. Unpublished doctoral dissertation, University of North Dakota, 1963.

Levitt, E. E.   Problems of experimental design and methodology in psychopharmacology research. In Report of the Conference on Mental Health Research, French Lick, Indiana. Indianapolis: The Association for the Advancement of Mental Health Research and Education, 1959.

Lindquist, E. F.   *Design and analysis of experiments in psychology and education.* Boston: Houghton, Mifflin, 1953.

Little, K. B., & Shneidman, E. S.   Congruencies among interpretations of psychological test and anamnestic data. *Psychol. Monogr.,* 1959, **73**, No. 6.

Loevinger, J., & Ossorio, A.   Evaluation of therapy by self-report: A paradox. *J. abnorm. soc. Psychol.,* 1959, **58**, 392–394.

Lorr, M., McNair, D. M., Michaux, W. W., & Raskin, A.   Frequency of treatment and change in psychotherapy. *J. abnorm. soc. Psychol.,* 1962, **64**, 281–292.

Luborsky, L.   Psychotherapy. *Annu. Rev. Psychol.,* 1959, **10**, 317–344.

Mandler, G., & Sarason, S. B.   A study of anxiety and learning. *J. abnorm. soc. Psychol.,* 1952, **47**, 166–173.

Martin, B., Lundy, R. M., & Lewin, M. H.   Verbal and GSR responses in experimental interviews as a function of three degrees of "therapist" communication. *J. abnorm. soc. Psychol.,* 1960, **60**, 234–240.

Matarazzo, J. D.   Prescribed behavior therapy: Suggestions from noncontent interview research. In A. J. Bachrach (Ed.), *Experimental foundations of clinical psychology.* New York: Basic Books, 1962. Pp. 471–509.

McConnell, J. V., Cutler, R. L., & McNeil, E. B.   Subliminal stimulation: An overview. *Amer. Psychologist,* 1958, **13**, 229–242.

Merrill, R. M.   On Keet's study, "Two verbal techniques in a miniature counseling situation." *J. abnorm. soc. Psychol.,* 1952, **47**, 722.

Mischel, W.   Preference for delayed reinforcement and social responsibility. *J. abnorm. soc. Psychol.,* 1961, **62**, 1–7.

Mowrer, O. H.   Changes in verbal behavior during psychotherapy. In O. H. Mowrer (Ed.), *Psychotherapy: Theory and research.* New York: Ronald Press, 1953. Pp. 463–545.

Orne, M. T.   On the social psychology of the psychological experiment. *Amer. Psychologist,* 1962, **17**, 776–783.

Pascal, G. R.   *Behavioral change in the clinic—a systematic approach.* New York: Grune & Stratton, 1959.

Pascal, G. R., & Zax, M.   Psychotherapeutics: Success or failure. *J. consult. Psychol.,* 1956, **20**, 325–331.

Patterson, C. H.   Methodological problems in evaluation. *Pers. Guid. J.,* 1960, **270**, 274.

Paul, G. L.   Effects of insight, desensitization, and attention-placebo treatment of anxiety: An approach to outcome research in psychotherapy. Unpublished doctoral dissertation, University of Illinois, 1964.

Peters, H. N., & Jones, F. D.   Evaluation of group psychotherapy by means of performance tests. *J. consult. Psychol.,* 1951, **15**, 363–367.

Powers, B., & Witmer, H.   *An experiment in the prevention of delinquency.* New York: Columbia Univer. Press, 1951.

Reznikoff, M., & Toomey, L. C.   *Evaluation of changes associated with psychiatric treatment.* Springfield, Ill.: Charles C. Thomas, 1959.

Rogers, C. R., & Dymond, R. F.   *Psychotherapy and personality change.* Chicago: Univer. of Chicago Press, 1954.

Rosenzweig, S.   A transvaluation of psychotherapy: A reply to Hans Eysenck. *J. abnorm. soc. Psychol.,* 1954, **49**, 298–304.

Schramm, W., Lyle, J., & Parker, E. B.   *Television in the lives of our children.* Stanford: Stanford Univer. Press, 1961.

Shapiro, A. K.   A contribution to a history of the placebo effect. *Behav. Sci.,* 1960, **5**, 109–135.

Shapiro, M. B., Marks, I. M., & Fox, B.   A therapeutic experiment on phobic and affective symptoms in an individual psychiatric patient. *Brit. J. soc. clin. Psychol.,* 1963, **2**, 81–93.

Shlien, J. M., Mosak, H. H., & Dreikurs, R.   Effect of time limits: A comparison of two therapies. *J. counsel. Psychol.,* 1962, **9**, 31–34.

Sidman, M.   *Tactics of scientific research.* New York: Basic Books, 1960.

Snyder, R., & Sechrest, L.   An experimental study of directive group therapy with defective delinquents. *Amer. J. ment. Def.,* 1959, **63**, 117–123.

Solomon, R. L.   An extension of control-group design. *Psychol. Bull.,* 1949, **46**, 137–150.

Sommer, R.   The distance for comfortable conversation—a further study. *Sociometry,* 1962, **25**, 111–116.

Spence, K. W.   The nature of theory construction in contemporary psychology. *Psychol. Rev.,* 1944, **51**, 47–68.

Spielberger, C. D., & Weitz, H.   Improving the academic performance of anxious college freshmen: A group-counseling approach to the prevention of underachievement. *Psychol. Monogr.,* 1964, **78**, No. 13.

Spielberger, C. D., Weitz, H., & Denny, J. P.   The effects of group counseling on the academic performance of anxious college freshmen. *J. counsel. Psychol.,* 1962, **9**, 195–204.

Strupp, H. H.   Some comments on the future of research in psychotherapy. *Behav. Sci.,* 1960, **1**, 60–71.

Taylor, J. W.   Relationship of success and length in psychotherapy. *J. consult. Psychol.,* 1956, **20**, 332.

Underwood, B. J. *Psychological research.* New York: Appleton-Century-Crofts, 1957.

Watson, P. D., DiMascio, A., Kanter, S. S., Suter, E., & Greenblatt, M.   A note on the influence of climatic factors on psychophysiological investigations. *Psychosom. Med.,* 1957, **19**, 419–423.

Webb, E., Campbell, D. T., Schwartz, R. J., & Sechrest, L.   *Resourceful measurement: Cooperation-free, non-reactive measures in social science.* Chicago: Rand-McNally, 1966, in press.

II

INDIVIDUAL PSYCHOTHERAPY

3

RELATIONSHIP:
INCREASING INTERPERSONAL
ATTRACTION

Viewed from a broad perspective, the historical development of individual psychotherapy may be accurately characterized in terms of the marked diversity of theoretical viewpoints put forth, the varied nature of specific techniques recommended, and, in general, the numerous different paths this development has followed. Basic concepts utilized to explain patient behavior, the time period of the patient's life focused on, the nature of the therapist's interventions, the overt and implicit characteristics of the tasks required of the patient, and the very language of the therapeutic give and take are but a few general examples of such diversity. Agreement on basic aspects of the therapeutic transaction by proponents of different therapeutic "schools" is far less common. On one point, however, the degree of theoretical and operational convergence is marked, namely the centrality accorded the interpersonal relationship between therapist and patient.

Perhaps the most salient feature of both classical and more recently developed forms of psychoanalytic therapy, despite certain basic orientational differences among them, is their overriding focus on transference and countertransference phenomena. The psychoanalytic "law of Talion," which stresses the reciprocity of transference and countertransference, is of similar relevance. The concept of "tele," defined in broader and more inclusive interpersonal terms than transference-countertransference, has long been a central construct in the psychodramatic therapy movement initiated and sustained by Moreno and his co-workers (1945). Snyder's (1961) largely eclectic orientation toward psychotherapy similarly places heaviest emphasis on the interpersonal traffic between therapist and patient. In Snyder's terms, the therapy relationship is viewed as ". . . the reciprocity of various sets of affective attitudes which two or more persons hold toward each other in psychotherapy" (p. 270). Closely similar interpersonal emphases are apparent in Grinker's (1961) transactional model of psychotherapy, Jackson's (1961) interactional approach, Libo's (1957, 1959) focus on therapist-patient attraction, Wolberg's (1954) more directive brand of psychotherapy, and the Rogerian (1961) concern with "unconditional positive regard." Murray (1963) and Shoben (1963) point out that such an interpersonal emphasis emerges even from a close inspection of the actual operations of deconditioning, desensitization or, more generally, "mechanotropic" therapeutic models offered by Wolpe (1958), Lazarus (1961), and Rachman (1959). A score of these examples might readily be noted. It will suffice, perhaps, to place ourselves in agreement with Bordin (1959) who has commented:

> The key to the influence of psychotherapy on the patient is in his relationship with the therapist. Wherever psychotherapy is accepted as a significant enterprise, this statement is so widely subscribed to as to become trite. Virtually all efforts to theorize about psychotherapy are intended to describe and explain what attributes of the interactions between the therapist and the patient will account for whatever behavior change results (p. 235).

It is clear then that the vast majority of theoretical approaches to psychotherapeutic treatment, despite their marked diversity on other grounds, come together in the extent of their common emphasis on interpersonal constructs mediating between patient and therapist. However, the specific nature of these constructs remains unclear, and hence their more effective use is inhibited. Transference, countertransference, interaction, transaction, relationship—these are the primary terms of concern here. Not only do they differ from one another in ways which remain to be clarified, but different writers use the same term to include differing ranges of phenomena. As Snyder (1961) notes with regard to "relationship," the construct of major interest to the present chapter, "The importance of the relationship is continually mentioned in the literature, although different authors mean quite different things by the term" (p. 271). Loevinger (1963) underscores the vagueness and multiplicity of meanings associated with relationship. She notes:

> Relationship, interaction, transaction: in the child guidance clinic these are the terms for that process in which, as Gillispie says, "everything blends

into everything and nothing may ever be defined." . . . in one or another cognate term relationship . . . is the cliche of the child guidance clinic (p. 246).

We are thus faced with a dilemma. We find wide agreement on the centrality to be accorded the therapist-patient relationship in the overall therapeutic process, yet there is much definitional diversity and lack of agreement concerning the specific nature and implications of this relationship. The task demanded seems clear; increased understanding and greater usefulness in the direction of therapeutic outcomes should follow from clarification and specification of the relationship construct. The present chapter will attempt a first approximation toward such clarification and specification by briefly examining ways in which the relationship construct has already been defined by relevant therapy research, and then by proposing in some detail a series of relationship hypotheses based upon findings from nonclinical research domains.

RELATIONSHIP RESEARCH—OUTCOME STUDIES

With regard to "outcome" investigations of relationship, a small but concurring number of studies have examined the widely, but not unanimously (e.g., Eaton, 1959) held belief that a "favorable" or "good quality" therapist-patient relationship is essential for a positive therapeutic outcome. In perhaps the earliest study of this type, Bown (1954) focused on the patient-therapist relationship developed in 20 sessions of nondirective therapy with six patients. Q-sort ratings of the quality of the relationship were obtained from each patient-therapist pair at four points during treatment. For therapy characterized as successful, in terms of independent outcome ratings and continuance, Bown reports that "the quality of the actual relationship as perceived by both therapist and client was substantially different from the quality of the relationship in unsuccessful therapy" (p. 43). It is of additional interest to note that the client's perception of the relationship more accurately distinguished between the successful and unsuccessful cases than did those of the therapist. Of further relevance is Bown's finding that the degree of similarity or congruence in the client's and therapist's perception of their relationship was positively correlated with rated success. The greater the agreement on the nature of their relationship, the greater the degree of rated improvement. As is true of other pioneering studies, the rudimentary nature of Bown's measures and the small size of his sample suggest caution in the generalization of his findings.

However, confirming evidence from other investigators was not long in coming.

Parloff's (1961) research effort toward this end was conducted in a group psychotherapy context. Relationship was operationally defined in terms of Fiedler's (1950, 1953) 75-item Q-sort deck. This deck consists of 25 items aimed at the therapist's ability to communicate with and understand the patient, 25 items describing the "emotional distance" between therapist and patient, and 25 items dealing with the area of "status" as reflected in the therapist's behavior toward the patient. The sortings by observers who sat in on the meetings of the three participating groups were completed for each of the 21 patients as paired with his therapist. These sortings or arrays were then correlated against the Fiedler ideal therapeutic relationship standard. The higher the correlation with the standard, the "better" the relationship between patient and therapist was assumed to be. Parloff's change or outcome criteria were a series of scales purportedly measuring patient comfort, effectiveness and objectivity. These scales were administered to each patient, to other members of each patients' group, and to the research staff before or early in therapy and again at the end of the 20-session course. Results indicate a significant degree of association between the quality of the therapeutic relationships on the one hand and certain of the change criteria on the other. More specifically, as Parloff notes,

> The data indicate that the better the patient-psychotherapist relationship, the greater the symptomatic relief experienced by the patient, the more likely it was that fellow group members would describe the patient as having become more dominant (leader), and the greater the increase in objectivity attributed to the patient by the research staff (p. 35).

A study conducted by Hunt, Ewing, LaForge, and Gilbert (1959) in a university counseling center also sought to examine the therapeutic relationship as a possible influence on therapeutic outcome. Six therapists and approximately 200 patients participated in therapy of varying lengths during the two-year period of data collection. Relationship was defined in terms of (1) the degree of correspondence between each therapist's description of his clients and his description of his own ideal self, and (2) the degree of correspondence between each therapist's description of his various clients and his description of his ideal client. Thus, relationship defined in this manner reflects only the therapists' viewpoints.

The outcome criteria employed were continuance in therapy and independent ratings on the Hunt-Kogan Movement Scale (Hunt & Kogan, 1950). Hunt et al.'s results indicate a significant relationship between their first derived relationship score and patient improvement for two of the six participating therapists—and a positive but non-significant association with outcome for their second index of quality of relationship. A number of factors may be responsible for the more equivocal nature of these results, compared with those reported by Bown and Parloff. It will suffice to note that the differing and more inferential nature of Hunt et al.'s definition of relationship may well be one such factor.

Gendlin, Jenny, and Shlien (1960) report a study bearing on treatment outcome and the therapist-patient relationship. Quality of relationship and patient change were operationalized in terms of therapist ratings obtained after the seventh and final therapy sessions for each of the 39 participating patients. The particular emphasis of this study was on the outcome implications of the extent of patient "focus on the relationship" during therapy. More specifically, results confirmed the hypothesis that outcome ratings are significantly associated with the extent to which the therapist rated his patient as (1) finding his relationship with the therapist relevant to his general interpersonal difficulties, (2) deriving from the relationship itself new and significant experiences, and (3) expressing his feelings directly rather than reporting them. Once again, therefore, relationship considerations—measured in ways differing from earlier reported studies—appear to relate significantly to the outcome criterion. Concurring findings pointing toward this general conclusion are reported by Holt and Luborsky (1952), Sapolsky (1965), Truax (1961), and Van der Veen (1961).

We do not attempt to be exhaustive in our coverage of relationship outcome studies. Our dual reason for their inclusion is already evident. In a manner strikingly parallel to the *theoretical* status of the relationship construct noted earlier, research evidence is generally unequivocal in its demonstration of a positive influence of the therapy relationship upon treatment outcome. Equally apparent, however, is the scant degree of overlap in the various operational definitions of "relationship."

RELATIONSHIP RESEARCH—PROCESS STUDIES

Process-oriented relationship studies reaffirm the generalization that as a mediating influence relationship appears crucial but its research definitions are variable to the point of being nearly study-specific. One early exception to this tendency for each investigator to define "relationship" in somewhat different measurement terms is Fiedler's Q-sort deck, described earlier in connection with Parloff's (1961) investigation. Fiedler's (1950, 1953) pioneering relationship studies are particularly well known, and need not detain us here. In general terms he provided evidence to indicate that:

. . . all psychotherapies have as their effective core the interpersonal relationship rather than the specific methods of treatment, and that the relationship is created by the therapist who must convey feelings to the client rather than concentrate on method (p. 285).

In addition to Parloff's and Fiedler's relationship studies, Quinn (1950) and Heine (1950) have made fruitful use of this early relationship operationalization. Quinn's results suggested, as had Fiedler's, that it is the therapist and not the patient who plays the major role in determining the nature of their consequent relationship. Heine asked patients who had been treated by therapists of differing orientations to describe the changes they had experienced as a result of therapy and the aspects of the treatment to which they attributed these changes. His results indicated that patients of therapists from different "schools" describe the factors leading to change in terms of different treatment methods but also in terms of the same treatment relationship.

In a series of investigations reported by Ashby, Ford, Guerney, and Guerney (1957), relationship was defined in different terms. The investigators constructed two questionnaires, The Client Personal Reaction Questionnaire (CPRQ) and The Therapist Personal Reaction Questionnaire (TPRQ). Each instrument consisted of two subscales, one reflecting positive and one negative reactions toward the therapy and the therapist (CPRQ) or the client (TPRQ). The main theme of this group of studies involved a series of comparisons between reflective and leading types of psychotherapy. Among the major findings was an interaction effect in which the clients' views of the therapeutic relationship were a joint function of individual characteristics of their therapists and the kind of therapy administered. Goldstein and Heller (1960) used essentially the same relationship items in a study examining the influence of therapist role expectations (regarding their own anticipated within-therapy behavior) upon the relationship subsequently formed. In addition to modified CPQR's and TPRQ's, an analogous instrument, the Supervisor's Reaction Questionnaire (SRQ), was completed by an observer who viewed each therapeutic interview.

These supervisor relationship ratings varied significantly in a positive manner with the degree of therapist model expectancy* and in a negative manner with the extent to which the therapist anticipated he would behave in a nurturant manner.

Snyder (1961) placed heaviest emphasis on affective components in his measures aimed at relationship. Using several of Bown's and Ashby et al.'s items and many of his own, he constructed two related scales. Termed the Client's Affect Scale and the Therapist's Affect Scale, they aimed at identifying quality of relationship in terms of the participants' evolving feelings toward one another. Snyder's major finding was a highly significant positive relationship between these two sets of scores over the course of therapy. He comments:

It is evident that transference and countertransference are highly related. Racker described this relationship as the "Law of Talion," which we have here demonstrated statistically, perhaps for the first time (p. 239).

A different approach is reflected in studies by Libo (1957) and Heller and Goldstein (1961) in which relationship was given measurement expression in terms of interpersonal attraction. Operationally, the instrument involved was Libo's Picture Impressions Test (1959), a projective test consisting of four cards illustrating therapylike situations to which the client is requested to respond in a manner analogous to TAT administration. The relationship score is expressed in terms of attraction to the therapist and the therapy process as judged from the protocols. In Libo's investigation, the test was administered to a series of patients immediately following their initial psychotherapeutic interview. As he hypothesized, the attraction-relationship score predicted with a statistically significant degree of accuracy whether or not a patient would return for his second interview. The more attracted a patient was, in Picture Impressions terms, the more likely he was to return. In the Heller and Goldstein (1961) study, support was obtained for the prediction of a significant positive correlation between quality of the relationship as viewed by the patient (Picture Impressions Attraction Score), and (1) patient pretherapy dependency and (2) patient over-therapy movement toward independence. The interpersonal attraction construct, with its deep roots in social psychological research, will be examined in considerable depth later in this

---

* A therapist who expects neither to judge nor to evaluate his patients; to be a permissive listener; to be neither protective nor critical (Apfelbaum, 1958; Goldstein & Heller, 1960).

chapter as we attempt a start at reformulation and clarification of "relationship" largely in interpersonal attraction terms.

Other definitional emphases may be abstracted from further relationship studies. Coons (1957) and Mendelsohn (1957) stress, as did Snyder, strong positive affect between therapist and patient as the heart of a good therapeutic relationship. Raush and Bordin (1957) in partial contrast underscore commitment to therapy, effort to understand, and spontaneity. Mellinger's (1956) research describes relationship in terms of interpersonal trust, and similarly, Jourard and Lasakow (1958) point to freedom in self-disclosure. Others (Patterson, 1958; Rosenthal, 1955; Schrier, 1953) have defined relationship for research purposes in terms of reciprocal need patterns of patient and therapist. Still other definitions of the therapy relationship are provided by theoretical discussions of the therapist-patient interaction. Rotter (1954), for example, suggests that the favorableness of the relationship as viewed by the patient is a direct function of the amount of positive reinforcement the patient has received from the therapist or has expectations of receiving. Frank (1959) and Goldstein (1962) have emphasized congruence or mutuality of therapist and patient expectations as the major foundation on which the relationship rests and, much earlier, Adler (1924) stressed mutuality of goals and goal-directions as the crux of the therapy relationship. Haley (1963) and Shands (1960), both speaking from the perspective of communications theory, have discussed the therapist-patient interaction in terms of symmetrical and complementary communicative relationships. Collier (1957) has taken yet a different tack, and characterized the relationship in terms of his theory of "stress-defense dynamics."

Our largely representative samples of theoretical and research material rather clearly converge. Relationship does indeed appear to be a most central and powerful psychotherapeutic variable. Of what consequence, one may ask, is the diversity and frequent ambiguity of the various theoretical and research definitions of relationship? Since research has unequivocally demonstrated its centrality, why need one be concerned about a lack of precision and agreement in "its" definition? As our initial chapter indicated, much more is at stake here than just "intellectual neatness." Our view of contemporary psychotherapy is of a process that is clearly inefficient in several major respects. Length of treatment, number of patients seen, and types of persons "admitted" to patient status are but some of the major dimensions of inefficiency. If greater precision in definition and use of major psychotherapeutic forces can be achieved, treatment can be shortened, more patients can participate, and a broader range of persons can be viewed as acceptable in terms of their potential for change. Further, and perhaps of greater consequence, the development of completely new approaches to altering patient behavior may be encouraged. It is with this as our motivation that the following start at reconceptualization of the meaning and therapeutic uses of relationship is offered. Above all we hope that this start at redefinition and our suggestions for new therapeutic usages to which the therapist-patient relationship may be put will encourage others to consider and examine psychotherapy from a perspective unrestrained by the parameters of present day "standard" psychotherapeutic practices and traditions.

SPECIFICATION OF RELEVANT PATIENTS

The psychotherapeutic relationship is viewed in the remainder of this chapter in terms of a variable of long-standing interest to those involved in social-psychological and personality research. This variable is interpersonal attraction. Of equal relevance, as we demonstrate, is a prime consequent of interpersonal attraction, that is, interpersonal influence. Our major contention is that psychotherapeutic efficiency may be markedly enhanced by increasing the degree of therapist influence over the patient. Manipulation of a major component of the therapy relationship, that is, patient attraction to the therapist, is offered as the primary means for increasing the level of therapist influence. Stated otherwise, *our general proposition is that by heightening the favorableness of patient attraction toward his therapist, to that degree does the patient become more receptive to therapist influence attempts.* One major task remains, however, before we examine (1) the relatedness of attraction and influence, and (2) our extrapolated hypotheses regarding attraction manipulation in the therapeutic context, to specify more precisely with what classes of patients we are concerned. For what types of patients is increased receptivity to therapist influence a desirable and often necessary objective?

Many years ago, Freud (1957) observed:

When are we to begin making our communications to the patient? When is the moment for disclosing to him the hidden meaning of the ideas that occur to him, and for initiating him into the postulates and technical procedures of analysis? The answer to this can only be: not until an effective transference has been established in the patient, a proper rapport with him. It remains the first aim of the treatment to attach him to it and to the person of the doctor. To ensure this, nothing need be done but to give him time.

If one exhibits a serious interest in him, *carefully clears away the resistances that crop up at the beginning* and avoids making certain mistakes, he will of himself form such an attachment. . . . (p. 140) (italics ours).

To paraphrase Freud, the early psychoanalytic view held that clearly favorable feelings on the patient's part toward the therapist are a precondition to patient receptivity to therapist communications and "instructions"; such patient feelings, Freud held, would be a natural consequent of such factors as the passage of time, therapist interest, and *working through of initial resistances*. However, from its very beginnings, and continuing unabated to the present, psychoanalytic and most other forms of psychotherapeutic treatment have been exceedingly restrictive in the kinds of persons admitted to therapeutic participation. Whether by diagnostic classification, institutional status, overt behavior, chronological age, or other criteria, a great many types of persons are clearly stamped "excludable" by contemporary psychotherapeutic lore. With regard to these "other criteria for exclusion," Schofield's (1964) survey of large and representative samples of psychiatrists, psychologists and social workers practicing psychotherapy is revealing. He comments:

What is the identification of the emotionally ill person whom the psychotherapists do not expect to be able to reach effectively through therapeutic conversation? Extreme youth (under age 15) or age (over 50) appears to be undesirable. A widowed or divorced status apparently does not contribute to an attractive patient. Limited education (less than high school) or too much education (postgraduate training) is equally rejected by social workers, psychologists, and psychiatrists. Employment in services, agriculture, fishery, forestry, semi-skilled or unskilled labor is not associated with being a "preferred risk."

. . . there are pressures toward a systematic selection of patients, pressures that are perhaps subtle and unconscious in part and that, in part, reflect theoretical biases common to all psychotherapists. These selective forces tend to restrict the efforts of the bulk of social workers, psychologists, and psychiatrists to clients who present the "Yavis" syndrome—young, attractive, verbal, intelligent, and successful (p. 133).

In broader terms, the basis of this exclusion process seems to be therapist inability or anticipation of inability to, as Freud put it, "clear away the resistances that crop up at the beginning." Thus, by a sort of fiat based on an admixture of clinical reports and therapeutic traditions, persons labeled psychopathic, sociopathic, delinquent, antisocial, unmotivated, unsuitable, nonverbal, or "involuntary" in other ways rarely find their way into psychotherapeutic participation. The number of contemporary therapists and therapy researchers who have responded to this lowering of therapeutic efficiency via categorical exclusion of certain classes of patients by offering constructive means for broadening the applicability of psychotherapy is remarkably small (e.g., Eissler, 1949; Gendlin et al., 1960; Slack, 1960; Strean, 1961).

Although our relationship hypotheses will aim in part at such "involuntary" patients, it is important to note that our hypothesized means of increasing patient attraction to the therapist and receptivity to his influence attempts are not aimed solely, or even primarily, at the "involuntary" patient candidate. Not only can therapeutic efficiency be enhanced by causing more *kinds* of persons to be accessible to the therapist's efforts, but the reciprocal goals of shortened duration and more patients seen in an absolute sense can be partially met to the extent that the crucial therapeutic steps through which a patient must pass on his way to successful termination can be telescoped in time. Freud's early dictum, as well as the theoretical and research material presented in earlier sections of this chapter, concur in pointing to the formation of a satisfactory therapist-patient relationship as one of the most important of these crucial therapeutic steps. Thus the great mass of *participating* psychotherapy patients, whose early session behavior may be accurately described as of varying degrees of resistiveness, ambivalence, or equivocation with regard to continued participation and openness to therapist influence, may participate in more rapid and perhaps, more effective psychotherapy to the extent that procedures are instituted to moderate or eliminate this initial resistance, ambivalence, or equivocation. Strupp (1962) speaks of the same issue:

    ... from the beginning of any psychotherapy, the therapist must succeed in sparking strivings in the patient—sometimes called "the will to recovery," "motivation for therapy," the striving for "self-realization," and the like which enable him to cooperate with the therapist and to oppose the neurotic forces within himself. Undoubtedly, no single combination of attributes will yield the answer. Much would depend, one suspects, on the patient's capacity to identify with the therapist as a "good parent." As yet, we know little about the dynamics of this process, in patients or in children, but it may well turn out to be the fulcrum upon which effective therapy turns (p. 583).

In a sense we have proposed here what might be considered a continuum of patient "involuntariness." At one extreme one might find the individual who is literally sentenced to psychotherapy by a court. His view of the therapist and therapeutic participation is likely to be singularly negative. The greater punishment of a period in prison may serve as his sole motivation for attendance at an initial therapy interview. Reversing the approach and avoidance gradients, the (likely hypothetical) patient at the voluntary end of the continuum is both willing and able with regard to therapeutic participation. Willing in the sense of genuine motivation for change; able in the sense of complete absence of the several diagnostic, behavioral, or intellectual "liabilities" currently used as bases for exclusion.

The great bulk of patients remaining would be distributed along this continuum, although our hunch would be of a tendency toward a bunching up on the ambivalent, equivocal half of the distribution. As Strupp (1964) has noted in this regard (and also of relevance to our hypothesized manipulations of patient attraction),

> Every neurotic patient is unconsciously committed to maintain the status quo, and psychotherapy, particularly if aimed at confronting the patient with his inner conflicts, proceeds against the obstacle of powerful unconscious resistances. Therefore, unless there is a strong conscious desire to be helped and to collaborate with the therapist, the odds against a favorable outcome may be insuperable (p. 6).

It is then the fully involuntary, the quasi-involuntary, the resistive, and the ambivalent patient with whom the present chapter is concerned.

Clara Thompson (1954) has accurately observed that before the 1920's the generally agreed on *therapeutic* use of transference involved attempting to make the patient more attracted to the therapist so that he might (directively) have more influence upon the patient. After that date relationship or transference, to be used *therapeutically,* became more a matter of something for patient and therapist to inspect jointly as it were, as it reflected the patient's other (real life) interpersonal relations. We do not take exception to this major psychotherapeutic development. Except for the crucial beginning stages, the hypotheses we propose do not suggest that psychotherapy need become more directive or authoritarian, that patient attraction need be manipulatively increased, or that the therapist's influence must be enhanced. However, in the beginning make or break sessions, for the classes of patients relevant to this chapter, these are precisely our general recommendations. This same theme is reflected more generally in Frank's (1959) observation:

> It might be objected that the therapist's direct use of influence tends to intensify the patient's dependency and thereby impede genuine progress. There is no question as to the desirability of helping patients to independence,

but the real problem is to determine when this goal is better achieved by freely accepting their initial dependency and using it, and when by resisting this attitude from the start. It is easy for patient and physician to become absorbed in a struggle over this issue, to the detriment of therapeutic movement. For example, sometimes giving a patient a symptomatic remedy he requests may improve the therapeutic relationship and permit discussion to move to more fruitful topics, whereas withholding it impedes all progress. In order to become genuinely self-reliant, a child needs to feel securely dependent on his parents. From this he develops the confidence in the dependability of others which enables him to forge ahead. The same consideration may often apply to patients (pp. 38-39).

Heller and Goldstein's (1961) finding noted earlier, that the more attracted a patient is toward his therapist the more (1) dependent he is pretherapy, and (2) the more independent he grows over therapy, would seem to support this contention. Of course, the position just offered in favor of active, early session manipulation of the patient's contribution to the therapeutic relationship does not constitute *evidence* for such an approach with the classes of patients we have specified as relevant to this chapter, any more than does clinical lore provide *evidence* in support of the prevalent opposing viewpoint. It is clear that the therapeutic value of the kinds of attraction-manipulating interventions that our hypotheses propose must first be established in a research context. Let us now turn to investigations of the general attraction-influence relationship and then to our extrapolated research hypotheses.

INTERPERSONAL ATTRACTION AND INTERPERSONAL INFLUENCE

The notion that A's interpersonal attraction toward B increases A's receptivity to influence by B is, research evidence aside for the moment, a significant point of convergence among four major contemporary cognitive theories. We refer here to the "balance" theories offered by Osgood and Tannenbaum (1955), Festinger (1957), Heider (1958), and Newcomb (1943, 1956). The first authors, for example, observe that "attitude change for a given object of judgment in the direction of the assertion is an approximately linear function of the favorableness of the original attitude toward the other object of judgment with which it is associated" (p. 54). Festinger has described this relationship in terms of cognitive dissonance reduction; Heider in terms of change toward balanced states; and Newcomb has viewed the attraction-influence alignment as a "strain toward symmetry." Of relevance for our purposes is the common theoretical implication that for A to be attracted to B and yet be nonreceptive to B's influence attempts causes more imbalance, asymmetry, or cognitive dissonance than would A's acceptance of B's influence efforts. When A is attracted to B and is simultaneously nonreceptive to B's influence, thus experiencing imbalance, a major means, as we shall see, of imbalance, dissonance, or strain reduction is in terms of an increase in receptivity to B's influence. It is of more than passing interest to note that Levy (1963), using the same theoretical material, comments:

> . . . the more favorable the source is regarded, the more favorable will be the consideration given any assertions by it. . . . The implication for psychotherapy is that for an interpretation to be given favorable consideration by the patient, the therapist must be favorably regarded (p. 267).

One of the earliest experimental tests of this general attraction-influence relationship is reported by Back (1951). A particularly salient aspect of this study is Back's success at inducing interpersonal attraction in three distinctly different ways; that is, attraction based on (1) personal liking, (2) task importance, and (3) group prestige. More specifically, his subjects were constituted into randomly assigned pairs, each of his seven experimental conditions having assigned to it ten such pairs. In one condition, the "negative treatment," all three bases for attraction were minimized. The other six conditions were attempts at inducing high or low levels of attraction based on the three attraction sets. Thus, with personal liking as the basis for attraction, the low attraction premeeting instructions contained the statement: "We tried to find a partner with whom you could work best. Of course, we couldn't find anybody who would fit the description exactly, but we found a fellow who corresponded to the main points, and you probably will like him." In contrast, members of high attraction pairs for this set of conditions were told: "Of course, we usually cannot match people the way they want, but for you we have found almost exactly the person you described. As a matter of fact, the matching was as close as we had expected to happen once or twice in the study, if at all. You'll like him a lot. What's more, he described a person very much like you. . . . you should get along extremely well." In an analogous manner, in the high and low attraction conditions based on task importance, the importance to the subjects of task results was varied. In the group prestige conditions attraction was varied in terms of amount of emphasis on the value of belonging to the group. The experimental task was one in which each subject, before meeting his partner, was given a set of three pictures about which he was to write a story. Although each subject was led to believe that he and his partner had responded to the same set of pictures, there were in fact slight differences between the sets. After completion of the initial story-writing, the subjects were brought together for a discussion which was structured as an opportunity to improve their own stories. Back notes, "necessity for influence was specifically denied." After the pair had met, each member, working apart once again, rewrote his story as he wished. Influence, the major dependent variable, was reliably measured in terms of changes from the preliminary to the final story which were in the direction of the subject's partner's preliminary story. Results demonstrated significantly more influence attempts and successful influence in the high attraction conditions. As Back observes,

> . . . the results show that an increase in cohesiveness [attraction], *independent of its nature,* will produce the following: . . . in the highly cohesive groups the discussion was more effective in that it produced influence, that is, group members changed more toward the partner's positions than they did in the less cohesive groups (p. 22).

Burdick and Burnes (1958) supply additional evidence. A group of seventeen subjects was gathered for the purpose of hearing a speaker discuss a case study of a juvenile delinquent and, as a second discussion topic, the proper dress for college men on campus. Before the speaker's arrival each subject read the case history and responded to a questionnaire eliciting opinions on the two topics. For example, they were required to indicate whether the boy himself or the boy's environment should be considered responsible for a crime he had committed. Subsequently, the speaker "spoke pleasantly" for an hour about the case that each S had read, taking the position that the boy's environment was totally responsible for the crime. The subjects again responded to the questionnaires and also to a scale indicating how well they liked the speaker. The speaker then returned to the group, supposedly to discuss the second topic, college clothing. Instead, he proceeded to berate the Ss for their docility and submissiveness when confronted by an authority. In general, he attempted to make himself disliked with no reference to the discussion topics. At the end of the second hour the Ss again filled out the opinion questionnaires and the one on their liking for the speaker. Results on the two administrations of this last questionnaire indicated that after the first hour 14 of the 17 Ss had strong feelings of liking for the speaker and that after the second hour 14 of them had decreased in their positive feelings toward him. Thus the initial experimental induction of liking for the speaker and the subsequent attempt to reduce these feelings were successful. Regarding the influence attempt, as represented by the opinion questionnaire, eight of the Ss shifted in their opinions, from premeeting to first hour, in the direction of the speaker's position (environmental responsibility). At the end of the second (dislike-induction) hour, during which no discussion of the topics took place, six Ss changed from their first hour opinions, five of them in a direction away from that originally presented by the speaker. Thus although the main effect of interest here was demonstrated for only a portion of the sample, it is of special interest to note that those subjects whose opinions did change under "like" and/or "dislike" inductions were those who were also high on need affiliation. Low need affiliation Ss were apparently unresponsive to the influence attempt under both conditions. The investigators conclude:

> . . . the attractiveness of the person serving as a source of communication was directly manipulated. Subjects who reported that they 'liked' him tended to change their opinions toward more agreement with him. When they were subsequently induced to "dislike" him, they tended to change their opinions toward greater disagreement. Evidence is presented that this change of opinion is related to need for affiliation (pp. 369-370).

Two verbal conditioning investigations conducted by Sapolsky (1960) also provide evidence bearing on the attraction-influence relationship. Of special interest in these otherwise identical studies is the fact that in one, subject attraction to the influence source was experimentally induced by using Back's (1951) procedures. In the second study attraction was established by naturalistic pairing of compatible subjects and experimenters. With both types of pairing for attraction, Sapolsky found substantial support for a positive effect of interpersonal attraction on acceptance of influence. Let us examine these studies more closely. Thirty subjects, randomly assigned to receive instructions designating the experimenter as either attractive or unattractive, participated in the first study. The same experimenter was used for both conditions. Before being introduced to E, each S was informed by the investigator that this was an experiment that required the two persons who would be working together to be congenial. The subjects then took the FIRO-B (Schutz, 1958), a scale requiring ratings of behavior which one desires to find in social situations. Ss assigned to the high-attraction condition were then told, "Usually, we can't match people exactly, but in your case this will be possible." In contrast, low-attraction Ss were instructed, "Usually we can match people quite well, but in your case we're going to have some trouble. It is going to take too long to locate somebody for you, so I am assigning you to Miss C. She may irritate you a little, but do the best you can." All subjects then met individually with E and participated in a standardized verbal conditioning task. The task involved presenting S with a series of verbs in combination with one of six personal pronouns; S then had to construct sentences with each of these two word sets. For *all* subjects, after 20 base rate trials, "E provided reinforcement by saying 'mmm-hmm' in a flat, unemotional tone at the end of any sentence that began with the 'I' or 'We' pronouns." Following the conditioning trials, as a check on the effectiveness of the attraction inducing instructions, a self-anchored sociometric scale (Gardner & Thompson, 1956) was administered to all Ss. This check demonstrated that the two groups of Ss did in fact differ significantly in their attraction to E. Results indicated a similarly significant difference between the two groups in terms of response to the conditioning trials. Ss in the high-attraction condition used the reinforced pronouns significantly more frequently than did low-attraction Ss.

Thirty (new) subjects and five experimenters took part in the second study. All responded to the FIRO-B scale described above. Rather than experimentally inducing attraction, as in the first study, each E was paired with three compatible and three incompatible Ss based on the FIRO-B scale. In this "naturalistic" manner two 15-subject groups were constituted—one highly compatible and one highly incompatible with its Es. In all other respects the study followed procedures identical to those already noted. Once again, a subsequent sociometric check demonstrated the success of the pairing procedure for establishing levels of attraction, and, also once again, results indicated significantly different conditioning levels for the attracted and unattracted Ss. Thus the relation between interpersonal attraction and receptivity to influence is given added support. Sapolsky (1960) concludes:

> Krasner has pointed out the similarity between the verbal reinforcement by E in conditioning procedures and the therapist's use of "mmm-hmm" in the psychotherapy setting. The findings of the present study suggest that the subtle cues provided by a therapist's use of "mmm-hmm" are likely to be effective only when the interpersonal relationship between him and the patient is positive or compatible (p. 246).

Very substantial additional support for this attraction-influence relationship is provided by a number of studies in the group dynamics area. Of particular interest here are studies of intermember influence and group cohesiveness, the latter variable being characteristically defined in terms of interpersonal attraction among group members.* In one of the earliest of these several investigations Festinger, Schacter, and Back (1950) examined the relationship between group cohesiveness in a housing project (how attractive the group was for its members) and how effectively a group standard relevant to the functioning of the group was maintained. A correlation of .72 was obtained between these two variables. Stated otherwise, the greater the attractiveness of the group for its members, the greater the amount of influence the group could successfully exert on each member.

French and Snyder (1959) sought to identify some of the factors that determine the influence a noncommissioned officer actually has on the performance of his men. In particular, they focused on the degree to which the officer was liked by his men. As a first step, questionnaire information was obtained from several Air Force crews regarding their personal feelings toward their officers including the "degree of liking." With this serving as the basic pretask information, each officer and three of his subordinates participated in a two-condition experiment. The first was designed so that the officer would initially disagree with his men concerning a problem solution which the subordinate members of the group had agreed upon. The interactions of the four-member groups were recorded and reliable information was obtained regarding how much influence the officer attempted and the degree to which his influence attempts were successful. Results indicated that the well-liked officers, in comparison to those less well-liked, more frequently sought to influence the subordinate group members and more frequently succeeded in doing so. The second experimental condition was structured so that it was possible to hold constant from group to group the amount of influence attempted by the officer. In essence, this condition was instituted to answer the question, "Would the better-liked officers be more successful in their influence even if they made precisely the same number and kind of influence attempts as the less well-liked officers?" Every officer was physically separated from his group but communicated to the other members by written notes asking them to modify their behavior in certain ways. These notes were identical for all groups. The study's findings revealed that such a standardized influence attempt, when apparently coming from

---

*Chapter 9 explores the group cohesiveness variable in considerable detail, particularly as it offers implications for the functioning of therapy groups.

a better-liked officer, resulted in greater actual influence than the same attempt coming from a less well-liked officer. In short, the French and Snyder study falls directly in line with the several investigations noted earlier: interpersonal attraction increases receptivity to interpersonal influence. Perhaps at this point it is sufficient to note that a number of other group dynamics investigations provide unequivocal support for this relationship (Gerard, 1954; Gordon, 1952; Newcomb, 1943; Seashore, 1954; Rasmussen & Zander, 1954). The basic relationship on which our hypotheses rest having been established, we can now proceed to a detailed presentation and examination of these hypotheses. The studies already discussed made a small beginning at clarifying the "stuff attraction is made of." Our hypotheses will aim at further clarification of this type, building toward a start at an attraction-based definition of the therapy relationship.

COGNITIVE DISSONANCE THEORY

Our discussion of the relationship between interpersonal attraction and influence receptivity touched on the relevance to this relationship of a series of recently developed cognitive "balance" theories, one of which was Festinger's (1957) theory of cognitive dissonance. Since the three hypotheses to be developed in the present chapter represent attempts to arouse dissonance in the classes of patients we have identified as relevant to these hypotheses and to channel the means by which such dissonance is reduced, a closer look at the core postulates of cognitive dissonance theory is required.* Festinger defines cognitive dissonance, in a broad sense, as a psychological tension having motivational characteristics. The theory speaks primarily about the conditions that arouse dissonance in an individual and the various ways in which dissonance reduction may take place. The focus of the theory is on cognitive elements and the relationship between them. Cognitive elements are items of information or cognitions about oneself, one's behavior, or one's environment. Two cognitions are said to be consonant if they are mutually consistent, that is, if one follows from, implies, or is compatible with the other. Knowledge that one does not wish to participate in psychotherapy, or marked reluctance regarding such participation, and participation in a resistive manner

---

* It is of interest to note in passing that to date only a single therapy investigation has made use of cognitive dissonance theory as a basis for its hypotheses. We refer to Bergin's (1962) study of therapist interpretations as dissonance-arousing messages.

are consonant elements. Consonance would also be represented by the cognition that one is highly attracted to the therapist and behaviors indicative of openness to therapist influence attempts. Dissonance is said to exist when two cognitive elements, occurring together, are mutually inconsistent; that is, one follows from the obverse of the other or is incompatible with the other. The cognition that one does not wish to participate in psychotherapy, or marked reluctance regarding such participation, and participation in a nonresistive manner are dissonant elements. A low level of patient attraction to the therapist would be dissonant with a high level of responsiveness to therapist influence attempts. The central hypothesis of the theory holds that the presence of dissonance gives rise to pressure to reduce that dissonance, and the strength of this pressure is a direct function of the magnitude of the existing dissonance. Thus, with reference to the involuntary or resistive patient, the theory would predict that the less he wished to participate in psychotherapy and the more in fact he participated in a nonresistive manner, the more dissonance he would experience and the greater the pressure to reduce it. In contrast, the less he wished to participate in psychotherapy and the more his participation was resistive in nature, the less dissonance he would experience and the less pressure would exist for dissonance reduction. It is this state of affairs that describes the consonance-dissonance status of the patients we are concerned with in this chapter. To the extent that termination of therapy is made difficult, early session resistive behavior is compatible with the wish not to participate in psychotherapy. In broadest terms, this statement may be considered an initial rationale suggesting dissonance *arousal* as the major manipulation for the experimental test of our three relationship hypotheses.

The patient with whom we are concerned, who is coming for psychotherapeutic treatment on an involuntary or quasi-voluntary basis and is resistive to participation in any of the ways characteristically considered therapeutic, may be said, to the extent that he continues to come for treatment, to be physically participating in psychotherapy, but not in a change-enhancing manner. The therapist, to return to our earlier quotation from Freud, has been fully or partially unsuccessful in working through the patient's early resistances. Intervention at this point needs to be directed toward two ends: (1) continuing his physical participation (keep him coming) and (2) increasing his psychological participation (by decreasing resistiveness and increasing receptivity to therapist influence attempts). Not to intervene at this early point in psychotherapy with such patients is, from our perspective, equivalent to accepting the inevitability of this therapy-lengthening, inefficiency-increasing stage of psychotherapy. The patient behaves resistively; his attraction to the therapist and the therapy process and his openness to therapist influence attempts are low. If he continues to come for treatment, his behavior in the absence of direct intervention will continue to be characterized as psychologically nonparticipative. This state of affairs, this typical working through of initial resistances, not only persists for an unnecessarily long period of time, thus lengthening the total duration of treatment, but also adds to the likelihood of premature termination by the patient. We hold, therefore, that something should be done to upset this unproductive and nontherapeutic level of patient participation, this unfavorable therapeutic relationship. We must *arouse* further cognitive dissonance in the patient, dissonance in the sense that the inconsistency of "coming" but not "doing" becomes a salient and unsatisfactory state of affairs for the patient. Such increased dissonance, by definition, leads to pressure for dissonance reduction. The patient, with this increased motivation for getting off his therapeutic fence is, we predict, likely to stop "coming" or start "doing" in a nonresistive manner or to reduce his dissonance by other means.

Festinger proposes three major avenues of dissonance reduction. The person may, he suggests, change one or more of the cognitions involved in the dissonant relationship. Thus, to the extent that relevant dissonance is aroused, the nature of our resistive patient's feelings toward the therapist and therapeutic participation may become more favorable; that is, his resistance may decrease and his attraction toward the therapist may increase, or, changing the opposing cognition in the original dissonant relationship, his resistance may increase to the point at which he terminates his therapeutic participation. Our hypotheses will not only offer means by which dissonance may be aroused in these consonantly resistive patients but will suggest ways in which dissonance reduction for such patients may be routed along the path that leads to increased attraction toward the therapist (hence increased influence receptivity) and routed away from alternative means of dissonance reduction such as changing cognitions by terminating therapy or the other alternatives we now discuss.

Festinger offers, as a second general means of dissonance reduction, the addition of new cognitive elements. Our dissonant patient, coming to therapy more and, because of our manipulations arousing dissonance, enjoying it less, may seek other elements, "knowledges," reasons or rationalizations to lessen the dissonant nature of his participation paradox. He may, for example, reconceptualize his participation as a duel with authority and justify (perhaps even enjoy) continuance on this dissonance-reducing basis. He may find added *justification* for continuance; that is, an element consonant with attendance by seeking and finding various secondary gains associated with his being labeled a patient. We emphasize the term justification in this example because it labels a concept which has assumed major importance in much of contemporary cognitive dissonance research. This notion has been given expression in dissonance theory by such statements as,

> . . . with other factors held constant, the greater the number and/or importance of positive attributes (consonant cognitions) associated with the chosen alternative, the less the magnitude of dissonance resulting from a choice (Brehm & Cohen, 1962, p. 24).

Thus, as demonstrated by dissonance studies we shall examine, if two groups of subjects are paid large and small sums of money, respectively, to write an essay presenting a view discrepant with their private opinions, more dissonance will be aroused in the subjects paid the *lesser* amount. Less dissonance is aroused in subjects paid at the higher rate because the greater amount of money provides more positive attributes, more consonant cognitions, more *justification* for writing in a discrepant manner. Subjects paid at the lower rate are provided less justification (fewer consonant cognitions) for their discrepant behavior. Thus greater dissonance is aroused and, since dissonance leads to dissonance reduction attempts, greater attitude change toward the discrepant position is likely to ensue. In like manner, our patient equivocally participating in therapy experiences dissonance whenever he participates in a nonresistive manner (since resistive behavior is consonant with his wish to avoid therapy). Such dissonance may be reduced the way we would wish, that is, by a decrease in resistiveness. Unless procedures are introduced to preclude it, other justifications may be sought by the patient for coming (e.g., "duel" with the therapist or seeking secondary gain).

The patient may seek dissonance reduction by a third general route, which Festinger describes as decreasing the subjective importance of the cognitions involved in the dissonant relationship. In a sense, what is involved in this third route is reduction of the dissonant conflict as a conflict without altering the *relationship* between dissonant elements. For example, a patient of the type we have been discussing may have made his initial contact with a therapist largely as a result of continued pressure from relatives, a parole officer, or others, and such pressure may have been reduced by his compliance with their duress. He may therefore view continuance in therapy as less stressful, less dissonance arousing, than a reinstatement of the earlier pressure from others to get him into therapy. His relationship with the therapist is, in this example, less dissonance arousing than the cognition of re-establishing his pretherapy relationships with others urging him into therapy. Stated otherwise, continuance in therapy is made more acceptable by being viewed by the patient as the lesser of two evils.

With these alternative means of dissonance reduction in mind, our hypotheses must also deal with means of increasing the probability that favorable change in patient attitude or feeling toward the therapist and therapeutic participation will be the most likely means of reducing dissonance. In doing so we must attend not only to avoiding those means of dissonance reduction exemplified by our discussion of justification, but, for reasons including minimizing the chances of dissonance reduction by premature termination, we must concern ourselves with the variable of *commitment*. Brehm and Cohen (1962) observe:

> . . . commitment, which we consider to occur when a person engages in an activity or when he decides on one thing rather than other, increases the resistance to change of the corresponding cognitive element, for it increases the resistance to change of the reality to which the element corresponds. . . . The role of commitment, then, in the theory of cognitive dissonance is, first, to aid the specification of psychological implication and hence the determination of what is consonant and what is dissonant and, second, to aid in the specification of the ways in which a person may try to reduce dissonance. . . . Where a person can be clearly committed to a given behavior or decision, information that is unambiguously inconsistent with that commitment should create dissonance and the individual should manifest attempts to reduce that dissonance (pp. 8-9).

Thus, to the extent that procedures are instituted to increase patient commitment to the act of coming for therapy, say, by having him pay for a dozen sessions in advance and indicating that half or all of his fees for these sessions will be returned to him if he misses no sessions, our dissonance arousing manipulations are less likely to result in dissonance reduction by termination of therapy and more likely to result in reduction by change in attitude toward therapy. Commitment and justification are related constructs in that justification may provide the basis for commitment. Thus under many circumstances the degree of justification, incentive, inducement, or coercion provided the patient largely determines his level of commitment to discrepant behavior. Our earlier discussion of justification indicated that, "the greater the number and/or importance of positive attributes (consonant cognitions) associated with the chosen alternative, the *less* the magnitude of dissonance." It follows that the optimal amount of justification to be provided a patient to achieve both commitment to a discrepant position *and* maximal dissonance arousal, is the minimal amount necessary to get him to engage in the discrepant behavior. Justification beyond this minimal amount adds dissonance-inhibiting positive cognitions. Thus the finding noted earlier that subjects paid at a high rate for writing a discrepant essay experience *less* dissonance than those paid a lesser amount.

Commitment and its effects may also be illustrated with reference to the dissonance arousing manipulation itself. One of the classes of such manipulations involved in the first hypothesis to follow is patient role playing; that is, requesting a consonantly resistive patient to "act as if" he very much wanted to participate in psychotherapy. In an inpatient setting such a role play procedure could readily be carried out in front of other patients who are candidates for psychotherapy. As studies examined later will indicate, such "public" position taking may greatly increase the individual's commitment to the position taken.

A third major construct, also often related to the amount of justification provided for engaging in discrepant behavior, is the degree of *choice* or *volition* the person perceives as associated with his decision to participate in or commit himself to discrepant behavior. Several studies to be considered later clearly suggest that the less justification (pressure, incentive, inducement, coercion, etc.) provided an individual for engaging in or commitment to discrepant behavior the more he perceives his decision to do so to be a volitional one and the more dissonance is aroused. When justification, coercion, or inducement is high, a greater number of positive attributes are associated with the decision to take a discrepant position, and thus the choice of entering into the discrepant behavior is low and minimal dissonance is aroused. Brehm and Cohen (1962) comment with regard to research supporting this viewpoint:

The interpretation of each study requires that a commitment be identified in order for there to be a clear case of dissonant cognitions. Once a commitment is identified, and assuming the existence of one or more important cognitions discrepant with that commitment, the degree of volition will control the magnitude of dissonance, at least in part. Where the degree of volition is low, the magnitude of dissonance will necessarily be small.

Where the degree of volition is high, the magnitude of dissonance will be large . . . (p. 218).

In summary, the three hypotheses that follow will not only point toward increasing patient attraction to the therapist by cognitive dissonance arousal and channeling of dissonance reduction, but will give consideration to the three interrelated variables we have indicated as playing a major role in dissonance arousal and reduction attempts. These variables are *commitment,* which specifies what is dissonant and reduces chances of dissonance reduction by change in the committed position; *choice,* which appears to influence the magnitude of the dissonance aroused; and *justification,* which influences both commitment and choice and which appears, depending on its magnitude, to permit dissonance reduction in channels which are, for our purposes, nonpreferred. In short, the hypotheses will have increased potential to the extent that they provide that patient participation in discrepant behavior is based on maximal commitment and choice, with minimal justification for such commitment and choice.

INCREASING ATTRACTION VIA PARTICIPATION

HYPOTHESIS 3.1: **Patient attraction to the therapist may be increased by cognitive dissonance induced by patient participation in overt behaviors discrepant with resistive behavior.**

This hypothesis predicts that certain procedures instituted early in the course of treatment of resistive, negatively attracted patients may by way of dissonance arousal and reduction result in a more favorable therapeutic relationship—at least as far as the patient's contribution to the relationship is concerned. This more positive patient perception of the therapist and therapeutic participation, as noted earlier, greatly increases patient openness to therapist influence attempts. In this important sense, therefore, heightened attraction to the therapist in such patients reduces the likelihood of wasted therapeutic hours and increases the likelihood of a more rapid and satisfactory therapeutic outcome. With these potential rewards in mind, let us turn to an examination of the specific dissonance-arousing interventions which research suggests as the most appropriate means of putting hypothesis 3.1 to experimental test. The first such intervention is patient participation in role playing procedures. In broad terms, this procedure requires the negatively attracted patient to act, in a literal sense, as if he were positively attracted to his therapist and to therapeutic participation. Although the manner in which such procedures lead to attitude change in the direction of the attitude position of the played role has only recently been clarified in the light of cognitive dissonance theory, the occurrence of such attitude change as an empirical phenomenon has long been recognized. For example, early suggestive studies by Harrow (1951) and Jones and Peters (1952) with schizophrenic patients, and by Sause (1954) and Maier (1952) with normal persons all pointed in the direction of progressive favorable change in the direction of the attitudes and behaviors represented by the roles played, as the role-play procedure continued. As is true of many research areas, however, early studies such as these lacked control groups, used very small samples, and on other grounds provided direction-pointing rather than definitive results. In like manner Kelly, Blake, and Stromberg (1957) found evidence suggesting that role-play experience increases the skill with which new roles can be taken, and, though also to a suggestive rather than statistically significant degree, Lieberman (1956) provided results in support of our basic theme, the influence of role playing on attitude change in a direction initially discrepant with the subject's own attitudes. Other research of this early, suggestive type is reviewed by Krasner (1959) and Mann (1956).

Before turning to more contemporary studies of the effects of role playing, it may be noted that role-play procedures have a long, if somewhat muddy, history of use in psychotherapy. The major use of such procedures in a therapeutic context has been in connection with psychodrama, although, as Krasner (1959) notes, the suggested use of drama for therapeutic purposes can be traced back to Aristotle. In modern times, but well before Moreno's (1945) psychodramatic movement, Reil (Zilboorg & Henry, 1941) in 1803 made use of role-play procedures with institutionalized mental patients. Conceiving of his procedures as a form of "noninjurious torture" he advocated that a special theater be established in mental hospitals in which patients would be urged to portray scenes from their earlier lives and in which the hospital staff would act as judges, prosecutors, etc., and point out to each actor-patient the "folly of his ways." Moreno's psychodramatic use of role playing, usually dated from 1911, has led to a huge mass of relevant professional literature. The overwhelming proportion of this literature consists of intuitive, clinical, nonresearch claims and counterclaims. Although Moreno's contribution to the group dynamics literature has led to a definitive body of research findings, the psychodrama literature has very clearly led in other directions. Thus, although in many respects psychodramatic use of role playing appears to hold major potential for a demonstration of the relation of role playing to attitude or behavior change, such a psychodramatic demonstration must, in spite of its long history and massive literature, continue to be considered as only suggestive in nature. Less cultish, more dispassionate examinations of psychodramatic role playing are called for.

A second major psychotherapeutic approach centered on role play techniques is Kelly's (1955) fixed role therapy. In this treatment approach the initial diagnostic study of the patient is used by a panel of treatment staff to construct a fixed-role sketch. This sketch, or carefully planned but sparsely detailed role play "script," is oriented toward the types of behavior it would appear desirable for the patient to assume; that is, to assume temporarily during the two weeks or so of role playing and more permanently to the extent that the role play experience mediates adoption by the patient of the role played attitudes and behaviors as "his own." The behaviors and attitudes comprising the sketch are characteristically in marked contrast to (or discrepant with) those the patient brings with him at the start of therapy. The role playing itself, in contrast to psychodrama, goes on outside the treatment clinic providing the patient with the major opportunity of "trying on" new behaviors and observing the types of interpresonal reactions such behaviors pull from other real figures in his interpersonal world. Two aspects of fixed role therapy are of particular interest. One is what Kelly terms the protective mask, that is, the fact that throughout the weeks of role playing and even during the therapeutic sessions (rehearsals) both patient and therapist maintain the make believe quality of the behaviors played. The rationale of this stipulation rests on the added safety and supposed increased likelihood of eventual patient role acceptance when the role behaviors can be tried out as if they really were not his own. Thus Kelly offers as an advantage of the protective mask the fact that the patient is enabled ". . . to explore his world without wholly and irrevocably committing himself" (p. 373). Although Kelly may be correct in this regard, our earlier discussion of cognitive dissonance theory has hinted, and our later discussion attempts to demonstrate, that when an individual can uncommit himself from a role-played position with relative ease, the likelihood of dissonance arousal and subsequent adoption of that position as his own is relatively low.

The second aspect of fixed-role therapy which will require our attention later in this chapter is the manner in which the sparsely detailed nature of the fixed-role sketch explicitly leaves room for patient spontaneity or improvisation in its enactment. Here, as is true of psychodrama, the amount of patient spontaneity or improvisation in filling in the details of the behaviors described generally in the fixed-role sketch appears to hold a direct influence on the degree of subsequent adoption by the patient of the role-play behaviors as his own. As Kelly notes:

> When the client shows signs, either in rehearsal or outside, that he has momentarily forgotten that he was just acting, the therapist may assume that true elaborative behavior is taking place. This means that a process is in motion which tends to interweave the client's new role constructs with the fabric of his main construction system. This is a good sign (p. 410).

As far as degree of direct validational support for the efficacy of fixed-role therapy is concerned, there are only a few, small sample, suggestive studies, such as those by Edwards (1940) and Robinson (1940). In all, therefore, the largely nonresearch literature on psychodrama and fixed role therapy combine to suggest the marked but as yet undemonstrated potential of role-play procedures for bringing about patient change. This suggestion is enhanced by further impressionistic reports of the value of role play procedures in other psychotherapeutic contexts [i.e., Deutsch and Murphy's (1955) sector therapy, Alexander and French's (1946) "corrective emotional experience," and the behavior therapy described by Wolpe (1958)]. With this as background, let us turn to the nonclinical research evidence underlying this hypothesis.

Investigations of Role Playing

One of the first experimental role-play studies is reported by Rosenberg (1952) who used three role-playing situations with three groups of 15 subjects each. Within each group of subjects there were three experimental tasks or positions through which all subjects were rotated: (1) role player, (2) identifier, in which S was instructed to identify with or empathize with the role players, and (3) active observer, in which S was instructed to watch the action unfold as objectively as possible. A separate group of control observers was simply instructed to watch the role playing. Dependent variable data were secured on post-role-play session questionnaires and a postsession group discussion. The major finding was a relationship between degree of participation or involvement in the role-play material and degree of attitude change in the direction of the discrepant role-play material. More specifically, change in attitude toward material with which they had initially disagreed was greatest in role players, next in identifiers, less in active observers, and least in control observers.

Two investigations conducted by Janis and King (1954) are of major interest. In their first study college student subjects were asked to listen to a speech presented by another student while at the same time they read the speech outline, or to give a speech on the assigned topic themselves. In the speech-giving condition subjects were instructed to play the role of a sincere advocate of the given point of view. Three topics were assigned in such a manner that each subject spoke on (role played) one topic and was passively exposed to the other two. In all instances the position of the speech disagreed with the initial position of both the speaker and the listeners. A questionnaire was administered to measure subject attitudes toward each of the three topics both before and after the experimental tasks. Attitude change scores derived from these questionnaires indicated that speech givers showed more change toward the discrepant position represented by the speech than did the listeners. Thus Rosenberg's (1952) major finding was replicated. Of added interest, Janis and King report that the speech givers who showed most attitude change also tended to have engaged in greater improvisation in their talks and to have been more satisfied with their performances in giving the talks. Thus, as is true of many careful investigations, this study answers one question (active participation via role playing *does* increase attitude change) and raises another (improvisation versus satisfaction as means of augmenting such attitude change). The investigators' second study was responsive to this new question, that is, it was designed to gather evidence on the separate effects of satisfaction and improvisation in producing attitude change. General instructions and type of subjects used were the same as in their first study. Also, as before, the subject's task was structured as a means of assessing oral speaking ability. Unlike the earlier investigation, role play subjects in this study did not talk to a group of other subjects but instead made a tape recording which they were told would be presented later to a group of judges. Three experimental conditions were instituted. In the first group subjects were asked to read the speech silently; in the second, to read it aloud; and in the third, to read it silently and then present it aloud as an impromptu speaker would. Questionnaire data revealed that subjects who presented the improvised speech were less satisfied with their performance than were subjects who simply read the speech aloud. Thus if improvisation increases attitude change from discrepant persuasion attempts, the improvisation group should show more attitude change; but, if satisfaction with performance is the more potent attitude change variable, the nonimprovisation group should evidence greater attitude change. Results indicated greater change in the direction of the speech in the improvisation condition. No difference was present when nonimprovisation and silent reading controls were compared in terms of attitude change.

Returning to hypothesis 3.1, then, experimental procedures which require or at least leave room for patient improvisation in his enactment of the attraction to the therapist role playing would appear to increase the likelihood of obtaining the desired, attraction-heightening effect. It may be noted in passing that a few explanatory bases have been offered for this augmenting effect of improvisation on attitude change. Hovland et al. (1953) propose and partially reject a "reformulation-comprehension" explanation of the improvisation effect. They comment,

> One of the salient characteristics of improvisation is that the individual reformulates the communication in his own words. It is possible that reformulation per se may give rise to a marked gain in comprehension of the content and thereby augment the chances that the persuasive communication will be influential. Opinion change may be facilitated by the mere act of translating the content into a more familiar vocabulary (pp. 233–234).

"Implicit labeling responses" form a second possible improvisation explanation offered by Hovland et al. Here the distinction between acceptability of direct suggestions from others versus those which appear to be spontaneously originated by oneself is relevant. To the extent that the latter may be assumed to be a more powerful basis of attitude acceptance, as it purportedly is for the acceptance of therapeutic interpretations, such implicit labeling responses (e.g., "This is my own idea") suggest a basis for the improvisation effect. Finally, and also at a speculative level, Brehm and Cohen (1962) have offered the following dissonance theory basis for the effects of improvisation:

> It will be recalled that, with the initial attitude strength and inducing force held constant, the greater the strength of discrepant verbal behavior, the greater will be the magnitude of dissonance and consequent attitude change. If it can be assumed that an increase in improvisation represents an increase in strength of verbalization, then the magnitude of dissonance and consequent attitude change will be a direct function of the amount of improvisation. . . . Thus, at the theoretical level, the improvisation effect may be a special case of dissonance theory (p. 256).

A number of other investigations of role playing are appropriate for our consideration. Each one demonstrates the basic relationship between engaging in behavior discrepant with one's private attitudes (role playing) and change in these private attitudes. In addition, each study specifies one or more conditions which enhance the likelihood of such attitude change occurring. Culbertson (1957) reports a study of this type. Subjects were assigned to three conditions: active participants, observers, and nonparticipating and nonobserving controls. The role-playing procedure, structured as a human relations discussion, involved the issue of community planning to encourage housing integration in the face of a large (hypothetical) influx of Negroes into the community. Subjects met in groups of six, each group consisting of three active participants and the observer assigned to each participant. Presession and postsession questionnaires were administered to all subjects regarding their specific attitudes toward housing integration and their more general attitudes toward Negroes. Results indicated that attitude change was significantly greater in role players than in either observers or control subjects. These differences were found for *both* role-play attitudes (pro-housing integration) and more general, favorable attitudes toward Negroes—attitudes that in a sense were not directly involved in the role-play procedure. To the extent that this suggestion of a generalization effect is given support by subsequent research, the potential value of role playing in psychotherapy for attraction-enhancing purposes becomes a potentially more potent therapeutic intervention; that is, we are primarily proposing the use of role playing and other possible means of increasing the attraction of the therapist in the eyes of resistive patients early in therapy for enabling, potentiating or reorienting purposes. We wish to change such patients' "set" toward the therapist. However, should such a manipulation be successful, it would still be incumbent on the therapist to "pick up the ball," to sustain the heightened level of patient attraction and influence receptivity, and to turn it to psychotherapeutic advantage. This sustaining of increased attraction and its therapeutic implications are, we would hold, made more likely to the extent that the role play or other intervention alters not only the specific attraction-to-the-therapist attitude involved in the manipulation itself, but also alters or generalizes to, as in Culbertson's study, the cluster of more general attitudes in which the manipulated attitude is embedded. Finally, Culbertson found significantly greater favorable change in attitude toward housing integration in low authoritarian subjects, compared with those with high F scale scores.

The role play-attitude change study conducted by Harvey and

Beverly (1961) is also of interest. Their theoretical rationale resembles the "implicit labeling responses" explanation of improvisation effects in Hovland et al. (1953). Harvey and Beverly note:

Various theoretical positions are doubtless consonant with the effects of role playing: especially ones that envisage a direct and more or less causal connection (even synonymity) between such internal structures as attitudes, on the one hand, and behavior, on the other. The present study, however, arises from theoretical considerations of a cognitive sort that have found validation in research on the effects of labeling. From the assignment of a label to an object or class of events stems a tendency to attribute characteristics to the object that are consistent with the label even though such attributions may be quite inappropriate to the "real nature" of the thing to which the name is affixed (p. 125).

Thus Harvey and Beverly might say, with reference to persons of concern to the present hypothesis, that the resistive patient's labeling of himself, via role playing, as attracted, cooperative, or nonresistive, leads to overt intherapy behaviors consistent with (or following from) these labels. Subjects in their study were students at a small, religiously-sponsored college. It is noted that "This population was selected because of its strong religious opposition to the sale and drinking of alcohol, the attitude issue of the study" (p. 126). After pretesting on attitudes toward this issue, all subjects were exposed to a speech that favored the sale of alcohol. Attitude postesting took place for half the subjects immediately after exposure to this persuasive speech. The other subjects, before posttesting for attitude change, were asked to record the best reasons they themselves could muster in favor of the sale and use of alcohol. Once again the predicted difference was obtained: greater change in the direction of initially discrepant attitudes occurred in role play than in simple exposure subjects. Of added interest, and in direct contrast to Culbertson's finding, Harvey and Beverly report that *high* authoritarian role players changed significantly more on the attitude issue than did *low* authoritarian role play subjects. We can only speculate on the bases for these two directly opposing findings. Perhaps differences in the kinds of subjects used, the type of role-play task imposed, or the difference in "experimenter bias" may be pointed to as the responsible factor or factors. More likely, and more parsimoniously, the differential results may be a simple function of the different authoritarianism measures used in the two studies. Regardless of basis, our inclusion of these discrepant findings serves to underscore once again the need for extrapolations such as those represented by hypothesis 3.1 to be to further research in a therapeutic context, and not directly to therapeutic practice.

Such prerequisite experimental verification in the therapy setting is given added support by a role-play study conducted by Scott (1957). His subjects were induced to engage in debates on three different issues, taking sides opposite to those they had indicated as their own in an attitude pretest. Half the subjects were rewarded in a predetermined order by a purported vote that proclaimed them the better debaters; the other half were punished by presumably losing the debate. A third group of subjects served as controls and did not participate in the debates. Results indicated significantly more attitude change in the direction of the initially discrepant attitudes in winning debaters, compared with both losing (nonrewarded) debaters and controls. The difference between losing debaters and controls was not significant, and neither of these two groups appeared to evidence significant attitude change. Thus Scott's study suggests that reward, satisfaction, or related constructs may be a valuable means of stabilizing whatever attitude changes result from role playing or related manipulations. Note, however, our earlier report of the King and Janis' (1956) study in which subject satisfaction with his role enactment did *not* serve to augment the degree of attitude change. On the other hand, a cognitive dissonance study reported by Weick (1963) found that procedures analogous to Scott's reward condition, when applied to his own subjects after the dissonance arousal manipulation, served "to validate and stabilize attitude change." Thus experimental tests of hypothesis 3.1 should include examination of various therapist behaviors which may serve to sustain, and perhaps even heighten, the increased level of patient attraction to which the dissonance arousal manipulations may have led.

A cognitive dissonance investigation by Cohen and Latané (Brehm & Cohen, 1962) sheds further light on the parameters of role playing as a means of effecting attitude change. The role-play position involved in this study required subjects to advocate that a compulsory religion course be added to the curriculum at their university. Pre-role-play testing ensured that all subjects selected for the study were initially strongly opposed to the addition of such a course. Following this testing, subjects were approached by a second experimenter who indicated he worked for the university's news bureau and was seeking ideas regarding the compulsory religion course. Subjects were then asked if they would help by tape recording their views and were also told that the news bureau had many statements against the course and were now seeking ideas on the other side, favoring the course. At this point in the experiment, and still before the taping of subjects' opinions, the experimenter manipulated the degree of subject choice. It will be recalled that our earlier sketch of dissonance theory suggested that the greater the perceived choice with which a person commits himself to discrepant behavior, the greater the magnitude of dissonance aroused and the greater the subsequent attitude change in the direction of the initially discrepant position. It is just this theoretical statement which the Cohen and Latané study sought to examine. Half the subjects, those assigned to the low choice condition, were asked to make the discrepant speech. The microphone was placed in their hands and they were given no chance to decline. The high choice subjects, in contrast, were told that ideas favoring the proposal were needed, but "the matter is entirely up to you." In effect, high choice structuring involved both subtle pressure to take the pro position and an attempt to create the impression that *S* was free to refuse. Subjects in both choice conditions, in addition to having their names and addresses noted by *E,* were given the impression that their ideas favoring the course would indeed be made public to the news bureau staff. This public stand, as later posttesting confirmed, resulted in a high level of commitment for subjects in both conditions. Posttesting of attitudes toward the compulsory religion course, after the dissonance-arousing tape recording was made, revealed significantly greater attitude change in a direction favoring the course in the high choice condition. Thus because both groups were equated in terms of initial (anticourse) attitudes and in level of commitment (difficulty of disowning the ideas presented), the investigators accurately concluded:

. . . the data support the assumption that variation in choice in taking a stand discrepant from one's attitudes produces variations in attitude change toward that discrepant position, so that the greater the choice, the greater the attitude change (p. 91).

Since this conclusion is clearly supported by a number of other cognitive dissonance studies (Brock, 1962; Cohen, Terry, & Jones, 1959; Davis & Jones, 1960), the most meaningful implementation of the relationship hypothesis being considered should clearly include examination of the degree of patient perceived choice in participating in the discrepant behavior.

The role-play studies we have examined provide, we feel, a large measure of the extrapolatory justification necessary to make experimental scrutiny of this implementation of hypothesis 3.1 worthwhile.

Examination of one final role-play study is necessary, however. The investigations explored thus far, whether in a dissonance context or not, have dealt with role-play situations whose content bears little direct similarity to patient attraction in psychotherapy. Thus, although we have held that the attitude change effects of role playing are potentially applicable to our resistive patients, we would feel on safer extrapolatory grounds if this effect were demonstrated with reference to interpersonal attitudes and feelings, that is, behaviors more relevant to the concern of our hypothesis than compulsory college courses, the sale of alcohol, and so forth. An investigation reported by Davis and Jones (1960) provides just such relevant interpersonal data. In addition this study gives explicit support to the need for concern with patient choice and commitment in dissonance arousal attempts via role-playing techniques. With reference to the operation of these two variables in an interpersonal context, the investigators comment:

In situations where one individual (A) has, for whatever reason, behaved toward another (B) in a manner which is discrepant with his private feelings about B, we might well expect the production of dissonance and a consequent change in A's attitude toward B. At least dissonance theory alerts us to this possibility and suggests the conditions under which such attitude change might occur. If person A is pressured by strong incentives or imperative role demands to behave in an overly warm or overly hostile fashion toward B, we would expect little change in A's private impression of B. If, however, A is less certain about what is expected and perceives alternative ways of responding to B, the same extreme behavior would likely produce corresponding changes in attitude toward B through the mechanism of dissonance reduction. Thus, the "degree of choice" variable seems quite applicable to situations of interpersonal action and perception.

There are, however, occasions similar to the interaction depicted above where A is operating under restraints or incentives which are only temporarily effective. Thus, the role requirements are not immutable and A can behave in a different fashion at a later time. . . . the dissonance research attempts to create dissonance by inducing the S to act in a way that is discrepant from his beliefs, have treated the S's behavior as irrevocable. S reads the unpleasant information, he agrees to copy the random numbers, he propagandizes the "naïve" subject, he eats the unpleasant vegetable, etc. In all these cases the S sees little prospect of taking back or in a public way canceling out the discrepant behavior. Whether or not S actually goes through on his commitment to behave in a certain way, he does not anticipate any simple way of neutralizing the behavioral act. It seems logical to suggest that dissonance reduction through attitude change is dependent on the absence of such anticipations. Thus, we would expect little dissonance in forced compliance situations where the unpleasant, alien, discrepant behavior can be withdrawn or neutralized (pp. 402-403).

With this position on choice and commitment as background, Davis and Jones conducted a study in which subjects were either cajoled (choice) or assigned (no choice) to read aloud a negative evaluation of a stimulus person (*SP*) who could hear but not see the subject. Half of the subjects expected to meet the *SP* later with the experimenter, at which time *S*'s role and the deception involved would be explained to *SP* (low commitment condition). The remaining subjects were led to believe that such a meeting was impossible and that the *SP* would not be disabused (high commitment condition). In line with the reasoning presented, the main experimental prediction was that dissonance would be greatest in the condition in which *S* had the illusion of choice and was not given the opportunity to neutralize his behavior. Thus the attitudes of these choice-high commitment *S*s should change most in the direction of the discrepant evaluation. Experimental results confirmed this prediction, leading the investigators to conclude:

> The results of the present experiment indicate the conditions under which a person, whose behavior toward another departs from his initial attitudes toward the other, changes his attitudes to make it consonant with his behavior. The person or actor must (a) feel that he has some freedom *not* to behave in the discrepant manner, and (b) realize that he cannot easily disclaim the behavior in the eyes of the target person. According to the findings presented above, the combination of these two conditions is necessary and sufficient to produce enough dissonance to motivate attitude change. In the absence of either condition, the amount of attitude change is negligible and significantly less than when both are present. We assume in this general statement that it is merely the amount of discrepancy between behavior and initial attitude which is important and not the direction of discrepancy. Since the present experiment only involved behavior which was more negative than the initial attitude, the generality of the present results is contingent on further empirical investigation (p. 409).

In summary, the first class of dissonance-arousing manipulations we are suggesting as overt behaviors discrepant with resistive behavior for hypothesis 3.1 is patient role playing. The content of such a role should focus on favorable attraction to the therapist which is, for resistive patients, largely discrepant with their own private attitudes. For maximal attitude change in the form of heightened attraction to occur, it seems important that this procedure include high levels of (1) patient *choice* regarding participation in the role playing, (2) patient *commitment,* in the sense that undoing, disowning or uncommitting himself from his discrepant behavior is made difficult, (3) patient *improvisation* (the role-play structuring should be in outline form, requiring that the role player fill in the specifics himself), and (4) post* role playing patient *reward,* that is, approval, reinforcement or other means of stabilizing the patient's new perspective toward his psychotherapist.

The variables (choice, commitment, improvisation, and reward) play a directly analogous role in the second class of discrepant behaviors we will now examine as another means of implementing the experimental test of hypothesis 3.1. Although we need not focus on each of these four variables in detail again, our earlier discussion of their influence also applies directly to this second class of discrepant behaviors.

Investigations of Essay Writing

A second class of overt behaviors relevant to hypothesis 3.1 is the writing of discrepant essays. Just as role playing by resistive, negatively attracted patients is hypothesized to lead to attitude change in the direction of less resistance and more positive attraction to the therapist, this is anticipated with respect to patient participation in a task that calls for a written description of how and why the patient might find himself more favorably predisposed toward his psychotherapist. A number of studies appear to offer direct evidence in extrapolatory support of this essay writing effect. For example, we refer to the cognitive dissonance studies conducted by Cohen, Brehm, and Fleming (1958), Rabbie, Brehm, and Cohen (1959), and Brock and Blackwood (1962). In all three investigations it was first established by questionnaires that all subjects uniformly favored a given attitude position (e.g., continuance of intercollegiate athletics, maintenance of current college tuition rates). Control subjects in each study did not

---

* Note that according to dissonance theory such reward or approval must be provided *after* the role play induced attitude change has taken place. Reward provided before the role playing or other manipulation, especially if offered as inducement for participating in the manipulation, would, dissonance theory suggests, serve as heightened justification. The greater such justification the smaller the degree of patient perceived choice, the smaller the dissonance aroused, and the smaller the attitude change that would take place. However, evidence on this point is not unequivocal. See, for example, Rosenberg, M. J., When dissonance fails, *J. pers. soc. Psychol.,* 1965, **1,** 28–42.

write an essay, but simply responded to the attitude questionnaire a second time. Experimental subjects, those who did write an essay against their own private attitudes on the issue, were of two types. Low justification experimental subjects were given few or minimal reasons as inducement for agreeing to write the discrepant essay. In contrast, high justification subjects were provided with several additional bases for participation in such a task. Results in all three studies indicated attitude change toward the initially discrepant position that was greatest in low justification subjects, smaller in high justification subjects, and least in control subjects. A majority of the predicted between-condition differences reached statistically significant levels. Thus we have additional evidence that participation in overt behaviors discrepant with one's private attitudes leads to attitude change away from these private attitudes. Furthermore, the more incentive, inducement, or justification one is given for such participation (beyond the absolute minimum necessary to induce the behavior itself), the less cognitive dissonance is aroused and the less attitude change takes place.

Studies by Kelman (1953) and Brehm and Cohen (1962) provide clear confirmation of both findings. In both studies essay writing of the type outlined above led to attitude change in the predicted direction, and the magnitude of such change varied inversely with justification provided for participation. In addition, the Kelman study demonstrated the attitude change augmenting effect of improvisation noted earlier in connection with role playing investigations. Brehm and Cohen's demonstration of the effects of justification in this research context represents a more powerful demonstration than the two-level, high-versus-low justification comparisons noted above. Subjects were paid at four different rates for writing the discrepant essay. These rates, and the mean attitude change score associated with each rate, were $10.00 (2.32), $5.00 (3.08), $1.00 (3.47), and $.50 (4.54). Thus these results indicate an inverse monotonic relationship between justification and attitude change. Finally, and also consonant with our examination of role playing, Brock (1962) reports evidence on the effects of choice on dissonance arousal by writing of discrepant essays. Non-Catholic college students were given high or low choice in whether to comply with Brock's request that they write an essay on "Why I would like to become a Catholic." Change in attitude toward Catholicism, as measured by pre- and postessay writing questionnaires, increased as choice increased. As Brehm and Cohen (1962) note: "These results, in addition to supporting the hypothesized effect of choice on dissonance, show that dissonance can affect attitudes on a strong social issue" (p. 45).

Our discussion of hypothesis 3.1 to this point has proposed two classes of behavior (role playing and essay writing about high attraction to the therapist and psychotherapy), which, when employed with resistive patients in such a manner that certain relevant variables are considered (choice, commitment, justification, improvisation, and reward) are hypothesized to lead to change in such patients in the direction of more favorable attitudes toward the therapist and psychotherapy. Clearly, these two types of overt discrepant behavior are but examples, and many other tasks might be hypothesized to lead to similar effects on attitude change. There is, for example, the possibility of having a resistive patient attempt to "sell" the virtues and benefits of therapeutic participation to a second resistive patient. In a study directly relevant to such a task, Festinger and Carlsmith (1959) had their subjects perform a boring and tedious task and then asked each S to tell the next S that the task was interesting and enjoyable. Results indicate that participation in the task of selling others something one does not initially believe in oneself leads to private attitude change in which the boring and tedious task is privately viewed as more interesting and enjoyable.

Before turning to our second relationship hypothesis, a comment seems necessary regarding practical issues that must be faced in testing hypothesis 3.1 in a psychotherapeutic context. How, one might ask, may patient participation in such discrepant behaviors be fitted in in the most meaningful and least artificial manner. It was noted earlier that role play procedures have already found a place, although for somewhat different purposes, in two types of contemporary psychotherapy. There appears to be, however, no need to restrict ourselves to the psychotherapist alone when it comes to deciding when and by whom the role playing, essay writing, selling others, etc., is to be instituted. There are at least three other members of most treatment staffs who have or can have commerce with each patient. We refer to the intake interviewer, the psychological tester, and one or more research persons. In interaction with any of these persons a patient may be asked about his private attitudes, hopes and fears about the future, feelings about the kind of therapist he has or would like to have, and so forth. In short, we are suggesting that the discrepant behaviors may be instituted meaningfully not only by the patient's psychotherapist but also by one or more of the other members of the treatment team.

INCREASING ATTRACTION VIA EXPOSURE

HYPOTHESIS 3.2:   **Patient attraction to the psychotherapist may be increased by cognitive dissonance induced by patient exposure to information discrepant with resistive behavior.**

This second relationship hypothesis parallels hypothesis 3.1 in several respects. In our first relationship hypothesis the word "participation" was central, and patients were to be induced to actual physical participation in overt behaviors discrepant with their attitudes toward psychotherapy. In hypothesis 3.2 "exposure" is the key term. In broadest terms, this hypothesis predicts that more favorable patient attitudes toward the therapist and therapeuic participation may follow from being exposed to communications which are inconsistent with continuance of resistive, nontherapeutic participation in psychotherapy. As was true for the participation hypothesis, our prediction regarding the consequences of exposure must consider the influence on such exposure effects of the interacting or extenuating variables of choice, commitment, justification, and reward. An exposure study conducted by Cohen, Terry, and Jones (1959), discussed below, will make this readily apparent, as far as the choice variable is concerned. In addition, a major issue in studies of attitude change, opinion conformity, and counterpropaganda concerns the effect on attitude change of the magnitude of the discrepancy between S's initial private attitudes and the position advocated by the persuasive message to which he is exposed. This relationship is of direct relevance to the patients of concern to the present hypothesis. The more resistive the patient, the greater the discrepancy between his own position and a message involving positive attraction to therapy and the therapist. Does this large discrepancy make it more or less likely that the desired attitude change in the form of heightened attraction will follow from exposure to such discrepant information? As will become apparent, and as is often the case when research in an area has progressed to the multivariate stage, the answer to this question is "it depends." Under certain circumstances we may predict that the more resistive the patient initially, the less resistive he will become following exposure. However, when other variables (such as choice) are not provided for in the procedures, what has been termed a "direct persuasion effect" may be expected to follow; that is, the greater the discrepancy between prior opinion and new information, the *greater* the resistance to attitude change (e.g., our resistive patient becomes even more resistive). Following the more or less standard design of cognitive dissonance exposure studies, Cohen et al. asked their subjects to take part in a "survey." A prequestionnaire on the attitude dimension involved was administered. A randomly selected half of the subjects were then given a high choice whether or not they wished to hear information contrary to the attitude position they had taken; low choice subjects were read the information with no opportunity to decline such exposure. Degree of discrepancy was a direct function of the distance between S's own initial attitudes and the position taken in the discrepant communication which was read to all subjects. Results, as the investigators note, support the conclusion that:

> Under the conditions of Low Choice, the relationship between discrepancy and attitude change may be conceived of as one of direct persuasion. The more extreme a person is in his own opinion the more he may be expected to resist counterarguments. Because he has had no choice in exposure, there is little dissonance between his cognitions (initial opinion) and behavior. . . . However, when a person has chosen to expose himself to the counter-communication, dissonance is produced between his cognitions (initial opinion) and behavior (choice of listening to discrepant information). In addition, the more discrepant the information, the more dissonance should be produced. In a situation in which he has chosen to take a stand contrary to his cognitions, the dissonance can be reduced by making those cognitions consistent with the behavior (i.e., changing his attitude to conform with the new information). And we would expect, the more the dissonance, the greater the pressure to reduce it and, therefore, the greater the consequent attitude change (p. 390).

A study reported by Brehm and Leventhal (Brehm & Cohen, 1962), in addition to providing a demonstration of the basic effect of exposure to discrepant information on attitude change, highlights the role of commitment in this process. As was true in the various "forced compliance" studies examined earlier, commitment in this investigation served to specify what is dissonant and reduce the likelihood of dissonance reduction by change in the position to which S was committed. Stated otherwise, the function of commitment in the exposure paradigm is to increase the difficulty of S's not going through with, summarily rejecting, or denying the fact of his exposure to discrepant information. We need not dwell on these variables further. It is sufficient, perhaps, to note that considerations such as choice and commitment apparently play as crucial a role in the implementation of this exposure hypothesis as they did in the possible experimental tests of our participation hypothesis.

It is instructive to consider at this point three possible implementations of the present hypothesis in a therapy research context. In the first, our resistive patient has ambivalently arrived for his therapy session and is seated in the therapist's waiting room. Also present is an individual who is apparently another waiting patient but who in reality is an accomplice planted by the therapist-researcher for purposes of delivering discrepant information to the "real" patient. The accomplice engages the patient in conversation aimed at direct exposure of the positive value of the therapist and psychotherapeutic participation. We call this implementation the "direct plant." A second possible set of procedures would largely resemble those for the direct plant, but instead of an accomplice speaking directly to the patient two accomplices would be present and they would be speaking *to each other*. In this manner the patient is exposed to the discrepant information (the conversation between the two accomplices) by *overhearing* it. We will call this possible means of examining hypothesis 3.2, the "overheard plant." A third possibility for exposing the patient to discrepant information grows from a suggestion made by Small (Psychology in the States, 1963) in another context. Small proposed, on strictly clinical grounds, that patients participating in psychotherapy be requested to have an annual "status and improvement" consultation with a therapist other than the one treating them as a periodic means of obtaining relatively independent information regarding patient change. For our purposes, we would suggest the possibility that our patients, while in the waiting room to see such a consultant therapist, be exposed to the discrepant information by overhearing this therapist deliver the message to another "consulting patient" (an accomplice), perhaps as a doorstep-threshold conversation as this other "patient" is leaving. Of course, there is no need to consider this particular implementation only in terms of Small's suggestion. The common patient waiting rooms in outpatient clinics and in suites of private offices provide equally opportune physical circumstances for the same exposure procedures. For reasons to be made apparent later, we call this potential implementation of the hypothesis, the "credible plant." Let us turn to the research bearing on these three possibilities. The studies to be examined not only highlight the possible rewards and hazards of each approach, they also provide further support for the basic effect of exposure to discrepant information on attitude change.

The Direct Plant

In an indirect but clearly relevant sense a study conducted by Centers (1963) provides evidence to support the direct plant approach.

Centers attempted to both replicate and extend Verplank's (1955) finding that operant conditioning procedures, instituted in the course of apparently ordinary conversations with subjects, successfully led to the conditioning of subject opinions. In Center's study subjects arriving at the laboratory waiting room were informed by another "subject" already there (actually the investigator's research assistant) that E had told him there would be about a half-hour delay in starting the experiment because of an equipment breakdown. A subsequent postexperimental check revealed that in all cases the actual subjects accepted the plant as another subject. The half-hour of waiting, which actually constituted the experiment itself, was divided into three 10-minute periods. For the first 10 minutes (the operant period) the accomplice generally permitted the subject to talk as much as he wished, showing interest in what S had to say but attempting to be noncommittal in response. Following this initial "base-rate" period was the second 10-minute period (the reinforcement period). Here the accomplice agreed with or paraphrased all of the subject's opinion statements. When extended silences occurred during either of these first two periods, the accomplice asked a neutral question as an attempt to get the subject talking again. During the last 10 minutes (the extinction period) the accomplice either disagreed with the subject's opinions or remained silent following subject opinion statements. Results clearly indicated that such conversational operant conditioning significantly increased the number of opinion statements in the reinforcement versus operant periods, and significantly decreased such statements in the extinction period as compared to the reinforcement phase. Levin and Shapiro (1962) have essentially replicated this finding. It is clear, therefore, that "conversational conditioning" does exist as a possible technique of relevance to the direct plant implementation of hypothesis 3.2. Such face-to-face attempts at exposing resistive patients to information discrepant with resistiveness, however, have no great likelihood of success in the form of subsequent attitude change; that is, the very nature of face-to-face persuasive attempts enhances the likelihood that the persuasive message will result in patient behavior *other than* attitude change in the direction of the discrepant communication. This is particularly true when the communicator of the discrepant information is viewed as another patient. There are three investigations relevant here, all of which provide evidence against such a direct plant approach, and in support of the hypothesis implementation we have called the "overheard plant."

The Overheard Plant

Jones, Hester, Farina, and Davis (1959) conducted a study in which pairs of subjects listened to two stimulus persons, allegedly conversing in an adjacent room, evaluate the personality of one member of the pair. One of the stimulus persons made derogatory remarks about the "involved" member; the other was more noncommittal and even mildly sympathetic toward the subject being evaluated. In one experimental condition the derogating stimulus person was pre-identified to the subjects as being maladjusted, the nonderogator as well-adjusted. In the other condition the identifications were reversed. After the pair of subjects had heard the evaluations, they rated the stimulus persons on a number of traits. The result of interest to us here concerns the differential subject reaction to derogation from the well-adjusted versus the maladjusted stimulus persons. Derogated Ss liked the maladjusted derogator better than did the nonderogated member of each pair and liked the well-adjusted derogator less. However, derogated Ss paid more attention to the derogatory comments made by these well-liked stimulus persons. The investigators' comment with regard to this last finding is of interest:

> When he is attacked by the well-adjusted derogator, it is difficult to take refuge in the thought that the derogator is highly inaccurate, a victim of projection, and so forth. Faced with the maladjusted derogator, however, he may console himself with the thoughts that (a) the derogator's judgments of others are distorted since they are colored by his own problems, and (b) the derogator is not fully responsible for the act of judgment, being a victim of a traumatic past history (p. 364).

Thus a resistive patient exposed in his therapist's waiting room to discrepant messages regarding the therapist by another "patient" may, this study suggests, readily reduce any dissonance aroused by the discrepant information by derogation of the message source, and not by private attitude change. We return to this theme when we consider research on communicator credibility. First, however, let us examine two studies conducted by Walster and Festinger (1962) bearing on the direct plant and overheard plant implementations.

In their first investigation, student subjects were informed that as part of their course they were required to take a 15-minute tour of the social psychology laboratory's observation room. Subjects toured in groups of two to four. As they walked to the observation room, the experimenter mentioned that because the laboratory was frequently not in use for experiments; graduate students often used it for a lounge.

One half of the groups (regular condition) were then told, "A couple of graduate students are in there now. I'll tell them we are coming through." (E then did so.) For the other groups of Ss (overheard condition), E said instead, "I think a couple of graduate students are in there now. If we are quiet, we can probably get into the observation booth without their hearing us." In both conditions, as subjects watched the graduate students talking, E described and demonstrated some techniques of "blind listening." Subjects were then told to try it, curtains were drawn over the observation mirrors, and earphones were passed around to each S. The conversation each S then heard was actually a taped persuasive communication in which two speakers attempted to present a strong case against an association between smoking and lung cancer. A week later, assessment was made of the subjects' degree of agreement with the persuasive communication and their evaluation of the tour. Results were as follows. Subjects in both the regular and overheard conditions agreed significantly more with the communication than did a control group which had not taken the tour. This finding supports the basic effect of exposure to discrepant information on attitude change. Subjects in the overheard condition agreed with the communication to a greater degree than did regular condition subjects. Further, all overheard condition subjects rated the speakers as more honest and sincere than did those in the regular condition. Thus we find added evidence in support of our suggestion of exposure by overhearing.

Walster and Festinger, in appropriate response to the somewhat marginal level of confidence ($p < .08$) associated with their finding that overheard condition Ss agreed with the communication more than regular condition Ss, carried out a second and more definitive study. As will be made apparent, this second investigation provides a clear and unequivocal demonstration of the superiority for attitude change purposes of overheard versus face-to-face or direct persuasive communications. Further, this study sought to determine the interaction of this communication source effect with the degree to which S is involved in the content of the communication. Two groups of persons, wives of college students living in an on-campus housing development and junior and senior women students living in dormitories, were used as subjects in the experiment. Two persuasive communications were selected. One of them, "Student husbands should spend a great deal more time at home," was expected (and proved to be) an involving issue primarily for the married women and not for the coeds. The other communication, "Junior and senior women should be allowed to live off campus if they desire," was relevant and involving only for unmarried students living in dormitories. Experimental procedures provided for all subjects to hear both communications, but, in a manner analogous to the first study, half of the subjects were led to believe the communicators knew they were listening, and the other half that they were overhearing the conversation unknown to the communicators. Postexposure data indicated that when the issue was one in which subjects were strongly involved there was a large and significant difference in the predicted direction between the regular and overheard conditions. Differences between conditions were negligible when the issue was not involving for the subject. The investigators speculate that this between-condition difference may be partly attributable to the fact that (when the issue is involving) regular condition Ss, but not overheard condition Ss, may "feel that the speaker is . . . attempting to influence him and has ulterior motives." Such a suspicion, they note, may partly nullify the potential effectiveness of the communication. Regardless of the adequacy of this speculation, it does highlight the issue of *communicator intent,* an issue we will need to explore further as an aspect of communicator credibility as we turn to the possibility of implementing the present hypothesis by use of a "credible plant."

The Credible Plant

It will be recalled that evidence was cited to indicate that the success in terms of attitude change of direct plant, face-to-face discrepant communications, may be attenuated by derogation of the "patient" communicator by the resistive patient. Exposure by overhearing the discrepant message, in partial contrast, makes the communicator's intent less suspect and, therefore, makes derogation of the communicator a less likely means of dissonance reduction and increases the chances of dissonance reduction by attitude change in the intended direction. Nevertheless, the overheard plant implementation does involve "patient" accomplices, and thus the possibility of dissonance reduction by rejection of the source remains; that is, even though overhearing the discrepant message may make it less likely, our resistive patient may still respond to the message by discounting the planted "patients" as noncredible message sources. We are thus led to seek a means of implementing the exposure hypothesis by using a message source potentially more credible than other "patients," while still retaining the apparent advantages for attitude change purposes of overheard message delivery. Stated otherwise, we are led to the credible plant implementation.

The best known studies dealing with the influence of credibility of the communicator on the acceptance of a communication were conducted by Hovland, Janis, and Kelley (1953). In their investigations, credibility was defined as consisting of two components:

(1) the extent to which a communicator is perceived to be a source of valid assertions (his "expertness") and (2) the degree of confidence in the communicator's intent to communicate the assertions he considers most valid (his "trustworthiness").

In one study of this series Hovland and Weiss (1951) varied source credibility through the use of communicators differing in trustworthiness. The general procedure consisted of presenting an identical communication to two groups of subjects, in one case from a source of high credibility and in the other from one of low credibility. Opinion questionnaires were administered before, immediately after, and a month after the communication. Affirmative and negative versions of four different communications were used. For example, an affirmative communication dealing with the question, "Should the antihistamine drugs continue to be sold without doctor's prescription?" was presented as emanating from the New England Journal of Biology and Medicine (high credibility source) or from a mass circulation monthly pictorial magazine (low credibility source). Results indicated that the four high credibility sources were judged to be trustworthy by 81 to 95 per cent of the subjects, the low credibility sources by 1 to 21 per cent. Opinion change in the direction advocated by the communicator, measured immediately after the communication, occurred significantly more often when it originated from a high credibility source than when from a low one. This differential source effectiveness, however, had disappeared by the time of the one-month follow-up.

A second, closely related study was conducted by Kelman and Hovland (1953). In the course of a regular high school program a guest speaker was introduced, who proceeded to give a talk favoring extreme leniency in the treatment of juvenile delinquents. Three different versions of the introduction to the speaker were used. In the positive version he was identified as a juvenile court judge; in the neutral introduction he was identified as a randomly selected member of the studio audience; and in the negative version he was represented as coming from the audience but also as a person who had been a delinquent as a youth and was currently out on bail. As in the earlier study, pre-post opinion questionnaires revealed significantly more opinion change toward leniency in both the positive (judge) and neutral communicator positions in comparison to the negative source. Once again, however, the differences between groups had disappeared on follow-up a few weeks later. In yet a third related investigation, Hovland and Mandell (1952) failed to find this influence effect, although their high credibility communication was judged more "fair and honest" than was the low credibility source. Hovland et al. (1953) comment:

> In summary, the research evidence indicates that the reactions to a communication are significantly affected by cues as to the communicator's intentions, expertness, and trustworthiness. The very same presentation tends to be judged more favorably when made by a communicator of high credibility than by one of low credibility. Furthermore, in the case of two of the three studies on credibility, the immediate acceptance of the recommended opinion was greater when presented by a highly credible communicator. From the results, it is not possible to disentangle the effects of the two main components of credibility—trustworthiness and expertness—but it appears that both are important variables (p. 35).

This basic finding, that acceptance of persuasive communications increases with increases in communicator credibility, has been reported by Arnett, Davidson, and Lewis (1931), Kulp (1934), Haiman (1949), Aronson and Golden (1962), as well as by other investigators. It is a solid finding, and stands in clear support of our recommendation that hypothesis 3.2 be tested by use of a credible plant.

One final consideration should be examined before we conclude our discussion of the present hypothesis. It was noted earlier that under conditions of high choice the greater the discrepancy between an S's initial attitude position and the position taken by the communication to which he is volitionally exposed, the greater the attitude change toward the communication. When the discrepancy is large (as it may well be when a highly resistive patient is exposed to the type of message we have been suggesting) and lies outside of the subject's "latitude of acceptance" (Hovland et al., 1953), the bulk of attitude change research would predict negative change; that is, rather than responding to a highly discrepant communication by change *toward* that communication, S rejects the communicator and holds even more firmly to his initial position. With regard to the highly resistive patient, such negative change might find expression by derogating the therapist and therapeutic participation even more and even by terminating therapy. Not only does the Cohen et al. (1959) study discussed earlier indicate that providing S with high perceived choice for exposure largely minimizes the likelihood of such a "boomerang" effect (Brehm &

Cohen, 1962), but an investigation conducted by Aronson, Turner, and Carlsmith (1963) demonstrates that source credibility further reduces the possibility of this negative boomerang effect. Some of their subjects were exposed to a persuasive communication by a highly credible source; others heard the same communication from a mildly credible source. The extent of the discrepancy between the subject's opinions and that represented by the communication was also varied. Subjects then reported their attitudes a second time. The results showed that for the highly credible source the amount of opinion change *increased* with increasing discrepancy; for the mildly credible source opinion change *decreased* with increasing discrepancy; and subjects in the large discrepancy condition who did not change in their attitudes disparaged the (mildly credible) communicator.

Our examination of research relevant to hypothesis 3.2 is thus concluded. This examination has sought to illustrate the conditions and procedures whose utilization in a therapy research context may serve to maximize the likelihood of resistive patient reorientation following exposure to a communication which places his therapist and therapeutic participation in a favorable light. As we moved from the direct to the overheard and on to the credible plant implementations of the hypothesis, evidence was noted which underscored the desirability of such procedures as increasing the patient's perceived choice in exposing himself to the communication, overhearing rather than face-to-face message delivery, a highly credible message source, and so forth. We will be the first to acknowledge, however, that practical considerations often make it difficult in a therapy-research context to institute all the procedures and conditions that nontherapy research has demonstrated as enhancing (and, in some instances, necessary for) the attitude change effects of exposure to discrepant information. Perhaps our most adequate response to this reality issue is suggested by our earlier discussion of therapy research design and methodology. In effect, we would propose that the relative importance in a therapy context of such variables as choice, overhearing, credibility, discrepancy and the other variables elaborated more fully in conjunction with hypothesis 3.1 (commitment, justification and reward) be examined in a *series* of studies, a research program in which these diverse and potentially consequential variables are systematically examined.

Let us assume that such future tests of this hypothesis in a therapy setting converge on a positive research outcome; that is, most of the research attempts at exposure succeed in a reorientation of the resistive patients involved. Although it may then be true that such heightened patient attraction to his therapist, such a more favorable therapeutic relationship, may mean heightened patient receptivity to therapist influence attempts and, more generally, more "therapeutic" therapy participation by the patient, there is no evidence to suggest that in the absence of further attraction-enhancing or attraction-sustaining intervention the patient will continue in this nonresistive manner. Even if our basic manipulation were successful, is there any reason to suspect its effects may be anything but temporary? We have no evidence on either side of this issue, although it is clear that it must eventually be faced. As noted earlier, we view the relationship manipulations suggested by this chapter's hypotheses as enabling, potentiating, or reorientational procedures and as a means of *temporarily* inducing a more favorable psychotherapeutic relationship. It may well be that what naturalistically follows such experimentally heightened patient attraction is the "good therapy" that Freud implies follows from naturalistically heightened patient attraction, via gradual working through of early resistances, but on the other hand, a return to resistiveness may ensue. Although we have touched on means of stabilizing changed attitudes following dissonance arousal and reduction in a nontherapy context, there is a general absence of research pointing to such procedures as they might be extrapolated to psychotherapy. In all, therefore, we raise the question of what procedures must follow successfully manipulated patient attitudes about therapy to underscore the current absence of and the potential need for answers in the hope that subsequent relevant research will be encouraged.

Finally let us assume that research examinations of the present hypothesis are generally negative; that is, not only does attitude change toward the communication not take place, but the research patients hold even more strongly to their preexposure resistive attitudes and behavior. In one sense, we can partially beg this question of undesirable effects on patients and therapeutic relationships by reemphasizing our stance that extrapolation be to therapy research and not to therapy practice. Yet, if we are urging here that these cognitive dissonance and attitude change research findings be tested in a *therapy research* context, real patients may be involved whether this context is called research or practice, and whether the experimenter calls himself researcher or psychotherapist. As this book's introduction makes clear, we are ethically comfortable with the risks implied by hypotheses such as these on the grounds that (1) contemporary psychotherapeutic practice is in many major respects a grossly inefficient technique, thus fairly demanding new perspectives and research orientations, and (2) this hypothesis rests, as we feel all our hypotheses do, on a generally sound, nonclinical research base. We leave it to each investigator to decide for himself, with regard to any of our hypotheses stirring his research interest, whether or not the attendant risks outweigh the potential rewards of positive results for the advance of psychotherapy; we ask only that such decisions be a function of realistic appraisals of the nature of psychotherapy as it really exists, and as it might ideally exist, and not as a function of what much of contemporary psychotherapeutic lore would have us believe.*

Our third hypothesis dealing with the patient-therapist relationship may now be considered. Although it represents our final attempt in the present chapter to extrapolate to psychotherapy largely from cognitive dissonance research, we hope that it is apparent to the reader at this point that many other implications for the therapy transaction may exist in research attempts aimed at examining dissonance theory and related "balance" models of cognitive behavior.

INCREASING ATTRACTION VIA OVERCOMPENSATION

HYPOTHESIS 3.3:   **Patient attraction to the therapist may be increased by cognitive dissonance induced by overcompensation provided the patient for therapeutic participation.**

In broad terms this hypothesis proposes the arousal of cognitive dissonance in resistive patients by providing them not with "reward" for continuing to come for therapy but with "overreward." This overreward may take several forms: special arrangements may be made, or purportedly be made, in the patient's behalf with regard to particularly convenient (for the patient) meeting times. The patient may be moved to the head of a waiting list, be permitted to choose his own therapist

---

* Some of our readers may feel inclined to reject our suggestions for the utilization of a credible plant on the grounds that it is unethical to mislead patients, to imply a promise of cure, or to suggest the possibility of a breach of confidentiality by allowing a patient to overhear someone else's "therapy" being discussed in a public waiting room. We do not make light of these ethical concerns and indeed suggest that a further discussion of the ethics of treating resistant patients is definitely in order. We further suggest, however, that the ethical alternatives are not so clear as they may initially appear. For example, is it ethical for a therapist to withhold treatment if society judges the patient in need of psychological help, but the patient himself does not voluntarily accept treatment? Or, is it ethical for a therapist to refrain from building confidence in treatment, when he strongly suspects that if he does not do so, the patient will leave therapy prematurely? For an amplification of these points, see pp. 148 to 150 in the next chapter.

from those available, or be assigned to a particularly prominent and respected therapist. The therapist may intervene with others of significance in the patient's life, he may ask especially low fees or, heresy of all heresies, even pay the patient for coming to therapy! Singly or in combination, procedures such as these clearly follow from the obverse of resistive patient behavior. Overreward provided the patient for behaving "nontherapeutically" is, therefore, a probable dissonance-arousing state of affairs. To label such interventions as departures from current practice is the grossest of understatements. Certain of these specific procedures are examined in detail, but a more appropriate beginning for this hypothesis requires that we first examine the broader rationale and specific nonclinical research behind the concept and the consequences of overcompensation. The bulk of this material is provided by Adams and his research group in their cognitive dissonance studies of what they term, "the psychology of inequity."

The inequity conceptualization grew initially from concern in business and industry with determining fair and appropriate worker compensation. Concretely, what is a fair day's wage for a fair day's work and, in contrast, what wage-work relationships are inequitable? Two relevant classes of considerations are "inputs" and "outcomes." In our industrial example inputs are the individual's (worker's) contribution to the work-for-wage exchange and include his education, experience, skill, seniority, degree of effort expended, and so forth. As Adams stresses, these inputs are defined as perceived by their contributor (or receiver) and are not necessarily isomorphic with the perception of the other party to the exchange. On the other side of the exchange are the rewards received by an individual for his services or inputs, termed "outcomes," and in the industrial setting might include pay, seniority benefits, job status, rewards intrinsic to the job, and such tangibles as a rug on one's office floor, a key to the executive washroom, and, symbol of symbols, a reserved parking spot that remains empty when one is not using it. In a manner analogous to inputs, outcomes are defined as perceived by the parties to the exchange. Adams comments that although his conceptualizations regarding inequity and inequitable exchanges grow primarily from wage inequities,

. . . the theoretical notions advanced are relevant to any social situation in which an exchange takes place, whether the exchange be of the type taking place between man and wife, between football teammates, between teacher and student, or even between Man and his God (Adams, 1963, p. 422).

Hypothesis 3.3, therefore, suggests the addition of "between patient and his therapist" to this series of interpersonal exchange possibilities. For the involuntary, quasi-involuntary, or resistive patient, his primary input is his physical attendance at the psychotherapy sessions. In the absence of overcompensating therapist interventions, his (perceived) outcomes are minimal or nonexistent, that is, the patient feels that he is "getting very little out of coming for therapy." In a real sense, from the patient's perspective, this would be a balanced, consonant, or equitable exchange. Because both inputs and outcomes are low, little if any (perceived) inequity exists and little if any cognitive dissonance is aroused. However, as evidence to be examined will allow us to predict, should the therapist provide "low-input" patients with one or more "high-outcomes" in the form of the kinds of procedures listed earlier, an inequitable exchange will occur, inconsistency between cognitions will exist, and "satisfactory" cognitive dissonance will be aroused in the patient.

Two further aspects of the inequity formulation are relevant to our use of it. The first is *relativity*. Adams observes:

There exist normative expectations of what constitute 'fair' correlations between inputs and outcomes. The bases of the expectations are the correlations obtaining for a reference person or group, a co-worker or colleague, a relative or neighbor, a group of co-workers, a craft group, an industry-wide pattern (p. 424).

Thus, Adams notes, when the normative expectations of the person making social comparisons are violated, when he finds his inputs and outcomes are not in balance in relation to those of others, feelings of inequity result. This concept of relativity finds expression in Adams' formal definition of inequity. Labeling "Person" as any individual for whom equity or inequity is perceived to exist and "Other" as any individual or group used by Person as a referent when he makes social comparisons of his inputs and outcomes, Adams writes: "Inequity exists for Person whenever his perceived job inputs and/or outcomes stand psychologically in an obverse relation to what he perceives are the inputs and/or outcomes of Other" (p. 424). Thus implementation of hypothesis 3.3 involves not only providing the patient with overcompensation by the therapist but awareness by the patient that other patients (of his therapist or in general) are *not* treated similarly. It is of interest to note that Parloff's (1961) study of the therapy relationship, discussed earlier, may be a demonstration of the role of relativity and social comparisons in inequitable therapy exchanges. Parloff reports:

Premature termination of therapy by a patient appears to be related to his perception of the "goodness" of the relationship he has established with his therapist *relative* to the general level of patient-therapist relationships within his [therapy] group. Individuals having the poorer relationships in a group tended to drop out of therapy irrespective of the *absolute* goodness of their therapeutic relationship (p. 37).

It seems reasonable to rephrase Parloff's conclusion in inequity terms by proposing that the patients in question (premature terminators), in their comparisons of their relationships with the therapist to the relationships they perceived existed between the therapist and other (Other) patients, felt they were receiving less in the way of Outcomes (a good relationship) for their inputs (therapeutic participation) than other patients (Other) were for theirs, and feelings of inequity resulted. One major means of reducing cognitive dissonance (here labeled inequity) is by rejection of the communicator or, more generally, by rejecting or derogating one of the major sources of cognitions involved in the dissonant relationship. Thus the patients terminated their therapeutic participation.

The second feature of inequity we wish to examine is *additivity*. Adams proposes that both inputs and outcomes are additive. He notes:

A given total of Person's inputs may be achieved by increasing or decreasing any one or more separate inputs; similarly, a given total of Person's outcomes may result from increasing or decreasing one or more separate outcomes (pp. 426-427).

As Adams illustrates, if in an industrial setting Person found it necessary to increase his inputs in order to reduce inequity, he could do so not only by increasing his effort, but by acquiring additional training or education. He states further:

. . . if greater outcomes were required to achieve equity, obtaining new status symbols might be equivalent to an increase in compensation, or a combination of improved job environment and increased discretionary content of the job might be (p. 427).

We include this brief discussion of additivity for its relevance to subsequent research decisions regarding which specific overcompensating procedures, and how many, the therapist might provide the patient. While these are questions answerable by research only, Adams' position on additivity suggests that a satisfactory demonstration of hypothesis 3.3 is most likely to follow an implementation which includes the use of several frequently used, overcompensating procedures by the therapist.

Investigations of Inequitable Reward

With these considerations regarding relativity and additivity in mind, let us examine the research directly underlying the inequity formulation. Adams and Rosenbaum (1962) sought to test the proposition that when Person is overpaid in relation to Other, he may reduce the resultant feelings of inequity by increasing his inputs. (Hypothesis 3.3, in its bare esesntials, is this last proposition cast into psychotherapeutic terms.) Subjects in this investigation were university students hired to serve as opinion interviewers. They were constituted into two experimental groups, one in which overcompensation was provided and one which was equitably compensated. All subjects were paid at the same hourly rate, but overcompensation subjects were made to feel markedly unqualified to earn at this rate because of their lack of interviewing training and experience and related reasons. The equitably compensated Ss were made to feel qualified to earn the same wage, by being informed that they were far better educated than census takers, that education and intelligence were the prime requisites of interviewing, and so forth. Thus the referent Others for all subjects were trained interviewers at large, not a specific, known person. The prediction that overcompensated subjects would attempt to increase their inputs could not find concrete expression by their seeking to get more training, experience, and so forth. In short, the major avenue of dissonance or inequity reduction for these Ss was to increase their productivity. Results clearly supported this prediction; overcompensated Ss obtained significantly more interviews per unit time than did equitably compensated Ss.

Directly comparable results are provided by Day (1961). His subjects were children who were given training trials in which they had to push a plunger mechanism to obtain M&M candies. The number of candies received on each trial varied between 1 and 6, and was a direct function of the magnitude of pressure exerted on the plunger. After response level had stabilized, 25 M&Ms were provided each S on each of five trials regardless of the pressure exerted. A significant number of Ss responded to the increased reward by increased pressure on the overrewarded trials. In terms of the inequity model, the children were comparing their inputs (pressure) and outcomes (M&Ms) during the overcompensation trials with those during the base rate trials. The latter trials define for the subject what constitutes "equity," and thus the subsequent overpayment is perceived of as inequitable. We see, therefore, that in overcompensating a given patient the therapist may utilize the patient himself, as he was compensated earlier, as the referent Other, and not only other specific patients or patients at large. This possibility increases in saliency when we note that the resistive patients of concern to this chapter have often, and unsuccessfully, made the "therapeutic rounds"; that is, it is far from uncommon for such patients to have sought therapeutic help elsewhere, with little in the way of "therapeutic success" or high therapeutic outcomes. It seems likely that the more resistive or "involuntary" the patient has been in the past, the less likely were his past therapists inclined to treat him as "special" in a positive sense, to have provided him with overcompensation naturalistically. In short, we propose that the resistive patient, more than the voluntary, less ambivalent patient, may come to psychotherapy with a ready-made perceptual base for judging equitable and inequitable behavior toward him by his therapist, and that the more his resistive interactions with earlier therapists have led to his being "undercompensated" by them the less actual overcompensation a new therapist need provide to establish a patient perception of inequity.

A study by Arrowood (1961) provides an additional, and perhaps more powerful, demonstration of the effect of inequitable outcomes on increased inputs. In Adams and Rosenbaum's study, Arrowood held, overcompensated subjects may have worked harder not because of overcompensation per se but because the induction of overcompensation led them to feel unqualified and unsure of holding their jobs. (All Ss thought they were going to be employed as interviewers for several weeks.) If this assumption is correct, Arrowood states, the same results might not have emerged if subjects were convinced that their employer would have no knowledge of their productivity. On the other hand, if the effect of overcompensation on inputs is not an artifact, overcompensated subjects should produce more than equitably compensated controls whether or not they thought the employer would learn of their productivity. Arrowood's experimental groups and procedures were identical to Adams and Rosenbaum's, except that overcompensated subjects were split into two subgroups, public and private. The public were led to believe that their employer would be aware of their interview productivity (their work was submitted to the employer directly by them), the private overcompensated subjects were under the impression that the employer would never learn of their productivity rate (work was mailed by Ss in preaddressed envelopes to a firm in a distant state). In *both* the public and private conditions overpaid subjects produced significantly more than equitably paid controls. Thus further evidence is provided for the influence of overcompensation as a means of increasing an individual's productivity.

To the extent that increased productivity from overcompensation, in the literal sense in which productivity is used in these studies, has extrapolatable implications for the "productivity" of resistive patients in psychotherapy, we must also focus on the quality of this increased productivity. That is, hypothesis 3.3 seeks to suggest a means of inducing the patient not only toward *more* therapeutic behavior in an absolute sense but also toward better quality therapeutic behavior (e.g., a more positive affective contribution to the therapeutic relationship). Two final studies reported by Adams speak directly on this issue of quality of inputs.

In the first study (Adams & Rosenbaum, 1962) it was hypothesized that whereas subjects overpaid *by the hour* would produce more than equitably paid controls, subjects overpaid *on a piecework basis* would produce less. The rationale for this piecework prediction was that since inequity was associated with each *unit* produced, feelings of inequity or the input-outcome discrepancy would increase as work proceeded. Hence, the investigators note, subjects would strive not so much to reduce inequity as to avoid increasing it by restricting production. Results provided clear confirmation of the hypothesis. Overpaid hourly subjects produced significantly more than controls; overpaid piecework subjects produced significantly less than controls. However, although results support the prediction, an explanation for them other than avoiding increases in inequity by restricting production exists. This explanation brings in the quality-of-production variable, as our final inequity study illustrates.

Adams (1963) observes:

> There is, however, an alternative explanation that would account for the same manifest behavior. It is entirely possible for subjects to *reduce* dissonance by increasing their effort on the production of each unit, for example, by increasing the quality of their work, which would have the effect of increasing the production time per unit and, therefore, have the consequence of reducing productivity. . . . This explanation assumes that pieceworkers would reduce their dissonance by increasing their inputs, very much as the hourly workers. Only the mode of increasing inputs varies: whereas hourly workers increase inputs on a quantitative dimension, pieceworkers increase them on a qualitative basis (p. 434).

With this as rationale, it was hypothesized that pieceworkers who perceive that they are inequitably overpaid will perform better quality work and have lower productivity than pieceworkers paid at the same rate who perceive they are equitably paid. The same interview task used in the earlier studies was employed, along with a modification permitting the measurement of quality of work. This modification was the addition of certain open-ended items. As before, productivity was defined in terms of the number of interviews obtained per unit of interviewing time. As predicted, the overpaid pieceworkers produced less work than their equitably paid counterparts, but what they did produce was of significantly higher quality, as these variables have been defined. Thus we are provided with additional clarification of the potential impact of cognitive dissonance arousal via induced inequity as a means of altering work inputs in an industrial setting and, by extrapolation, patient inputs in psychotherapy. We now return to an examination of some of the concrete means we have suggested as procedures a therapist might utilize for providing overcompensation to the resistive patient. This examination focuses on altering by overcompensation those patient inputs that involve his attraction to the psychotherapist and, more generally, the therapy relationship.

Inequitable Reward in Psychotherapy

Therapist payment to the patient for the latter's attendance at psychotherapy clearly appears to be the grossest departure from current clinical practices of the various overcompensation procedures listed earlier, and is therefore an appropriate procedure to examine first. As might be suspected, there is far from a wealth of relevant research dealing with this procedure, but what does exist provides support for the contention that payment provided patients can be a powerful means of favorably influencing the quality of the therapeutic relationship. Two studies are considered; in both the patients involved were clearly of the type we have described as involuntary and highly resistive to therapeutic participation. Slack (1960), who conducted the first study, comments on one likely basis for relationship difficulties with one subclass of such patients or potential patients:

> The doctor-patient relationship is, after all, a very special transaction . . . it takes years of conditioning, cultural processing and even interested study in popular literature before the middle class child understands what doctors can and cannot do. We cannot expect the working class delinquent to respond to a treatment which begins only after a fairly realistic understanding of this situation develops (p. 241).

Slack argues, as we have been urging throughout, that because typical procedures for "indoctrinating" patients into meaningful therapeutic participation and for sustaining such particicipation are characteristically unsuccessful or highly inefficient with persons such as the late adolescent delinquents he has studied, there is a major need for new approaches. Slack's response to this need is, as we shall see, both imaginative and provocative. As a substitute for a role model based on a conceptualization of the doctor-patient relationship, his procedures for approaching his delinquent subjects are rooted in the relationship typically obtaining between an experimenter and his subjects. Thus his procedures are labeled, "experimenter-subject psychotherapy." His subjects were eleven "hard-core delinquents with long police records going back to early years. They were truly recalcitrant individuals . . ." (p. 247). All of these subjects, Slack adds, shared a marked, explicitly stated resistance to participating in psychotherapeutic treatment. Experimenter-subject psychotherapy, in its early and middle stages, is at least formally conceptualized as a job and not as psychotherapy. Thus Ss are hired as research subjects and are not referred to as patients. Experimenter-subject meetings in fact are devoted to research activities. The nature of these research activities, however, is what eventually permits the inclusion of "psychotherapy" in experimenter-subject psychotherapy. Slack observes:

In the very early stages of research . . . it is not uncommon for psychologists of even the strictest behavioristic bias to sit down with the subject and listen very carefully to what he says about his experiences. At this point both the experimenter and the subject are phenomenologists and introspectionists, and although what is communicated is heuristic and cannot often pass for scientific fact, it is of the utmost utility as far as discovery is concerned (p. 244).

The research activities in which the subject participated consisted primarily of discussions with the experimenter about the S's personal reactions to and feelings about results of various tests administered to each S or of other research procedures in which S participated. It is this major introspective feature of the purported research tasks, combined with a supportive, nurturant, nonthreatening atmosphere which, Slack reports, leads more and more over time to an experimenter-subject relationship that, in fact if not in name, is describable as a highly positive therapist-patient relationship. As Slack describes it:

In E-S psychotherapy the inquiry and evaluation part of the experimental session is lengthened, elaborated, and expanded into almost unrecognizable proportions. It becomes the main body of the experiment, may last for years, and provides the structure of a relationship which can be as completely psychotherapeutic as circumstances such as the skill of the experimenter-therapist will allow (p. 244).

By way of results, he reports that with all the subject-patients in-volved so far a highly satisfactory interpersonal relationship with the experimenter-therapist did in fact develop and that Ss were engaged actively and meaningfully in the experimental-therapeutic introspec-tive tasks that constituted their "job duties." Although it is obviously correct to label this research report as "only impressionistic," and al-though the positive relationships that developed may be "real" but only a "Slack-effect," that is, therapist-specific, the key point remains: not only would involvement in a seemingly positive therapeutic rela-tionship not have taken place for these delinquent Ss had they not been paid, but no participation or involvement of any kind would have occurred.

A second and less impressionistic study, reported by Schwitzgebel and Schwitzgebel (1963), yielded evidence bearing not only on the effects of this approach on the experimenter-subject relationship, but also on certain criteria of therapeutic outcome. More important for our present purposes, the study provides grounds for the appropriate-ness of construing such participation-for-pay as "over-compensation." Stated otherwise, it appears that the subjects felt their outcomes to be inequitably higher than their inputs.

Forty subjects participated in the study. Twenty were controls who were carefully matched with the twenty experimental subjects on relevant criteria, and used for comparative purposes on the indices of therapeutic outcome. The control Ss did not participate in the ex-perimenter-subject therapy procedures. The experimental subjects, average age 17, had all spent six months or more in prison. For the most part they were of a lower-lower socioeconomic level, and eleven of them had histories of active refusal to participate in psychotherapeu-tic treatment. In the typical initial contact the investigator approached a group of boys on a streetcorner in an "appropriate" neighborhood and indicated the availability of jobs as experimental subjects if any of them qualified. In the investigator's terms from one such initial contact:

> We are from college and trying to find out what kids think about cops and teachers and school and stuff like that. Instead of reading a bunch of books we decided just to go out and ask the kids themselves. We usually pay a dollar an hour for kids to talk into a tape recorder. . . . We want kids who know what they are talking about—not just a bunch of bull. You've got to have a record or know what you're talking about (pp. 4-5).

The degree to which subjects perceived the initial input-outcome exchange as inequitable in the direction of overreward is evident in the investigator's statement:

The offer of cash for what appeared to be a very easy job ("just talkin") had a great attraction. Ss were reminded that they could quit the job whenever they wished if they didn't like it and that they could talk about anything they wanted. As the project became known and gained considerable gang prestige, the problem was not one of recruitment, but of deciding on what basis volunteers should be turned away. . . . The Es have generally been reluctant to hire volunteers in order to avoid the possibility that petty crimes might be committed in order to meet project "qualifications" (pp. 5-6).

In a manner not unlike Slack's procedures, experimental Ss in this study participated in a series of sessions in which they discussed primarily their own feelings and behaviors. Sessions lasted an hour, two to five times a week, and took place for nine months to a year for each S. Further seemingly overcompensatory rewards were provided as the Ss participation continued. Specifically, in addition to the payment for participation immediately following each session, Ss were given cash bonuses (twenty-five cents to one dollar) for exceptionally "good" interviews as determined by E. Such bonuses, or small unexpected gifts, were also given to S for certain socially desirable behaviors that occurred during the interviews. Nonmonetary rewards were also provided, such as acquiescing to S's requests for the opportunity to participate in activities under E's control other than the usual interviews (e.g., group discussions or building electronic equipment). These activities, the investigators note, were scheduled to meet the desire on the part of Ss to spend more time in the laboratory. The detailed description provided by the investigators of the course of E-S therapy with their Ss clearly suggests the development and stabilization of decidedly favorable interpersonal relationships between Es and Ss. A comparison of experimental subjects with their "untreated" controls revealed significant treatment outcome differences favoring the experimental subjects in terms of the mean number of subsequent arrests during a three-year follow-up period. Further, among the Ss in both conditions who were arrested during the follow-up period, experimental Ss spent on the average significantly shorter terms in prison, suggesting that their crimes were less negative from a penal viewpoint. Thus the investigators concluded:

The employment of delinquents as experimental Ss, opens, we believe, several interesting avenues of exploration. This procedure suggests that certain segments of the population usually highly resistant to any form of psychological intervention are quite ready to accept and to profit from such intervention when there are (from the viewpoint of the "patient") definite, concrete, short-term rewards (p. 11).

What may we say in summary of these two studies of experimenter-subject psychotherapy? Unlike the nonclinical studies of Adams and his research group, no direct comparisons are made of equitably and inequitably paid subjects undergoing experimenter–subject psychotherapy. We have held it quite likely that subjects in both *E–S* studies perceived themselves to be overcompensated, but the evidence for this contention is largely anecdotal or inferential, hence must be considered suggestive. The relationship and outcome findings in these studies, however, clearly add credence to the potential value of more extended rigorous research examination of overcompensation by payment to the patient. We hope that this examination would focus not only on the genuinely involuntary patient, as in the studies by Slack, and Schwitzgebel and Schwitzgebel, but would encompass more fully the range of resistive, ambivalent, or equivocal psychotherapy patients.

In addition to the pay-for-participation implementation of hypothesis 3.3, we listed earlier a number of other special, overcompensatory procedures that a therapist might institute with a resistive patient. No doubt a large number of still other procedures might be suggested. The psychotherapy literature yields but a single study which examines the consequences of some of these additional procedures. This final investigation of what appears to possibly be overcompensation-in-psychotherapy, conducted by Stevenson (1962), is clinical-impressionistic in design and largely positive in its results. His ten-patient sample was diagnosed psychoneurotic, and his investigative goal was, as in ours, to find means of accelerating patient change in psychotherapy. Stevenson comments:

> The modification of incentives forms an important part of many efforts to influence behavior. "Time off" for good behavior in prison, payment of workers for "piecework," "incentive bonuses" for business executives, and examinations for students illustrate the manipulation of incentives to influence behavior (p. 21).

This framework combined with Stevenson's observation that in ". . . recoveries from psychoneurosis without treatment, . . . recovery had sometimes become initiated or accelerated when new incentives for different behavioral responses confronted the patient" (p. 20) suggested to him the possibility that more rapid behavioral change in his therapy patients might follow from providing them with concrete incentives for change. In addition, as indicated later, under certain circumstances deterrents and punishments were instituted in series with or instead of rewards or incentives. The patient behaviors which these procedures sought to induce were willingness to be exposed to phobic stimuli, assertiveness in highly submissive patients, punctuality in tardy patients, increased social activity in withdrawn or shy patients, and lessened sleep in somnolent patients. Incentives included a reduction or cancellation of the fee for one or more sessions, the company of the therapist during exposure of the patient to a stressful situation, helping the patient to obtain the approval of a particularly significant and respected superior, and other interventions in the patient's behalf vis à vis significant persons in the patient's extratherapy world. Deterrents took the form of such procedures as raising the fee for one or more sessions, postponement of the next appointment until completion of an assigned extratherapy task, reproof by a respected superior, and so forth. In nine of the ten patients with whom such procedures were instituted Stevenson reports that the desired behavioral response occurred. He concludes:

I believe that occasions arise when the therapist can manipulate incentives to the benefit of his patients. Many patients, especially those with severe behavior disorders, may prove unamenable to conventional psychotherapy. It fails to provide them with sufficient incentives for change. . . . But even with patients who come readily to therapy and seem amenable to its usual devices, we may occasionally shorten the duration of treatment by increasing their therapeutic experiences through judicious handling of incentives (p. 26).

It is not quite clear from the nature of Stevenson's comments whether his patients perceived his interventions as equitable or inequitable, as just reward or overcompensation. Thus one must be cautious in viewing his impressions as further evidence of inequity. Nevertheless, his findings are provocative and, when viewed in combination with the Slack (1960) and Schwitzgebel and Schwitzgebel (1963) findings, provide a clear suggestion that the therapeutic value of overcompensatory procedures, if they do exist, may not be limited to the resistive patient we have focused on throughout this chapter.

THERAPIST ATTRACTION

The three hypotheses presented in this chapter have sought to describe means with the potential for increasing patient attraction to the therapist; that is, on the face of it, we have focused exclusively on the patient's contribution to the therapy relationship. We propose, however, that an additional contribution to an improved therapeutic relationship may result from manipulations such as these. There is considerable evidence to assume that manipulation of the inputs of either participant in the therapeutic interaction is equivalent to manipulation of the inputs of *both* participants. Therefore, it is proposed that manipulation of patient attraction to the therapist is, in fact, also manipulation of the therapist's attraction toward the patient. Jones and Thibaut (1958), in their classification of diverse two-person interactions, have discussed what they label "reciprocally contingent" interpersonal relationships. In such relationships *both* participants function as variable responders acting as a partial cause of the other's behavior. In the two-person interaction called individual psychotherapy this reciprocal contingency model would find expression in a variety of concrete ways, including the position that the therapist's behavior and feelings toward a given patient are in large measure a function of that patient's own behavior toward and feelings about his therapist, rather than being standardized across a series of patients for that therapist. With regard to reciprocity of attractiveness, one of the writers (Heller et al., 1963) has in fact demonstrated that friendly clients "pull" significantly more therapist friendliness than do non-friendly clients. In this investigation four actors were rigorously trained to serve as (1) dominant-friendly, (2) dominant-hostile, (3) dependent-friendly, and (4) dependent-hostile therapy clients. Each client-actor was presented in counterbalanced order to 34 psychotherapists-in-training for half-hour interviews. In all cases the therapists perceived their interviewees as genuine clients. Each interview was observed by a judge trained to rate the therapists on the same dimensions which had previously been built into the client-actors' roles. Results showed that "client friendliness was judged to have evoked significantly more interviewer friendliness than was the case for client hostility" (p. 11). As a further demonstration of the reciprocally contingent nature of the therapist-patient interaction, dominant client behavior was judged to have evoked significantly more interviewer dependency than was true of dependent behavior.

This influence of the patient upon his psychotherapist's feelings and behavior is further illustrated by a number of other investigations. For example, the degree of therapist attraction toward a given patient-candidate and his expressed interest in taking the patient into treatment has been shown to correlate significantly with ratings of patient prognosis (Affleck & Garfield, 1961; Wallach & Strupp, 1960), patient motivation to enter therapy (Raskin, 1961) and ratings of patient ego strength, insight and social adjustment (Wallach & Strupp, 1960). Negative patient behavior or characteristics may also be reciprocated by the therapist. Russell (1961) found that negativistic patients generated significantly greater anxiety in their therapists than did more positively oriented patients. Bandura, Lipsher and Miller (1960) demonstrated that in the face of patient hostility directed toward him the therapist who tends to express his own hostility directly and who is low in need for approval permits and encourages further expressions of patient hostility; therapists less directly expressive of their own hostility and higher in need for approval are less likely to respond with permissiveness on encouragement in reaction to patient hostility. Other aspects of the therapist's behavior toward his patient have been shown to be responsive to patient characteristics. A study reported by Cutler (1958) found that when behavior exhibited by the patient is similar to behavior that has been identified as conflictual for the therapist, the therapist's responses to this behavior will be judged less adequate for therapeutic purposes than his responses to material that is relatively nonconflictual for him. These studies combine to demonstrate rather clearly that both positive and negative therapist feelings and behaviors may be elicited by specific positive and negative patient characteristics. Investigations reported by Barrington (1961), Peterson et al. (1958), Saslow and Matarazzo (1959), Shapiro (1962), and Van der Veen (1965) are among several studies that provide further confirmation of the reciprocally contingent nature of individual psychotherapy. Studies such as these, when combined with the increased clinical interest in counter-transference effects in recent years, have led to a corresponding increase in acceptance of this reciprocal contingency viewpoint. Thus Marmor (1960) comments with regard to the therapist-patient relationship in psychoanalysis, ". . . the analytic relationship is seen more and more as a dynamic two-way interaction rather than as the analysand's relationship to the analyst" (p. 569). In all, therefore, there is strong reason to suspect that procedures introduced into psychotherapy to increase patient attraction to the therapist would, to the extent they are successful, lead to the therapist having a more favorable view of the patient. Thus the impact of such procedures on the therapy relationship may be a dual impact. In the final analysis, of course, the accuracy and significance of this reciprocal contingency position, as well as of the three relationship hypotheses we have presented, will have to be determined by direct research examination.

REFERENCES

Adams, J. S.   The measurement of perceived equity in pay differentials. Unpublished manuscript, General Electric Co., Behavioral Research Service, 1961.

Adams, J. S.   Toward an understanding of inequity. *J. abnorm. soc. Psychol.,* 1963, **67**, 422–436.

Adams, J. S., & Rosenbaum, W. B.   The relationship of worker productivity to cognitive dissonance. *J. appl. Psychol.,* 1962, **46**, 161–164.

Adler, A.   *The practice and theory of individual psychology.* New York: Harcourt, Brace, 1924.

Affleck, D. C., & Garfield, S. L.   Predictive judgments of therapists and duration of stay in psychotherapy. *J. clin. Psychol.,* 1961, **17**, 134–137.

Alexander, F., & French, T. M.   *Psychoanalytic therapy.* New York: Ronald Press, 1946.

Apfelbaum, B.   *Dimensions of transference in psychotherapy.* Berkeley: Univer. of California Press, 1958.

Arnett, C. E., Davidson, H. H., & Lewis, H. N.   Prestige as a factor in attitude changes. *Sociol. soc. Res.,* 1931, **16**, 49–55.

Aronson, E., & Golden, B. W.   The effects of relevant and irrelevant aspects of communicator credibility on opinion change. *J. Pers.,* 1962, **30**, 137–146.

Aronson, E., Turner, J. A., & Carlsmith, J. M.   Communicator credibility and communication discrepancy as determinants of opinion change. *J. abnorm. soc. Psychol.,* 1963, **67**, 31–36.

Arrowood, A. J.   Some effects on productivity of justified and unjustified levels of reward under public and private conditions. Unpublished doctoral dissertation, University of Minnesota, 1961.

Ashby, J. D., Ford, D. H., Guerney, B. G., Jr., & Guerney, L.   Effects on clients of a reflective and a leading type of psychotherapy. *Psychol. Monogr.,* 1957, **7**, 1–32.

Back, K. W.   Influence through social communication. *J. abnorm. soc. Psychol.,* 1951, **46**, 9–23.

Bandura, A., Lipsher, D. H., & Miller, P. E.   Psychotherapists' approach-avoidance reactions to patients' expressions of hostility. *J. consult. Psychol.,* 1960, **24**, 1–8.

Barrington, B. L.   Prediction from counselor behavior of client perception and of case outcome. *J. counsel. Psychol.,* 1961, **8**, 37–42.

Beir, E.   Client-centered therapy and the involuntary patient. *J. consult. Psychol.,* 1952, **16**, 332–337.

Bergin, A. E.   The effect of dissonant persuasive communications upon changes in a self-referring attitude. *J. Pers.,* 1962, **30**, 423–438.

Bordin, E. S.   Inside the therapeutic hour. In E. A. Rubinstein & M. B.

Parloff (Eds.), *Research in psychotherapy.* Washington: American Psychological Association, 1959. Pp. 235–246.

Bown, O. H.   An investigation of therapeutic relationships in client-centered psychotherapy. Unpublished doctoral dissertation, University of Chicago, 1954.

Brehm, J. W., & Cohen, A. R.   *Explorations in cognitive dissonance.* New York: Wiley, 1962.

Brehm, J. W., & Leventhal, G. S.   An experiment on the effects of commitment. In J. W. Brehm & A. R. Cohen, *Explorations in cognitive dissonance.* New York: Wiley, 1962. Pp. 192–198.

Brock, T. C.   Cognitive restructuring and attitude change. *J. abnorm. soc. Psychol.,* 1962, **64,** 264–271.

Brock, T. C., & Blackwood, J. E.   Dissonance reduction, social comparisons, and modification of others' opinions. *J. abnorm. soc. Psychol.,* 1963, **65,** 319–324.

Burdick, H. A., & Burnes, A. J.   A test of "strain toward symmetry" theories. *J. abnorm. soc. Psychol.,* 1958, **57,** 367–370.

Centers, R.   A laboratory adaptation of the conversational procedure for the conditioning of verbal operants. *J. abnorm. soc. Psychol.,* 1963, **67,** 334–339.

Cohen, A. R., Brehm, J. W., & Fleming, W. H.   Attitude change and justification for compliance. *J. abnorm. soc. Psychol.,* 1958, **56,** 276–278.

Cohen, A. R., & Latané, B.   An experiment on choice in commitment to counter-attitudinal behavior. In J. W. Brehm & A. R. Cohen, *Explorations in cognitive dissonance.* New York: Wiley, 1962. Pp. 88–91.

Cohen, A. R., Terry, H. I., & Jones, C. B.   Attitudinal effects of choice in exposure to counter-propaganda. *J. abnorm. soc. Psychol.,* 1959, **58,** 388–391.

Collier, R. M.   Consciousness as a regulatory field: a theory of psychotherapy. *J. abnorm. soc. Psychol.,* 1957, **55,** 275–282.

Coons, W. H.   Interaction and insight in group psychotherapy. *Canad. J. Psychol.,* 1957, **11,** 1–8.

Culbertson, F. M.   Modification of an emotionally held attitude through role playing. *J. abnorm. soc. Psychol.,* 1957, **54,** 230–233.

Cutler, R. L.   Countertransference effects in psychotherapy. *J. consult. Psychol.,* 1958, **22,** 349–356.

Davis, K., & Jones, E. E.   Changes in interpersonal perception as a means of reducing cognitive dissonance. *J. abnorm. soc. Psychol.,* 1960, **61,** 402–410.

Day, C. R.   Some consequences of increased reward following establishment of output-reward expectation level. Unpublished master's thesis, Duke University, 1961.

Deutsch, F., & Murphy, W. F.   *The clinical interview.* New York: International Universities Press, 1955.

Dreikurs, R. The Adlerian approach to psychodynamics. In M. I. Stein (Ed.), *Contemporary psychotherapies.* New York: Free Press, 1961, 60–79.

Eaton, J. W. The client-practitioner relationship as a variable in the evaluation of treatment outcome. *Psychiatry,* 1959, **22,** 189–195.

Edwards, E. D. Observations of the use and efficacy of changing a patient's concept of his role—a psychotherapeutic device. Unpublished master's thesis, Fort Hays Kansas State College, 1940.

Eissler, K. R. Some problems of delinquency. In K. R. Eissler (Ed.), *Searchlights on delinquency.* New York: International Universities Press, 1949. Pp. 3–25.

Festinger, L. *A theory of cognitive dissonance.* Stanford: Stanford Univer. Press, 1957.

Festinger, L., & Carlsmith, J. M. Cognitive consequences of forced compliance. *J. abnorm. soc. Psychol.,* 1959, **58,** 203–210.

Festinger, L., Schachter, S., & Back, K. *Social pressures in informal groups.* New York: Harper, 1950.

Fiedler, F. E. The concept of an ideal therapeutic relationship. *J. consult. Psychol.,* 1950, **14,** 39–45.

Fiedler, F. E. Quantitative studies on the role of therapists' feelings toward their patients. In O. H. Mowrer (Ed.), *Psychotherapy theory and research.* New York: Ronald Press, 1953. Pp. 296–315.

Frank, J. D. The dynamics of the psychotherapeutic relationship. *Psychiatry,* 1959, **22,** 17–39.

French, J. R. P., Jr., & Snyder, R. Leadership and interpersonal power. In D. Cartwright (Ed.), *Studies in social power.* Ann Arbor: Institute for Social Research, 1959. Pp. 118–149.

Freud, S. *The standard edition of the complete psychological works of Sigmund Freud.* London: The Hogarth Press, 1957.

Gardner, E. F., & Thompson, G. G. *Social relations and morale in small groups.* New York: Appleton-Century-Crofts, 1956.

Gendlin, E. T. Initiating psychotherapy with "unmotivated" patients. *Psychiat. Quart.,* 1961, **35,** 1–6.

Gendlin, E. T., Jenny, R. H., & Shlien, J. Counselor ratings of process and outcomes in client-centered therapy. *J. clin. Psychol.,* 1960, **16,** 210–213.

Gerard, H. B. The anchorage of opinions in face-to-face groups. *Hum. Relat.,* 1954, **7,** 313–325.

Goldstein, A. P., & Heller, K. Role expectations, participant personality characteristics, and the client-counselor relationship. Unpublished manuscript, August, 1960.

Gordon, R. L. Interaction between attitude and the definitions of the situation in the expression of opinion. *Amer. sociol. Rev.,* 1952, **17,** 50–58.

Grinker, R. R. A transactional model for psychotherapy. In M. I. Stein (Ed.), *Contemporary psychotherapies.* New York: Free Press, 1961. Pp. 190–213.

Halman, F. S.   An experimental study of the effects of Ethos in public speaking. *Speech Monogr.*, 1949, **16**, 190–202.

Haley, J.   *Strategies of psychotherapy.* New York: Grune & Stratton, 1963.

Harrow, G. S.   The effects of psychodrama group therapy on role behavior of schizophrenic patients. *Grp. Psychother.*, 1951, **3**, 316–320.

Harvey, O. J., & Beverly, G. D.   Some personality correlates of concept change through role playing. *J. abnorm. soc. Psychol.*, 1961, **63**, 125–130.

Heider, J.   *The psychology of interpersonal relations.* New York: Wiley, 1958.

Heine, R. W.   An investigation of the relationship between changes and responsible factors as seen by clients following treatment by psychotherapists of the psychoanalytic, Adlerian and non-directive schools. Unpublished doctoral dissertation, University of Chicago, 1950.

Heller, K., & Goldstein, A. P.   Client dependency and therapist expectancy as relationship maintaining variables in psychotherapy. *J. consult. Psychol.*, 1961, **25**, 371–375.

Heller, K., Myers, R. A., & Kline, L.   Interviewer behavior as a function of standardized client roles. *J. consult. Psychol.*, 1963, **27**, 117–122.

Holt, R. R., & Luborsky, L.   Research in the selection of psychiatrists. *Bull. Menninger Clin.*, 1952, **16**, 125–135.

Hovland, C. I., Janis, I. L., & Kelley, H. H.   *Communication and persuasion.* New York: Yale Univer. Press, 1953.

Hovland, C. I., & Mandell, W.   An experimental comparison of conclusion-drawing by the communicator and by the audience. *J. abnorm. soc. Psychol.*, 1952, **47**, 581–588.

Hovland, C. I., & Weiss, W.   The influence of source credibility on communication effectiveness. *Publ. Opin. Quart.*, 1951, **15**, 635–650.

Hunt, J. McV., Ewing, T. N., LaForge, R., & Gilbert, W. M.   An integrated approach to research on therapeutic counseling with samples of results. *J. counsel. Psychol.*, 1959, **6**, 46–54.

Hunt, J. McV., & Kogan, L. S.   *Assessing the results of social casework: a manual on judging movement.* New York: Family Service Association of America, 1950.

Jackson, D. D.   Interactional psychotherapy. In M. I. Stein (Ed.), *Contemporary psychotherapies.* New York: Free Press, 1961. Pp. 256–271.

Janis, I. L., & King, B. T.   The influence of role playing on opinion change. *J. abnorm. soc. Psychol.*, 1954, **49**, 211–218.

Jones, E. E., Hester, S. L., Farina, A., & Davis, K. E.   Reactions to unfavorable personal evaluations as a function of the evaluator's perceived adjustment. *J. abnorm. soc. Psychol.*, 1959, **59**, 363–370.

Jones, E. E., & Thibaut, J. W.   Interaction goals as bases of inference in interpersonal perception. In R. Taguiri & L. Petrullo (Eds.), *Person perception and interpersonal behavior.* Stanford: Stanford Univer. Press, 1958. Pp. 151–178.

Jones, F. D., & Peters, A. N.   An experimental evaluation of group psychotherapy. *J. abnorm. soc. Psychol.,* 1952, **47**, 345–353.

Jourard, S. M., & Lasakow, P.   Some factors in self-disclosure. *J. abnorm. soc. Psychol.,* 1958, **56**, 91–98.

Kelly, G. A.   *The psychology of personal constructs.* New York: Norton, 1955.

Kelly, J. G., Blake, R. R., & Stromberg, C. E.   The effect of role training on role reversal. *Grp. Psychother.,* 1957, **10**, 95–104.

Kelman, H.   Attitude change as a function of response restriction. *Hum. Relat.,* 1953, **6**, 185–214.

Kelman, H. C., & Hovland, C. I.   Reinstatement of the communicator in delayed measurement of opinion change. *J. abnorm. soc. Psychol.,* 1953, **48**, 327–335.

King, B. T., & Janis, I. L.   Comparison of the effectiveness of improvised vs. non-improvised role-playing in producing opinion changes. *Hum. Relat.,* 1956, **9**, 177–186.

Krasner, L.   Role taking research and psychotherapy. Res. rep. of VA Palo Alto, 1959, No. 5.

Kulp, D. H.   Prestige as measured by single-experience changes and their permanency. *J. educ. Res.,* 1934, **27**, 663–672.

Lazarus, A.   Group therapy of phobic disorders by systematic desensitization. *J. abnorm. soc. Psychol.,* 1961, **63**, 504–510.

Levin, G., & Shapiro, D.   The operant conditioning of conversation. *J. exp. anal. Behav.,* 1962, **5**, 309–316.

Levy, L.   *Psychological interpretation.* New York: Holt, Rinehart & Winston, 1963.

Libo, L.   The projective expression of patient-therapist attraction. *J. clin. Psychol.,* 1957, **13**, 33–36.

Libo, L.   Picture impressions: a projective technique for investigating the patient-therapist relationship. Baltimore: University of Maryland Medical School, 1959.

Lieberman, S.   The effects of changes in roles on the attitudes of role occupants. *Hum. Relat.,* 1956, **9**, 385–402.

Loevinger, J.   Conflict of commitment in clinical research. *Amer. Psychologist,* 1963, **18**, 241–251.

Maier, N. R. F.   *Principles of human relations.* New York: Wiley, 1952.

Mann, J. H.   Experimental evaluations of role playing. *Psychol. Bull.,* 1956, **53**, 227–234.

Marmor, J.   The reintegration of psychoanalysis into psychiatric practice. *Arch. gen. Psychiat.,* 1960, **3**, 569–574.

Mellinger, G. D.   Interpersonal trust as a factor in communication. *J. abnorm. soc. Psychol.,* 1956, **52**, 304–309.

Mendelsohn, R. M., Yates, J. W., & Peterson, L.   The experimental aspect of psychotherapy. *Amer. J. Psychother.,* 1957, **11**, 254–261.

Moreno, J. L. *Group psychotherapy, a symposium.* New York: Beacon House, 1945.

Murray, E. J. Learning theory and psychotherapy: biotropic versus sociotropic approaches. *J. counsel. Psychol.,* 1963, 10, 250–255.

Newcomb, T. M. *Personality and social change: attitude formation in a student community.* New York: Dryden, 1943.

Newcomb, T. M. The prediction of interpersonal attraction. *Amer. Psychologist,* 1956, 11, 575–586.

Osgood, C. E., & Tannenbaum, P. H. The principle of congruity in the prediction of attitude change. *Psychol. Rev.,* 1955, 62, 42–55.

Parloff, M. B. Therapist-patient relationship and outcome of psychotherapy. *J. consult. Psychol.,* 1961, 25, 29–38.

Patterson,, C. H. The place of values in counseling and psychotherapy. *J. counsel. Psychol.,* 1958, 5, 216–223.

Peterson, A. O. D., Snyder, W. U., Guthrie, G. M., & Ray, W. S. Therapist factors: an exploratory investigation of therapeutic biases. *J. counsel. Psychol.,* 1958, 5, 169–173.

Psychology in the States. *Amer. Psychologist,* 1963, 18, 680–682.

Quinn, R. D. Psychotherapists' expressions as an index to the quality of early therapeutic relationships established by representatives of the non-directive, Adlerian, and psychoanalytic schools. Unpublished doctoral dissertation. University of Chicago, 1950.

Rabbie, J. M., Brehm, J. W., & Cohen, A. R. Verbalization and reactions to cognitive dissonance. *J. Pers.,* 1959, 27, 407–417.

Rachman, S. The treatment of anxiety and phobic reactions by systematic desensitization psychotherapy. *J. abnorm. soc. Psychol.,* 1959, 58, 259–263.

Raskin, A. Factors therapist associate with motivation to enter psychotherapy. *J. clin. Psychol.,* 1961, 17, 62–65.

Rasmussen, G., & Zander, A. Group membership and self-evaluation. *Hum. Relat.,* 1954, 7, 239–251.

Raush, H. L., & Bordin, E. S. Warmth in personality development and in psychotherapy. *Psychiatry,* 1957, 20, 351–363.

Redl, F., & Wineman, D. *Children who hate.* Glencoe, Ill.; Free Press, 1951.

Robinson, A. J. A further validation of role therapy. Unpublished master's thesis, Fort Hays Kansas State College, 1940.

Rogers, C. R. The characteristics of a helping relationship. In M. I. Stein (Ed.), *Contemporary psychotherapies.* New York: Free Press, 1961. Pp. 95–112.

Rosenberg, P. An experimental analysis of psychodrama. Unpublished doctoral dissertation, Harvard University, 1952.

Rosenthal, D. Changes in some moral values following psychotherapy. *J. consult. Psychol.,* 1955, 19, 431–436.

Rotter, J. *Social learning and clinical psychology.* New York: Prentice-Hall, 1954.

Russell, P. D. Counselor anxiety in relation to clinical experience and hostile or friendly clients. Unpublished doctoral dissertation, Pennsylvania State University, 1961.

Sapolsky, A. Effect of interpersonal relationships upon verbal conditioning. *J. abnorm. soc. Psychol.,* 1960, **60**, 241–246.

Sapolsky, A. Relationship between patient-doctor compatability, mutual perception, and outcome of treatment. *J. abnorm. Psychol.,* 1965, **70**, 70–76.

Saslow, G., & Matarazzo, J. D. A technique for studying changes in interview behavior. In E. A. Rubenstein & M. B. Parloff (Eds.), *Research in Psychotherapy.* Washington: American Psychological Association, 1959. Pp. 125–159.

Sause, L. M. Role playing the selected problems of student teachers. Unpublished doctoral dissertation, Teacher's College, Columbia University, 1954.

Schofield, W. *Psychotherapy, the purchase of friendship.* Englewood Cliffs, N.J.: Prentice-Hall, 1964.

Schrier, H. The significance of identification in psychotherapy. *Amer. J. Orthopsychiat.,* 1953, **23**, 585–605.

Schutz, W. C. *FIRO: A three-dimensional theory of interpersonal behavior.* New York: Rinehart, 1958.

Schwitzgebel, R., & Schwitzgebel, R. Therapeutic research: a procedure for the reduction of adolescent crime. Presented at American Psychological Association, Philadelphia, August, 1963.

Scott, W. A. Attitude change through reward of verbal behavior. *J. abnorm. soc. Psychol.,* 1957, **55**, 72–75.

Seashore, S. E. Group cohesiveness as a factor in industrial morale and productivity. *Amer. Psychologist,* 1954, **9**, 468 (Abstract).

Shands, H. C. *Thinking and psychotherapy.* Cambridge: Harvard Univer. Press, 1960.

Shapiro, S. B. Patient wisdom: an anthology of creative insights in psychotherapy. *J. Psychol.,* 1962, **54**, 285–291.

Shoben, E. J., Jr. The therapeutic object: men or machines? *J. counsel. Psychol.,* 1963, **10**, 264–268.

Slack, C. W. Experimenter-subject psychotherapy. *Mental Hyg.,* 1960, **44**, 238–256.

Snyder, W. U. *The psychotherapy relationship.* New York: Macmillan, 1961.

Sternbach, O., & Nagelberg, L. On the patient-therapist relationship in some "untreatable cases," *Psychoanalysis,* 1957, **5**.

Stevenson, I. The use of rewards and punishments in psychotherapy. *Comp. Psychiat.,* 1962, **3**, 20–28.

Strean, H. S. Difficulties met in the treatment of adolescents. *Psychoanal. psychoanal. Rev.,* 1961, **48**, 69–80.

Strupp, H. H.   Patient-doctor relationships. In A. J. Bachrach (Ed.), *Experimental foundations of clinical psychology*. New York: Basic Books, 1962. Pp. 576–615.

Strupp, H. H.   The outcome problem in psychotherapy research. *Psychotherapy*, 1964, 1, 1–13.

Symonds, A.   Special problems in the treatment of adolescents. *Amer. J. Psychother.*, 1963, 17, 596–605.

Thompson, C.   Introduction. In B. Wolstein, *Transference*. New York: Grune & Stratton, 1954.

Truax, C. B.   The process of group psychotherapy. *Psychol. Monogr.*, 1961, 75, Whole no. 511.

Van der Veen, F.   The perception by clients and by judges of the conditions offered by the therapist in the therapy relationship. *U. Wisc. Psychiat. Inst. Bull.*, 1961, 1, No. 10.

Van der Veen, F.   Effects of the therapist and the patient on each other's therapeutic behavior. *J. consult. Psychol.*, 1965, 29, 19–26.

Verplank, W. S.   The control of the content of conversation: reinforcement of statements of opinion. *J. abnorm. soc. Psychol.*, 1955, 51, 668–676.

Wallach, M. S. & Strupp, H. H.   Psychotherapists' clinical judgments and attitudes toward patients. *J. consult. Psychol.*, 1960, 24, 316–323.

Walster, E., & Festinger, L.   The effectiveness of "overheard" persuasive communications. *J. abnorm. soc. Psychol.*, 1962, 65, 395–402.

Weick, K. E.   The reduction of cognitive dissonance through task enhancement. Presented at American Psychological Association, Philadelphia, August, 1963.

Wolberg, L. R.   *The technique of psychotherapy*. New York: Grune & Stratton, 1954.

Wolf, S.   Effects of suggestion and conditioning on the action of chemical agents in human subjects. *J. clin. Invest.*, 1950, 29, 100–109.

Wolpe, J.   *Psychotherapy by reciprocal inhibition*. London: Oxford University, 1958.

Zilboorg, G. & Henry, G. W.   *A history of medical psychology*. New York: Norton, 1941.

4

RESISTANCE TO BEHAVIOR CHANGE

In many ways, psychotherapeutic treatment has reached a crossroads. Individual, verbal, insight-oriented psychotherapy has become a highly refined procedure with a fair degree of success for patients capable of meeting its entrance requirements. Unfortunately, as our introductory chapter highlighted, one major dilemma of present day psychotherapy is that despite the refinements of technique too many troubled individuals are considered unsuitable for this treatment. The reasons for this incompatibility between present treatment methods and populations in need of psychological help are varied, but looking at the problem from a broad perspective, several important factors stand out. To begin with, despite refinements in technique, psychotherapy, even when successful, remains an inefficient and overly time-consuming endeavor. Further, even with maximal efficiency, verbal insight-oriented psychotherapy cannot be the treatment of choice for many individuals because they either lack the ability to perform the patient's task as presently conceived in most contemporary psychotherapies or are of such rigid personality structure that behavior change for them is not possible as long as the treatment approach requires confessional-like explorations that emphasize faults and weaknesses. Hopefully, we should have the ingenuity to develop techniques which would help these persons change their maladaptive behaviors by the use of treatment procedures that more easily overcome these deficiencies. Finally, we must consider that because of the way in which psychotherapy is conducted the nature and structure of the treatment itself may impose barriers to effective communication. In particular we intend to consider whether the structure of therapeutic communication and the manner in which therapeutic messages are delivered handicap the therapist in his attempt to reach certain classes of patients.

146

We have labeled this chapter "Resistance to Behavior Change" because of our conviction that behavior change in psychotherapy can be made more effective not only by considering factors responsible for therapeutic success but by paying careful attention to the reasons why psychotherapy is *not* effective. A study of these resistances should help to overcome them. As has been true of our other chapters, our concern here is to highlight nonpsychotherapy research in behavior change, seeking from this material unifying hypotheses to suggest new and different ways of altering patient behavior. In this chapter our emphasis is on factors responsible for overcoming resistance to behavior change.

It should be clear from the outset that the manner in which we use the term resistance is not limited to its typical psychoanalytic meaning as an ego function whose purpose is to prevent the discharge of intense unconscious phenomena, or in more succinct analytic terms, "everything that prevents the patient from producing material derived from the unconscious is resistance" (Fenichel, 1945, p. 27). For the psychoanalyst the term resistance implies that some aspect of the patient's personality is preventing him from accepting the "truth" being voiced by the psychotherapist. Even more specifically, the concept implies that resistance represents an active force within the patient preventing him from learning the true but threatening causes of his symptoms. Although we are willing to accept the possibility that some forms of resistance to psychotherapy are motivated by the patient's approach to what have been up until now inhibited and painful thoughts, it seems both restricting and naïve to consider that barriers to communication in psychotherapy are produced only because the patient is fighting the uncovering of his traumatic past. We agree with Kelly's position when he states, "If a client does not construe things the way we do, we assume that he construes them in some other way, not that he really must construe them the way we do but is unaware of it" (1955, p. 467). The psychoanalytic view provides no leeway to consider alternate reasons for a patient's unwillingness to accept a particular communication from his therapist, reasons that may reside completely within the realities of the therapeutic situation. Confronted with patient "resistance" we should immediately consider alternate explanations that could account for the patient's unwillingness to accept the therapist's message. Perhaps poor cognitive ability on the part of the patient prevents him from grasping the full intent of the therapist's remarks, or the frame of reference used by the therapist may be so discrepant from that used by the patient that the very meaning of words is not the same for both. Finally, the manner in which the therapist presents his comments may blind the patient from 'understanding his full intent. These possibilities, all quite different from the analyst's "fear of uncovering" hypothesis, could contribute to patient resistance.

THE RESISTANT PATIENT AND THE ETHICS
OF BEHAVIOR MANIPULATION

On the bases of the manipulations of patient behavior we are suggesting in this book, there undoubtedly will be some therapists who will view as unethical the changing of patient behavior without the full awareness and consent of the patient himself. These arguments, which have already been raised against behavior therapy, we suspect will also be applied to our own suggested hypotheses. Therefore we must deal with the ethical issues involved in behavior change.

We have reserved our primary discussion of ethics for this chapter because the ethical issues inherent in therapeutic practice become much more accentuated when a therapist is confronted by a resistant and reluctant patient. Although motivation for treatment is said to be a desirable characteristic of all patients, the psychotherapist frequently finds himself facing a patient who has not solicited treatment of his own free will. More and more patients who have been given little choice in the decision to seek help are being referred by the courts and other social agencies. They may even incur severe punishment if they do not comply with the court's orders. Children and hospitalized psychotics may also be classified as involuntary patients, for in these cases it is typically some other involved party who makes the decision that the patient's behavior is inappropriate and that he needs help. The patient has not voluntarily consented to treatment.

Although recognizing the difficulties of dealing with inadequately motivated patients, therapists are often more concerned with the problems of trying to reach these patients than whether they should be talking to an involuntary patient at all. For example, Wolberg notes with regard to involuntary patients that "it is impossible to establish the kind of working relationship that permits of the achievement of meaningful therapeutic goals" (1954, p. 275) and "the great problem is to convince the patient to continue in treatment in spite of his doubts" (Wolberg, 1954, p. 288); yet he claims that he would leave the choice of participation up to the patient. Here we have the dilemma of a patient being forced to talk to a therapist against his will and being "sold" a treatment he does want; yet somehow we manage to consider this a practical rather than an ethical issue. It seems hypocritical to argue that attempting to treat resistant individuals who face severe punishment if they do not comply (e.g., imprisonment or continued hospitalization) is more ethical than a behavioral and openly manipulative therapy.

One might argue that treating a reluctant patient can be perfectly ethical, for the therapist can make it clear to the prospective patient that he will attempt to help him achieve more adjusted behavior. The patient is then said to be free to resist these influence attempts if he chooses. The essence of this argument is that as long as the patient is aware of the therapist's intent any therapeutic work is justified. However, we wonder just how much choice a patient actually has even here. Aside from the negative consequences of noncompliance which already greatly restrict his freedom of choice, we also suspect that the patient is typically unaware of the nuances of the therapist's attempts to "win him over." The patient might resist if he were aware of the purpose of some of the therapist's machinations, but he is usually not given the opportunity to become aware. For example, Wolberg presents an excerpt of a treatment session to illustrate the manner in which a therapist might "create incentives for therapy." In this example the therapist asks questions such as: "Are you completely satisfied with your present life and adjustment?" "Your mother thinks you ought to get treatment; I wonder why." and "But there must be *some* area in which you aren't completely happy" (Wolberg, 1954, p. 281). These are certainly not subtle attempts to influence a patient by continuously suggesting to him that he is unhappy and needs treatment, but examples of more subtle influence are not hard to find. Dean (1958) suggests that going for "cokes" and fraternizing with adolescent delinquent patients may be essential activities in building therapeutic rapport. Even though this may be a desirable activity, probably no therapist would tell his patient, "I am going to have a coke with you so that you will like me better and be more willing to participate in other kinds of treatment that I have in mind." It is almost certain that this would be an unwise statement that would completely alienate the patient. Similarly, we have heard of analysts who tell their patients that they do not want them to read any books about psychoanalysis, for an awareness of the analytic method would provide fuel for further patient "resistance." Patients are not given full knowledge of treatment procedures in most therapy systems, yet most therapists do not consider themselves as engaging in unethical practice.

Finally, we must report that there is research evidence to indicate that awareness of an influence attempt can impede behavior change under certain conditions. In an early study of resistance to influence Frank (1944) found very little resistance among experimental subjects to a task that required eating dry soda crackers. However, when the experimenter made the subjects aware of his attempts to influence their behavior by telling them that his job was to make them eat the crackers, resistance rose appreciably. Frank concluded that "resistance to an activity is readily aroused if doing so involves submitting to an arbitrary personal demand of someone else, and is thereby equivalent to a personal defeat" (1944, p. 40). Twenty years later Kanfer and Marston (1964) confirmed Frank's finding that subjects resist influence attempts of which they are made aware. In an interview setting in which subjects were required to talk about themselves on preselected topics Kanfer and Marston found that when subjects were aware of the interviewer's influence attempts they showed less willingness to listen to him when he disagreed with their remarks than subjects who were uninformed of the interviewer's purpose. In general, we believe that therapists should be more open about the rationale for their activities, keeping ambiguities in treatment to a minimum (see hypotheses 4.2a and 5.4a), but we suspect that there are times when influence attempts must be covert if they are to be successful.

In summary, we conclude that therapy as now practiced is already covertly manipulative, even though it may not be recognized as such by its practitioners. Thus therapists should learn more about therapeutic influence and consider carefully the ethical responsibilities associated with clinical practice. This means that the therapist must take full responsibility for his actions and can no longer escape consideration of ethical issues by hiding behind the platitude that it is the patient alone who determines the course of treatment. This is certainly not true for the involuntary and resisting patient. But it should also be clear that accepting therapeutic manipulations openly does not necessarily mean that the patient should be seen as a passive lump of clay who is shaped at will by his therapist. We hope that close examination of the specific hypotheses proposed in this book will reveal that many of these hypotheses involve manipulating the conditions of treatment in such a way that patients will become more active in their own treatment. Helping a patient who is trapped by his symptomatology to accept alternate modes of behavior should make him better able to cope with his problems. To us, this represents an ethical alternative.

OVERVIEW OF THE CHAPTER

Our purpose in this chapter is to discuss the varieties of resistances to behavior change in psychotherapy and to group them according to a communication model proposed independently by Hartley and Hartley (1952) and Cohen (1964). These authors consider communication to be a basic social process, since it is "the means by which one person influences another, and is in turn influenced by him, it is the actual carrier of social process" (Cohen, 1964, p. 16). Because the mode of operation in psychotherapy involves verbal communication, the therapist could be conceptualized as a communicator who initiates therapeutic communiques intended to change the behavior of the patient who is the communicant or recipient of the communication. A breakdown in communication can occur as a function of the characteristics of communicator or communicant or of the nature of the communiqué. We shall now discuss these breakdowns as resistances to effective communication and the hypotheses aimed at overcoming them.

RESISTANCE AS A FUNCTION OF COMMUNICANT CHARACTERISTICS

Resistance in psychotherapy has many determinants, not the least of which is that the personality characteristics of many patients make them poor risks for treatment. Although many theorists phrase their entrance requirements differently, in practice there seems to be near unanimity in the selection of "good" patients. We have already referred (Chapter 3) to Schofield's (1964) survey of randomly selected practicing psychiatrists, psychiatric social workers, and clinical psychologists, and his finding that the nonpreferred candidates for psychotherapy are clearly identifiable and are similar for all three professions. From Schofield's large list of poor risk characteristics (see p. 82) we can distill three broad categories under which many of the individual poor risk traits could probably be included. *Inability to form a close interpersonal relationship, poor verbal ability,* and *high defensiveness* seem to be the main deficiencies that poor risk patients demonstrate. Each of these liabilities, standing alone, would be a sufficient basis on which to predict a poor prognosis. Unfortunately, too many potential patients possess all three undesirable traits. For example, many "inaccessible" juvenile delinquents are persons who are suspicious of close contact with others, are unpracticed in verbal introspection, and cannot assume any personal responsibility for their difficulties. One problem then is to develop treatment procedures that would not handicap these individuals.

When patients with these therapeutic liabilities enter traditional psychotherapy, their course of treatment is usually unsuccessful and they are often branded as "resistant." The psychotherapist confronted with such resistant patients should not assume that the only or preferred solution to his problem is to develop better selection criteria so that he can screen out "bad" patients more efficiently. If a patient is resistant, it is often because our techniques are inadequate to handle the special therapeutic problems he brings to the consulting room. Further, it is clear that if he continues the current practice of attempting to apply the same methods of psychotherapy indiscriminately to all comers, the therapist will find himself judged obsolete by a society whose larger mental health needs are not being met; he will be considered a too-expensive luxury. It is incumbent on the therapist to investigate his lack of success with certain classes of patient, working toward the goal of developing new techniques and improving old ones to expand his usefulness beyond its present narrow range. However, before modifications in practice can be suggested, we need a more detailed understanding of the kinds of persons for whom our present treatment techniques are insufficient.

If we hypothesize that resistance to therapeutic messages can be a function of characteristics of the communicant, or the receiver of the message, we must first determine whether there are in fact communicant characteristics which are regularly associated with the rejection of messages. The area of research often labeled "persuasibility" or "conformity" comes close to our main interest, even though the emphasis in these studies is primarily on communicant characteristics associated with message *acceptance,* not rejection. For example, Blake and Mouton (1961) reviewing the literature on characteristics of subjects susceptible to conformity pressures, offer the following conclusion:

Results show that those who are more susceptible to conformity pressures are more likely to be submissive, low in self-confidence, show less nervous tension, score higher on authoritarian scales, be less intelligent, less original, and to score on the simplicity end of the dimension of the complexity-simplicity scale. They are more likely to be characterized as low in need achievement, high in need for social approval, conventional in values and to have a greater inner conformity need. In addition, they show greater dependence on the perceptual field and are more compliant in social situations. . . . Finally, in several investigations it has been reported that on an individual-by-individual basis conformity tendencies are *general* across several tasks administered under conditions of social contradiction, thus showing personal consistency to conformity behavior. (pp. 19-20).

In contrast to the extensive work that has been done to determine characteristics of conformity, surprisingly little interest has been generated in studying the characteristics of those who are resistant to influence. To begin with, noncompliant persons are usually less willing subjects in psychological research and are thus less readily available for study. Further, more often than not, resistance to influence is considered a positively valued trait in our culture, at times indicating "productive nonconformity" (Pepinsky, 1961) or perhaps patriotic resistance to interrogation (Bidermann & Zimmer, 1961). Whether resistance to influence is considered a culturally desirable trait often depends on the nature of the conformity pressure. Rokeach (1961) expresses this point of view:

There is really nothing so ugly about authority, only certain kinds of authority. And there need be no inherent contradiction between reliance on authority and reliance on reason, so long as we use independent reason to guide us in selecting the authorities we choose to influence us and so long as we use reason to tell us when to throw overboard one authority in favor of another (p. 234).

Thus neither compliance nor resistance in itself would indicate reason for concern, except that when an individual finds himself in need of professional help of any kind it is the compliant individual who is more likely to seek out such help. One of us (Heller, 1963) has already observed that successful psychotherapy patients bear a striking resemblance to descriptions of subjects susceptible to experimental influence and that, although the extent of their psychopathology might be great, hyperindependent persons usually resist influence whether it occurs in the laboratory or in the psychotherapeutic relationship. Although the hyperindependent person might need help, he is less likely to seek it voluntarily.

Janis and Hovland (1959) provide a conceptual scheme for categorizing the extremes of high and low persuasibility. These authors note that individual differences in *attention, comprehension,* and *acceptance* of messages will give rise to different degrees of susceptibility to persuasion. If an individual persistently avoids attending to certain classes of messages, he will remain relatively uninfluenced. Similarly, if a person does not comprehend a message and fails to grasp its import, he will remain uninfluenced, even though in this case the message might have been attended to. Finally, a person may attend to a message and comprehend its significance but still remain uninfluenced if he fails to accept the message. When confronted with a resistant individual in psychotherapy, we often assume that our message was attended to and comprehended and that we have a failure in message acceptance because of some motivational factors within the communicant; however, faulty attention or comprehension may be responsible for the communication breakdown. For example, Janis and Hovland list several disorders of attention and comprehension of interest to the therapist. These include hyperactive and distractible patients whose attention quickly shifts before the full message is received, patients whose fantasy life is so extensive that they pay little attention to the communications of those about them, patients for whom failures in comprehension are caused by differences in cultural patterns between themselves and their therapists, and "hysterical" patients whose blocking of associations produce misunderstandings, distortions, and other failures in comprehension. Janis and Hovland correctly note that failures in attention, comprehension, and acceptance of communications are not always due to motivational factors but may represent deficiencies in cognitive and interpersonal *abilities*. Thus, when we describe poor-risk psychotherapy patients as persons who find interpersonal relationships difficult, whose verbal skills are unpracticed, and who prefer the status quo to the threat inherent in change, we must also note that we may be dealing with motivated resistance or deficiencies in ability. We should not suspect motivated resistance too quickly.

Considering the different forms that resistance to the therapist's message can take (inattention, miscomprehension, rejection) and the varied sources responsible for that resistance (poor ability, motivated resistance) we may indeed wonder whether any one therapeutic suggestion could be sufficient to deal with such a variety. Yet, when we consider typical therapeutic practice, we see that even for the nonresistant patient therapy is often narrow and restrictive, based on one particular model of psychopathology. Even though schools of psychotherapy differ in their conceptualizations of the therapeutic process, their theories are too often based on a psychology of the inhibited neurotic, on an anxiety-avoidance model of psychopathology which assumes that what went wrong initially in the patient's life was that strong fear blocked free undistorted self-expression. The patient many years later continues to repress, deny, and distort experience to prevent the re-emergence of intense anxiety. The behaviors that were associated with strong anxiety are avoided, and the patient never learns that the danger that may have existed in childhood is no longer present. Learning theorists have put the problem rather succinctly by stating that fear associated with inhibited responses cannot be extinguished, for if the response does not occur the individual has no way of knowing whether the danger is still present. The inhibited neurotic avoids the expression of behavior that at one time produced extreme anxiety, even though the danger associated with that behavior is no longer present. Thus he is never free from his internalized anxiety.

An important derivative of an anxiety-avoidance model of psychopathology is that the patient cannot be forced to experience the feared situation prematurely, lest he be overwhelmed by internal anxiety. The therapist is cautioned to avoid premature interpretations in psychotherapy, for even though his analysis of his patient's dynamics may be correct the anxiety that such an interpretation would engender would be so great that the patient would be panicked; or if his defensive structure were operating properly, the interpretation would be immediately denied or distorted. Thus the therapist is advised that it will do little good to force or "trick" the patient into giving up his symptomatology too early or engaging in the feared behavior too soon.

The clearest example of an anxiety-avoidance conflict model is presented by Dollard and Miller (1950). We shall focus our discussion on the dynamics of approach-avoidance conflicts as presented by these authors, for the situation in which a person has strong tendencies to approach and avoid the same goal contains the type of conflict that confronts the neurotic when he is prevented by his inhibitions from responding appropriately to his environment. A graphic representation of an approach-avoidance conflict as presented by Dollard and Miller is shown in Fig. 2.

Note that it does little good to raise the gradient of approach, to motivate the individual to come closer to the feared object, as long as strong fear has not been diminished. Attempting to increase motivation to approach is often characteristic of the counsel the inhibited neurotic receives from well-meaning friends and family members, but as long as strong fear remains approach can only increase the patient's misery. Thus Dollard and Miller's admonition to the therapist is to concentrate on the fears motivating avoidance rather than to try to increase the motivation to approach the feared goal. We can see from this description that psychotherapy with the inhibited neurotic, although maintaining a fairly high probability of final success, by its very nature remains a lengthy and time-consuming endeavor. To extinguish inhibited fears the patient must first emit them in therapy with some fair degree of frequency in order for extinction (based on the permissiveness of the therapist) to occur.

But does a system of psychotherapy based on the psychopathology of the inhibited neurotic contain within it procedures of sufficient generality to be adequate for other forms of disorders? We think not and further submit that other models of behavior change need to be developed to help those individuals whose personality characteristics

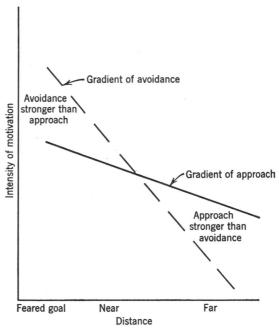

Figure 2. Approach-avoidance conflict in which the avoidance gradient is steeper than the approach gradient (adapted from Dollard and Miller, 1950).

cause them to be labeled as "poor risks" or "resistors" in conventional psychotherapy. Alternate models of behavior change have already been proposed by behavior therapists (Ullman & Krasner, 1965; Wolpe, Salter, & Reyna, 1964) and others (Fairweather, 1964). At present we shall consider the implications of a model of behavior change put forth by Herbert Kelman (1961) in his discussion of the relationship between induced action and attitude change. We are taking the liberty of extrapolating Kelman's model to the clinical situation.

Kelman notes that in a classical approach-avoidance conflict in which the avoidance gradient is steeper than the approach gradient (as in the model proposed by Dollard and Miller) any attempt to induce positive association is likely to be unsuccessful. As soon as the momentary forces inducing approach are removed, the person tends to revert to his earlier level of association with the feared object. As long as strong, unextinguished fear remains, forced compliance procedures that do not in some way reduce the level of the avoidance gradient can pro-

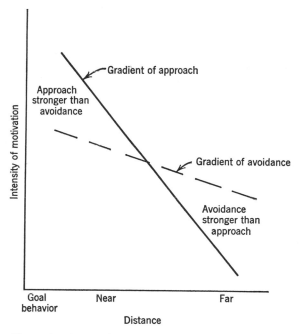

Figure 3. Approach-avoidance conflict in which the approach gradient is steeper than the avoidance gradient (adapted from Kelman, 1961).

duce only temporary results. However, Kelman proposes that there is no reason to assume that the gradients of approach and avoidance must always be structured as in the Dollard and Miller model. Consider the possibility that the approach gradient is steeper than the avoidance gradient, as in Fig. 3. The labels on this diagram have been modified from Kelman (1961, p. 93) to aid comparison with the Dollard and Miller model. A person whose relationship with an object is as described in the diagram would probably not find himself in a situation of *overt* conflict, for he would tend to stay away from any association with the object in question. He would not voluntarily move toward the point of equilibrium, for as long as he is beyond that point the avoidance gradient is higher than the approach gradient. Suppose, however, that he can be induced to take an action that takes him past the point of intersection of the two gradients; he would find himself in a region in which his approach tendencies would outweigh his avoidance tendencies. If this happened, even with the inducement removed, he would continue to associate with the object.

Is this a reasonable model to explain pathological behavior? Although we know of no evidence on this question, we can visualize examples in which the negative behaviors confronting the therapist have no underlying or deep-rooted fears associated with them. In fact, we can seriously conceive of the possibility that for the majority of potential patients their pathology might be better fitted by Kelman's model than by the classical model proposed by Dollard and Miller. This would be particularly true for cases in which the individual has both positive and negative tendencies toward an object, but through experience the negative tendencies have come to prevail. The individual then appears to be negative and resistant. Inducing these individuals to form positive associations should, if successful, strengthen approach tendencies to the point at which the negative arm of the conflict could be completely overcome. In Chapter 3 we suggested such procedures; we hypothesized that by inducing attraction to the therapist the resistant patient's negative reaction to therapy can be overcome. However, if the previous level of the patient's approach tendencies is too low, attraction inducement, although successful in overcoming initial negative attitudes, still might not provide the necessary motivation for the patient to be able to continue in psychotherapy. Also, patients who lack effective self-control systems are not likely to benefit from the unconditional permissiveness inherent in most therapeutic relationships, which may instead lead to the inadvertent strengthening of deviant behavior (Bandura & Walters, 1963). Therefore, we feel the need to consider alternate forms of therapy that do not require the initial formation of a close interpersonal and verbal therapeutic interaction.

HYPOTHESIS 4.1: Psychotherapy with resistant patients should be oriented toward accepting and utilizing the role behaviors in which the patients are already proficient.

Our recommendation is simple and, as we shall document shortly, has already been antedated by some therapy practitioners. We propose that different therapeutic tasks be chosen according to the behaviors already available to the patient. We have previously indicated that patients are resistant in psychotherapy for varied reasons and that each patient deficiency may need its own remedy. It is now time to consider two alternative therapeutic procedures that might provide these remedies.

HYPOTHESIS 4.1a: **Impersonal and machine therapies are recommended initially for those patients who are avoidant of close interpersonal relationships.**

HYPOTHESIS 4.1b: **Action therapies are recommended initially for patients unpracticed in introspection.**

There are some individuals whose developmental history shows the nonreinforcement or direct punishment of affiliative behavior. This pattern can occur when parents thwart dependency responses while at the same time providing an aggressive model from whom the child can learn aggressive means of responding in interpersonal situations (Bandura & Walters, 1963). Because of fear of retaliation, the child may never counteraggress in his parents' presence, but he may use aggressive techniques exclusively to cope with others. Fear of dependency combined with such easy access to aggression can effectively shut off possible correction by other more benevolent societal agents since they are automatically alienated at first contact. For example, observing this pattern of poor verbal introspective ability and alienation from others often found in antisocial predelinquents, Redl and Wineman (1957) wryly note:

> Most of them are entirely nonverbal, would balk at playing "sissy stuff" like doll house, and find it face losing to ask for help from any adult, especially a kind one of the sissified middle class variety . . . when exposed to the interview room or play room situation, they usually unpack such a volume of immediately acted-out destructiveness that the psychiatrist who hoped to be kind and understanding finds himself forced against his will to restrain or even to hold them in their wild attacks. . . . In short, even under the best of conditions, these youngsters produce so much aggression so fast that we don't even have time to unpack the medicine we brought with us for their cure (Redl & Wineman, 1957, p. 25).

In contrast, the developmental history of the typical neurotic shows a strong attachment to others to the point of overincorporation and internalization of all societal standards. The neurotic suffers but he is well practiced in turning to others for help and finds much less difficulty in relating to the therapist. In the case of the predelinquent, Redl and Wineman specifically warn against overwhelming him with a close, "loving" relationship and suggest that a benevolent but somewhat impersonal and objective style of interaction is most likely to lead to success, particularly in the early stages of contact. These authors have developed a therapeutic approach which relies heavily on programmed activities suited to the capabilities of the children under treatment. Interviewing is kept to a minimum and is never held on a regular basis for a fixed length of time. Within the context of the residential treatment home and its program, they talk to the child when his behavior in the programmed activity seems to need discussion. In other words, they discuss a child's behavior with him only when his "ego" seems strong enough to stand the stress and when his distortion of reality and his acting out of distorted perceptions are current and immediate.

Others working with aggressive delinquents have gone even further in their de-emphasis of a close relationship. Schwitzgebel and Schwitzgebel (1961), Slack (1960), and Stollak and Guerney (1964) all report procedures in which there is little initial relationship. For example, in the study by Stollak and Guerney, the subject was requested to talk into a tape recorder in a room by himself. The only contact with the experimenter was the minimal interchange that occurred before and after the recording sessions when the subject was being led back to his ward. (Subjects were inmates in a diagnostic center for juvenile delinquents.) It is interesting to note that a positive relationship with the experimenter did form, but with the subject determining the pace of its development. Every subject talked into the tape recorder as if he were talking to the experimenter, often referring to him by name. Whenever the experimenter walked through the ward, most of the subjects would seek him out and exchange a greeting, asking when the next experimental session would occur. Since their work is still in its preliminary stages, Stollak and Guerney do not report whether this experience had any effect on patient symptomatology. However, Schwitzgebel and Kolb (1964), reporting on a follow-up of patients participating in "experimenter-subject" psychotherapy, which also involved delinquents talking into a tape recorder, found that after three years subjects in the experiment showed a significant reduction in the frequency and severity of crime when compared with a matched-control group. In both the Stollak and Guerney and the Schwitzgebel and Kolb studies positive relationships with the experimenter did develop, but the relationship was not forced by the experimenter, nor was the ability to form a relationship a precondition for treatment. Sechrest and

Strowig (1962) note that teaching machines can have similar advantages in a classroom setting. They suggest that students, recalcitrant to normal teacher instruction, might not have their antagonisms toward education aroused to the same degree by an impersonal, nonauthority figure such as a teaching machine.

We are suggesting that the psychotherapist refrain from attempting to force a close interpersonal relationship, not only with the aggressive delinquent patient, but with any patient for whom close contact is initially threatening. Our ability to help a troubled individual should not be predicated on his ability to relate to a benevolent therapist, even though in the history of psychotherapy it has been a prime requirement. For example, another type of patient often found inaccessible to treatment because of his poor ability to relate to the therapist is the withdrawn schizophrenic who was considered untreatable by early psychoanalysts. Freud, in particular, felt that treatment should be limited to the "transference neuroses" (hysteria, anxiety hysteria, and obsessional neurosis) and that persons suffering from "narcissistic" disorders (e.g., schizophrenia) are not treatable because they have no capacity for transference. In referring to these individuals Freud noted:

> They turn from the physician, not in hostility, but in indifference. Therefore they are not to be influenced by him, what he says leaves them cold, makes no impression on them, and therefore the process of cure which can be carried through with others, the revivification of the pathogenic conflict and the overcoming of the resistance due to the repressions, cannot be effected with them. They remain as they are. They have often enough undertaken attempts at recovery on their own account which have led to pathological results; we can do nothing to alter this. . . . They produce no transference, and are, therefore, inaccessible to our efforts, not to be cured by us (Freud, 1953, p. 455).

Others working with schizophrenics, particularly those in the group heavily influenced by Harry Stack Sullivan (1953), did not accept this pessimistic note about the prognosis of schizophrenia. They set about to demonstrate that schizophrenics were not inaccessible to treatment and with patience and persistence demonstrated their ability to reach and relate to withdrawn schizophrenics. Their emphasis was on the necessity for establishing a therapeutic relationship before the proper work of analysis could begin. However, the years of work required with carefully selected individual patients has not spoken well for the efficiency of this treatment. Slowly coaxing the withdrawn patient to the point at which some rudimentary relationship with the therapist can be tentatively established is not an effective way of dealing with a significant number of mental hospital patients, even assuming that once such a relationship were established success would be probable.

As a group, the behavior therapists are perhaps most willing to treat patients with poor motivation and ability by devising therapeutic tasks suited to their intact skills. The Skinnerian concept of "shaping" implies that in working for the emergence of a particular behavior not yet in the response repertoire of the individual the experimenter reinforces those available responses that can lead successively in the desired direction. Thus Isaacs, Thomas, and Goldiamond (1960) were able to reinstate speaking in a mute catatonic schizophrenic by successively reinforcing, with chewing gum, the sequence of behavior consisting of eye, facial, and lip movements, vocalizations, word utterance, and finally meaningful speech.

Much of the recent work in behavior therapy has been reviewed by Ullman and Krasner (1965) and need not be detailed here. Some of it is still at the single case study stage with only limited changes in behavior noted. For example, in the work reported by Isaacs, Thomas, and Goldiamond only two patients participated in the therapeutic procedures, and in each case clinical improvement did not proceed beyond the point of producing increased verbalization. Similarly, the work of Ferster and DeMyer (1962) has demonstrated that severely disturbed autistic children can be taught to respond to impersonal reinforcement (machine-delivered), but it has not yet shown any generalization of behavior outside the experimental room. However, such is not the case for all behavior therapists; at least a few report sustained clinical improvement in well-controlled studies (e.g., Lang, 1965; Paul, 1964). Let us consider in detail one controlled experiment.

King, Armitage, and Tilton (1960) compared a group of chronic, severely withdrawn patients receiving "operant-interpersonal" therapy with similar groups receiving "verbal" therapy, "recreational" therapy, and no therapy. Operant-interpersonal therapy required patients to respond to a large reinforcement-delivering machine in the presence of the therapist. At first patients undergoing this procedure on an individual basis made simple operant responses for rewards of candy, cigarettes, and colored slides. More complex psychomotor, verbal, and interpersonal components were systematically incorporated into the procedure. As the patient became proficient in simple problem solving, the problems became more complex. Requests for simple verbal responses were then introduced by the therapist, after which cooperative problem solving was required first with the therapist, then with other patients. Eventually the entire group receiving this form of therapy met together to take turns working the machine in two-man teams while other members of the group sat around the machine as an audience. Results of the experiment indicated that the operant-interpersonal method was more effective than all other forms of therapy in promoting clinical improvement based on both ward observations and interview assessment. Significant differences in favor of the operant-interpersonal method were found for the level of patient verbalization, motivation to leave the ward, interest in occupational therapy, transfer to better wards, and decrease in frequency of enuresis. A follow-up six months later indicated a persistence in the improved ward behavior demonstrated by the operant-interpersonal group. In contrast, the verbal therapy group showed no significant differences from the no-therapy group and much less improvement than either the operant-interpersonal or the recreational therapy groups. The authors conclude that, in initiating therapy with chronic withdrawn schizophrenics, "verbal communication should not be emphasized, at least as an initial procedure" (King, Armitage, & Tilton, 1960, p. 284).

Some therapists might be willing to consider a behaviorally oriented procedure as an initial step in building a therapeutic relationship that would then allow traditional verbal therapy to ensue, but they might insist that an impersonal or action therapy could not be maximally beneficial, for there might never be any working through of inner conflicts. The alternate hypothesis about psychopathology underpinning our current therapy suggestions concerning impersonal and action therapies is that the investigation of inner conflicts may not be feasible, desirable, or necessary for many patients. Evidence is accumulating that patient change can occur more effectively for certain classes of patient when absolutely no attempt is made to exhume inner conflicts. Some of this work has already been discussed; a further example can be found in the work of Fairweather (1964) and his associates.

Noting a growing concern for the infantilization of the hospitalized patient, even among some progressive treatment-oriented institutions (e.g., Stanton & Schwartz, 1954), Fairweather hoped to develop a treatment program that would maximize the patient's usefulness as a therapeutic agent. Fairweather assumed that patients are taught to become permanent residents of mental hospitals by methods of treatment that require excessive conformity and that when properly reinforced by hospital personnel produce "good" patients with little initiative to leave the hospital. He comments on the dilemma of patient adjustment to hospital routine as follows:

From many observations, a chronic mental patient can be described as an individual who has not demonstrated the minimal behaviors required for assuming a community role which is rewarded by his social group. For this reason he is rejected by the community and enters the mental hospital. Upon entering the hospital, his grossly deviant behaviors diminish and he frequently demonstrates an adequate adjustment within the hospital social system. He has, in fact, established himself in a role within the hospital which he was unable to do in the community. This role has an attending social position with rights and duties which provide the patient with an expected set of behaviors which, in turn, stabilizes him. For those who have had the most difficulty in adjusting to society, the establishment of such a role is frequently time consuming and seemingly arrived at by trial and error. Nonetheless, a role is created for each individual in the hospital. The patient may, for example, establish himself as a leader on the ward, a follower, a preoccupied hermit, a clown, or the like. The behaviors acompanying his hospital role identify him as an individual and define him as a specific person.

Once this stabilizing role has been established and reinforced by the hospital social system, it is exceedingly difficult for the patient to leave the hospital and successfully return to the community. Not only must he discard those aspects of his role behavior through which he has gained attention and social status but he must also be prepared for the negative reception afforded feared minority group members. Under these conditions, many patients tend to remain in the hospital and those who stay longest continue to stay. Even if the "long-termer" leaves the hospital, he usually quickly returns (Fairweather, 1964, pp. 24-25).

To counteract the debilitating effects of traditional hospital care and the dependency-inducing effects of psychotherapy within such a setting, Fairweather set out to construct an action-oriented, nonintrospective therapy based on developing patient role behaviors in the institution that would be consistent with those to be used in later community living. Thus patient-led, autonomous work groups were created in which patients had responsibility for their own management and welfare. When a patient was admitted to this program, he was immediately assigned to a small group of patients who oriented him to the hospital and introduced him to ward procedures. It became the group's job to ensure that each patient learned appropriate personal care, remained punctual on his work assignments, and behaved appropriately when given hospital passes. The group had the responsibility of recommending how each member's money, privileges, and job assignments should be handled. When recommending realistic and meaningful courses of action, the group itself would be rewarded. (For a full description of group structure and duties see Fairweather, 1964, pp. 171-209.)

This small-group treatment program was compared with a traditional ward of patients matched for age, diagnosis, and length of previous hospitalization. Patients on the traditional ward received the usual medication, recreational activities, work assignments, and ward meetings. Results indicated that patients participating in the small-group treatment program, compared with patients on the traditional ward, showed more social interaction with one another, looked to other patients rather than to the staff for help, had more positive expectancies about the future, spent less time in the hospital, and showed a better adjustment to the community, as measured by employment records and established friendships. However, rate of return to the hospital was not changed by the experimental program. In both the small-group and the traditional wards the rate of recidivism was determined mostly by the chronicity of previous hospitalization. Although this last finding represents some degree of disappointment, the authors claim to have predicted it at the onset of the study, since patients lost their reference group membership at the time of departure from the hospital often returning to a lonely real-life environment (e.g., more than 70% of the sample were either single, divorced, or separated).

What seems to be needed is a mechanism to bridge the gap between the hospital setting and the more rigorous demands of community life. Procedures for accomplishing this transition have been suggested by Fairweather and by Cumming and Cumming (1963). Essentially, their suggestions coincide in recommending continuation of milieu therapy and group self-help beyond the point of hospital discharge to provide a more protected transition from hospital to community. For example, one can conceive of "alumni night" at a community hospital in which the small groups originally constituted in the hospital might continue to meet together for therapeutic support, in a manner perhaps similar to the weekly meetings of Alcoholics Anonymous. The possibility of programmed activities should also not be overlooked. Informal meetings with police officers were found by Cumming and Cumming to increase communication between patients and police, overcoming the prejudices and misconceptions of both groups. This suggestion has particular merit because the police are usually the first to be called at the time of impending hospitalization. For some patients who have only frightened or angry words with the police these meetings could help to correct distorted perceptions of authority figures. From the policeman's point of view, having mental patients participate in his training could easily help change his attitude toward them.

In this section we have tried to demonstrate that traditional, verbal, insight-oriented psychotherapy is not the treatment of choice for many patients and that a more appropriate therapeutic strategy would be to build treatment techniques more attuned to the patients' actual intact behaviors. We have concentrated our attention on those procedures that would overcome the requirements found in traditional psychotherapy, namely introspective ability and the ability to form a close interpersonal relationship with the therapist. We have used a model originally proposed by Kelman (1961) to illustrate that if negative avoidant behavior can be overcome many otherwise resistant persons will become accessible to prosocial training. It is our contention that resistance in psychotherapy is often situation-specific, developed by ideal therapeutic tasks that require abilities not found in the response repertoire of many patients. Further, the procedures we have discussed sharply call into question the restricted training that many psychotherapists now receive. To some extent, the psychotherapist needs to become a "behavioral engineer" (Kanfer, 1965), an expert in the psychology of behavior change, ready with particular techniques designed to overcome specific patient problems. One of us has recently expressed this point of view:

> Our crucial need at the present time is not to demonstrate that all therapies are in fact the same, all operating by similar principles. While this knowledge might increase the efficiency of already established therapeutic procedures, it would do little toward expanding the scope of treatment possibilities to include those individuals now found not suitable for psychotherapy. Unhampered by parochial affiliations to "schools" of therapy, we need to investigate procedures that facilitate or inhibit behavior change specifying the exact conditions under which they operate. We should insist that our therapy theorists not delude us, or themselves, into thinking that the new treatments they would propose represent a panacea equally appropriate for all disorders. For increased therapeutic effectiveness we need precision rifles, not broad gauge shotguns (Heller, 1965, p. 7).

So far our attention has been focused on individuals who appear resistant because of poor verbal and interpersonal skills. We have reserved our suggestions for dealing with communicant resistance because of excessive defensiveness so that we may deal with procedures to reduce defensiveness and threat as a separate issue. This discussion follows.

RESISTANCE AS A FUNCTION OF THE NATURE OF THERAPEUTIC COMMUNICATIONS

A dilemma for some psychotherapy patients is that they are driven by the discomfort of their symptoms to seek help while resisting any change in values or behavior. In this regard the psychotherapy patient is not unlike any other person who finds himself in the position of having to give up old behavioral patterns because they are no longer sufficient to cope with the new stresses arising around him. One need only observe the behavior of those committed to the old order as political systems change, or the behavior of older citizens as social morals change to see that what is threatening is change itself. This point of view is most succinctly presented by George Kelly who defines threat as "the awareness of imminent comprehensive change in one's core structures" (Kelly, 1955, p. 489). With regard to psychotherapy, this definition implies that as long as the patient feels that his symptomatology can be relieved without any other behavior change on his part, he will consider the therapy situation safe. Therapy becomes threatening when the therapist persists in suggesting to the patient that it is the patient himself who must be the locus of change. In commenting on people with personal problems who seek professional help, Gurin et al. (1960) note in their survey of American attitudes toward mental health:

It appears that people who go for help are, in most cases, not seeking any change in themselves but rather are looking for comfort, reassurance, and advice (p. 323).

These authors note further

Twenty-five per cent of the group who went for help attribute the blame for their personal problems to another person; only twenty-three per cent specifically trace the difficulty to some defect in themselves. In terms of the motivation for therapy, then, it appears that going for help does not necessarily imply any self-insight or readiness to change (p. 306).

Hence we see a dilemma of psychotherapy: the patient wants and expects help, but resists change.

As therapy proceeds beyond the initial phases of problem elaboration and specification, the therapist is faced with the problem of determining the extent of new points of view he will present to his patient. He can, like the client-centered therapist, offer no new ideas beyond those that the patient himself has already presented. In this way he may perhaps minimize threat, but at the same time the patient may never change his perceptions unless he somehow develops the ability to extricate himself from his difficulties by his own efforts. However, if the therapist wishes to present a position in some way discrepant from that already held by the patient, that is, if he wishes to influence his patient, he must recognize that he may be producing threat. In a sense then threat may be almost unavoidable if the patient is to move forward in considering new points of view about himself. Guided by this view, we are now ready to propose our first hypothesis.

Resistance and Threat

HYPOTHESIS 4.2:   **Resistance in psychotherapy is reduced as the threat value of therapeutic communications is decreased.**

How can threat be reduced when the therapist sees a clear need to go beyond the restricted conceptualization of his patient? Traditional therapists have been well aware of the necessity for proper timing of therapeutic interpretations and the need to carefully avoid "deep" interpretations, that is, interpretations that are too discrepant from the patient's original conceptualization. Before suggesting answers to this question we must first establish that threatening messages are, in fact, less readily accepted.

The effect of threatening communication has been a traditional concern of propaganda researchers. For some time the view prevailed that fear-arousing messages were effective because, when emotional tension is aroused, the audience becomes more highly motivated to accept the reassuring beliefs or recommendations advocated by the communicator. This orientation has been the underlying assumption determining the nature of many propaganda appeals used in time of war, to combat venereal disease and smoking, and to provide impetus for safer driving and the purchase of seat belts. However, although research data are not completely conclusive (e.g., Leventhal, Singer, & Jones, 1965; Rosenblatt, 1965), there is a general trend in the literature to indicate that the opposite is true, that fear-arousing appeals retard message acceptance.

There are two main reasons why the results of experiments on the effects of fear-arousing appeals have not always produced consistent results. To begin with, these appeals are often not distinguished from the more general class of "emotional" appeals which usually also includes the effects of aggression-arousing messages. Second, even if one were to concentrate on the more restricted classes of communication which involve fear-arousal only, their effects on message acceptance can occur in more than one way. Hovland, Janis, and Kelley (1953) mention at least three different response measures that might be differentially affected by fear-arousing appeals. Fear arousal can effect attention to the verbal content of the communication, comprehension of the message involved, or acceptance of the conclusions advocated by the communication. Blocking of attention would retard comprehension and message acceptance, but it is also possible that the message might be fully attended to and comprehended but rejected. Not only must we ask whether fear-arousing appeals enhance or retard communication but, if there is a diminution in the effectiveness of the appeal, we must also determine which response modality is responsible for the loss.

The program of research conducted by Janis and his associates provides the most direct evidence that threatening messages are resisted. Janis and Feshbach (1953) found that strong fear appeals were equally effective in communicating dental hygiene information as minimum threat communications but were least effective in producing behavior change. Immediately after presentation of the messages there were no significant differences between the groups receiving strong or minimal threat communications with regard to their comprehension of the message. A questionnaire administered one week later showed that the greatest change in dental practice occurred for the group receiving the communication with the least amount of fear-arousing material. This study was further confirmed in a replication by Janis and Feshbach (1954) in which they discovered that subjects already predisposed toward high anxiety are most resistant to fear-arousing communications. Further confirmation comes from Janis and Terwilliger (1962), who found that a strong threat appeal was less effective in changing attitudes toward smoking than a mild threat appeal. The strong threat appeal seemed to induce subjects to avoid thinking about the threatening aspects of the communication while the message was being presented. From this study and from the work of Janis and Milholland (1954) we can conclude that attending to a message and learning its rational content can also be impeded by threat arousal.

The relationship between fear arousal and message rejection found by Janis and his collaborators has been replicated by others with similar results. Nunnally and Bobren (1959) found that high anxiety messages about mental health depress public interest, and Blomgren and Scheuneman (1961) found that fewer seat belts are purchased when advertising campaigns emphasize extreme bodily injury and death. However, other factors have also been known to mediate the relationship between fear arousal and message rejection. Goldstein

(1959) observed that fear appeals receive greater acceptance among "copers" (those capable of relating tension-producing stimuli to themselves) than among "avoiders" (those incapable of relating tension-producing stimuli to themselves). This result was largely due to the marked differential effectiveness of the two appeals on the avoider group and not to any differential acceptance by the copers. Berkowitz and Cottingham (1960) demonstrated that the nature of the message is also an important variable mediating between fear arousal and acceptance. These authors found that if a message was uninteresting to the subject a strong fear appeal was facilitative, for by dramatizing the message the subject's attention was captured. However, if the message was personally relevant, minimal fear arousal increased message acceptance. These studies indicate that the relationship between fear arousal and message rejection is complex but in general confirm that threat can be a factor in retarding message acceptance.

If threat retards message acceptance, why are not all therapeutic messages rejected immediately? Unfortunately, this does happen in many cases and may partly account for the high termination rates associated with psychotherapy. What keeps most patients continuing in therapy despite the threat is that they are suffering or experiencing "misery" (Dollard & Miller, 1950). Hence the therapist must find a balance between the threat produced by his messages and the suffering they are intended to alleviate. In his book *Psychological Interpretation* Levy (1963) presents this point as a formal postulate in his theory of interpretation. Levy reasons that since all interpretation is productive of dissonance (there would be no point in making an interpretation if it did not differ in some way from a position held by the patient), and since dissonance is aversive (Festinger, 1957) the stage would be set for quick rejection were it not for the fact that the therapist is reducing dissonance. Levy's postulate can be stated as follows:

> To the extent that the dissonance induced by interpretation (post-interpretation dissonance) is greater than that existing prior to its presentation (pre-interpretation dissonance), the interpretation will either be rejected or distorted, or the therapist will be devalued. To the extent that the reverse is the case, the interpretation will be accepted as intended and the therapist will not be subjected to devaluation (Levy, 1963, p. 285).

We can now see why all interpretations are not immediately rejected. Despite his general reluctance to change, the patient is often in a state of conflict when he enters therapy. There are aspects of his behavior that he does not understand and which make him uncomfortable. By helping the patient "make sense" out of his experience, the therapist is helping to reduce already existing dissonance. However, if his interpretation produces more dissonance than it reduces, the therapist runs the risk that he himself and the entire therapy situation will acquire aversive qualities. Note that in order for post interpretation dissonance to be less than preinterpretation dissonance some degree of dissonance within the patient must be present before the interpretation is made. This last requirement is difficult to meet when dealing with reluctant patients who have not come for help voluntarily. In these cases threatening interpretations have an even greater adverse effect, for with preinterpretation dissonance at a minimal level message rejection is highly likely. Therefore it is necessary to consider procedures that would reduce threat for highly defensive patients.

Ambiguity and Message Threat

The effect of ambiguity as a therapeutic variable has remained a controversial topic from the time when psychotherapists started to question the value of Freud's original behind-the-couch technique. In the Freudian model the entire therapy situation was designed to minimize the intrusion of the therapist into the field of consciousness of the patient. The therapist sat behind his patient so that his personal reactions to the patient's remarks would not be seen, he said little, and the instructions to the patient, "Tell me whatever comes to your mind," gave no direction to the course the patient was to follow. The sum total of these procedures produced maximum therapeutic ambiguity which according to Bordin (1955) was justified on the following theoretical grounds. To begin with, therapeutic ambiguity was considered a prerequisite for the development of free association. Like an unstructured projective situation, the client's reaction to ambiguity was said to lead to inferences about the general nature of his conflicts and defenses. Furthermore, ambiguity was considered necessary for the development of transference phenomena. For example, Fenichel (1945) suggests that a therapist cannot be certain that transference reactions are being manifested if he does not eliminate the reality basis for the patient's reaction. Only thus can he demonstrate to himself as well as to the patient that the patient's reactions to him are controlled by irrational, infantile feelings.

Thus we see that for the traditional Freudian psychotherapist ambiguity was a prerequisite for the therapeutic work of free association and the development and interpretation of transference phenomena. However, Frank (1961) suggests that ambiguity is an important ingredient of all methods of influence, whether they be called thought reform, "brain-washing," or psychotherapy. Frank notes that like the interrogators in thought reform psychotherapists give their patients the impression that they know what is wrong with them but that the patient must find out for himself in order to be helped. In both procedures ambiguity is heightened even further because the end point of the process is indeterminant; that is, like the prisoner-of-war, the patient must keep trying until he is "cured," but he does not know when this will be because the criteria that demonstrate that cure has been achieved are never clearly specified. Hence, forced to rely on a therapist who is constantly "permissive" but never directive, the patient finds himself naturally turning to the therapist for cues and guidelines. Being eager for some feedback, however minimal, the patient is considered by Frank to be much more under the therapist's influence than he ever could be in a clearer, more structured, and less anxiety arousing situation.

Despite the wide use ambiguity has received in clinical practice, we offer the following hypothesis:

HYPOTHESIS 4.2a: **Unambiguous messages decrease the threat value of therapeutic communications.**

If ambiguity produces such powerful results in changing behavior, as its proponents would have us believe, why do we consider ambiguity to be one of the factors that increase threat and subsequent patient resistance? To answer this question properly we must turn to a consideration of the nonpsychotherapy research on the effects of ambiguity.

The effects of ambiguity on anxiety seem clear from the literature. Ambiguity has been found to increase anxiety in a clinical interview (Dibner, 1958), in a group setting (Smith, 1957), and in the context of a psychological experiment (Dittes & Zemach, 1964). That ambiguity increases anxiety has never really been disputed, even by the proponents of its use in psychotherapy. For example, Frank agrees that the ambiguity of the traditional psychotherapy situation makes patients more anxious but goes on to suggest that this effect should heighten patient suggestibility so that the patient's motivation to seek relief from the therapist will also be increased. This last assumption—that anxiety created by an ambiguous situation should lead to greater affiliation with the therapist—needs further examination, and for this reason experiments by Rabbie (1963) and the previously mentioned work by Dittes and Zemach are considered in greater detail.

In the Rabbie experiment subjects were told that they were participating in an experiment involving their "emotional and physiological reactions to certain kinds of stimuli," as dummy electrodes were attached to their hands and arms. A high degree of fear was aroused in all subjects by telling them that they might receive painful electric shocks. Ambiguity was induced by varying the probability that a subject would receive a shock. In the high ambiguity condition subjects were told that only one out of four persons consider the shocks to be painful, whereas in the low ambiguity condition subjects were told that all persons consider the shocks quite painful. The main dependent variable of the experiment was affiliative tendencies measured by asking the subjects to indicate their preference for waiting alone or together while the experimental room was put in order. Rabbie found that when they were told that they would be allowed to talk to each other while waiting, those in the ambiguous condition produced a significantly greater preference to affiliate or wait together with another subject. Here, then, is the first bit of evidence to indicate that subjects in a threatening situation respond to ambiguity with increased affiliation toward other subjects. When considering the relevance of this experiment to psychotherapy one must ask whether affiliation *toward the therapist* would occur if he is seen as the source of the threat.

A second study of relevance is that of Dittes and Zemach (1964) in which subjects were presented with two surrealistic paintings and were then given explanatory comments for each picture. For half the subjects the commentary was "at least as surrealistic as the painting itself," whereas the other half received rather clear, literal, and detailed interpretations. As in the preceding experiment, subjects were told that there would be a delay of a few minutes and were asked to indicate whether they would prefer waiting alone or with others. Again, those subjects exposed to the ambiguous condition, that is, presented with the unclear commentary, indicated a preference for waiting with others. Subjects were then given a further choice of either waiting with a group like themselves who had just seen the paintings and commentaries or with a group described as being hand picked for their congeniality, compatibility, and friendliness, purportedly waiting for another experiment. Presumably, the first group could best satisfy the subject's need for cognitive clarity, for they had supposedly shared the experience. Social comparison would be facilitated in the first group, but the second group merely involved waiting with congenial and friendly people. The results demonstrated that subjects exposed to an ambiguous commentary indicated a desire to avoid others who had shared their experience and evidenced a strong preference for waiting with "congenial" people.

The results of this experiment are not completely clear because it is difficult to know what the subjects might have expected in the group that had seen the same painting and heard the same commentary. It would be almost impossible for subjects in the ambiguous condition to understand either painting or commentary, but what was their prediction of the performance of other subjects? If they thought that the others had found the material as confusing as they had, perhaps the subjects would have been more willing to share their experience, but if they thought that they alone had had difficulty understanding the material they might have been unwilling to risk talking about the paintings and exposing their ignorance. At any rate, we see that subjects exposed to ambiguity show increased affiliative tendencies but not with others who could expose them to further threat. In our opinion, then, if the therapist is seen as the source of threat, closer affiliation with him would probably not occur.

We suspect that the threatening aspects of ambiguity do not drive all prospective patients away because some enter therapy strongly attracted to the therapist as a "healer." For these individuals, who are already susceptible to influence, almost any form of treatment would produce beneficial results. However, we are proposing that for those who are initially resistant to influence therapeutic ambiguity will make the process of behavior change more difficult and may represent at least one factor which is responsible for traditional psychotherapy not having achieved even wider applicability. With regard to some restricted therapist operations ambiguity is desirable, but the general clinical setting needs more structure for many resistant patients, and the therapist must present clearer messages than has been the case in the traditional clinical interview. At this point, however, two topics need further elaboration: the effects of ambiguity on learning, and the ease of projection of internal need states in ambiguous situations.

In two experiments by Kanfer and Marston (1961, 1962), the effects of ambiguity on learning and transfer in a verbal conditioning situation were studied. Both studies noted that when ambiguity was decreased, faster learning and greater transfer were obtained. The first study provides some clues as to how ambiguity may operate in a clinical interview, so it will be described in some detail.

Kanfer and Marston note that there are at least three sources of ambiguity in the typical verbal conditioning procedure: the instructions might be ambiguous, the reinforcing stimulus might be presented ambiguously, and the distinctiveness of the stimulus materials might vary in clarity. In their experiment, all three types of ambiguity were investigated. Ambiguity in the instructions was varied in the following manner. Some subjects were told that each correct response would receive a point and were asked to work for points. Subjects in another group were not given any information about the scoring of responses. In another group, ambiguity of the reinforcing stimulus was studied by using either a neutral physical stimulus (e.g., a light) or a meaningful social reinforcer (e.g., "good"). The subject's task was to pronounce one of two words appearing on a card, with each word pair containing one neutral and one hostile word. Stimulus discriminability was varied by increasing the discrepancy in the degree of hostile connotation between the two members of a stimulus pair by using hostile words which were either mildly or intensely hostile. The experimenters found that learning and transfer occurred most slowly in the groups presented with ambiguous instructions. Ambiguity in the reinforcing stimulus and lack of distinctness of the stimulus materials also slowed learning so that the group for which all three variables were ambiguous (no instructions with regard to scoring, a light as the reinforcing stimulus, and mildly hostile words) showed no learning at all. This last group came as close to total ambiguity as is possible in this experimental setting and probably bears closest resemblance to the ambiguity of the traditional Freudian interview described earlier.

The Kanfer and Marston studies demonstrate that ambiguity may retard learning because when confronted with ambiguous messages, subjects may not know what is expected of them and hence may be unable to respond effectively. Thus less intelligent subjects or those for whom the experimenter's frame of reference is foreign may have greatest difficulty. This point has relevance for psychotherapy because several investigators have demonstrated that dropout rates among lower class patients are much greater than among patients who do not have to cross socioeconomic or communication barriers to reach effective understanding with their therapists (Heine and Trosman, 1960). That message clarity can help a therapist reach intellectually less capable patients can be demonstrated by research concerned with "stating a conclusion" (Cohen, 1964). In general, stating a conclusion enhances message acceptance more than a communication which leaves the conclusion to be drawn completely to the audience (Hovland & Mandell,

1952). The effects of stating a conclusion are enhanced with less intelligent listeners (Thistlethwaite, deHaan, & Kamenetsky, 1955) and when the issue under discussion increases in complexity (Krech, Crutchfield, & Ballachey, 1962). Thus we conclude that a therapist should keep his message simple and unambiguous under these conditions.

We have yet to deal with what may be considered the primary theoretical justification for the use of ambiguity in psychotherapy. We refer here to the Freudian assumption, mentioned earlier, that ambiguity is necessary for the proper development of transference reactions in the patient. This proposition, which bears some similarity to assumptions implicit in most unstructured projective tests, claims that only in ambiguous situations can the patient's needs and desires be properly projected. We do not wish to enter the controversy concerning the assumptions and uses of projective tests, but we must point out that research in attitude change (Manis, 1961) as well as some work with projective tests (Murstein, 1963) have not found that ambiguity automatically increases projection of internal need states. Even so, we must recognize that for the therapist whose theoretical orientation requires the analysis of transference phenomena an ambiguous therapy setting may be essential. However, what is disturbing to us is that this therapy ingredient has been adopted indiscriminantly, even by those who do not describe their therapy in traditional transference terms. It is these individuals, we feel, who have unnecessarily burdened their therapy with a threat-producing procedure.

It should be noted that we are not advocating complete structure along all possible dimensions in psychotherapy. Bordin (1955) notes that it is possible to conceive of three areas in which ambiguity can be found in psychotherapy. These are the topics appropriate for patient discussion, the closeness and degree of explicitness of the relationship between the patient and therapist, and the goals toward which the therapist feels he and the patient should work. Of the three, the therapist's broad, long-term goals may remain ambiguous, for it is possible that some patients would have difficulty comprehending these even if they were elucidated. If a therapist feels that his patient needs to learn to express hostility more openly, it does little good, and may perhaps do harm, to broadcast this to the patient at the beginning of treatment. This is consistent with our previously stated opinion that opinion that awareness of an influence attempt may retard its effectiveness. But on the other two therapeutic dimensions, namely the patient's task with regard to the topics to be considered at any given moment and the nature of the therapeutic relationship, we feel greater clarity and structure will enhance behavior change. Contemporary psychotherapy theory seems to be moving in this direction and we welcome this development. An interesting example of this kind of change can be represented by Rogerian therapy. Early client centered therapists quickly abandoned "simple acceptance" as their primary mode of behavior and began increasing their "clarification" and "restatement" techniques. Current Rogerian emphasis on "empathic understanding" represents a further decrease in ambiguity with the therapeutic relationship being made explicit by the therapist trying to demonstrate his understanding by putting into words the message that he thinks the patient is trying to communicate.

We may summarize this section on message ambiguity by restating our contention that reducing ambiguity in therapy will decrease threat and increase the likelihood that the therapist's remarks will be understood and accepted. This point is particularly relevant for patients who are not initially attracted to therapy and are hence more resistant to therapeutic influence. However, even in the case of a complaint patient, the therapist may find that when anxiety starts to increase beyond what he would consider to be optimal bounds increased clarity and structure could prove effective weapons in lowering that anxiety.

Delayed Compliance and Message Threat

If the threat value of a therapeutic message is too great, it may become so easily distorted or denied by the patient that it is never even considered by him. Such action by a patient may occur frequently when an interpretation by the therapist seems to imply the necessity of immediate action. Patients for whom any change is threatening would resist such messages. Rejection of the therapist's message would also occur fairly frequently by those patients who interpret all relationships, including therapy, as a contest for supremacy. These individuals, who need to maintain an image of complete independence and self-reliance, are not often seen in a therapist's office, and if forced to present themselves for treatment are not likely to experience success. This is at least partly because the dependent, help-seeking, acquiescent patient's role is so difficult for them to assume. It is for these two groups of resistant patients, those for whom any change is threatening and for whom any implied suggestion or advice is threatening, that we suggest the adoption of therapeutic procedures that permit and even actively encourage delayed compliance.

Encouraging the patient to actively suspend or hold in abeyance his evaluation of a remark or interpretation by the therapist has no advocates in any of the traditional therapy schools. If anything, there are suggestions in some of the analytic models that anything short of immediate recognition of the truth of the therapist's interpretation must be treated as resistance. When one is engaged in conversion procedures with compliant persons, forced compliance has much to recommend it. Early and public commitment to an idea has been found to be an effective procedure for changing attitude even though initial belief in the espoused position is minimal. This point developed from experiments by Festinger and his associates (Brehm & Cohen, 1962; Festinger, 1957) assumes that the subject can be made to take a public stand advocating a position which he himself does not accept. It is only after he has taken such a stand that cognitive dissonance theory predicts attitude change. The possible utility of cognitive dissonance research for psychotherapy has been discussed in Chapter 3 where we have suggested procedures by which cognitive dissonance arousal can change resistant attitudes by increasing patient attraction to the therapist. At this point we would like to emphasize the multiplicity of alternatives available for dealing with resistant behavior and are ready to suggest that offering messages which actively encourage delayed compliance is one such procedure. This hypothesis can be formally stated as follows:

HYPOTHESIS 4.2b: **Messages that encourage delayed compliance decrease the threat value of therapeutic communications.**

The basic research from which this hypothesis was extrapolated involves experiments which have observed increases in opinion change over time which have been labeled "the sleeper effect." The finding of interest here is that while the advantage of communications coming from highly credible sources decrease with time, those coming from low credible sources increase with time, that is, the effectiveness of communication from high credible sources shows a decay effect, decreasing in effectiveness over time as might be expected from a normal process of forgetting. What has proved of particular interest in the research on "sleeper effects" is that while opinion change produced by low credible sources is initially low, their effectiveness in inducing opinion change increases with the passage of time. If we were to conceptualize the therapist as a communicator of low credibility for the typical resistant patient we may begin to see why communications encouraging delayed compliance might take advantage of possible "sleeper effects." Before we can speculate further about how this hypothesis would be implemented in psychotherapy a more complete description of the research demonstrating the existence of "sleeper effects" is in order.

One of the pioneering studies concerned with the effects of a communication over time was conducted by a group of investigators working for the United States Army during the Second World War (Hovland, Lumsdaine, & Sheffield, 1940). The study of interest to us was part of a larger investigation dealing with the effectiveness of films and other mass communication devices. We shall focus on the part of their work dealing with the effectiveness of an orientation film called "The Battle of Britain." The effects of the film were studied at two points, one week after the film's presentation, and nine weeks after the showing. The design of the study involved four groups of three companies each. All groups were administered an opinion and fact questionnaire before the showing of the film while two of the groups, the experimental groups, received a second version of the questionnaire either one week or nine weeks after the showing. The two control groups took the questionnaires at the same time as their respective experimental groups but did not see the film.

While the factual content of the film was retained less well after a nine-week period, the surprising result of this study was that many of the opinion items which were not accepted one week after the film's presentation were accepted nine weeks later—viewers seemed more willing to accept opinions espoused in the film that were not so readily accepted shortly after its presentation even though the factual content upon which these opinions rested had been forgotten to a greater extent. In explaining their results, the investigators speculated that there may have been aspects of the film which were resisted at first but which were found more acceptable with the passage of time. The investigators added that the source of an item of opinion is more quickly forgotten than the material itself, and if the source is initially discounted as presenting a biased view, the material presented by that source may be assimilated and accepted at a later date when its association with the biased source becomes lessened. We shall see that this same explanation is used by Hovland and his associates in their further studies of "the sleeper effect."

The most immediate followup of the original Hovland, Lumsdaine, and Sheffield finding was in a study by Hovland and Weiss (1951). In this study, a college class was presented with written messages (e.g., Should anti-histamine drugs continue to be sold without a doctor's prescription?) attributed to high or low trustworthy sources (e.g., New England Journal of Biology and Medicine versus monthly pictorial magazine). There was significant opinion change in favor of the positions advocated by the trustworthy sources and against those held by the untrustworthy sources when opinion questionnaires were administered immediately after the communication. However four weeks later when the class was tested again there was a decrease in agreement with the trustworthy sources, and an increase in agreement with the untrustworthy sources. This finding was further validated by Kelman and Hovland (1953) who in addition were able to demonstrate that "reinstating" the communicator by reminding the subjects of the source of the communication caused the "sleeper effect" to all but disappear. For the groups in which the communicator was reinstated, the extent of agreement with the positive source and disagreement with the negative source was the same three weeks later as it was immediately following the communication.

In considering the applicability of the studies just reported to the practice of psychotherapy, the first point that becomes clear is that these studies taken together suggest therapeutic procedures that would be quite different for compliant and resistant patients. When the communicator is already considered in a positive light, the effect of his prestige is greatest immediately on presenting a message. Thus for patients already positively oriented toward their therapists, a message which suggests immediate compliance should benefit from whatever therapist prestige is associated with it. But for many resistant patients, therapist prestige is low and hence not available to enhance the therapist's message. It is in these instances that we suggest the therapist encourage delayed compliance so that the content of his message might be retained and acted on more favorably when the association with its therapeutic source has been lessened. Thus, in implementing this hypothesis, the therapist would suggest to his patient that he purposely not take action upon the message just delivered but that he simply "think about it." We can picture a therapist telling his resistant patient "I don't want you to believe it just because I said so; look the situation over for yourself and then come to a decision." This would allow the patient to accept parts of the therapist's message, or to accept the message entirely, but in either case make it his own— a goal toward which all therapies claim they strive.

Our suggestions come close to and are consonant with those presented by Haley (1963) who goes further than suggesting delayed compliance by actively inviting the patient to disobey the therapist. Haley interprets the therapeutic situation as a struggle for influence, with the therapist hoping to influence his patient and the patient in turn, by his symptomatology and defensive behavior, attempting to keep some control of therapy. For many resistant patients this conceptualization has much to recommend it, for their entire history has been one of keeping themselves from being controlled by others. Haley's therapy presents paradoxical directives which make it appear that the patient is actually complying when he engages in what would normally be considered resistant behavior. For example, if refusing to approach the therapist is resistance, then telling the patient to stand still and not move toward the therapist is directing him to resist. Hence in order to resist this directive the patient has little choice but to engage in more acceptable behavior. Since the resistance becomes therapist initiated, its continued practice is a sign of acquiescence; hence it is abandoned.

In summary then, we are suggesting that research on the "sleeper effect" has relevance for psychotherapy in that it suggests that therapists whose patients are not attracted to them may increase their influence by offering interpretations which encourage delayed compliance. We see this maneuver as one which should decrease the threat many resistant patients feel when required to immediately acquiesce to a therapist's suggestion. We would not at all be surprised if the therapist found that by allowing and encouraging this period of grace, his work would proceed more smoothly since he has now made the patient's role behavior in therapy less threatening.

Immunization Against Counterarguments

Traditionally, psychotherapy theorists have paid little attention to the real world of the patient. Advocates of family therapy (Ackerman, 1958; Jackson, 1959) are correcting this deficiency in part, as are milieu therapists (Cumming & Cumming, 1962) and patient self-government proponents (Fairweather, 1964). But the psychotherapist practicing individual, insight-oriented psychotherapy too often seems immune to these new developments.

Traditional psychotherapy theory often assumes that patient pathology has its origins in past traumatic events and that the patient continues to respond to situations with defensive behaviors perhaps necessary at one time but now no longer adaptive. The assumption is often made that the real world no longer contributes to the patient's difficulties and that were the patient's environment to continue to be aversive, psychotherapy would probably be impossible. Thus the emphasis in psychotherapy has been that with the new perceptions produced by a working through of old conflicts the patient should become free to deal effectively with his current environment and any new stresses still residing therein.

This position has characterized Freudian psychoanalysis both in its traditional format (Fenichel, 1945) and as revised by Dollard and Miller (1950). Consider the following quotation from the latter authors:

> Most generally stated, the problem is to keep the patient's behavior up to date, to keep it in accord with current conditions of life. In order to modernize the neurotic patient he must frequently learn to try out new responses appropriate to new conditions and, in order to get him to try out these responses, he must clearly see that the conflicts and repressions from which he suffers are not justified by the current conditions of reward and punishment. He must further learn that the conditions in the past which produced these conflicts are sharply dissimilar from those of the present, thanks to age-grading and often to original mistraining. He must notice that many of his current habits are similar to those which he had in childhood and were learned in childhood under childhood conditions.
>
> As a result of noting these similarities and differences, the patient becomes convinced that his neurotic behavior is functionally obsolete, and this conviction gives him the courage, which he has not had, to try new responses. If he tries such responses and, if they are rewarded, the neurotic impasse is broken up and the patient begins to learn anew (p. 305).

Dollard and Miller go on to note that the conditions of real life must be favorable if new responses are to be learned; if the patient's real life does not permit resolution of his neurotic conflict, psychotherapy will not help. However, Dollard and Miller offer no suggestions concerning how a therapist might prepare a patient for an unsympathetic environment.

Psychoanalysts are not unique in ignoring the possibility that a therapist may need to take direct measures to ensure that his work will not be undone by environmental agents. Rogers assumes that as a client achieves greater inner congruence others in his environment recognizing his growth and increased maturity will react to him more favorably, helping to perpetuate the favorable growth cycle started in psychotherapy. No new technique must be instituted to handle real life adjustment since "changes in behavior keep pace with the changes in the organization of self" (Rogers, 1951, p. 195). Ford and Urban (1963) describe Rogers' emphasis in the following way:

> Rogers assumes that changes in behaviors outside of the therapy interview will follow automatically upon changes in the self-evaluative thoughts and associated emotions during the therapy hour. Changes in the self-evaluative

thoughts and their emotional concomitants result in reduced anxiety, improved discrimination among situational events and responses, more accurate symbolization of them, and greater confidence in one's own decisions. These provide the conditions from which more appropriate instrumental and interpersonal responses will naturally grow (p. 435).

What can a therapist do when encountering a real life environment that does not facilitate patient growth? We have already mentioned the possibilities of including important members of the patient's environment in the treatment process (family therapy) or reconstituting that environment (milieu therapy, community social planning, etc.). In the next chapter we also state our conviction that the therapist must help the patient deal with current environmental stress more actively than a completely officebound treatment would permit. At this time, we would like to emphasize procedures that would make the therapist's messages more immune to counter-arguments by others in the patient's environment whose views if accepted by the patient would perpetuate maladaptive perceptions and behavior. We are thus in a position to offer the following interrelated hypotheses:

HYPOTHESIS 4.3: **Resistance in psychotherapy is reduced by messages which immunize the patient against subsequent counter-argument.**

HYPOTHESIS 4.3a: **Therapeutic messages preceded by weak counter-arguments immunize the patient against other stronger arguments.**

The issue to which these hypotheses are directed is whether a communicator should mention ideas opposed to those he wishes to present. For some time a commonly held point of view in the field of propaganda was that in appealing for acceptance of any specific belief or policy no opposing arguments should be discussed because mentioning rival ideas invites comparison, hesitation, and doubt. It is our subjective impression that many psychotherapists operate as did these early propagandists, either ignoring other points of view or treating them as examples of resistance if initiated by the patient. While this procedure may serve effectively in dealing with compliant patients, we hope to illustrate by the research material to be presented that other procedures are necessary for those aware of or committed to points of view opposed by the therapist.

We again begin our discussion of research with the early group of studies by Hovland, Lumsdaine, and Sheffield (1949). The study to be reported here was conducted in 1945, when the Second World War was drawing to a close in Europe and army officials were becoming concerned about the prevalent overoptimism of their men concerning ment, each of two experimental groups of 214 soldiers listened to one of two specially prepared radio transcriptions describing why the war with Japan would be a long one. Beliefs about the issue were tested before and immediately after the communication for both experimental groups, and for a control group of 197 men who participated in the testing but did not hear the programs. One program, the one-sided message, only included the arguments for thinking that the war with Japan would be a long one. The other program, presenting the two-sided message, included the same arguments as the first program but also considered some argument on the other side, emphasizing Japan's weakness.

In order to evaluate the effectiveness of the two programs, subjects were asked to estimate the probable length of the war with Japan. Both programs were effective in convincing the men that the war with Japan would be difficult, but no advantage of one program over the other was found for the audience as a whole. However, there were important differences between the subjects depending on their initial points of view. The program presenting the one-sided picture was more effective only for those subjects initially favoring the position taken in the communication; the two-sided program was more effective in changing the opinion of those initially opposed to the communication. The authors also evaluated their results in terms of the educational level of the subjects. They found that the two-sided communication was more effective among the better educated subjects regardless of initial position, whereas the one-sided presentation was primarily effective "with those who were already convinced among the less well educated group." Thus the Hovland, Lumsdaine, and Sheffield study provides strong evidence in support of the view that when faced with a listener who is known to be initially resistant to his message a communicator needs to indicate an awareness of the relevant counter-arguments.

While the above experiment assumes an opinion on the part of the listener, one can legitimately ask whether a similar effect would be observed in an initially neutral listener who was exposed to a counter-communication at a later date. In other words, what are the effects of one-sided versus two-sided communications in producing "immunization" against *subsequent* opposing messages? Lumsdaine and Janis (1953) sought to answer this question by presenting different high school classes with one of two versions of a recorded radio program in both of which a commentator took the view that "it would be at least five years before Russia could produce A-bombs in quantity." (This study was conducted in 1953, several months before the announcement that Russia had produced an atomic explosion.) The one-sided presentation contained only the arguments supporting the conclusion while the two-sided message contained these points but also discussed arguments on the other side of the issue. Different groups heard each of these programs and one week later half of each group was exposed to a counter-communication and the other half was not. The counter-message consisted of a second communication in which the same issue was discussed by a different commentator who took a position opposite from the first, that Russia had probably already developed an atomic bomb. Which group would prove to be more resistant to the counter-message? The results of the experiment clearly indicated that it was the subjects who received the two-sided message who were able to maintain the attitude adopted in the first communication. Compared to subjects who received the one-sided message, subjects receiving the two-sided message were relatively unaffected by the later communication. In explaining their results the authors conclude:

> Regardless of initial position, a convincing one-sided communication presenting only positive arguments will tend to sway many members of the audience farther in the direction advocated by the communicator. However, when these persons subsequently hear the opposite point of view, also supported by cogent-sounding arguments, their opinions tend to be swayed back in the negative direction, especially if the new arguments appear to offset the previous positive arguments. But if the initial communication is, instead, a two-sided one it will already have taken into account both the positive and negative arguments and still have reached the positive conclusion. When the listener is then subsequently exposed to the presentation of opposing arguments in the counter-propaganda, he is less likely to be influenced by them. He is not only familiar with the opposing point of view, but has been led to the positive conclusion in a context in which the negative arguments were in evidence. In effect, he has been given an advance basis for ignoring or discounting the opposing communication and, thus "inoculated," he will tend to retain the positive conclusion (Lumsdaine & Janis, 1953, p. 318).

Thus far we have seen that a two-sided communication is more effective than a one-sided one when the listener initially disagrees with the communicator's position and when regardless of initial opinion the listener is later exposed to counter-messages. However, we still have to know how much of the counter-argument should be mentioned in the initial message for it to have immunizing properties. While the two-sided messages in the experiments cited above acknowledge the counter-argument, should the communicator elaborate these counter-arguments at length? If the communicator presents an elaboration of all the "facts on the other side" he might strengthen the position of the already opposed listener. On the other hand, if he mentions all the relevant counter-arguments the opposed listener might have less of a tendency to dismiss his ideas as emanating from a biased source. This issue was investigated by Thistlethwaite and Kamenetzky (1955), who found that a two-sided message with no elaboration of counter-arguments was more effective in changing attitudes than a similar two-sided message in which the counter-arguments were elaborated. However the authors point out that although their experiment did not provide full data on this point, they suspect that an important variable to be considered before the full effects of elaboration of counter-arguments is known is whether the elaborated facts are already known to the listener. If the opposed listener is not aware of all the facts supporting his position, an elaboration of them would probably strengthen his opposition; however, if he is already aware of these facts, their inclusion would make him more susceptible to influence since he would probably see the communicator who mentions these facts as unbiased and fair.

Any description of research results on the topic of immunization to counter-messages would be incomplete if it did not include mention of the extensive work of McGuire and Papageorgis (McGuire, 1961a, 1961b, 1962; McGuire & Papageorgis, 1961, 1962; Papageorgis & McGuire, 1961). These studies as well as others on this topic were reviewed by McGuire (1964) who proposes an "inoculation theory" similar to that proposed by Hovland, Lumsdaine, & Sheffield to account for the increased resistance to counter-persuasion that can be provided by "supportive" and "refutational" defenses (McGuire's terms which overlap in meaning with one-sided and two-sided messages, respectively). The biological analogy from whence the term "inoculation theory" originates has been stated by McGuire as follows:

In the biological situation, the person is typically made resistant to some attacking virus by pre-exposure to a weakened dose of the virus. This mild dose stimulates his defenses so that he will be better able to overcome any massive viral attack to which he is later exposed, but is not so strong that this pre-exposure will itself cause the disease. Alternatively, biological resistance can be augmented by supportive therapy such as adequate rest, good diet, and vitamin supplements. Inoculation is likely to be superior to supportive therapy to the extent that the person has previously been brought up in a germ-free environment. It is a seeming paradox that individuals raised aseptically tend to appear vigorously healthy (even without supportive therapy) but are highly vulnerable when suddenly exposed to massive doses of the disease virus. (1964, p. 200)

It can be seen that inoculation theory predicts that while supportive defenses appear to strengthen an initial belief, in fact such noninoculated attitudes are least resistant to subsequent attack, a finding consistently replicated by McGuire.

McGuire demonstrated further that inoculation produces greatest resistance to counter-influence in situations in which an individual is not motivated to develop a defense because he assumes that belief to have obvious validity and is thus unpracticed in defending his belief. In order to motivate him to develop adequate defenses for his belief, inoculation theory suggests exposing the individual to a weakened form of the attacking arguments he is likely to encounter.

In the McGuire experiments, the subject's initial belief is vulnerable because it is a "cultural truism," a belief so widely shared within the person's social milieu that he would not have heard it attacked and might consider an attack on it impossible. Hence he is unmotivated and unpracticed in its defense. In psychotherapy, the ideas we wish to inoculate are not cultural truisms but new points of view being presented by the therapist. Even so, there is some similarity between the two situations in that like McGuire's experimental subjects the psychotherapy patient is probably unpracticed in defending his newly acquired beliefs. He, too, would be vulnerable to counter-influence unless helped to achieve an appropriate defense.

We feel confident in concluding that a review of the research indicates that two-sided messages are most effective in situations in which the communicant himself is opposed to the message or an undefended belief is vulnerable to subsequent attack. In the first case the increased receptivity in an otherwise opposed individual is probably caused by the message being seen in a more objective manner; in the latter case, the two-sided message helps establish a defense against counter-influence. Some words of caution are in order at this point. There is much about the operation of immunizing arguments that is still unknown. For example, the immunization process can raise anxiety by exposing the individual to ideas discrepant with his new beliefs or by forewarning him of subsequent attack. It is expected that the threat associated with immunization would be less than would occur if the individual were exposed to the subsequent attack unprepared, but we do not know the kinds of messages for which prior immunization is most effective. McGuire used cultural truisms, Hovland and his associates worked with controversial beliefs, and Manis (1965) studied immunization as a function of favorable versus unfavorable messages; but no investigator has tried immunization procedures on the personal, self-oriented beliefs which are most relevant to psycho-therapy. Another unresolved question concerns the extent to which the communicant should actively engage in the immunization procedure. The studies of forced compliance mentioned earlier indicate that active participation in an activity generally increases one's commitment to it, but Manis and Blake (1963) and McGuire (1961) report no increases in immunization effectiveness when the S participates more actively in the defense. A third unresolved issue concerns the order of presenta-tion of the arguments for effective immunization. Hovland, Lumsdaine, and Sheffield (1949) recommend that for maximum immunization the order of presentation of the full message should be "positive argument leading, objection raised by an opposed counter-argument, and then positive argument offsetting the objection" (p. 205). However, the re-search on order effects in persuasive messages when both sides of an issue are to be presented successively indicates that neither "primacy" nor "recency" show consistent superiority. Factors such as degree of public commitment, anxiety arousing properties and complexity of the message, degree of attention and motivation to learn, as well as other factors have been shown to affect the results of experiments dealing with order of presentation (Cohen, 1964; Hovland, 1957; Hovland, Janis, & Kelley, 1953). With such known complexity, direct test in the clinical situation itself is in order.

Bearing these cautions in mind, we feel that it is safe to conclude that as a general procedure to reduce initial resistance and to prevent later weakening of an implanted idea, immunization procedures have much to recommend them to the clinician for his research considera-tion. Although these procedures may seem clinically unorthodox, they are based on a fairly large body of empirical evidence and should be investigated in a clinical setting. We hope that a consideration of these hypotheses will lead others to develop methods for dealing with that too often neglected aspect of a patient's life—the nontherapeutic environment.

RESISTANCE AS A FUNCTION OF COMMUNICATOR CHARACTERISTICS

It has been known for some time that the personal characteristics of a communicator can affect the reception that his message will receive. How the communicant perceives the communicator can be influenced by such communicator characteristics as vividness of personality, status, the expertise attributed to him, and the stake he has in the issue under discussion. Similarly, the communicant may be motivated by such attitudes as affection and admiration for the communicator, fear and awe of him, trust and confidence in his sincerity, fairness, and credibility (Cohen, 1964, p. 23). In general, research has demonstrated that communicators with positively valued characteristics are more effective than those with negative characteristics (Aronson & Golden, 1962; Hovland & Weiss, 1951; Kelman & Eagly, 1965; Kelman & Hovland, 1953; Weiss & Fine, 1956). The problem in psychotherapy is that for many resistant patients the therapist is often not seen as a positive communicator.

Although the influence of the personal characteristics of the therapist on the treatment process was recognized early in the history of psychoanalysis, little systematic study was given to this variable. Strupp (1960) notes that Freud seemed ambivalent about the extent to which the therapist as a person should intrude into the treatment process. On one hand the therapist was instructed to keep the analytic field clean and uncontaminated since the cathartic properties of the therapy situation were said to depend on the patient's ability to unravel a long stream of associations that would in a deterministic manner lead to the causal trauma. The patient was driven to perform in this manner and the therapist's function was to provide the opportunity for the associations to occur undistorted by his instrusions. On the other hand, Freud very quickly realized that the patient's attitude toward the therapist made quite a bit of difference in the efficacy of the treatment and that in a number of cases, "the personal equation of the doctor" was enough to overcome patient resistance (Freud, 1937, p. 214). Still, with the discussion of the therapist's personal contribution to the treatment process limited to conceptions of transference and countertransference, little attention was given to the real stimulus qualities of the therapist. The patient's reaction to the therapist was not considered to be due to aspects of the therapist's real behavior but was assumed to be merely a reflection of the patient's inner life and his unresolved feelings toward other significant persons in his past.

It is only within the last two decades that serious attempts have been made to systematically investigate the effects of the personal characteristics of the therapist on the patient. Much of this work was influenced by the theories of Harry Stack Sullivan (1953; 1954). Sullivan's concept of *participant observation* implied that the therapist could consider the patient's behavior in therapy only in relation to the stimulus characteristics of himself as a person; that "his principal instrument of observation is his self—his personality, him as a person" (Sullivan, 1954, p. 3). Thus, being able to see himself as he really is and how he looks to his patient has become an important task for the therapist.

Although many therapists would now agree that their personality characteristics play an important part in the treatment process, so far only a few have attempted to investigate this question (e.g., Bandura, Lipsher, & Miller, 1960; Cutler, 1958; Holt & Luborsky, 1958; Russell & Snyder, 1963; Strupp, 1960). However, the clinical literature is filled with many descriptions of the ideal therapist. In reviewing this literature, Krasner has observed that the ideal therapist has been variously described as:

> . . . mature, well-adjusted, sympathetic, tolerant, patient, kindly, tactful, non-judgmental, accepting, permissive, non-critical, warm, likeable, interested in human beings, respectful, cherishing and working for a democratic kind of interpersonal relationship with all people, free of racial and religious bigotry, having a worthwhile goal in life, friendly, encouraging, optimistic, strong, intelligent, wise, curious, creative, artistic, scientifically oriented, competent, trustworthy, a model for the patient to follow, resourceful, emotionally sensitive, self-aware, insightful of his own problems, spontaneous, having a sense of humor, feeling personally secure, mature about sex, growing and maturing with life's experiences, having a high frustration tolerance, self-confident, relaxed, objective, self-analytic, aware of his own prejudices, nonobsequious, humble, skeptical but not pessimistic or self-deprecatory, trustworthy, dependable, consistent, open, honest, frank, technically sophisticated, professionally dedicated, and charming (Krasner, 1963, pp. 16-17).

We agree with Krasner that no real therapist, or any human being, could possess all the above qualities. Going even further, we wonder whether the concept of an ideal therapist personality, suitable in all treatment settings, has much meaning. Particular therapist personality traits might enhance therapeutic technique with some patients but prove a hindrance with others. In a series of studies, Whitehorn and Betz (summarized by Betz, 1962) were able to demonstrate that certain therapists (Type A) consistently achieved better results with schizophrenic patients than other therapists (Type B) and that therapist type could be reliably distinguished by a 23-item scale developed from the Strong Vocational Interest Blank. The possibility that A therapists had greater therapeutic aptitude in general was ruled out by the investigators for "both groups did equally well with other types of patients than schizophrenic" (Betz, 1962, p. 44). However, this last finding was questioned by McNair, Callahan, and Lorr (1962) who used the

A-B scale with a sample of 40 VA psychotherapists. Patients in this study were VA outpatients, and with this group *B* therapists were superior. Thus neither *A* nor *B* therapist personality characteristics are ideal for all patients. Further confirmation of this point comes from Carson, Harden, and Shows (1964), who demonstrated that in a series of experimental interviews the performance of student interviewers classified according to the Whitehorn and Betz *A-B* typology could be differentiated. *A* interviewers could obtain more personal information from subjects in whom a suspicious and distrusting set had been induced; *B* interviewers were more successful with subjects in whom a friendly and trusting expectation had been induced. Carson et al. conclude that it is only when interviewee characteristics are considered that meaningful differences which can be associated with *A-B* interviewer types emerge.

Unfortunately, patients are not selected for therapy on primarily rational bases. Personal preferences of therapists, often covert and disguised, play a large and too often unrecognized part of the selection procedure. Rarely does one hear a therapist say, "I can't work with this patient"; more likely is the remark, "This patient is not a suitable candidate." Yet the congruence between personal characteristics of therapists and successful patients is remarkable (Heine & Trosman, 1960; Hollingshead & Redlich, 1958; Sharaf & Levinson, 1957). Observation of this congruence has led Levinson to propose a "homophilic hypothesis," that is,

in selecting patients for psychotherapy, the therapist tends to prefer candidates who resemble him in social background, outlook, and personality. He tends to reject candidates who differ markedly in most of these respects (Levinson, 1962, p. 23).

If a homophilic hypothesis is in fact in operation in the selection of patients for psychotherapy, who will provide help for the non-preferred therapy candidates—those who, unlike their middle-class therapists, are not verbal, introspective, or highly educated? One possibility is that a new profession may be called for, which unlike present-day psychology and psychiatry does not put a premium on academic skills and upward social mobility. Such a suggestion has been made by Gordon (1965) as a method of reaching out-of-work, out-of-school youth growing up in extreme poverty. Gordon recommends the use of subprofessionals from the same milieu as the clients to be served. These trained, indigenous workers can communicate instantly with the suspicious and distrustful client in a way that many middleclass professionals cannot do, particularly since the latter are often seen as part of the system against which the hostile, anomic youth is fighting.

We recognize the desirability of Gordon's proposal for well-trained indigenous subprofessionals, particularly since the traditional helping professions alone could never meet the mental health needs of so large a proportion of our population. However, it seems wasteful to suggest that existing professionals cannot cross class boundaries. With an awareness of the problems to be encountered in treating resistant patients, therapists motivated to do so should be able to overcome their homophilic tendencies.

How can a therapist encourage the resistant patient to see him as a positive communicator? We have already discussed methods of attraction inducement (Chapter 3). At this point we will consider an alternate proposal which would more directly utilize the personal qualities of the therapist.

HYPOTHESIS 4.4: **Resistance in psychotherapy can be reduced by training the patient to view the therapist as a positive but discriminating reinforcer.**

This hypothesis suggests that the initial distrust of the therapist exhibited by the resistant patient might be lessened through prior training oriented toward changing the patient's negative perception of the therapist. Asocial and antisocial patients are the primary candidates for this hypothesis, for it is these individuals who exhibit deficiencies in social training caused by the avoidance of close personal relationships. However, this suggestion would be applicable for anyone whose social history reflects a chronic inability to form and maintain stable affectional ties to others. Cairns and Lewis (1962) found that in a group of college students, those who were high dependency inhibitors (who inhibited the development of close interpersonal relationships) evaluated a simple verbal reinforcement such as "mmhmm" in nonpositive terms. Further, evaluation of the reinforcement stimulus was related to the amount of verbal conditioning that occurred, so that there was markedly less conditioning for those who evaluated the reinforcement stimulus in nonpositive terms. Similar deficits in learning among antisocial individuals have been demonstrated in investigations by Lykken (1957) and Cairns (1961). The latter study is of particular interest because it involved an interview task in which "confiding" responses were to be reinforced. A confiding response was defined as "any personal reference that the S made to his home or family, e.g., references to parents, siblings, foster- or step-parents, relatives, and generalized references to the home" (Cairns 1961, p. 472). Ss, all adolescents being detained in a juvenile institution, did not differ initially in the amount of personal information they confided to the experimenter. However, unlike "low dependency inhibition" subjects who responded to verbal approval by accelerating their production of reinforced responses, subjects high in dependency inhibition produced fewer and fewer confiding responses as reinforcement continued. Cairns concluded that in retraining children high in dependency inhibition, social rewards (e.g., approval, friendliness, etc.) will have a disruptive rather than a facilitative effect unless the anxiety associated with dependent behavior is reduced.

For asocial and antisocial patients who are not yet ready to respond to others as social reinforcers, procedures to help the patient learn to want the interest and approval of the therapist are in order. We have in mind procedures in which the therapist would be associated with the delivery of primary rewards so that the person of the therapist acquires rewarding properties. Once the patient has learned to want the interest and approval of the therapist, these reinforcers may be used to promote the acquisition of new positive habits (Bandura, 1961).

The work of Cairns (1962) is noteworthy as an illustration of the manner in which a patient might be trained to view the therapist as a positive reinforcer. In this study, 6- to 7-year-old children were assigned to one of three conditions: a condition in which they were reinforced for making dependency responses (i.e., paying attention to and seeking help from the experimenter); a reinforcement control condition in which the same number of reinforcements was presented as in the first group but in which presentation of the reinforcement was not contingent upon the occurrence of help seeking responses; and a condition in which subjects received no reinforcement but were mildly punished. Subjects were brought into a room in which a toy cabinet was in prominent display. For the first group the glass doors of the cabinet were closed and the child was required to ask the experimenter for help in order to receive a toy. For the second group the doors of toy cabinet were open so the child could get the toys himself, and any request for help was answered in a politely noncommittal manner (e.g., "You can get it"). For both groups the experimenter sat in a chair turned so as to face the child and conversed with the child in a friendly manner. However, for the third group, which was slightly punishing, the subjects were not allowed to play with the toys in full view in the closed toy cabinet and were ignored by the experimenter who appeared to be working busily at his desk. Following this experimental manipulation, each child participated in a two-choice motor conditioning task with a second experimenter. Only in the first group, those previously rewarded for seeking help from the experimenter, was a significant conditioning effect obtained. The performances of both the control and frustrated groups were significantly below that of the group reinforced for dependency. Cairns concluded that the "greater effectiveness of the reinforcer for the group rewarded for dependency was due primarily to the S's greater attentiveness to and awareness of the verbal and behavioral responses of the E" (Cairns, 1962, p. 4).

McCoy and Zigler (1965) also found that a prior positive experience with an experimenter increased the subject's willingness to participate with him in a monotonous task. But Zigler and Kanzer (1962) caution that the effectiveness of a social reinforcer is not constant across all populations and that a particular positive social reinforcer cannot be considered the functional equivalent of any other positive social reinforcer. Thus, these authors demonstrated that "praise" reinforcers (e.g., "good") were more effective than "correct" reinforcers (e.g., "right") among lower-class children. These authors further suggest that lower-class children are less influenced by abstract, symbolic rewards than are middle-class children. We conclude from this and other supporting work (Terrell, Durkin, & Wiesley, 1959) that the therapist should become associated with the dispensing of concrete, primary rewards if he is to acquire characteristics of an effective social reinforcer for many resistant patients.

A powerful primary reward is food, and Janis, Kaye, and Kirschner (1965) confirmed an earlier finding by Razran (1940) that acceptance of persuasive messages increases when the messages are presented as the subject is being fed. This suggestion has received support from experimenters who have used feeding techniques with psychotic patients. Peters and Jenkins (1954) administered subshock injections of insulin to schizophrenic patients to stimulate a hunger drive. They then encouraged the patients to solve a series of graded problem-solving tasks using fudge as a reward. Tasks of gradually increasing difficulty were administered in which the experimenter personally mediated the primary rewards. After several weeks, the insulin injections were discontinued and social rewards, which by this time had become more effective, were used in solving interpersonal problems that the patients were likely to encounter in their daily activities both inside and outside the hospital. Others have demonstrated that the behavior of psychotics can be shaped by the use of primary rewards such as food (Ferster & DeMyer, 1962; Sherman, 1965), but the importance of the Peters and Jenkins study is that it demonstrates that dispensing primary rewards can increase the social reward value of the therapist and approval from him can then influence subsequent behavior.

Dispensing food to patients is not the only activity that a therapist can use to increase his impact as a social reinforcer. Any task whose successful completion depends on cooperative effort by patient and therapist will enhance the image of the therapist, provided the task goal is initially highly valued by the patient and the cooperative effort leads to success (Berkowitz, 1957; Kidd & Campbell, 1955). Thus, the reinforcing properties of the therapist can be increased by activities ranging from successful participation in a basketball game, to helping the patient obtain a valued job, or helping prepare a progress report for a parole board.

It is important for the reader to recognize that we are not advocating that the therapist be unconditionally accepting. Our hypothesis suggests that the patient be trained to view the therapist as a positive *but discriminating* reinforcer, a goal not synonymous with a totally accepting attitude. To begin with, unconditional acceptance is virtually impossible to achieve even by its advocates, as has been demonstrated by Truax (1965). Mild disapproval, silence and nonresponsiveness, and avoidance of specific topics are used by almost every therapist to channel the patient's behavior (Bandura & Walters, 1963). This is particularly important in the treatment of antisocial patients, for in these cases there exists the very real danger that unconditional permissiveness would unleash a flood of uncontrolled aggression. Berkowitz (1962) has suggested that the free expression of hostility might weaken frustration-induced aggression but not hostility habits. Thus while complete permissiveness might be of value in the treatment of overinhibited, frustrated patients, this procedure would not be appropriate for those whose life-style has made aggression a prepotent response.

We note further that *unconditional* acceptance and approval have not been found to enhance learning (Kelley & Ring, 1961) or provide a free atmosphere for the open discussion of problems in all instances (Heller, Davis, & Saunders, 1964). In the Kelley and Ring study it was demonstrated that when a trainer is always "trusting," that is, when he assumes that the trainee has made a correct response unless presented with contrary evidence, the trainee is encouraged to conceal his behavior. In other words, if an individual can get approval without showing his responses to another, he will not be motivated to present his behavior for public inspection as long as the possibility exists that it may be incorrect. We can visualize some psychotherapy patients who might act in a similar manner with an indiscriminately permissive therapist in that they would have little motivation to say "bad" things about themselves if they could receive indiscriminate approval without having to do so. Some patients overcome this tendency because they are motivated for self-examination by the press of their symptoms, but for the patient who enters therapy reluctantly and is unmotivated for treatment, indiscriminate approval provides little motivation to learn new, possibly painful responses.

In an experimental interview, Heller, Davis, and Saunders (1964) found that interviewer friendliness, when presented indiscriminately, regardless of the content of the interviewee's remarks, did not encourage self-disclosure as measured by the number of problems subjects were willing to attribute to themselves. The one exception to this finding was that subjects who readily admitted problems on personality inventories did speak about personal problems in the interview when the interviewer was passively friendly. Again we see that while indiscriminate friendliness might have some value in psychotherapy with "good" patients who are ready and willing to explore personal problems, we have found no evidence to recommend its use with resistant and reluctant patients.

We can summarize this section by reviewing our suggestions that the therapist can increase his influence with resistant patients by procedures that encourage the patient to see him as a positive communicator. This can be accomplished by training procedures which associate the therapist with powerful primary reinforcers or which provide the patient with a highly valued success experience contingent on intervention by the therapist. The indiscriminate permissiveness often associated with the psychotherapy of the inhibited neurotic has no place in the treatment of most resistant patients, as it provides an invitation to aggression by the habitually hostile and a poor basis for learning by the unmotivated and the chronically asocial.

We are now ready to propose a second way in which the personal qualities of the therapist can be utilized to maximize behavior change in psychotherapy.

HYPOTHESIS 4.5: **Resistance in psychotherapy can be reduced by maximizing the opportunities for imitation learning by the patient.**

Many patients do not possess within their response repertoires the behaviors necessary for successful psychotherapy or for productive real-life behavior; limited experience, not an unwillingness to carry through therapeutic suggestions, makes them appear resistant. These patients are frustrating to work with and are often judged inaccessible when in fact, what they need is the opportunity to learn prosocial behavior. Some therapists do not believe it is their function to correct deficiencies in background and training and that "psychotherapy cannot enable anyone to 'begin over'—it can only help the patient to make the best of what is at hand" (Dollard & Miller, 1950, p. 345). We cannot accept this view and agree with Bandura that the therapist should not only be a source of reinforcements (as is suggested in hypothesis 4.4) but should also be "a source of behavioral repertoires" (Bandura, 1965, p. 339). Therefore we suggest that one way of maximizing behavior change for patients with impoverished behavioral repertoires is for the therapist to encourage imitation learning.

The efficacy of imitation learning as a method of inducing behavior change has been well illustrated by Bandura and his associates; their large program of research has been summarized on several occasions (Bandura, 1961; 1962; 1965; Bandura & Walters, 1963) and has demonstrated many important effects. Models can help the observer acquire new responses that did not previously exist in his behavioral repertoire. Exposure to models can facilitate the emergence of previously learned responses. Finally, exposure to models may strengthen or weaken inhibitory responses in the observer as a function of rewarding or punishing response consequences to the model. Thus imitation learning can help establish the timing of responses and provide a means of learning inhibitory controls. All of these effects are important for the psychotherapy patient. He must learn new responses, recover, and be ready to reinstitute previously learned responses, as well as learn proper response control so that he is responding appropriately to the environment.

Much of the work of Bandura and his associates has been done with nursery school children among whom overt imitative behaviors are prepotent. Therefore, in suggesting imitation learning as a therapeutic strategy one must seriously question whether resistant adults would be motivated to imitate a therapeutic model. As Bandura has pointed out, merely providing a model for imitation is not sufficient.

"Even though the therapist exhibits the kinds of behaviors that he wants the patient to learn, this is likely to have little influence on him if he rejects the therapist as a model" (Bandura, 1961, pp. 151-152). Preliminary work may be necessary to establish the therapist as a positive reinforcer before learning through imitation can be successful. However, there are several reasons why imitation learning is particularly suited to overcome resistances in therapy. Modeling effects do not depend on verbal mediation and so are suited to nonverbal and nonintrospective patients; modeling procedures need not require immediate compliance and are therefore ideal for highly defensive patients who would resist more direct attempts at conversion; and once the therapist's behavior has acquired rewarding properties, imitation learning can be a powerful tool in establishing prosocial responses.

Although there have been reports of patients being treated by modeling procedures, these have usually involved young children (e.g., Chittenden, 1942; Jack, 1934; Page, 1936). One significant exception is an unpublished report by Staples, Wilson, and Walters (reported in Bandura & Walters, 1963). In this study, regressed schizophrenics whose verbal behavior was minimal were shown slides with instructions to talk about what they saw. Some patients were exposed to a talkative model who freely described and commented on the slides between the exposures of the first and second series. These patients showed a marked increase in verbal responsiveness from the first to the second trial when compared with patients who listened to music between the two slide presentations. Preliminary results also suggested that exposure to a model was more effective in increasing verbal productivity than was the dispensing of cigarettes as rewards for speaking.

What characteristics should a therapist have if he is to serve as a successful model? Research has demonstrated that models having high prestige are more likely to serve as sources of imitative behavior than those having low prestige (Asch, 1948; Lefkowitz, Blake, & Mouton, 1955); powerful and rewarding models are imitated more than those who are recipients of rewards (Bandura, Ross, & Ross, 1963); and models who exhibit a warm, nurturant personality are more influential than those who behave in a distant, nonrewarding fashion (Bandura & Huston, 1961). Thus, we might predict that therapists should be seen as powerful, rewarding, nurturant, and successful. However, there has been some work to indicate that subjects who believe themselves to be similar to models in some attributes are more likely to match other classes of model responses than are subjects who believe themselves to be unlike the models (Burnstein, Stotland & Zander, 1961; Stotland & Patchen, 1961). This finding suggests that while therapists should be positive figures, the discrepancy between patient and therapist should not be too large. There should be some common bond on which iden-tification can be built. For example, while subjects who are high in self-esteem identify more readily with successful models, low self-esteem subjects identify with poor models and with the negative attributes of these models (Dabbs, 1964; Stotland & Cottrell, 1962; Stotland & Dunn, 1962; Stotland & Hillmer, 1962). A matching of patient and therapist seems to be in order except that if they are too similar, there would be few new responses to imitate. Confirmation of this point is offered by Carson and Heine (1962) who found that extreme similarity and extreme dissimilarity between patient and therapist, as measured by a similarity score derived from the MMPI, were associated with poorer treatment outcome. These authors note that while excessive dissimilar-ity might make it difficult for the therapist to understand the patient, excessive similarity might also make the therapist ineffective by virtue of his overidentification with the patient and his problems. We expect quite naturally that patients and therapists would be different in many ways, but if modeling effects are to be enhanced, some similarity must exist for identification to occur.

We can conceive of modeling procedures instituted in the thera-pist's office, in the patient's natural environment, or even in the therapist's own home, and shall consider each possibility in turn. Dur-ing the course of traditional psychotherapy, the patient is exposed to many incidental cues involving the therapist's values, attitudes, and behavior. For example, Rosenthal (1955) reports that in spite of the precautions taken by therapists to avoid imposing their own values on their patients, patients who were judged as showing the greatest im-provement were those whose moral values became more like the values held by their therapist; patients who were less improved became less like the therapist in values. We are suggesting that the therapist can change what is now an incidental and haphazard learning situation by more active behaviors which would aid modeling by revealing more about the therapist's beliefs and attitudes. Lennard and Bernstein (1960) report that among four psychotherapists studied intensively over a period of almost one year, those who were active did a better job of teaching their patients what to expect in therapy. They spent more time discussing the patient's role during the initial sessions and as a group, their interviews showed less "system strain" as measured by discontinuance of treatment, broken appointments, and patient complaints. The work of Heller, Davis, and Saunders (1964) as well as the program of research of Matarazzo and his collaborators (reviewed by Matarazzo, Wiens, & Saslow, 1965) have also demonstrated that active interviewers increase the verbal productivity of their interviewees. Our first suggestion then is that imitation learning in psychotherapy can be enhanced by active therapist behaviors and that there exists a matching phenomenon in interviews such that as one participant becomes more verbose and open, the other participant is encouraged to do likewise.

Even with more active attempts by the therapist to present himself as a model for the patient, an interview setting provides only a minimal number of therapist behaviors that can be modeled. The patient can learn something of the therapist's values and style of thinking, but an interview is not the best place for modeling real-life overt behaviors. For this reason we would encourage therapists interested in maximizing imitation learning to enter the patient's natural habitat and allow the patient to reciprocate in kind. We recognize some of the reasons therapists have been reluctant to do this in the past. Although the very early analysts saw patients in their own homes, increased professionalization among therapists and the desire to keep the patient's transference reactions uncontaminated combined to produce an excessively asceptic treatment. Some current therapists are trying to overcome this (for example, Gendlin, 1961; Rogers, 1961; 1962; Truax, 1965). Quite naturally, we recognize the dangers inherent in relying on modeling procedures exclusively. The patient should not become so involved in observing the therapist he has little time to live his own life. Furthermore caution must be exercised that the discrepancy between the behavior of the model and that of the observer is not too great, particularly for the resistant patient. Research on attitude change as a function of the amount of change advocated has demonstrated that when subjects are presented with a communication from a highly credible source, greater opinion change occurs when the opinion is presented as more discrepant from their own. However, for less credible sources, as the discrepancy between the communicator and the communicant increases, opinion change by the communicant decreases (Aronson, Turner, & Carlsmith, 1963; Bergin, 1962; Hovland, 1959). Thus, as long as the therapist remains a negative communicator a large discrepancy between his style of life and that of the resistant patient may seem so insurmountable to the patient that he may reject the therapist as a model. For this reason, a procedure such as exposing the patient to the therapist's home life may have to wait for a later stage in therapy for some patients.

Modeling procedures are common in some corrective institutions where it is hoped that resistant patients will be motivated to imitate prosocial behavior by observing other patients receive rewards and privileges for good conduct; sometimes a therapeutic staff member who lives with the inmates can also be utilized as a model. But why should the opportunity for obtaining rewards by imitating prosocial behavior exist only within an institution, with the patient left completely to his own resources in an inhospitable environment both preceding and following incarceration?

We conclude this section of the chapter by noting again that there is little systematic experimental work studying the effects of imitation learning in psychotherapy. Although the results of nonpsychotherapy studies seem quite promising, much is still unknown and open to speculation, for example, little is known concerning which behaviors are least appropriate for imitation learning and which receive little attention from adolescent or adult observers. We suggest modeling procedures as an area for future clinical research because we can think of few better ways of maximizing the personal impact of the therapist.

SUMMARY

In this chapter we have tried to indicate some of the varied sources responsible for resistance to behavior change in psychotherapy. We have taken the position that much resistant behavior occurs because current treatment practices have not been successfully adapted to the varied forms that pathological behavior takes. Many current psychotherapy systems require patient behaviors that are unavailable to many persons in need of help. Our suggestions in this chapter have been oriented toward procedures that would overcome these deficiencies by focusing on asocial and antisocial patients, highly defensive patients, and those with impoverished response repertoires. Unlike traditional analytic interpretations of resistance, we have placed the primary responsibility for overcoming these handicaps not with the patient, but with the therapist. The latter is called on to develop new forms of treatment with less exclusive entrance requirements. This chapter can be seen as a small beginning in this direction.

We know of no better way of closing this chapter than to reproduce a description of two cases reported by Hollingshead and Redlich (1958), for they will illustrate what we feel are some of the deficiencies in current treatment practices, particularly because it is our firm conviction that psychotherapists can do more for those who have up until now been excluded from treatment.

The case histories of two compulsively promiscuous adolescent females are drawn on to illustrate the differential impact of class status on the way in which lay persons and psychiatrists perceive and appraise similar behavior. Both girls came to the attention of the police at about the same time but under very different circumstances. One came from a core group class I family, the other from a class V family broken by the desertion of the father. The class I girl, after one of her frequent drinking and sexual escapades on a weekend away from an exclusive boarding school, became involved in an automobile accident while drunk. Her family immediately arranged for bail through the influence of a member of an outstanding law firm, a powerful friend telephoned a newspaper contact, and the report of the accident was not published; within twenty-four hours the girl was returned to school. In a few weeks the school authorities realized that the girl was pregnant and notified her parents. A psychiatrist was called in for consultation by the parents with the expectation, expressed frankly, that he was to recommend a therapeutic interruption of the pregnancy. He did not see fit to do this, and instead recommended hospitalization in a psychiatric institution to initiate psychotherapy. The parents, although disappointed that the girl would not have a "therapeutic" abortion, finally consented to hospitalization. In due course the girl delivered a healthy baby who was placed for adoption. Throughout her stay in the hospital she received intensive psychotherapy and after being discharged continued in treatment with a highly regarded psychoanalyst.

The class V girl was arrested by the police after she was observed having intercourse with four or five sailors from a nearby naval base. At the end of a brief and perfunctory trial the girl was sentenced to a reform school. After two years there she was paroled as an unpaid domestic. While on parole she became involved in promiscuous activity, was caught by the police, and was sent to the state reformatory for women. She accepted her sentence as deserved "punishment" but created enough disturbance in the reformatory to attract the attention of a guidance officer who recommended that a psychiatrist be consulted. The psychiatrist who saw her was impressed by her crudeness and inability to communicate with him on most subjects and alienated by the fact that she thought masturbation was "bad," whereas intercourse with many men whom she hardly knew was "OK." The psychiatrist's recommendation was to return the girl to her regular routine because she was not "able to profit from psychotherapy" (Hollingshead & Redlich, 1958, pp. 175-176).

REFERENCES

Ackerman, N. W. *The psychodynamics of family life: Diagnosis and treatment of family relationships.* New York: Basic Books, 1958.

Aronson, E., & Golden, B. W. The effect of relevant and irrelevant aspects of communicator credibility on opinion change. *J. Pers.,* 1962, **30,** 135–146.

Aronson, E., Turner, J. A., & Carlsmith, J. M. Communicator credibility and communication discrepancy as determinants of opinion change. *J. abnorm. soc. Psychol.,* 1963, **67,** 31–36.

Asch, S. E. The doctrine of suggestion, prestige and imitation in social psychology. *Psychol. Rev.,* 1948, **55,** 250–276.

Bandura, A. Psychotherapy as a learning process. *Psychol. Bull.,* 1961, **58,** 143–159.

Bandura, A. Social learning through imitation. In M. R. Jones (Ed.), *Nebraska symposium on motivation: 1962.* Lincoln: Univer. of Nebraska Press, 1962. Pp. 211–215.

Bandura, A. Behavioral modifications through modeling procedures. In L. Krasner & L. P. Ullman (Eds.), *Research in behavior modification.* New York: Holt, Rinehart & Winston, 1965. Pp. 310–340.

Bandura, A., & Huston, A. C. Identification as a process of incidental learning. *J. abnorm. soc. Pschol.,* 1961, **63,** 311–318.

Bandura, A., Lipsher, D. H., & Miller, P. E. Psychotherapists' approach-avoidance reactions to patients' expressions of hostility. *J. consult. Psychol.,* 1960, **24,** 1–8.

Bandura, A., Ross, D., & Ross, S. A. A comparative test of the status envy, social power, and secondary reinforcement theories of identificatory learning. *J. abnorm. soc. Psychol.,* 1963, **67,** 527–534.

Bandura, A., & Walters, R. H. *Social learning and personality development.* New York: Holt, Rinehart & Winston, 1963.

Bergin, A. The effect of dissonant persuasive communications upon changes in a self-referring attitude. *J. Pers.,* 1962, **30,** 423–438.

Berkowitz, L. Effects of perceived dependency relationships upon conformity to group expectations. *J. abnorm. soc. Psychol.,* 1957, **55,** 350–354.

Berkowitz, L. *Agression: a social psychological analysis.* New York: McGraw-Hill, 1962.

Berkowitz, L., & Cottingham, D. R. The interest value and relevance of fear-arousing communications. *J. abnorm. soc. Psychol.,* 1960, **60,** 37–43.

Betz, B. J. Experiences in research in psychotherapy with schizophrenic patients. In H. H. Strupp & L. Luborsky (Eds.), *Research in psychotherapy.* Washington: Amer. Psychol. Assoc., 1962. Pp. 41–60.

Biderman, A. D., & Zimmer, H. *The manipulation of human behavior.* New York: Wiley, 1961.

Blake, R. R., & Mouton, J. S. Conformity, resistance and conversion. In I. A. Berg & B. M. Bass (Eds.), *Conformity and deviation.* New York: Harper, 1961. Pp. 1–37.

Blomgren, G. W., Jr., & Scheuneman, T. W. Psychological resistance to seat belts. Research project report RR-115, The Traffic Institute, Northwestern University, 1961.

Bordin, E. S. Ambiguity as a therapeutic variable. *J. consult. Psychol.,* 1955, **19**, 9–15.

Brehem, J. W., & Cohen, A. R. *Explorations in cognitive dissonance.* New York: Wiley, 1962.

Burnstein, E., Stotland, E., & Zander, A. Similarity to a model and self-evaluation. *J. abnorm. soc. Psychol.,* 1961, **62**, 257–264.

Cairns, R. B. The influence of dependency inhibition on the effectiveness of social reinforcement. *J. Pers.,* 1961, **29**, 466–488.

Cairns, R. B. Antecedents of social reinforcer effectiveness. USPHS Project Report No. M-4373(a), 1962.

Cairns, R. B., & Lewis, M. Dependency and the reinforcement value of a verbal stimulus. *J. consult. Psychol.,* 1962, **26**, 1–8.

Carson, R. C., Harden, J. A., & Shows, W. D. A-B distinction and behavior in quasi-therapeutic situations. *J. consult. Psychol.,* 1964, **28**, 426–433.

Carson, R. C., & Heine, R. W. Similarity and success in therapeutic dyads. *J. consult. Psychol.,* 1962, **26**, 38–43.

Chittenden, G. E. An experimental study in measuring and modifying assertive behavior in young children. *Monogr. soc. Res. child Develpm.,* 1942, **7**, No. 1 (Serial No. 31).

Cohen, A. R. *Attitude change and social influence.* New York: Basic Books, 1964.

Cumming, J., & Cumming, E. *Ego and milieu.* New York: Atherton Press, 1963.

Cutler, R. Countertransference effects in psychotherapy. *J. consult. Psychol.,* 1958, **22**, 349–356.

Dabbs, J. M., Jr. Self-esteem, communicator characteristics, and attitude change. *J. abnorm. soc. Psychol.,* 1964, **69**, 173–181.

Dean, S. I. Treatment of the reluctant client. *Amer. Psychologist,* 1958, **13**, 627–630.

Dibner, A. S. Ambiguity and anxiety. *J. abnorm. soc. Psychol.,* 1958, **56**, 165–174.

Dittes, J. E., & Zemach, M. The effect of cognitive ambiguity on anxiety and affiliative preference. Presented at Amer. Psychol. Assoc., Los Angeles, 1964.

Dollard, J., & Miller, N. E. *Personality and psychotherapy.* New York: McGraw-Hill, 1950.

Fairweather, G. W. *Social psychology in treating mental illness: an experimental approach.* New York: Wiley, 1964.

Fenichel, O. *The psychoanalytic theory of neurosis.* New York: W. W. Norton & Co., 1945.

Ferster, C. B., & DeMyer, M. K. A method for the experimental analysis of the behavior of autistic children. *Amer. J. Orthopsychiat.,* 1962, **32**, 89–98.

Festinger, L. *A theory of cognitive dissonance.* Stanford: Stanford Univer. Press, 1957.

Ford, D. H., & Urban, H. B. *Systems of psychotherapy.* New York: Wiley, 1963.

Frank, J. D. Experimental studies of personal pressure and resistance: I. Experimental production of resistance. *J. gen. Psychol.,* 1944, **30**, 23–41.

Frank, J. D. The role of influence in psychotherapy. In M. I. Stein (Ed.), *Contemporary psychotherapies.* New York: The Free Press of Glencoe, 1961. Pp. 17–41.

Freud, S. The psychotherapy of hysteria. In J. Breuer & S. Freud, *Studies in hysteria.* Boston: Beacon Press, 1937. Pp. 190–232.

Freud, S. *A general introduction to psychoanalysis.* New York: Doubleday, 1953.

Gendlin, E. T. Initiating psychotherapy with "unmotivated" patients. *Psychiat. Quart.,* 1961, **35**, 1–6.

Goldstein, M. J. The relationship between coping and avoiding behavior and response to fear-arousing propaganda. *J. abnorm. soc. Psychol.,* 1959, **58**, 247–252.

Gordon, J. E. Project CAUSE, the Federal Anti-Poverty Program, and some implications of subprofessional training. *Amer. Psychologist,* 1965, **20**, 334–343.

Gurin, G., Veroff, J., & Feld, S. *Americans view their mental health.* New York: Basic Books, 1960.

Haley, J. *Strategies of psychotherapy.* New York: Grune & Stratton, 1963.

Hartley, E. L., & Hartley, R. E. *Fundamentals of social psychology.* New York: Alfred A. Knopf, 1952.

Heine, R. W., & Trosman, H. Initial expectations of the doctor-patient interaction as a factor in continuance in psychotherapy. *Psychiatry,* 1960, **23**, 275–278.

Heller, K. Experimental analogues of psychotherapy: the clinical relevance of laboratory findings of social influence. *J. nerv. ment. Dis.,* 1963, **137**, 420–426.

Heller, K. A broader perspective for interview therapy. Presented at Midwestern Psychol. Assoc., Chicago, 1965.

Heller, K., Davis, J. D., & Saunders, F. Clinical implications of laboratory studies of interpersonal style. Presented at Midwestern Psychol. Assoc., St. Louis, 1964.

Hollingshead, A. B., & Redlich, F. C. *Social class and mental illness.* New York: Wiley, 1958.

Holt, R. R., & Luborsky, L. *Personality patterns of psychiatrists.* New York: Basic Books, 1958.

Hovland, C. I. (Ed.). *The order of presentation in persuation.* New Haven: Yale Univer. Press, 1957.

Hovland, C. I. Reconciling conflicting results derived from experimental and survey studies of attitude change. *Amer. Psychologist,* 1959, 14, 8–17.

Hovland, C. I., & Janis, I. L. (Eds.). *Personality and persuasibility.* New Haven: Yale Univer. Press, 1959.

Hovland, C. I., Janis, I. L., & Kelley, H. H. *Communication and persuasion: psychological studies of opinion change.* New Haven: Yale Univer. Press, 1953.

Hovland, C. I., Lumsdaine, A. A. & Sheffield, F. D. *Experiments on mass communication.* Princeton: Princeton Univer. Press, 1949.

Hovland, C. I., & Mandell, W. An experimental comparison of conclusion-drawing by the communicator and by the audience. *J. abnorm. soc. Psychol.,* 1952, 47, 581–588.

Hovland, C. I., & Weiss, W. The influence of source credibility on communication effectiveness. *Publ. Opin. Quart.,* 1951, 15, 635–650.

Isaacs, W., Thomas, J., & Goldiamond, I. Application of operant conditioning to reinstate verbal behavior in psychotics. *J. speech. hear. Disord.,* 1960, 25, 8–12.

Jack, L. M. An experimental study of ascendant behavior in preschool children. *Univer. Ia. Stud. Child Welf.,* 1934, 9, 3–65.

Jackson, D. D. Family interaction, family homeostasis and some implications for conjoint-family psychotherapy. In J. H. Masserman (Ed.), *Science and psychoanalysis.* Vol. 2. *Individual and family dynamics.* New York: Grune & Stratton, 1959. Pp. 122–141.

Janis, I. L., & Feshbach, S. Effects of fear-arousing communications. *J. abnorm. soc. Psychol.,* 1953, 48, 78–92.

Janis, I. L., & Feshbach, S. Personality differences associated with responsiveness to fear-arousing communications. *J. Pers.,* 1954, 23, 154–166.

Janis, I. L., Kaye, D., & Kirschner, P. Facilitating effects of "eating-while-reading" on responsiveness to persuasive communications. *J. pers. soc. Psychol.,* 1965, 1, 181–186.

Janis, I. L., & Milholland, H. C., Jr. The influence of threat appeals on selective learning of the content of a persuasive communication. *J. Psychol.,* 1954, 37, 75–80.

Janis, I. L., & Terwilliger, R. F. An experimental study of psychological resistances to fear-arousing communications. *J. abnorm. soc. Psychol.,* 1962, 65, 403–410.

Kanfer, F. H. Implications of conditioning techniques for interview therapy. Presented at Midwestern Psychol. Assoc., Chicago, 1965.

Kanfer, F: H., & Marston, A. R. Verbal conditioning, ambiguity and psychotherapy. *Psychol. Rep.,* 1961, 9, 461–475.

Kanfer, F. H., & Marston, A. R. The effect of task-relevant information on verbal conditioning. *J. Psychol.*, 1962, **53**, 29–36.

Kanfer, F. H., & Marston, A. R. Characteristics of interactional behavior in a psychotherapy analogue. *J. consult. Psychol.*, 1964, **28**, 456–467.

Kelley, H. H., & Ring, K. Some effects of "suspicious" versus "trusting" training schedules. *J. abnorm. soc. Psychol.*, 1961, **63**, 294–301.

Kelly, G. A. *The psychology of personal constructs.* Vol. 1. New York: W. W. Norton & Co., 1955.

Kelman, H. C. The induction of action and attitude change. Proceedings of the XIV International Congress of Applied Psychology, Copenhagen, 1961, 81–110.

Kelman, H. C., & Eagly, A. H. Attitude toward the communicator, perception of communication content, and attitude change. *J. pers. soc. Psychol.*, 1965, **1**, 63–78.

Kelman, H. C., & Hovland, C. I. "Reinstatement" of the communicator in delayed measurement of opinion change. *J. abnorm. soc. Psychol.*, 1953, **48**, 327–335.

Kidd, J. S., & Campbell, D. T. Conformity to groups as a function of group success. *J. abnorm. soc. Psychol.*, 1955, **51**, 390–393.

King, G. F., Armitage, S. G., & Tilton, J. R. A therapeutic approach to schizophrenics of extreme pathology: an operant-interpersonal method. *J. abnorm. soc. Psychol.*, 1960, **61**, 276–286.

Krasner, L. The therapist as a social reinforcer: man or machine. Presented at Amer. Psychol. Assoc., Philadelphia, 1963.

Krech, D., Crutchfield, R. S., & Ballachey, E. L. *Individual in society.* New York: McGraw-Hill, 1962.

Lang, P. J. Psychotherapy, pseudotherapy and behavior therapy. Presented at Midwestern Psychol. Assoc., Chicago, 1965.

Lefkowitz, M., Blake, R. R., & Mouton, J. S. Status factors in pedestrian violation of traffic signals. *J. abnorm. soc. Psychol.*, 1955, **51**, 704–706.

Lennard, H., & Bernstein, A. *The anatomy of psychotherapy.* New York: Columbia Univer. Press, 1960.

Leventhal, H., Singer, R., & Jones, S. Effects of fear and specificity of recommendations upon attitudes and behavior. *J. pers. soc. Psychol.*, 1965, **2**, 20–29.

Levinson, D. J. The psychotherapist's contribution to the patient's treatment career. In H. H. Strupp & L. Luborsky (Eds.), *Research in psychotherapy.* Washington: Amer. Psychol. Assoc., 1962. Pp. 13–24.

Levy, L. H. *Psychological interpretation.* New York: Holt, Rinehart & Winston, 1963.

Lumsdaine, A. A., & Janis, I. L. Resistance to "counterpropaganda" produced by one-sided and two-sided "propaganda" presentations. *Publ. Opin. Quart.*, 1953, **17**, 311–318.

Lykken, D. T.   A study of anxiety in the sociopathic personality. *J. abnorm. soc. Psychol.,* 1957, **55**, 6-10.

Manis, M.   The interpretation of opinion statements as a function of message ambiguity and recipient attitude. *J. abnorm. soc. Psychol.,* 1961, **63**, 76–81.

Manis, M.   Immunization, delay and the interpretation of persuasive messages. *J. pers. soc. Psychol.,* 1965, **1**, 541–550.

Manis, M., & Blake, J. B.   Interpretation of persuasive messages as a function of prior immunization. *J. abnorm. soc. Psychol.,* 1963, **66**, 225–230.

Matarazzo, J. D., Wiens, A. N., & Saslow, G.   Studies in interview speech behavior. In L. Krasner & L. P. Ullmann (Eds.), *Research in behavior modification.* New York: Holt, Rinehart & Winston, 1965. Pp. 179–210.

McCoy, N., & Zigler, E.   Social reinforcer effectiveness as a function of the relationship between child and adult. *J. pers. soc. Psychol.,* 1965, **1**, 604–612.

McGuire, W. J.   The effectiveness of supportive and refutational defenses in immunizing and restoring beliefs against persuasion. *Sociometry,* 1961a, **24**, 184–197.

McGuire, W. J.   Resistance to persuasion conferred by active and passive prior refutation of the same and alternative counterarguments. *J. abnorm. soc. Psychol.,* 1961b, **63**, 326–332.

McGuire, W. J.   Persistence of the resistance to persuasion induced by various types of prior belief defenses. *J. abnorm. soc. Psychol.,* 1962, **64**, 241–248.

McGuire, W. J.   Inducing resistance to persuasion. In L. Berkowitz (Ed.), *Advances in experimental social psychology.* Vol. 1. New York: Academic Press, 1964. Pp. 191–229.

McGuire, W. J., & Papageorgis, D.   The relative efficacy of various types of prior belief-defense in producing immunity against persuasion. *J. abnorm. soc. Psychol.,* 1961, **62**, 327–337.

McGuire, W. J., & Papageorgis, D.   Effectiveness of forewarning in developing resistance to persuasion. *Publ. Opin. Quart.,* 1962, **26**, 24–34.

McNair, D. M., Callahan, D. M., & Lorr, M.   Therapist "type" and patient response to psychotherapy. *J. consult. Psychol.,* 1962, **26**, 425–429.

Murstein, B. I.   *Theory and research in projective techniques.* New York: Wiley, 1963.

Nunnally, J. C., & Bobren, A. M.   Variables governing the willingness to receive communications on mental health. *J. Pers.,* 1959, **27**, 38–46.

Page, M. L.   The modification of ascendant behavior in preschool children. *Univer. Ia. Stud. Child Welf.,* 1936, **9**, 3–65.

Papageorgis, D., & McGuire, W. J.   The generality of immunity to persuasion produced by pre-exposure to weakened counterarguments. *J. abnorm. soc. Psychol.,* 1961, **62**, 475–481.

Paul, G. L.   Effects of insight, desensitization, and attention-placebo treatment of anxiety: an approach to outcome research in psychotherapy. Unpublished doctoral dissertation, University of Illinois, 1964.

Pepinsky, P. N.   Social exceptions that prove the rule. In I. A. Berg, & B. M. Bass (Eds.), *Conformity and deviation*. New York: Harper, 1961. Pp. 380–411.

Peters, H. N., & Jenkins, R. L.   Improvement of chronic schizophrenic patients with guided problem-solving motivated by hunger. *Psychiat. Quart. Suppl.*, 1954, **28**, 84–101.

Rabbie, J. M.   Differential preference for companionship under threat. *J. abnorm. soc. Psychol.*, 1963, **67**, 643–648.

Razran, G. H.   Conditioned response changes in rating and appraising sociopolitical slogans. *Psychol. Bull.*, 1940, **37**, 481.

Redl, F., & Wineman, D.   *The aggressive child*. Glencoe: The Free Press, 1957.

Rogers, C. R.   *Client-centered therapy*. Boston: Houghton Mifflin, 1951.

Rogers, C. R.   *On becoming a person*. Boston: Houghton Mifflin, 1961.

Rogers, C. R.   Some learnings from a study of psychotherapy with schizophrenics. Paper presented at a conference on "Psychotherapy of schizophrenia: adults and children," Temple Univer. Medical Center, Philadelphia, March 15, 1962.

Rokeach, M.   Authority, authoritarianism, and conformity. In I. A. Berg & B. M. Bass (Eds.), *Conformity and deviation*. New York: Harper, 1961. Pp. 230–257.

Rosenblatt, P. C.   Enhancement of persuasion by threat. Presented at Midwestern Psychol. Assoc., Chicago, 1965.

Rosenthal, D.   Changes in some moral values following psychotherapy. *J. consult. Psychol.*, 1955, **19**, 431–436.

Russell, P. D., & Snyder, W. U.   Counselor anxiety in relation to amount of clinical experience and quality of affect demonstrated by clients. *J. consult. Psychol.*, 1963, **27**, 358–363.

Schofield, W.   *Psychotherapy: the purchase of friendship*. Englewood Cliffs, N. J.: Prentice-Hall, 1964.

Schwitzgebel, R., & Kolb, D. A.   Inducing behavior change in adolescent delinquents. *Behav. Res. Ther.*, 1964, **1**, 297–304.

Schwitzgebel, R., & Schwitzgebel, R.   Reduction of adolescent crime by a research method. *J. soc. Ther.*, 1961, **7**, 212–215.

Sechrest, L. B., & Strowig, R. W.   Teaching machines and the individual learner. *Educ. Theory*, 1962, **12**, 157–169.

Sharaf, M. R., & Levinson, D. J.   Patterns of ideology and role-definition among psychiatric residents. In M. Greenblatt, D. J. Levinson, & R. H. Williams (Eds.), *The patient and the mental hospital*. Glencoe: Free Press, 1957. Pp. 263–285.

Sherman, J. A.   Use of reinforcement and imitation to reinstate verbal behavior in mute psychotics. *J. abnorm. Psychol.*, 1965, **70**, 155–164.

Slack, C. W.   Experimenter-subject psychotherapy: a new method of introducing intensive office treatment for unreachable cases. *Ment. Hyg.*, 1960, 44, 238–256.

Smith, E. E.   The effects of clear and unclear role expectations on group productivity and defensiveness. *J. abnorm. soc. Psychol.*, 1957, 55, 213–217.

Stanton, A. H., & Schwartz, M. S.   *The mental hospital.* New York: Basic Books, 1954.

Staples, F. R., Wilson, F. S., & Walters, R. H.   Increasing the verbal responsiveness of chronic schizophrenics. Unpublished research, Ontario Hospital, New Toronto, and University of Waterloo, 1963. (Cited in A. Bandura & R. H. Walters, *Social learning and personality development.* New York: Holt, Rinehart & Winston, 1963.)

Stollak, G. E., & Guerney, B., Jr.   Exploration of personal problems by juvenile delinquents under conditions of minimal reinforcement. *J. clin. Psychol.*, 1964, 20, 279–283.

Stotland, E., & Cottrell, N. B.   Similarity of performance as influenced by interaction, self-esteem and birth order. *J. abnorm. soc. Psychol.*, 1962, 64, 183–191.

Stotland, E., & Dunn, R. E.   Identification, "oppositeness," authoritarianism, self-esteem and birth order. *Psychol. Monogr.*, 1962, 76, No. 9, Whole No. 528, 1–21.

Stotland, E., & Hillmer, M. L.   Identification, authoritarian defensiveness, and self-esteem. *J. abnorm. soc. Psychol.*, 1962, 64, 334–342.

Stotland, E., & Patchen, M.   Identification and changes in prejudice and in authoritarianism. *J. abnorm. soc. Psychol.*, 1961, 62, 265–274.

Strupp, H. H.   *Psychotherapists in action.* New York: Grune & Stratton, 1960.

Sullivan, H. S.   *The interpersonal theory of psychiatry.* New York: W. W. Norton, 1953.

Sullivan, H. S.   *The psychiatric interview.* New York: W. W. Norton, 1954.

Terrell, G., Jr., Durkin, D., & Wiesley, M.   Social class and the nature of the incentive in discrimination learning. *J. abnorm. soc. Psychol.*, 1959, 59, 270–272.

Thistlethwaite, D. L., de Haan, H., & Kamenetsky, J.   The effects of "directive" and "nondirective" communication procedures on attitudes. *J. abnorm. soc. Psychol.*, 1955, 51, 107–113.

Thistlethwaite, D. L., & Kamenetsky, J.   Attitude change through refutation and elaboration of audience counterarguments. *J. abnorm. soc. Psychol.*, 1955, 51, 3–12.

Truax, C. B.   Behavior therapy and psychotherapy: toward a constructive encounter. Presented at Midwestern Psychol. Assoc., Chicago, 1965.

Ullmann, L. P., & Krasner, L. (Eds.), *Case studies in behavior modification.* New York: Holt, Rinehart & Winston, 1965.

Weiss, W., & Fine, B. J.   The effect of induced aggressiveness on opinion change. *J. abnorm. soc. Psychol.*, 1956, 52, 109–114.

Wolberg, L. R. *The technique of psychotherapy.* New York: Grune & Stratton, 1954.

Wolpe, J., Salter, A., & Reyna, L. J. *The conditioning therapies.* New York: Holt, Rinehart & Winston, 1964.

Zigler, E., & Kanzer, P. The effectiveness of two classes of verbal reinforcers on the performance of middle- and lower-class children. *J. Pers.,* 1962, **30**, 157-163.

5

TRANSFER OF THERAPEUTIC
LEARNING

The field of learning is one of the areas of greatest investment of
research money and energy in all of psychology, and the implications
of knowledge about learning for psychotherapy research are, or should
be, obvious. Yet it seems to us that a mine of ore which would assay
high is going largely unexploited. Research on verbal conditioning
(Krasner, 1962), on aversive conditioning (Kushner, 1965; McGuire &
Vallance, 1964; Meyer & Crisp, 1964; Miller et al., 1964; Sanderson et
al., 1964; Thorpe et al., 1964), on counterconditioning (Wolpe, 1958),
and on a wide variety of other procedures primarily based on conditioning research (Krasner & Ullman, 1965; Ullman & Krasner, 1965)
has pointed the way to the development of new methods in psychotherapy and new ways of looking at some of the older procedures; but
there are vast sections of the research literature on learning which are
being completely ignored. One searches in vain even in new treatises
on psychotherapy for integration of ideas stemming from discrimination learning, concept attainment, reinforcement schedules, and a host
of other topics of research interest in the field of learning. Whatever
consideration is given to learning is slight. Instead, the same tired and
threadbare "dynamics" are trotted out to do their service once more.
A recent book on psychotherapy which purports to be founded in psychological theory (Holland, 1965) and is considerably nearer the banks
of the mainstream of psychology than most books, indexes a total of
five pages of text dealing with learning, two pages with reinforcement
and motivation, three pages for generalization and none at all for
transfer; but there are thirteen pages indexed for transference alone.

We do not look with favor on any claim that most of the research on learning has nothing to do with psychotherapy. We believe that research on learning cannot be irrelevant to psychotherapy. The main difficulty to the present time has been the refusal, or at least the failure, to consider learning research from the standpoint of its import for psychotherapy. Whatever else it is, psychotherapy must be considered a learning enterprise. We need not specify too narrowly just what is to be learned in psychotherapy; it may be specific behaviors or a whole new outlook on life, but it cannot be denied that the intended outcome of psychotherapy is a change in an individual that can only be termed a manifestation of learning. It behooves us to think hard about the basic research on the learning process to discover what it implies for the field of psychotherapy. The point of view we are espousing is not original, nor is it new. Cameron and Magaret (1951) noted some time ago that, "The keystone of contemporary therapy is *learning in social interaction*" (p. 603). More recently Ford and Urban (1963) have attempted a systematic comparison of various approaches to therapy, and they not only maintain that therapy of necessity involves changes in behavior but assert that the study of therapy actually becomes a study of ways of changing behavior in specified directions.

Obviously, we cannot hope to cover the whole field of learning research. Entire books are written on learning, or even on narrow aspects of learning, and with justification, and research in the field proliferates at a high rate. We intend only to point to several hypotheses derived from learning research which we believe worthy of test in research more clearly oriented to psychotherapy and to stimulate further efforts in this direction.

TRANSFER OF TRAINING

One of the areas of great research activity which appears to have clear relevance for psychotherapy is transfer of training; that is, the effect of training in a particular task on acquisition and performance of subsequent tasks. Deese has said, "There is no more important topic in the whole of the psychology of learning than transfer of training" (1958, p. 213); yet in book after book and article after article on psychotherapy the topic is never mentioned. In many respects it is strange that so little systematic attention has been paid to transfer of training research as it might bear on psychotherapy. For one thing, transfer itself as a topic was developed out of very practical interests in possibilities for modifying behavior in education, motor learning, athletics, language skills, and the like, yet there has probably never been an attempt to make a theoretical construct of transfer. Second, the psychotherapy literature is replete with observations that clearly affirm the importance of transfer considerations. Many writers (e.g., Ford and Urban, 1963) have described the difficulties that arise in trying to ensure that what goes on in the interview will be carried over into extratherapy situations; and many others have described various problems in the psychotherapy situation that can clearly be viewed as constituting transfer of training problems. However, in spite of the recognition, both implicit and explicit, of the general relevance of the construct of transfer of training for psychotherapy, almost no attempt has been made to exploit the research to modify psychotherapy research in directions likely to produce favorable modifications in training. For example, in their review of systems of therapy Ford and Urban (1963) state that modification of behavior in nontherapy situations is the ultimate goal of all patients, but they find little evidence that originators of therapy systems have paid specific attention to transfer. Most simply seem to assume that habits acquired in therapy will be carried over into extratherapy situations. At best, there is the explicit recognition that what goes on outside therapy is really critical and that patients should be encouraged to try out new responses "in real life."

As a concept and a process, transfer of training is typically presented in association with proactive interference and facilitation and occasionally in association with discussions of generalization (Bugelski, 1956; Deese, 1958; Lawson, 1960). The justification for such a presentation lies in the near identity of the research designs necessary for a demonstration of any of the phenomena described. In its essentials the design is given as follows:

Experimental Group	Learn A	Learn B
Control Group	Rest	Learn B

With this design any discrepancy in the performance of the experimental and control groups on task B can presumably be attributed to the effects of having learned A. However, the distinction between generalization, transfer, and proaction seems to lie in the specific nature of the task at B. If the subject has learned task or response A, his first exposure to B will represent a test of generalization. If the experimental group makes a larger or more reliable response on the first trial, we are more likely to say that the response to A has generalized than that it has transferred or that proactive facilitation has occurred. Then if subjects are asked to *learn* to perform response B, any difference in *speed of acquisition* between the experimental and control groups is likely to be attributed to transfer of training. Finally, if having learned to perform *B*, subjects are asked after a period of time to perform *B* once more, any difference between experimental and control group subjects will be attributed to proactive facilitation or proactive interference (proactive effects refer specifically to *retention*). At least conceptually, the three effects are separable. Experimental subjects could learn a motor response and then be compared with controls on a different motor task. An initial difference in performance would be attributable to the (probably stimulus) generalization of the experimental group, and, depending on the appropriateness of the original response, the effects might be good or bad. However, an initial superiority of the experimental group would not ensure continued superiority, and by a criterion of speed of acquisition of the second response there might or might not be a difference between experimental and control subjects. Despite differences in initial level or in speed of acquisition, experimental and control subjects might differ in level of retention of the response. There have, in fact, been studies in verbal learning which show positive transfer but retroactive interference (Deese & Hardman, 1954).

For the purposes of this exposition we use the term "transfer" or "transfer of training" generically to denote all the various effects that the acquisition of one response may have on responses that must be acquired and/or emitted later. It seems probable to us that the effects we have described as transfer are of greater importance to the psychotherapy situation than either generalization or proaction as defined here. The "failure of discrimination" (Prokasy & Hall, 1963) which makes it probable that an individual will respond to some person outside the therapy situation in the same manner in which he has learned to respond to the therapist seems to us a weak and somewhat improbable way of accounting for the changes that may result from psychotherapy. Similarly, the specific problem of retention of responses acquired in therapy is not likely to be an issue of much importance, since the persistence of the responses depends on their subsequent reinforcement history. In particular, it seems questionable that responses learned in therapy would have any very powerful effects on retention of responses later acquired.

The typical analysis of the transfer of training problem has been in terms of a model that employs the ideas of stimuli and responses and the connections between them. Much of our empirical knowledge about transfer comes from studies of verbal learning analyzed almost exclusively in *S-R* units. We do no want to suggest that it is necessarily more than convenient to represent the transfer problem in such a manner; a representation featuring a more cognitive approach would be equally satisfactory. Still, we find it expedient to couch our discussion in the S-R terms which are familiar to psychologists and which articulate well with the majority of the research that has been done. We begin with the assumption that transfer of training is a phenomenon and that in theory it may take all values from completely $(+ 100\%)$ positive to completely $(- 100\%)$ negative. The evidence for the existence of transfer is extensive and need not be detailed here (Bugelski, 1956; Deese, 1958; Ellis, 1965; Lawson, 1960), but evidence for transfer effects has been about inversely proportional to the breadth or importance of the habit involved. Thus it has been easier to demonstrate effects for nonsense syllables than for vocabularies and for vocabularies than for critical thinking.

There have been two major conceptions of the way in which transfer may take place. One theory, attributable largely to E. L. Thorndike (Deese, 1958), is the theory of identical elements. On the basis of a variety of experiments Thorndike came to the conclusion that when there was a facilitative effect of one habit on another it was to the extent that and because they shared identical elements. The facilitating effects of the study of Latin on learning English, if they exist, occur only because Latin and English share certain elements. Thorndike's work and theory was directed mostly against the once popular theory of formal discipline which held that certain activities such as memorizing or reasoning were desirable because of the practice or exercise they afforded for various faculties of the mind. The theory of formal discipline was pretty much expunged from modern education by Thorndike and his followers, although the evidence against it was never much more weighty than the evidence in favor and it is in poor repute at present. One of our subsequent hypotheses, in fact, recommends "emotional sensitivity training," a procedure not far removed from the "exercising of a faculty" (see p. 297).

Still, if the idea of exercising faculties of the mind was weak, there was and is another theory about transfer of training that is not totally incompatible with some of the beliefs and practices of old-fashioned educators. Rather than supposing that transfer takes place on the basis of identical elements in two tasks, some writers and researchers have thought that transfer might occur in the learning of a general principle that could be applied in sundry situations. The first experiment testing such a notion was Judd's (1902) classic study on shooting darts at a target submerged in water. Judd found that boys who were instructed about the principle of refraction did better at the task than boys not so instructed. His findings have been replicated with air-rifle shooters by Hendrickson and Schroeder (1941). Transfer in such a situation was not a product of identical elements in two stimulus situations but was attributable to the acquisition of a principle presumably applicable in many situations. Other and broader experiments have been done. Woodrow (1927) was able to produce improved ability to memorize poetry, prose, and factual material by instructing subjects in specific techniques of memorization. Ulmer (1939) found that a special geometry curriculum designed to arouse critical thinking both connected and unconnected with geometry resulted in better performance on several later measures. We must conclude, then, that transfer can take place as a result of learning of a general principle. Current educational emphasis on the "New Math" is justified largely on the basis of the assumption of transfer of general principles.

The wonder is that the two conceptions of transfer have so often been viewed as incompatible. We can see neither the requirement nor the justification for a single theory of transfer effects. Research on verbal learning (Osgood, 1953; Underwood & Schulz, 1960) as well as in other areas certainly justifies the contention that transfer of training is proportional to identity of elements, but, just as certainly, other research, such as Judd's, points to the reality of transfer by way of general principles having no inherent similarity to the responses they facilitate (or could impede). Looking ahead to our discussion of psychotherapy, we would say that transfer from therapy to extratherapy situations may occur either by specific responses which would be emitted in the presence of stimuli similar to those of the therapy situation or by general principles applicable in various circumstances.

We should mention one additional variety of "transfer" that is utilized to a considerable extent by psychologically sophisticated psychotherapists (e.g., Dollard & Miller, 1950; Holland, 1965) and is unquestionably implicit in the views of many other writers. We are referring to "mediated generalization," by which is meant making diverse stimuli equivalent by attaching the same cue-producing response or label to them. For example, if a therapy patient can learn to recognize and label his feelings in certain situations as "hostile," then in any other situations in which the same label is employed the same responses should occur. A part of the task in therapy may be viewed as developing appropriate cue-producing responses. Obviously there may also be mediated discriminations; labels may be employed to enhance the distinctiveness of stimuli (e.g., when a patient learns to label certain of his fears as "unjustified" so that he distinguishes them from realistic fears). The relevance of the idea of mediated generalization and discrimination will be most apparent in our discussion of "advance organizers."

Analyses of the transfer situation are often couched in terms of similarity between stimulus and response members of the two tasks involved (see Ellis, 1965). In a very influential analysis of transfer of training and retroactive interference Osgood (1949) was able to plot transfer effects as a joint function of stimulus and response similarity. If we view the transfer situation in terms of the familiar S-R schema, we see that there are two distinct transfer problems. We assume that the initial learning consists of S_1—R_1. Subsequent learning would then be S_2—R_1 or S_1—R_2. For the first type of transfer the subject must learn to attach a familiar response to new but similar stimuli, or, to take an example from psychotherapy, he must learn to make the same response to people outside therapy that he learned to make to the therapist. In such a transfer situation it is pretty well agreed that transfer will be positive or that acquisition of the second habit will be facilitated (Bruce, 1933; Bugelski, 1956; Deese, 1958; Lawson, 1960; Osgood, 1949, 1953). Learning gets better when subjects give the same response repeatedly to different stimuli. A large part of the transfer effect just described may be attributable to the increase in availability of the relevant response, about which more will be said later. It may also be stated that if the responses are the same transfer will be positive if the two stimuli are similar (Bulgelski, 1956; Osgood, 1953).

In fact, the occurrence of transfer is probably not quite so simple as has just been implied. First, it is no simple matter to specify what constitutes a dimension of similarity for stimuli (Bugelski, 1956; Osgood, 1953). When nonsense syllables are used as stimuli and responses, similarity is defined in terms of identical elements, but for most other tasks it is difficult to decide in advance just what constitutes similarity. Razran (1939) studied generalization across dimensions of physical and meaningful similarity and found the gradient of meaning to be the strongest determinant of the response. However, other investigators have shown generalization along other dimensions than meaning (see Osgood, 1953), thus illustrating the problems of defining stimulus similarity. Presumably, the same considerations would apply to responses. In a verbal learning study Young and Underwood (1954) found that similarity of responses is not related to the occurrence of positive transfer unless there is high *intralist* similarity. Presumably, if within a series of responses those responses to be learned and transferred are diverse, then transfer from one list to another is not a function of the similarity of the response terms in the two lists. Nonetheless, following Osgood, it seems justifiable and necessary to conclude that *"the greater the similarity between practice and test stimuli, the greater the amount of positive transfer"* (Osgood, 1953, p. 525).

Transfer also seems to be a function of degree of original learning, with a high degree of original learning favoring positive transfer (Travers, 1963), although Bugelski (1956) notes that negative transfer may be greater when the original material is poorly learned. Evidence on both points is reviewed by Ausubel (1963). Thus to facilitate transfer initial learning should be thorough, even to the point of overlearning. Harlow (1959) has made the same point with respect to the establishing of learning sets, noting that early trials are critical; if learning is discontinued before the principle is well learned, little transfer will occur. We may take this to mean that learning should extend over more trials and more situations than are necessary merely to produce initial changes in behavior. If we wish to alter habitual responses to authority figures, many trials with many different authority stimuli may be required to ensure transfer beyond the original training situation.

Studies of generalization seem to have shown a rather different relationship between degree of original learning and probability of generalization. As training on the original stimulus proceeds, the generalization gradient is raised up to some medium point of training. If training on the original stimulus is carried to a very high level, the generalization of the response to other stimuli decreases in probability (Hovland, 1937). The complex nature of the relationship between level of original learning and generalization has been verified by Gagne and Foster (1949). Findings indicate that if generalization is desired training on the original stimulus should be kept at a moderate level. We cannot resist speculating on the implications of these findings for length of psychotherapy, especially for therapies interminable.

There are many situations in which the S_1—R_1, S_2—R_1 paradigm fails to convey the fact that S_1 and S_2 are only samples from a population of stimuli to which we wish R_1 to be given. In the usual verbal learning experiment S_1 may consist of a nonsense syllable such as XOR printed on a strip of paper and presented in the window of a memory drum, and that is the only form in which the stimulus ever appears. In situations with broader implications XOR might sometimes appear as xor, at other times as X O r, and at still others as XoR printed in red. In psychotherapy there is little inherent value in the patient's learning to make particular responses toward the therapist *qua* therapist. Rather the therapist is a representative of a large group of persons toward whom it is hoped the appropriate responses will be made. We should know, then, whether transfer is greater when original training is given to only one or a few of the possible stimuli (or on only one or a few of the possible responses) or when training is given on a variety of stimuli. Duncan (1958) has shown that on a perceptual-motor, paired associates task transfer is markedly enhanced by varied training. When the total amount of practice is constant, any amount of varied training, even with only two stimuli, is better than training on a single stimulus. Other investigators have obtained similar results in concept attainment tasks, showing that concepts are attained more readily when a variety of examples is presented (Callantine & Warren, 1955; Shore & Sechrest, 1961), although the latter investigators found some evidence favoring a moderate number of different examples repeated a few times each rather than a few examples repeated many times or many examples given only once. The implication is clear that in order to maximize positive transfer, training should provide for some sampling of the population of stimuli to which the response must ultimately be given.

Transfer of training is apparently related to "learning to learn" or to the formation of "learning sets." Harlow (1949) was able to show over a series of experiments that both monkeys and children manifest an increasing speed of learning on specific problems with increasing experience with the class of problems involved. Apparently the habits or orientations they acquire transfer to later problems in a series. Other investigators have found comparable improvement over successive experiences with the same general class of materials; for example, in verbal learning naïve subjects learn lists more slowly than experienced ones (Deese, 1958). Thus it appears that some general habits or modes of response may be acquired which make it possible for an individual to improve his capacity to solve certain kinds of problems or to acquire certain kinds of responses. These findings suggest that under proper conditions we may expect an individual gradually to get better at meeting the difficulties he encounters. Lennard and Bernstein (1960) have applied this notion to the psychotherapy situation and have employed the term "deutero" learning (Ruesch, 1957) to denote improvement in learning skill over time. There has been little work that suggests very specifically the conditions that contribute to the formation of learning sets, but sheer practice at problem solving seems to be sufficient.

Learning sets are evidently related to the idea of transfer through the learning of general principles. In fact, some sets are easily described in terms of general principles; for example, "continue to make the same choice until there is a failure of payoff, then shift to the opposite choice." To achieve maximum efficiency in performance it is desirable to induce learning sets whenever possible.

The question what is learned, hence what is transferred, has been asked in psychology for a long period of time and is still with us (e.g., Breger & McGaugh, 1965). We do not propose to give a definitive answer, but simply to suggest that there are many possible, perhaps correct, answers to the question raised and that the answers have different consequences. There is, of course, the obvious learning and transfer of simple behaviors. We learn to tie square knots with a small piece of rope in a particular circumstance and can later tie square knots with all kinds of materials and under many circumstances. Presumably a good bit of the learning that takes place in psychotherapy consists of the acquisition of fairly specific behaviors or behavior patterns that are emitted when the appropriate cues are given. Introspective responses are a good example. Many psychotherapy patients learn in therapy to examine their own behavior (e.g., their motives), and to the extent that transfer occurs they will be introspective in other situations as well. At a broader level, we may think of disinhibiting effects of learning, especially in relation to psychotherapy. A patient may become less inhibited about asserting himself in psychotherapy, and that disinhibition may transfer beyond the confines of therapy into other aspects of the patient's life. Transfer may take place as a result of the development of mediating responses in psychotherapy (i.e., the mediators may be learned in therapy). We think it reasonable to suppose that transfer may take place in any of the ways suggested and perhaps in other ways as well.

The matter of transfer of training is above all an issue of practicality, at least if our paramount interest is in performance on the second, or the transferred to, task. The question is simply whether, if we wish to facilitate performance on task B, time is better spent partly in practicing on A or whether greater returns will be obtained by concentrating on B. There are obvious instances in which the answer will almost certainly be that time had better be spent on the critical task. For example, if one wished to teach French to a group of children, it would be foolish to begin by teaching Latin; or, if one wanted to learn to play the flute, nothing would be gained by learning first to play a recorder. The time necessary to learn to play the recorder would be much better spent in practicing on the flute. Probably for a great many tasks the advantages of an oblique approach, of beginning with a to-be-transferred task, are nil.

There are circumstances, however, in which training on other than the ultimate, critical task becomes necessary or at least highly efficient. There are some tasks on which the consequences of error are too serious to risk direct practice in the early stages of learning. For example, the Link trainer and similar aeronautical devices have proved valuable in the training of pilots because the risks involved in direct training are simply too great. Neophytes in many fields may be trained with artificial devices or under artificial circumstances if there is danger of injuring themselves or others by inevitable errors. Not at all incidentally, we suggest that psychotherapy may provide a "safe" training ground in which the consequences of errors by the patient need not be serious. Far better for him to practice initially on the therapist.

In addition to the serious consequences of errors, the expense of training may justify indirect methods. Even inefficient training may be justified if it is markedly less expensive than the real thing, and by "expense" we mean to include the time of highly trained, scarce instructors. Riflemen would probably be somewhat better off doing all of their practicing with live ammunition, but the expense of ammunition and of arrangements for its safe use makes "dry runs" expedient. Similarly, if techniques of psychotherapy can be devised to minimize the need for specific attention from the therapist, they may be expedient even if they are not optimal.

Finally, training on tasks other than the critical one may be justified when the goals of training are general and perhaps even not completely known. It is unlikely that anyone would seriously propose teaching Latin for the sole purpose of facilitating the acquisition of English or a romance language; rather it is hoped that a broader, more general understanding of the nature of our language and our cultural heritage will be acquired. Also, Latin, as well as many other subjects and responses, may be taught because it is supposed that in some unanticipated way they may be useful in the future, that is, that they may facilitate other responses; or, as in Ulmer's (1939) study, geometry may be taught with the hope that not only will an area of mathematics be elucidated but more general effects of thinking will develop. If one can teach geometry *and* critical thinking, one had better do so. Similarly, it may be argued that in psychotherapy the aim is not simply to produce more adequate responses toward "mother" but to assist the patient to develop ways of responding that may be generally useful to him. Although it may be true that, viewed simply as a problem of relating to mother, the patient's efforts should be spent in interaction with her, or at least in dealing with the problem, most psychotherapists probably hope to accomplish a good deal more than that.

TRANSFER AND PSYCHOTHERAPY

Although it is probably unnecessary, we have pointed out and wish to remind the reader that transfer is ordinarily conceived of as an effect that can take values ranging from positive through zero to negative; that is, the acquisition of a particular response may facilitate later learning, may have nothing to do with later learning, or may actually impede later learning. It appears to us that whatever responses arc acquired in psychotherapy they may similarly facilitate, be irrelevant to, or impede performance outside the therapy situation. No more than in other disciplines (e.g., formal education), is it necessarily true that what is learned in psychotherapy will facilitate responses in other situations. Unpleasant though it may be to contemplate, there is even the possibility that responses learned in psychotherapy may actually have negative transfer for desirable extratherapy behaviors (e.g., the introspection that occurs in psychotherapy may not be desirable in many other situations). However, much of the outcome research on traditional psychotherapy suggests that the hypothesis of zero transfer is tenable.

It is of more than passing interest that the concept of transfer has long been considered highly relevant to psychotherapy, but in a strikingly diffcrcnt way; that is, in *negative transfer from real life to psychotherapy*. The habits that an individual has acquired before psychotherapy are transferred to (transference) the psychotherapy situation and keep him from forming a realistic relationship with the therapist. At least, that is the supposition. Sechrest (1962) has shown that the attitudes or reactions most likely to be transferred to the therapist are those formed in relation to other well-educated, professional persons. Whether such attitudes are unrealistic or not is difficult to say. The point is that the concept of transfer has clearly been thought relevant to psychotherapy. We simply propose to continue the relevance from therapy to the extratherapy or posttherapy life of the patient.

As in other fields, for example, education (Schulz, 1960), it is not sufficient merely to suggest the relevance of transfer to the psychotherapy situation and to imply that therapy should be carried on in a way that provides for transfer. We need specific knowledge of the conditions under which learning or other changes that take place in therapy will be carried over into extratherapy situations. Probably many of the observations that have been made of therapy or hospital cures which bear little relation to behavior on the outside are understandable in terms of a failure to transfer. We cannot assume that a behavior acquired in the therapy situation, however well learned, will carry over into other situations. Unquestionably the phenomena of therapy are orderly and lawful; they follow definite rules. We must, then, understand the rules that determine what responses will be generalized, or transferred, to other situations and what responses will not. As a first approximation to the rules obtaining in psychotherapy, we suggest the knowledge gained from study of transfer of other habits.

Let us consider some of the possible reasons for the failure of transfer. (For purposes of our discussion we shall ignore the possibility of negative transfer—that responses acquired in psychotherapy may actually be detrimental to performance in other situations.) We shall explore this question at greater length, but we begin by mentioning the obvious fact that the psychotherapy situation is markedly different as a stimulus situation from virtually every other situation in which the individual may be expected to perform. Moreover, the psychotherapist is, himself, unusual, if not unique, as a stimulus person, especially for those patients who come from a different socioeconomic background. We revert to the question of the stimulus characteristics of psychotherapy in our transfer hypotheses which follow.

It should be clear that under the best of circumstances there is a sharp distinction between the psychotherapy and extratherapy situations, and for a variety of reasons responses appropriate to both do not always carry over. (Responses characteristic in extratherapy situations do not always "transfer" to therapy either.) Among other differences, reinforcement schedules may be discrepant in the two situations. (For the sake of simplification, we speak of therapy and extratherapy as two distinct situations.) Whenever a consistent discrepancy exists, we may expect that the patient will at some level respond to it. Thus, if the behaviors reinforced in and outside of therapy are different, we may suppose that the patient will learn, probably quickly, the discrimination and respond to it. Just as a pigeon learns to make one responses in the presence of a green light and another in the presence of a red light, a patient learns to respond differently in various situations.

Even though the therapist reinforces some category of response such as "expression of hostility" in the therapy hour, there is no assurance that the response will be followed by the same reinforcement in other circumstances. A patient's husband may not be nearly so tolerant of her hostility as her therapist. When transfer of therapy learning fails, an important investigatory step is to find out what the reinforcement contingencies are outside of therapy. We note, even insist, that many aspects of the typical psychotherapy session make it very simple for the patient to make the discrimination between therapy and extra-therapy; for example, the regular hour of a regular day of the week, the special office of a singular person, and so forth. We have more to say on this point later.

Another aspect of the reinforcement schedule problem is that a distinction may exist between the regularity of reinforcements in the therapy and extratherapy situations that will make a discrimination not only likely but necessary. At an evident but superficial level it may seem desirable to ensure that the therapy patient meet with a consistent and benign environment in therapy. Thus, when the patient expresses hostility toward the therapist, the therapist is expected to reinforce such behavior regularly. It is regarded as a breach of good practice for the therapist to meet the patient's hostility with counter-hostility or even negative reinforcement. The therapist is expected to remain accepting and warm. Unfortunately, as we know, responses reinforced on a 100% schedule are not especially robust when negative reinforcement is encountered. Thus, despite the efforts of the therapist, the response he so patiently nurtures may prove weak by the criterion of resistance to extinction. Probably most patients realize, if their therapists do not, that psychotherapy is, after all, a very special experience, quite unlike "real life."

Transfer will tend to be minimal when the training stimulus is nonrepresentative of the population of stimuli to which the response is to be transferred. Nonrepresentativeness may occur because the stimulus is not drawn from the same population as the test or critical stimuli. In psychotherapy it is almost certainly true that for a large proportion of patients in treatment the psychotherapist is quite different from the extratherapy figures with whom he deals. It may not be readily apparent to a patient from a blue-collar environment that the responses he has developed to deal with the therapist will meet with the same success if applied to his peers. Nonrepresentativeness may also occur because the stimulus, even though drawn from the correct population, does not sufficiently represent the range or diversity of the population. To take an extreme example, an individual drawn randomly from the population of a city would almost certainly not be representative of the population of that city. Similarly, a therapist is only a single person with particular characteristics who cannot be expected to represent the diverse stimulus persons in a patient's environment. Therapists have been admonished to try to provide a "blank screen" on which a patient may project whatever stimulus characteristics he needs at a given moment, but it seems improbable that therapists can do more than slightly obscure their individuality.

Some Suggestions for Minimizing Transfer in Psychotherapy

If we wish to minimize the transfer of psychotherapy learning to extratherapy situations, a number of things may be done. First, a single therapist should provide some rather distinctive personal cues, such as appearance, dress, and manner, that would mark him as a rather special person, different from others. Second, an unvarying and powerful stimulus pattern should provide a context for the therapy, thus ensuring that whatever responses may be developed would become very strongly attached to the unique therapy stimuli. For example, the therapist would use one office for every situation. The furniture in the office would be distinctive and it would not vary from session to session. There should be some stimuli which would identify the office as such and mark it off from other places; for example, diplomas on the wall, bookshelves, and filing cabinets. And, not to belabor the point unduly, the therapy would be conducted on the same day of every week, at the same time of day, and for some standard length of time, say fifty minutes.

Although the picture we have just drawn may seem exaggerated, we are convinced that it is substantially justified. It is evident to us that the field of psychotherapy can profit greatly from a more intent look at its practices and possibilities from the standpoint of the concept of transfer of training. We now discuss some research hypotheses about therapy that stem more or less directly from considerations about problems of transfer and generalization.

HYPOTHESIS 5.1: **Transfer of learning from psychotherapy to extratherapy situations will be greater when the therapy stimuli are representative of extratherapy stimuli.**

We believe that if some way can be found to increase the similarity between the stimuli afforded by the psychotherapy situation, in the context of which new responses are acquired, and those in the patient's "real life," the transfer to extratherapy life of the patient will be facilitated. Some way must be found to increase the range of stimuli in psychotherapy and to make the stimuli more like those obtaining at the time the patient must make critical responses. Therefore, we are suggesting research examination of what, for want of a better term, we call "parkbench therapy."

HYPOTHESIS 5.1a: **Transfer of learning from psychotherapy to extra-therapy situations will be greater if therapy is conducted outside an office in a variety of situations in which the patient will ultimately have to respond.**

When we think about it, it seems remarkable that psychotherapy should have been confined to offices for so many years. Assuredly that is the way Freud began to practice, and there is no question that it is convenient for the therapist to sit in his office and wait for patients to come to him. Probably the analogy afforded by medical practice and the early domination of the field by persons with a medical orientation played no small part in keeping therapy within four diploma-covered walls. There are, however, as we have suggested, theoretical reasons for considering expanding the environment for therapy, and there are also existing practices and research that point in the same direction and offer hope of efficacy.

In practical, operational terms what we are suggesting is that therapy be carried out as much as possible in the patient's own extra-therapy environment, in the circumstances in which he is expected to respond. Thus some interviews may be carried out in the patient's home, others at his place of employment, still others may take place in bars, in automobiles, and even on park benches. The most appropriate place for an interview should depend on the topic of discussion, but it should be a place directly relevant to the discussion. Thus, if therapy is at the point of dealing with attitudes toward authority figures, it may help to hold sessions in places in which authority figures are actually visible, say in the presence of a policeman in the park or in situations in which the cues for authority are very strong, as in the patient's place of employment. When therapy deals with family figures, it may be conducted in environments strongly saturated with cues for the appropriate family figures.

There are two reasons why we believe that such therapy may be more efficacious than office-bound treatment. First, whatever responses there are would be connected more strongly with the relevant stimuli, for the responses would have occurred in actual contiguity with the stimuli. Second, the stimuli would presumably be considerably more vivid than if some attempt were made to produce them in an office. Although there is some likelihood that mental images may be aroused in the absence of particular stimuli, and such images may be rather powerful under the right conditions, mental images are scarcely ever likely to be as powerful as the real stimuli. Moreover, they are probably difficult to elicit on command, and they are ephemeral, disappearing with the slightest distracting stimulus. The presence of actual stimuli can be expected to facilitate the arousal of responses to a level at which they can become more clearly the focus of therapeutic efforts, as well as to facilitate transfer of new responses.

It is not necessarily the case that psychotherapy should begin on the park bench. There may be an initial period during which greatest progress can be made within an office setting, for example, in establishing the prestige and general reinforcement value of the therapist, perhaps a critical stage in therapy (Frank, 1961), and the issue of transfer of training may not be especially salient. Certainly in the later stages of therapy, however, we would expect an extended therapy environment to be of substantial value. Even if we view therapy primarily in terms of gaining insight or in terms of the value of establishing a good relationship with the therapist, there must come a time when attention is given to the problem of carrying over the insight or the attitudes gained in the relationship into the remainder of the patient's life. At that point, even if it is late in the total therapy process, we believe that it can increase the effectiveness of therapy to extend it into the patient's actual environment.

Although we are inclined to prefer moving therapy out of the office into a variety of real life situations, a good bit may be accomplished by enhancing certain stimuli within the office setting itself. For example, use may be made of pictures of a patient's wife and other family members, of his boss, his friends and other important figures in his life in order to increase their salience for him. Pictures may also be used that would symbolize certain of his special conflicts or problems, thus assisting his usual image-forming powers. In attempting to treat alcoholics by associating a noxious electric shock with ingestion of alcohol, Hsu (1965) has found it useful to construct a replica of a small bar in the treatment situation to increase the reality of the situation for the patients. The wearing of street clothing by nursing personnel can increase transfer value and has been shown to be a possible and desirable change (Jones, Kahn, & Wolcott, 1964). At the famous Herstedvester institution in Denmark for the treatment of difficult and chronic criminal offenders many efforts are made to develop a situation of work and life that is much like that the inmate would encounter should he improve enough to be released. As he works his way to freedom, the stimuli he faces become progressively closer approximations to the world outside the walls (Stürup, 1964).

A basis in prior practice and in research for park bench therapy is not entirely lacking, although it seems not to have been done in the way we are proposing. One of the first psychological studies reported that bears on our problem is the classic work in 1924 by Mary Cover Jones (1960) who attempted to cure a child of his fear of white, furry objects. She did not do so by talking to the child in her office. Instead she put the child into a room with three nonfrightened children who would provide good models for him and gradually introduced a white rabbit at closer and closer intervals. In addition, she introduced the rabbit while the child was in a pleasant state of mind induced by eating candy. This basic model for treatment has reappeared in the guise of counterconditioning or desensitization therapy (Wolpe, 1954, 1958, 1961). Although Wolpe seems in therapy sessions to rely largely on patients' mental images of the things they fear, he and other behavior therapists have been bold and apparently successful in treating patients in the presence of the objects they fear and sometimes *in situ*. Stevenson (1962) treated a patient *in* an elevator which aroused her fear; Lazarus (1960) treated a child with a fear of automobile accidents in an automobile; Rachman (1959) worked directly with feared objects and acts; Murphy (1964) ultimately got a patient with a fear of worms to go into the fields for desensitization; Lang and Lazovik (1963) utilized live snakes in their investigation; and Rudolf (1961) reports the recovery of a number of patients with severe anxiety while they were being exposed to repeated air attacks during World War II. Using only a slightly different approach, Walton and Mather (1963) dealt with a case involving stammering and phobias about people by having the patient gradually work into social situations involving closer and closer contact with other persons. What all of these cases have in common is that the treatment occurs in the context of the actual feared objects or acts and often in the very situations in which the ultimate response of assertiveness or nonfear is desired. The problem of transfer is largely obviated by the fact that the training occurs in relation to the critical stimuli. Ayllon and his associates (Ayllon & Azrin, 1964; Ayllon & Haughton, 1962; Ayllon & Michael, 1959) have used more direct positive and aversive reinforcement training, but also *in the situation* in which the response was desired and again with apparently good results.

However, there have even been therapists of more orthodox persuasion who have gone outside the office to carry on their work. In Amsterdam there is a community psychiatry program whose aim is to keep patients out of hospitals, and a great deal of the treatment takes place in their homes (Hurder, 1961). Much of the treatment is of an emergency nature and referrals to a regular clinic are often made, but the emphasis on home treatment is remarkable. (It is interesting how selective psychiatry and psychology have been in their borrowings from the medical model; the standard professional office is much admired, but house calls are not.) Another large and important group of therapists, in the United States, does the major portion of its therapeutic work in homes, at places of employment, and even on the street. We have in mind the pastoral psychologists or counselors who can only be said to work *out of* an office. Unfortunately, there is no special evidence of their effectiveness, but ministers, priests, and rabbis are highly regarded by the public at large and are often the first to be called when trouble arises. If we can believe the accounts we hear, they are often quite effective; and, of course, a great deal of the work of social workers is carried on outside offices, in some cases on the streets and probably literally on park benches when they are attempting to reach delinquents.

In the light of our previous recommendation that pictures be used to enhance the value of certain stimuli with which therapy is concerned, it is quite interesting to examine Cassell's (1965) research on puppet therapy with children about to undergo cardiac catheterization. Cassell noted that children subjected to strange and potentially traumatic hospital experiences often showed strong emotional responses but that little of any effectiveness was done to relieve their feelings. She believed that an important element in their obvious fear was the strangeness of the situation, their lack of understanding of what was going to happen to them. Therefore she developed a brief therapy designed in large part to produce some meaningful comprehension of cardiac catheterization or at least the parts of it of which the child would be aware. She built some ingenious miniatures of the operating table and fluoroscope equipment used with the important instruments and made some realistic puppets to represent the patient, parents, nurse, and physician. The therapy then consisted of going through the procedures with the child, including such important elements as swabbing him with alcohol, strapping the child puppet (encasing the child's hand) down to the operating table, turning on the red light, and so on. The results indicated substantial transfer from the puppet therapy to the actual catheterization, with the result that the children exposed to therapy were rated less disturbed than controls during the procedure. In a postcatheterization session the procedure was re-enacted with the child being given an opportunity to play the physician's role. Follow-up measures indicated that the treated children were significantly less reluctant to return to the hospital for further tests than were the controls who had been managed in the ordinary way. We consider Cassell's study a striking demonstration of planning for transfer, and although we cannot be sure that her results could not have been achieved by more conventional methods the burden of proof here is on those who think they could have been.

Earlier in this chapter we discussed the proposition, seemingly well supported in experimental literature, that transfer effects are greater when the subject is trained on a variety of stimuli rather than on a single stimulus, and it is partly for that reason that it seems worthwhile to us to test the outcome of therapy practiced in a wide variety of situations. However, an individual's environment certainly consists of more than the physical setting; in fact, the interpersonal environment may be of much greater importance than the physical environment. Therefore, it occurs to us that transfer might be facilitated if therapy took place in a somewhat broader interpersonal context. Our next hypothesis is addressed to this point.

HYPOTHESIS 5.2: **There will be greater transfer of learning from psychotherapy to extratherapy situations if therapy is provided by more than one therapist.**

One of our students suggested a variant on psychotherapy practice that takes advantage of the possibilities for elaborating the interpersonal context of therapy without introducing any inherent inefficiency (Holmes, 1965). He called his suggestion "round robin therapy." Most psychotherapy, all orthodox therapy, takes place in an office where one patient and one therapist spend many hours together. All the appointments for a particular patient are with the same therapist. Such arrangements may have much to recommend them, but they certainly do not correspond to expectations about what constitutes a good arrangement for transfer. It is suggested, therefore, that a patient have appointments with several different therapists. He might, for example, be seeing four different therapists simultaneously but see each of them only every other week; thus he would have two sessions each week.

The employment of several different therapists may (but not necessarily) greatly increase the breadth of stimuli or the complexity of the total stimulus pattern to which the patient is exposed. The different personalities, styles, and even appearances of the separate therapists should become stimuli or cues for the desired responses. Since, presumably, all the therapists would be reinforcing responses in the same general class, the response class would become conditioned to a variety of interpersonal stimuli, and, since the exact form of the response is assumed to vary more when emitted in the presence of varying stimuli, greater response generalization should occur, that is, a wider range of responses within a class would be emitted and reinforced. In addition, therapists differ in the particular responses they reinforce and would therefore contribute to the development of flexibility of response on the part of the patient.

A second possible basis for increased effectiveness of round robin therapy is that different therapists would reinforce responses in somewhat different ways and schedules, so that the desired response would not become contingent on a narrow class of reinforcers possibly employed by one therapist. Some therapists probably rely more heavily on verbal reinforcers, some on posture and gesture cues. When the patient leaves the therapy situation, he is susceptible to those reinforcements that have been employed by the therapist, partly because certain reinforcements have been selectively associated with others. For example, the therapist may tend to make a certain gesture when he is pleased and smiles. Thus a patient who has been exposed to several different therapists should be sensitive to a wider range of reinforcement possibilities. He is less likely to "miss" a reinforcement different from the ones used by a single therapist. Moreover, since different therapists are scarcely likely to provide the same *amount* of reinforcement for any particular response, the patient will learn more readily that people differ in real or apparent appreciation of given behaviors. He will not be so likely to experience a decrement in quantity of reinforcement as a qualitative change in reinforcement patterns.

To revert to a practical level, it is not supposed that in round robin therapy every therapist would operate in the independent manner characteristic of therapists operating alone. It would probably be wasteful for every therapist to begin with probing interviews or the formulation of therapeutic plans. We suggest that therapy begin with a series of interviews conducted by one therapist for the purpose of establishing the "target symptoms" to be dealt with, formulating a treatment plan, and setting the ground rules for therapy. After the initial interviews, the first therapist would communicate his findings and recommendations to the other members of the therapeutic "team," who would then begin seeing the patient. Each therapist would, in his own characteristic way, try to work with the patient toward the goals of the therapy, whether they are cast in terms of specific behavioral changes or in terms of the gaining of self-understanding. Round robin therapy should not require any more therapists or therapist time than is usually the case.

There has been one trial of something like round robin therapy which has come to our attention. Lipkin (1965) had one female patient see fifteen (!) different therapists for one interview each, with no contact among therapists. On self-ideal Q-sorts he found that she changed in the same way as patients being treated in the conventional manner. In fact, by the end of her treatment the correlation between her self and ideal Q-sorts had increased from a very low level to .80, a value well above the typical correlation of .55 or so generally found after therapy. Moreover, other measures, including behavioral criteria, showed great improvement in Lipkin's patient. Obviously the opportunity to employ several different therapists with the same patient should not be passed up in any research setting. In a psychiatric institute known to one of the writers a new clinic is being developed in which patients will be seen by the first available therapist if they express no preference and will be encouraged to come in for help irregularly, as they need it, rather than on the conventional schedule. Something akin to round robin therapy might become routine in such an outpatient clinic.

Group psychotherapy probably offers at least some of the advantages to be gained in seeing a number of different therapists. There is no evidence suggesting that group psychotherapy is any less effective than individual therapy, in spite of the dilution of the therapist's attention and influence. Perhaps some of the presumed effectiveness of group therapy is maintained by the multiplicity of figures with whom any particular patient can interact. The greatest disadvantages in comparison with round robin therapy are that, first, few if any of the members of a therapy group have the skills of a professional therapist in therapeutic interactions, and second, because of the number of persons in the therapy group it is probably true that for any patient contact with the therapist is less concentrated and less intensive than it would be in individual sessions.

From time to time the practice of psychotherapy with multiple therapists present has been suggested (e.g., Mullan & Sangiuliano, 1960; Whitaker, Malone, & Warkentin, 1956). Mintz (1963) has described what she believes to be the advantages of a cotherapist enabling the closer approximation to a family structure in therapy, but we would emphasize the advantage simply in terms of adding an additional person with whom the patient could interact. We are dubious about the possibility of advantages from simultaneous employment of more than one therapist simply on the ground that it seems unlikely that the increase in efficiency or efficacy would outweigh the added cost of multiple therapists.

Many patients in fact have multiple therapists in that they rely on such quasi-therapists as friends and relatives in addition to formal therapists. When they have more than one formal therapist, it is usually sequentially. The transferring of patients from one therapist to another is undoubtedly very frequent, and many patients "shop around" for a therapist whenever they feel they need one. No statistics seem to be available on the number or proportion of patients who have been treated by two or more different therapists, but it is safe to say that there are many such cases. Whether these cases especially benefit from treatment is not known, but they may be the more difficult patients to begin with.

Should there be some desire to begin with an approximation to round robin therapy to see how it works before beginning a full-scale program, we have a practical suggestion. It is common practice in the medical profession for physicians to substitute for one another. When, for whatever reason, it is necessary for a physician to miss an appointment with a patient, he does not usually cancel it; he simply gets a substitute from among his associates. It should be possible to do the same thing in psychotherapy. One natural situation in which to test some of the effects of round robin therapy would be to have psychotherapists substitute for each other when appointments cannot be kept. With a minimum of disruption in the usual routines of clinics and hospitals, a good bit of multiple therapy could be observed, even if the conditions for a good experiment could not be accomplished.

RESPONSE AVAILABILITY AND PSYCHOTHERAPY

We have alluded above to the fact that the probability of occurrence of a response at any particular time is in part a function of the availability of the response to the S. If an individual has never encountered and practiced a response, say, a foreign word, it cannot be available to him for use in situations in which it might be appropriate, except as it might occur as a random emission. One of the functions of much training and practice on learning tasks is simply to raise the level of availability of a particular response to the point at which it can readily be used. In learning the conversational use of a language a good bit of practice in pronouncing a word is necessary before the word really becomes available for use. People who are trying to learn a motor response such as a golf swing may spend hours practicing the correct response to make it smooth and automatic. We show that the probability of the occurrence of any response is a function of the frequency of its evocation, and we then point to some implications of such a research finding for psychotherapy.

Underwood and Schulz (1960) have made an especially clear statement of the frequency of evocation hypothesis which they call the "spew" hypothesis. In connection with the field of verbal learning, they and others have found that a subject will "spew" responses in an order that reflects frequency of prior experience and evocation. Therefore, the more frequent responses will be more available in the forming of new associations. As Underwood and Schulz put it, "Other things being equal, therefore, the more frequently a verbal unit has been experienced, the more quickly this will become a response in a new association connection" (p. 86). As an example of the research bases for such statements the investigation of Cohen, Bousfield, & Whitmarsh (described by Underwood & Shulz, 1960) can be cited. These investigators gave subjects category names, such as fish, male name, and color, and asked them to give the first four specific examples the category name made them think of. Their results showed a marked tendency for words with a high frequency of occurrence in ordinary use to be given most frequently by the subjects. Thus, as male names, John, Bob, and Joe were given quite often, whereas Vinton, Wallace, and Wesley were given only infrequently. Some investigators have used either frequent or infrequent words as response units in learning studies, but Underwood and Schulz present the results of several experiments in which they manipulated frequency of experience with nonsense syllables and showed that familiar syllables more readily enter into associative connections; that is, they are learned faster when they appear as response terms. Hovland and Kurtz (1952) also found that preliminary familiarization with specific nonsense syllables was helpful in later learning when the syllables were arranged in serial lists. The effectiveness of preliminary response training is not limited to verbal materials. Gagne and Baker (1950) had an experimental task which required subjects to move one of several switches when a particular one of several lights came on. Some subjects were given pretraining consisting of learning to associate each of the several lights with a letter, thus differentiating among the lights. The pretraining had a large facilitating effect on ability of subjects to learn to associate each switch with its corresponding light. Similar findings hold for the attainment of concepts (Hunt, 1962; Kendler & Karasik, 1958); when the concept category is a high dominance response, either by reason of historical or manipulated frequency, the concept is attained more quickly.

The research on availability of responses and speed of learning, especially when availability is determined by frequency, seems to us to have important implications for psychotherapy. We assume that the desired outcome of psychotherapy is some change in behavior, and the research just cited suggests that desired responses should be emphasized and practiced during the therapy sessions. Evidently what we have reference to is related to transfer of training, but we wish to emphasize the response term rather than the stimulus. *Other things being equal, the response which has been emitted most frequently in the past will be emitted on subsequent occasions.* When a patient leaves the therapy situation, the responses most available to him are the ones most often emitted in therapy, and those responses are most likely to occur in extratherapy settings. Therefore greatest practice in psychotherapy should be encouraged for the responses that are most desired.

HYPOTHESIS 5.3:   **Greater effectiveness of psychotherapy will be achieved if very strong emphasis is placed in therapy on emitting of responses considered desirable in other circumstances.**

Once the therapist, and presumably the patient, have decided on the kinds of responses they would like the patient to emit outside the therapy situation, those responses should be heavily practiced and differentiated from other responses. Contiguity learning theorists indicate that it is a mistake to permit any practice at all on erroneous or undesired responses on the ground that every emission of a response increases the tendency to give that response in the presence of appropriate stimuli. For example, few pedagogues would recommend that a child being taught French should be permitted to practice incorrect responses with the hope that they could be eliminated at some future time.

However, a good bit of psychotherapy practice is not based at all on learning models, but on one of the "dynamic" models that lead to very different suggestions. Thus many conceptions of psychotherapy have rather strong affinities for the "cathartic" concept which supposes that the way to get rid of undesirable responses is to "get them out of one's system" by free expression. The underlying model is hydraulic, and the idea is to relieve the pressure that supposedly builds up when people "bottle things up" inside. Other "insight" models for therapy assume that undesirable responses will persist until the reasons for them are comprehended, and good therapy consists of a detailed and extended examination of bad responses until their sources are understood. Then it is assumed that there will be no further "need" for such responses and they will cease.

There seems to be no current documentation for this, but it is our conviction that psychotherapy as it has traditionally been practiced has expended a grossly disproportionate amount of time and effort on responses to be eliminated eventually. No data exist to verify our conviction, but we have searched through voluminous therapy transcripts and countless diagnostic summaries and have encountered surprisingly few instances of concern for positive, "prosocial" responses, except perhaps in the case of individuals diagnosed as "psychopathic." Many records contain accounts of the difficulties patients have in expressing hostility, but few mention those of expressing positive feelings. We have read several therapy transcripts in which there were interpolations about the patient's "ambivalence" toward another person, but the therapeutic discussions concentrated heavily on the negative feelings. We believe that it many cases the heavy emphasis on negative feelings (which are assumed to be undesirable responses when carried outside or beyond therapy) and other undesirable responses may so heighten the availability of such responses that they become probable in conditions where they are certainly inappropriate.

HYPOTHESIS 5.3a: **Concentration on positive feelings and responses and exclusion of negative feelings and responses will result in an increase in the effectiveness of psychotherapy.**

Not at all facetiously we term the approach we are suggesting "love therapy" to contrast it with what appears to us to be the "hostility therapy" that is prevalent. We assume that the ultimately desired therapeutic outcome in many, probably a majority, of cases is the substitution of positive or prosocial responses for negative or antisocial ones. For example, suppose a patient enters treatment with feelings of strong hostility toward authority figures (e.g., teachers), which we see as having developed out of his poor relationship with his father; that is, his hostility toward authority replicates his hostility toward his father. Now we may not care whether the patient changes his feelings toward his father or not; his father may be living in another place or may even be dead. We assume, however, that most therapists would consider it desirable to replace the hostility toward teachers with an attitude of (discriminating, perhaps) respect. However, the way in which therapy usually seems to take place is that the patient's hostility toward his father is thoroughly explored and extensively elaborated. The patient is led to view his hostility in all its aspects and becomes more and more accomplished in recognizing and labeling his hostile feelings. At the same time, the connection between the "father" and the teachers is elaborated and explored until the patient sees clearly that, at least in his own mind, father and teacher are greatly equivalent as stimuli. Then, somehow, it seems to be hoped that when the connections are all made clear and when the hostility has been thoroughly understood, the "need" for hostility toward teachers will have disappeared. We wonder. Could it be that the therapist has produced a person so well practiced in the expression of hostility that it has become a highly available response, one with a high probability of occurrence anywhere? And does the emphasis on the associative connection between father and teacher actually weaken that association?

Let us at least consider an alternative approach to the example we have chosen. Suppose the therapist begins by finding a figure, perhaps an "authority" figure such as an uncle, toward whom the patient has predominantly positive feelings. Then let the investigation continue by an exploration of positive feelings, an elaboration of the feelings of love and respect so that the patient comes to recognize and label such feelings in himself without hesitation. Give him practice on the response that is ultimately desired. Then the therapist can attempt to develop an association between the uncle figure and the teacher figure, pointing out the similarities, mentioning them often in the same context. Finally the therapy may proceed to a consideration of the patient's positive (even if initially minimal) feelings toward teachers. By such tactics we would hope to avoid increasing the differentiation and availability of hostility as a response and also strengthen the association of teacher as a stimulus with other valued stimuli.

We would like to make it clear that we are not suggesting that hostility is an inappropriate or otherwise poor topic for psychotherapy discussion. What we have reservations about is the emphasis placed on negative feelings such as hostility at the expense of consideration of more positive responses. Obviously a good bit of therapy theory and practice is directed toward the inhibited neurotic individual who is assumed to be in difficulty because of problems in asserting himself and expressing hostility, and although we are inclined to believe that the inhibited neurotic has problems with other than negative, hostile feelings we grant that some practice in therapy on this hostility is justified. We are not convinced, however, that development of the capacity for open expression of hostility automatically leads to a more satisfying and effective way of life. We suppose that the longer term aims of psychotherapy must include the development of "prosocial" responses. Therefore, attention, specific attention, in therapy should be paid to them.

The research of Schachter and Singer (1962) on cognitive aspects of affective states may have some bearing on the therapy variations we are proposing. These authors induced a state of physiological arousal by injection of adrenalin and were then able to show that the affective state experienced by the subject was a function of his cognition of the state. *Exactly the same* physiological state seemingly could be experienced as anger or elation, depending on the cognitions of the subject induced by a model. The subjects were resistant to manipulation of their cognitions when they were aware that their physiological arousal had its origin in the injection they had received.

Thus in a situation in which an individual is subjected to an ambiguous affective state his reaction to that state will be in part a function of his labeling of it. Any training that substantially increases the availability of one label over another may well bias the direction of the individual's characteristic affective experience. Overemphasis on hostility, for example, may produce such awareness of it as a possible response and such a high tendency to emit it as a response that when subjected to some sort of ambiguous arousal the individual's customary cognitive reaction will be "I must be angry." It is of considerable interest in this connection to observe that during adolescence the "love" response becomes highly available, probably through frequency of experience, heightened expectancy, and the like, and the adolescent youngster is highly likely to interpret any sort of arousal he experiences in the presence of a member of the opposite sex as love. We are not here suggesting such an indiscriminate increase in availability of that response.

Although we have cast our discussion in the mold imposed by the love-hostility bipolarity, we believe that the suggestion made in hypothesis 5.3a is equally applicable to other responses. If one wishes to enhance self-esteem, self-esteem as a response should be explored and made highly available as a verbal response, rather than concentrating on an exploration of self-derogation. The consequences of the response, "I did better that time" are different from and probably better than, "There, I loused it up again!" Since we are not persuaded of the necessity for exposing all the "dynamics" of self-derogation, and since we expect that appropriate responses can establish benign cycles as well as inappropriate responses can establish vicious ones, the self-favorable response may often be much the better.

There is some precedent for what we are proposing here in "Morita" therapy in Japan, named for its founder, Dr. Seima Morita (Caudill, 1959). According to the recommendations of Morita the patient is kept isolated and prohibited from all activity for one week. After that he begins to keep a diary on which the therapist comments in writing several times each week. At the same time the patient is set to doing simple manual tasks that will bring him into contact with nature. Morita therapy grew out of Zen Buddhistic principles, and in it

Emphasis is on the treatment of the patient through his daily life experiences, and it is felt that *a direct approach to the constructive forces within the patient is to be preferred over an analytic approach to the obstructive, pathological conflicts in his personality* (Caudill, 1959, p. 237. Italics ours).

ADVANCE ORGANIZERS AND PSYCHOTHERAPY

When an individual must engage in some task, learn something, or acquire some skill, it may be very helpful to have available a cognitive structure that will enable him to make sense out of experience as it occurs. Some theorists have suggested that the absence of structure may produce anxiety (Kelly, 1955), and there is a wealth of empirical literature showing ways in which a prior structure or set can facilitate (or interfere with) learning and performance. We propose to examine certain aspects of this literature for its possible relevance to psychotherapy. We wish to pay special attention to the thinking and research of David P. Ausubel (1963) on the concept of "advance organizers" in learning. First let us state our general hypothesis.

HYPOTHESIS 5.4:   **A cognitive structure which enables an individual correctly to anticipate and organize his experience will facilitate learning and retention of new or more elaborate behavior sequences.**

We can begin at the level of very simple responses to show the importance of an initial set. We need not explore all the evidence in detail, but there is no question that an initial or anticipatory set can heighten perceptual sensitivity. Many investigators (e.g., Woodworth & Schlosberg, 1954) have shown that ability to detect and respond to a signal is increased if the subject knows the nature of the signal and when it should appear if it is going to. Speech is much more intelligible if the listener knows pretty well what to expect (Miller, Heise, & Lichten, 1951). Although the implications for psychotherapy of such simple phenomena are very limited, we do believe that the sensitivities of a therapy patient are important. His sensitivity in psychotherapy might be substantially increased if he knew in advance what he should look for. We refer later to "emotional sensitivity training" (p. 297), but here we are pointing toward preliminary training designed to make the patient sensitive to the therapeutic process and outcome.

Reaction time is almost certain to be enhanced by a preparatory set (Woodworth & Schlosberg, 1954). When a subject knows that he is expected to respond within a given period of time, his response occurs with greater speed than when he is not anticipating a signal to respond.

At a more complex level of behavior it has been shown that some form of prior structure facilitates performance on a variety of tasks. Even rats seem to show such effects. Forgus (1954, 1955) reared rats in a "complex" environment with many obstacles, blocks, etc., on the cage floor or in a very simple environment. One group of rats was allowed only *visual* experience with the complex environment; they were separated from it by glass. Nonetheless, when tested later in a maze-running task in which various objects like those in the complex environment provided impediments to free movement, *both* the motorically and visually experienced groups were superior to the group reared in the simple environment. The relationship of such findings to transfer of training is apparent, but we would stress the idea that the visually experienced group had been provided with prior structure that made it possible for them to interpret their later experience (i.e., we choose to view the experiment, heuristically, in such terms, we are not implying the literal existence of cognitive structure in those rats.) Incidentally, in the second experiment it was found that visual experience facilitated performance maximally only when visual cues were relevant. When tested in an environment impoverished in visual information, the group with actual complex motor experience was clearly superior.

We think that Judd's (1902) and Hendrickson and Schroeder's (1941) experiments on transfer as a result of training on general principles are meaningful in terms of the facilitating effect of prior structure. Providing an individual with an over-all scheme by means of which he is able to anticipate his experience correctly can result in a superior performance on a perceptual motor task. Of course, the subjects in experiments on dart or air rifle shooting at submerged targets are scarcely naïve when they begin. However, we assume that having had specific instructions about refraction of light waves passing through water sensitizes subjects to different aspects of their visual experience and enables them to understand what is happening, for example, when their missiles are off-target.

In his review of problem-solving research Duncan (1959) found that anticipatory sets and various preliminary structuring procedures had facilitating or detrimental effects on problem-solving, depending on the relationship of the preliminary activity to relevant problem-solving activity. For example, Goldbeck, Bernstein, Hillix, and Marx (1957) found that subjects who were taught a way of analyzing problems were better able to make use of a particular problem-solving technique which they were taught later. Without the prior structure provided by the knowledge of the analytical approach, the problem-solving technique was of no value. Various studies cited by Duncan indicate the superiority of providing training in "understanding" of problems in facilitating later problem solving.

Finally, it seems to us that the work of Ausubel and his associates on "advance organizers" in meaningful verbal learning is especially significant in its implications for psychotherapy. Ausubel (1963) has proposed that the existence of cognitive structure, which he defines as "an individual's organization, stability, and clarity of knowledge in a particular subject-matter field" (p. 26), is the major factor influencing learning and retention of meaningful new material. The cognitive structure provides a way of *subsuming* new material in one of two ways. When the new material is an instance of an established concept or is illustrative of a previous general proposition, subsumption is said to be *derivative,* but when the new learning is "an extension, elaboration, or qualification of previously learned propositions" subsumption is *correlative.* When an individual's cognitive structuring of a field is adequate, a basis for subsumption exists, and new material is better comprehended and retained. Ausubel puts the case as follows:

> . . . new ideas and information can be efficiently learned and retained only to the extent that more inclusive and appropriately relevant concepts are already available in cognitive structure to serve a subsuming role or to furnish ideational anchorage (p. 79).

He goes on to point out that although the principle seems self-evident it is rarely followed in textbooks or other materials. Nor, we would add, is it followed in psychotherapy.

A general organizational approach to the presentation of any field of learning is referred to by Ausubel as *progressive differentiation*. The more general and inclusive ideas of a discipline should be presented first, and they should then be progressively differentiated in detail and specificity. Ausubel believes that this organization actually corresponds to the natural and preferred way of structuring material in the mind of the learner. There is a hierarchy of concepts with the most inclusive at the apex.

One of the ways of providing for progressive differentiation is by the use of *advance organizers*. An advance organizer provides a cognitive framework or structure into which new material can be interwoven. The nature and inclusiveness of the advance organizer will depend on the subject's prior level of organization of concepts in the field in which he is learning. Ausubel believes that the more unfamiliar the material, hence the lower the level of differentiation of the individual's concepts, the more inclusive and general the organizer must be. Thus for a novice in a field the initial organizers must be broadly inclusive—the most general concepts in the field; for persons with some prior experience the organizers should be more specific. The organizer is introduced before the learning material and is at a higher level of abstraction and inclusiveness than the material to be learned.

An additional purpose of organizers is to achieve *integrative reconciliation,* by which is meant the specific reconciliation of previously learned material and cognitive structure with the new material to be learned. Advance organizers may make possible the systematic comparison of ideas, the analysis of relationships among them. Organizers may be used to point out the similarities or differences between existing cognitive structure and the new material to be acquired. Thus economy in cognitive structure is achieved, for the needless proliferation of concepts is avoided. Moreover, the real differences that exist between concepts may be sharpened and better discriminated.

Ausubel states his belief that,

. . . if an organizer can first delineate clearly, precisely, and explicitly the principal similarities and differences between the ideas in a new learning passage, on the one hand, and existing related concepts in cognitive structure on the other, it seems reasonable to postulate that the more detailed ideas and information in the learning passage would be grasped later with fewer ambiguities, fewer competing meanings, and fewer misconceptions suggested by the learner's prior knowledge of the related concepts; and that as these clearer, less confused new meanings interact with analogous established meanings during the retention interval, they would be more likely to retain their identity (p. 83).

At least a part of what is involved here is conveyed in Bruner's (1960) discussion of the need for teaching the "structure" as well as the content of a discipline.

There are two different kinds of organizers that may facilitate learning and retention of new material. The "expository" organizer is used with completely unfamiliar material to provide for immediate subsumption of the new material in terms that are already familiar to the learner. The expository organizer makes relevant a structure into which the new material may be fitted when no obvious structure exists. For example, in beginning a discussion of the eye and vision, many lecturers often introduce the camera as a model or example of visual apparatus. For relatively familiar material the need is for an organizer, called a "comparative" organizer, which will integrate new concepts with those that are basically similar in existing structure and will facilitate discrimination between new and existing concepts that are different but might easily be confused. As an example of the latter, a discussion of the Skinnerian concept of "reinforcement" might be preceded by a general presentation of ideas about reward and punishment.

Ausubel reviews and describes a considerable amount of research relevant to the effectiveness of advance organizers in facilitating learning; hence we need not review the work in detail here. However, it may be helpful to describe briefly some of the specific research procedures to illustrate more exactly what is meant by an advance organizer. In an early experiment Ausubel (1960) used rather complex and certainly unfamiliar material on the metallurgy of carbon steel as learning material. The advance organizer group was given an initial passage written at a much higher level of abstraction and inclusiveness than the learning passage itself. "It was designed to serve as an organizing or anchoring focus for the steel material and to relate it to existing cognitive structure" (p. 268). The organizing passage discussed metals and alloys and their properties in general terms so that the subjects were given relevant background concepts, but a preliminary test showed that the organizing material alone did not raise performance on the criterion test to a level above chance. Thus the advance organizer did not *itself* improve scores on the final test. The control group received a passage consisting of historically relevant material such as the evolution of methods of making iron and steel. Then both groups were exposed to a learning situation that required them to study the passage on carbon steel metallurgy, and all subjects were tested for retention three days later. (Note that in this experiment it is impossible to say whether the advance organizer affected learning, retention, or both.) The results showed a superiority in retention for the advance organizer group.

Another experiment of a similar nature has shown that general background knowledge in a subject matter area not only facilitated the learning of unfamiliar material but actually enhanced the effect of the organizer (Ausubel & Fitzgerald, 1962). Moreover, and this is a point especially important for psychotherapy research, these authors also showed that an advance organizer was especially helpful to those subjects relatively poor in verbal ability, perhaps because such persons are less likely to structure the material spontaneously in a useful way.

Advance organizers may be effective in part because they improve discrimination among concepts that are already present and those that are new. This would correspond to the "comparative" organizer function. Ausubel and Blake (1958) and Ausubel and Fitzgerald (1961) found that when subjects were asked to learn unfamiliar material about Buddhism those with the greatest knowledge of Christianity made higher scores on the learning measure, even when the effect of verbal ability was partialed out. They also found that when established ideas are already clear and stable, organizers are of little value, organizers that point specifically to the relationships between two sets of ideas increase discriminability and enhance learning and retention (Ausubel & Fitzgerald, 1961).

Now let us proceed to our specific psychotherapy hypothesis.

HYPOTHESIS 5.4a: Giving patients prior information about the nature of psychotherapy, the theories underlying it, and the techniques to be used will facilitate progress in psychotherapy.

We find it rather remarkable that psychotherapists have apparently been unwilling to impart to their patients more than a little of the process of psychotherapy. Some writers have made general suggestions about "structuring" of psychotherapy (e.g., Fromm-Reichmann, 1950; Holland, 1965; Rotter, 1954; Wolberg, 1954), but such suggestions have been rudimentary and sometimes even evasive. Many, perhaps most, other writers have ignored the whole question of just what patients should be told about psychotherapy. We believe that in many cases a fuller explication would be quite desirable.

Rather strangely, it has been certain of the "behavioral" therapists who have been most explicit with their patients (e.g., Wolpe, 1958), this despite contentions of some (e.g., Rogers, 1955; Jourard, 1959) that behavioristic approaches to therapy are manipulative and dangerous. Patients to be treated by desensitization are often given a definite rationale for the occurrence of the disorder as well as for the treatment to be employed. In effect, such patients are given a relevant, if brief, theory concerning the origins of their symptoms and a description of the treatment that is to ensue. The provision of that information produces a cognitive structure by means of which the patient can organize his experiences in therapy. Although we cannot show that the preliminary tactics of the desensitization therapist have any bearing on the outcome of treatment, the very favorable results reported (e.g., Paul, 1964; Wolpe, 1961) may reflect, in part, the advantages that may be obtained by providing better structure. Cassell's (1965) work in puppet therapy may also be viewed as having provided the children with prior structure concerning the trauma they were to experience.

For whatever reasons, few therapists would seem to be anywhere near as explicit as the behavior therapists, either about the theories they hold or about the techniques they employ. But it is unclear whether patients are kept uninformed because (1) it is not believed that informing them would be of any value, (2) desirable results are obtained only when the learning is by self-discovery, or (3) it is believed that the value of the technique and treatment would be impaired by the knowledge of the patient. We would call into question the second assumption and refer the reader to the cogent arguments and data given by Ausubel (1963) in refutation of the idea that really meaningful learning must come through self-discovery. We also note that all therapists who interpret the expressions of their patients are intervening in the learning process so that at most only the pacing of learning would be at issue.

It is more difficult to determine the legitimacy of the objection that making explicit the theories of therapy would undermine the effectiveness of the techniques used. It was noted in Chapter 4 that resistance to manipulation increases when the manipulative attempts are explicit. We would suggest, however, that there are many varieties of manipulation, and not all explicit manipulations fail. For example, it now appears that susceptibility to verbal conditioning is a direct function of awareness (Farber, 1963; Spielberger, 1962). Moreover, it has long been noted that the verbal conditioning paradigm is an inefficient way to increase probabilities of emission of various word classes. Simply telling people what is wanted is faster (Bandura, 1962). Kanfer and Marston (1961) showed that in a verbal conditioning situation both speed of acquisition and transfer are enhanced by clear instructions about the situation (e.g., telling Ss that their task was to get as many "points" as possible). We suspect that explicit manipulative attempts are likely to fail when they are viewed as irrational or arbitrary by the subject, when they involve some suggestion of challenge or competition, or when they are apparently asymmetrical in outcome in favor of the manipulator. A critical variable is the rationale or manner of presentation of the manipulative attempt.

For example, "reflection of feeling" as a technique in therapy is assuredly manipulative and intended to have some purpose. Even Rogers has admitted that all psychotherapists are in the business of influencing and controlling behavior (Rogers & Skinner, 1956). If patients were baldly informed that the therapist hoped, by using such a technique, to "manipulate" them in some manner, they might well have their resistance aroused. However, if the therapist told them truthfully that by reflecting the feelings, rather than the content, of the patients' statements he hoped to help them come to a better understanding of their feelings and themselves, it seems much less likely that any resistance at all would be aroused. Whether such a straightforward statement would decrease the effectiveness of reflection as a technique (assuming it has some) is an empirical matter. We suggest that it might actually increase the impact of reflection on the patient. For one thing, it might obviate some of the resistance that is aroused when the therapist reflects and the patient has no idea what he is doing. We suppose it quite possible that providing some prior understanding of the reason for the technique (i.e., some structure), would enhance it.

But we need not remain at the level of specific techniques. Patients might, for example, be informed about the theoretical basis for client-centered therapy as well as about the techniques. They might read Rogers' works or those of other proponents. Undoubtedly many psychoanalytic patients read a good bit in the field. We know of no pertinent evidence, but it is our informed guess that most therapists of most schools would be quite reluctant to inform their patients fully or have them informed by other means of the nature of and the theoretical basis for psychotherapy. Attempts by a patient to get information, at least in the therapy session, are often considered a manifestation of resistance, and extratherapy interest, as shown in reading, is thought to be "intellectualizing." Wolberg (1954), for example, in comparing various therapeutic approaches, states that adjunctive reading is never used in psychoanalytic insight therapy and even advises explicitly against it.

Probably a good bit of the "resistance" of psychotherapists to informing patients about psychotherapy theory and practice stems from the conviction that therapy would not work if the patient really understood it, at least in the beginning. In general, psychotherapy theorists place great emphasis, often implicitly, on learning carried on at a low level of awareness (e.g., see Fromm-Reichmann, 1950; Holland, 1965). This is another instance of the extensive divorcement of psychotherapy and psychology, for research clearly indicates that if learning without awareness exists it is slow and uncertain in comparison to learning taking place under conditions of high awareness (Farber, 1963). (The high level of awareness of the learning may be another factor accounting for the generally favorable results cited for desensitization therapies.) Thus we have therapists struggling along trying to convince their patients that they accept them, no matter what, but quite unwilling simply to say so. How odd we would consider a suitor who behaved in the same way! Note that we are not arguing that words are enough, any more than Ausubel would argue that the organizer is enough. Indeed, they are not. Many a young man has professed love before he felt it and before it would be truly credible. But, *in the light of structure provided by words,* actions take on a clarity and meaning that they do not otherwise possess.

There are examples, in addition to those provided by desensitization therapy, of the provision of advance organizing structure in psychotherapy. Most therapists would undoubtedly endorse the principle of communicating something about the nature of psychotherapy to patients. We go further by recommending that as much information as possible be given rather than as little as the therapist can get by with. Wolberg (1954) discusses structuring in several places in his large volume and, among other things, gets into questions of explaining the manner of communication in therapy, the general routine in therapy, the patient's responsibilities in psychotherapy, the role of the psychotherapist, and so on. He even indicates that it may be necessary (we believe it is certainly necessary) to explain how psychotherapy works and makes the interesting suggestion that the patient be given an illustrative case history to show how it has helped in other cases. However, he seems to think that only as much structuring as is forced on the therapist is desirable and makes specific recommendations only with respect to the poorly motivated or otherwise ill-prepared patient.

Fromm-Reichmann (1950) indicates that she thinks structuring should be quite limited, although she may give a patient what amounts to a rationale for psychotherapy (i.e., an explanation of what is to happen). She also indicates that structuring depends on the characteristics of the patient with the implication that it will be necessary primarily for the poorer candidates. Holland (1965), although stating that "Every patient has a right to know what the 'rules of the game' are, and no psychotherapist has the right to assume that he knows" (p. 242), adds that instructions regarding therapy are especially important with the young, less intelligent, naïve, uneducated person. We suggest that all evidence from other fields, for example, learning and education, shows uniformly that the training procedures which benefit the poor student benefit the good student even more. Analogously, we suggest that if structuring is good for the poor therapy prospect it is likely to be even better for the good one.

One of the more explicit writers about the nature and purpose of structuring in therapy is Rotter (1954), who describes the process of "successive structuring." He notes that structuring refers to all discussions about therapy and concerns the purposes, goals, plans, roles and responsibilities occurring in therapy. One of the purposes of structuring is to get the patient "to attend to, react to, or concern himself with the 'right' things in therapy" (p. 352). This statement is quite consistent with an important part of our position. Rotter does not believe that structuring is something that can and should be done once and for all in the beginning of therapy, a point on which most other therapists would concur (e.g., Holland, 1965); he suggests that structuring must occur repeatedly, that is, successively, during therapy, a position with which we would agree. We believe, in addition, that the effectiveness and efficiency of therapy may be improved by more and better initial structuring than is now usually the practice.

Hoehn-Saric et al. (1964) have explored the use of procedures quite similar to our recommendations. They developed a "role induction interview" designed to arouse realistic expectations of improvement, explain the therapist's behavior, tell the patient how he is expected to behave, and show him how to recognize and overcome resistance. The sample consisted of 40 neurotics, who had applied for outpatient treatment, divided into experimental and control groups. The therapists were psychiatric residents who were unaware of the nature of the study. The experimental patients proved to be higher on the therapy behavior scale after the third interview, had better attendance over the therapy period, and were rated better in "relationship" by their therapists. In addition, they scored higher on several outcome measures and showed significantly greater improvement in target symptoms. The rather deliberate and somewhat unusual structuring done in this experiment was of obvious benefit and points to the need for immediate and intensive study of similar advance organizers.

Exactly what should be done to provide "advance organizers" for psychotherapy is difficult to say at this point. We do not know of any readily available material and are not committed to one form of material. However, with an eye toward increasing the efficiency of therapy, we are inclined to suggest the use of written and tape-recorded material rather than having the therapist spend his time covering the same ground. Bibliotherapy, has usually had the form of stimulating reading to provide a focus for discussion in therapy or of reading of the "self-help" variety. We would like to see material made available for the specific purpose of preparing the prospective patient for psychotherapy by presenting a theory relevant to his disorder, a rationale for the treatment, and a description of the treatment to follow. Specific materials, such as case histories (Wolberg, 1954), might be very useful in making various important points concrete. We think it of great interest that Wolberg has stated that resistance to working with dreams in psychotherapy is sometimes alleviated by reading books that present a rationale of dream interpretation. A test and extension of his suggestion is clearly called for. Wolberg also gives an "outline of therapy" which presents the objectives, tasks, and processes of the various stages of therapy that may well provide a basis for the production of material essential to the specific purposes we have in mind.

SOME FURTHER POSSIBLE APPLICATIONS OF RESEARCH ON LEARNING TO PSYCHOTHERAPY

Obviously we have far from exhausted the field of learning as a source of hypotheses about psychotherapy. In fact, we have only scratched the surface a little around the general issue of transfer of training. There are many other areas of learning research that may be equally or even more fruitfully explored, and we would like, before concluding this chapter, to give a few examples of research that may be exploited in the service of improving psychotherapy. As in our other hypotheses, we offer the following suggestions in a heuristic rather than a dogmatic spirit. They are meant to illustrate the kind of thinking and analysis we would like to see take place more often, but we are sure that most readers will be able to develop more, and hopefully better, hypotheses of their own.

One of the recurrent problems in treatment of many patients is the overgeneralized response (e.g., the generalization of experience with an abusive father to the conclusion that "Men are no damn good"). The task of therapy is, then, to develop a discrimination among men as stimulus figures. Discrimination learning is a field with a considerable theoretical and empirical history in psychology, and there is a great deal of research that may be explored for ideas about ways in which discriminations can be effectively and efficiently taught. A perusal of Brogden's (1951) discussion of discrimination learning in animals might suggest any number of testable hypotheses having important implications for psychotherapy; for example, that discriminations will be acquired faster when responses to the stimuli are dissimilar. Thus discriminations among people may be acquired more rapidly if the individual employs one trait or dimension to describe one person and a very different dimension to describe others from whom the discrimination is to take place.

The area of concept attainment also may be an important source of hypotheses about psychotherapy. A great deal of what goes on in psychotherapy may be viewed from the perspective of concept learning; for example, the patient is expected to "learn" the concept of "resistance," whether the learning takes place before therapy as an advance organizer or during the course of therapy. Many aspects of research on concept attainment, then, are relevant to psychotherapy. We may begin with the effectiveness of positive and negative instances of concepts in concept attainment; that is, whether a given event is or is not a member of the category involved. Early work (Smoke, 1933) showed that people do not find the negative information that a given event is *not* a member of the concept category as useful as the positive information that it *is* an exemplar of the concept. It has since been shown that whether negative information is poorer than positive information depends on the type of concept problem involved (Hovland, 1952; Wallace & Sechrest, 1961). It has also been shown (Wallace & Sechrest, 1962) that under many conditions people may have serious difficulties in utilizing information they are given. This suggests the desirability of considerable guidance and cueing in learning. One of the most powerful determinants of difficulty for common concepts has been shown to be the number of irrelevant dimensions (Archer, Bourne, & Brown, 1955). From such a finding we can conclude that concept attainment will be faster when irrelevant factors are reduced to a minimum. Understanding of some of the difficult problems in psychotherapy might be advanced by analysis of and extrapolation from research in concept attainment.

The scheduling of learning in psychotherapy may not appear to be much of a problem, for so little deliberate planning for psychotherapy ever takes place. Nonetheless, it seems to us that there are persuasive reasons for supposing that some times are better than others for the introduction of particular topics and that a certain amount of planning for the sequence of events in therapy would not be amiss. We are inevitably reminded here of the problems of curriculum planning in education. There are many factors that might be related to scheduling of various kinds of therapeutic experience, but we would like merely to point here to the possible relevance of the Hull-Spence concept of "drive" and its effects on learning. Essentially, the Hull-Spence theory (Spence, 1956) of a multiplicative relation between drive and habit strength can be used to predict that under conditions of relatively high anxiety simple tasks will be acquired with relative speed, whereas low anxiety is more conducive to complex kinds of learning, learning in which there are many competing responses. We shall not detail the evidence that has been amassed in favor of the hypothesis as stated, but it is extensive. We should like to point to one recent study (Nakamura & Broen, 1965) in which a very low drive state was induced by means of a simple modification of progressive relaxation training and in which it was shown that competing, nondominant responses were facilitated. These findings, along with those of others, show clearly that the concept of drive is relevant to learning and to the scheduling of particular kinds of learning. For one thing, they suggest that in the earliest stages of therapy, when patients are presumably most anxious, or at any other time when there is a recrudescence of anxiety, the complexity of the therapeutic task should be reduced. Only relatively simple learning should be attempted. The subtler points of therapeutic learning should be saved for sessions in which anxiety is low.

Incentive is another factor of great importance in determining the performance of a response. Large incentives have a different effect from small incentives. For example, Hill and his associates (Hill, Cotton, & Clayton, 1962; Hill & Spear, 1962) have found that a large incentive produces faster acquisition of a habit and faster reversal when the large incentive is associated with the reversal rather than the original habit. Moreover, a larger incentive is also associated with greater resistance to extinction. Such findings have an obvious relevance to some aspects of psychotherapy. What may be of even greater importance in psychotherapy than absolute magnitude of incentive is relative magnitude of incentive resulting from shifts in incentive level from one situation to another. Crespi (1942) has reported "depression" and "elation" effects when incentive magnitude shifts upward or downward from the expected level. Thus, if subjects have been accustomed to a large incentive and are switched to a small one, their performance may drop below the level that would obtain had they been receiving a small incentive all along. Similarly, if they have been receiving a small incentive and are suddenly shifted to a large one, their performance may "overshoot" the level of subjects accustomed to the large incentive. Merely to point to one possible implication of Crespi's findings for psychotherapy, we wonder whether the general level of incentive for behavior during treatment is consistent with the level to be expected in extratherapy situations. If the incentives are considerably larger in the treatment situation, say, in terms of the amount of social approval gained, then when the patient is shifted to the smaller incentive obtaining outside treatment, where "normal" behavior is expected and is met with indifference, a "depression" effect may occur. Perhaps in a treatment center patients should be maintained on the smallest incentives consistent with the occurrence of desirable behaviors so that, if anything, extratherapy incentives will seem reasonable by comparison.

Finally, we should like to suggest that an important factor in the occurrence and maintenance of any response with complex outcomes is the scheduling in time of positive and negative reinforcements. It has been well established that a delay in the occurrence of any reinforcement seriously impairs its effectiveness (Renner, 1964). Mowrer and Ullman (1945) attempted to account for the so-called "neurotic paradox" in terms of the immediate positive reinforcement (anxiety reduction) but delayed negative reinforcement (punishment) of neurotic responses. They suggested that when the negative consequences of a response are long delayed, though the positive ones are immediate, the response is likely to persist. On the other hand, Renner (1964) concludes that relatively long periods of delay may be bridged by verbal or other mediating responses. We believe that there are important implications for psychotherapy in research on delay of reinforcement and in ways of altering reinforcement gradients.

With these few examples we conclude our discussion of the ways in which basic psychological research in the general area of learning may be exploited for the benefit of research in psychotherapy. We trust that the interested reader will be able to generate many additional hypotheses for himself.

REFERENCES

Archer, E. J., Bourne, L. E. & Brown, F. C.   Concept identification as a function of irrelevant information and instructions. *J. exp. Psychol.*, 1955, **49**, 153–164.

Ausubel, D. P.   The use of advance organizers in the learning and retention of meaningful verbal material. *J. educ. Psychol.*, 1960, **51**, 267–272.

Ausubel, D. P.   *The psychology of meaningful verbal learning.* New York: Grune & Stratton, 1963.

Ausubel, D. P., & Blake, E.   Proactive inhibition in the forgetting of meaningful school material. *J. educ. Psychol.*, 1958, **52**, 145–149.

Ausubel, D. P., & Fitzgerald, D.   The role of discriminability in meaningful verbal learning and retention. *J. educ. Psychol.*, 1961, **52**, 266–274.

Ausubel, D. P., & Fitzgerald, D.   Organizer, general background, and antecedent learning variables in sequential verbal learning. *J. educ. Psychol.*, 1962, **53**, 243–249.

Ayllon, T., & Azrin, N. H.   Reinforcement and instructions with mental patients. *J. exp. anal. Behav.*, 1964, **7**, 327–331.

Ayllon, T., & Haughton, E.   Control of the behavior of schizophrenic patients by food. *J. exp. anal. Behav.*, 1962, **5**, 343–352.

Ayllon, T., & Michael, J.   The psychiatric nurse as a behavioral engineer. *J. exp. anal. Behav.*, 1959, **2**, 323–334.

Bandura, A.   Social learning through imitation. In M. R. Jones (Ed.), *Nebraska symposium on motivation.* Lincoln: Univer. of Nebraska Press, 1962. Pp. 211–268.

Breger, L., & McGaugh, J. L.   Critique and reformulation of "learning-theory" approaches to psychotherapy and neurosis. *Psychol. Bull.*, 1965, **63**, 338–358.

Brogden, W. J.   Animal studies of learning. In S. S. Stevens (Ed.), *Handbook of experimental psychology.* New York: John Wiley, 1951. Pp. 568–612.

Bruce, R. W.   Conditions of transfer of training. *J. exp. Psychol.*, 1933, **16**, 343–361.

Bruner, J. S.   *The process of education.* Cambridge: Harvard Univer. Press, 1960.

Bugelski, B. R.   *The psychology of learning.* New York: Holt, 1956.

Callantine, M. F., & Warren, J. M.   Learning sets in human concept formation. *Psychol. Repts.*, 1955, **1**, 363–367.

Cameron, N., & Magaret, A.   *Behavior pathology.* Boston: Houghton-Mifflin, 1951.

Cassell, S. Effect of brief puppet therapy upon the emotional responses of children undergoing cardiac catheterization. *J. consult. Psychol.,* 1965, **29** 1–8.

Caudill, W. Observations on the cultural context of Japanese psychiatry. In M. K. Opler (Ed.), *Culture and mental health.* New York: Macmillan, 1959. Pp. 213–242.

Crespi, L. P. Quantitative variation of incentive and performance in the white rat. *Amer. J. Psychol.,* 1942, **55,** 467–517.

Deese, J. *The psychology of learning.* (2nd ed.) New York: McGraw-Hill, 1958.

Deese, J., & Hardman, G. W., Jr. An analysis of errors in retroactive inhibition of rote verbal learning. *Amer. J. Psychol.,* 1954, **67,** 299–307.

Dollard, J., & Miller, N. E. *Personality and psychotherapy.* New York: McGraw-Hill, 1950.

Duncan, C. P. Transfer after training with single versus multiple tasks. *J. exp. Psychol.,* 1958, **55,** 63–72.

Duncan, C. P. Recent research on human problem solving. *Psychol. Bull.,* 1959, **56,** 397–429.

Ellis, H. *The transfer of learning.* New York: Macmillan, 1965.

Farber, I. E. The things people say to themselves. *Amer. Psychologist,* 1963, **18,** 185–197.

Ford, D. H., & Urban, H. B. *Systems of psychotherapy.* New York: Wiley, 1963.

Forgus, R. H. The effect of early perceptual learning on the behavioral organization of adult rats. *J. compar. physiol. Psychol.,* 1954, **47,** 331–336.

Forgus, R. H. Early visual and motor experience as determiners of complex maze learning ability under rich and reduced stimulation. *J. compar. physiol. Psychol.,* 1955, **48,** 215–220.

Frank, J. D. *Persuasion and healing.* Baltimore: Johns Hopkins Press, 1961.

Fromm–Reichmann, F. *Principles of intensive psychotherapy.* Chicago: Univer. of Chicago Press, 1950.

Gagne, R. M., & Baker, K. E. Stimulus pre-differentiation as a factor in transfer of training. *J. exp. Psychol.,* 1950, **40,** 439–451.

Gagne, R. M., & Foster, H. Transfer of training from practice on components in a motor skill. *J. exp. Psychol.,* 1949, **39,** 47–68.

Goldbeck, R. A., Bernstein, B. B., Hillix, W. A., & Marx, M. H. Application of the half-split technique to problem-solving tasks. *J. exp. Psychol.,* 1957, **53,** 330–338.

Harlow, H. F. The formation of learning sets. *Psychol. Rev.,* 1949, **56,** 51–65.

Harlow, H. F. Learning set and error factor theory. In S. Koch (Ed.), *Psychology: a study of a science.* Vol. 2. New York: McGraw-Hill, 1959. Pp. 492–537.

Hendrickson, G., & Schroeder, W. H. Transfer of training in learning to hit a submerged target. *J. educ. Psychol.,* 1941, **32,** 205–213.

Hill, W. F., Cotton, J. W., & Clayton, K. N. Effect of reward magnitude, percentage of reinforcement, and training method on acquisition and reversal in a T maze. *J. exp. Psychol.,* 1962, **64**, 81–86.

Hill, W. F., & Spear, N. E. Resistance to extinction as a joint function of reward magnitude and the spacing of extinction trials. *J. exp. Psychol.,* 1962, **64**, 636–639.

Hoehn-Saric, R., Frank, J. D., Imber, S. D., Nash, E. H., Stone, A. R., & Battle, C. C. Systematic preparation of patients for psychotherapy. I. Effects on therapy behavior and outcome. *J. psychiat. Res.,* 1964, **2**, 267–281.

Holland, G. A. *Fundamentals of psychotherapy.* New York: Holt, Rinehart, & Winston, 1965.

Holmes, D. S. Round-robin therapy. Unpublished manuscript, Northwestern University, 1965.

Hovland, C. I. The generalization of conditioned responses: IV. The effects of varying amounts of reinforcement upon the degree of generalization of conditioned responses. *J. exp. Psychol.,* 1937, **21**, 261–276.

Hovland, C. I. A communication analysis of concept learning. *Psychol. Rev.,* 1952, **59**, 461–472.

Hovland, C. I., & Kurtz, K. H. Experimental studies in rote-learning theory: X. Pre-learning syllable familiarization and the length-difficulty relationship. *J. exp. Psychol.,* 1952, **44**, 31–39.

Hsu, J. J. Electro-conditioning treatment for alcoholics. *Quart. J. Stud. Alc.,* 1965, **26**, 449–459.

Hunt, E. B. *Concept learning.* New York: John Wiley, 1962.

Hurder, W. P. European mental health programs as viewed by mental health specialists and legislators. Atlanta: Southern Regional Education Board, 1961.

Jones, M. C. A laboratory study of fear: the case of Peter. In H. J. Eysenck (Ed.), *Behavior therapy and the neuroses.* New York: Pergamon Press, 1960. Pp. 45–51.

Jones, N. F., Kahn, M. W., & Wolcott, O. Wearing of street clothing by mental hospital personnel. *Int. J. soc. Psychiat.,* 1964, **10**, 216–222.

Jourard, S. I-thou relationship versus manipulation in counseling and psychotherapy. *J. indiv. Psychol.,* 1959, **15**, 174–179.

Judd, C. H. Practice and its effects on the perception of illusions. *Psychol. Rev.,* 1902, **9**, 27–39.

Kanfer, F. H., & Marston, A. R. Verbal conditioning, ambiguity, and psychotherapy. *Psychol. Repts.,* 1961, **9**, 461–475.

Kelly, G. A. *The psychology of personal constructs.* New York: W. W. Norton, 1955.

Kendler, H. H., & Karasik, A. D. Concept formation as a function of competition between response produced cues. *J. exp. Psychol.,* 1958, **55**, 278–283.

Krasner, L. The therapist as a social reinforcement machine. In H. H.

Strupp & L. Luborsky (Eds.), *Research in psychotherapy*. Washington: Amer. Psychol. Assoc., 1962. Pp. 61–94.

Krasner, L., & Ullman, L. P. (Eds.) *Research in behavior modification*. New York: Holt, Rinehart & Winston, 1965.

Kushner, M. The reduction of a long-standing fetish by means of aversive conditioning. In L. P. Ullman & L. Krasner (Eds.), *Case studies in behavior modification*. New York: Holt, Rinehart & Winston, 1965. Pp. 231–238.

Lang, P. J., & Lazovik, A. D. Experimental desensitization of a phobia. *J. abnorm. soc. Psychol.*, 1963, **66**, 519–525.

Lawson, R. *Learning and behavior*. New York: Macmillan, 1960.

Lazarus, A. A. The elimination of children's phobias by deconditioning. In H. J. Eysenck (Ed.), *Behavior therapy and the neuroses*. New York: Pergamon Press, 1960. Pp. 114–122.

Lennard, H. L., & Bernstein, A. *The anatomy of psychotherapy*. New York: Columbia Univer. Press, 1960.

Lipkin, S. Twenty therapists: twenty interviews. Presented at Amer. Psychol. Assoc., Chicago, 1965.

McGuire, R. J., & Vallance, M. Aversion therapy by electric shock: a simple technique. In C. M. Franks (Ed.), *Conditioning techniques in clinical practice and research*. New York: Springer, 1964. Pp. 178–188.

Meyer, V., & Crisp, A. H. Aversion therapy in two cases of obesity. *Behav. res. Ther.*, 1964, **2**, 143–148.

Miller, E. C., Dvorak, B. A., & Turner, D. W. A method of creating aversion to alcohol by reflex conditioning in a group setting. In C. M. Franks (Ed.), *Conditioning techniques in clinical practice and research*. New York: Springer, 1964. Pp. 157–164.

Miller, G. A., Heise, G. A., & Lichten, W. The intelligibility of speech as a function of the test materials. *J. exp. Psychol.*, 1951, **41**, 329–335.

Mintz, E. Transference in co-therapy groups. *J. consult. Psychol.*, 1963, **27**, 34–39.

Mowrer, O. H., & Ullman, A. D. Time as a determinant in integrative learning. *Psychol. Rev.*, 1945, **52**, 61–90.

Mullan, H., & Sanguiliano, I. Multiple psychotherapeutic practice: preliminary report. *Amer. J. Psychother.*, 1960, **14**, 550–565.

Murphy, I. C. Extinction of an incapacitating fear of earthworms. *J. clin. Psychol.*, 1964, **20**, 396–398.

Nakamura, C. Y., & Broen, W. E. Further study of effects of low drive states on competing responses. *J. exp. Psychol.*, 1965, **70**, 434–436.

Osgood, C. E. The similarity paradox in human learning: a resolution. *Psychol. Rev.*, 1949, **56**, 132–143.

Osgood, C. E. *Method and theory in experimental psychology*. New York: Oxford Univer. Press, 1953.

Paul, G. L.   Effects of insight, desensitization, and attention-placebo treatment of anxiety: an approach to outcome research in psychotherapy. Unpublished doctoral dissertation, University of Illinois, 1964.

Prokasy, W. F., & Hall, J. F. Primary stimulus generalization. *Psychol. Rev.*, 1963, **70**, 310–322.

Rachman, S.   The treatment of anxiety and phobic reactions by systematic desensitization psychotherapy. *J. abnorm. soc. Psychol.*, 1959, **58**, 259–263.

Razran, G.H.S.   A quantitative study of meaning by a conditioned salivary technique (semantic conditioning). *Science*, 1939, **90**, 89–90.

Renner, K. E.   Delay of reinforcement: a historical review. *Psychol. Bull.*, 1964, **61**, 341–361.

Rogers, C. R.   Persons or science: a philosophical question. *Amer. Psychologist*, 1955, **10**, 267–278.

Rogers, C. R., & Skinner, B. F.   Some issues concerning the control of human behavior: a symposium. *Science*, 1956, **124**, 1057–1066.

Rotter, J. B.   *Social learning and clinical psychology.* New York: Prentice-Hall, 1954.

Rudolf, G. de M.   Deconditioning and time-therapy. *J. ment. Sci.*, 1961, **107**, 1097–1101.

Ruesch, J.   *Disturbed communication.* New York: W. W. Norton, 1957.

Sanderson, R. E., Campbell, D., & Laverty, S. G.   An investigation of a new aversive conditioning treatment for alcoholics. In C. M. Franks (Ed.), *Conditioning techniques in clinical practice and research.* New York: Springer, 1964. Pp. 155–177.

Schachter, S., & Singer, J. E.   Cognitive, social and physiological determinants of emotional state. *Psychol. Rev.*, 1962, **69**, 379–399.

Schulz, R. W.   Problem solving behavior and transfer. *Harv. educ. Rev.*, 1960, **30**, 1, 61–77.

Sechrest, L.   Stimulus equivalents of the psychotherapist. *J. indiv. Psychol.*, 1962, **18**, 172–176.

Shore, E., & Sechrest, L.   Concept attainment as a function of number of positive instances presented. *J. educ. Psychol.*, 1961, **52**, 303–307.

Smoke, K. L.   Negative instances in concept learning. *J. exp. Psychol.*, 1933, **16**, 583–588.

Spence, K. W.   *Behavior theory and conditioning.* New Haven: Yale Univer. Press, 1956.

Spielberger, C. D.   The role of awareness in verbal conditioning. In C. W. Eriksen (Ed.), *Behavior and awareness—a symposium of research and interpretation.* Durham, N.C.: Duke Univer. Press, 1962. Pp. 73–101.

Stevenson, I.   The use of rewards and punishments in psychotherapy. *Comprehen. Psychiat.*, 1962, **3**, 20–28.

Stürup, G. K.   The treatment of chronic criminals. Presented at Menninger Foundation. Unpublished mimeo, 1964.

Thorpe, J. G., Schmidt, E., Brown, P. T., & Castell, D.   Aversion-relief therapy: a new method for general application. *Behav. res. Ther.*, 1964, 2, 71–82.

Travers, R. M. W.   *Essentials of learning: an overview for students of education.* New York: Macmillan, 1963.

Ullman, L. P., & Krasner, L. (Eds.)   *Case studies in behavior modification.* New York: Holt, Rinehart & Winston, 1965.

Ulmer, G.   Teaching geometry to cultivate reflective thinking: an experimental study with 1239 high school pupils. *J. exp. Educ.*, 1939, 8, 18–25.

Underwood, B. J., & Schulz, R. W.   *Meaningfulness and verbal learning.* New York: Lippincott, 1960.

Wallace, J., & Sechrest, L.   Relative difficulty of conjunctive and disjunctive concepts. *J. psychol. Stud.*, 1961, 12, 97–104.

Wallace, J., & Sechrest, L.   Assimilation and utilization of information in concept attainment under varying conditions of information presentation. *J. educ. Psychol.*, 1962, 53, 157–164.

Walton, D., & Mather, M. D.   The relevance of generalization techniques to the treatment of stammering and phobic symptoms. *Behav. res. Ther.*, 1963, 1, 121–125.

Whitaker, C. A., Malone, T. P., & Warkentin, J.   Multiple therapy and psychotherapy. In F. Fromm-Reichmann & M. Moreno (Eds.), *Progress in psychotherapy.* New York: Grune & Stratton, 1956. Pp. 210–216.

Wolberg, L. R.   *The technique of psychotherapy.* New York: Grune & Stratton, 1954.

Wolpe, J.   Reciprocal inhibition as the main basis of psychotherapeutic effects. *Arch. neurol. Psychiat.*, 1954, 72, 205–226.

Wolpe, J.   *Psychotherapy by reciprocal inhibition.* Stanford: Stanford Univer. Press, 1958.

Wolpe, J.   The systematic desensitization treatment of neuroses. *J. ner. ment. Dis.*, 1961, 132, 189–203.

Woodrow, H.   The effect of type of training upon transference. *J. educ. Psychol.*, 1927, 18, 159–172.

Woodworth, R. S., & Schlosberg, H.   *Experimental psychology.* New York: Holt, 1954.

Young, R. K., & Underwood, B. J.   Transfer in verbal materials with dissimilar stimuli and response similarity varied. *J. exp. Psychol.*, 1954, 47, 153–159.

6

FURTHER EXTRAPOLATIONS—
INDIVIDUAL THERAPY

Relationship, resistance, and therapeutic learning, three central dimensions of psychotherapy, have been examined and three sets of extrapolatory hypotheses have been proposed. They serve, it is hoped, as a start at illustrating the varied and potentially important ways in which nonclinical research findings may lead to more effective means of altering patient behavior. However, beyond these three dimensions of psychotherapy, there still remain a large number of ways in which current therapeutic practice and theory stand in need of major change. As this chapter demonstrates, much therapeutic inefficiency and "excess therapeutic baggage" has grounds for alteration or elimination in nonclinical behavior change research.

From the large number of possible hypotheses includable in a chapter such as this, we have chosen to present and develop four. These final attempts to extrapolate to individual psychotherapy were chosen primarily for illustrative purposes; that is, in addition to whatever these hypotheses may eventually offer the practitioner, we seek to provide the reader with a broader flavor of the range of behavior change research potentially usable by the investigator of psychotherapy. The hypotheses which follow, although very different from one another in the antecedent materials from which they grow and in the consequent changes in therapeutic practice toward which they point, are tied together with the thread of our common theme—the basic unity of psychotherapeutic and nonclinical attempts at behavior change.

VICARIOUS LEARNING ON THE WAITING LIST

In a large proportion of clinical settings the candidate for psychotherapy, after having cleared the hurdles associated with admission to candidacy, is placed on a waiting list. There he may stay for as brief a period as a few days or, more likely, several weeks or months. Perhaps more than any other time period in the interval from candidacy to therapy termination, the patient's stay on a waiting list provides an excellent and unexplored opportunity for instituting procedures which may accelerate behavior change. With extremely few exceptions, waiting list time is "do nothing" time, at least as far as *formal* psychotherapeutic interventions are concerned. Of course, if one feels bound by traditional therapeutic practices, if one feels that any interventions that take place must be conducted by the therapist, waiting-list time is destined to remain "do nothing" time, in any formal sense. On the other hand, evidence now exists that patients do change while on a waiting list, and that at least a portion of this change is attributable to the interventions of the treatment staff—interventions *not* intended to be therapeutic. For example, in an investigation of "unspontaneous remission" in psychotherapy Goldstein (1962) has demonstrated that patient consultations—with an intake interviewer, psychological tester, or other sequentially pretherapist member of the treatment staff—function as a sort of nonspecific therapy which has symptom reduction consequences. It appears that the interest and attention inherent in such consultative interventions is perceived by patients as treatment, to which they respond. Barron and Leary (1955) and Dymond (1954) provide corroborative evidence for this effect. If it is true that patient change occurs at the hands of members of the treatment staff other than the patient's eventual therapist *when no such change is deliberately being attempted,* it should be clear that purposeful, planned use of patient waiting-list time has substantially greater potential for bringing about patient change or, at minimum, "priming" him so that his therapy can proceed more rapidly and effectively when it does start. It is to just such a usage of patient waiting-list time that hypothesis 6.1 refers.

HYPOTHESIS 6.1: **Pretherapy vicarious learning opportunities provided to waiting-list patients will lead to a "telescoping" in time of behavior change-inhibiting stages of subsequent psychotherapy.**

As one concrete expression of this hypothesis, we propose that patients awaiting the start of their formal psychotherapy be asked to come to the treatment center at regular intervals. Either individually or in groups, the patient would spend each pretherapy visit viewing movies or video tapes of selected real or fictitious psychotherapy sessions. In broadest terms, the purpose of such an experience would be to provide the patient with an opportunity to learn "vicariously" something about the nature of psychotherapy, about appropriate patient role behaviors and, perhaps, about his presenting problems and their basis—thus shortening the time needed to do so *during* psychotherapy. In addition to the basic issue of the therapeutic purposes such viewing sessions might serve, an issue to which we return in some detail, several subsidiary questions are immediately evident. What is to be the nature of such movies or tapes? Will they be in any way individualized for each patient-viewer or simply shown to heterogeneously grouped patients? Is simple viewing all that need be involved, or must companion procedures be instituted? Our development of this hypothesis and its clinical-research implementation will be responsive to queries such as these. Our first task, however, is an examination of the nonclinical research from which the hypothesis grows.

Investigations of Vicarious Learning

The basic phenomenon in which we are interested here is the learning which may occur by a given individual (observer) when he sees (1) another individual (model) behaving and, (2) the model is reinforced for his behavior. A surprisingly large number of different but overlapping terms have been used to describe this process and its variants. Miller and Dollard (1941), in their pioneering *Social Learning and Imitation,* describe three such related processes: same behavior, copying, and matched-dependent behavior. Mowrer (1960) has discussed empathetic learning; De Charms and Rosenbaum (1960) have reported research dealing with observational learning; Campbell (1961) has invoked a conformity explanation; Maccoby and Wilson (1957) have relied on an identification model; and Bandura and Walters (1963) have examined the behavior of interest here in terms of modeling effects, inhibitory and disinhibitory effects, and eliciting effects. Although it appears unnecessary for our present purposes to compare and contrast these overlapping concepts, our choice of vicarious learning as the process underlying hypothesis 6.1 calls for definition and explanation. A statement by De Charms and Rosenbaum (1960) is of immediate interest:

In order to set the boundaries of what is to be considered as vicarious-ness, criteria for inclusion or exclusion should be designated. As the principal criterion for inclusion, one can designate those modifications in an individ-ual's response system that occur as a function of observation of another's behavior without any direct response made by the observer to the same en-vironmental stimuli and in which the response of the other or "vicar" has the same or similar effect on the characteristics of the observer *as if* the observer had performed the response himself (p. 267).

Similarly, Berger (1961) comments,

Vicarious reinforcement is defined as a change in the strength of an ob-server's response following his exposure to the presentation of a reinforcing stimulus to a performer, in the absence of direct reinforcement of the ob-server (p. 477).

While imitation is a process different from vicarious learning, the behavioral consequences of the two processes are the same. With direct relevance to the purpose of hypothesis 6.1, Miller and Dollard (1941) have observed:

Imitation can hasten the process of learning by forcing the subject to respond correctly to the proper cue more quickly than he otherwise would. In this way, a preliminary phase of imitation or copying is often useful in teaching a subject to respond independently to the proper environmental cues (p. 203).

Bandura and Walters (1963), who have made what may be the major recent research contribution to this area of learning by observa-tion, similarly note,

. . . imitation is an indispensable aspect of learning. Even in cases where some other stimulus is known to be capable of arousing an approximation to the desired behavior, the process of acquisition can be considerably short-ened by the provision of social models (p. 3).

This basic vicarious learning phenomenon is demonstrated in a verbal conditioning study conducted by Kanfer and Marston (1963). Four experimental groups were constituted, and the task of subjects in all groups was to say words intermittently with a taped, simulated group. Members of one experimental group were given direct rein-forcement. That is, E said "good" directly to S following words to be conditioned. Members of a second group were provided vicarious re-inforcement. They heard E say "good" whenever a taped S gave a critical response. Members of the third experimental group received both direct and vicarious reinforcement, and the fourth group was given neither. Results clearly indicated that vicarious reinforcement facilitated learning to an extent that was not surpassed by direct reinforcement. McBrearty, Marston, and Kanfer (1961), in a second study by this research group, similarly demonstrated that the amount of learning evidenced by observers given vicarious reinforcement can be as great as that shown by performers given direct reinforcement.

Concurring results emerge from a series of investigations reported by Berger (1961). In one of his studies, for example, subjects were told they were participating in an investigation of ESP. Some subjects were models (Sm), their task being to guess the number, from one to ten, that E had paired with a series of nonsense syllables which would be read to each subject. Other subjects served as observers (So), and their assigned task was to read the nonsense syllables to the Sm's. During the syllable reading E supposedly indicated whether a (number) response was "right" or "wrong," although he actually sought to reinforce certain syllables. After five presentations of the list, both model and observer subjects were asked to write down all the syllables they could recall. An examination of the number of syllables recalled according to the reinforcing stimulus with which they were associated revealed a significant degree of vicarious incidental learning by the Sos. In fact, the effect on syllable learning of E saying "right" or "wrong" to Sms' numerical responses was significantly greater for Sos than for the Sms themselves. Berger's (1961) subsequent research provides essential confirmation of these findings, as does a study reported by Lewis and Duncan (1958).

In short, as Bandura and Walters (1963) conclude from studies such as these,

> New responses may be learned or the characteristics of existing response hierarchies may be changed as a function of observing the behavior of others and its response consequences without the observer's performing any overt responses himself or receiving any direct reinforcement during the acquisition period (p. 47).

With these demonstrations of the occurrence of vicarious learning as our base, we shall further examine issues relevant to hypothesis 6.1. In the discussion that follows we are particularly interested in specific variables involved in the research implementation of this hypothesis. In addition, we shall draw on further vicarious learning research in an effort to identify factors that either augment or retard such acquisition.

Two particularly central issues are film content and specification of the patients for whom these procedures are intended.

Film Characteristics

In attempting to specify the desirable characteristics of what may be called "psychotherapeutic vicarious learning films," we find ourselves ill-equipped to detail features that may be considered "technical." Fortunately, information regarding such technical dimensions of learning films are available elsewhere; for example, May and Lumsdaine's *Learning from Films* (1958). There are, however, certain important requisites for such films that can be specified here. First, however, the question must be raised, "What is it we wish the patient to learn?" In a broad sense, there are two possible answers to this question. We may wish the patient to learn something vicariously from his viewing sessions which *all* patients must learn to enhance the possibility of successful and more rapid treatment, or we may intend the films to teach him something that only he and patients very similar to him need to learn. Thus we speak here of patient-general and patient-specific films.

As a hypothetical example, a patient-general film appropriate for viewing by all therapy patients might be titled, "What is Psychotherapy," or "The Patient Role in Psychotherapy." Such a film would have the potential to teach the patient-to-be what it means to be a patient, what his rights and obligations are, and how he and the therapist are expected to meet these rights and obligations; in short, what he can expect of treatment. Goldstein (1962) has elsewhere examined in detail the implications of therapist and patient expectancies regarding their own and each other's behavior. The implications of mutuality of such expectations for the length and outcome of treatment are very marked. For example, investigations reported by Chance (1959), Gliedman et al. (1958), Heine and Trosman (1960), and Lennard and Bernstein (1960), converge in the finding that incongruent or nonmutual therapist and patient expectancies regarding their respective role behaviors result in a poor therapeutic relationship, premature termination, and/or little patient change. Others (Hankoff, Englehardt, & Freedman, 1960; Riessman, 1963) have reported the same finding as it occurs in an outpatient clinic when the psychiatrist offers verbal-participatory, insight-oriented psychotherapy, and the "unstructured" patient expects to be ministered to, given advice, medication, and so forth. Hoehn-Saric et al. (1964) report a study in which half of all post-intake (but pretherapy) patients had a second "intake" interview devoted solely to structuring their therapy-relevant expectancies. Control patients did not participate in this Role Induction Interview. On a number of subsequent process and outcome criteria the structured patients performed better than the controls. Other studies have recognized the need for increasing the congruence of therapists' and patients' expectancies. Rotter (1954) has urged that "successive structuring" be incorporated into all therapeutic courses. Here the therapist and patient would periodically and repeatedly devote a portion of their time to a purposeful mutual attempt to share and understand their expectancies regarding their own and each other's behavior. Frank (1961), Goldstein (1962), Orne (1964), and Riessman (1963) have taken similar positions. If the purpose of the viewing sessions is to teach material of this "applicable-to-all" type, waiting-list patients can be grouped heterogeneously and view the films together. In such a procedure the specific nature of the movie patient's (model) problems assumes relatively little direct importance.

In contrast, in advance of the start of formal treatment one may wish to focus directly on the problems of the waiting-list patient. Let us assume for the moment that a review of the intake records constituting a hypothetical waiting list reveals six phobic patients among those waiting. Perhaps a film could be selected or developed for these patients, in which the symptomatology of the movie patient was phobic in nature. With proper film selection, and perhaps subsequent group discussion with a member of the clinic staff, such viewing could begin teaching the patient that others have problems highly similar to his, that the therapist is likely to respond to such psychopathology in a nonthreatening, change-encouraging manner, and so forth. There is, of course, no need to choose between these two types of films. Ideally, waiting-list patients will view *both* patient-general (e.g., structuring of expectancies) and patient-specific (e.g., the treatment of phobic reactions) films. At minimum, the vicarious learning that may follow from both types of film viewing can clearly save later therapeutic time for the patients, and provide more therapist time for patients who might otherwise not be seen.

A further aspect of film content is worth noting. Regardless of the general or specific orientation of a film, a number of features should be incorporated into the film to enhance the likelihood of vicarious learning taking place. One such augmenting film characteristic involves the response consequences to the film model. If the film model is rewarded for his behavior by the therapist or by someone else, is vicarious learning by the observer of that behavior more likely to occur? Several investigations have examined precisely this issue. In an investigation reported by Bandura, Ross, and Ross (1963b) children observed a film in which an adult (model) exhibited a series of aggressive behaviors. One group of observers then saw the model receive severe punishment. In a second group the model was generously rewarded with approval and food, and the third condition involved no response consequences to the model. As Bandura notes,

> During the acquisition period the children neither performed any overt responses nor received any direct reinforcement and, therefore, any learning that occurred was purely on an observational or vicarious basis (p. 57).

A postexposure test of imitative behavior revealed that the differential consequences to the model for his aggressive behavior led to differential amounts of imitative behavior by the observers. Children in the model-punished condition performed significantly fewer responses than children in both the model-rewarded and the no-consequence groups. Bandura, Ross, and Ross (1963c) report a successful replication of this investigation.

Walters, Leat, and Mezei (1963) report a concurring study. Kindergarten age subjects were assigned to one of three groups: (1) model-rewarded for deviation, (2) model-punished for deviation, and (3) a control group to whom no model was presented. All Ss were first shown a number of attractive toys with which they were forbidden to play. The model-rewarded group then saw a film in which a child was playing with the forbidden toys and was subsequently rewarded for doing so. In the model-punished group the child was scolded for playing with the toys. Following the movie viewing, children in all three groups were left with the toys for fifteen minutes, with nothing else to occupy their attention. Children who had seen the model rewarded played with the toys more readily and more often than children who had seen the model punished, and control children exhibited an intermediate amount of such "deviation."

In a similar manner research reported by Berger (1961) demonstrated that punishment meted out to a model in the presence of an observer can vicariously establish a conditioned fear response in the latter. Observers in one group were informed that the model they were viewing would receive a shock whenever a light dimmed. The dimming of the light was preceded on each trial by a buzzer. A second observer group was instructed that the model would make a voluntary arm movement whenever the light dimmed but that the model was receiving no aversive stimulation. The frequency of observers' GSRs to the buzzer was the measure of vicarious conditioning. As predicted, observers who viewed the model being "shocked" displayed vicariously conditioned emotional reactions to a significantly greater degree than observers treated otherwise.

Investigations such as these lead us to conclude, as have Bandura and Walters (1963):

> There is evidence, then, that social response patterns, both deviant and conforming, can be readily transmitted through the influence of a model and that imitation is facilitated if the model receives rewards. On the other hand, if the model is known to receive punishments, the observer may refrain from making novel deviant responses or even be restrained from performing deviant acts that he has already learned (p. 84).

It is clear, therefore, that vicarious learning by the observing waiting-list patient would be enhanced by reward provided the patient model in the film. Such reward may be provided by things said or done by the film therapist, by communications made by the film patient, or by "outcomes" described by a staff member leading a postviewing group discussion of a film.

In addition to whether or not the film model is rewarded for his behavior, there are several other considerations relevant to the model that influence the degree of vicarious learning by the observer. From the findings of a number of investigations in this area, Campbell (1961) has proposed the following generalizations:

1. The more similar a novel model is to observed past rewarded models, the greater the vicarious learning.
2. The more recently observed the model's behavior, the greater the vicarious learning.
3. The more numerous the model's modeling the same act, the greater the vicarious learning.
4. In the absence of observer knowledge about reward to the model in a given instance, the more previous reward the model has received, the greater the vicarious learning.

Observer Characteristics

In this section we examine the observer characteristics that are relevant for maximizing the occurrence of vicarious learning. Maccoby and Wilson (1957) report two investigations bearing on the matching of observer and film characteristics. Their general hypothesis was that the amount and kind of material that a viewer learns from a film is partly determined by his choice of the film character with whom he identifies. They anticipated that viewers would tend to identify with film characters similar to themselves in sex and social status. Movies in which more than one character were presented in favorable terms were shown to 25 classes of seventh-grade children. Using a measure of identification developed for the studies, the researchers found that viewers did in fact identify most frequently with like-sex film characters. With respect to similarity of social class, however, viewers strongly tended to identify with the character whose social class corresponded to the viewer's aspired social class, rather than his actual current status. Learning was measured in terms of memory of movie content. Viewers remembered best the behaviors and statements of the characters with whom they had identified. Other studies confirm these findings with regard both to sex (Bandura, Ross, & Ross, 1963a; Rosenblith, 1959; Rosenblith, 1961) and social status (Asch, 1948; Lefkowitz et al., 1955; Lippitt et al., 1952) of viewer and model. These findings hold a clear message for the selection or development of vicarious learning films for waiting-list patients. Descriptive information (e.g., sex, social class) about the viewing patients should influence film selection in the sense of determining with whom among the film characters we wish the viewer to identify, and from whom we wish him to learn. For example, all else being equal, a lower-middle-class female patient on the waiting list should be shown a movie in which the patient is also female, but of a higher socioeconomic level. This, of course, is a too literal extrapolation—all else is never equal. Thus the role of viewer and model sex and social status must be examined in tests of hypothesis 6.1, along with many other descriptive and substantive characteristics of both viewer and model.

There are, however, a number of observer characteristics that appear likely to maximize vicarious learning, regardless of film characteristics and therefore must be considered in deciding which patients among those awaiting psychotherapy are to be selected for vicarious learning procedures.

De Charms and Rosenbaum (1960) tested the hypothesis that vicarious expression of hostility would be equivalent to direct hostile expression in terms of hostility reduction. Their design permitted subjects who were attacked verbally either to respond directly to the attacker or to observe an attack on the original aggressor by another person. A measure of residual hostility served as the dependent variable. Another group of verbally attacked subjects, controls, were not permitted either to respond to being attacked or to observe another person so respond. Results indicated that most residual hostility was shown by these nonresponding, nonobserving control subjects. Significantly less residual hostility was evidenced by the observing subjects, and still less (but not significantly so) by those subjects permitted a direct response to the aggressor. However, the between-condition differences noted reached statistically significant levels *only for subjects with low self-esteem*. Research reported by Gelfand (1962), Lesser and Abelson (1959), and Rosenbaum, Horne, and Chalmers (1962) all concur in pointing to low self-esteem as an enhancer of vicarious learning— thus directing us to one important observer characteristic in selecting patients for vicarious learning procedures.

Other such variables have been identified. Highly dependent persons have been shown to be particularly prone to imitative behavior following observation of a rewarded model (Jakubczak & Walters, 1959; Miller & Dollard, 1941; Schein, 1954). Observers who are led to believe that they are similar to models in a number of background and attitudinal dimensions prove significantly more likely to match responses made by the models than observers not so instructed (Burnstein et al., 1961; Stotland & Dunn, 1963). Persons who have been previously rewarded for matching behavior are more likely to do so again in a new situation (Lanzetta & Kanareff, 1959; Miller & Dollard, 1941; Schein, 1954). The level of the observer's emotional arousal appears to be another relevant variable. Emotional arousal of moderate intensity seems to predispose the observer to significantly greater degrees of matching behavior than do either high or low levels of arousal (Schachter & Singer, 1962; Schacter & Wheeler, 1962; Walters, Leat, & Mezei, 1960). The review by Campbell (1961) notes that the degree of vicarious learning will be greater (1) the more frequently, strongly, consistently and recently the observer has been reinforced for imitating a given model, (2) the more similar the response of the model to responses for which the observer has been reinforced for imitating previously, (3) the more recently the model's behavior has been observed, and (4) the more models for which the observer has been rewarded for imitating.

Psychotherapeutic Applications

A number of anecdotal and experimental efforts have dealt with variables relevant to vicarious learning in the context of psychotherapy. The absolute number of such efforts is small, however, and their relevance to psychotherapy, although real, is more typically accidental than purposeful. As Bandura and Walters (1963) note,

In spite of the prevalence of imitative learning in the acquisition of social behavior, it has rarely been deliberately and systematically used in the treatment of behavior disorders. Its incidental use is, however, apparent in many descriptions of traditional and social-learning treatment procedures . . . (p. 242).

Such accidental or incidental use of vicarious learning principles has occurred in connection with both individual and group psychotherapy.

One early example in an individual therapy context is Rosenthal's (1955) investigation of patient and therapist moral values. In spite of apparent therapist efforts to avoid imposing their values on their patients, patients judged as improved changed their values in the areas of sex, aggression, and authority in the direction of the values held by their therapists. Patients judged unimproved became less like their therapists in these respects. This investigation and others like it (e.g., Sheehan, 1953) are clearly open to a modeling or imitative learning interpretation.

Staples, Wilson, and Walters (1963) report a similarly relevant study. Highly nonverbal, chronic schizophrenics were their subjects. Two series of slides depicting landscapes, animals, and other stimuli were presented to these patients, and they were instructed to discuss their reactions to the pictures. One group of patients was exposed to a talkative model between the first and second series of slides. They discussed and described their reactions to the first slide series freely and in detail. A second patient group had only music interposed between the two series of slides. As the investigators had predicted, the subsequent verbal responsiveness of subjects exposed to the talkative model was significantly greater than that of patients not so exposed. In addition, there was some evidence that exposure to the model was effective in increasing patient verbalization than direct reinforcements (cigarettes for speaking).

Chittenden (1942) conducted an investigation that perhaps comes closest of those considered so far to the idea of using vicarious learning techniques in psychotherapy. Her subjects, highly aggressive children, were assigned to either a "training" or a control condition. Children in the training condition observed a series of "plays" in which dolls representing preschool children exhibited both aggressive and cooperative reactions to frustrating circumstances—circumstances very similar to those encountered by the children in their everyday activities. Following the presentation of each pair of alternative responses, E and the child discussed the social situation presented in the play and reached a joint decision concerning the appropriateness of the social responses made by the dolls. Test trials were interspersed among the plays, trials in which the children were required to provide their own solution to an interpersonal conflict involving two dolls. In comparison to control group children, training group subjects showed a significant decrease in aggressive responses from initial to final test. Furthermore, this between group difference was apparent from independent ratings made of the children's within-school behavior before, immediately after, and one month after the training sessions. Bandura and Walters (1963) comment in relation to this investigation:

> This study is noteworthy for its demonstration that *observational discrimination learning*, coupled with reasoning, fostered cooperative behavior which was incompatible with the initially prepotent aggressive responses, thus leading to their inhibition. In this study, reasoning consisted in part of drawing attention to the adverse consequences of antisocial behavior, to both participants in the symbolic social situations. The outcome therefore provides an excellent example of vicarious learning through observation of response consequences to a model (p. 245).

Chittenden's use of plays immediately suggests that there may be vehicles in addition to films through which vicarious learning procedures can be conducted with waiting-list patients. As in Chittenden's plays, patients could be asked to view "live" therapy sessions—either real or fictitious. Such a procedure, however, would be costly in terms of time and, more important, would offer an insufficient degree of opportunity for control by the treatment staff of such variables as what behaviors will be displayed as "learning models." Live sessions and films of sessions do not, however, exhaust the possibilities.

Aural tapes and typescripts appear potentially useful, as does a procedure recently described by Kagan, Krathwohl, and Miller (1963) which they call Interpersonal Process Recall. Here therapy sessions are video taped. Immediately after each session or after periodic sessions, therapist and patient proceed to separate rooms to view and listen to a playback of their interview. Each is joined in his respective room by an interrogator, who encourages him to describe his feelings, interpret statements, and translate body movements viewed during the replay. The interrogator, the therapist, or the patient may stop the playback at any time to discuss it. Whenever such a stop is made, the tape is automatically stopped for the other team. Thus both parties to the interaction may simultaneously examine the same aspects of their interview. We propose that these procedures, with modifications, are clearly appropriate for vicarious learning purposes—with another patient serving as model for the waiting-list patient or with the patient serving as his own model when the patient is already in formal psychotherapy. The major technical modification required would be editing of tapes to select parts of interviews considered modelable. The therapist need not participate in viewing sessions; an interrogator would. His primary role would be to draw the patient's attention to behavior (of the patient) on the tape which was rewarded by the therapist and which is worthy of further modeling. The major conceptual modification implied by this scheme when used for patients already undergoing treatment is that the patient serves as his own model. Such a procedure is not without precedent. Our discussion of overcompensation in Chapter 3 involved a patient considering how he had been compensated previously when deciding whether a current outcome was equitable or inequitable. Bandura and Walters (1963) suggest that the patient serves as his own model in role play-post role play and hypnosis-posthypnotic sequences. These instances, combined with findings in such studies as Kanfer, Bradley, and Marston's (1962) demonstrating the occurrence of self-reinforcement, suggest the apparent feasibility of the procedures outlined above.

The use of aural tapes for vicarious learning purposes is illustrated by a study, reported by Truax (1963), which serves as an independently derived initial test of hypothesis 6.1. Subjects in this investigation of Vicarious Therapy Pretraining were patients in a mental hospital setting who were to participate in group psychotherapy. Experimental patients listened to a 30-minute tape recording of excerpts of "good" patient therapy behavior. Truax notes, "The tape itself illustrates in a very concrete manner how clients often explore themselves and their feelings. It provides both cognitive and experiential structuring of 'how to be a good client'" (p. 863). Control patients did not listen to this tape, but were treated like the experimental patients in all other respects. A comparison of the early session behavior of these two groups of patients revealed that patients from therapy groups which had undergone pretraining showed significantly higher levels of intrapersonal exploration or, in Truax's terms, "deeper levels of therapeutic process." Thus the initial experimental test of the usefulness of vicarious learning procedures in the therapeutic context has yielded positive results.

Still further support for these procedures is provided, in a less direct manner, in research reported by Geocaris (1960) in which patients were required to listen to recordings of their sessions for a number of hours equal to the number of hours they had spent in therapy; in Walz and Johnston's (1963) study in which therapists viewed video-taped playbacks of their therapy sessions; and in a series of investigations of self-confrontation reported by Nielsen (1964) in which sets of persons viewed and responded to a movie of their own interactions with one another under stress conditions.

Finally, the group psychotherapy literature also provides several bits of anecdotal information which give added credence to our suggestion that vicarious learning procedures have already found a place in contemporary psychotherapy. For example, Bach (1954) and others have proposed as one of the major therapeutic advantages of open groups (new patients entering as vacancies occur), ". . . many newcomers quickly learn to identify with the prevailing group level of discourse" (p. 34). Thus, Bach suggests, there are several aspects characteristic of the development of a therapy group which inhibit improvement. Their resolution takes time. Hypothetically, let us assume that "speaking freely," defined in some operational way, takes eight months for the typical group therapy patient to accomplish. Let us further assume an open therapy group in which all the members have been in attendance eight or more months. Vicarious learning research suggests that a new patient joining this group would take *less than* eight months to reach what Bach terms "the prevailing group level of discourse." That is, with the other patients serving as models and with the therapist and other patients serving as dispensers of rewards (for modeling verbalizations), vicarious learning occurs in the new patient, thus shortening the time necessary for *his* psychotherapy. This often observed phenomenon is essentially responsible for the term "telescoping" in hypothesis 6.1.

Other types of vicarious learning occur in group psychotherapy. Whitaker and Lieberman (1964) refer to "spectator therapy," in which change occurs in a given patient via his opportunity to observe and listen to the productions of other patients with problems similar to his. Bach (1954) reports a similar phenomenon as it occurs within two-person group therapy subgroups, that is, "recovery à deux" or "identification with the pace setter." Or, as Corsini and Rosenberg (1955) observed, anxiety reduction and reassurance may occur through a phenomenon they term "universalization," in which the patient's observation of other patients leads him to recognize the degree to which his psychopathology is not unique. Frank (1955) has described this process in terms of "mirror reactions." Slavson (1950) makes frequent use of modeling techniques in his group therapy with children and adolescents. For example, at the end of an activity group therapy session, rather than telling the group members to clean up, Slavson will start doing so himself. The more "modelable" group members will follow his example first, and they in turn provide models for the remaining group members who will follow suit. Finally, Kadis et al. (1963) make use of films during their group therapy sessions. They comment:

> When patients recognize the part played by anxieties and defenses, via their identification with characters and situations in the films, they often find it easier to start coping with their own resistances and to reinforce each other's motivation for psychotherapy (p. 51).

In all, therefore, vicarious learning principles, though not labeled as such, have begun to find a place in contemporary psychotherapy. This largely anecdotal material, when combined with research bearing directly upon vicarious learning phenomena, appears to underscore the credibility of hypothesis 6.1 and its potential therapeutic impact.

INDIVIDUALIZED TIME LIMITS

The major temporal dimensions of psychotherapy have received a large and perhaps disproportionate amount of research scrutiny. We suspect that the large number of studies examining the duration of therapy, the frequency of sessions, session length, and related time considerations is at least in part based on the appeal of these precisely quantifiable time variables as they contrast with the difficult-to-quantify nature of most independent variables in psychotherapy research. Thus much of this research very carefully and exactly leads nowhere as far as improved understanding and practice of the psychotherapeutic process is concerned. There are, however, several exceptions to this theme, particularly when the findings from several studies in a given areas are viewed in combination. As background for our development of hypothesis 6.2, let us now look briefly at these studies of psychotherapeutic time dimensions.

Duration of psychotherapy has clearly received the most attention of variables of this type. Several investigators (Mensh & Golden, 1951; Myers & Auld, 1955; Seeman, 1949; Standel & Van Der Veen, 1957; Sullivan et al., 1958) report a significant relationship between duration of therapy and various criteria of patient improvement. The multiple basis for this unsurprising finding is clearly suggested by other duration studies which report a reliable positive association between length of treatment and (1) therapist expectation of degree of patient improvement (Goldstein, 1962), (2) patient attraction to the therapist (Heller & Goldstein, 1961), (3) patient socioeconomic status (Gallagher & Kanter, 1961; Myers & Auld, 1955; Rubinstein & Lorr, 1956; Schaffer & Myers, 1954), (4) patient self-dissatisfaction (Rubinstein & Lorr, 1956; Taulbee, 1958), (5) patient educational level (Garfield & Affleck, 1959; Rubinstein & Lorr, 1956), (6) patient intelligence (Auld & Eron, 1953; Gibby et al., 1954), (7) patient anxiety (Gibby et al., 1954; Kotkov & Meadow, 1953; Lorr et al., 1958), (8) patient verbal productivity (Gibby et al., 1954; Gallagher, 1954), (9) patient dependency (Taulbee, 1958; Hunt et al., 1959), (10) patient motivation for therapy (Blair, 1950; Kutash & Dengrove, 1950; McCladdie, 1950) and a significant negative correlation with patient rigidity and patient impulsivity (Rubinstein & Lorr, 1956). Affleck and Garfield (1961), Heilbrun (1961), and particularly Lorr, Katz, and Rubinstein (1958) have made effective use of findings such as these in developing criteria and measures for predicting length of patient stay in psychotherapy.

Two investigations of treatment frequency reported by McNair and Lorr (1960) further underscore the importance of the duration variable. Their findings clearly indicate that it is the *length of time* a patient is in treatment which relates to patient change, and not the absolute number of sessions in which the patient participates during this period of time. Thus although patients differing in number of months of treatment differed on criteria of improvement, patients in therapy for the same number of months but seen twice a week, once a week or biweekly did not differ significantly on these same criteria. While the findings of these studies are of interest in their own right, perhaps the most noteworthy aspect of the McNair and Lorr studies is the fact that the relevant time dimension—treatment frequency—was manipulated. Clearly, a naturalistic, observational research approach to tests of the influence of treatment frequency is simply not adequate to the task.

Much the same point might be made for the single study of session length which has been reported. Its manipulative, experimental nature clearly provided the most adequate means of assessing the research questions involved. Imber et al. (1957) randomly assigned patients to one of three types of treatment: (1) group therapy one and one-half hours per week, (2) individual therapy one hour per week, or (3) individual "minimal contact" therapy one-half hour every two weeks. These differential session lengths, while perhaps confounded by the differing types of psychotherapies associated with them, failed to produce differential effects on the major criterion of improvement. Thus whether sessions lasted one and one-half hours, one hour or one half hour biweekly appeared to make no difference as far as amount of reduction in patient subjective discomfort was concerned. By implication, we have here further evidence that it may be duration, and not other time dimensions, that is of most consequence for the therapeutic outcome. Taken together, the various studies noted suggest that patients remaining in therapy for only a small number of sessions do not improve a great deal—and clearly do not improve as much as patients in therapy for longer periods of time.

Time-Limited Psychotherapy

There is, however, a fly in the therapeutic ointment. Assuming a naturalistic approach to therapy research, in which variables are unmanipulated and therapy is kept "traditional," it does indeed seem to be true that, within limits, the longer the duration, the greater the improvement. A very different picture emerges, however, when tradition is left behind and we examine research in which the duration of therapy itself is manipulated. More concretely, we speak here of *time-limited psychotherapy*—treatment in which the patient is informed in the first session or two that his treatment will be limited to a given number of sessions. When this number of sessions is reached, treatment in fact terminates. While time-limited psychotherapy has a very short research history, its occasional use has been commented upon for a number of years. Freud (1957) took a somewhat ambivalent position regarding such a therapeutic maneuver:

I have employed the method of fixing a date for termination of analysis in other cases and I have also inquired about the experience of other analysts in this respect. There can only be one verdict about the value of this blackmailing device. The measure is effective, provided one hits the right time at which to employ it. But it cannot be held to guarantee perfect accomplishment of the task of psychoanalysis. On the contrary, we may be quite sure that, while the force of the threat will have the effect of bringing part of the material to light, another part will be held back and buried, as it were, and will be lost to our therapeutic efforts (p. 319).

Rank's (1936) "end-setting" technique also represents an early use of time limits in psychotherapy. With separation anxiety serving as a major focus of Rankian therapy, the issue of termination of treatment assumed more than its usual importance. The therapist, in collaboration with the patient, set a tentative termination date. This was kept open to revision and, Rank notes, such end-setting was highly individualized—although he offers very few clues to the basis for such individualization:

The patient's reaction to the therapist's decision to end therapy, if properly handled, will lead to a final resolution of the conflict between wanting to be independent and self-reliant versus being dependent and have another take the responsibility for one's life and happiness (p. 26).

With very few exceptions, most notably Taft (1933), the use of time limits on the length of psychotherapy disappeared from the therapeutic scene in the years following the appearance of Rank's writings. It is true that Jung (1954) has written about setting limits on session frequency, and Rogers (1942) has spoken about limits on session length, but aside from indirectly relevant writings about brief psychotherapy, little attention until lately has been focused on limiting the duration of psychotherapy.

Recently however, Shlien (1957) reported an investigation aimed directly at evaluating time-limited psychotherapy. Patient improvement on a number of criteria was examined for patients assigned to two treatment groups:

1. Time-limited therapy—patients were told at the start of treatment that their therapy would be limited to 20 sessions.
2. Time-unlimited therapy—patients assigned to this condition continued in treatment until voluntary termination.

Patients in both groups were carefully matched on relevant demographic variables. Results indicated that time-limited patients improved as much or more in their 20 sessions on a variety of change measures than did the time-unlimited patients in an average of 55 sessions. Furthermore, at the end of the latter period, time-limited patients had maintained their level of improvement, in spite of being out of treatment for several months. Henry and Shlien (1958) and Gendlin and Shlien (1961) report further findings from this project, again encouraging in nature as far as the therapeutic value of time-limited treatment is concerned. With direct relevance to hypothesis 6.2, which proposes nonclinical temporal criteria for individualizing time limits, Shlien (1957) comments:

. . . the next step in research on time limits in therapy will be to undertake a project in which the limit is not arbitrary, but is adjusted to the needs and situation of the client as well as the counselor, and in which the client participates in the decision to set the termination in advance. This, it is believed, will retain all the demonstrated values of time limits, and eliminate any detriments which stem from the arbitrariness of the uniform limits in the present experiment (p. 321).

Although we most strongly agree with Shlien's proposal for research on individualizing time limits, the "next step" in the development of this research area was more appropriately an independent replication of the basic phenomenon; that is, would others also find time-limited treatment to be as valuable as or more valuable than treatment unlimited in duration? An investigation by Lorr, McNair, and Goldstein (in process) sought to provide this independent replication. As in the Shlien study, patients in this investigation were randomly assigned to time-limited treatment (20 sessions) or treatment unlimited in duration. Each participating psychotherapist saw two patients, one from each of the treatment conditions. At the end of 20 sessions the time-limited patients reported significantly less somatic distress, tension, depression, confusion and fatigue. Time-unlimited patients did not. Further, therapist ratings at this point in time indicated significantly greater distress relief for time-limited patients. To what extent this superiority of time-limited patients on these several change criteria is sustained will be determined when the unlimited patients have all terminated their treatment. In all, however, Shlien's findings are clearly upheld. Time-limited psychotherapy is as efficient as or more efficient than therapy not limited in duration in effecting patient change. Two recent studies, reported by Muench (1965) and Wright, Gabriel, and Haimowitz (1961) provide essentially confirming results. Further, this patient responsiveness to "speed of improvement expectations" communicated by treatment personnel is evident in Rioch's (1960) study of combat psychiatry and Davis' (1958) research with physically disabled patients. If it is correct, then, to accept the position that limiting the duration of therapy not only fails to retard patient progress but instead speeds it up, we are led to what must be the next logical investigative step—individualizing time limits. We thus come to our next hypothesis.

HYPOTHESIS 6.2: **The imposition of individualized time limits based on patient characteristics associated with differential responses to temporal events will enhance the effectiveness of psychotherapy.**

It is research dealing with such variables as time perception, time estimation, time perspective, and judgments of time duration from which we now wish to draw evidence for this hypothesis. None of this evidence deals directly with psychotherapeutic events and thus, as before, the evidence bears upon psychotherapy only by extrapolation. In a real sense, we hope with this hypothesis to make a start at what may be called a "clinical multiple regression equation" predictive of patient response to time-limited psychotherapy and the most appropriate length of such therapy for a given patient. The components of such an equation are patient characteristics identified as associated with one or another class of response to various temporal events or dimensions. Unfortunately, research in the areas indicated above is not yet advanced enough to provide us with full knowledge of appropriate components for our prediction of patient response to treatment or most appropriate time limits. Nevertheless, some very promising directions are suggested by these studies, and it is these directions which we will now examine.

A Goal Gradient Effect

It will be instructive if a portion of this nonclinical research is invoked for purposes of speculating why time-limited therapy works as it does. What is there about the anticipation of treatment coming to a close at a definite point in time which serves literally to speed up the rate of patient change? The goal gradient phenomenon, first systematically examined by Hull (1943) appears to represent an important part of the answer to this question. Hull's investigations of the strength of responses at different distances from the goal revealed that the rat increases its speed of running with decreasing distance from the goal. This speed of locomotion gradient, when combined with the concept of secondary reinforcement led to the idea of a goal gradient. For our purposes, the important aspect of this conceptualization is that the animal's speed increases the closer he comes to the goal—both spatially and temporally. Although the major portion of goal gradient research has focused upon spatial gradients, temporal gradients have not been ignored. On a general level, Cohen (1953) notes:

Spatial gradients are easier to study experimentally than temporal ones. That is perhaps why so few attempts . . . have been made to study temporal gradients with human subjects although human situations very commonly have a temporal character. Instances of temporal situations in which a person's behavior probably corresponds to a gradient are an examinee awaiting his examination or its results, a patient awaiting a tooth extraction, a bride awaiting the marriage ceremony, and a pregnant woman awaiting a birth of her infant. One cannot retreat from a temporal goal, so movement towards it is inexorable, unlike behavior corresponding to spatial gradients where there may be a possibility of withdrawal (pp. 305-306).

It seems quite clear from these examples that the patient participating in time-limited therapy is indeed involved in a temporal gradient. If this is the case, the effect of anticipation of termination should be to call forth increased patient and therapist effort toward the therapeutic goal, that is, patient change. Studies of subject "output" in the face of temporal goal gradients bolster this interpretation. Katz (1940), for example, has demonstrated that the frequency of resumption of interrupted tasks increases as the point of interruption approaches completion of the task. Cohen (1954) has demonstrated essentially the same phenomenon in a study in which recall was the criterion. Earlier studies by Zeigarnik (1927) and Ovsiankina (1928) are consistent with these findings.

A study by Farber (1953) is also relevant to this effect of anticipation of temporal goals. The studies noted above involved the effect of temporal goals on various work or output criteria. Farber, in contrast, was interested in the effects of such goals on affective states or feeling tone. Quite simply, his subjects were asked to rank the days of the week in order of preference, to indicate in detail how they felt about each day, and why. For the entire sample, the order of preference was: Sat., Fri., Sun., Thurs., Wed., Tues., Mon. If one considers which days of the week are, or precede, recreational or leisure time days and which are characteristically less pleasant, work days, this ordering makes immediate sense. Farber comments:

> Saturday is the favorite day of the week. The reasons given for this choice stress, of course, that it is a free day. . . . However, mention is also made of the fact that it is liked because it is *followed* by a free day, i.e., the *future outlook* on Saturday is favorable. . . . Monday is the least favorable day. . . . Since the actual work performed on Monday does not in general differ from that performed on the other week-days, the dislike of Monday cannot be attributed to the activities on that day. The explanation is again to be found in the future time perspective, as revealed in one typical comment: "On Monday the whole week of work stretches ahead of you."
>
> From Monday through Friday a neat gradient exists with steadily rising outlook. The week-end might conceptually be viewed as a goal, with a goal-gradient of feeling-tone as it is approached (p. 235).

Two other investigations by Farber (1944, 1951), as well as an independent study reported by Cason (1931), confirm this apparently affective and perhaps motivational effect of future time perspective. These studies may well have direct implications for the day-of-week scheduling of therapy interviews. More important, however, they combine with goal gradient research to suggest that when time limits are set for a given patient's treatment course not only should they be strictly adhered to but, to have maximal effect, the end point should constantly be kept in the patient's awareness.

Time Perception and Psychopathology

If the foregoing discussion is an adequate partial explanation of the manner in which therapy with a predefined duration has its rapid therapeutic impact, a patient's characteristic future time perspective becomes a material consideration in determining whether a time limit should be set for him and, if so, for how many sessions. Research demonstrates a number of interesting relationships between future time perspective and type of patient psychopathology. Although we share with many others a lack of enthusiasm for reliance upon diagnostic labels, they clearly are not devoid of information. Thus the association of diagnosis and aspects of future time perspective will permit us to include patient diagnosis as the first major component in our "equation" predicting optimal length for time limited psychotherapy.

A number of early investigations have pointed to one or another type of time distortion as a frequent feature of schizophrenic processes. For example, Dobson (1954), Guertin and Rabin (1960), Johnston (1939), and Adler (1954) report that schizophrenic patients are more variable than normals in estimating length of time spans. Fischer (1929), Fraisse (1963) and Israeli (1936) speak of a schizophrenic "loss of time sense." DuBois (1954), Minkowski (1933) and Horanyi-Hechst (1943) are others who point to temporal confusion and distortion in schizophrenics. Pearl and Berg (1963) have reported that schizophrenic Ss exhibit significantly greater distortion in estimating time duration when the stimuli involved are relevant to their major conflicts than when nonconflictual stimuli are presented. Two recent investigations of this general type are particularly relevant to hypothesis 6.2.

De la Garza and Worchel (1956) compared temporal orientation of a group of 50 schizophrenic subjects with that of 50 carefully matched normals. On two rather different tests of time orientation, schizophrenic subjects performed at a significantly poorer level. Of special interest here, however, are certain within-test findings. An item analysis revealed that schizophrenic subjects had not done equally poorly on all types of test items. Items passed by almost all schizophrenic Ss included "How many minutes in an hour?" "What day follows Thursday?" "Is it morning or afternoon?" and a request to re-order correctly "May, March, April." Items such as these are "easy" in the sense not only of having been overlearned but of having either concrete referents ("Is it morning or afternoon?") or being successively related ("May, March, April"). Items characteristically failed by this patient group included "What day of the week is it?" and being asked to re-order correctly "Tuesday, Saturday, Friday" or "September 17, 1951, April 10, 1950, December 29, 1952." This last item is more difficult in that it contains three elements (months, days, years) to be considered simultaneously. The Tuesday-Saturday-Friday series is complicated by the fact of being nonadjacent days, and in the remaining item no immediate referents are available to help the patient determine what day of the week it is. The investigators comment:

> When some frame of reference is required that is not given in the immediate perceptual field, that is, contained within the series itself, the schizophrenic seems to find it difficult to orient the elements properly (p. 193).

A closely related study is reported by Wallace (1956). He compared a schizophrenic and a normal group on three tests of future time perspective: (1) an ordering of 10 likely future events, (2) story construction aimed at determining the length of time represented in each story, (3) estimates of the subject's own age when a series of future events were likely to occur. Wallace was particularly interested in comparing groups in terms of two major features of future time perspective: extension and coherence. Extension was defined as the length of future time span conceptualized by an individual. Coherence refers to the degree of organization of events within this time span. Results indicated both a significantly shorter and significantly less well organized future time perspective in the schizophrenic subjects.

The findings of these two investigations suggest a number of possibilities regarding the use of time-limited psychotherapy with schizophrenic patients. First, it may simply not work; that is, the structuring of time limits may not be understood and 20 sessions of time-limited therapy with such a patient may prove no better and no worse than 20 sessions of standard, time-unlimited treatment. At this stage of our knowledge, of course, this remains an unanswered, empirical question. Another possibility is that such structuring would have an impact, but an impact arousing different kinds of expectancies and behaviors than those that seem to characterize a neurotic, time-limited therapy population. We know of no research speaking directly to this point, but it does not seem farfetched to propose a different class of response in schizophrenic versus nonschizophrenic subjects to pressures implicit in a goal gradient. Wallace's findings may also suggest that the limit be set not at the beginning of treatment but more toward the (heretofore unmentioned) end. In any event, it seems quite clear that the structuring of time limits with schizophrenic patients must be particularly concrete, detailed, and frequently repeated.

It appears that the perception of the passage of time and future time perspective may also be idiosyncratically associated with other psychopathological groups. In Strauss's (1947) terms, there may be a more or less consistent "ego time" for such patient groups, in contrast to more widely held "world time." Manic and depressive patients, for example, have long been characterized in terms of distorted time perspectives. Strauss (1947) has described depressive patients as "forever tied to the past" and the manic as strikingly (dis)oriented toward the future. Kloos (1938) has proposed a similar distinction. Fraisse (1963) comments that "the euphoria of a manic is . . . bound up with this shrinking of his temporal horizon: neither the weight of the past nor the uncertainty of the future can influence his mood, which depends entirely on the present" (p. 185). DuBois (1954) describes the depressed patient as someone "who states that since things have been so bad in the past and the road to the future is blocked, there is no reason to do anything in the present" (p. 49). Minkowski (1933) similarly describes manic and depressive disorders in terms of faulty future time perspective. Further, in a time estimation study reported by Solomon (1950), manic patients overestimated time passage to an extent significantly greater than depressed patients. Again we may speculate about the possible implications of these findings for time-limited treatment. If the future time perspective findings noted are to be accepted literally, it may be that time-limited psychotherapy is an inappropriate treatment choice for both manic and depressive patients; or, as seems possible with the schizophrenic patient, the structuring of limits may fail to evoke a "goal gradient effect," and the patient in fact will participate in a limited number of "standard" therapy sessions. As before, issues such as these await research examination.

Somewhat less attention has been devoted to temporal considerations in research dealing with nonpsychotic psychopathological groups. Studies by Barndt and Johnson (1955) and Brock and Del Giudice (1963) demonstrate shorter future time perspectives in psychopathic as compared to normal subjects. DuBois (1954) and Meerloo (1948) have discussed distortions in time perspective in neurotic patients in terms of a rebellion against authority figures. Although they interpret the expression "killing time" a bit too literally for our tastes, their interpretation does raise the importance of patient perception of the therapist for decisions regarding time-limited therapy. In analogous ways,

Coheen (1950) and Fraisse (1963) have examined temporal distortions in organic patients, and Brower and Brower (1947) and Gothberg (1949) have noted important distortions in future time perspective in feeble-minded patients. In all, therefore, these studies combine with research noted earlier to suggest that type of patient psychopathology is one important determinant both of over-all response to time-limited treatment and the most appropriate specific length for such treatment.

Time Perception and Motivation

A second variable of potential use for specifying individualized time limits is patient motivation for therapy or, stated in terms more characteristic of nonclinical temporal research, strength of patient motivation to reach the goal or successfully complete the experimental task. Our discussion of psychopathological groups and time limits has revealed that the impact of such treatment may be partly contingent on the patient's idiosyncratic interpretation of the passage of time or of his future time perspective. There has been research to demonstrate that task motivation similarly influences the perception of time passage and time perspective. In an early investigation of this type, Filer and Meals (1949) found clear support for their hypothesis that "individuals motivated to complete a task will believe they have worked longer at the task than individuals not so motivated . . . after both groups have worked an equal amount of time" (p. 329). Their interpretation of this finding is of direct relevance to our goal gradient interpretation of the influence of time limits in psychotherapy and furthermore underscores the likely role of patient motivation.

Wright, Irwin and Gebhard, and others have presented evidence that psychological distance tends to affect the attractiveness of a goal. It seems likely that the attractiveness of a goal will affect the psychological distance one must travel to reach that goal. The experimental groups in our study were motivated so that they desired the completion of a time interval. Thus, when they were interrupted and asked how long they had been working, they by their estimation placed themselves closer to the end of the ten-minute interval than Ss who presumably had no special desire for the time to be completed (p. 330).

Related findings have been provided by other investigators. Rosenzweig and Koht (1933) report that when subjects are highly motivated their time estimates are shorter than when under low motivation. Hindle (1951) has found that perceived time is inversely related to perceived progress rate through a task. In a series of investigations, Meade (1959, 1960, 1963) drew on the latter investigations to demonstrate that when subjects are motivated to reach a goal their time estimates are inversely related to their perceived progress. This relationship did not hold under conditions of low subject motivation. These various findings combine to suggest that patient motivational level may be a relevant variable in determinations about the over-all appropriateness of time-limited therapy for a given patient and the specific length of such treatment.

Other Temporal Relationships

A small number of studies in each of a large number of research areas have suggested several other variables of likely predictive relevance for our hypothetical multiple regression equation. Burns and Gifford (1961), Falk and Bindra (1954) and Siegman (1962) have shown that highly anxious subjects overestimate the passage of time. Buck (1946) constructed the Time Appreciation Test as a measure of intelligence, thus proposing a relationship of intellectual level to correctness of time estimations and perspective. McDougall (1904), Yerkes and Urban (1906), Axel (1924) and Gulliksen (1927) have all independently demonstrated a greater degree of time overestimation by women subjects, when males and females are compared on a variety of time estimation tasks. Frank (1939) and Gilliland, Hofeld, and Eckstrand (1946) have reported culturally based differences in future time perspective. And finally, in two separate studies, Thor (1962a, 1962b) has shown that subjects' time perspective either early or late in the day is significantly longer than estimates obtained around midday, thus suggesting that even the time of day at which the therapy session is scheduled may be a relevant variable.

We have, then, suggested a number of variables of possible use for individualizing decisions about time-limited psychotherapy. These have included patient diagnosis, motivation for therapy, anxiety level, intelligence, sex, cultural background and time of day set for the patient's session. All of these variables are offered suggestively and by extrapolation only. To date none has been examined as they relate to temporal variables in a psychotherapeutic context. It is just such examination which tests of hypothesis 6.2 can provide.

SOCIAL ISOLATION AND SUSCEPTIBILITY TO INFLUENCE

In our earlier discussion of the therapist-patient relationship we hypothesized certain procedures as a means of enhancing the degree of patient responsiveness to therapist influence attempts. In that instance we specified at some length the classes of patients for whom we felt such procedures were appropriate. In addition to this specification of the involuntary or highly resistive patient, we further proposed that the procedures outlined would likely be used most appropriately only at the early stages of a course of psychotherapy. In contrast to these delimiting suggestions, hypothesis 6.3 proposes a procedure aimed toward similar goals, but with considerably less restriction on the classes of patients or stages of therapy for which it is intended.

HYPOTHESIS 6.3:   **Patient susceptibility to therapist influence attempts may be increased by patient participation in presession social isolation.**

With this hypothesis we are suggesting that therapy patients spend a brief period before each (or several) therapy session in a condition of isolation or deprivation. Such a procedure may have several consequents; that is, in addition to heightening susceptibility to influence, this and related procedures may enhance the reinforcing value of interpersonal approval, increase suggestibility and, of relevance to both individual and group therapy, increase need affiliation. It is this multiple possible outcome of social isolation experiences which permits us to go beyond the restrictions of our relationship hypotheses (involuntary patient and early stages of therapy only) and propose the broader applicability of hypothesis 6.3. Research dealing directly with social isolation and its consequents is examined here, and problems that have arisen in the interpretation of a number of these studies are considered. Finally, we note briefly the role already played by isolation and deprivation procedures in psychotherapy.

Investigations of Deprivation

A number of early studies of sensory and social deprivation, many of which were of a broad, exploratory nature, yielded leads pointing toward both influenceability and interpersonal consequents of deprivation procedures. Heron (1961) and Bexton, Heron, and Scott (1954), for example, report that sensory deprivation, as operationalized in their studies "increased susceptibility to propagandization." Myers, Murphy, and Smith (1960) found that deprivation subjects, in contrast to nondeprived controls, were highly responsive to social pressure as evidenced by predeprivation to postdeprivation opinion change. Hebb (1961) reports similar findings. Cobb and Shor (1964) found that sensory-isolation procedures significantly increased subject responsiveness under subsequently induced hypnosis. An increase in need for contact with other people is reported by Kubzansky (1961). Lilly (1956) and Brownfield (1964) suggest similar deprivation consequences in their general discussions of stimulus hunger. Such early direction-pointing investigations led to a number of studies directly aimed at the impact of social isolation upon interpersonal influence and related dependent variables.

Gewirtz and Baer (1958a) raised the question, "does the incidence of behavior for social contact with other people increase following a period of social deprivations?" They comment:

. . . relevant stimuli (e.g., food, water) acquire maximal reinforcing value for an organism only subsequent to its recent deprivation of them. Other reinforcers of no apparent biological importance, like that provided by the opportunity to make a brief observation response, appear also to be raised in effectiveness following preceding periods of deprivation. In this context, it is a provocative question whether *social* reinforcers (those dispensed by people) postulated to possess reinforcing value through a history of conditioning, respond in a similar manner to deprivation (p. 49).

As they had hypothesized, the investigators, using children as subjects, found that the effectiveness of adult approval as a reinforcer was reliably enhanced by a preceding period of 20 minutes of social isolation—relative to its effectiveness for the same Ss when not isolated. Using the same gamelike task as that in the first study, Gewirtz and Baer (1958b) report a second, confirming investigation.

Subjects were 102 first- and second-grade children. Before playing the game, Ss were subjected to one of three experimental conditions: (1) 34 Ss were subjected to a 20-minute period of social isolation, (2) 34 Ss played the game immediately, a condition described by the investigators as nondeprivation, and (3) the final group of 34 Ss devoted 20 pregame minutes to drawing and cutting out designs, while E maintained a stream of friendly conversation with them, expressing frequent approval of their artistic efforts. This third condition was labeled satiation (for approval and social contact). All subjects then played the experimental game, which involved placing marbles in one of two holes in a toy which had been constructed for the study. E observed S's play for a four-minute, baseline period, during which no approval or other reinforcement was dispensed. This baseline period was followed immediately, for all subjects by a 10-minute test of reinforcer effectiveness, that is, E proceeded at this point to dispense the approval reinforcement ("good," "hmm-hmm," "fine," etc.) according to certain predetermined fixed ratios whenever S dropped a marble into the "correct" hole—defined as the hole preferred least during the last (fourth) minute of the baseline period. The major dependent variable, therefore, was the number of marbles dropped in the correct and incorrect holes during each minute of the 10-minute trial period. In addition to this reinforcer effectiveness score, the number of spontaneous social initiations by subjects made during the baseline period were noted, and judgments were made about the apparent intensity of such social interactions. As predicted, the reinforcing effectiveness of approval was relatively greatest after isolation, intermediate after nondeprivation, and least after satiation. Although between-condition differences were statistically significant, approval served as a reinforcer in all three conditions. Additional findings were that, following isolation, there was a significantly greater frequency of initiation of social interactions and a significantly larger proportion of Ss exhibiting apparently intense social interactions, as compared to nondeprivation and satiation subjects.

When viewed together, these two investigations by Gewirtz and Baer clearly seem to launch us on our way with nonclinical support for hypothesis 6.3. Other investigations permit us to continue in this direction.

Stevenson and Odom (1962) observed that in the two studies discussed above, isolated subjects were deprived of not only social but also other types of stimuli. Their results, therefore, may have been due to general stimulus deprivation, and not only deprivation of social stimuli. In a direct attempt at clarification, three groups of subjects participated in the same gamelike task as above. Preceding this trial period, the first subject group (social deprivation) played alone for 15 minutes in a room containing a variety of interesting toys. The second group (general stimulus deprivation) was left alone for 15 minutes with no toys. A third (control) group received no pre-experimental treatment. The social deprivation (isolation with toys) group showed the greatest responsiveness to subsequent interpersonal reinforcement, and the control group showed the least. The general stimulus deprivation group did not differ significantly from the social deprivation group in this regard, but both were significantly more "reinforceable" than the controls. The investigators conclude,

The results are interpreted as tentatively supporting the hypothesis that the increased effectiveness of social reinforcement following isolation is primarily dependent upon the deprivation of social stimuli rather than upon more general stimulus deprivation (p. 431).

Further supportive evidence is provided in a study by Zigler (1961), in which social deprivation was more naturalistically defined.

His subjects were institutionalized feebleminded children. Pre-institutional social deprivation was defined in terms of independent judgments made from subjects' case histories. The hypothesis was advanced that interaction with an adult and adult approval provide greater reinforcement for the responses of feebleminded subjects who have experienced a greater amount of social deprivation than for those who have experienced a lesser amount. On three independent "response to reinforcement" criteria, this hypothesis was clearly upheld. Corroborative results for this general finding are reported by still other investigators (Suedfeld, 1964; Walters & Quinn, 1960).

Were the studies presented to be all the essential research bearing on hypothesis 6.3, we could conclude our discussion at this point with a recommendation that brief periods of social isolation be provided therapy patients as a means of enhancing therapist influence (reinforceability), patient need affiliation, and so forth. Although our complete presentation of this hypothesis in fact permits us to conclude with this research recommendation, a series of studies have appeared which markedly alter the meaning of the findings presented above. It is these studies we now wish to consider.

An Anxiety Interpretation

A number of investigations reported by Walters and his research collaborators are particularly relevant. The first two studies in this series, reported by Walters and Karal (1960), were straightforward attempts to demonstrate the effects of social deprivation on susceptibility to influence in two adult populations. Contrary to the consistent positive findings noted earlier, no such effect was demonstrable in these two studies. The design of the studies was such that alternative explanations were not testable, and thus a third investigation was conducted.

Walters and Ray (1960) reason that perhaps ". . . Gewirtz and Baer aroused anxiety by their isolation procedure, and that the findings attributed to the arousal of a social drive could, in fact, have been due to the arousal of anxiety" (p. 1). They note further that such an explanation would be consistent with Schachter's (1959) demonstration that under anxiety-arousing conditions subjects tend both to seek out the company of others and to become increasingly susceptible to social influence. Further, Taylor and Spence's (1952) position that anxious (high-drive) subjects perform more effectively than nonanxious subjects on simple tasks, and Brown's (1953) notion that the important motivating component of many acquired drives appears to be anxiety are also, Walters and Ray note, consistent with their anxiety interpretation. In a direct test of this possibility, they conducted a replication of the Gewirtz and Baer study (1958b) but, in lieu of a simple comparison of isolated and nonisolated subjects, both groups were further divided experimentally into anxious and nonanxious subgroups. Anxiety was induced in subjects by the manner in which S's teacher introduced him to E and the manner in which E structured the experimental task. The nature of this task was identical in all respects to Gewirtz and Baer's procedures. With responsiveness to reinforcement again serving as the dependent variable, results indicated a highly significant difference between isolated anxious and isolated nonanxious subjects and a small, but also statistically significant difference between isolated and nonisolated subjects. Walters and Ray comment, "The results of this study give strong support to the hypothesis that anxiety, not isolation by itself, is the major factor affecting rate of conditioning" (p. 5). Thus we are provided with an initial bit of evidence that the effects of isolation upon conditioning, influenceability, and so forth, while quite real, may be more parsimoniously conceptualized as an anxiety effect, and not as an isolation effect per se. One final study reported by this research group provides even stronger support for such a position.

Walters, Marshall, and Shooter (1960) assigned 36 adolescent boys to one of four conditions: isolated anxious, isolated nonanxious, nonisolated anxious, nonisolated nonanxious. Each subject was tested for suggestibility in the autokinetic situation before and after exposure to his experimental condition. Anxious subjects showed a significantly greater increase in suggestibility, in response to contrary judgments, than the nonanxious. They were also more quickly conditioned to give a specific class of judgments. No differences were found between the isolated and nonisolated. Subjects' self-reports indicated that the anxiety arousing condition had produced its intended effect. The investigators conclude:

> The results were interpreted as supporting a theory advanced by Walters and Karal that social isolation has, in itself, no effect upon susceptibility to social influence, but that under anxiety-arousing conditions, which sometimes are produced by social isolation, Ss can be more readily influenced than when anxiety is not present (p. 9).

A number of independent investigations shed further light on the question whether social isolation directly enhances susceptibility to influence or whether, as Walters et al. claim, anxiety is the responsible mechanism with social isolation serving as but one of several possible means of arousing anxiety. Paivio (1963) examined social isolation and subject anxiety as possible determinants of the degree to which an audience influences a speaker. His subjects were divided into two groups, high and low audience anxiety—defined as a tendency to be anxious about performing before others. Subjects were required to tell stories to an audience either with or without prior exposure to a brief period of social isolation. Results demonstrated that isolated subjects high in audience anxiety told significantly shorter stories than did nonisolated high anxiety subjects. The stories of isolated and nonisolated low anxiety Ss did not differ in length. Paivio comments, ". . . the data of the present study thus provide more support for an anxiety than a 'deprivation' interpretation of the effects of an experimental social isolation procedure" (p. 253). Thus we find here further evidence of anxiety as the responsible agent, with isolation apparently serving to augment subject anxiety.

Results of other studies, though not providing direct tests of isolation versus anxiety effects, are consistent with this conclusion. Byrne (1961) reports, as did Schachter (1959), that subject anxiety increases affiliative needs. Staples and Walters (1961) found that increases in anxiety heighten subject susceptibility to social influence. Reitman and Cleveland (1961) report that social isolation increased anxiety in a nonpsychotic population, but that an opposite result obtains with schizophrenic subjects. Taken in combination, these studies and those examined earlier in connection with hypothesis 6.3 lead one to conclude that social isolation *may* have the desired influenceability-enhancing effect predicted by the hypothesis. If so, the major mediational mechanism appears to be the arousal of subject anxiety. We are thus led to two questions. Is anxiety arousal for influenceability (or any) purposes an appropriate procedure to consider when dealing with psychotherapy patients? If so, what procedures can be instituted to maximize the probability of such arousal taking place? It is to these two questions to which we must now turn.

It will be recalled that at the beginning of our discussion of this hypothesis it was held that the procedure to be recommended was intended to have wide applicability regarding the types of patients and stages of psychotherapy to which it applied. If an isolation-anxiety arousal sequence leads, as research has demonstrated, to heightened susceptibility to influence, affiliativeness and reinforceability, one can readily conceive of numerous therapeutic circumstances for which such heightening would be most desirable. Yet anxiety reduction is one of the most central intermediate (and often ultimate) goals for which treatment is undertaken in the first place. Then why set out purposefully to increase patient anxiety level? The answer is clear. Regardless of theoretical orientation, the vast majority of contemporary therapists consider a moderate amount of patient anxiety to be an absolutely necessary patient characteristic, both for purposes of staying in therapy and doing the "work" of therapy. Luborsky (1962) describes Freud's (1957) position:

> . . . [Freud] believed an optimum level of "suffering" is conducive to change; premature improvements can reduce the motive for change. The therapist's focus, therefore, should not be upon making life pleasant for the patient. The role of anxiety is especially clear in the treatment of patients with phobias. For cure to occur, Freud recommended that the patient put up with the anxiety of engaging in the activities which arouse the phobic anxiety (p. 127).

Rogers (1957), viewing psychotherapy from a very different stance, has similarly included among the patient characteristics which he considers preconditions for therapeutic change, ". . . the client is in a state of incongruence, being vulnerable or anxious." Schofield (1964) has demonstrated how very widely this position is held among psychotherapists of diverse training and orientation, and Luborsky (1962), and Siegal and Rosen (1962) provide experimental evidence indicating a relationship between patient improvement and level of anxiety. The learning research cited earlier pointing to motivational properties of anxiety clearly supports this position. Anxiety arousing procedures, such as social isolation, thus become appropriate for patients who can be identified as "anxiety-deficient."

In spite of the fact that it is now largely clear that anxiety is a more significant variable for our purposes than is social isolation per se, we continue here to recommend social isolation as the anxiety arousal procedure of choice for three reasons: (1) social isolation procedures are not difficult to implement in a psychotherapeutic setting, (2) research shows several protherapeutic consequents of isolation-induced anxiety (influenceability, affiliativeness, etc.), at least some of which *may* be attributable to isolation and not anxiety, and (3) social isolation procedures have already been used to advantage in a psychotherapeutic context. A brief examination of the basis for this last statement will serve to illustrate further, albeit indirectly, the appropriateness of social isolation-anxiety arousal procedures for psychotherapy, as proposed by hypothesis 6.3. It is to be noted, however, that these studies, even as a group, cannot be construed as an already conducted test of this hypothesis. Their small number and general clinical-exploratory nature preclude such a conclusion. That they provide further encouragement of the potential value of hypothesis 6.3 is clear, however.

Deprivation in Psychotherapy

Goldfried (1960), Lilly (1956) and Robertson (1961) have written in general, speculative terms about likely therapeutic consequences of sensory and social deprivation. Azima (1955) reports an exploratory study in which 15 hospitalized psychotic and neurotic patients were subjected to periods of isolation, which led to an "increase in motivation, socialization and self assertiveness." In a second similarly impressionistic study Azima, Vispo, and Azima (1961) report much the same conclusion. Smith and Lewty (1959) report a temporary alleviation of certain types of symptoms in schizophrenics subjected to sensory deprivation procedures. Harris (1959) isolated 12 schizophrenic subjects for periods up to two hours and found that their hallucinations became less intense and their over-all symptomatology either improved or showed no change. Cohen (1960) and Lawes (1963) report similar impressions. Gibby, Adams, and Carrera (1960) exposed psychiatric patients to a few hours of social deprivation and, they report, this led to ". . . less overt symptomatology, enhanced ego functioning, greater capacity to relate to others, improved reality testing and more effective intellectual functioning" (p. 74). Gibby and Adams (1961), in a second study with a similar patient group, found support for their hypothesis that "sensory deprivation increases receptivity, acceptance, and assimilation of meaningful verbal material" (p. 78). And so it is evident that clinical-impressionistic studies stand in clear support of hypothesis 6.3. We may now turn to the final issue we wish to consider in relation to this hypothesis.

Expectancy Effects

At a number of points throughout this book we present evidence that patient expectations are a major determinant of their future behavior. As we draw discussion of hypothesis 6.3 to a close, we wish to touch upon one important aspect of its research implementation. This expectancy effect will be its focus. More specifically, whether anxiety is aroused by the isolation procedure, and whether the isolation-anxiety sequence leads to increased susceptibility to influence, will be shown to be in part a function of what S expects the isolation procedure, and its consequents, to be like. Pollard, Uhr, and Jackson (1963) emphasized the role of pre-isolation instructions as an influence upon isolation effects. They found that subjects with three hours of sensory deprivation plus the pre-isolation suggestion that they would experience peculiar cognitive and perceptual reactions reported significantly more such effects than subjects who had received eight hours of sensory deprivation but neutral pre-isolation instructions. Jackson and Kelley (1962) report directly parallel findings. Schachter (1959) appears to have dealt with the same class of expectancy effects when he distinguished between voluntary and nonvoluntary subjects in isolation experiments. Kandel, Myers, and Murphy (1958) compared the effects of two sets of instructions on the reporting of visual sensations during two minutes of darkness. They found that one group, which was told that the experiencing of such sensations was to be expected under these conditions, reported significantly more visual sensations than did another group not so instructed. In a rather different manner, Orne and Scheibe (1964) have demonstrated the influence of subject pre-isolation expectancies on their isolation and post-isolation behaviors. Such effects are made particularly evident by this last study.

Based on their earlier studies of "demand characteristics" involved in hypnosis experiments, Orne and Scheibe suggest:

> The results of any experiment involving human subjects are seen to include at least two distinct components. The first, which may be called the true experimental effect, is entirely contingent upon the antecedence of the independent variable. The second is induced by the social cues that attend the experimental situation and is unrelated to the independent variables. . . . Research findings on sensory deprivation are likely to be subject to the kind of bias here described (p. 4).

In addition to investigations such as we have described, Orne and Scheibe point to sensory and social deprivation studies in which a "panic button" is clearly in view in the experimental room (Vernon et al., 1961; Zubek et al., 1961) or in which S is required to sign a forbidding release form prior to participation (Freedman et al., 1961). Such procedures are clearly potent means of structuring subjects' expectancies toward the anticipation of a negative experience. Two groups of subjects were employed by Orne and Scheibe in their own study. The experimental subjects, in a variety of verbal and nonverbal ways, were led to expect that the four hours they were about to spend in an isolation chamber would lead to a full array of sensory deprivation effects.

Specifically, they were told the experiment would be performed in a psychiatric hospital. On arrival, S met E who was dressed in a white coat. A medical history was taken. An aura of great seriousness was maintained throughout. An "emergency tray" (so labeled) of drugs and medical instruments was in full view of the subjects. Instructions to subjects included the request that they report any visual imagery, fantasies, unusual feelings, difficulties in concentration, hallucinations, feelings of disorientation, and so forth. They were further told that, "Such experiences are not unusual under the conditions to which you are to be subjected. If at any time you feel very discomforted, you may obtain release immediately by pressing the button which I will show you once we enter the chamber . . . Should you feel upset, or should anything untoward happen, a physician is immediately at hand." Finally, experimental subjects were also asked to sign a medical release form. Most of these instructions were omitted for control subjects. E wore a business suit, no emergency tray was present, no medical history was taken, no "panic button" existed in the isolation room, and so forth. These Ss were informed that they were part of a control group for a sensory deprivation experiment. Subjects from both groups spent four hours in the identical "isolation chamber." (Identical save for the "panic button.") The actual nature of this isolation chamber was very different from that typically used in sensory deprivation studies. It was a large, quiet, well lit room containing a desk, food and water, writing paper and implements, and a few other objects. Voices, footsteps and other outside noises could be heard in the room. Subjects were not prohibited from walking around or from other activities. Thus experimental and control subjects were treated very differently in terms of pre-isolation instructions and, it appears, the kinds of pre-isolation expectancies which were induced. Experimental and control subjects were treated identically during the "isolation" period. On a large number of experimental-control comparisons, the experimental Ss exhibited a significantly greater number of sensory deprivation effects. The investigators conclude:

In any experiment, the subject's reaction may be viewed as resulting from both the actual treatment (restriction of sensory input by means of gauntlets, goggles, special chambers, etc.) and the social situation created by the setting in which the experiment is conducted, the instructions used, and the cue characteristics of the treatment operations themselves. For example, in our particular experiment the treatment was not that of sensory deprivation, but, rather of 4-hour isolation. At the same time, the situation (demand characteristics) was deliberately varied for the control and the experimental groups. We interpret our data to mean that four hours of isolation coupled with differing sets of demand characteristics yield different experimental results (p. 11).

It is clear, therefore, that the implementation of hypothesis 6.3 need devote major attention to pre-isolation instructions. When properly framed, such instructions can lead to a maximization of the pro-therapeutic effects predicted by the hypothesis.

EMOTIONAL SENSITIVITY TRAINING

In a recent provocative paper entitled "The Other 109 Hours," Wright (1961) draws attention to a very important opportunity for enhancing efforts aimed at changing patient behavior—an opportunity for the most part ignored by contemporary approaches to psychotherapy. Specifically, his title refers to the number of hours in a patient's week, minus 56 for sleeping and three for formal psychotherapy. His theme is a plea that more therapeutic use be made of these between session hours; that is, just as our hypothesis 6.1 proposes that waiting time before the start of formal psychotherapy can and should be used in the service of therapeutic goals, Wright suggests that such ends can be served by procedures interpolated between formal therapy sessions. He comments:

. . . the interaction of the organism with its environment is. a far more powerful factor in the modification of behavior than many hours of individual psychotherapy. Just as it is inefficient to teach chemistry or anatomy by the lecture method alone, so it is inefficient to teach adequate behavior patterns in only a two or three hour a week session with a therapist—intense though it may be. I believe the three therapy hours should be closely related to the 109 lab hours in order to further intensify the stimulus value of both. It must be remembered that psychotherapy is not available at all for the great majority of the people anyway, nor is it likely to be. This extension of therapy to include the social milieu is more easily applied in institutional settings such as prisons, NP hospitals, and universities (pp. 36-37).

We most strongly agree with the position Wright has taken. It is of course true that not all therapeutic approaches fully ignore these "109 hours." Many therapists will, on occasion, assign specific tasks for patients to accomplish between sessions. For others, between-sessions time is made therapy-relevant by being viewed as assimilation time, during which the interpretations and other substance of the therapeutic hour can "sink in" or, at least, be mulled over by the patient. A few therapeutic approaches, a very few, do involve the level of systematic use of between session time which hypothesis 6.4 will suggest. Kelly's (1955) fixed role therapy quite clearly falls into such a category, as do the therapeutic approaches by Herzberg (1947) and Stevenson (1959). However, the majority of contemporary psychotherapists make extremely little, if any, use of such between-session time in anything approaching a planned, systematic manner.

Standing unnoticed by those responsible for the state of affairs just described are a number of studies unequivocally demonstrating that special, circumscribed training sessions can successfully teach patient groups a number of specific skills which are clearly relevant to their everyday interpersonal and social functioning; that is, non-therapy training sessions can and do provide "patient-pupils" with some of the behavioral skills that their psychotherapy seeks to achieve. Morton (1955), for example, was able to successfully train patients to seek alternative problem solutions for problems relating to their daily functioning. Schroder and Rotter (1952) report a similar finding plus generalization of alternative-seeking behavior to new problem situations. In a real sense, they trained patients to be less rigid and more flexible in their problem solving efforts. Spohn and Wolk (1963) trained chronic schizophrenic subjects for increased social and interpersonal participation. Their effort was successful and, further, such behavior generalized to newly made contacts with strangers in new situations. Peters and Jenkins (1954) and Tilton (1956) report concurring findings. Early but well-controlled studies by Jack (1934) and Page (1935) demonstrated the success of training for greater ascendant behavior in child subjects. Keister (1937) and Grosslight and Childs (1947) report similar results in training for more persistent behavior. These and similar studies immediately suggest the possibility of training sessions for psychotherapy patients during "the other 109 hours." For a number of reasons, including the fact that the skills which could be taught in such sessions are discreet skills in need of integration with other aspects of the patient's functioning, and because of the uncertainty of generalization in the absence of specific efforts in that direction, we do not propose that training sessions be considered a possible substitute for psychotherapy sessions. It is only in a complementary role that we wish to cast them, interspersed among more formal treatment sessions. To develop this theme more fully, hypothesis 6.4 considers in detail one possible type of training session. It should be made clear, however, that there are a great many personal and interpersonal skills which may be conceptualized in this manner.

HYPOTHESIS 6.4: **Patient change in psychotherapy will be enhanced by the provision of between-session training in emotional sensitivity.**

A recent and major development in psychological research has been an extensive focus on interpersonal perception. Literally scores of such studies have appeared. Interpersonal accuracy, assumed similarity, leadership, small group behavior, generality of interpersonal judgments, interpersonal prediction as a function of judge and object characteristics, and comparisons of diagnostic groups in terms of their interpersonal perceptions are but a few of the "person perception" subareas which have been examined. Early, apparently simple methodological problems have often proved severely more complicated and resistant to easy solution as research findings have come in. In all, however, important findings have emerged and the promise for more of the same seems substantial. Although relatively little of this material has yet found its way into the psychotherapeutic context, what follows may clearly be considered a step in this direction.

One subarea of interpersonal perception research has been the interpersonal communication of emotional meaning. Included here are studies of facial and vocal affective expression, the cues involved in communication of such expression, individual and group differences in accuracy of interpretation of emotional expression and, of most direct relevance to hypothesis 6.4, training to increase individual sensitivity in communicating and reading emotional expression. We have chosen this particular skill area as the means of illustrating hypothesis 6.4 because it clearly reflects an area of psychotherapeutic concern almost always characteristic of both neurotic and psychotic patients. That is, almost all major forms of psychopathology may be described as including inaccuracy or distortion in the patient's perception of both his own and others' emotional communications. Thus whether the distortion takes form in oversensitivity, hyposensitivity, lack of sensitivity, qualitative misperceptions, or confusion, it is clear that almost all classes of psychotherapy patients are in need of change in this regard. Cadman, Misbach, and Brown (1954) have described this need as follows:

> If the individual has failed to apprehend adequately the common phenomenal experiences which characterize his subculture, his ability to communicate will be handicapped. The degree of his handicap will be proportionate to the uniqueness of his "phenomenal meanings" for the emotional experiences, language symbols, and objects prevailing in his culture. In our conception, communication may be briefly described as a process of transmitting appropriate cues and responding appropriately to the cues of other individuals in

a continuous endeavor to approach satisfaction of needs. But communication can be adequate (need-satisfying) only to the extent that there exists a common phenomenal understanding of the "experiences" to be communicated and of the cues, and responses to cues, appropriate to these experiences. Hence, the greater the common phenomenal understanding, the greater the ease of adequacy of communication, and vice versa.

Failure to acquire a commonly accepted and appropriate set of behavioral responses, for use within social situations, prevents the individual from making his intentions understandable to others. Inability to respond appropriately to social cues also deprives the individual of opportunity to elicit from others continuing attempts to communicate their motives. Thus, attainment of mutual comprehension of motives, without which behavior is in considerable part desocialized, is very much dependent upon utilization of skill in responding to social cues (p. 2).

Psychotherapy may accomplish such changed sensitivity toward emotional communications. Special training sessions, we predict, when combined with formal treatment, can accomplish such goals more rapidly and effectively.

Investigations of Emotional Sensitivity Training

The investigations which provide the essential evidence from which this extrapolated proposal is made are all successful demonstrations that brief, formal training in the analysis and interpretation of facial or vocal expressions can lead to increased sensitivity or accuracy in such emotional communication. In the first, ground-breaking study of this type, Allport (1924) gave a test of facial expression interpretation to 12 subjects. Each S then spent 15 minutes studying a "chart of expressions" in which a number of facial expressions and their components were depicted as associated with various affective states. The Facial Expressions Test was then repeated, with a pretraining versus posttraining comparison of test results revealing a significant improvement in identification and interpretation of facial expressions in the large majority of subjects. While it may simply be a straightforward regression effect, it is worth noting that in this and two confirming studies reported by Allport in which "sensitivity training" yielded increased accuracy, the least efficient Ss gained the most from the training; Ss most efficient on pretraining tests gained the least. The psychotherapy patient, to whom this hypothesis is addressed, clearly falls at the least efficient extreme of an emotional sensitivity dimension.

Guilford (1929) reports an extension of this last study which attempts to determine whether longer periods of training would result in corresponding increments in "emotional sensitivity." His subjects were 15 students who were tested and trained over a 10-day period. Four equivalent picture sets of 24 faces each were made up from those developed by Rudolf (1903) and refined by Langfeld (1918). Each set contained expressions reliably judged as depicting (1) pain-grief, (2) surprise-fear, (3) anger, (4) disgust, and (5) pleasure. The over-all training procedure consisted in essence of alternating a number of test and training trials, with the results of a given test serving as the substance of the training session following this test. On each test, S was required to write down the name of the emotion which he felt best described the expression, and to add whatever he could by way of qualifying adjectives. A plot to test-to-test changes in accuracy reveals a marked, progressive increase in subject accuracy over the five trials for all subjects, with those least accurate initially showing the greatest increment.

Jenness (1932) also reports concurring research results, in which he replicated Allport's findings by using not only the same length of training session as Allport (15 minutes) but also a 45-minute training session. In yet a third study a group of subjects undergoing 15 minutes of emotional sensitivity training were compared for gain in accuracy to a matched control group for whom a 15-minute rest period, rather than a training session, was interpolated between the two testing sessions. The marked superiority of experimental subjects in terms of gain in accuracy clearly indicates that such gain is attributable to the training itself, and not practice effects from the first testing.

These concurring studies by Allport, Guilford, and Jenness are not of recent vintage. All were conducted thirty or more years ago. Research interest in emotional expressiveness has continued since that time, but in a quantitatively low key. That is, not many studies have been conducted, but with the recent burgeoning of research interest in person perception, studies of facial and vocal expressiveness have begun to appear more frequently. Of these studies, only one has spoken directly to the issue of sensitivity training. We consider this investigation first.

Mattis (Davitz, 1964) recently reported an investigation of means of increasing sensitivity to emotional expressions. It resembles Jenness' last study in several essential respects, except that here vocal rather than facial expression was under investigation. Subjects were 44 undergraduate college students, half of whom served as controls. As their first task the control Ss listened to a tape developed by Beldoch (Davitz, 1964) and attempted to identify the emotional expressions recorded. They then took a 15-minute coffee break and repeated the tape-judging procedure. In contrast, between pretesting and posttesting, experimental subjects were divided into subgroups of three or four each. They first listened to a practice tape in which speakers recited the alphabet, attempting to express each of the emotional meanings presented on the Beldoch tape. Subjects tried to identify the emotional meanings expressed on this practice tape. The tape was replayed, and before each item Ss were told which emotional meaning the speaker was trying to express. Following this, each experimental S himself attempted to express each emotional meaning contained in the tape. Finally, these expressions were discussed by the other members of each S's subgroup. The posttest was then administered. Results were clearcut. Experimental Ss improved in accuracy significantly more than did control Ss. A discussion by Davitz (1964) of Mattis' results is of interest:

> The possibility of teaching people to be more sensitive to emotional communication is encouraged by Mattis' results. In the schools, of course, and in most informal education situations in our culture, discursive communication, primarily in the verbal mode, is emphasized. Ability to understand nonverbal expressions of emotional meaning develops largely without formal tuition, and in light of the complexity of this kind of communication, it is somewhat surprising that people perform as well as they do in understanding the messages expressed. Nevertheless, Mattis' results offer some hope that directed, planned experiences in nonverbal communication can influence a person's sensitivity in this area. For those involved in the training of clinical psychologists, psychiatrists, social workers, and other professionals concerned with emotional communication, fostering emotional sensitivity through some sort of educational experience is an exciting possibility (pp. 155-156).

The studies examined thus far have centered upon the central theme of hypothesis 6.4, that is, training to increase emotional sensitivity. Many other aspects of emotional expressiveness have come under examination during the relatively long history of this research area. A partial sample of such topics would include: (1) the relative ranking of different classes of emotions in terms of the accuracy with which they are characteristically identified, (2) comparisons of posed and unposed pictures, films and live actors as stimuli, (3) patterning of cues versus specific facial features as aids to identification, (4) the effect on accuracy of knowledge of the situation in which the emotion is expressed, (5) innate versus acquired determinants of expressiveness, (6) the effects on expressive judgments of familiarity with the communicator, (7) the effect on accuracy of such judge characteristics as sex and level of intelligence, (8) the effect on judgments of vocal expressions of emotion of rate, pitch and related speech characteristics, (9) personality and cognitive correlates of emotional sensitivity, (10) the influence of emotional sensitivity upon interpersonal relationships, and (11) cultural differences in emotional expressiveness. Several of these investigative subareas are of relevance for the research implementation of the present hypothesis. They have all been discussed in depth in recent reviews by Davitz (1964), Kramer (1963), and Woodworth and Schlosberg (1954); thus most of these topics need not detain us further here. For illustrative purposes, however, we present the studies which follow. Each is drawn from a different subarea listed above. Each serves as an example of the manner in which extrapolation or tentative generalization of findings from emotional expressiveness research may aid in the implementation of hypothesis 6.4.

Blau (Davitz, 1964) sought to compare blind and sighted subjects on a number of affective judgment dimensions, including accuracy of judgments of vocally expressed emotions and degree of tendency to note affect in spoken dialogue in the absence of explicit instructions to do so. His subjects were congenitally blind adolescents and a matched group of sighted adolescents. Contrary to expectations, no significant difference emerged between subject groups in terms of accuracy of judgments. Blind subjects, however, were significantly more attentive than were sighted subjects to the affective component of speech, were more attentive to specific affective details, and were more active in interpreting everyday sounds. Two concluding comments by the investigator are particularly relevant for our purposes:

> Quite aside from the issue of accuracy, blind Ss seem to show a readiness to note affect, and it is interesting to speculate that something akin to this phenomenon may have led to the popular notion of "sensitivity" in the blind. The sighted S, because he can "tell by looking," has less need to develop the habits of listening which the blind S apparently manifests (p. 123). . . . Educators of the sighted may find pause for thought in the evidence that many of their charges are probably failing to maximize the information available in their auditory environment. The results of this study give added weight to the view (that) . . . the blind child is forced to turn to senses other than sight to explore his world. Such avenues are equally open to people with normal vision, although they are less used or understood because of the sighted person's preoccupation with visual stimuli (p. 126).

Blau's results and their interpretation suggest one important concrete means by which emotional sensitivity training with psychotherapy patients may be conducted—via screening out of visual cues during training for sensitivity to *vocal* emotional expression, and screening out of auditory cues during training for sensitivity to *facial* emotional expression.

A study reported by Hornstein (Davitz, 1964) suggests a possible unanticipated consequence of the types of training for emotional sensitivity recommended by hypothesis 6.4. If the patient can "read" the therapist *too* well, their relationship may suffer. Hornstein used college students living in a dormitory as subjects. High and low compatible roommate pairs were identified. Low compatible pairs were defined as former roommates who had requested a change of roommates after living together for one semester, and whose combined preferences for each other on three sociometric devices were below the median for the total sample. High compatible pairs were defined as roommates who had lived together for at least one semester without requesting any change and whose combined preferences for each other on the sociometric devices were above the median for the total sample. Following a standardized procedure, each subject attempted to communicate, to the other member of her pair, a series of emotional meanings (affection, anger, boredom, cheerfulness, impatience, joy, sadness, satisfaction and neutral). Results took the form of a clearly curvilinear relationship between compatibility and sensitivity. Both very high and very low sensitivity were associated with low compatibility. High compatible pairs were consistently in the middle of the sensitivity distribution. The research report concludes:

> Perhaps interpersonal compatibility requires some minimal level of sensitivity to each other; without this minimal level, it seems likely that conflicts would occur simply as a result of ignorance of each other. On the other hand, too great a sensitivity to each other may interfere with interpersonal functioning; perhaps some "blindness" or "interpersonal repression" of information is necessary for getting along together in daily living (p. 152).

Whether Hornstein's results hold for subject pairs other than college roommates, such as therapist-patient pairs, is yet to be determined. If subsequent research yields an affirmative answer, questions then arise regarding optimal, as opposed to maximal, levels of emotional sensitivity toward which psychotherapy patients should be trained.

Davitz (1964), who has been a major contributor to emotional sensitivity research, sought to identify personality, perceptual, and cognitive correlates of emotional sensitivity. In his first study, 80 graduate student subjects, divided into two 40-member groups for cross-validation purposes, were administered an emotional sensitivity test and a battery of personality tests. None of the 33 personality variables measured held up as significant correlates of emotional sensitivity. The new approach thus called for was reflected in a second study in which perceptual and cognitive correlates of emotional sensitivity were sought. In this instance, a very different result emerged. A highly significant relationship was present between the criterion variable, emotional sensitivity, and each of the four predictor variables: (1) verbal intelligence, (2) abstract symbolic ability, (3) auditory discrimination, and (4) knowledge of vocal characteristics. A multiple correlation combining these four variables against the emotional sensitivity measure was .60. Davitz observes:

> The findings lend credence to a conceptualization of emotional sensitivity in terms of complex stimuli, intervening perceptual and symbolic processes, and subsequent verbal responses. Some previous theoretical discussions of emotional sensitivity have involved mysterious terms such as the 'third ear,' and other obscure hypothetical constructs without measurable referents, unfortunately, such conceptualizations have hindered, rather than promoted meaningful empirical research in this area (p. 66).

The major implication of Davitz' findings for psychotherapy appears to lie in the domain of selection of patients for sensitivity training. That is, assuming such training cannot be made available to all patients, those most likely to profit from emotional sensitivity training appear to be those patients high in verbal intelligence, abstract symbolic ability, and so forth. Selection of patients for such purposes, therefore, would do well to reflect these predictor variables. Whether to select patients high in these characteristics—because they can benefit from training most, or as we prefer, patients low in these characteristics—because they perhaps need such training most, is a decision we leave to the personal choice of each investigator.

Our presentation of hypothesis 6.4, as well as Chapter 6, is thus concluded. The four hypotheses presented, although superficially unrelated, hold together when viewed as attempts to illustrate further the wide diversity of nonclinical research findings of potential usefulness to the researcher interested in individual psychotherapy. At this point in our presentation, we trust it is abundantly clear that yet other such extrapolatable research areas exist. With the hope that this major message has been communicated, we now turn to a consideration of group psychotherapy.

REFERENCES

Adler, N. The perception of time as a function of self-organization. Unpublished doctoral dissertation, University of California, Berkeley, 1954.

Affleck, D. C., & Garfield, S. L. Predictive judgments of therapists and duration of stay in psychotherapy. *J. clin. Psychol.,* 1961, **17**, 134–137.

Allport, F. H. *Social psychology.* Boston: Houghton-Mifflin, 1924.

Asch, S. E. The doctrine of suggestion, prestige, and imitation in social psychology. *Psychol. Rev.,* 1948, **55**, 250–276.

Auld, F., & Eron, L. D. The use of Rorschach scores to predict whether patients will continue psychotherapy. *J. consult. Psychol.,* 1953, **17**, 105–109.

Axel, R. Estimation of time. *Arch. Psychol.,* 1924, **12**, No. 74.

Azima, H. Prolonged sleep treatment in mental disorders. *J. ment. Sci.,* 1955, **101**, 593–602.

Azima, H., Vispo, R., & Azima, F. J. Observations on anaclitic therapy during sensory deprivation. In P. Solomon (Ed.) *Sensory deprivation.* Cambridge: Harvard Univer. Press, 1961. Pp. 143–160.

Bach, G. R. *Intensive group psychotherapy.* New York: Ronald Press, 1954.

Bandura, A., Ross, D., & Ross, S. A. Imitation of film-mediated aggressive models. *J. abnorm. soc. Psychol.,* 1963a, **66**, 3–11.

Bandura, A., Ross D., & Ross, S. A. Vicarious reinforcement and imitation. *J. abnorm. soc. Psychol.,* 1963b, **67**, 601–607.

Bandura, A., Ross, D., & Ross, S. A. A comparative test of the status envy, social power, and the secondary-reinforcement theories of identificatory learning. *J. abnorm. soc. Psychol.,* 1963c, **67**, 527-534.

Bandura, A., & Walters, R. H. *Social learning and personality development.* New York: Holt, Rinehart & Winston, 1963.

Barndt, R. J., & Johnson, D. M. Time orientation in delinquents. *J. abnorm. soc. Psychol.,* 1955, **51**, 343–345.

Barron, F., & Leary, T. Changes in psychoneurotic patients with and without psychotherapy. *J. consult. Psychol.,* 1955, **19**, 239–245.

Berger, S. M. Incidental learning through vicarious reinforcement. *Psychol. Rep.,* 1961, **9**, 477–491.

Bexton, W. H., Heron, W., & Scott, T. H. Effects of decreased variation in the sensory environment. *Canad. J. Psychiat.,* 1954, **8**, 70–76.

Blair, M. L. Criteria for screening applications to a mental hygiene clinic, *Smith Coll. Stud. soc. Wk.,* 1950.

Brock, T. C., & Del Giudice, C. Stealing and temporal orientation. *J. abnorm. soc. Psychol.,* 1963, **66**, 91–94.

Brower, J. F., & Brower, D. Relation between temporal judgment and social competence in the feebleminded. *Amer. J. ment. Def.,* 1947, **51**, 619–623.

Brown, J. S. Problems presented by the concept of acquired drives. In *Current theory and research in motivation: a symposium.* Lincoln: Univer. of Nebraska Press, 1953.

Brownfield, C. A. Deterioration and facilitation hypotheses in sensory-deprivation research. *Psychol. Bull.*, 1964, **61**, 304–313.

Buck, J. N. The time appreciation test. *J. appl. Psychol.*, 1946, **30**, 388–398.

Burns, N. M., & Gifford, B. C. Time estimation and anxiety. *J. psychol. Stud.*, 1961, **12**, 19–27.

Burnstein, E., Stotland, E. & Zander, A. Similarity to a model and self-evaluation. *J. abnorm. soc. Psychol.*, 1961, **62**, 257–264.

Byrne, D. Anxiety and the experimental arousal of affiliation need. *J. abnorm. soc. Psychol.*, 1961, **63**, 660–662.

Cadman, W. H., Misbach, L., & Brown, D. V. An assessment of round-table psychotherapy. *Psychol. Monogr.*, 1954, **68**, Whole No. 384.

Campbell, D. T. Conformity in psychology's theories of acquired behavioral dispositions. In I. A. Berg & B. M. Bass (Eds.) *Conformity and deviation.* New York: Harper, 1961. Pp. 101–142.

Cason, H. General curves and conditions of feeling. *J. appl. Psychol.*, 1931, **15**, 126–148.

Chance, E. *Families in treatment.* New York: Basic Books, 1959.

Chittenden, G. E. An experimental study in measuring and modifying assertive behavior in young children. *Monogr. Soc. Res. Child Develpm.*, 1942, **7**, No. 31.

Cobb, J. C., & Shor, R. E. Development of techniques to maximize hypnotic responsiveness. Presented at Eastern Psychol. Assoc., Philadelphia, 1964.

Coheen, J. Disturbances in time perception in organic brain disease. *J. nerv. ment. Dis.*, 1950, **113**, 121–129.

Cohen, B. D., Luby, E. D., Rosenbaum, G., & Gottlieb, J. S. Combined sernyl and sensory deprivation. *Comprehen. Psychiat.*, 1960, **1**, 345–348.

Cohen, J. The concept of goal gradients: A review of its present status. *J. gen. Psychol.*, 1953, **49**, 303–308.

Cohen, J. The experience of time. *Acta psychol.*, 1954, **10**, 207–219.

Corsini, R. J., & Rosenberg, B. Mechanisms of group psychotherapy. *J. abnorm. soc. Psychol.*, 1955, **51**, 406–411.

Costello, C. G. *Psychology for psychiatrists.* New York: Pergamon Press, 1965.

Davis, F. Polio in the family. Unpublished doctoral dissertation, University of Chicago, 1958.

Davitz, J. R. *The communication of emotional meaning.* New York: McGraw-Hill, 1964.

De Charms, R., & Rosenbaum, M. E. The problem of vicarious experience. In D. Willner (Ed.) *Decisions, values and groups.* New York: Pergamon Press, 1960. Pp. 267–277.

De la Garza, C., & Worchel, P. Time and space orientation on schizophrenia. *J. abnorm. soc. Psychol.*, 1956, **52**, 191–194.

Dobson, W. R. An investigation of various factors involved in time perception as manifested by different nosological groups. *J. genet. Psychol.*, 1954, **50**, 277–298.

Dubois, F. S.   The sense of time and its relation to psychiatric illness. *Amer. J. Psychiat.,* 1954, 111, 56–61.

Dymond, R. F.   Adjustment changes over therapy from self-sorts. In C. R. Rogers & R. F. Dymond (Eds.) *Psychotherapy and personality change.* Chicago: The Univer. of Chicago Press, 1954. Pp. 76–84.

Falk, J. L., & Bindra, D.   Judgment of time as a function of serial position and stress. *J. exp. Psychol.,* 1954, 47, 279–282.

Farber, M. L.   Suffering and time-perspective of the prisoner. *Univ. Iowa Stud. Child Wel.,* 1944, 20, 153–227.

Farber, M. L.   The Armageddon complex: Dynamics of opinion. *Pub. opin. Quart.,* 1951, 15, 217–224.

Farber, M. L.   Time perspective and feeling—tone: a study in the perception of the days. *J. Psychol.,* 1953, 35, 253–257.

Filer, R. J., & Meals, D. W.   The effect of motivating conditions on the estimation of time. *J. exp. Psychol.,* 1949, 39, 327–331.

Fischer, F.   Zeitstruktur und schizophrenie. *Z. ges. neurol. Psychiat.,* 1929, 121, 544–574.

Fraisse, P.   Time relationships and their pathological disintegrations. *Encephale,* 1952, 41, 122–142.

Fraisse, P.   *The psychology of time.* New York: Harper & Row, 1963.

Frank, J. D.   Some values of conflict in therapeutic groups. *Group Psychother.,* 1955, 8, 142–151.

Frank, J. D.   *Persuasion and healing.* Baltimore: The Johns Hopkins Press, 1961.

Frank, L. K.   Time perspectives. *J. soc. Phil.,* 1939, 4, 293–312.

Freedman, S. J., Grunebaum, H. U., & Greenblatt, M.   Perceptual and cognitive changes in sensory deprivation. In P. Solomon (Ed.), *Sensory deprivation.* Cambridge: Harvard Univer. Press, 1961. Pp. 58–71.

Freud, S.   *The standard edition of the complete psychological works of Sigmund Freud.* London: The Hogarth Press, 1957.

Gallagher, E. B., & Kanter, S. M. S.   The duration of outpatient psychotherapy. *Psychiat. Quart.,* 1961, 35, 312–331.

Gallagher, J. J.   Test indicators for therapy prognosis. *J. consult. Psychol.,* 1954, 18, 409–413.

Garfield, S. L., & Affleck, D. C.   An appraisal of duration of stay in outpatient psychotherapy. *J. ner. ment. Dis.,* 1959, 129, 492–498.

Gelfand, D. M.   The influence of self-esteem on rate of verbal conditioning and social matching behavior. *J. abnorm. soc. Psychol.,* 1962, 65, 259–265.

Gendlin, E. T., & Shlien, J. M.   Immediacy in time attitudes before and after time-limited psychotherapy. *J. clin. Psychol.,* 1961, 17, 69–72.

Geocaris, K.   The patient as listener. *Arch. gen. Psychiat.,* 1960, 2, 81–88.

Gewirtz, J. L., & Baer, D. M.   The effects of brief social deprivation on behaviors for a social reinforcer. *J. abnorm. soc. Psychol.,* 1958a, 56, 49–56.

Gewirtz, J. L., & Baer, D. M.   Deprivation and satiation of social reinforcers as drive conditions. *J. abnorm. soc. Psychol.*, 1958b, **57**, 165–172.

Gibby, R. G., & Adams, H. B.   Receptiveness of psychiatric patients to verbal communication. *Arch. gen. Psychiat.*, 1961, **5**, 366–370.

Gibby, R. G., Adams, H. B., & Carrera, R. N.   Therapeutic changes in psychiatric patients following partial sensory deprivation. *Arch. gen. Psychiat.*, 1960, **3**, 33–42.

Gibby, R. G., Stotsky, B. A., Hiler, E. W., & Miller, D. R.   Validation of Rorschach criteria for predicting duration of therapy. *J. consult. Psychol.*, 1954, **18**, 185–191.

Gilliland, A. R., Hofeld, J. B., & Eckstrand, G.   Studies in time perception. *Psychol. Bull.*, 1946, **43**, 162–176.

Gliedman, L. H., Nash, E. H., Jr., Imber, S. D., Stone, A. R., & Frank, J. D.   Reduction of symptoms by pharmacologically inert substances and by short-term psychotherapy. *Arch. neurol. Psychiat.*, 1958, **79**, 345–351.

Goldfried, N.   Psychoanalytic interpretation of sensory deprivation. *Psychol. Rec.*, 1960, **10**, 211–215.

Goldstein, A. P.   Patient's expectancies and non-specific therapy as a basis for (un)spontaneous remission. *J. clin. Psychol.*, 1960, **16**, 399–403.

Goldstein, A. P.   *Therapist-patient expectancies in psychotherapy.* New York: Pergamon Press, 1962.

Gothberg, L. C.   The mentally defective child's understanding of time. *Amer. J. ment. Def.*, 1949, **53**, 441–455.

Grosslight, J., & Childs, I. L.   Persistence as a function of previous experience of failure followed by success. *Amer. J. Psychol.*, 1947, **60**, 378–387.

Guertin, W. H., & Rabin, A. I.   Misperception of time in schizophrenia. *Psychol. Rep.*, 1960, **7**, 57–58.

Guilford, J. F.   An experiment in learning to read facial expressions. *J. abnorm. soc. Psychol.*, 1929, **24**, 191–202.

Gulliksen, H.   The influence of occupation upon the perception of time. *J. exp. Psychol.*, 1927, **10**, 52–59.

Hankoff, L. D., Engelhardt, D. M., & Freedman, N.   Placebo response in schizophrenic outpatients. *Arch. gen. Psychiat.*, 1960, **2**, 33–42.

Harris, A.   Sensory deprivation in schizophrenia. *J. ment. Sci.*, 1959, **105**, 235–237.

Hebb, D. O.   Introduction to: Heron, W. Cognitive and physiological effects of perceptual isolation. In P. Solomon (Ed.) *Sensory deprivation.* Cambridge: Harvard Univer. Press, 1961. Pp. 6–33.

Heilbrun, A. B.   Client personality patterns, counselor dominance, and duration of counseling. *Psychol. Rep.*, 1961, **9**, 15–25.

Heine, R. W., & Trosman, H.   Initial expectations of the doctor-patient interaction as a factor in continuance in psychotherapy. *Psychiat.*, 1960, **23**, 275–278.

Heller, K., and Goldstein, A. P.   Client dependency and therapist expectancy as relationship maintaining variables in psychotherapy. *J. consult. Psychol.*, 1961, **25**, 371–375.

Henry, W. E., & Shlien, J. M.   Affective complexity and psychotherapy: Some comparisons of time-limited and unlimited treatment. *J. proj. Tech.*, 1958, **22**, 153–162.

Heron, W.   Cognitive and physiological effects of perceptual isolation. In P. Solomon (Ed.) *Sensory deprivation*. Cambridge: Harvard Univer. Press, 1961. Pp. 6–33.

Herzberg, A.   *Active psychotherapy*. New York: Grune & Stratton, 1947.

Hindle, H. M.   Time estimates as a function of distance travelled and relative clarity of a goal. *J. Pers.*, 1951, **19**, 483–501.

Hoehn-Saric, R., Frank, J. D., Imber, S. D., Nash, E. H., Jr., Stone, A. R., & Battle, C. C.   Systematic preparation of patients for psychotherapy. I. Effects on therapy behavior and outcome. *J. psychiat. Res.*, 1964, **2**, 267–281.

Horanyi-Hechst, B.   Zeitbeuresstsein und Schizophrenie. *Arch. Psychiat.*, 1943, **116**, 287–292.

Hull, C. L.   *Principles of behavior*. New York: Appleton-Century, 1943.

Hunt, J. Mc V., Ewing, T. N., La Forge, R., & Gilbert, W. M.   An integrated approach to research on therapeutic counseling. *J. counsel. Psychol.*, 1959, **6**, 46–54.

Imber, S. D., Frank, J. D., Nash, E. H., Jr., Stone, R. S., & Gliedman, L. H. Improvement and amount of therapeutic contact: an alternative to the use of no treatment controls in psychotherapy. *J. consult. Psychol.*, 1957, **21**, 309–315.

Israeli, M.   *Abnormal personality and time*. New York: Science Press, 1936.

Jack, L. M.   An experimental study of ascendant behavior in preschool children. *Univ. Iowa Stud. Child Wel.*, 1934, **9**, 7–65.

Jackson, C. W., Jr., & Kelley, E. L.   Influence of suggestion and subjects' prior knowledge in research on sensory deprivation. *Science*, 1962, **132**, 211–212.

Jakubczak, L. F., & Walters, R. H.   Suggestibility as dependency behavior. *J. abnorm. soc. Psychol.*, 1959, **59**, 102–107.

Jenness, A. F.   The effect of coaching subjects in the recognition of facial expressions. *J. gen. Psychol.*, 1932, **7**, 163–178.

Johnston, H. M.   A comparison of time estimation of schizophrenic patients with that of normal individuals. Unpublished master's thesis, Brown University, 1939.

Jung, C. G.   The practice of psychotherapy. *Collected works*, Vol. XVI. New York: Pantheon, 1954.

Kadis, A. L., Krasner, J. D., Winick, C., & Foulkes, S. H.   *A practicum of group psychotherapy*. New York: Harper & Row, 1963.

Kagan, N., Krathwohl, D. R., & Miller, R.   Stimulated recall in therapy using video tape. *J. counsel. Psychol.*, 1963, **3**, 237–243.

Kandel, E. J., Myers, T. I., & Murphy, D. B.   Influence of prior verbalization and instructions on visual sensations reported under conditions of reduced sensory input. *Amer. Psychologist*, 1958, 13, 334.

Kanfer, F. H., Bradley, M. M., & Marston, A. R.   Self reinforcement as a function of degree of learning. *Psychol. Rep.* 1962, 10, 885–886.

Kanfer, F. H., & Marston, A. R.   Human reinforcement: vicarious and direct. *J. exp. Psychol.*, 1963, 65, 292–296.

Katz, E.   Some factors affecting resumption of interrupted activities by preschool children. *Inst. Child Wel. Monogr. Ser.*, No. 16, 1940.

Keister, M. E.   The behavior of your children in failure. *Univ. Iowa Stud. Child Wel.*, 1937, 14, 29–82.

Kelly, G. A.   *The psychology of personal constructs.* New York: W. W. Norton, 1955.

Kloos, G.   Stoerungun des zeiterlebens in der endogenen depression. *Nervenarzi*, 1938, 11, 225–244.

Kotkov, B., & Meadow, A.   Rorschach criteria for predicting continuation in individual psychotherapy. *J. consult. Psychol.*, 1953, 17, 16–20.

Kramer, E.   Judgment of personal characteristics and emotions from nonverbal properties of speech. *Psychol. Bull.*, 1963, 60, 408–420.

Kubzansky, P. E.   The effects of reduced environmental stimulation on human behavior: A review. In A. D. Binderman & H. Zimmer (Eds.) *The manipulation of human behavior.* New York: Wiley, 1961.

Kutash, S., & Dengrove, E.   Why patients discontinue treatment in a mental hygiene clinic. *Amer. J. Psychother.*, 1950, 4, 457–462.

Langfeld, H. S.   The judgment of emotion by facial expression. *J. abnorm. soc. Psychol.*, 1918, 13, 172–184.

Lanzetta, J. T., & Kanareff, V. T.   The effects of a monetary reward on the acquisition of an imitative response. *J. abnorm. soc. Psychol.*, 1959, 59, 120–127.

Lawes, T. G.   Schizophrenia, sernyl and sensory deprivation. *Brit. J. Psychiat.*, 1963, 109, 243–250.

Lefkowitz, M. M., Blake, R. R., & Mouton, J. S.   Status factors in pedestrian violation of traffic signals. *J. abnorm. soc. Psychol.*, 1955, 51, 704–706.

Lennard, H. L., & Bernstein, A.   *The anatomy of psychotherapy.* New York: Columbia Univer. Press, 1960.

Lesser, G. S., & Abelson, R. P.   Personality correlates of persuasibility in children. In I. L. Janis & C. I. Hovland (Eds.) *Personality and persuasibility.* New Haven: Yale Univer. Press, 1959, 187–206.

Lewis, D. J., & Duncan, C. P.   Vicarious experience and partial reinforcement. *J. abnorm. soc. Psychol.*, 1958, 57, 321–326.

Lilly, J.   Effects of physical restraint and of reduction on ordinary levels of physical stimuli on intact, healthy persons. *Group adv. Psychiat.*, 1956, No. 2.

Lippitt, R., Polansky, N., Redl, F., & Rosen, S.   The dynamics of power:

a field study of social influence in groups of children. *Hum. Rel.,* 1952, **5,** 37–64.

Lorr, M., Katz, M. M., & Rubinstein, E. A. The prediction of length of stay in psychotherapy. *J. consult. Psychol.,* 1958, **22,** 321–327.

Lorr, M., McNair, D. M., Michaux, W. M., & Raskin, A. Frequency of treatment and change in psychotherapy. *J. abnorm. soc. Psychol.,* 1962, **64,** 281–292.

Lorr, M., McNair, D. M., & Goldstein, A. P. A comparison of time-limited and time-unlimited psychotherapy (in process).

Luborsky, L. The patient's personality and psychotherapeutic change. In H. H. Strupp & L. Luborsky (Ed.) *Research in psychotherapy.* Washington: Amer. Psychol. Assoc., 1962. Pp. 115–133.

Maccoby, E. E., & Wilson, W. C. Identification and observational learning from films. *J. abnorm. soc. Psychol.,* 1957, **55,** 76–87.

May, M. A., & Lumsdaine, A. A. *Learning from films.* New Haven: Yale Univer. Press, 1958.

McBrearty, J. F., Marston, A. R., & Kanfer, F. H. Conditioning a verbal operant in a group setting: direct vs. vicarious reinforcement. *Amer. Psychologist,* 1961, **16,** 425.

McCladdie, R. E. A comparison of referred and self-referred psychotic patients in a Veterans Administration Mental Hygiene Clinic. Unpublished M. S. W. thesis, University of Southern California, 1950.

McDougall, R. Sex differences in the sense of time. *Science,* 1904, **19,** 707–708.

McNair, D. M., & Lorr, M. Therapists' judgments of appropriateness of psychotherapy frequency schedules. *J. consult. Psychol.,* 1960, **24,** 500–506.

Meade, R. D. Time estimates as affected by motivational level, goal distance, and rate of progress. *J. exp. Psychol.,* 1959, **58,** 275-279.

Meade, R. D. Time estimates as affected by need tension and rate of progress. *J. Psychol.,* 1960, **50,** 173–177.

Meade, R. D. Effect of motivation and progress on the estimation of longer time intervals. *J. exp. Psychol.,* 1963, **65,** 564–567.

Meerloo, A. M. Father time. *Psychiat. Quart.,* 1948, **22,** 587–608.

Mensh, I. N., and Golden, J. M. Factors in psychotherapeutic success. *J. Mo. Med. Ass.,* 1951, **48,** 180–184.

Miller, N. E., & Dollard, J. *Social learning and imitation.* New Haven: Yale Univer. Press, 1941.

Minkowski, E. Le problème du temps en psychopathologie. *Rech. Phil.,* 1933, **2,** 231–256.

Morton, R. B. An experiment in brief psychotherapy. *Psychol. Monogr.,* 1955, **66,** Whole No. 1.

Mowrer, O. H. *Learning theory and behavior.* New York: Wiley, 1960.

Muench, G. A. An investigation of the efficacy of time-limited psychotherapy. Presented at Amer. Psychol. Assoc., Los Angeles, 1965.

Myers, J. K., & Auld, F., Jr.   Some variables related to outcome of psychotherapy. *J. clin. Psychol.,* 1955, **11,** 51–54.

Myers, T. I., Murphy, D. B., & Smith, S.   Progress report on studies of sensory deprivation. Human Resources Research Office, 1960.

Nielsen, G.   *Studies in self confrontation.* Cleveland: Howard Allen, 1954.

Orne, M. T.   The anticipatory socialization interview. Unpublished manuscript, Institute of the Pennsylvania Hospital, Philadelphia, Pennsylvania, 1964.

Orne, M. T., & Scheibe, K. E.   The contribution of nondeprivation factors in the production of sensory deprivation effects. *J. abnorm. soc. Psychol.,* 1964, **68,** 3–12.

Overall, B., & Aronson, H.   Expectations of psychotherapy in patients of lower socioeconomic status. *Amer. J. Orthopsychiat.,* 1963, **33,** 421–430.

Ovsiankina, M.   Die wiederaufnakme unterbrochene handlungen. *Psychol. Forsch.,* 1928, **11,** 302–379.

Page, M. L.   The modification of ascendant behavior in preschool children. *Univ. Iowa Stud. Child Wel.,* 1935, **12,** 1–69.

Paivio, A.   Audience influence, social isolation, and speech. *J. abnorm. soc. Psychol.,* 1963, **67,** 247–253.

Pearl, D., & Berg, P. S. D.   Time perception and conflict arousal in schizophrenia. *J. abnorm. soc. Psychol.,* 1963, **66,** 332–338.

Peters, H. L., & Jenkins, R. L.   Improvement of chronic schizophrenic patients with guided problem-solving motivated by hunger. *Psychiat. Quart. Suppl.,* 1954, **28,** 84–101.

Pollard, J. C., Uhr, L., & Jackson, C. W., Jr.   Studies in sensory deprivation. *Arch. gen. Psychiat.,* 1963, **8,** 435–454.

Rank, O.   *Will therapy.* New York: Alfred A. Knopf, 1936.

Reitman, E. E., & Cleveland, S. E.   The effect of reduced environmental stimulation on various behavior modalities for schizophrenic and non-psychotic subjects. Unpublished manuscript, VA Hospital, Houston, Texas, 1961.

Riessman, F.   New models for a treatment approach of low-income clients. Presented at Amer. Orthopsychiat. Assoc., Washington, 1963.

Rioch, D. McK.   Recent contributions of neuropsychiatric research to the theory and practice of psychotherapy. *Amer. J. Psychoanal.,* 1960, **20,** 115–129.

Robertson, M. H.   Sensory deprivation and some therapeutic considerations. *Psychol. Rec.,* 1961, **11,** 343–347.

Rogers, C. R.   *Counseling and psychotherapy.* New York: Houghton-Mifflin, 1942.

Rogers, C. R.   The necessary and sufficient conditions of therapeutic personality change. *J. consult. Psychol.,* 1957, **21,** 95–103.

Rosenbaum, M. E., Horne, W. C., & Chalmers, D. K.   Level of self-esteem and the learning of imitation and non-imitation. *J. Pers.,* 1962, **30,** 147–156.

Rosenblith, J. F. Learning by imitation in kindergarten children. *Child Develpm.*, 1959, 30, 69–80.

Rosenblith, J. F. Imitative color choices in kindergarten children. *Child Develpm.*, 1961, 32, 211–223.

Rosensweig, S., & Koht, A. The experience of duration as affected by need-tension. *J. exp. Psychol.*, 1933, 16, 745–774.

Rosenthal, D. Changes in some moral values following psychotherapy. *J. consult. Psychol.*, 1955, 19, 431–436.

Rotter, J. B. *Social learning and clinical psychology.* New York: Prentice-Hall, 1954.

Rubinstein, E. A., & Lorr, M. A comparison of terminators and remainers in outpatient psychotherapy. *J. clin. Psychol.*, 1956, 12, 345–349.

Rudolph, H. *Der ausdruck der gernutsbewegungen des mensclen.* Text and atlas. Dresden: Kuehtmann, 1903.

Schachter, S. *The psychology of affiliation.* Stanford: Stanford Univer. Press, 1959.

Schachter, S., & Singer, J. E. Cognitive, social and physiological determinants of emotional states. *Psychol. Rev.*, 1962, 69, 379–399.

Schachter, S., & Wheeler, L. Epinephrine, Chlorpromazine, and amusement. *J. abnorm. soc. Psychol.*, 1962, 65, 121–128.

Schaffer, L., & Myers, J. M. Psychotherapy and social stratification. *Psychiat.*, 1954, 17, 83–93.

Schein, E. H. The effect of reward on adult imitative behavior. *J. abnorm. soc. Psychol.*, 1954, 49, 389–395.

Schofield, W. *Psychotherapy, the purchase of friendship.* Englewood Cliffs, N.J.: Prentice-Hall, 1964.

Schroder, H. M., & Rotter, J. B. Rigidity as learned behavior. *J. exp. Psychol.*, 1952, 44, 141–150.

Seeman, J. An investigation of client reactions to vocational counseling. *J. consult. Psychol.*, 1949, 13, 95–104.

Sheehan, J. G. Rorschach changes during psychotherapy in relation to personality of the therapist. *Amer. Psychologist*, 1953, 8, 434–435.

Shlien, J. M. Time-limited psychotherapy: an experimental investigation of practical values and theoretical implications. *J. counsel. Psychol.*, 1957, 4, 318–322.

Siegal, R. S., & Rosen, I. C. Character style and anxiety tolerance. In H. H. Strupp & L. Luborsky (Eds.) *Research in psychotherapy.* Washington: Amer. Psychol. Assoc., 1962. Pp. 206–217.

Siegman, A. W. Anxiety, impulse control, intelligence and the estimation of time. *J. clin. Psychol.*, 1962, 18, 103–105.

Slavson, S. R. *Analytic group psychotherapy with children, adolescents, and adults.* New York: Columbia Univer. Press, 1950.

Smith, S., & Lewty, W. Perceptual isolation using a silent room. *Lancet*, 1959, 2, 342–348.

Solomon, A.   The relation of time estimation to personality traits. Unpublished master's thesis, University of Kentucky, 1950.

Spohn, H. E., & Wolk, W.   Effect of group problem solving experience upon social withdrawal in chronic schizophrenics. *J. abnorm. soc. Psychol.*, 1963, **66**, 187–190.

Standel, S. W., & Van Der Veen, F.   Length of therapy in relation to counselor estimates of personal integration and other case variables. *J. consult. Psychol.*, 1957, **21**, 1–9.

Staples, F. R., & Walters, R. H.   Anxiety, birth order, and susceptibility to social influence. *J. abnorm. soc. Psychol.*, 1961, **62**, 716–719.

Staples, F. R., Wilson, F. S., & Walters, R. H.   Increasing the verbal responsiveness of chronic schizophrenics. Unpublished manuscript, Ontario Hospital, New Toronto, Canada, 1963.

Stevenson, H. W., & Odom, R. D.   The effectiveness of social reinforcement following two conditions of deprivation. *J. abnorm. soc. Psychol.*, 1962, **65**, 429–430.

Stevenson, I.   Direct instigation of behavioral changes in psychotherapy. *Arch. gen. Psychiat.*, 1959, **1**, 99–107.

Stotland, E., & Dunn, R.   Empathy, self-esteem, and birth order. *J. abnorm. soc. Psychol.*, 1963, **66**, 532–540.

Strauss, E. W.   Disorders of personal time in depressive states. *South. Med J.*, 1947, **40**, 154–158.

Suedfeld, P.   Attitude manipulation in restricted environments. *J. abnorm. soc. Psychol.*, 1964, **68**, 242–247.

Sullivan, T. R., Miller, C., & Smelser, W.   Factors in length of stay and progress in psychotherapy. *J. consult. Psychol.*, 1958, **22**, 1–9.

Taft, J.   *Dynamics of therapy in a controlled relationship.* New York: Macmillan, 1933.

Taulbee, E. S.   Relationship between certain personality variables and continuation in psychotherapy. *J. consult. Psychol.*, 1958, **22**, 83–89.

Taylor, J. A., & Spence, K. W.   The relationship of anxiety level to performance in serial learning. *J. exp. Psychol.*, 1952, 44, 61–64.

Thor, D. H.   Time perspective and time of day. *Psychol. Rec.*, 1962a, **12**, 417–422.

Thor, D. H.   Diurnal variability in time estimation. *Per. mot. Skills,* 1962b, **15**, 451–454.

Tilton, J. R.   The use of instrumental motor and verbal learning techniques in the treatment of chronic schizophrenics. *Dissert. Abstr.*, 1956, **16**, 1180–1181.

Truax, C. B.   Depth of intrapersonal exploration on therapeutic process in group psychotherapy with and without vicarious therapy pretraining. Wisconsin Psychiatric Institute, 1963, mimeograph.

Vernon, J. A., McGill, T. E., Gulick, W. L., & Candland, D. K.   The effect of human isolation upon some perceptual and motor skills. In P. Solomon

(Ed.) *Sensory deprivation.* Cambridge: Harvard Univer. Press, 1961. Pp. 41–57.

Wallace, M. Future time perspective in schizophrenia. *J. abnorm. soc. Psychol.,* 1956, **52**, 240–245.

Walters, R. H., & Karal, P. Social deprivation and verbal behavior. *J. Pers.,* 1960, **28**, 89–107.

Walters, R. H., Leat, M., & Mezei, L. Response inhibition and disinhibition through empathetic learning. *Canad. J. Psychol.,* 1963, **16**, 235–243.

Walters, R. H., Marshall, W. E., & Shooter, J. R. Anxiety, isolation, and susceptibility to social influence. *J. Pers.,* 1960, **28**, 518–529.

Walters, R. H., & Quinn, M. J. The effects of social and sensory deprivation on autokinetic judgments. *J. Pers.,* 1960, **28**, 210–219.

Walters, R. H., & Ray, E. Anxiety, social isolation, and reinforcer effectiveness. *J. Pers.,* 1960, **28**, 258–267.

Walz, G. R., & Johnston, J. A. Counselors look at themselves on video tape. *J. counsel. Psychol.,* 1963, **10**, 232–236.

Whitaker, D. S., & Lieberman, M. A. *Psychotherapy through the group process.* New York: Atherton Press, 1964.

Woodworth, R. S., & Schlosberg, H. *Experimental psychology.* New York: Holt, 1954.

Wright, B. A. *Physical disability, a psychological approach.* New York: Harper, 1960.

Wright, F. H. The other 109 hours. In F. J. Shaw (Ed.) *Behavioristic approaches to counseling and psychotherapy.* Birmingham: Univer. of Alabama Stud., 1961.

Wright, K., Gabriel, E., & Haimowitz, N. Time-limited psychotherapy: Advantages, problems, outcomes. *Psychol. Rep.,* 1961, **9**, 187–190.

Yerkes, R. M., & Urban, T. Time estimation in its relation to sex, age and physiological rhythms. *Harv. psychol. Stud.,* 1906, **2**, 405–430.

Ziegarnik, B. Uber das behalten von erledigten und unerledigten handlungen. *Psychol. Forsch.,* 1927, **9**, 1–85.

Zigler, E. Social deprivation and rigidity in the performance of feebleminded children. *J. abnorm. soc. Psychol.,* 1961, **62**, 413–421.

Zubek, J. P., Pushbar, D., Sansom, W., & Gowing, J. Perceptual changes after prolonged sensory isolation (darkness and silence). *Canad. J. Psychol.,* 1961, **15**, 83–100.

III

GROUP PSYCHOTHERAPY

7

GROUP COMPOSITION AND
INITIAL STRUCTURE

INTRODUCTION

As has been our intent in earlier chapters, our focus on group psychotherapy will emphasize the identification and development of hypotheses whose investigation offers the potential for a firmer underpinning
of important psychotherapeutic variables. This general emphasis
assumes considerable additional importance in this and the remaining
chapters when we note that the sphere of psychotherapy to which they
are addressed currently suffers from the weakest research foundation of
all areas considered thus far. With only a few exceptions, the structure
of contemporary group psychotherapy practice rests on a body of professional literature consisting overwhelmingly of anecdotal, case history,
and related impressionistic reports. Although we are quick to pay
homage to the need for material at this level of observation, for its
hypothesis-generating potential, if nothing else, such accord on our
part is largely tempered by the gross absence of evidence, over an
appreciable time period, of any significant movement or development
among most individuals currently interested in group psychotherapy,
toward research activity characterized as hypothesis testing, manipulative, experimental, or as more than purely descriptive. Thus group
psychotherapy literature as a whole has remained at the earliest and
most primitive level of observation and inquiry. From several perspectives the potential offered by this treatment approach is considerable,
a fact that demands efforts aimed at greater understanding, control,
and teachability of the group psychotherapy process. The plateau of
descriptiveness which the current group psychotherapy literature represents must be built on, developed, and elaborated. How is this to

come about? What sources of research hypotheses can most profitably be drawn on? The potential utility of several bodies of information is readily apparent. As indicated above, the generally descriptive group psychotherapy literature is one such hypothesis generating source, and indeed it will be drawn upon as the present chapter's hypotheses are developed. Research focused on individual psychotherapy similarly suggests much of potential importance for the group therapy process, as do studies of verbal conditioning, interpersonal communication and attraction, and, more generally, dyadic interaction. All of these bases for extrapolation have been considered in depth in earlier chapters aimed at other dimensions of psychotherapy. Although we do not, therefore, draw heavily on such material in the present and succeeding chapters, we do so to an extent that makes clear that their relevance to group phenomena is both real and important. A further source of potential information and clarification of group psychotherapy, the one to which most of our attention will be devoted, is the group dynamics or small group research literature. Under these terms are subsumed a very large number of carefully conceived and conducted investigations inquiring into the composition, functioning, or structural dimensions of problem-solving, training, and other not intentionally therapeutic small groups. In essence, therefore, the discussions which follow assume a position consistent with our earlier chapters; the aspects of psychotherapy toward which our hypotheses are aimed will become most usable by the practitioner, most teachable to the student, most meaningfully manipulatable by the researcher, and most understandable by all to the extent that such hypotheses depend for their development on the most judicious use of both clinical and nonclinical research reports. Since our interpretation in the present instance of judicious use of research material will lead to heavy reliance on group dynamics or small group research, it is important that this decision be examined in greater detail.

Cartwright (1951), a leading contributor to the group dynamics movement, provided an important early, if indirect, paper on this issue of extrapolation. Drawing on a series of small group studies, he formulated eight principles by which group characteristics are held to influence attitudinal and behavioral change in group members. Though not oriented toward therapy groups, this formulation was clearly a significant first step toward bridging the conceptual gap between problem-solving and therapy group interactions. Bach (1954) carries matters a bit further by presenting a strong a priori case for the relevance of these group dynamics influences in therapy groups. He suggests that small group variables such as cohesiveness, clique formation, norm development, and so forth—all of which operate in a largely specifiable manner in problem-solving groups—have counterpart influences in group psychotherapy. Hunt (1964), Lorr (1963), and Schneider (1955) are others who have developed a cogent a priori case for the process of group dynamic to group psychotherapy extrapolation. Let us, however, underscore the a priori nature of the foregoing. With a few exceptions, largely in the form of studies meaningfully applying Bales Interaction Process Analysis to therapy groups,* such extrapolations have neither been developed nor placed under experimental scrutiny. Thus, although we clearly lean toward this extrapolatory position, confirming evidence is yet to become available. Further, there are others who hold that group dynamic considerations are wholly irrelevant to psychotherapeutic interactions.

Locke (1961) for example, representing a psychoanalytic viewpoint, comments:

> Group psychotherapy does not employ the so-called group dynamics. Although these may be present in the psychoanalytic groups, as in any group, they play no conscious or directed part in the therapy. Further, it is the individual who is being treated, not the group (p. 37).

Lowrey (1944) and Wolf and Schwartz (1962) have favored a similar view. The latter authors take their stand against group dynamics with a remarkable degree of vehemence and apparently base it on a misperception of the manner in which group dynamics principles and therapist orientation to the group as a whole influence the resulting therapeutic interaction. They comment:

> The group dynamic emphasis tends to homogenize the membership, to create an apparency of psychologic uniformity and so to block the emergence of . . . healthy differentiation. The group dynamic point of view sponsors a false belief in the value of mediocrity. The group dynamic orientation is anti-rational and anti-multidimensional. It emphasizes structure and neglects content and process. The stress on group dynamics is anticlinical and anti-therapeutic . . . (p. 218).

As Parloff (1963) observes, and our presentation thus far hints, this debate can best be understood more generally in terms of an analogous "individual-oriented" versus "group-oriented" split among contemporary group psychotherapists. He comments:

*These studies are examined in Chapter 10.

Members of these two schools react quite differently to the specific variables with which the group dynamicist is concerned. The individual-oriented
group therapist rejects many of the variables described by students of small
groups as being either irrelevant to group therapy or actually dangerous
to group therapy and, therefore, to be avoided. . . . The individual-oriented
group therapist postulates that group therapy does not involve significantly
more than the techniques, goals and theory of individual psychotherapy.
He deals with individual psychodynamics and the influence of the behavior
of the members and the therapist on each other. The group is merely viewed
as the setting in which these events occur . . . .

The second . . . school of group therapy focuses on the group as a unit
and is therefore in principle more accessible to the influence of group dynamics research. In a sense, these therapists have developed a philosophy
which effectively reduces the therapy group to a single unit, that is, a single
individual (pp. 4–6).

A key point here, however, is that viewing contemporary group
psychotherapists in such a dichotomous manner is clearly an exaggera-
tion, as Parloff acknowledges. It is no doubt true that there are in fact
therapists who adhere strictly to an individual-oriented or group-
oriented perspective; but it is more important to note that the large
majority of contemporary group psychotherapists lean toward a more
moderate or modal position. Although most psychotherapists will tend
to favor either an individual, leader-centered approach or a group-
oriented, group-centered viewpoint, attention to *both* individual
psychodynamics and group characteristics is the rule, not the exception. The writings of Bach (1954), Foulkes and Anthony (1957), Frank
(1957), Liff (1952), and many others amply illustrate this point.

We have briefly examined the nature of the therapist's operating
orientation, at this point in our discussion, for its relevance to therapist
acceptance or rejection of group dynamics concepts. We return to this
topic at some length in our next chapter to deal with group psychotherapist orientation and operations. At that point we shall attempt
to develop psychotherapy relevant hypotheses from the considerable
group dynamics leadership research inquiring into the consequences
of leader-centered and group-centered structures in problem-solving
groups.

With the foregoing as background, our position on group psychotherapy may be stated as follows: group dynamics research literature
appears to have much to offer the researcher and clinician interested
in group psychotherapy. The extrapolation process, however, must be
selective and subject to research examination. Extrapolations must be

to further formal or clinical research, and not directly to psychotherapeutic practice. As Durkin (1957) aptly states:

> . . . if we are to compare normal with therapeutic groups and to consider
> applying the experimental findings which have been made on the former to
> the management of the latter, then we must qualify those findings according
> to the specific requirements deriving from the differences between their
> separate goals . . . the final solution must come through further experimen-
> tation with therapeutic groups (p. 125). . . . scientific validation should shed
> further light on the relationship between the group processes and the thera-
> peutic process; minimize errors in the application of results from one type
> of group to another; most important increase the mutual understanding and
> eventual integration of the knowledge produced by these two main ap-
> proaches to the understanding of the nature of groups (p. 130).

GROUP COMPOSITION AND INITIAL STRUCTURE

The first general question which must be faced by the prospective
group therapist concerns the manner in which his group is to be
constituted. What classes of patients are to be included and how
many? On what grounds is patient selection to be made most effectively? Do the intake or initiation procedures in which the patient-
candidate participates on his way to group membership influence his
subsequent within-group behavior? These are the types of issue to
which our hypotheses will speak as we focus on several specific aspects
of therapy group composition.

Functional Selection of Group Membership

Perhaps one of the most enduring issues in the group psychotherapy literature relevant to group composition relates to homogeneous versus heterogeneous group membership. Opinions are varied
and often heated. Within groups of proponents of either viewpoint
we find differing bases for homogeneity or heterogeneity. Although
diagnostic category is the prevailing type of criterion, relevant research
is rare. A sampling of these diverse stances is of interest. Slavson (1957),
leans toward the homogeneity pole of this continuum. He comments:

> . . . identification is particularly important in therapy groups for it makes
> possible vicarious catharsis and spectator therapy. It is for this reason that
> patients assigned to the same age group should have, as far as possible, com-
> mon central or nuclear problems even though their symptoms and clinical
> diagnoses may be at variance or dissimilar" (p. 116).

Rosow and Kaplan (1954) agree and report that selection for their therapy groups is guided by interpatient similarity in terms of symptoms, personality characteristics, and degree of insight. Grouping patients on these bases, they add, enhances the extent to which patients are enabled to empathize with one another and provide each other with meaningful insights and interpretations. Furst (1951) offers the following compilation of supposed advantages from a series of writers favoring homogeneous versus heterogeneous group composition.

1. More rapid, mutual identification.
2. More rapid development of insight.
3. Shortened duration of psychotherapy.
4. More regular attendance.
5. Decreased resistance and destructive behavior.
6. Less frequent development of cliques and subgroups.
7. More rapid symptom removal.

Proponents of a heterogeneous group structure, in contrast, claim that with diversity of composition:

1. Therapy is deeper.
2. Reality testing is more thorough.
3. Intragroup transferences are more readily formed.
4. Groups are more easily assembled.

Wolf and Schwartz (1962), perhaps the most ardent champions of the heterogeneity viewpoint, comment:

> One aim of psychotherapy is to confront the patient with alternatives to the compulsion which leaves him no choice. When the therapist limits the patient to others similarly compelled blindly to pursue a course, the reinforced, unhealthy custom tends to prevail. Where the patient is witness to many optional ways of being . . . the wholesome exercise of some discrimination is enhanced (p. 60). The therapists' preferences for the homogeneous or heterogeneous medium is some indication of his values. Treating people as if they were identical is sectarian. Differentiating them is humanitarian. Homogeneity sees disagreement as irreconcilable. Heterogeneity sees disagreement as a basis for fruitful exchange. Homogeneity breeds egocentricity, the inability to tolerate complementarity. The heterogeneous group is a practice-ground that helps the patient become secure with the stranger (p. 59).

And so, in several quarters, the argument continues, waxing, waning, and remaining unclarified. Many, if not most, group psychotherapists have recognized, however, that the heterogeneity-homogeneity controversy is in many respects a pseudocontroversy, a false polarization, an irrelevant misdirection of energy. More and more they are clinically experimenting with the more consequential issue of achieving a "balanced" group. Rather than asking "Which is more therapeutically effective, a homogeneous or heterogeneous group?" they are more correctly directing attention toward clinically isolating those *specific* interpatient similarities and differences leading to the most interactive, compatible and mutually responsive psychotherapy group. From our perspective this is certainly a step in the right direction. As will be seen later, our extrapolated hypotheses in this area continue in this direction by proposing potentially more effective and rigorous means of avoiding group compositional generalities and suggesting procedures for composing potentially more therapeutic group structures. Locke (1961), one advocate of this balanced approach to group composition, observes:

> Balancing of groups seems to be the most popular method of group composition. Groups are established by balancing active and passive patients, or by balancing diagnostic category, or personality characteristics, or whatever else the therapist regards as decisive (p. 245).
>
> The guiding factor is communication. Whatever the characteristic, if the imperative of communication be kept to the fore there will be no difficulty of decision. If the spread is too great between group members in any characteristics . . . if there is no common meeting ground because of the difference, there can be no communication and therefore no interaction (p. 246).

This redirection of orientation away from gross heterogeneity-homogeneity considerations in favor of more discriminating attention to efforts aimed at composing therapy groups on the basis of patient characteristics more relevant to their likely compatibility and interaction is also reflected in the writings of Powdermaker and Frank (1953), Bach (1954), and Hinkley and Hermann (1951). Peer and authority relationships, competitiveness, tolerance for aggression from others, and ability to expose one's weaknesses before others are the characteristics of the type reported useful by Powdermaker and Frank (1953). Bach's (1954) exclusion from his therapy groups of "chronic monopolists," patients with insufficient reality contact, and potentially disruptive psychopathic patients similarly highlights the implicit attempts currently being made to compose balanced groups on the basis of likely interaction and communication characteristics of group members.

Although there may be a growing degree of agreement on the position that therapy groups should be constituted to maximize the intermediate goals of maximal group interaction and compatibility of membership, as well as the ultimate goal of patient improvement, there is far less agreement on the methods by which such compositional decisions should be made. It is clear that at present most decisions to exclude or include a given individual stem from material gleaned from individual interviews and from psychological testing. The predictive accuracy of such procedures has not, however, proved to be satisfactory. Bach (1954), holding to this viewpoint, observes:

> Evidence concerning the psychological interdependency of human organisms makes it clear that it is impossible to predict the behavior of the group reliably on the basis of diagnostic evaluations of the individual members. . . . The faith that adequate selection is a major assurance of therapeutic efficiency in group psychotherapy is consequently bound to remain an unfulfilled, naive, professional wish. At present we cannot go beyond making a few broad and obvious principles for grouping (pp. 17-18).

Completely accurate prediction of an individual's behavior in a group not yet convened is obviously an all but unattainable goal, but we take issue with Bach's contention that only "a few broad and obvious principles for grouping" are derivable. We feel, in fact, that aspects of his own approach to this very problem have the potential for yielding criteria for selection and grouping much more predictive of subsequent within-group behavior than follow from standard interview and testing procedures. We refer here to Bach's use of the MAPS Figure Grouping, the Life Space Drawing, visiting within the group, and similar techniques which shift the locus of patient factors to be evaluated away from relatively isolated, intrapsychic concerns and in the direction of more group-related testing procedures demanding less inference and generalization to later within-group behavior. Research findings reported by Schutz (1958) also have much to offer in this regard. In particular, we refer to his development in both theoretical and operational terms of the concept of interpersonal compatibility. Of even more direct relevance are his studies successfully predicting level of group productivity in experimentally constituted groups composed of members said to be either compatible or incompatible in terms of their individual orientations to interpersonal relations. Further, use of psychodramatic techniques for group composition purposes, as well as such situational tests as Del Torto and Corneytz's (1944) Projective and Expressive Action Test, Crutchfield's (1951) Group Squares Test, and Heller's (1959; Heller & Goldstein, 1961) behavioral modification of The Rosenzweig PF study (1947) are other worthwhile possibilities. From our viewpoint, this is the direction patient selection for group psychotherapy must follow. Predictiveness of subsequent group performance, we hold, is increased to the degree that the bases for prediction correspond to, or at least are more directly similar to, the subsequent group interaction itself.

Although there is little reference in the group psychotherapy literature to the potential utility of prediction from "overt behavior-to-overt behavior" (or from group-oriented testing to within therapy group behavior) as a method of selecting and grouping patients, it is of interest to note in passing that the few such available references that approximate this position represent a series of very diverse theoretical orientations. The earliest and most developed of these, not initially aimed at therapy groups in particular, is represented by sociometric measurement.

In the typical sociometric procedure, in barest outline, the nature of the group involved is made explicit to all members and all members are asked to choose or reject an unspecified number of other group members in terms of certain preselected criteria. It is important to note that this type of measurement, especially Moreno's (1934; Moreno & Jennings, 1944) early use of it, was not only a means of identifying a group's sociogrammatic or interpersonal choice structure but also the basis for reorganization and restructuring of the group. Thus, although what is represented here is not quite the behavior to behavior-predictive method of group composition we propose, it is a close approximation.

Locke (1961), writing from the perspective of his psychoanalytic group therapy practice, comments:

> The most fruitful procedure by which patients can be selected is not in terms of diagnosis, but rather in terms of behavior. This makes the manner in which the patient operates, the manner in which he functions, the prime consideration. When this approach is taken, the therapist cuts through the structural rigidities of nosology and comes right to the dynamics of the patient himself . . . .
>
> Such a selection is functional, not structural, as would be an approach from the point of view of diagnosis. When a functional selection is made, the very patient described as presenting a poor prognosis, paradoxically enough, can do well in a group. The basis for this is the effect one given person can have on the other persons in the group, and in turn, the counter-effect. That is, determination should be made of the impact that this given individual has on the others in the group because of his particular kind of functioning. When this is the criterion for selection, the group becomes a more cohesive unit (pp. 242-243).

A large-scale investigation of nondirective group psychotherapy, conducted by Gorlow, Hoch, and Telschow (1952) yielded the not unrelated finding of a

> . . . statistically significant relationship between each member's behavior in the first two sessions and his behavior during the remainder of the therapy cycle (which) suggests the feasibility of altering a group's composition on the basis of initial behavior (pp. 111-112).

Deer and Silver (1962) report a relevant predictive study in which the therapy administered was described as "verbal, alternatively directive and nondirective, and occasionally deep although generally superficial." Their subjects, 24 adolescents in group psychotherapy, were each administered a number of projective tests. A subsequent attempt to demonstrate relationships between 42 scores derived from this test battery and therapist ratings of patient within-therapy behavior was singularly unsuccessful. The investigators conclude:

> . . . clinicians' failure to consistently predict group behavior on the basis of individual dynamics may be indirect evidence of the power of the group to shape and control the behavior of its members contrary to their personal predilections. If such a finding is borne out by other research it would point to the futility of making predictions about an individual's behavior in a group other than on the basis of what he does in a group similar or identical to a group in which his behavior is to be predicted (pp. 324-325).

It may also be noted that Stone, Parloff, and Frank (1954), in their investigation of "diagnostic therapy groups," provided partial support for this conclusion.

Finally, representing a psychoanalytic background combined with a very group-centered operating orientation, Foulkes (1949) has made occasional use of "the group as a test" for selection purposes. In addition to other bases, his justification for this selection procedure rests on the lessened degree of inference necessary in predicting to future member behavior within the therapy group itself and, as Foulkes comments, ". . . such a selection does justice to the fact that an individual who is not compatible with a particular group, might well be with another one" (p. 60).

Our first hypothesis aimed at group therapy has begun to emerge. Let us state it formally at this point, after which we will turn to the group dynamics research literature for its development and elaboration.

HYPOTHESIS 7.1: **On a variety of interactive, communicative and compatibility criteria, prediction of subsequent within-group behavior will be more accurate when based on direct behavioral measurement than on interview or psychometric measurement.**

In essence, this hypothesis proposes a comparison between two methods of selecting and grouping patients for group psychotherapy. Our preference for the behaviorally oriented approach rests, we feel, both on sound measurement principles involving minimization of inference or undue generalization and on a strong body of group dynamics research findings. We now present these findings and later suggest a variety of ways this hypothesis and its implications may be investigated.

Investigations of Behavioral Selection

Borgatta and Bales (1955b) report a clearly relevant study. Their subjects were 126 Air Force enlisted personnel who were divided into batches or subgroups of nine men each. Three-man group meetings were held within each batch according to a procedure which resulted in each subject participating in a total of four group meetings. Rotation of subjects across groups was such that each man met with every other subject in his batch only one time. Each session involved discussional and role playing tasks. Member interaction was observed and classified in terms of Bales' Interaction Process Analysis. The investigators' examination of subject and group rates and patterns of interaction yielded results important to our hypothesis. They found that the interaction rate actually demonstrated by a given member was an inverse function of the characteristic rates of his co-participators. Although the total rate achieved by a given group was in large measure a function of the summed characteristic rates of the participants, the total rate was also found to reflect the degree of differentiation of the characteristic rates of the individual group members.

More specifically, when groups were reconstituted with members all of whom had previously demonstrated high interaction rates in different, earlier groups, results indicate that members clearly tended to depress each others' rate of interaction. When the newly constituted group consisted of all low participators from earlier sessions, each members' interaction rate was elevated. The highest group interaction rates were in evidence in differentiated groups, those constituted of members high, low, and moderate in their earlier group session interactions. The investigators conclude:

The results of this study indicate that it may be possible to use diagnostic sessions to estimate characteristic rates of particular individuals and from this information to predict certain aspects of performance of the individual in a particular group if we have estimates of the characteristic performance of each of the individuals based on previous diagnostic sessions (p. 397).

Blake, Mouton, and Fruchter (1954) similarly provide evidence of the utility of behavioral observation of group sessions for predicting individual behavior in later, reconstituted groups. In this investigation 33 subjects participated in two completely independent interactional situations. Changes between the two group situations included the tests on which the members worked, the composition of the group, and the identity of the group observer. Their results support the hypothesis that

. . . reliable judgments of short-term interaction can be made even when the two situations are different. Items that permit consistent assessment from both the between- and within-sessions point of view include leadership, contribution to group decision, and dominance. . . . These results support the view that direct-assessment data can serve as one basis for evaluating personal and social characteristics that cannot be satisfactorily measured by other techniques (p. 578).

Bell and French (1955) designed a study to determine the extent to which individuals maintain consistent leadership status in a series of informal discussion groups made up of different members. Their subjects were 25 male college students who were unacquainted with one another at the outset of the investigation. Over a six-week period each S participated in six five-man discussions, each time including four other men whom he had not met previously. Thus in the course of the study each S met once and only once with every other S. Results in the form of an average correlation of .75 on leadership behavior initiated across groups led the investigators to conclude: ". . . it would seem that individual characteristics are responsible for somewhat over half of the variance in leadership status within the average group" (p. 277).

The three preceding studies provide direct and clearcut evidence of the value of "diagnostic" or "tryout" group sessions for predicting individual and group behavior in subsequently constituted groups. The studies which follow speak to this same point by showing individual consistency on several crucial group-relevant dimensions across a series of group meetings. It is important to note as we examine these investigations that the group or other behavioral task on which the predictions involved are made typically bear a strong structural similarity to the group situation being predicted. This is an important consideration underlying our later suggestion that one possible implementation of hypothesis 7.1 be in terms of diagnostic or tryout group sessions which are structurally similar to our predictive interest, the group psychotherapy session.

Haythorn (1955) conducted an investigation aimed at identifying member influences on group characteristics. His design involved systematic rotation of individuals through five groups, reconstituted each time to accomplish unique membership composition. Subjects were college sophomores who met in groups of four on each trial. The three group tasks involved reasoning, mechanical, and discussional emphases. Two independent observers viewed each session and recorded member behavior in terms of a category system developed by Carter (Carter, Haythorn, Meirowitz, & Lanzetta, 1951). In general, results supported the conclusion that

. . . there are significant relationships between the behavior of individual group members and the characteristics of the total group, and that these relationships can be experimentally isolated" (pp. 338-339).

The generally accepted view, based on a large number of investigations in the area of leadership behavior, is that such behavior is jointly determined by intra-individual and situational considerations. Thus on the average only a moderate correlation will be obtained between the degree of leadership behavior demonstrated by an individual across varying group situations, but such a correlation will tend to be substantial if the two situations are similar in important respects. For example, Bass and Norton (1951) report a correlation of .90 between successful leadership behavior displayed in leaderless group discussions held a week apart. Group composition and task were held constant. A change in the task for one of the sessions caused the correlation across sessions on leadership behavior to drop to .86, and later to .75 when two members of each participating group received special coaching. Arbous and Maree (1951) obtained a median correlation of .67 between the extent to which administrative candidates displayed successful leadership when appointed discussion leaders and the extent of such behavior in initially leaderless discussions. However, when group composition and discussion topic were systematically varied, the between-situations correlation of successful leadership behavior dropped to .58. Similarly, data collected in the screening of OSS candidates demonstrated that the correlation between rated performance in leaderless group discussions and leadership ratings obtained from situational tests decreased consistently as the latter became more dissimilar from free discussion. As Bass (1955, 1960) reports, rated leadership behavior in a leaderless group discussion correlates .56 with leadership displayed in a debate, .48 with leadership in a personal interview, .47 with leadership in solving a problem of crossing a brook, and .30 with leadership in cooperatively constructing a giant toy.

The group dynamics investigations examined so far point to certain classes of within-group behavior, all of which are relevant to the psychotherapeutic encounter and which occur with sufficient intraindividual consistency across similar group situations to be considered predictively useful for our present purpose. Characteristic interaction rate, member contribution to group decision, and leadership behavior were the member behaviors so considered. To these may be added conformity to group norms and ascendance-submission behavior. Gilchrist (1959) reviewed a series of studies all pointing to the joint conclusion that Ss conforming to group norms in a given situation will similarly tend to yield in related group tasks. One final study further reinforces, albeit indirectly, the potential value of composing groups in terms of behavioral or group interactional measurement, rather than measurement of the individual "out of context" as it were. Breer (1960), using 25 college students as his experimental subjects, found clear support for his hypothesis that "A prediction based on pre-interaction measures of the subject and the other person (would be) superior to one based on attributes of the subject alone" (p. 181). His results were most striking in the case of ascendance-submission. When both the subject's and the other person's scores on this variable were considered together, it was possible to account for 37 per cent of the variance in the subject's ascendance toward the other person ($r = .62$). Predicting from pre-interaction ascendance of the subjects alone yielded a correlation of .46. Breer concludes by noting,

Thus it was possible to account for approximately 21 per cent of the variance in the subjects' behavior toward others solely on the basis of what was known about the others (p. 182).

Weislogel and Schwartz (1955), in their examination of situational testing methodology, summarize much of our position by their emphasis on the "principle of consistency." They interpret this to mean that

. . . a subject will respond to similar environmental situations in a similar manner. Hence, the tasks to be assigned in the testing should correspond to tasks normally encountered in the . . . activity itself . . . . (p. 40).

Their discussion of other major considerations in situational testing is of major relevance to our present development of hypothesis 7.1. They state:

Thus, the first criterion for a situational test is that it must provide a measure of the testee's typical performance. . . . The second criterion is closely related to this one. . . . For predictions of typical performance to have any value in selection, they must be related to a definition of job success. Situational test performance must, therefore, be preceded by a behavioral definition of job success; that is, a definition capable of direct comparison with the measures obtained from the test. This is the second criterion.

The third criterion derives from considerations applicable to all types of predictors. It is necessary that the scoring procedures be as objective as possible; that is, independent of the specific observer. This is particularly important in situational tests, where the scoring is based on observations of test performance (pp. 40-41).

These three criteria, (1) typical performance or consistency, (2) relation to task success, and (3) objective observation, provide the basic framework of choice for tests of the hypothesized superiority of behavioral-observational versus interview-psychometric bases for therapy group composition.

1. *Consistency.* Our discussion of group dynamics research findings up to this point may be viewed essentially as an attempt to support the consistency principle as it applies to the group context. Two general procedures appear to possess satisfactory experimental design characteristics for the translation of the consistency principle to group psychotherapy composition.

(A) *Trial groups.* One possible approach would make use of a series of trial or tryout groups. This approach is particularly applicable in settings in which a large pool of potential group therapy members may exist, such as day care centers and mental hospitals. For illustrative purposes let us assume that in a given setting a number of such potential therapy patients are available. Use of the method of rotating patients through reconstituted groups can provide an opportunity to obtain information relative to characteristic patient interaction rate, leadership behavior, and so forth. Since the trial group tasks can readily be structured along lines similar to those characteristic of early therapy sessions, and since the trial and subsequent "real" therapy sessions are similar in several other central group dimensions (patient population, setting of meetings, and presence of therapist), we may be reasonably confident that the "tests-to-real task" consistency requirement is adequately met.

(B) *Simulation.* Whenever the available patient population is insufficient for a trial groups design, the somewhat more rigorous but more artificial (less "consistency of test-to-task") alternative of simulation may be an appropriate procedure. Credit is due Blake and Brehm (1954) for their pioneering use of tape recordings to simulate groups. In their procedure each subject is placed in an isolated booth to listen to a tape recording that he is led to believe is a group interaction in progress and that he is a part of the group. Every participant therefore receives identical stimulation. Although Blake and Brehm focused on the variable of susceptibility to influence and Bass (1960) suggests that the technique is easily modifiable for study of reaction to various types of group leadership, it is readily apparent that the technique is potentially adaptable for a wide range of group variables of major importance for group psychotherapy.

2. *Relation to task success.* As applied to therapy groups, this criterion may be reframed by asking, "Which group composition considerations are positively related to a favorable therapeutic outcome for group members?" Clearly, this is the overriding issue for this hypothesis. Further, improved likelihood of a favorable therapeutic outcome is obviously the major raison d'etre for interest in not only group composition but any other therapy group characteristic. We have suggested throughout that interview and psychometric information concerning patient personality, diagnosis, or status characteristics are inadequate to the task of most efficiently defining group member characteristics and group composition most predictive of subsequent patient improvement. We have begun to describe experimental procedures by which these as yet unspecified, potentially more effective predictors may be measured. Although variables noted earlier, such as characteristic rate of interaction and leadership behavior are a small beginning toward the kind of dimensions we feel may have most predictive utility for constituting *therapeutic* therapy groups, much more must be said and considerably more predictive research must be undertaken before we are satisfied that an approximation to the full range of such potential dimensions is available.

Fuller identification of such predictors is clearly a high priority task for future investigations. Several promising paths which such research may do well to follow will be apparent in our later discussions of therapist orientation, group cohesiveness and related therapy group dimensions.

3. *Objective observation.* Assuming the possibility of trial therapy sessions and the identification of a series of member characteristics

potentialy relatable to both group composition and therapeutic outcome, how are we to proceed?

A series of behavioral rating systems have been developed by researchers interested in group dynamics. Their usefulness in any given research subarea has proved to be a joint function both of considerations essentially internal to the rating system (degree of observer inference required, number of acts to be rated per unit time, typical level of associated interrater reliability, etc.) and external factors (task complexity, size of group, nature of criteria being predicted, etc.). Thus their potential usefulness for trial psychotherapy sessions or at other points in the group therapy transaction is a function of similar considerations internal and external to the rating system. Systems which may profitably be explored as potentially of value for recording diverse patient behaviors in trial and group therapy sessions will now be considered briefly. Note that it is the basic *orientation* of each system that we are recommending for exploration, acknowledging that in each instance specific category and, perhaps, procedural modifications may well be necessary before such systems can be meaningfully used with therapy groups.

(A) *Bales—Interaction process analysis* (Bales, 1950, 1954). We consider the Bales system first not only because it has been used more than any other observational rating system in group dynamics research but also because it—or a modification of it—appears to be of highest potential value for reliably rating the classes of variables that we feel to be most consequential for this and several of our other hypotheses. In capsule form the rating system is interaction process centered, not content oriented. Twelve categories of group member behavior are represented, that is, the positive and negative aspects of orientation, evaluation, control over others, decision, tension management, and integration. The simple sentence is the unit of observation in this system. In addition, in its typical application, certain classes of nonverbal behavior are scored at one-minute intervals. Scores derived are primarily the number of acts of a given kind in each category (by individuals or groups) and ratios of such scores. Interrater reliability coefficients, with trained raters, have ranged from .75 to .95.

Our interest in this particular rating system's potential is reflected in our later detailed consideration of it, especially in the form of therapy-oriented research findings.

(B) *Carter—Leadership-oriented rating system* (Carter, Haythorn, Meirowitz, & Lanzetta, 1951). Studies utilizing this rating system have focused for the most part on leadership behavior. Seven principal dimensions are represented: proposes and initiates action, disagrees and argues, shows a personal feeling of . . . , nonproductive behavior, and so forth, with a large number of subcategories within each principal rating area. In addition to this within-session categorization of member behavior, observers complete postsession ratings of 15 personal traits and 4 group-oriented traits for each group member. Included here are member authoritarianism, leadership, submissiveness, and insight. Carter reports an average correlation between two observers' postmeeting ratings across all traits as .68.

(C) *Heyns—Conference problem-solving category system* (Heyns, 1948). This 12-category group observational system was developed for examination of problem-solving processes in decision-making conferences. The categories are essentially cognitive in nature, that is, goal setting, problem proposals, information giving or seeking, summarizing, and so forth. Reported reliability coefficients range from .64 to .97.

(D) *Steinzor—Social interaction category system* (Steinzor, 1949). Steinzor's stated aim in developing this rating system was to focus on "group atmosphere." His 18 categories (activate and originate, structure and delimit, defend, conciliate, conform, etc.) are scored from a motivational point of view; that is, verbal behavior is scored primarily in terms of its inferred intent as well as in terms of the loci of intent (self, group, or issue). No doubt, largely as a result of the degree of inference required by the task of judging intent, low interrater reliabilities are reported for this system.

(E) *Fouriezos, Hutt, and Guetzkow—Self-oriented need observational system* (Fouriezos et al., 1950). This approach also focuses on participant motivation, though in a manner very different from Steinzor's. It is applied primarily at decision-making conferences, in which observers, using a cue manual, record behavioral cues of participants related to dependency, status, dominance, aggression, and catharsis. Based on this recorded or tallied within-session information, raters make final member by member ratings of global "self-oriented" versus "group-oriented" need behavior. Although the degree of inference required by this category system approaches that of Steinzor, associated reliability coefficients are considerably higher, a difference likely resulting from the more global nature of the final rating.

(G) *Benne and Sheats—Functional role categories* (Benne & Sheats, 1948). This category listing, though not associated with any developed observational or rating procedure, is nevertheless of very real potential importance for the concept of functional composition of therapy groups. These authors have essentialy been concerned with identifying and describing a variety of functional role categories. Primarily with problem-solving groups in mind, they describe the "energizer," who prods the group to action, the "information seeker," the "information giver," the "initiator," who proposes new ideas, the "elaborator," who spells out suggestions, and other member-in-action role behaviors. In addition, they suggest the importance of a series of group building and maintenance roles, such as the "harmonizer," "expediter," and "encourager." We feel progress in understanding and measurement along such functional lines to be, as our hypothesis indicates, central to more efficient procedures for constituting therapy groups.

(H) Finally, there is an additional, rather broad group of rating systems which, in modified form, could be put to advantageous use in the group psychotherapy context. Almost all have found use so far only in individual psychotherapy or other two-person interactions. Included here is the category system originated by Chapple (1940, 1949) and developed further by Saslow and Matarazzo (1959), as well as the content-analysis and observational rating systems of Murray (1956), Snyder (1945), and Strupp (1955).

It is of interest to note that Gorlow et al. (1952) were able to make effective use in the group therapy context of the approach developed by Snyder, after first making certain modifications in the system to increase its applicability to psychotherapy with groups.

To recapitulate, in our development of the present hypothesis we turned first to an examination of the heterogeneity-homogeneity issue in group-therapy composition. We hold that continued focus on such a dichotomous approach is a misdirection of professional energy, a focus that will likely continue to prove unfruitful in attempting to maximize *therapeutic* patient groupings; that efforts on the part of many contemporary group therapists to constitute a "balanced" group are clearly a step in the right direction, but that their almost exclusive reliance on individual interviews and psychological testing to obtain information for balancing purposes does not appear to be the most efficient choice of those procedures potentially available for patient selection and grouping. Reference to a series of group dynamics research findings points to the predictive value of utilizing group interaction itself as the basis for estimating subsequent group member behavior in reconstituted groups. We hypothesized that such group behavior-to-group behavior prediction can more effectively lead to interactive, communicative, compatible groups than can predictions about group behavior based upon interview-psychometric information. We then considered the possible implementation of this hypothesis in terms of the situational test development principles of consistency, relation to task success, and objective observation of member behavior.

GROUP SIZE

An examination of current group therapy practice with regard to the number of patients to be accepted into any given therapy group yields proponents of groups size 3 (Dreikurs, 1950), 6 (Hobbs, 1951), 8 (Goldfarb, 1953), 10 (Cavanagh & Gerstein, 1949), 6 to 8 (Kelman, 1948), 5 to 10 (Kew & Kew, 1950), 7 to 8 (Foulkes, 1949), 8 to 10 (Ebaugh, 1951), 8 to 12 (Altshuler, 1940), 6 to 20 (Dynes & Hamilton, 1945), and so forth. It seems apparent that three interrelated factors are responsible for this bewildering array of diverse recommendations. First, all such recommendations find their basis largely in the clinical experience of the various proponents. Little effort is made at comparison with other viewpoints or at obtaining more circumspect examination of the size variable. Second, in many instances group size is considered as a single variable influencing subsequent therapeutic outcome. For example, it is often proposed, without reference to other group characteristics, that group size X most frequently leads to positive therapeutic results, whereas a group composed of Y number of patients is generally less therapeutic. Lastly, many such recommendations are tied to differing therapeutic approaches. Thus proponents hold that for a type A group therapy, X number of patients per group is most efficacious, but with therapy of a B orientation groups size Y are better. Thus impressionistic, simplistic, and approach-bound considerations result in a wide variety of recommendations as to the "best" size for therapy groups. Let us briefly examine these three considerations further. We have commented earlier on the reliance on personalized, nonverified clinical impressions as the sole or major source of group-relevant decisions. The eventual degree of clarification that such an approach will provide in regard to group size or other group characteristics is clearly limited.

Considering group size as a variable that by itself is a major influence on outcome is, we feel, a similarly limited and unproductive viewpoint. We offer evidence in later sections of our discussion that will point to the basic weaknesses of this simple, univariate approach. The perspective on group size that we feel holds some potential for more effective group psychotherapy is hinted at by the third consideration. Viewing size as related to therapeutic approach is a first step in what might be termed a functional-interactional approach to group size. That is, rather than being a single determinant of later therapeutic events, group size as an influence in psychotherapy becomes meaningful only when viewed as an interactional variable. Thus to speak of the influence on therapeutic outcome of group size *as it interacts with* therapeutic approach is, we feel, a step in the right direction, albeit a very nonspecific one. Recourse to the group dynamics research literature will provide us with more concrete and manipulatable means of exploring the interaction of group size and other group dimensions as they bear on the outcome of the group's task. Evidence will be presented which permits the ensuing attempt at hypothesis construction to be viewed as a functional approach to the group size variable, in much the same sense as our development of hypothesis 7.1. Our present hypothesis may be stated as follows:

HYPOTHESIS 7.2: **Decisions as to the optimal size of a given therapy group will yield better patient within-group performance and better therapeutic outcome when such decisions are based on the interaction of group size with behavioral patient characteristics rather than on nonbehavioral patient characteristics such as age, sex, and diagnosis.**

Let us now turn to some of the relevant group dynamics research findings.

Member Interaction

As the size of problem-solving groups is increased, the following is noted:

1. The differences between the relative interaction rates of members tend to disappear (Stephan & Mishler, 1952).
2. The difference between the relative interaction rates of the group leader and the average member becomes greater (Stephan & Mishler, 1952).
3. The absolute rate of interaction for any given member tends to decrease because the interaction rate for each member is inversely related to the rates of the other group members (Borgatta & Bales, 1955c).
4. The proportion of very infrequent contributors to the group interaction increases (Kelley & Thibaut, 1954).
5. An increasing proportion of the members report feelings of threat and inhibition regarding participation (Gibb, 1954).

Bales and Borgatta (1955a) have examined the group size-group interaction relationship via Interaction Process Analysis. As the size of problem-solving groups increases from two to seven, they report, the rate of giving information and suggestions increases, whereas the rates of asking for opinions and showing agreement decreases. As an explanatory hypothesis for such interactional changes, the investigators suggest that as group size increases, there is a tendency toward a more mechanical method of introducing information, less sensitive exploration of the viewpoints of others, and more direct attempts to control others and reach a solution, all of which are associated with the increasing constriction of time available per member.

Leadership

The following are among the more substantial findings emerging in group dynamics research to suggest the interaction of group size with the nature of group leadership that develops. As groups increase in size, the following is noted:

1. An increasing proportion of the verbalizations in the group tends to be addressed to the group leader and a decreasing proportion to other members. In turn, as size increases, the group leader tends to address more and more of his remarks to the group as a whole and less and less to specific individuals within the group. In essence, "the communication pattern tends to 'centralize' around a leader through whom most of the communication flows" (Miller, 1950, p. 439).
2. The demands on the leader's role become greater and more numerous (Hemphill, 1950).
3. Tolerance on the part of group members for leader-centered direction becomes greater (Hemphill, 1950).
4. There is less opportunity for any one individual to adopt a position of leadership (Hemphill, 1950).
5. There is an increasingly high intercorrelation among member leadership initiative, auhoritarianism, and insight. Carter, Haythorn, Shriver, & Lanzetta (1951) comment:

   In the group of four, each individual has sufficient latitude or space in which to behave and thus the basic abilities of each individual can be expressed; but in the larger group only the more forceful individuals are able to express their abilities and ideas, since the amount of freedom in the situation is not sufficient to accommodate all the group members (p. 260).

Intermember Relations

A third group dimension which appears to be influenced by group size and which acts with it as a joint influence upon task success is the interpersonal relations among group members. Miller (1950) reports that larger conference groups are more disruptive than smaller ones. Rated "sense of belonging" in these groups correlated -.44 with group size, and, further, lack of opportunity to talk, itself positively related to size of group, correlated .52 with reported feelings of frustration. Hare (1952) provides evidence that the amount of consensus is lower, and degree of dissatisfaction with sessions higher, in 12-man versus 5-man discussion groups. Seashore (1954) reports small groups to be more cohesive than larger ones. Hare (1962) indicates that as groups increase in size there is a corresponding tendency for the increased formation and solidification of subgroups and cliques. Also, member status and the over-all group hierarchy becomes more resistant to change with increasing group size. Coyle (1930) and Kinney (1953) report a strengthening of the affectional ties between members as groups become smaller.

In studies of an interesting aspect of the group size-member interaction relationship groups composed of an uneven number of members have generally proved to be more harmonious than groups consisting of an even number of members. Borgatta and Bales (1955c), for example, report significant differences between groups with an even or odd number of members on several such dimensions. Even-sized groups (four or six members) are characterized by more disagreement and antagonism and less asking for suggestions or showing agreement than are odd-sized groups (three, five, or seven). The investigators attribute these differences to the opportunity present in even sized groups for two antagonistic subgroups with an equal number of members to form. Thus, in contrast to groups with an odd number of members, in even sized groups the probability of a majority and a minority developing around a given issue is lower, and the probability of a deadlock or stalemate forming is higher.

Finally, it may be noted that studies by Hare (1952), Bales and Borgatta (1955), and Slater (1958) all agree in their evidence that from the group members' perspective five-member groups are most frequently reported to be the most harmonious problem-solving groups.

Our consideration of group size so far clearly indicates that, in the group dynamics research area at least, size is most profitably viewed as an influence on task success only to the extent that it influences or interacts with the nature and rates of member interaction, group leadership structure, and member-to-member interpersonal relations. Hypothesis 7.2 proposes that group size may be utilized most meaningfully in the psychotherapeutic context if it is viewed in *analogous* functional and interactional terms. We underscore analogous here in recognition of the likelihood that, as we noted from Durkin (1957) earlier, the differing nature of the group goals and related considerations will influence the degree of carry-over or "extrapolatability" of group size (and other) findings in the group dynamics context to size influences in therapy groups. For example, since group consensus is much less of a necessity in therapy groups than is the case in problem-solving groups, perhaps future research will indicate that the odd-even effect does not operate, or operates only in unimportant ways, in therapy groups. Similarly, although it seems likely that interaction, leadership, and interpersonal relations among members are among the important member, leader, and group variables interacting with group size in *both* types of groups, it is equally likely that in many instances the exact nature of this interaction of variables will differ from problem-solving to therapy groups. It is self-evident, however, that this possibility should serve as a spur to, and not an inhibition of, continued research on group size. As a most appropriate way of closing this development of our group size hypothesis, let us briefly examine a study conducted by Castore (1962). It clearly serves as one of many possible examples to reinforce our major contention that group size assumes meaning in the group therapy context only when it is considered functionally as interacting with and influencing other key group dimensions. Castore (1962) comments:

> The aim of a therapeutic group is the improvement of the patient. Conditions which increase rate, depth, reliability of growth that is deemed desirable would generally be accepted as of value. One of these conditions would be opportunity for verbal expression. Opportunity is related to many facets of group interaction. . . . The emergence of subgroups makes verbal expression more difficult for the individual members of a group. Groups which are too small may find that practices such as establishing of norms . . . and holding to stereotyped patterns of interaction, act along with other behaviors to reduce over-all interaction between members. Large groups possess as many objections (p. 456).

With this as his implied motivation, Castore set out to determine the group size representing optimal growth value for members in terms of the interactional variable: number of different member-to-member verbal relationships initiated. This measure, instead of focusing on frequency of participation, reflects the spread or diffusion of interaction among group members; it is the number of other members to whom each individual in the group directed at least one remark during an hour's session. In a group of seven members, for example, perfect diffusion would be obtained if each member directed at least one comment to each of the six other members.

Castore's subjects consisted of members of 55 therapy groups in inpatient mental hospital settings. Member age varied from 14 to 70; males and females were distributed approximately equally across groups, and, Castore notes, all types of diagnostic categories were represented. Groups ranged in size from 5 to 20 patients, with 34 of the 55 groups composed of 11 to 18 patients each. After a rather straightforward rating procedure which permitted reliable recording of initiation and direction of patient verbal behavior, a marked reduction in the percentage of member verbal interrelationships was noted when group size reached nine members. A second marked reduction occurred when 17 or more members were present. Castore comments:

> Based on these data a desirable level of verbal interaction would be determined by the aims of a particular group. Obviously, for those who are quite reticent and interact with extreme difficulty, more opportunity should arise in a group with less than 9 members (p. 457).

Before summarizing our position on group size, we observe in passing that it is exactly that kind of behavioral selection and grouping of group therapy patients discussed under hypothesis 7.1 which has the potential for making the most meaningful use of group-size considerations such as Castore's reference to reticent and noninteractive patients.

To recapitulate briefly, in our examination of the size dimension of therapy groups we began by noting the very diverse recommendations for optimal group size forthcoming from contemporary group psychotherapists. To a very large extent, such recommendations derive from the clinical-impressionistic level of evidence with which we have previously taken issue. As an alternative, we proposed a conceptualization of group size in which size assumes meaning for group psychotherapy only as it influences and interacts with other patient, therapist, and group characteristics which, in turn, appear to influence therapeutic outcome. Group dynamics literature clearly suggests that in the nontherapy group context, some of the important variables mediating between group size and task success are member verbal interaction rate, group leadership structure, and member interpersonal relationships. Although we acknowledge that these variables may not function in exactly the same mediating role in group therapy—because of differing group goals—we nevertheless believe they are the most promising starting point for tying together group size and therapeutic outcome. A study by Castore relating size to verbal interrelatedness in therapy groups was cited as an important beginning in this direction.

INITIATION INTO THE THERAPY GROUP

In our discussion of the first two group therapy hypotheses it was readily apparent that wide variability exists among contemporary group psychotherapists in terms of both the type and size of group they attempt to constitute. This degree of variability is similarly in evidence when we examine the nature and number of tests, interviews, and other hurdles over which the patient-candidate must pass on his way to acceptance into the group. The extremes of what may be termed a "severity of initiation" dimension are represented by Bach (1954) and Fink (1956). Patient-candidates being considered for (and considering) therapy group membership with Bach characteristically participate in most of the following: (1) standard and group-oriented psychological testing; (2) an individual interview focusing on test results; (3) an interview centered on the nature of group psychotherapy, often including the reading by the patient of protocols of past meetings; (4) the reading and discussion of a "preparation sheet" covering such matters as extra office meeting, ethical considerations, group goals, and so forth; and (5) a trial attendance at a meeting of an ongoing open group which permits the candidate to decide on the appropriateness of a given group for him, and which also permits already accepted group members to vote on the particular patient-candidate's acceptance or rejection. In marked contrast to this formidable initiation or screening procedure, Fink (1956) implies that a single, individual interview frequently will be sufficient for screening purposes and, further, "On rare occasions, a person is allowed to enter the group directly if he is referred by another therapist who can give some indication of the patient's readiness for group experience" (p. 4). The initiation into group membership described by Wolf and Schwartz (1962) probably represents the more typical approach to this compositional issue. Their patient-candidates typically participate in a single, largely projective psychological testing session and a variable but small number of individual interviews. We propose in the development of the following hypothesis that such initiation procedures influence the degree of attraction with which the group is viewed by the patient-candidate. The more patient effort included in screening procedures or the more severe the initiation into membership, the more attractive the anticipated membership status will be to the patient. More formally, our hypothesis may be stated:

HYPOTHESIS 7.3:   **The degree of effort required of the patient-candidate to gain therapy group membership will positively influence the subsequent initial attractiveness of membership status to him if he persists in completing the required premembership tasks. At the upper limit of this relationship, a curvilinear or asymptotic pattern will emerge.**

This hypothesis predicts that the initial attractiveness of therapy group membership will on the average be highest for Bach's patients whose screening hurdles are numerous; next highest for those screened in terms of Wolf and Schwartz's more typical procedures; and lowest for those passing through Fink's minimal screening. Beyond a yet to be determined point the amount of patient effort required by initiation and screening procedures will likely become a negative influence on attraction to the group or, at best, a point of diminishing returns at which further testing, interviewing, or other screening procedures add little to patient involvement or commitment, hence little to attraction. This is the a priori basis for the second part of hypothesis 7.3, which predicts the eventual emergence of a curvilinear or asymptotic relationship between screening procedures required and patient attraction to group. Let us now turn to the research foundation for this predicted influence of severity of initiation on attraction to group membership.

Investigations of Severity of Initiation

A study by Aronson (1961) demonstrates a strong positive relationship between the degree of effort expended by subjects on an experimental task and the relative attractiveness of the task. Working from a dissonance theory base, it was predicted that an individual striving for a goal unsuccessfully will experience dissonance; that is, the cognition that he is expending effort is dissonant with S's cognition that he is unrewarded. One means of dissonance reduction in this context would be for S to find something about the situation (other than goal attainment) to which he could attach value. In Aronson's laboratory test of this proposition his independent variables were conditions classified as effortful or easy in terms of degree of effort required of S in his attempts at goal attainment. On each trial all subjects obtained a container. On rewarded trials the containers were red and contained money. On unrewarded trials the containers were green and empty. All subjects were required to rate the relative attractiveness of the two colors both before and after the experimental trials. As already suggested, each time a subject received an unrewarded container under effortful conditions his cognition that it was empty would be dissonant with his cognition that he had exerted effort to obtain it. It was predicted that in order for dissonance reduction to occur S would attach value to the color of the unrewarded container. Results clearly supported this prediction. A large, significant difference emerged between effortful and easy conditions in relative preference for the two colors. Subjects working under the easy set shifted in preference toward red, the rewarded color. Subjects in the effortful set shifted toward green to an extent marked enough to counterbalance any like shift toward red, the reward-associated color.

Aronson and Mills (1959) conducted a related investigation, one more directly relevant to group considerations. In this second study college women who had volunteered to participate in discussion groups were randomly assigned to one of three experimental conditions: a severe initiation condition, a mild initiation condition, and a control condition. As a precondition to joining the group, severe condition subjects were required to read some material likely to cause feelings of marked embarrassment. Subjects assigned to the mild condition read material unlikely to cause embarrassment. No pre-admission procedures were required of control subjects. Each subject then listened to a tape recording which appeared to be an ongoing discussion being conducted by the group, and then completed a questionnaire evaluating the discussion and the participants. Results provided clear support for their hypothesis. Subjects in the severe initiation condition perceived the group as being significantly more attractive than did either mild initiation or control subjects.

These two investigations combine to suggest that the degree to which a task is made effortful for an individual will influence his perception of the attractiveness of the task. It is also relevant to note more generally that studies by Cohen (1959), Yaryan and Festinger (1961), and Zimbardo (1960), all of which were aimed at evaluating aspects of cognitive dissonance theory, demonstrate a clear effect of degree of effort upon subsequent attitude change. Cohen (1959) had his subjects work on a communication which supported a viewpoint opposed to their own, informing some subjects that understanding of the arguments would be easy, and informing other subjects that such understanding would be difficult to accomplish. Measurement of subjects' attitudes subsequent to their reading of the communication revealed that those who had initially held a rather extreme view showed positive attitude change in proportion to the amount of difficulty they were led to expect in understanding the communication. Yaryan and Festinger (1961) presented all their subjects with a standard set of instructions concerning the probability of their having to take an examination in the future. Those subjects in the high preparatory effort condition had to commit to memory a list of difficult symbolic definitions in preparation for the test they might have to take. Subjects in the low preparatory effort condition were merely asked to look over the definitions and get a rough idea of their nature. Subsequent to this memorization or perusal, each subject was asked whether she believed she was one of the persons selected to take the test. Results clearly demonstrated that high preparatory effort subjects more frequently believed that they would have to take the test. Finally, Zimbardo (1960) had 20 university students, all of whom were very much in favor of a numerical grading system, read a report which was a series of arguments against such a grading system. Half of the subjects read the report under high effort conditions, half under low effort conditions. Degree of effort was manipulated, respectively, in terms of a relatively long or a very brief duration of delayed auditory feedback while reading the report. Post-report measurement regarding attitudes toward the grading system revealed that the high effort subjects became significantly more opposed to the numerical grading system than the low effort subjects.

In addition to this direct basis for extrapolation from the group dynamics research area, supporting material is also available in less direct form from research on individual psychotherapy. Studies by Barron and Leary (1955), Goldstein (1960), and Heller and Goldstein (1961) indicate that intake screening and in-therapy status measurement of patients is interpreted by many if not most patients as concrete evidence of genuine interest and concern on the part of professional personnel. Not only do these procedures apparently relate to symptom reduction but probably also color the patient's initial perception of the treatment setting and personnel along distinctly favorable lines. The finding reported by Goldstein and Shipman (1961) that the nature of the patient's referral to individual psychotherapy significantly influences his confidence in the treatment clinic and its staff provides further indirect evidence of this contention. It may be noted in passing that some support for this notion grows from Skinner's (1953) classification of attention as a generalized reinforcer. The attention of other people, he proposes, is reinforcing because it is a necessary condition for receiving other more specific reinforcements from them. Krasner (1955, 1962), building upon this theme in a manner which dovetails with the findings noted above, notes that the very presence of the therapist "is supplying generalized reinforcement at all times in the therapy situation, irrespective of the particular technique or personality involved" (1962, p. 68).

Thus we have proposed two potential bases for the predicted influence of initiation into group on attractiveness of group to the patient-candidate. The group dynamics research basis rests on degree of effort involved in the initiation or screening process. The individual psychotherapy research basis rests on degree of attention involved in these initial procedures. Both bases lead to the prediction of heightened attraction of group membership in the eyes of the patient-candidate as a function of increasing degrees of elaborateness of initiation into the group.

It appears, therefore, that research aimed at exploring hypothesis 7.3 could consider several issues in addition to the basic test of the predicted screening procedure—attraction to group relationship. For example, assuming that support is found for this prediction, use in practice can follow only on systematic attempts at identifying the initiation procedures that are most important in influencing attractiveness to group. Perhaps as a more meaningful question, what types of screening-procedure administrators, conducting these procedures in what manner, are most influential in increasing patient-candidate attraction to group membership? What is the point at which task, task administrator, and task-procedure characteristics combine to reach an asymptote or, in fact, decline in their influence on attraction; that is, when is the point of diminishing returns or a negative influence on attraction reached? To what extent can evidence be provided that points differentially to either effort or attention (or something else) as the mechanism responsible for the screening procedure-attraction to group relationship, assuming that this relationship is in fact demonstrable in the group therapy setting? These, then, are but a few of the salient issues that arise in consideration of the influence of candidacy stage procedures on patient perception of the yet to be joined therapy group.

VOTING IN NEW MEMBERS

Our final hypothesis dealing with group composition concerns that special compositional decision made after a group has been established initially, a decision left largely in the hands of patient members of the group. We refer to the voting-in procedure characteristic of many "open" therapy groups, a procedure whereby patients already constituting the group are given a major voice in the decision as to whether a given patient-candidate is to be accepted as a member of their therapy group.

There are, it appears, several criteria in use along which the procedure of having group members vote on new patient-candidates may be structured. A most useful one, from our perspective, is that developed by Bach (1954). He comments:

> Criteria of group dynamics governing the selection of one or two newcomers or replacements for therapy in a relatively stable group will differ widely, depending on what kind of roles are open in a particular group at a particular time. One group may at a certain time have an opening for an aggressive male, while another group would reject such an individual, seeking instead to add to the team a passive-dependent female patient . . . In our regime, the group of patients who belong at the time of selection actively participate in gauging the nature of the group dynamic state of affairs. Thus, selection is made not only with respect to clinical personality consideration, but selection procedures take cognizance of the need of the group to increase its role repertoire, in order to obtain better complementation between roles (p. 25).

As is no doubt obvious at this point in our discussion, such emphasis on functional patient roles as the major basis of the voting-in procedure quite readily dovetails with the functional approach to group composition underlying our earlier hypotheses. Our present hypothesis, however, is oriented more toward the circumstance in which the therapist provides more structural or status-oriented information to his group about the patient-candidate, when the basis of the vote is essentially centered on case history, descriptive, attitudinal, diagnostic, or other nonfunctional, nonbehavioral information about the patient to be voted on. Under this circumstance we propose the following hypothesis:

HYPOTHESIS 7.4: **Open therapy groups in which members are permitted to vote on the acceptability for membership of new patient-candidates, based on structural, nonbehavioral information about such candidates, will tend to become increasingly homogeneous on relevant structural dimensions with continued use of the patient voting procedure.**

This hypothesis rests primarily on the group dynamics and interpersonal behavior research finding which quite consistently indicates the high degree of relatedness of, on the one hand, attitudinal and cognitive similarity between two individuals and, on the other hand, their interpersonal attraction. To the extent that interpersonal attraction finds overt expression in a vote for acceptance of a given patient-candidate, this series of findings will provide support for our prediction that the group will become increasingly homogeneous on these attitudinal and related dimensions the more the group members are permitted this major role in patient selection.

Investigations of Attraction and Similarity

As early as 1937 Winslow (1937) found a high positive relationship between friendship choices and attitudinal similarity in a wide variety of attitudinal areas. Richardson (1940) was similarly able to demonstrate the high degree of interrelatedness of friendship patterns and similarity of basic values or orientation, as was Bonney (1946) in terms of vocational interests. Forsyth and Katz (1946), Precker (1952), Shapiro (1953), and Smith (1952) report similar findings. Lindzey and Borgatta (1954) summarize much of this research with their comment:

> In general, this research suggests that within certain groups maintenance of particular attitudes is correlated with sociometric status and, further, that individuals who choose one another tend to be similar in their attitude structure (p. 432).

Zander and Havelin (1960), working in another area of individual functioning, were able to demonstrate concurring trends. Cartwright and Zander (1960), reviewing a series of such studies, comment:

> . . . persons preferred to associate with those close to them in ability (rather) than with ones divergent from them in ability. *The result of the tendency for like to join like in group association is an eventual increase in similarity among the members* (p. 81) (italics added).

In addition to focus on attitudinal and ability dimensions, a series of studies has examined the relationship between interpersonal attraction and dyadic similarity along a variety of personality dimensions. Flemming (1935), provided an early demonstration of the relationship of friendship choice and similarity on such personality dimensions as intraversion-extraversion, and social adjustment. Pintner, Forlano, and Freedman (1937), however were generally unable to replicate this finding in a younger age group. Van Dyne (1940) reported low but significant correlations between sociometric friendship choices and similarity between the chooser and chosen in terms of dominance and stability. In general, the findings in this area of personality similarity and interpersonal attraction present a generally consistent picture which, while to a fair extent trait-specific, suggests a low but stable positive relationship between interpersonal attraction and personality trait similarity. Let us examine a few recent studies in this general area of interpersonal attraction and dyadic similarity in greater detail. These studies will permit a somewhat closer look at the nature and dynamics of the voting-in procedure.

Lundy, Katkovsky, Cromwell, and Shoemaker (1955) had each of

54 college students describe himself, his ideal self, and his best-liked and least-liked fellow student on a multiple-choice personality questionnaire. A score representing self-acceptability was obtained for each subject in terms of the number of questionnaire items on which his self- and ideal self-descriptions were the same. A self-unacceptability score was derived in terms of the number of items on which the self- and ideal self-descriptions differed. Comparisons were then made between the self-description acceptability and unacceptability scores and descriptions of positive and negative sociometric choices. As hypothesized, the investigators report that descriptions of positive sociometric choices were more similar to the S's acceptable self-descriptions than to their unacceptable self-descriptions. The converse tended to characterize S's negative sociometric choices. In general, Ss were found to describe persons they liked best as more similar to themselves than persons they liked least. Thus this investigation not only provides support for our basic contention but, in addition, points to a potentially important psychodynamic basis on which interpersonal choice decisions are made.

The studies examined so far quite consistently point to a strong positive relationship between interpersonal attraction and interindividual similarity, particularly on attitudinal dimensions. For purposes of identifying evidence which justifies extrapolating from this material to the voting-in procedure in group psychotherapy it is important that the causal aspect of this relationship be considered; that is, to what extent does research evidence suggest that attitudinal similarity, in fact, *determines* interpersonal attraction? The relevance of the research we are considering for hypothesis 7.4 stands or falls, it would appear, on the extent to which this directionality of causation can be specified, because, in a very real sense, the hypothesis rests on the assumption that attitudinal similarity with the patient-candidate, as perceived by the patients already constituting the group, determines their attraction toward him and hence their vote.

Newcomb (1961), in an imporant longitudinal study of the development of interpersonal attraction, reports substantial evidence indicating that the relationship between attitudinal agreement and mutual attraction is an interdependent one, changes in either inducing changes in the other. He comments further:

Thus several quite diverse sets of data all provide support for the general hypothesis that, following but not before adequate opportunity for pair members to become familiar with each others' attitudes, pair attraction is predictable from actual agreement (p. 96).

A study by Byrne (1961) is also clearly relevant. With the general aim of examining the proposition that attitude similarity has a causative influence on the degree of interpersonal attraction, he hypothesized: (1) a stranger who is known to have attitudes similar to those of the subject is better liked than a stranger with attitudes dissimilar to those of the subject, and (2) a stranger who is known to have attitudes similar to those of the subject is judged to be more intelligent, better informed, more moral, and better adjusted than a stranger with attitudes dissimilar to those of the subject. An attitude scale representing 26 opinion areas was administered to a class of 64 college student subjects. Two weeks later all subjects were falsely informed that the attitude scale had been given as part of a study in interpersonal prediction. They were told that individuals in another class had been given the same scale that they took, that students in the two classes had been matched, and that they were to be given each other's tests in order to determine how much they could learn about one another from this information alone. The questionnaire responses they actually received at this time were, in fact, made up by the experimenter. On a random basis, subjects received questionnaires from "their matched partners" whose responses were identical to or opposite from their own attitude questionnaire responses. Each subject then responded to a rating scale aimed at measuring the degree of interpersonal attraction toward this (fictitious) other person; that is, they were told to indicate how much they felt they would like this person and whether they believed they would enjoy working with the person as a partner in an experiment. In addition, each subject completed four evaluation scales in which he judged the other person's intelligence, knowledge of current events, morality, and adjustment. Byrne's hypotheses received strong support. The group of subjects who received attitude scales which were filled out in the same way as their own indicated significantly more positive feelings toward the stranger than did the group that received scales reflecting dissimilar attitudes. Further, the similar attitudes group rated the stranger significantly higher than did the dissimilar attitudes group on intelligence, knowledge of current events, morality, and adjustment.

Thus both the Newcomb and Byrne studies clearly point to a causative effect of attitudinal similarity on interpersonal attraction. As Byrne notes in closing, and as we believe also applies to the aspect of group psychotherapy we are considering,

> It should be possible now to study the effect of attitude differences less extreme than those in the present study and to combine this variable with

the others that influence interpersonal attraction in order to determine inter-action effects (p. 715).

In addition to this suggested line of research, and the basic test of the effect of the voting-in procedure on therapy group homogeneity, there are certain other aspects of the voting-in process of interest in the psychotherapeutic context whose examination is suggested by group dynamics and interpersonal behavior research.

Other Aspects of Voting-In

It was noted earlier that Bach (1954) emphasizes functional roles needed by the group, roles whose nature is partially decided upon by the existing members, as the suggested basis for group member voting on the patient-candidate. Bruner (1941) comments: "Whether members of a group perceive a newcomer as facilitating or obstructing may be determined, at least in part, by the needs of the group" (p. 122). Ziller and Behringer (1960) have in fact demonstrated this to be the case with regard to conditions of group success and failure. The knowl-edgeable newcomer tended to be more effective and influential in failure groups than in successful groups. In general, this study provided evidence suggesting that members of failure groups perceive the new-comer as a possible resource, a stimulus to needed change, whereas successful groups tend to perceive him as a restriction, a stimulus to potentially disruptive change. These findings suggest that there may well be other characteristics of therapy groups which influence be-havior toward the patient-candidate. Perhaps therapy groups low in cohesiveness respond to newcomers in a manner analogous to Ziller and Behringer's successful groups, with highly cohesive therapy groups more negatively oriented toward the newcomer. Cartwright and Zander (1960) note that

. . . on the basis of several studies it appears that those who are not members but who are strongly attracted to membership act as members do, and in some cases may outdo the members, apparently in order to prove their suitability for acceptance by the group (p. 89).

This group dynamics finding clearly suggests the importance of considering the degree to which the patient-candidate's behavior, on which group members base their acceptance-rejection decision, is open to deliberate or unintentional distortion in the direction of the patient-candidate's conception of greater acceptability. Investigations of within-group status hierarchies, between-member power differentials, and subgrouping have all assumed an important role in group dy-namics research. To the extent that such group structural factors operate in therapy groups, one must wonder about their influence on the decision regarding candidates for admission. Do some more powerful group members, in effect, stuff the ballot box while other, less influential patients are "disfranchised?" Voting sequence may also be a relevant consideration. Hare (1962) notes that "Since the first persons to vote publicly are often the ones who are most confident of their opinions . . . some of these early responders will influence later responses" (p. 35). Although the major determiner of the acceptability of a new patient is and should be the therapist, to what extent do his own preferences unintentionally influence the decision of group members? Does such therapist influence differ in leader-centered and group-centered therapy groups? Is the essentially democratic voting-in procedure feasible in therapy groups conducted in an encapsulated, authoritarian setting, such as a prison? If so, what are the implications, if any, for group cohesiveness and other group characteristics of such a procedure utilized in this setting?

REFERENCES

Altshuler, J. M.   One year's experience with group psychotherapy. *Ment. Hyg.,* 1940, **24**, 190–196.

Arbous, A. G., & Maree, J.   Contribution of two group discussion techniques to a validated test battery. *Occup. Psychol.,* 1951, **25**, 73–89.

Aronson, E.   The effect of effort on the attractiveness of rewarded and unrewarded stimuli. *J. abnorm. soc. Psychol.,* 1961, **63**, 375–380.

Aronson E., & Mills, J.   The effects of severity of initiation on liking for a group. *J. abnorm. soc. Psychol.,* 1959, **59**, 177–181.

Bach, G. R.   *Intensive group psychotherapy.* New York: Ronald Press, 1954.

Bales, R. F.   *Interaction process analysis: a method for the study of small groups.* Cambridge, Mass.: Addison-Wesley, 1950.

Bales, R. F.   In conference. *Harv. Bus. Rev.,* 1954, **32**, 44–50.

Bales, R. F., & Borgatta, E. F.   Size of group as a factor in the interaction profile. In A. P. Hare, E. F. Borgatta, & R. F. Bales (Eds.), *Small groups: studies in social interaction.* New York: Alfred A. Knopf, 1955. Pp. 396–413.

Barron, F., & Leary, T.   Changes in psychoneurotic patients with and without psychotherapy. *J. consult. Psychol.,* 1955, **19**, 239–245.

Bass, B. M.   Interrelations among measurements of member and group performance. Tech. Rep. 4, Contract N70NR 35609, Louisiana State University, Baton Rouge, 1955.

Bass, B. M.   *Leadership, psychology and organizational behavior.* New York: Harper, 1960.

Bass, B. M., & Norton, F. M.   Group size and leaderless discussion. *J. appl. Psychol.*, 1951, 35, 397–401.

Bell, G. B., & French, R. L.   Consistency of individual leadership position in small groups of varying membership. In A. P. Hare, E. F. Borgatta, & R. F. Bales (Eds.), *Small groups.* New York: Alfred A. Knopf, 1955. Pp. 275–280.

Benne, K. D., & Sheats, P.   Functional roles of group members. *J. soc. Issues,* 1948, 4, 41–49.

Blake, R. R., & Brehm, J. W.   The use of tape recording to simulate a group atmosphere. *J. abnorm. soc. Psychol.,* 1954, 49, 311–313.

Blake, R. R., Mouton, J. S., & Fruchter, B.   The consistency of interpersonal behavior judgments made on the basis of short-term interactions in three-man groups. *J. abnorm. soc. Psychol.,* 1954, 49, 573–578.

Bonney, M. E.   A sociometric study of the relationship of some factors to mutual friendships on the elementary, secondary, and college levels. *Sociometry,* 1946, 9, 21–47.

Borgatta, E. F., & Bales, R. F.   The consistency of subject behavior and the reliability of scoring in interaction process analysis. In A. P. Hare, E. F. Borgatta, & R. F. Bales (Eds.), *Small groups.* New York: Alfred A. Knopf, 1955a. Pp. 300–304.

Borgatta, E. F., & Bales, R. F.   Interaction of individuals in reconstituted groups. In A. P. Hare, E. F. Borgatta, & R. F. Bales (Eds.), *Small groups.* New York: Alfred A. Knopf, 1955b. Pp. 379–396.

Borgatta, E. F., & Bales, R. F.   Size of group as a factor in the interaction profile. In A. P. Hare, E. F. Borgatta, & R. F. Bales (Eds.), *Small groups.* New York: Alfred A. Knopf, 1955c. Pp. 397–413.

Breer, P. E.   Predicting interpersonal behavior from personality and role. Unpublished doctoral dissertation, Harvard University, 1960.

Bruner, J. S.   Personality dynamics and the process of perceiving. In R. R. Blake & G. V. Ramsey (Eds.), *Perception: an approach to personality.* New York: Ronald Press, 1941. Pp. 123–142.

Byrne, D.   Interpersonal attraction and attitude similarity. *J. abnorm. soc. Psychol.,* 1961, 62, 713–715.

Carter, L. F., Haythorn, W., Shriver, E., & Lanzetta, J.   The behavior of leaders and other group members. *J. abnorm. soc. Psychol.,* 1951, 46, 589–595.

Carter, L. F., Haythorn, W., Meirowitz, B., & Lanzetta, J.   A note on a new technique of interaction recording. *J. abnorm. soc. Psychol.,* 1951, 46, 258–260.

Cartwright, D.   Achieving change in people: some applications of group dynamics theory. *Hum. Rel.,* 1951, 4, 381–392.

Cartwright, D., & Zander, A. (Eds.)   *Group dynamics.* Evanston, Ill: Row, Peterson & Co., 1960.

Castore, G. F.   Number of verbal interrelationships as a determinant of group size. *J. abnorm. soc. Psychol.,* 1962, 64, 456–457.

Cavanagh, J. R., & Gerstein, S.   Group psychotherapy in a naval disciplinary barracks. *Nav. med. Bull.,* 1949, **49,** 645–654.

Chapple, E. D.   Measuring human relations: an introduction to the study of the interaction of individuals. *Genet. psychol. Monogr.,* 1940, **22,** 1–147.

Chapple, E. D.   The interaction chronograph: its evolution and present application. *Personnel,* 1949, **25,** 295–307.

Cohen, A. R.   Communication discrepancy and attitude change: a dissonance theory approach. *J. Pers.,* 1959, **27,** 386–396.

Corsini, R. J.   *Methods of group psychotherapy.* New York: McGraw-Hill, 1957.

Coyle, G. L.   *Social process in organized groups.* New York: R. R. Smith, 1930.

Crutchfield, R. S.   Assessment of persons through a quasi group-interaction technique. *J. abnorm. soc. Psychol.,* 1951, **46,** 577–588.

Deer, J., & Silver, A. W.   Predicting participation and behavior in group therapy from test protocols. *J. clin. Psychol.,* 1962, **18,** 322–325.

Del Torto, J., & Corneytz, P.   Psychodrama as expressive and projective technique. *Sociometry,* 1944, **8,** 356–375.

Dreikurs, R.   Techniques and dynamics of multiple psychotherapy. *Psychiat. Quart.,* 1950, **24,** 788–799.

Durkin, H. E.   Toward a common basis for group dynamics: group and therapeutic processes in group psychotherapy. *Int. J. grp. Psychother.,* 1957, **7,** 115–130.

Dynes, J. B., & Hamilton, F. J.   Group psychotherapy of psychiatric war casualties. *Nav. med. Bull.,* 1945, **44,** 549–597.

Ebaugh, F. G.   Group therapy. *Neuropsychiat.,* 1951, **1,** 19–32.

Fink, H. K.   Some therapeutic departures in group therapy. *Psychol. Newsletter,* 1956, **8,** 1–11.

Flemming, G.   A factor analysis of the personality of high school leaders. *J. appl. Psychol.,* 1935, **19,** 597–605.

Forsyth, E., & Katz, L.   A matrix approach to the analysis of sociometric data: preliminary report. *Sociometry,* 1946, **9,** 340–347.   ·

Foulkes, S. H.   *Introduction to group-analytic psychotherapy.* New York: Grune & Stratton, 1949.

Foulkes, S. H., & Anthony, E. J.   *Group psychotherapy: the psychoanalytic approach.* London: Penguin Books, 1957.

Fouriezos, N., Hutt, M., & Guetzkow, H.   Measurement of self-oriented needs in discussion groups. *J. abnorm. soc. Psychol.,* 1950, **45,** 682–690.

Frank, J. D.   Some determinants, manifestations, and effects of cohesiveness in therapy groups. *Int. J. grp. Psychother.,* 1957, **7,** 53–63.

Furst, W.   Homogeneous versus heterogeneous groups. *Int. J. grp. Psychother.,* 1951, **1,** 120–123.

Gibb, C. A.   Leadership. In G. Lindzey (Ed.), *Handbook of social psychology.* Cambridge, Mass.: Addison-Wesley, 1954. Pp. 877–920.

Gilchrist, J. C.   Social psychology and the group processes. In P. R. Farnsworth and Q. McNemar (Eds.), *Annual review of Psychology*. Palo Alto, Calif.: Annual Reviews, Inc., 1959. Pp. 233–264.

Goldfarb, W.   Principles of group psychotherapy. *Amer. J. Psychother.*, 1953, **7**, 418–432.

Goldstein, A. P.   Patient's expectancies and non-specific therapy as a basis for (un)spontaneous remission. *J. clin. Psychol.*, 1960, **16**, 399–403.

Goldstein, A. P., & Shipman, W. G.   Patient expectancies, symptom reduction and aspects of the initial psychotherapeutic interview. *J. clin. Psychol.*, 1961, **17**, 129–133.

Gorlow, J., Hoch, E. L., & Telschow, E. F.   *Non-directive group psychotherapy*. New York: Teacher's College Studies in Education, Columbia University, 1952.

Hare, A. P.   A study of interaction and consensus in different sized groups. *Amer. soc. Rev.*, 1952, **17**, 261–267.

Hare, A. P.   *Handbook of small group research*. New York: The Free Press of Glencoe, 1962.

Haythorn, W.   The influence of individual members on the characteristics of small groups. In A. P. Hare, E. F. Borgatta, & R. F. Bales (Eds.), *Small groups*. New York: Alfred A. Knopf, 1955. Pp. 330–341.

Heller, K.   Dependency changes in psychotherapy as a function of the discrepancy between conscious self-report and projective test performance. Unpublished doctoral dissertation, Pennsylvania State University, 1959.

Heller, K., & Goldstein, A. P.   Client dependency and therapist expectancy as relationship maintaining variables in psychotherapy. *J. consult Psychol.*, 1961, **25**, 371–375.

Hemphill, J. K.   Relations between the size of the group and the behavior of "superior" leaders. *J. soc. Psychol.*, 1950, **32**, 11–22.

Heyns, R. W.   *Functional analysis of group problem solving behavior*. Ann Arbor, Mich.: Conference Research, Department of Psychology, University of Michigan, 1948 (mimeo).

Heynes, R. W., & Lippitt, R.   Systematic observational techniques. In G. Lindzey (Ed.), *Handbook of social psychology*. Cambridge, Mass.: Addison-Wesley, 1954. Pp. 370–404.

Hinkley, R. G., & Hermann, L.   *Group treatment in psychotherapy*. Minneapolis: University of Minnesota, 1951.

Hobbs, N.   Group-centered psychotherapy. In C. R. Rogers, *Client centered psychotherapy*. Boston: Houghton-Mifflin, 1951.

Hunt, J. McV.   Concerning the impact of group psychotherapy on psychology. *Int. J. grp. Psychother.*, 1964, **14**, 3–31.

Kelley, H. H., & Thibaut, J. W.   Experimental studies of group problem solving and process. In G. Lindzey (Ed.), *Handbook of social psychology*. Cambridge, Mass.: Addison-Wesley, 1954.

Kelman, H.   Group therapy. *Amer. J. Psychoanal.*, 1948, **8**, 144–153.

Kew, C. E., & Kew, C. J.   Group psychotherapy in a church setting. *Pastoral Psychol.,* 1950, 1, 36–39.

Kinney, E. E.   A study of peer group social acceptability at the fifth grade level in a public school. *J. educ. Res.,* 1953, 47, 57–64.

Krasner, L.   The use of generalized reinforcers in psychotherapy research. *Psychol. Rep.,* 1955, 1, 19–25.

Krasner, L.   The therapist as a social reinforcement machine. In H. H. Strupp & L. Luborsky (Eds.), *Research in psychotherapy.* Washington: Amer. Psychol. Assoc., 1962. Pp. 61–94.

Liff, Z. A.   *Group dynamics and psychotherapy.* New York: Postgraduate Center for Psychotherapy, 1952 (mimeo).

Lindzey, G., & Borgatta, E. F.   Sociometric measurement. In G. Lindzey (Ed.), *Handbook of social psychology.* Cambridge, Mass.: Addison-Wesley, 1954. Pp. 405–448.

Locke, N. M.   *Group psychoanalysis.* New York: New York University Press, 1961.

Lorr, M.   Research problems in group psychotherapy. Paper read at Amer. Grp. Psychother. Assoc., Washington, January, 1963.

Lowrey, L. G.   Group therapy for mothers. *Amer. J. Orthopsychiat.,* 1944, 14, 589–592.

Lundy, R. M., Katkovsky, W., Cromwell, R. L., & Shoemaker, D. J.   Self acceptability and descriptions of sociometric choices. *J. abnorm. soc. Psychol.,* 1955, 51, 260–262.

Matarazzo, J. D.   The interaction chronograph as an instrument for objective measurement of interaction patterns during interviews. *J. Psychol.,* 1956, 41, 347–367.

Miller, N. E.   Effects of group size on group process and member satisfaction. Process of Adm. Conf., University of Michigan, Ann Arbor, 1950.

Moreno, J. L.   *Who shall survive?* Washington: Nervous and Mental Disease Publishing Co., 1934.

Moreno, J. L., & Jennings, H. H.   Sociometric methods of grouping and regrouping: with reference to authoritative and democratic methods of grouping. *Sociometry,* 1944, 7, 397–414.

Murray, E. J.   A content analysis method for studying psychotherapy. *Psychol. Monogr.,* 1956, 70, Whole No. 420.

Newcomb, T. M.   *The acquaintance process.* New York: Holt, Rinehart & Winston, 1961.

Parloff, M. B.   Group dynamics and group psychotherapy: the state of the union. Paper read at Amer. Grp. Psychother. Assoc., Washington, January, 1963.

Pintner, R., Forlano, G., & Freedman, H.   Personality and attitudinal similarity among classroom friends. *J. appl. Psychol.,* 1937, 21, 48–65.

Powdermaker, F., & Frank, J. D.   *Group psychotherapy.* Cambridge: Harvard Univer. Press, 1953.

Precker, J. A.   Similarity of valuings as a factor in selection of peers and near-authority figures. *J. abnorm. soc. Psychol.,* 1952, **47**, 406–414.

Richardson, H. M.   Community of values as a factor in friendships of college and adult women. *J. soc. Psychol.,* 1940, **11**, 303–312.

Rosenzweig, S.   *Rosenzweig picture-frustration study: revised form for adults, test and manual.* St. Louis: Author, 1947.

Rosow, H. M., & Kaplan, L. P.   Integrated individual and group therapy. *Int. J. grp. Psychother.,* 1954, 4, 381–392.

Saslow, G., & Matarazzo, J. D.   A technique for studying changes in interview behavior. In E. A. Rubinstein & M. B. Parloff (Eds.), *Research in psychotherapy.* Washington: Amer. Psychol. Assoc., 1959. Pp. 125–159.

Schneider, L.   A proposed conceptual integration of group dynamics and therapy. *J. soc. Psychol.,* 1955, **42**, 173–191.

Schutz, W. C.   *FIRO.* New York: Rinehart & Co., 1958.

Seashore, S. E.   *Group cohesiveness in the industrial workgroup.* Ann Arbor: University of Michigan, 1954.

Shapiro, D.   Psychological factors in friendship choice and rejection. Unpublished doctoral dissertation, University of Michigan, 1953.

Skinner, B. F.   *Science and human behavior.* New York: Macmillan, 1953.

Slater, P. E.   Contrasting correlates of group size. *Sociometry,* 1958, **21**, 129–139.

Slavson, S. R.   Are there "group dynamics" in therapy groups? *Int. J. grp. psychother.,* 1957, **7**, 131–154.

Smith, A. J.   Similarity of values and its relation to acceptance and the projection of similarity. *J. Psychol.,* 1952, **43**, 251–260.

Snyder, W. U.   An investigation of the nature of non-directive therapy. *J. gen. Psychol.,* 1945, **33**, 193–223.

Steinzor, B.   The development and evaluation of a measure of social interaction. *Hum. Relat.,* 1949, **2**, 103–122.

Stephan, F. F., & Mishler, E. G.   The distribution of participation in small groups: an experimental approximation. *Amer. soc. Rev.,* 1952, **17**, 598–608.

Stone, A. R., Parloff, M. B., & Frank, J. D.   The use of "diagnostic" groups in a group therapy program. *Int. J. grp. Psychother.,* 1954, 4, 274–284.

Strupp, H. H.   An objective comparison of Rogerian and Psychoanalytic techniques. *J. consult. Psychol.,* 1955, **19**, 1–7.

Van Dyne, V. E.   Personality traits and friendship formation in adolescent girls. *J. soc. Psychol.,* 1940, **12**, 291–303.

Weislogel, R. L., & Schwartz, P. A.   Some practical and theoretical problems in situational testing. *Ed. Psychol. Meas.,* 1955, **15**, 39–46.

Winslow, C. N.   A study of the extent of agreement between friend's opinions and their ability to estimate the opinions of each other. *J. soc. Psychol.,* 1937, **8**, 433–442.

Wolf, A., & Schwartz, E. K.   *Psychoanalysis in groups.* New York: Grune & Stratton, 1962.

Yaryan, R., & Festinger, L.   Preparatory action and belief in the probable occurrence of future events. *J. abnorm. soc. Psychol.,* 1961, **63**, 603–606.

Zander, A., & Havelin, A.   Social comparison and interpersonal attractiveness. *Hum. Relat.,* 1960, **13**, 21–32.

Ziller, R. C., & Behringer, R. D.   Assimilation of the knowledgeable newcomer under conditions of group success and failure. *J. abnorm. soc. Psychol.,* 1960, **60**, 288–291.

Zimbardo, P. G.   Involvement and communication discrepancy as determinants of opinion change. *J. abnorm. soc. Psychol.,* 1960, **60**, 86–94.

8

GROUP PSYCHOTHERAPIST
ORIENTATION

At the outset of our consideration of the composition of therapy groups we suggested that a prime determinant of the degree to which a given group psychotherapist is open to consideration of group dynamics research findings relates to his basic orientation toward therapy groups. The therapist whose theoretical orientation and therapeutic techniques lies in the direction of leader or therapist-centeredness and who conducts individually oriented group psychotherapy tends to perceive the group dynamics body of research as largely irrelevant to his psychotherapeutic task. In contrast, the therapist whose orientation and operations favor more of a group-oriented, group-centered approach tends to be receptive to the potential usefulness of group dynamics evidence for purposes of helping to clarify and make more effective his functioning as a group psychotherapist.

The present section will focus on potentially useful comparisons of these two group leadership orientations and the ways in which they find expression other than in attitudes toward group dynamics research, but it is most important to note at the ouset that for most group psychotherapists, adherence to a therapist-centered or group-centered viewpoint is more of a "leaning toward" orientation than a fixed, extreme position. As noted earlier, group psychotherapists in action characteristically attend to *both* group forces or influences and individual psychodynamics. It is the degree to which reliance is placed on one or the other of these two orientations that is at issue here. The therapist-centered, individual orientation leans toward psychotherapy of people *in* groups. The group-centered viewpoint is more one of psychotherapy *through* groups. The therapist-centered position is more directive, interpretive, and focused on the psychodynamics of indi-

361

vidual members. The group-centered psychotherapist is less overtly active, more of a catalyst or encourager of member-to-member and not member-to-therapist interaction and more oriented toward groupwide influences on individual patients. As Semon and Goldstein (1957) observe:

> The leader-centered method, or therapy in a group, assumes that the therapeutic potential is resident in the relationship formed between each member and the leader with the result that the focus of treatment is on the individual within the group. In the group-centered method, or therapy through a group, the assumption is that the motivation for change is contained within the emotional relationship established among the members of the group. In this method, the focus of treatment is on the group (p. 317).

To repeat, we deal here with a continuum and clearly not a dichotomy. Although its theoretical poles, for heuristic purposes, may be described as therapist- or leader-centered and group-centered, we find that operationally most group therapists cluster near the middle of the continuum, leaning toward one approach or the other but agreeing much more than they differ.

Several years ago, Gorlow, Hoch, and Telschow (1952) commented: "How much should a group leader participate? This is perhaps the greatest single problem in group psychotherapy" (p. 15). In somewhat extended form we agree with the importance they accord this variable. The basic orientation of the group psychotherapist, expressed, among other ways, by his degree of participation, was and indeed still is a major problem in need of resolution for the advance of group psychotherapy. Following the Gorlow et al. (1952) series of investigations, only a few studies have centered on this group therapist orientation problem. Speculation and theorizing have been in abundance. Relevant research has not. Let us now turn to some of these "position papers" in more detail. We do so by starting at the leader-centered, individual-oriented pole of our proposed continuum of therapist orientations, follow by consideration of what is more or less its opposite, the group-centered, group-oriented viewpoint, and finally examine the large middle ground into which most contemporary viewpoints currently fall.

A CONTINUUM OF GROUP THERAPIST ORIENTATIONS

Several group psychotherapists have rather clearly stated their preference for an approach to the group psychotherapy interaction that emphasizes active leadership behavior and primary focus on individual group members as the major vehicles mediating patient change. As Lowrey (1944) comments:

... the essential point is that the lines of the treatment relationships are from each individual to the therapist. In other words, this is therapy in the group, rather than therapy by the group. Group interaction does occur, and it has a therapeutic effect, but this is definitely a secondary mechanism ... (p. 11).

Wolf and Schwartz (1962) champion a similar viewpoint:

It is looming as an important task in group psychotherapy to re-emphasize the necessity to attend to the patient if we wish to treat him. We need, despite our enthusiasm for therapy in a group, to return to the psychoanalytic emphasis upon the individual, the individual in interaction. It is not possible to treat a group. We need to keep the patient the center of attention, not an abstraction lost in a sociologic ideal (p. 72).

Their individual-oriented viewpoint finds direct expression in a series of leader-centered therapeutic operations and procedures, largely in the form of more or less standard psychoanalytic techniques. This orientation toward the individual, coupled with its logical consequent, use of therapist-centered, active, therapist procedures also finds expression and development in the type of "group psychoanalysis" propounded by Locke (1961). He notes:

It must be re-emphasized that the individual is being treated, not the group. The group is the place where the individual displays all the characteristics of his neurosis. The therapist takes advantage of this presentation of the individual's conflict, and works with the individual in a group setting. The group, as such, does not exist (p. 23).

Thus the writings of Lowrey (1944), Wolf and Schwartz (1962), and Locke (1961) may be viewed as defining the leader-centered, individual-oriented pole of a group psychotherapist orientation continuum. Although all three of the generally concurring viewpoints just presented are psychoanalytic in origin, it will become clear later in our discussion that many attempts to utilize psychoanalytic principles and techniques in the group therapy context have not eventuated in such a directly translated active and interpretive approach. First, however, let us examine the opposite of the polar extreme we have just described. We refer to the early application of nondirective individual therapy to the group context, as represented by Hobbs (1951). He comments:

The most challenging new element in the group situation is the possibility of releasing the therapeutic potential of the group itself. *Group therapy,* and not individual therapy in a group, is the goal. If the therapist is skillful, the group itself becomes a therapeutic agent and gathers momentum of its own . . . (p. 305).

In the initiation of the group-centered approach, at least in its early, nondirective form, "the therapist proceeds with the assumption that the group can get started and work out directions without his guidance" (Hobbs, 1951, p. 294). Following from this orientation, heaviest reliance was placed on the standard, nondirective techniques of reflection and clarification of feeling, restatement of content, and simple acceptance and so forth. Hobbs adds:

> The concern with diagnosis is minimal, interpretation is not relied on as a therapeutic instrument, insight is not considered to be an essential change-agent in the process of learning, transference attitudes are handled just like all other affect-laden expressions . . . (Hobbs, 1951, p. 289).

Thus, although the more contemporary nondirective approach to group psychotherapy has moved to some extent away from this polar position, its early framing by Hobbs clearly serves the heuristic purpose of defining the group-centered pole of our therapist orientation continuum. The nondirective viewpoint espoused by Gorlow, Hoch, and Telschow (1952), as well as the essentially leaderless group approach proposed by Bion (1959), are also representative of this more extremely group-centered therapist orientation.

With the limiting poles of group psychotherapist orientation thus defined, we are in a position to turn to the several viewpoints more centrally located on this continuum. It will be apparent that some lean a bit toward an active, interpretive approach, and several rely more on group forces and characteristics as mediators of patient change. With reference to those leaning toward leader-centeredness, a statement by Corsini (1957) seems to capture very well the marked degree of variability among many therapists working from a psychoanalytic background.

> . . . the final common objective of analytic methods is to analyze; the analysis may come from the participants but more usually comes from the therapist, who is regarded as the final judge in most cases.
>
> The therapist may assume varying degrees of authority, ranging from complete control to passive participation . . . he may, for example, find it advantageous to pull together the discussion, lecturing on some topic and indicating how each of the members may be working on the basis of some principle. He may offer dream interpretations. He may initiate discussions on some topic and may then act as a facilitator, using techniques of encouragement and reflection (p. 63).

Redl's (1942) active, interpretive approach to group therapy with children appears to be but one example of this moderately leader-centered orientation. In a directly analogous manner there are some who generally cluster near the middle of our therapist-orientation continuum and lean toward the group-centered orientation but who also demonstrate variability among themselves in this respect.

The writings of Bach (1954), growing from a selective use of psychoanalytic and Lewinian field theory concepts, represent such a qualified group-oriented leaning. In essence, his approach during the early, formative sessions of a given therapy group is primarily oriented toward discouraging the development of a leader-centered, therapist-dependent group structure. Once this essential group orientation is established, Bach feels the therapist is free to operate in a manner which, still emphasizing a group-centered orientation, involves mutually planned programmatic activities and a moderate degree of therapist activity. Most of the wide variety of therapist operations utilized by Bach share the characteristics of being essentially group-oriented and at times involving a moderate level of intervention by the therapist. Thus a major effort is made to avoid procedures which intensify the centrality of the therapist's role. Although use is made of concurrent individual therapy sessions, these sessions consistently have as their prime referent events and feelings directly related to the group experience. Similarly, organized group activities and procedures, initially introduced by the therapist and thus ". . . temporarily [having] the undesirable effect of strengthening the central or power position of the therapist-leader" (p. 76), gradually shift to a procedure in which decisions regarding their use are determined more and more by the group members. Bach (1954) notes:

> If this is done correctly, group cohesiveness is furthered and leader-dependency actually weakened. After initiation by the leader, a group routine can become established independent of leader-direction" (p. 76).

Bach's perspective on dream interpretation affords yet another example of his modified group-centered viewpoint. His behavior involves participation with the group in its "basic emotion of wonderment" of what a dream may mean. If the group therapist yields to the always present dependency wishes of the group to have him interpret dream material, Bach cautions, he is then contributing to an expectation of leader-centeredness on the part of the group membership.

Thus, in sum, we may characterize Bach's over-all position as modified group-centered, a position which in many essential respects also generally characterizes the writings of Foulkes (1946), Frank (1957), Hinkley and Hermann (1951), Liff (1952), and others. Foulkes (1946), for example, who reserves the terms "leader" and "leading" to represent "active and manifest exertion of influence upon the group" and substitutes the perhaps more neutral term "conductor" to describe the group therapist, pictures his orientation as follows:

> Thus a conductor may or may not lead the group. The guiding principle for him is always the therapeutic function. In the best interest of this function, he has sometimes to assume the role of a leader. Most of the time, according to our opinion, his therapeutic role is better served the more he refrains from leading and, indeed, it is essential that he should not identify the task of conducting the group with that of leading it (p. 133).

Foulkes, too, directs his efforts in early sessions at weaning the group from its need to be led. Going somewhat further than Bach toward group-centeredness, he refrains from use of set topics or planned discussion areas and emphasizes, instead, "free-floating discussion" which he describes as the group counterpart of free association.

To the extent that therapist orientation and operations influence patient change in group psychotherapy, the variability in approach we have highlighted so far clearly indicates the importance of research aimed at identifying the general type of orientation, or the elements of each orientation, that most effectively result in patient change. A small series of group psychotherapy investigations, and a larger number of related studies in the context of individual psychotherapy, have aimed at this basic therapist-centered versus group-centered comparison and the related pairings of psychoanalytic versus nondirective therapy, leading versus reflective therapy, and, more generally, therapist activity level. We shall now examine these studies, particularly in terms of the future research directions to which they point. Following this, we shall turn to the considerable group dynamics research material which points to potential means of identifying the most therapeutically effective group therapist orientations and operations.

Investigations of Therapist Orientation

An investigation by Singer and Goldman (1954) contrasted two therapy groups of ten schizophrenic patients each. Psychotherapy was conducted weekly for a five-month period, under one of two therapist orientations. One group met under generally directive authoritarian conditions, with lectures by the leader-therapist functioning as the major therapist intervention. The second group, more democratic in leadership orientation, received encouragement for free expression and participation of group members. Intergroup comparisons in the form of rating of group cohesiveness, relevance of material discussed, and nature of interpersonal communication all demonstrated the superiority, for this sample, of the more group-centered leadership approach.

Ends and Page (1957) contrasted the effectiveness of psychoanalytic (patterned after Alexander and French) and client-centered group psychotherapy in a population of male alcoholic patients. Sixteen groups of six patients each were formed. Sessions were held three times weekly for five weeks, with each participating therapist conducting a group under each experimental condition (therapist orientation). Q-sort comparisons of patients receiving therapy under the therapist orientations of concern to us here revealed significant but different types of personality changes under the different orientations. Change in patients in the psychoanalytically oriented groups was reflected only in the present-self Q-sort responses. In contrast, in the client-centered groups, patient change was expressed in both present and ideal self-terms. The investigators note,

> If one believes that misbehavior, mental illness or maladjustment are manifestations of the whole personality, rather than of one aspect of it, then the process of coordinated restructuring seems to represent sounder therapeutic movement or personality growth (p. 274).

In a study not utilizing therapy groups, but clearly most relevant to such groups, Bovard (1951) examined the effects of group-centeredness and leader-centeredness on communication of feeling, identification, and clinical insight. Two matched sections of an elementary psychology course, with 25 students in each, served as experimental subjects. The major leader orientation difference distinguishing the conduct of the two groups was that the amount of member-to-member verbal interaction was maximized in meetings of the group-centered section, and minimized in the leader-centered section. After each section had met for 39 class hours under these conditions, it was asked to discuss, with the leader not participating, a human relations problem made explicit by a movie they were shown on "the feeling of rejection." Typescripts of each group's discussion were rated blindly by two independent judges. The group-centered section, in contrast to their leader-centered counterparts, evidenced greater communication of feeling, more identification with the movie character, and greater clinical insight into her personality dynamics.

Let us stop for a moment to see where these studies are taking us. So far matters appear largely one-sided. In the three comparative studies examined to this point the group-centered class of conditions appears to affect subject or patient behavior more favorably than the more directive leader-centered approach. Although, as a generalization, this superiority of the group-centered approach will be bolstered by several lines of research which we examine later, closer inspection will reveal some necessary qualifications and several issues in need of further research. For example, in the Ends and Page (1957) study discussed above, an additional finding was that *both* the psychoanalytic and nondirective groups were superior to the control group on clearcut behavioral followup criteria. The nature of the control group condition was essentially that of a leaderless discussion group, that is, a group functioning in large measure under a very minimally leading leadership orientation, one not unlike the early nondirective approach to groups we used as defining the group-centered pole of our therapist orientation continuum. The superiority of the analytic and contemporary nondirective approaches to this leaderless approach causes one to wonder not so much about the broad question of leader-centered versus group-centered orientations but, instead, about the perhaps more meaningful question, "What is the optimal amount of leader-therapist participation?" What may be most efficacious in this regard is an approach such as Bach's (1954). That is, an essentially group-oriented approach that makes selective, carefully considered use of therapist interventions and involves therapist activity under selected circumstances; but activity used in such a manner that the basic group-centered orientation is not disturbed. Such a balanced, selective approach is also hinted at by Gorlow et al. (1952):

If he (the therapist) participates extensively, . . . interaction among the members is limited and the experience is apt to become similar to individual therapy. On the other hand, if he participates minimally, the meetings may take on the character of a "bull session" with consequent argumentativeness rather than an atmosphere of sympathetic understanding (p. 15).

Not inconsistent with this viewpoint are the early research findings of Hobbs and Pascal (1946). Their comparison of group therapist orientations indicated "that both client-centered and eclectic responses by the therapist were more highly associated with positive therapeutic statements by the patients than didactic-authoritarian responses by the therapist" (p. 2). Further, in a study conducted by Truax (1961), the degree of leadership behavior on the part of the therapist was significantly related to three independent measures of the extent of patient self-exploration. At first glance this finding appears to support a leader-centered, perhaps directive, therapist orientation only, but closer inspection of Truax's definition of "leadership" reveals a degree of support for the modified, group-centered approach upon which we have been focusing. He defines a low level of leadership as one in which ". . . the therapist is little more than a participating member; when the atmosphere is laissez-faire; when other members have assumed the leadership role" (p. 10). A high level of leadership, in contrast, includes *both* the kinds of active leader-centeredness examined previously and ". . . a very permissive leadership when it is clear that the therapist is leading, rather than just participating as a member" (p. 10). This last statement seems to approach quite closely at least one central aspect of a modified group-centered approach, such as Bach's; whereas Truax's low level of leadership is much closer to the early nondirective orientation or Bion's leaderless group approach. Taken as a group, however, these investigations provide as much confusion as clarification. The Hobbs and Pascal (1946) study, as well as some of the other investigations we have noted, generally indicate a group-centered orientation on the part of the therapist to be more efficacious than a leader-centered approach. The Truax (1961) study, in contrast, is readily interpretable in opposite terms: the more leadership provided by the therapist the more patient self-exploration took place. And, to round out the picture of possible outcomes of such orientational comparisons, a study by Semon and Goldstein (1957) and to a large extent, the Ends and Page (1957) investigation, report no differences following from these contrasting therapist orientations. What appears to be called for in this regard is a series of investigations in which group therapist leadership behavior is systematically measured or operationalized by a series of therapist activities representing a graduated range from intervention to nonintervention. Under these conditions, we may well find that the broad relationship between leadership orientation and patient change is curvilinear. Perhaps, in support of the possible superiority of a modified group-centered orientation, therapist intervention to a point not disturbing a basic group-centered orientation is facilitative; beyond this point it serves to inhibit patient change. However, these conflicting results point to a much more important research issue, an issue which is highlighted further by the investigations comparing therapist orientations in individual psychotherapy.

In several of our earlier discussions, on group size for example, we underscored the necessity for research aimed at identifying consequents of varying group size to be *interactional* in nature. That is, size becomes an important group characteristic only when viewed as it interacts with other patient, therapist or relationship variables, for example, unmet functional roles in the group. This same general need for multivariate, interactional research clearly applies to investigations of therapist orientation. Thus the group psychotherapy studies noted earlier which contrast two or more therapeutic approaches are characteristically far too simple in design. Though they represent an important first step, their exclusive focus on a single therapeutic dimension, in abstraction, as it were, fails to reflect the reality of the therapeutic transaction. Clearly, sufficient research now exists to indicate that such investigations, aimed at determining the influence of therapist orientation and techniques on therapeutic outcome, must also take into account a host of other potentially relevant patient, therapist, and relationship variables.

We lay stress on the importance of this interactional, multivariate approach to research aimed at group therapist orientation because it is central to the two major hypotheses we present and develop in this chapter. Thus, although these hypotheses will be framed in terms of "orientation *A* will be more effective than orientation *B*" in producing a particular therapeutic effect, the reader should add, in each case, that the implementation of the hypotheses must reflect attention to other potentially relevant patient and therapist variables that may interact with therapist orientation to influence the nature of the consequent effect. Studies aimed at contrasting therapeutic orientation in the context of individual therapy have demonstrated the key importance of this interactional approach. Ashby, Ford, Guerney, and Guerney (1957), for example, report a series of carefully designed and executed investigations which examine a leading versus a reflective type of individual psychotherapy. The ten participating psychotherapists each saw two patients for twice-weekly individual therapy sessions. On a random basis, one patient in each pair received psychotherapy of a leading, interpretive, active type; the other patient in the pair was seen under reflective, generally nondirective therapy conditions. Among their major findings, both the positive and defensive aspects of the therapeutic relationship, as viewed by the client, were related to the interaction of the therapist with the type of therapy (leading or reflective) in which the patient was participating.

A series of investigations conducted by Strupp (1955a, 1955b, 1960) similarly point to (1) specific differences following from different therapist orientations, and (2) the need for such investigations to assume a more multivariate, interactional design. He comments:

> The results of this investigation leave little doubt that adherence to the Rogerian frame of reference is an important determinant of a psychotherapist's techniques, transcending professional affiliation and experience level. Also . . . psychoanalytically oriented psychologists, psychiatrists and social workers form a rather homogeneous group with respect to their therapeutic operations. Future investigations must refine these analyses and specify the conditions under which a given technique achieves a particular effect (1955a, p. 6).

Several of the participants at both the Washington (Rubinstein & Parloff, 1959) and Chapel Hill (Strupp & Luborsky, 1962) conferences on psychotherapy research, as well as a number of other investigators (e.g., Goldstein, 1962; Ford, 1959), have similarly underscored the need for research of an interactional type, in which patient change is conceptualized as resulting from the interaction of a variety of patient, therapist, and relationship variables. Findings from the investigations of Howe and Pope (1961) on therapist activity level and from a series of studies (e.g., Harway et al., 1953; Raush et al., 1956; Speisman, 1959) of "depth of interpretation" further suggest that the complex influence of these variables, which in turn are very much a function of the therapist's operating orientation, may best be clarified by recourse to the multivariate, multilevel research advocated above.

To summarize briefly our presentation so far, examination of the theoretical positions assumed by contemporary group psychotherapists reveals a continuum of orientations whose poles are describable as leader or therapist-centered and group-centered. Modal positions, with leanings in one direction or the other, seem to be most characteristic at the present time. The little research which has been conducted regarding identification of the orientation(s) that most effectively lead to patient change has produced a conflicting picture. Although there is some evidence to suggest that a modified group-centered approach may more frequently than other therapist orientations lead to a favorable therapeutic outcome, the over-all research picture is far from unequivocal. Studies examining therapist orientation in the context of individual therapy have focused more on process considerations. Their main contribution thus far appears to lie in the degree to which they emphasize the need for research in which therapist orientation is viewed as interacting with other central patient, therapist, and relationship variables as they jointly influence therapeutic outcome. This central consideration, overlooked all too often in what little group psychotherapy research has been conducted, is emphasized in the hypotheses that follow.

THERAPIST ORIENTATION IN EARLY SESSIONS

A broad overview of a course of group psychotherapy reveals, particularly when the therapist leans toward a group-centered approach, two basic leadership stages from the patients' perspective. During the early sessions, perhaps the first dozen or so, the patients' pretherapy and early therapy expectations and needs lead them characteristically to anticipate and desire that their group be actively led and directed by the therapist. Such an outlook dovetails for the most part with most of their earlier experiences with nonpsychotherapeutic groups, which have led to the expectation of a leader-centered group. Thus, their motivational state is largely one of wanting their problems to be administered to along lines of the traditional doctor-patient relationship. As we note, upsetting this expectancy in early sessions and failing to meet this patient need has negative effects on the participating patients. Group-centered therapists hold that it is the therapist's job to wean the patient away from this early set toward a potentially more productive group-centered orientation, that is, toward the second stage of group leadership.

Foulkes (1946) and Bach (1954) are among the many contemporary observers of the group psychotherapy scene who view matters in this manner. As Bach indicates, it is common for group therapy patients, during early sessions in particular, to direct their comments almost exclusively to the therapist. These comments are frequently of a dependent, deferent type, and reflect the patients' implicit expectations and efforts to pull leadership behavior from the therapist. This patient orientation is countered by proponents of a group-centered therapist approach in a manner such as Foulkes' "leadership by default." In essence, this involves a consistent refocusing of patient queries by inviting the patient himself, or other group members, to provide tentative replies to such questions. As Bach (1954) describes this process:

> Thus, the therapist, through his own initiatory act of not using his leadership position in a directive or didactic way, gives behavioral notice that the group has to handle its own problems. In our example regime this attitude is not maintained in the rigid form suggested by Foulkes beyond the first twenty meetings, during which, however, it is rigidly maintained. . . . This

"defaulting" role carries this message to the groups . . . "I am throwing your dependency needs back to you. I, the therapist, refuse to fulfill your assumptions that I will or can lead you into mental health via the road of dependency" (p. 38).

As much of the material on leader-centered therapist orientations noted earlier indicates, such an effort to shift the prevailing patient orientation away from the leader and toward fellow group members does not characterize the leader-centered therapy group. Let us propose, therefore, two hypotheses, both firmly rooted in group dynamics and related research findings, whose test would represent an important start at more accurately understanding the effects of diverse therapist orientations and the patient reactions they appear to elicit. Cautioning as we have before that what we propose must also take into account other patient, leader, and related variables, the following may be predicted:

HYPOTHESIS 8.1:   **In the early stages of a course of group psychotherapy a leader-centered therapist orientation will be associated with less patient hostility and more patient attraction to the therapist and to the group than will a group-centered therapist orientation.**

In those instances in which the therapist, by defaulting his leadership role or by related techniques, manages successfully to shift the prevailing patient orientation toward group-centeredness, we predict:

HYPOTHESIS 8.2:   **In the later stages of a course of group psychotherapy a leader-centered therapist orientation will be associated with more patient hostility and less patient attraction to the therapist and to the group than will a group-centered approach.**

Considering the early stage hypothesis first, two broad lines of research appear to provide substantial support for its further examination. The first such body of research involves studies aimed at the consequences of mutually shared versus discrepant therapist-patient role expectancies in individual psychotherapy and the broader area of mutuality of role expectancies in dyads. The second series of relevant findings pertains to the consequences of unclear or ambiguous goals in problem solving and other nonpsychotherapeutic small groups. Our introduction to hypothesis 8.1 suggests that the expectancies of patients anticipating active and directive therapy group leadership will generally be congruent with the leader-centered therapist's own expectancies and generally discrepant with those held by the therapist who has a group-centered orientation. In a broad sense the hypothesis itself (as well as hypothesis 8.2—as will be seen) predicts that congruent therapist-patient expectancies lead to a more favorable patient affective state than do more discrepant participant expectancies.

Investigations of Role Expectancies

Lennard and Bernstein (1960) studied a large series of individual psychoanalytic therapy sessions, with particular emphasis on participant expectations, communication, and relationship. One of their major findings was a highly significant association between the degree of discrepancy in therapist and patient role expectations and the degree of disharmony or strain in their interpersonal relationship:

> When both members of a dyad are in agreement regarding their reciprocal obligations and returns, there is consensus or similarity of expectations, and harmony or stability occurs in their interpersonal relations. . . . But when there is any degree of discrepancy or lack of consensus between the participants, and their expectations are dissimilar . . . manifestations of strain appear in their interpersonal relations. If expectations are too dissimilar, the . . . system disintegrates unless the differences can be reconciled (p. 153).

Other investigations aimed at expectational influences in individual psychotherapy have yielded concurring findings. Chance's (1959) study, for example, led her to conclude that ". . . mutuality of expectation may be one of the prerequisites to therapy" (p. 105). Goldstein (1962), in a review of this line of investigation, similarly was led to emphasize the centrality of mutuality of therapist and patient role expectancies. It appears, further, that the significance of such shared expectations goes well beyond the psychotherapeutic context. Janis (1958), for example, has demonstrated that upsetting expectancies in the direction of more stress than anticipated consistently leads to hostile, aggressive behavior under certain doctor-patient interactions. Wright (1960) reports concurring results. A directly relevant investigation in the group dynamics setting is reported by Berkowitz and Levy (1956). They studied 72 decision-making conferences in a variety of business and industrial settings. All conferences were observed and rated in terms of Heyns' (1948) system. Conference participants were later interviewed and also completed questionnaires aimed at determining their attraction to the conference leadership and satisfaction with the meeting. Results indicated that members' satisfaction increased: (1) the more the conference chairman controlled the group's operations, (2) the more functionally differentiated the chairman was from the other group members, and (3) the greater the proportion of interaction directed toward the chairman, as opposed to other members. Satisfaction also increased the less the members participated or proposed solutions relative to the sum of these behaviors in the group.

One of their findings is of special interest in that his elaboration of it provides a glimpse at the issues we shall consider when we turn to later session therapist orientation and also underscores the need for considering group variables as they interact or combine with one another. We have noted that a given conference member's satisfaction with the conference proceedings increased as the amount of participation by other members decreased; that is, the more leader-centered the conference, the greater the member satisfaction. However, drawing on his own further results and those of Heyns (1948), Berkowitz and Levy (1956) note quite a different pattern of member satisfaction and attitudes toward other group members as the urgency of the problem at hand changes. When the group's problems are relatively urgent, solution proposing by members increases under permissive leadership with resultant increases in cohesiveness and satisfaction. As Berkowitz and Levy comment:

> The group's motivation to reach a problem solution as quickly as possible thus appears to be stronger than its motivation to conform to the expectancies concerning role differentiation.

In sum, these diverse studies focusing on leadership expectancies in psychotherapy and other settings appear to converge in the general conclusion that the more discrepant the expectancies, the less the attraction to the group, the less the satisfaction of group members, and the more the strain or negative affect between leader and led or therapist and patient. One final study focusing on role expectancies serves both to reinforce this conclusion and provide transition to our second basis for hypothesis 8.1, investigations of clarity of group goals. Smith (1957) established a series of five-member problem-solving groups which were to function under two experimental and two control conditions. Two of the five members of each experimental group were accomplices, paid to remain silent during the group's efforts at task solution. Under the first experimental condition, "ambiguous role expectations," it was predicted that the influence of the two silent accomplices would reduce group satisfaction and productivity and increase member defensiveness. These predictions were confirmed. In the second experimental condition, "unambiguous role expectations," all procedures were the same save for the fact that group members were informed in advance of the meeting that the two members usually were "listeners" in group meetings. As Smith (1957) hypothesized, this clarification of role expectancies served to restore group satisfaction and productivity (but not defensiveness) to control group levels. Thus Smith's results add further evidence to one aspect of the central point presently being examined, expectational clarity is an important influence on group satisfaction and productivity. Further, his demonstration of the positive effects of clarifying ambiguous role expectations will be an important consideration as we later move from early session therapist orientation, through transitional leader defaulting techniques and on to later session therapist orientation.

Investigations of Goal Clarity

Our basis for predicting the more favorable effects on patients of early session leader-centeredness rests, in addition to factors of mutuality of expectations, on studies of the clarity of group goals. Raven and Reitsema (1957) report a significant investigation in this area. Their 78 subjects were divided into two experimental groups. For one, the group goal and the means of achieving it were made explicit; for the other, both goal and goal path were made ambiguous. The experimental comparisons consisted essentially in contrasting these differently treated groups on a series of group-relevant characteristics. Results indicated that subjects operating under unambiguous goal conditions were more attracted to their group, less hostile toward fellow group members, more willing to be influenced by other members, and as a group were more cohesive than subjects with unclear goal instructions. These findings, particularly those oriented toward member hostility and attraction to group, obviously bear importantly on hypothesis 8.1.

The hostility-goal ambiguity relationship is also suggested by a study by Hamblin (1960). His procedures were such that group members could, if they saw fit to do so, replace the group leader with someone else from their ranks. Twelve of his 24 groups participated in a crisis situation for which no solution existed. Hamblin's (1960) findings indicate that ". . . groups tend to replace their old leader with a new leader if the old leader does not have an obvious solution to a crisis problem" (p. 584).

Related to this is Smock's (1955) finding that groups under stress demonstrated a greater tendency than nonstress groups to seek structure in an ambiguous group situation. Further, they also tended to maintain their perceived structure longer, in spite of increasing incongruity between their view and the stimuli involved.

Other relevant investigations have been reported. Cohen (1959), for example, provides evidence that his subjects with an unclear versus clear or apparent path to goal attainment "were less secure, had lower self-evaluations, were less motivated, and worked less efficiently" (p. 39). Cohen, Stotland, and Wolfe (1955) and Wolfe, Snoek, and Rosenthal (1961) report a negative relationship between clarity of the group experience and member frustration. Equally important, and once again underscoring our repeated emphasis on interactional, multivariate research, both of these studies found this relationship to hold most markedly for subjects with a high need for cognitive structure. What do these several studies tell us? They combine, it appears, with the previously noted series of expectancy studies to indicate the variety of negative consequences that consistently follow from unclear ambiguous group structural characteristics. Taken as a whole, they pointedly provide basic evidence for the prediction of more favorable patient response to a leader-centered versus a group-centered therapist orientation in the early stages of group psychotherapy. May all these studies, therefore, be taken as evidence suggesting that a leader-centered approach to group psychotherapy is the approach of choice? Were our discussion to stop here, this question would obviously have to be answered affirmatively. However, in spite of its less favorable early effects, there is a considerable body of group dynamics research suggesting that the group-centered approach is very likely to result in patient behavior much more highly related to a favorable therapeutic outcome than would be the case if an essentially leader-centered approach persisted beyond the first 10 to 20 therapy sessions. Thus hypothesis 8.2, to which we will now turn, predicts the long-term superiority of the group-centered approach on several key therapeutic dimensions.

THERAPIST ORIENTATION IN LATER SESSIONS

The hypothesis just considered predicted the early session superiority of a leader-centered therapist approach partly on the basis that such an approach would be more congruent with early session patient expectancies than a group-centered orientation. The hypothesis to be examined now is similarly predictable from the same research evidence. Note on page 373 that we qualify this hypothesis with the stipulation that we predict it to hold "in those instances in which the therapist, by defaulting his leadership role or by related techniques, manages successfully to shift the prevailing patient orientation toward group-centeredness." This stipulation simply proposes that the group-centered orientation will be superior *if* the therapist manages success-fully to re-orient the prevailing patient expectancies in a direction more congruent with his own expectancies. To the extent that leader-ship defaulting accomplishes this re-orientation, the therapist's and patient's expectancies are mutually shared and the positive effects of such compatibility noted earlier on their relationship, group cohesive-ness, hostility reduction, and interpersonal attraction should follow. It may be noted in passing, before turning to a second body of research underlying hypothesis 8.2, that more than one technique exists which may accomplish this expectational re-orientation. The procedure already noted, leadership by default, is essentially an implicit tech-nique in which the therapist attempts to illustrate, by example of his overt verbal behavior, that he does not choose to respond directly to member questions or to actively lead the group. Although it is the clinical impression of Bach (1954), Foulkes (1946), Gordon (1955), and others that this is the most efficient procedure available for accom-plishing patient re-orientation toward the leader's role, an alternative does exist. We have in mind the "successive structuring" advocated by Rotter (1954) for the individual therapy context. He describes this more explicit procedure as a continuous process in which parts of several periodic sessions with the patient are spent in discussion and exploration of ". . . the purposes and goals of the therapy, the plans of the therapist, the respective roles and responsibilities of the patient and therapist and the attitudes both have toward the therapy at any time" (pp. 351-352). Thus, though leadership by default is an implicit, largely unverbalized technique, successive structuring is more explicit and overtly verbalized. Gordon (1955) reports that his own experience with groups, as well as his impression of the experience of the client-centered approach, leads him to conclude that:

> Such structuring . . . is seldom effective. . . . The members find this strange new leader role foreign to their previous experience, or . . . they do not really believe that the leader can honestly carry out this kind of role. Unsuccessful attempts to structure with groups run parallel to the experience of client-centered therapy. . . . Apparently it is so unlike other relationships that it can be understood only by actually experiencing it over a period of time, in contrast to merely hearing about it (p. 172).

Gordon's position may accurately reflect the likely consequences of such overtly stated structuring, but the importance of expectational re-orienting procedures is such, especially in a group-centered ap-proach, that we feel this should not be considered a closed issue.

Research comparing the two procedures, and perhaps also aimed at seeking an optimal blending of both, appears to be well worthwhile. The potential value of such research is enhanced when one notes, in contrast to Gordon, that Lennard and Bernstein (1960) provide evidence of the relationship-enhancing value of a technique in individual psychotherapy similar to Rotter's successive structuring and also to the findings of Smith (1957) discussed earlier in which explicit clarification of previously ambiguous member role expectations served to heighten group satisfaction and productivity. Further, studies by Salzberg (1961, 1962) and Heckel, Froelich, and Salzberg (1962) suggest that a blending of these re-orientational approaches in the form of a judicious combination of therapist silence and redirection may serve to influence favorably both the nature and substance of the therapy group's interaction.

Investigations of Leader Orientation

To turn more directly to the evidence upon which hypothesis 8.2 is based, we note that the research findings which follow relate to the hypothesis in an indirect manner, in the sense that the studies involved typically do not examine groups meeting over a period of time, that is, groups with earlier or later stages, but instead focus on temporarily constituted groups meeting only for a few sessions. There are exceptions, however. Zimet and Fine (1955), for example, conducted an investigation in which a group of school administrators met for 16 weekly sessions of five hours each. Each session was divided into two parts, differing in the nature of the group's leadership. The first two hours of each session may be characterized as leader-centered: a professor of education lectured to the group and led the group discussion. After a dinner hour, the second two hours were spent in a group-centered, self-directed discussion. After the eleventh meeting, at the urging of the group members themselves, the leader-centered orientation of the first two hours was dropped and replaced by a group-centered approach. Bearing on both hypotheses 8.1 and 8.2, the investigators report that the group-centered climate, although initially arousing more defensiveness, subsequently demonstrated more rapid and sustained member gain than either the content-centered or lecture-centered approaches. The content-centered group climate did not show statistically significant gain in member interaction until it had shifted to a group-centered orientation.

Thus the Zimet and Fine study points to the initially more negative but subsequently more positive group functioning associated with a group-centered leadership approach. Gordon (1955) has reviewed a long series of related investigations. His summary comment on the longitudinal impact of group-centered leadership is of interest:

> The initial impact of group-centered leadership . . . is often a kind of disorganization for the group and frustration for group members. . . . This initial phase might be characterized as a period of destructuring, during which the old patterns of group organization and behavior break down and the group finds itself sorely needing new patterns. . . . Once the group has weathered the stormy period of destructuring, it soon begins to restructure itself through learning new ways of organizing its activities and solving its problems. It emerges from its initial disorganization and confusion into a period of constructive development (p. 227).

A large number of studies have been reported that represent direct comparisons of varying leadership styles in problem-solving, decision-making, training, or other small groups. The Lewin, Lippitt, and White (1939) studies in this area have functioned in many ways as the keynote investigations, giving impetus to an extended series of related studies which followed. In these initial studies, three group leadership orientations were compared on a wide variety of criteria.

1. Authoritarian leadership—Group policy was determined by and actively carried out under the complete direction of the group leader. He did not participate as a group member and was personal in his praise and criticism of each member's work. Work partner pairings were decided by the leader.
2. Democratic leadership—Group policy derived from group discussion and decisions, with the leader's encouragement and assistance. The leader provided a general sketch of the path to the group goal and responded to member help-seeking by presenting alternative solutions from which the group could choose. Work partner pairings were determined by the group members. The leader attempted to function as a regular group member, but allowed members to do the group work.
3. Laissez-faire leadership—Group members were given complete freedom in all major respects. The leader took no part in setting group structure and participated only very minimally, and only when asked, in answering questions or otherwise moving the group towards its goal. No attempt was made by the leader to appraise or regulate the group's progress.

In one of the main studies in this series, a number of 5-member groups of 10-year-old boys constituted the study sample. The groups were roughly equated on a number of interpersonal, socioeconomic and intellectual variables. Four adult group leaders were trained to a level of proficiency in the three leadership orientations. The leaders were shifted from group to group every six weeks, each time changing leadership style at the time of this transition. In this manner, each group was exposed to the range of leaders and leadership orientations.

Before turning to their findings, it may be noted that in a rough sense, the authoritarian, democratic and laissez-faire leadership approaches, when translated to the group psychotherapy context, approximate, respectively, the polar leader-centered, modified group-centered and polar group-centered therapist orientations discussed earlier.

In contrast to the other leadership orientations, the authoritarian approach resulted in the greatest group productivity in terms of quantity, the most member hostility and discontent, the most dependent behavior, more demands for attention, more destruction of property and more scapegoating behavior. Democratic leadership in this study produced the highest quality productivity, the highest task motivation in the leader's absence, more originality, friendliness, and group cohesiveness, low dependence on the leader and most sharing of property. Laissez-faire leadership resulted in the lowest level of productivity, the poorest quality product, the most play, little dependence upon the leader and intermediate productivity. Taken as a whole, these investigations seem to represent an early demonstration of the superiority in the areas other than quantity of group productivity of a leadership orientation described by Lewin, Lippitt, and White as "democratic" and held by us as closely analogous to a modified group-centered psychotherapist approach.

Asch (1946), Fox (1957), and Solem (1958) report concurring findings. Groups led on a democratic basis were more satisfying to the membership but less efficient than autocratically led groups. Faw (1949), in partial contrast, reports the superiority, in an educational setting, of a group-centered approach on both satisfaction *and* productivity dimensions. Flanders (1951) finds a learner-centered teaching approach to produce less hostility, anxiety and withdrawal than a teacher-centered orientation. Perkins (1950) finds such a group-centered orientation in the training of teachers to result in more objective and insightful teacher behavior than that following a leader-centered type of training. Gordon (1955) has evaluated a number of educational leadership comparison studies. He comments:

In summarizing the results of these eleven studies of leadership, all carried out in educational settings, it can be stated with a high degree of confidence that group-centered leadership in the classroom situation is not only possible but also beneficial in many respects. Students seem to learn as much or more factual information; they participate more; they enjoy the experiences, and they acquire certain other important learnings, such as clinical insight, greater personal adjustment, socially integrative behavior, skills of working cooperatively with others, and the freedom to communicate their deeper feelings and attitudes. Finally, when these student groups are given certain tasks requiring group judgment or group decisions, those with group-centered leadership demonstrate more effectiveness in altering individual judgments in the direction of a group norm, than do groups with directive or leader-centered leadership. The members of group-centered classes also are more satisfied with the decisions reached by their groups (pp. 99-100).

In addition to these early field studies and investigations in educational settings, a closely related series of studies similarly suggests that behavior change is more effectively accomplished via a participatory style of group leadership. Under the impetus of wartime conditions, a number of investigations classifiable as action research were initiated to answer such questions as, "What is the best way to convince housewives to buy low-priority foods which they are not accustomed to eating?" These studies, as well as later ones which followed, consistently indicated that such mundane matters as increasing production of pajamas, eating more sweetbreads, increasing milk consumption, giving infants more cod liver oil, and switching from white to whole wheat bread are all more effectively accomplished through participation in a group discussion, rather than the more leader-centered approach involving a lecture by a relevant expert (Lewin, 1943). Analogously, Willerman (1943) has demonstrated that members are less motivated to reach goals set by external figures than goals set through discussion and decision within the group. Preston and Heintz (1949) report comparable findings, as does Hare (1955), who concludes from a series of studies like the foregoing that:

. . . if one wishes to change attitudes and the subsequent behavior of a group, discussion and decision where all members participate as directly as possible tend to be more effective than "enlightenment" or "persuasion" by the lecture method, or by an unqualified order from above (p. 287).

Investigations of Communication Networks

There is yet another area whose concern is largely centered on comparisons of group leadership styles. We refer to the several investigations of communication networks in small groups. The relationship of these studies to the investigations of leadership orientation examined at length earlier is readily apparent when one notes that the central concern of communication network studies involves examination of the effects on group functioning and intermember relationships of manipulation of communication channels open to group members and the "centrality" of each member in the total group communication pattern. Although a number of such communication networks have been explored in the broad manner indicated above, only relatively few of them are of direct interest to our present discussion. These are presented in Figure 4.

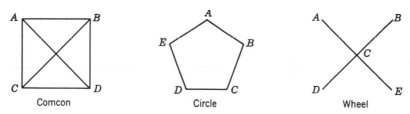

Figure 4. Communication networks relevant to group therapy leadership.

Each letter in these networks represents a different group member or network position and each line represents a two-person communication linkage. It is immediately apparent from inspection of Figure 4 that marked variability exists among these communication networks in the degree to which members of each are free to communicate with each other. Group member B, for example, is free to communicate with all other group members in the comcon (or all-channel) network, with two other members (A and C) in the circle network, and with only one member (C) in the wheel network. It may also be noted that differences exist among members or positions in each network with respect to how many lines of communication are tied to each and how far, in terms of number of links, each member is from each other member. Viewing the various networks in this manner leads us to the key communication network concept of centrality. In the wheel network, member C clearly is most central. Within the two other networks, all members are, in a sense, equally central or peripheral. Although several other communication networks, involving more intermediate levels of group member centrality, have been subjected to experimental scrutiny, we have chosen to focus on those networks representing the extremes of organizational centrality for heuristic reasons based upon their marked similarity to group-centered (comcon and circle) and leader-centered (wheel) leadership orientations. Let us, therefore, pursue the ramifications of these networks further.

The initial studies examining these and more intermediate (in terms of centrality) communication networks were conducted by Bavelas (1960) and Leavitt (1951). With varying opportunities for intermember communication, groups of five members each were constituted and instructed in a problem-solving task. More specifically, each member was independently provided with a set of cards with a symbol on each. The problem to be solved, by written communication among the members for whom the network permitted communication, was to determine which symbol all group members had in common. The problem was considered solved when every member indicated he knew this shared symbol. The comcon network was not included in these early studies. Comparisons among networks reveal several important findings. In broad terms, the more centralized the network the more efficient it was—sending fewer messages, solving the problem faster, and making fewer errors. Yet it is equally important to note that the members of less centralized networks made fewer unanimous errors, corrected a greater proportion of the errors they did make, were more satisfied with their group experience, and in general evidenced higher morale than did members of more centralized groups. A second finding of note, later confirmed by Goldberg (1955), was the consistent tendency for the individual occupying the most central position in a pattern to be recognized as the group leader. Those in the more peripheral positions of centralized nets tended to be dissatisfied with their group experience. Leavitt (1951) notes in summary:

. . . the circle, one extreme, is active, leaderless, unorganized, erratic and yet is enjoyed by its members. The wheel at the other extreme, is less active, has a distinct leader, is well and stably organized, is less erratic and yet is unsatisfying to most of its members (p. 46).

These early investigations directly parallel the leadership comparison studies of Lewin et al. (1939), Asch (1946), Fox (1957), and Solem (1958) noted earlier. The group-centered, less centralized orientation to problem-solving and related groups results in less efficiency and more favorable group-associated member affect.

Note, however, that the group-centered orientation in these early investigations is represented by the circle communication network which, while to a fair extent communicatively permissive, still permits each member only two communication linkages. The comcon network, in contrast, with all channels open, goes considerably further toward representing the type of group organization which characterizes group-centered group psychotherapy. Hence findings relevant to this open network, particularly as its influence contrasts with more centralized networks, are perhaps of greater relevance to the comparisons implied in hypothesis 8.2. Shaw and his coworkers have been active in this comparative area. They report three studies (1954a, 1954b, 1956) that demonstrate the comcon net to result in less time for problem solution, fewer errors, and more member satisfaction than more centralized communication networks. Heise and Miller (1955) and Guetzkow (1960) have both confirmed this finding. In contrast to the earlier communication network studies, therefore, these later investigations suggest that a fully open network is *both* more efficient and more satisfying to group members. Of additional interest, and bearing upon our later discussion of isolate or marginal members in therapy groups, Shaw and Rothschild (1956) have confirmed the earlier findings of Bavelas (1960) and Leavitt (1951) to the effect that "centrality [of a given group member] varied . . . directly with individual morale" (p. 275). Others have found similar results, leading Hare (1955) to conclude:

> . . . positions in the communication network, especially those with one-way and limited connection restrictions, are related to frustration and antagonism on the part of the disadvantaged members and to satisfaction and leadership status for the central members (p. 277).

One study, by Cohen, Bennis, and Wolkon (1962), examined the longitudinal effects of participation in a series of communication networks. Subjects participating in a wheel network for a period of time and then reorganized into a circle network are in many ways undergoing the same type of leadership-reduction transition evident in the leader-centered to group-centered shift which takes place as group-centered therapy groups move from early to later sessions. The investigators report that individuals moving from a wheel to circle network performed better on the study's task and were more satisfied with their group experience than were individuals who operated in only circle groups throughout the study. On the same criteria, members of wheel networks throughout were superior to members starting in a circle network and later shifting to a wheel. These findings, in the view of the investigators are explainable in terms of the concept of relative deprivation. Wheel to circle groups were released from the severe operating restrictions and communication inequality of the wheel network, hence, they suggest, their greater relative satisfaction when compared to subjects remaining in a circle network throughout. Analogously, circle to wheel groups underwent change from a less restricted network to one characterized by considerably more communication inequality, and hence their lesser degree of satisfaction when compared to subjects in a wheel network throughout.

Taken as a group, the many studies of communication networks and leadership orientation that we have examined consistently demonstrate that in diverse laboratory, industrial, educational, and other field settings a group-centered leadership orientation results in more favorable member affective reactions and attitudes toward the group than does a leader-centered orientation. Successful accomplishment of the group task also appears more often to follow from group-centered leadership, although this result is somewhat more equivocal.

There are, of course, some exceptions to this finding of the superiority of a group-centered approach. In addition, it is clear that at least some of the investigations demonstrating the advantages of group-centeredness suffer from important methodological weaknesses. Further, a few studies have been reported in which no differences between the two major leadership orientations emerged on criteria in which we have been interested.

Nevertheless, in spite of these dissenting bits of evidence, the broad superiority of group-centeredness over leader-centeredness appears to be a firm conclusion. We must recall, however, that although group-centeredness clearly seems to be the most effective leadership orientation in problem solving, training, and many other types of non-psychotherapy groups, the comparatively small amount of leadership research conducted in the group psychotherapy context is essentially equivocal in this regard. The contrasting nature of findings from these two classes of investigative contexts underscores once again that group dynamics research should lead to group psychotherapy research, and not to direct translation into psychotherapeutic practice. Later research may well demonstrate that a group-centered or modified group-centered therapist orientation most efficiently leads to change in group therapy patients, yet it may turn out that, as we quoted Durkin (1957) earlier, the differing nature of group goals in therapy and non-therapy groups markedly influences the applicability to group psychotherapy of research findings derived from studies of other classes of groups. Broadly speaking, the discussions of communication networks by Hare (1955), Heise and Miller (1955), and Riecken and Homans (1954), all touch on this same issue by indicating that network efficiency is to a very large degree a function of the task the group is facing. Thus we can perhaps best conclude our discussion of group therapist orientation by indicating that the considerable research we have examined points most clearly to the major need for direct research examination of group therapist orientation from a perspective which also considers the interacting influence of stage of therapy, patient and therapist personality and behavioral characteristics, therapist and patient goals, and related variables.

REFERENCES

Asch, S. E. Forming impressions of personality. *J. abnorm. soc. Psychol.*, 1946, 41, 258–290.

Ashby, J. D., Ford, D. H., Guerney, B. G., & Guerney, L. F. Effects on clients of a reflective and a leading type of psychotherapy. *Psychol. Monogr.*, 1957, 71, No. 453.

Bach, G. R. *Intensive group psychotherapy.* New York: Ronald Press, 1954.

Bavelas, A. Communication patterns in task-oriented groups. In D. Cartwright & A. Zander (Eds.), *Group dynamics.* Evanston, Ill.: Row, Peterson & Co., 1960. Pp. 667–682.

Berkowitz, L., & Levy, B. Pride in group performance and group task motivation. *J. abnorm. soc. Psychol.*, 1956, 53, 300–306.

Bion, W. R. *Experiences in groups.* New York: Basic Books, 1959.

Bovard, E. W. The experimental production of interpersonal affect. *J. abnorm. soc. Psychol.*, 1951, 46, 521–528.

Chance, E. *Families in treatment.* New York: Basic Books, 1959.

Cohen, A. M., Bennis, W. G., & Wolkon, G. H. The effects of changes in communication networks on the behaviors of problem-solving groups. *Sociometry*, 1962, 25, 177–196.

Cohen, A. R. Situational structure, self-esteem, and threat-oriented reactions to power. In D. Cartwright (Ed.), *Studies in social power.* Ann Arbor, Mich.: Research Center for Group Dynamics, 1959. Pp. 35–52.

Cohen, A. R., Stotland, E., & Wolfe, D. M. An experimental investigation of need for cognition. *J. abnorm. soc. Psychol.*, 1955, 51, 291–294.

Corsini, R. J. *Methods of group psychotherapy.* New York: McGraw-Hill, 1957.

Durkin, H. E. Toward a common basis for group dynamics: group and therapeutic processes in group psychotherapy. *Int. J. grp. Psychother.*, 1957, 7, 115–130.

Ends, E. J., & Page, C. W. A study of three types of group psychotherapy with hospitalized male inebriates. *Quart. J. stud. Alc.*, 1957, 18, 263–277.

Faw, V.   A psychotherapeutic method of teaching psychology. *American Psychologist,* 1949, **4**, 104–109.

Flanders, N. A.   Personal-social anxiety as a factor in experimental learning situations. *J. educ. Res.,* 1951, **45**, 100–110.

Ford, D. H.   Research approaches to psychotherapy. *J. counsel. Psychol.,* 1959, **6**, 55–60.

Foulkes, S. H.   Principles and practice of group therapy. *Bull. Menninger Clin.,* 1946, **10**, 85–89.

Fox, W. M.   Group reaction to two types of conference leadership. *Hum. Relat.,* 1957, **10**, 279–289.

Frank, J. D.   Some determinants, manifestations, and effects of cohesiveness in therapy groups. *Int. J. grp. Psychother.,* 1957, **7**, 53–63.

Goldberg, S. E.   Influence and leadership as a function of group structure. *J. abnorm. soc. Psychol.,* 1955, **51**, 119–122.

Goldstein, A. P.   *Therapist-patient expectancies in psychotherapy.* New York: Pergamon Press, 1962.

Gordon, T.   *Group centered leadership.* Boston: Houghton-Mifflin, 1955.

Gorlow, L., Hoch, E. L., & Telschow, E. F.   *Non-directive group psychotherapy.* New York: Teacher's College Studies in Education, Columbia University, 1952.

Guetzkow, H.   Differentiation of roles in task-oriented groups. In D. Cartwright and A. Zander (Eds.), *Group dynamics.* Evanston, Ill.: Row, Peterson & Co., 1960. Pp. 683–704.

Hamblin, R. L.   Leadership and crises. In D. Cartwright & A. Zander (Eds.), *Group dynamics.* Evanston, Ill.: Row, Peterson & Co., 1960. Pp. 571–585.

Hare, A. P.   Small group discussions with participatory and supervisory leadership. In A. P. Hare, E. F. Borgatta, & R. F. Bales (Eds.), *Small groups.* New York: Alfred A. Knopf, 1955. Pp. 556–560.

Harway, N. I., Dittman, A. T., Rausch, H. L., Bordin, E. S., & Rigler, D.   The measurement of depth of interpretation. *J. consult. Psychol.,* 1953, **19**, 247–253.

Heckel, R. V., Froelich, R. E., & Salzberg, H. C.   Interaction and redirection in group therapy. *Psychol. Rep.,* 1962, **10**, 14.

Heise, G. A., & Miller, G. A.   Problem solving by small groups using various communication nets. In A. P. Hare, E. F. Borgatta, & R. F. Bales (Eds.), *Small groups.* New York: Alfred A. Knopf, 1955. Pp. 353–367.

Heyns, R.   Effects of variation in leadership on participants behavior in discussion groups. Unpublished doctoral dissertation, University of Michigan, 1948.

Hinkley, R. G., & Hermann, L.   *Group treatment in psychotherapy.* Minneapolis: University of Minnesota, 1951.

Hobbs, N.   Group-centered psychotherapy. In C. R. Rogers, *Client-centered therapy.* Boston, Mass.: Houghton-Mifflin, 1951. Pp. 278–319.

Hobbs, N., & Pascal, G.   A method for the quantitative analysis of group psychotherapy. *American Psychologist,* 1946, 1, 297.

Howe, E. S., & Pope, B.   An empirical scale of therapist verbal activity in the initial interview. *J. consult. Psychol.,* 1961, 25, 510–520.

Janis, I. L.   *Psychological stress.* New York: Wiley, 1958.

Leavitt, H. J.   Some effects of certain communication patterns on group performance. *J. abnorm. soc. Psychol.,* 1951, 46, 38–50.

Lennard, H. L., & Bernstein, A.   *The anatomy of psychotherapy.* New York: Columbia Univer. Press, 1960.

Lewin, K.   Forces behind food habits and methods of change. *Bull. Nat. Res. Council,* 1943, 108, 35–65.

Lewin, K., Lippitt, R., & White, R.   Patterns of aggressive behavior in experimentally created "social climates." *J. soc. Psychol.,* 1939, 10, 271–299.

Liff, Z. A.   Group dynamics and psychotherapy. New York: Postgraduate Center for Psychotherapy, 1952. (mimeo.)

Lindzey, G. (Ed.).   *Handbook of social psychology.* Cambridge, Mass.: Addison-Wesley, 1954.

Lippitt, R.   An experimental study of the effect of democratic and authoritarian group atmospheres. *Univ. Iowa Stud. in Child Welfare,* 1940, 16, No. 3.

Locke, N. M.   *Group psychoanalysis.* New York: New York Univer. Press, 1961.

Lowrey, L. G.   Group therapy for mothers. *Amer. J. Orthopsychiat.,* 1944, 14, 589–592.

Parloff, M. B., & Rubinstein, E. A.   Research problems in psychotherapy. In E. A. Rubinstein & M. B. Parloff (Eds.), *Research in psychotherapy.* Washington: American Psychological Assoc., 1959. Pp. 276–293.

Perkins, H. V., Jr.   The effects of climate and curriculum on group learning. *J. educ. Res.,* 1950, 44, 269–286.

Preston, M. G., & Heintz, R. K.   Effects of participatory versus supervisory leadership on group judgment. *J. abnorm. soc. Psychol.,* 1949, 44, 345–355.

Raush, H. L., Sperber, Z., Rigler, D., Williams, J., Harway, N. I., Bordin, E. S., Dittman, A. T., & Hays, W. L.   A dimensional analysis of depth of interpretation. *J. consult. Psychol.,* 1956, 20, 43–48.

Raven, B. H., & Reitsema, J.   The effects of varied clarity of group goal and group path upon the individual and his relation to his group. *Hum. Relat.,* 1957, 10, 29–45.

Redl, F.   Group emotion and leadership. *Psychiat.,* 1942, 5, 573–596.

Riecken, H. W., & Homans, G. C.   Psychological aspects of social structure. In G. Lindzey (Ed.), *Handbook of social psychology.* Cambridge, Mass.: Addison-Wesley, 1954. Pp. 786–832.

Rotter, J. B.   *Social learning and clinical psychology.* New York: Prentice-Hall, 1954.

Rubinstein, E. A., & Parloff, M. B.   *Research in psychotherapy.* Washington: American Psychological Association, 1959.

Salzberg, H. C.   Manipulation of verbal behavior in a group psychotherapeutic setting. *Psychol. Rep.,* 1961, **9**, 183–186.

Salzberg, H. C.   Effects of silence and redirection on verbal responses in group psychotherapy. *Psychol. Rep.,* 1962, **11**, 455–461.

Semon, R. G., & Goldstein, N.   The effectiveness of group psychotherapy with chronic schizophrenic patients and an evaluation of different therapeutic methods. *J. consult. Psychol.,* 1957, **21**, 317–322.

Shaw, M. E.   Some effects of problem complexity upon problem solution efficiency in different communication nets. *J. exp. Psychol.,* 1954a, **48**, 211–217.

Shaw, M. E.   Some effects of unequal distribution of information upon group performance in various communication nets. *J. abnorm. soc. Psychol.,* 1954b, **49**, 547–553.

Shaw, M. E., & Rothschild, G. H.   Some effects of prolonged experience in communication nets. *J. appl. Psychol.,* 1956, **40**, 281–286.

Singer, J. L., & Goldman, G. D.   Experimentally contrasted social atmospheres in group psychotherapy with chronic schizophrenics. *J. soc. Psychol.,* 1954, **40**, 23–37.

Smith, E. E.   The effects of clear and unclear role expectations on group productivity and defensiveness. *J. abnorm. soc. Psychol.,* 1957, **55**, 213-217.

Smock, C. D.   The influence of stress on the "Intolerance of Ambiguity." *J. abnorm. soc. Psychol.,* 1955, **50**, 177–182.

Solem, A. R.   An evaluation of two attitudinal approaches to delegation. *J. appl. Psychol.,* 1958, **42**, 36–40.

Speisman, J. C.   Depth of interpretation and verbal resistance in psychotherapy. *J. consult. Psychol.,* 1959, **23**, 93–99.

Strupp, H. H.   An objective comparison of Rogerian and psychoanalytic techniques. *J. consult. Psychol.,* 1955a, **19**, 1–7.

Strupp, H. H.   Psychotherapeutic technique, professional affiliation, and experience level. *J. consult. Psychol.,* 1955b, **19**, 97–102.

Strupp, H. H.   Nature of psychotherapist's contribution to treatment process. *Arch. gen. Psychiat.,* 1960, **3**, 219–231.

Strupp, H. H., & Luborsky, L. (Eds.).   *Research in psychotherapy.* Washington: American Psychological Assoc., 1962.

Truax, C. B.   The process of group psychotherapy. *Psychol. Monogr.,* 1961, **75** Whole No. 511.

White, R., & Lippitt, R.   Leader behavior and member reaction. In D. Cartwright & A. Zander (Eds.), *Group dynamics.* Evanston, Ill.: Row, Peterson & Co., 1960. Pp. 527–553.

Willerman, B.   Group decision and request as means of changing food habits. In K. Lewin (Ed.), *Forces behind food habits and methods of change.*

Bull. Natl. Res. Council, Washington, 1943, **108,** 35–65.

Wolf, A., & Schwartz, E. K. *Psychoanalysis in groups.* New York: Grune & Stratton, 1962.

Wolfe, D. M., Snoek, J. D., & Rosenthal, R. A. Report to company participants on 1960 University of Michigan research project. Ann Arbor, Mich.: Institute for Social Research, 1961.

Wright, B. A. *Physical disability—a psychological approach.* New York: Harper, 1960.

Zimet, C. N., & Fine, H. J. Personality changes with a group therapeutic experience in a human relations seminar. *J. abnorm. soc. Psychol.,* 1955, **51,** 68–73.

9

GROUP COHESIVENESS

In the two preceding chapters we dealt with the composition of psychotherapy groups and the orientation and operations of the group psychotherapist. In both earlier discussions our prime intent was to develop and present hypotheses which related in important ways to apparently crucial aspects of the group therapy encounter and served to illustrate the predictive relevance for these hypotheses of research findings in areas other than group therapy research itself, especially in the group dynamics research literature. Because of the very great number of group dynamics and other research findings of potential import for group psychotherapy, and the almost equally numerous aspects of group psychotherapy in need of research examination, no effort was made in the earlier sections to be exhaustive in our consideration of relevant material. Instead of attempting to examine all possible bases for extrapolation of group psychotherapy research, we chose to probe certain selected and apparently important areas in considerable depth. This approach to research materials will also characterize the discussion and hypotheses that follow. Rather than attempting to explore many aspects of intragroup relations in group psychotherapy in depth, we have chosen to center on the one variable of this general class that has clearly assumed the most prominent role in the group dynamics research literature. Other intragroup relational dimensions are examined briefly later, but our prime concern here is this central variable, group cohesiveness. In general terms, it is our contention that group cohesiveness in psychotherapy groups is *potentially* of a level of importance equal to its prominence in the group dynamics context.

DEFINITIONS OF COHESIVENESS

A brief examination of the conceptual and mensurational development of the group cohesiveness construct, and the resolved and unresolved problems associated with this development, will place our use
of the term in proper perspective. Both Cartwright and Zander (1960)
and Golembiewski (1962) note that early studies of small group cohesiveness in fact used three different, if overlapping, definitions of the
cohesiveness concept:

1. The attraction of a group for its members.
2. The motivation of members to participate in the group's activities.
3. The coordination of the efforts of group members.

As Golembiewski (1962) observes, however, the latter two definitions relate primarily to group productivity and member achievement
motivation, whereas the first involves generalized group property
and motivation for membership per se. Cartwright and Zander (1960)
relegate the second definition of cohesiveness to the category of group
goal, and the third, coordination of effort, to noncohesiveness areas of
group functioning as well. The tendency to split off productivity-
related definitions of cohesiveness from definitions resting on attraction
to the group grew from several investigations (e.g., Schachter et al.,
1960) which demonstrated that groups toward which members are
highly attracted may develop norms resulting in low group productivity, low achievement motivation, low degree of effort for goal achievement.

These and related research findings led, therefore, to a narrowing
of the range of phenomena to be subsumed under the cohesiveness
concept. Member attraction to the group became the central focus of
group cohesiveness. Festinger et al. (1950), for example, defined cohesiveness at this stage in its development as, ". . . the total field of forces
which act on members to remain in the group . . . and may be
(operationally) defined as the average for all members of the resultant
force toward remaining in the group." (p. 37) Perhaps the most telling
fault in the initial *applications* of this early definition of cohesiveness
lay in the use of member sociometric choices as its sole measurement
basis. As Golembiewski (1962) comments:

Cohesiveness is defined as a group property, or "the total field of forces."
But the most available sources of data are the individuals in interaction who
make up the group. Hence the operational definition suggested is an individ-

ual measure whose precise relation to cohesiveness as a group concept is unclear (p. 152).

In spite of this methodological drawback, a great deal of research has been conducted that operationalized group cohesiveness sociometrically. Gross and Martin (1952) and Van Bergen and Koekebakker (1959) reviewed much of this material and pointed to the conceptual and operational clarification which grew from it as well as the problems to which it gave birth. One important such clarification was provided by Schachter (1951). Avoiding much of the difficulty of sociometric measurement (when used for cohesiveness-measuring purposes), Schachter placed greater emphasis on the "resultant" aspect of attraction to the group. In a study in which varying degrees of cohesiveness were successfully induced, and later related to intragroup communication patterns, Schachter had his Ss respond to a postexperimental cohesiveness questionnaire asking:

1. Do you want to remain a member of this group?
2. How often do you think this group should meet?
3. If enough members decide not to stay, so that it seems this group might discontinue, would you like the chance to persuade others to stay?

Golembiewski (1962) comments with regard to this shift in measurement of the cohesiveness concept:

The "resultant" measure of attraction-to-group implies several advantages. Schachter thus not only avoided the particularistic deficiencies of such commonly used operations as sociometric choice. He was also able to determine independently the degree to which his cohesiveness-inducing experimental manipulation (varying task attractiveness) was successful. Finally, the "resultant" approach has the advantages of tapping attraction to a specific group. This is in contrast to measures such as the sociometric (p. 155).

Thus, to bring matters up to the present point in small group research, cohesiveness is defined conceptually by most current small group researchers in a manner not unlike that of Festinger et al. (1950) more than a decade ago, "The cohesiveness of a group is the resultant of all forces acting on all members to remain in the group." This definition has generally withstood the tests of time and experimental usefulness, and its most adequate operationalization has, to a moderate extent, shifted from a sociometric to a more "resultant measurement" base. Nevertheless, much remains to be done in the way of resolving problems of measurement and conceptualization which still exist. Basic research aimed at clarifying some of the following issues is highly important. Regarding the common procedure of averaging individual attraction-to-group scores, to what degree is cohesiveness represented by such a group mean inaccurate for failure to reflect spread or within-group attraction differences? How may such facts of group life as group status hierarchies and member power differentials be reflected in over-all group cohesiveness scores, in contrast to the more usual procedure of giving each member's attraction-to-group score equal weighting? Several yet-to-be-resolved questions center on the variety of sources of member attraction to the group. Are varying sources of attraction equally powerful in building group cohesiveness? Are attraction scores from differing sources additive? Should they be given equal weightings? These are issues clearly in need of resolution as a precondition to continued understanding and manipulation of small group cohesiveness.

We have thus briefly considered the development of group cohesiveness as a general concept and in measurement terms. A few group psychotherapists have also recognized the central role that may be played by the cohesiveness dimension in the functioning of therapy groups.

COHESIVENESS IN THERAPY GROUPS

Both Bach (1954) and Frank (1957), for example, have presented carefully considered views on the probable role of group cohesiveness in psychotherapy groups. Bach (1954) comments on Cartwright's (1951) first principle for the application of group dynamics research to changing individual behavior. This principle holds that "if the group is to be used effectively as a medium of change, those people who are to be changed and those who are to exert influence for change must have a strong sense of belonging to the same group" (pp. 347-348). Bach asserts:

This principle of cohesiveness is most relevant to the therapy group, for much of the therapeutic process is mediated by all members. The most unique feature of group therapy is the cotherapeutic influence of peers, not of the doctor alone. Traditionally, the doctor is thought of as having the most influence, but in group therapy this is actually not necessarily so, because the relatively low degree of cohesiveness between doctor and patient as compared with the often very deeply involved peer relationships between the patients gives the co-patient a greater power of effective influence (1954, p. 348).

Bach's perspective on the cohesiveness of therapy groups is a beginning at establishing the basis for the central role we are according it. As Bach hints, there may be justification for viewing cohesiveness in group psychotherapy as analogous to "relationship" in individual psychotherapy in the apparent centrality of each for patient change.

Frank (1957) notes:

Experimenters with small groups have distinguished four general sources of group cohesiveness which can be manipulated, and therefore have implications for the management of therapeutic groups. They have found that a member tends to find a group attractive to the extent that (1) he perceives it as potentially meeting a personal need; (2) he likes the other members; (3) he likes the group activities; and (4) he sees the group as conferring prestige or status because of its relation to its social environment (pp. 57-58).

We are in accord with Frank's view that it is to a large extent the criteria of manipulatability which determine the potential usefulness to group psychotherapy of any given determinant of group cohesiveness.

Frank (1957) further comments:

The thesis of this paper is that interactions of members of a therapy group may be understood in part as manifestations of properties of the group per se rather than exclusively determined by personal characteristics of the members . . . . The therapeutic relevance of group cohesiveness lies clearly in the fact that the more a group's members are attracted to it, the more they are influenced by its standards. If these approve diversity of outlook, nondefensive expression of feelings and honest attempts at self-examinations; if they reward maintenance of communication . . . then the more cohesive the group is, the more likely it is to induce therapeutic changes in its members (p. 63).

A very important aspect of this statement frequently misunderstood by those leaning toward an individual-oriented view of group psychotherapy is that group cohesiveness and resultant conformity to group norms is *not* necessarily equivalent to uniformity, standardization of behavior, or lack of diversity. Wolf and Schwartz (1962), for example, are in error when they note, "Behind the group dynamic concept of cohesion, identification and belonging lies a pressure for . . . homogeneity and a denial of the right to deviate" (p. 224). As Frank (1957) observes, however, it is of importance to distinguish between conformity and uniformity. It is common, they note, for a group's norm to encourage members to be as different from one another as possible along important dimensions. Conformity to this value would result not in uniformity of behavior, but in nonuniformity. They suggest that this is frequently characteristic of psychotherapy groups. It is also pertinent that the single study (Truax, 1961) aimed largely at cohesiveness as a potential influence in psychotherapy groups found significant relationships between group cohesiveness and both degree of patient self-exploration and degree of patient insight. Truax notes:

> These results indicate that cohesion, long a central concept in the analysis of small group behavior, is also of importance in the analysis of group psychotherapy: successful group psychotherapy groups are cohesive . . . . These findings not only suggest the fruitfulness of applying knowledge of attitude change obtained from studies of experimental groups, but, also point to a variable unique to the group setting and one which is susceptible to external manipulation (p. 16).

With cohesiveness as it operates in therapy groups thus introduced, we now turn to a brief examination of group dynamics research findings exploring the consequents of group cohesion. Examination of this material will permit us to return later to the therapeutic context to frame hypotheses potentially leading to more adequate harnessing of group cohesiveness in the service of patient change.

CONSEQUENTS OF GROUP COHESIVENESS

In a broad sense, we may dichotomize group dynamics research oriented toward cohesiveness in terms of those variables demonstrated to function as antecedent to or as determinants of group cohesiveness, and those consequent to or following from cohesive group structure. As noted earlier, our formal hypotheses will be oriented toward group and individual variables whose manipulation is potentially cohesiveness-enhancing. As a means of indicating the centrality of cohesiveness in small group functioning, we list the following typically replicated findings from small-group studies which have demonstrated that members of highly cohesive groups, in contrast to members of groups low in cohesiveness, will:

1. Be more open to influence by other group members.
2. Be more accepting of member hostility.
3. Place greater value on the group's goals.
4. Find more anxiety reduction.
5. Be more equal participants in group discussion.

6. Be more active participants in group discussion.
7. Exert more pressure on deviates or marginal group members.
8. Be less susceptible to disruption as a group when a member terminates his membership.
9. Be more in agreement regarding member status hierarchy.
10. Use "we" more than "I" in their group discussions.
11. Remain in the group longer.
12. Be absent less often from group meetings.

This listing of findings regarding the consequents of group cohesiveness clearly suggests that cohesive group structure and functioning —at least as far as nontherapeutic groups are concerned—is indeed a powerful influence on individual member behavior, an influence finding expression in an array of cognitive, interpersonal, and overt behavioral areas of group member functioning. Because our chosen task leads us to center on determinants of group cohesiveness, we do not wish to dwell at length on its consequents, save for the above indication of its varied and considerable influence. However, a comment regarding the relevance of this large body of research to group psychotherapy is in order. Taken as a whole, these studies call for careful and considered "replication" in the context of group psychotherapy. The following hypotheses, as well as the more general extension of group dynamics-initiated cohesiveness concepts to group psychotherapy, take on meaning *only* to the extent that research can demonstrate that group cohesiveness is a significant influence on members of therapy groups. There is little basis at this point in the development of group psychotherapy research for predicting the degree of congruence between already-conducted group dynamics research and yet-to-be-conducted group therapy research on the consequents of cohesiveness. The latter class of research must as its first step generally demonstrate the influence of group cohesiveness on member behavior. Failing this, our hypotheses pertaining to the manipulation and enhancement of group cohesiveness obviously have little point. Thus the first experimental forays aimed at the effects of attraction to the therapy group on member communication, anxiety reduction, expression of hostility, absenteeism, or what have you, must demonstrate a significant causal influence as a precondition to further meaningful experimentation on the antecedents of cohesiveness in therapy groups. In essence, it must be demonstrated that cohesiveness matters. We strongly suspect, extrapolating from evidence cited above, that it matters very much. But we underscore the fact that, save for the Truax

(1961) study, research demonstrating this general point has yet to be conducted. We are not, of course, proposing that the nature of the causal relationships such research may identify will be or necessarily should be identical to those already identified as operative in non-therapy groups. In fact, the ways in which the operation of cohesiveness differs from therapy to nontherapy groups is of prime interest in its own right. This is true for a variety of reasons, especially for the leads such comparisons may provide regarding the group conditions under which group dynamics-to-group therapy research extrapolation is appropriate. This need too, therefore, demands basic research efforts aimed at specifying the nature and degree of influence of group cohesiveness in psychotherapy groups. In addition to this general need for research demonstration of the power of cohesiveness in therapy groups, there are several broad questions toward which we propose that such consequents-of-cohesiveness research in group psychotherapy may fruitfully be directed. Besides the obvious central concern, the influence of therapy group cohesiveness on therapeutic outcome or patient change, several intermediate issues are apparent. Are there meaningful differences between therapy groups varying in degree of cohesiveness in terms of:

1. The rate of verbal interaction for a given patient, in comparison both with other patients and the therapist?
2. The rate and nature of verbal interaction directed at marginal group members?
3. The development and influence of within-group status hierarchies?
4. The development and influence of within-group cliques or subgroups?
5. The expression and resolution of intermember and member-to-therapist hostility?
6. The degree of consistency of patient in-therapy behavior and earlier trial session behavior?
7. Communication toward and acceptance of new group members in open groups?
8. Degree of acceptance of patient-initiated interpretations?
9. Degree of acceptance of therapist-initiated interpretations?
10. Depth of therapist and patient-initiated interpretations?
11. Development, maintenance, and influence of "member-as-therapist" behavior?
12. Degree of member-to-member influence on verbal behavior?
13. Ease of defaulting of leadership role by the therapist?

14. Usefulness of postsession (withous therapist) group meetings?
15. Duration of group and member attendance?

To summarize our discussion so far, we have attempted to take a comprehensive view of the small-group concept of cohesiveness, both from historical and contemporary perspectives. Although there is considerable evidence of its very central influence in nonpsychotherapy groups it has received some recognition, but little relevant research scrutiny, in the therapeutic context. The first step in such an examination should deal with the influence therapy group cohesiveness may have on the interaction and therapeutic progress of patient members. We have sketched above several broad research questions that appear to be promising paths for such initial cohesiveness-consequents research to follow. Our discussion of cohesiveness may now turn to antecedent considerations and our extrapolated hypotheses.

INCREASING ATTRACTION BY STRUCTURING INITIAL EXPECTANCIES

Hypothesis 7.3, which focused on the potential increment in patient attraction to group resulting from the degree and nature of effort required to gain group membership, was our first hypothesis aimed specifically at group therapy by focusing on the issue of increasing attraction or cohesiveness via deliberate manipulation. There is a second such manipulative procedure that may be considered at this premembership stage of the therapeutic transaction, one that also offers the potential for increasing the attractiveness of membership for the patient. We speak here of the opportunity available to the group psychotherapist during this premembership stage to structure the patient's expectancies in the direction of increased attraction to other group members.

Manipulation of Patient Expectancies

Although no reference is made in the group psychotherapy research literature to manipulation of patient expectancies or the consequences of expectational differences among patients, a great deal of attention has been devoted to such matters by researchers interested in individual psychotherapy. Both Frank (1959) and Snyder (1946), for example, have suggested that the nature of the patient's referral to psychotherapy will significantly influence his initial attitudes toward the treatment process. Goldstein and Shipman (1961) provide evidence supporting this contention. They report a significant effect of favor-ableness of referral source upon patient's initial confidence in the treatment clinic and its personnel. Heine and Trosman (1960) have indicated related findings. These investigations both point to the influence of pretherapeutic involvement experiences on the subsequent attractiveness of therapeutic participation for the patient. Further, a large number of studies (e.g., Frank et al., 1959; Goldstein, 1962) have demonstrated a positive relationship between patients' pretherapy expectations of improvement and subsequent patient change. Several studies (e.g., Frank, 1959; Goldstein, 1962) also convincingly demon-strate the influence of patient pretherapy expectancies regarding the nature of psychotherapy on their subsequent in-therapy behavior. These two classes of studies, focusing on patient prognostic expec-tancies and role expectancies respectively, combine to underscore the general point that attitudes held by patients about their anticipated therapeutic experience have a clearly demonstrable influence on their later within-therapy behaviors and perceptions. Perhaps even more to the point, a study by Heller and Goldstein (1961) demonstrated a significant positive relationship between the degree of patient pre-therapy attraction toward the therapist and the therapeutic process and the extent to which the patient subsequently described himself as becoming more independent over the course of his psychotherapeu-tic participation. This now-substantial body of individual psycho-therapy research findings serves, therefore, as our initial basis for hypothesis 9.1.

HYPOTHESIS 9.1: **Therapy group cohesiveness may be increased by manipulation of premembership structuring of patient therapy-relevant expectancies.**

Structuring for Attraction

Cartwright and Zander (1960) provide a general introduction to the group dynamics research basis for this hypothesis with their state-ment:

> The general principle may be derived that the valence of a group will be increased by heightening the awareness of a member (or a potential mem-ber) that he can fulfill his needs by belonging to the group . . . it is . . . common for organizations to attempt to strengthen various sources of attrac-tion for the membership by dramatizing the value of the group's properties or the gains to be derived from belonging (p. 78).

Similarly, Bass (1960) comments: "A group is more attractive, the greater the rewards which may be earned by membership in the group and the greater the anticipation or expectancy of earning them" (p. 60).

An investigation conducted by Schachter, Ellertson, McBride, and Gregory (1960) bears directly on our hypothesized means of increasing patient attraction to the therapy group. This study was designed to examine the influence of group cohesiveness on member susceptibility to influence and group productivity. The nature of their influence and productivity findings are not of central concern to the issue being considered, but their manner of manipulating cohesiveness is most relevant. Their subjects were 25 college students, unknown to one another, in groups composed of three subjects each. As the first stage of their participation, each S completed personality questionnaires designed ostensibly to yield detailed personality information. On arriving for the group session, but before meeting the other group members, each S was interviewed individually by one of the experimenters. During this interview, whose *stated* intent was simply to obtain routine information, each subject in the high cohesiveness condition was told she was a member of an extremely congenial group and that "there is every reason to expect that the other members of the group will like you and you will like them." Subjects in the low cohesiveness condition were told that because of scheduling difficulties it had been impossible to bring together a congenial group and that "there is no particular reason to think that you will like them or that they will care for you." After the group session each S responded to a questionnaire aimed at assessing the success of the cohesiveness manipulation. Using a scaled response format, it contained the following questions:

1. How did you like your team?
2. If you were taking part in another experiment, how much would you like to work with these same girls?
3. How much do you think you would like to see your teammates?

A comparison of subjects in high and low cohesiveness conditions demonstrated significant differences on all three items, thus attesting to the success of the cohesiveness manipulation via the investigator's simple and straightforward instructions to subjects.

Festinger et al. (1950) report related findings. In their investigation an attempt was made to induce varying degrees of group cohesiveness based on anticipated attitudinal similarity with other group members. This second manipulable basis for attraction relates very closely to research material discussed in support of hypothesis 7.4, voting-in of new members. In this experiment each subject was first required to indicate his opinion on a given issue. He was then provided with a predetermined tabulation of the supposed opinions on the same issue held by other group members. In this procedure some subjects were given the impression that the opinions of most of the other group members were congruent with their own, while other subjects were led to believe that the opinions held by most other group members were considerably different from theirs. Following the actual group meeting, all subjects were asked how well they liked the other members of their group. A clear difference emerged across the two classes of experimental groups. Subjects anticipating that other members of their group held opinions divergent from their own were significantly less attracted to the group than were subjects anticipating more congruent member opinions.

In a related manner, Back (1951) was able to successfully manipulate mutual attraction in pairs of subjects by a series of premeeting structuring variations. While his main experimental purpose, to demonstrate the differing consequences of differing bases for attraction, is also of relevance for our present discussion, his independent variable manipulation is more to the point we are now considering. Back was able to manipulate the degree of within-pair cohesiveness by telling each subject, before he met his partner, that they would or would not (1) like each other, (2) receive a prize for the best group performance, or (3) serve as a model of a highly productive group. Thus this study's findings not only reinforce the feasibility of within-group cohesiveness manipulation through premeeting structuring, but further indicate that there are several dimensions of relevance to group functioning along which this manipulation may take place.

There are several studies in the research area broadly termed "interpersonal perception" that similarly demonstrate that attraction toward another individual is readily manipulable by premeeting structuring or expectancies. In one such investigation, Asch (1946) provided groups of students with two lists indicating a series of personal characteristics of an hypothetical individual. The first list consisted of: intelligent, skillful, industrious, warm, determined, practical, and cautious. The second list was identical except "cold" was substituted for "warm." Subjects were then instructed to write personality sketches of the two persons described by the trait lists, and also to select from a checklist of pairs of opposite traits the terms that best fit their impression of each person. In general, analysis of the personality sketches and trait selections indicated marked differences in subject perception of "warm" and "cold" persons.

In a more "real-life" setting Kelley (1950) demonstrated essentially the same effect as Asch. His subjects were 65 college students in three classes. A person unknown to the subjects was introduced to each class as a temporary replacement for their regular instructor. Half of the members of each class were given biographical information about the substitute instructor which included the statement that he was rather "cold." The remaining subjects were independently given identical information exception for the substituted statement that the instructor was "very warm." The instructor then led each class in a twenty-minute discussion, and a record was kept of each student's participation. Afterwards, first impression ratings of the instructor were obtained from all subjects. Comparison of the warm- and cold-expectation groups indicated that subjects provided the expectation of interpersonal warmth rated the instructor as more considerate of others, less formal, more sociable and more humorous than did their cold-expectation classmates. They also participated more in the class discussion than did the subjects with the cold expectation.

Thus we are provided with evidence that premeeting expectational structuring may find expression both in several dimensions of interpersonal perception and in overt verbal behavior. Beilin (1960), Mensh and Wishner (1947), and Wishner (1960) report concurring findings. In addition, based on studies conducted by himself and by Alexander and Drucker (1960), McGrath (1962) notes:

> We have shown that interpersonal perception which individuals bring with them into a new group are the key to initial formation of positive interpersonal relations. Alexander and Drucker found that interpersonal perceptions can be deliberately altered by experimental means, and that they ultimately aid the adjustment of teammates. At this stage of our knowledge, therefore, it would seem . . . profitable to attempt the assembly of 'quasi-therapeutic' groups by selecting or training group members to perceive teammates in a favorable way . . . (p. 373).

Finally, it may be noted that DiVesta and Bossart (1958) report evidence for their hypothesis that expressed attitudes in their subjects vary according to the labels attached by someone else to the situation in question. Bieri (1953) has demonstrated that first-impression attitudes held toward other persons, once formed, are strongly resistant to change. Both Raven and Reitsema (1957) and Smith (1957), as noted in our earlier discussion of therapist orientations, have shown that clarity of group structure and functioning serves to increase group cohesiveness. Raven and Reitsema, for example, report that subjects with a clear picture of group goals and the basis for group procedures were more group-oriented and less interpersonally hostile than subjects ambiguously oriented in these respects. Thus the clarity provided by premeeting structuring, its contents aside, may itself serve as cohesiveness-enhancing.

It appears that the series of investigations just described, when viewed in combination with the several studies noted earlier pertaining to referral source and expectancies in individual psychotherapy, provide ample encouragement for research examinations of hypothesis 9.1. In broad terms, we have implicitly suggested by the studies described above that the implementation of this hypothesis would likely be a simple and straightforward affair. Perhaps all that is necessary to enhance a patient's initial attraction to membership in a given therapy group is to tell him, prior to the first session, that there is reason to believe that he will like the other group members, get along well with them, and find them most helpful in his efforts to deal with the problems bringing him to therapy. In reality, however, matters are far from this simple. Research exists pointing to two additional major considerations which must be dealt with in successfully testing hypothesis 9.1, and there may well be more such issues. Let us assume we have established a therapy group of eight members and, in so doing, have structured the expectations of each member in the direction of highly favorable intermember attraction. If such an effort is uniformly confirmed, if each member does in fact subsequently perceive all other members in a distinctly favorable light, we may anticipate little initial difficulty as far as group cohesiveness is concerned. Alternatively, however, let us assume that following such efforts aimed at creating favorable initial attraction in therapy patients, their perceived reality of the first meeting leads four of the group members to feel that their favorable interpersonal expectancies have been upset or disconfirmed. Janis (1958) has demonstrated in considerable detail that individuals exposed to more stress than anticipated in certain situations will strongly tend to react with hostility on becoming aware of the disconfirmation of their expectations. Wright (1960) reports similar findings. Thus if we attempt pretherapy structuring of patient expectancies leading them to anticipate a highly congenial, interpersonally comfortable, or problem-resolving group, we run the risk that the disconfirmation of this structuring attempt will eventuate in a level of group cohesiveness which may be even less satisfactory than that which might have developed had not attempts at manipulating attraction-to-group been made.

In addition to the functional composition of therapy groups suggested earlier, there is a basis, or the beginning of one, for handling or controlling this possibility of differential patient responsiveness to in-therapy events relevant to their attraction expectancies. We have in mind here those studies yielding evidence regarding personality correlates of successful and unsuccessful attempts at attraction induction. The study by Heller and Goldstein (1961) noted earlier, for example, demonstrated on two levels of measurement that more dependent individuals tend to view their anticipated therapeutic experience with markedly higher attraction than do their more independent counterparts. Dittes (1959) has demonstrated a similar effect of level of patient self-esteem. In his investigation some subjects were led to anticipate they would be well accepted by other group members; others that they would be poorly accepted. As predicted, the high acceptance condition resulted in significantly greater attraction to the group. However, significant differences also emerged *within* the group of high acceptance Ss. Those with high self-esteem were not nearly as attracted to the group because of their acceptance by it as were (highly accepted) subjects with low self-esteem. Dittes interpreted this finding as reflecting a strong need for acceptance among this latter group of Ss.

Thus we have pointed to two variables which must be kept in mind in any research implementation of hypothesis 9.1. Marked upsetting of favorable expectancies may be predicted to result in lowered attraction-to-group. Dependency and self-esteem are but two of several patient personality characteristics which partially determine patient responsiveness to later attraction-relevant events. It appears, therefore, that the most appropriate initial attempts at testing efforts to structure heightened attraction in group therapy patients should consider the interaction effects of patient characteristics such as those identified above, and also to aim at structuring such attraction to a fairly high but not unlikely level.

INCREASING ATTRACTION BY INTERGROUP COMPETITION

The hypothesis we deal with next, and those remaining in our consideration of cohesiveness, focus on manipulations which are potentially cohesiveness-enhancing after the therapy group has begun to meet. In the present instance there appear to be no directly relevant research reports or even speculations in the group psychotherapy literature. We shall proceed, therefore, to state the hypothesis and then examine its group dynamics research basis.

HYPOTHESIS 9.2:   **Therapy group cohesiveness may be increased by intergroup competition.**

Allport's (1954) observations regarding outgroup influences on ingroup cohesiveness provide, to some extent, an historical background for research material we shall consider. Allport states:

> The French biologist, Felix Le Dantec, insisted that every social unit from the family to the nation could exist only by virtue of having some 'common enemy' . . . In favor of Le Dantec's view is the well known Machiavellian trick of creating a common enemy in order to cement an in-group.
>
> Hitler created the Jewish menace not so much to demolish the Jews as to cement the Nazi hold over Germany. At the turn of the century the Workingman's Party in California whipped up an anti-Oriental sentiment to consolidate its own ranks which, without a common enemy, were indifferent and wavering. School spirit is never so strong as when the time for an athletic contest with the traditional 'enemy' approaches. Instances are so numerous that one is tempted to accept the doctrine.
>
> Now there is no denying that the presence of a threatening common enemy will cement the in-group sense of any organized aggregate of people . . . but the psychological emphasis must be placed primarily on the desire for security, not on hostility itself (pp. 41-42).

Investigations of Intergroup Competition

The central investigations of the effects of intergroup competition on within-group cohesiveness are the experimental camp studies conducted by Sherif and Sherif (1953). The first study in this series, conducted in 1949, took place in a camp in northern Connecticut. Twenty-four boys, all approximately aged twelve and homogeneous on a variety of background criteria, were selected as the camp members. The study may be viewed in three stages.

1. *Informal Grouping.* This opening stage was oriented toward providing a maximum of freedom for the 24 subjects to form informal groups, subgroups and friendships of their own choosing. All activities were campwide, thus avoiding any attempts at grouping initiated by the camp staff (the investigators). The investigators note: "Thus it became possible to single out budding friendship groups and, more or less, to equate the weights of such personal factors in the two experimental groups of stage 2" (p. 239).

2. *Formal Grouping.* The second phase of the study centered on the composition of two essentially similar groups of twelve boys each and the development of well defined ingroup structure. Observation of developing friendship groupings during stage 1, and sociometric preference ratings obtained at the end of this first experimental period served as the major bases for composition of the two experimental groups. That is, observational and sociometric information were utilized deliberately to split the friendship groups which had begun to emerge during the self-directed initial grouping phase of the study. Thus at the point at which the two experimental groups were formed, the number of friendship choices given to members of the experimental ingroup was less than the number of friendship choices assigned to members of the experimental outgroup. During the course of this second stage, each group, separated physically from one another, participated in a variety of groupwide camp activities. The variety of such activities permitted all members of each group to participate and do well in several. All rewards during this period, however, were given on a group basis, and not to particular individuals. The investigators comment: "The major outcome of these participations in both groups during stage 2 was the formation of well-defined in-group organizations or structures" (p. 248). In addition, they report the development during this second experimental period of ". . . strong in-group feelings of loyalty and solidarity within the group . . ." (p. 260). Finally it may be noted of this stage that by its close there was a marked shift in friendship choices away from the outgroup and toward other members of the subjects' ingroup.

3. *Intergroup Relations.* The third and final phase of the investigation was planned to examine the within- and between-group effects of bringing the two groups into contact in a series of competitive and frustrating situations. Sherif and Sherif observe:

> The consequence of these intergroup relations in competitive situations and in frustrating situations which members of one group perceived as being caused by the other group was first to solidify the in-group belongingness and solidarity, to enhance in-group democracy, and to strengthen in-group friendship. Qualifications must be added that during the period of repeated defeats suffered by the Red Devils there were signs of disorganization and internal feuds in this group. But in the face of broadside attacks by the Bull Dogs there was closing ranks in the Red Devil Group (p. 284).

From this investigation, as well as later replications with child (Sherif & Sherif, 1953) and adult (Blake & Mouton, 1961) populations, we find substantial support for the proposition that intergroup competition functions to increase within-group cohesiveness. Although this finding appears to be more unequivocally applicable to the "winning" group than to the "losing" group, the findings suggest that the "intergroup competition-increased ingroup cohesiveness" relationship will also find expression under as yet unspecified conditions in the group doing less well competitively. Subsequent to this keynote series of investigations, other researchers have reported studies aimed at the cohesiveness-intergroup competition relationship and, more generally, internal group behavior under threat conditions.

Myers (1962) reports an investigation in which 60 three-man teams comprised of 180 ROTC students participated in a rifle-shooting tournament. Six teams in each of five leagues engaged in a face-to-face, 25-bout, round-robin competition. Thirty other teams fired against certain preset standards, and not against the performance of other teams. Adjustment to group, the study's dependent variable, was operationalized in terms of measures of esteem for and acceptance of other group members. The study's findings indicated that team adjustment was highest under the experimental condition combining competition and task success. Further, competition combined with little success at the group's task also led to better team adjustment than did that characterizing the low-success, noncompetitive teams. As Myers notes, "It was concluded that the competitive experience not only engendered good adjustment under favorable conditions (success) but that it acted as a prophylactic against poor adjustment in unfavorable situations" (p. 332). Thus we are provided with further evidence of the favorable influence of intergroup competition on the quality of member-to-member interpersonal perception. In addition, failure in such competitive situations, at least in this investigation, seems to generate a similar, if less strong, positive effect.

In a related study Wilson and Miller (1961) report a significant increase in attraction toward teammates following competitive interaction with other groups. An unexpected finding was a smaller, but also significant increase in attraction toward members of the opposing team. Further, there was no significant difference between the two types of attraction increases. Lanzetta, Haefner, Langham, and Axelrod (1954) were interested in the more general question of the effects of situational threat on group behavior. In contrast to nonthreatened

410   GROUP PSYCHOTHERAPY

groups, they found that "threat groups showed less behavior that would result in tension and friction within the group and more behavior oriented toward group acceptance" (p. 452). Pepitone and Kleiner (1957) and Thibaut (1950) report similar effects of threat upon intragroup interactions and perceptions.

Following from this series of investigations, hypothesis 9.2 suggests that cohesiveness of therapy groups may potentially be increased via bringing such groups into competitive interaction with other (not necessarily psychotherapy) groups. Though this general class of manipulations may be somewhat less feasible in an outpatient group therapy setting, it appears to be a reasonable approach to consider in such inpatient or quasi-inpatient settings as mental hospitals, prisons, day-care centers, and the like. Such intergroup competition could, though not necessarily, take the form of an athletic competition. Although this form of competition has the advantage of being similar or identical to usual institutional recreational activities in many instances, the therapist-investigator instigating the competition has little control over its outcome. The research we have examined suggests that even failure under competitive circumstances may increase ingroup cohesiveness, but findings also point to a much stronger and more reliable positive effect on cohesiveness growing from competition between groups when one is on the winning side. Thus a more appropriate implementation of hypothesis 9.2 may well involve the type of competitive intergroup interaction in which the outcome of the competition is not immediately apparent but, instead, must first pass through "scoring" or other manipulable procedures in the hands of the therapist-investigator. In addition to this common means of controlling outcome of intergroup competition, we may also point to the several studies of group behavior which relied on use of stooges (e.g., Asch, 1952; Smith, 1957; Wilson & Miller, 1961) or simulation techniques (e.g., Blake & Brehm, 1954; Guetzkow, 1951) as a means of assuring controlled manipulation of independent variables.

INCREASING ATTRACTION BY TEMPORARY INCLUSION OF A "DEVIANT PLANT"

Our previous hypothesis discussed the potential increment to group cohesiveness which might follow from subjecting the therapy group to a competitive experience with another group or, more generally, subjecting the group to "threat," broadly defined. The hypothesis to which we now turn rests on a directly analogous base, with the key difference being the locus of the source of "threat" or disruption to the group. This hypothesis may be stated as follows:

HYPOTHESIS 9.3:   **Therapy group cohesiveness may be increased by the temporary inclusion within the therapy group of a "deviant plant."**

In essence, we are proposing that for a period of a relatively few sessions, the therapist add to the group membership a "plant," or "accomplice" whose within-group behavior is intentionally deviant. The essential task of such an accomplice would be to explicitly and repeatedly state and defend a nonnormative or deviant position on important group-relevant issues, about which the other group members have previously reached a general consensus. Over the course of his brief group membership (whose ending could be explained to the group in terms of an "unplanned environmental event"), the accomplice would gradually slide from his discrepant viewpoint toward the group norm. Our hypothesis predicts that a therapy group provided with the opportunity of jointly expressing mutually shared affect and attitudes toward such a deviant plant will, via this expressive behavior and their success in "winning him over," function at—or have increased potential for functioning at—a higher level of group cohesiveness than was true before the accomplice joined the group.

The Deviant Group Member

Reference to group dynamics research literature readily indicates that the deviate or marginal group member has received a considerable amount of investigative attention. Much of this attention has centered on within-group communication and interaction involving deviant group members. Several investigations have demonstrated that a greater number of communications, particularly in the form of influence attempts, are directed by group members toward the deviant member, the one whose statements or position is most discrepant from the modal group position. These influence attempts continue to increase in number and then drop off sharply when the deviate is either won over or given up as a lost cause and rejected by the other group members. Schachter (1951) has demonstrated that the more deviant a member's position is, the more these effects will be in evidence. His subjects were divided into 32 discussion groups of five to seven members each. Three plants, perceived by the group as regular members, were introduced into each group. These accomplices had as their task playing the role of "mode," "slider" or "deviate." The modal role player maintained consistent agreement with the modal group opinion on the discussion topic throughout. The slider, whose behavior corresponded to that suggested by hypothesis 9.3, began his participation by supporting a position widely discrepant from the prevailing group position, and gradually shifted his position by degrees toward the modal group opinion as if he had been persuaded. The deviant plant maintained a marked difference between his expressed opinion and the modal group opinion throughout. Postmeeting sociometric choice measures clearly demonstrated the success of the role playing in that the deviates were consistently least chosen (most rejected), followed by the sliders, and then the modes. As indicated earlier, a continuously increasing number of communications were directed toward the deviate, only to fall off after reaching a peak amount. Compatible with this was the continuously decreasing number of communications directed toward the sliders as they shifted from deviant to modal positions.

In a related study, Festinger et al. (1952) established two degrees of opinion perceived as deviant: one a single step removed from the general opinion of the group and the other three steps removed. The other group members directed proportionately more of their communications toward the extreme deviate than toward the slight deviate.

The several investigations in this specific area, such as those described, combine to convincingly demonstrate the powerful effect on within-group communication patterns wrought by the presence of a deviant group member. However, there are other group characteristics which serve to determine the manner and extent to which these deviate-caused communication effects will occur. One such characteristic is group cohesiveness. In the study by Schachter (1951) discussed above, which has since been replicated on more than one occasion, the more cohesive the group, the more steep was the rise in communication rate toward the deviate and the earlier was the point at which such interactions began to fall off. Berkowitz (1954) has shown that the proportion of communications to the deviate early in group discussion increases with the degree of interdependence among the group members. Similarly, Hall (1955) has provided evidence that the greater the group's cohesiveness, the stronger are the pressures on the occupant of any given role to act in terms of the other group member's expectations. Emerson (1954), Festinger, Schachter, and Back (1950), Horowitz, Lyons, and Perlmutter (1951), and Moreno (1954) are among the several other group dynamics researchers whose findings point to a significant effect of group cohesiveness on communication and acceptance-rejection of deviant group members. The hypothesis now under consideration, however, speaks to the converse of this relationship, the effect of the presence of a deviant group member on group cohesiveness. Thus although the research evidence discussed to the present point serves as important background material, we must have recourse to a different body of research findings for more direct encouragement of the appropriateness of hypothesis 9.3.

Similarity and Attraction

It will be recalled that as part of our examination of group composition we focused on the process of group members voting on the acceptability of new patient-candidates for their group. It was our contention that continued use of such a procedure results in an increasingly homogeneous group. As support for this contention, we cited a series of investigations which found that individuals are more attracted to others who hold similar rather than dissimilar attitudes. Further, evidence was introduced that indicated that attitudinal similarity is a determinant of interpersonal attraction.

Studies by Newcomb (1961), Byrne (1961), and Smith (1957) all pointed to a causal effect of intermember similarity on their subsequent attraction to one another. As Bass (1960) notes, ". . . if we see others sharing our attitudes, we increase in our attraction to them" (p. 70). Thus in the case of hypothesis 7.4 we predicted a causal chain in which patient-candidates similar to (or giving the appearance of being similar to) members already constituting the group would be perceived as more attractive by the group members and be voted into group membership on the basis of this similarity-caused attraction, resulting in an increasingly homogeneous (similar) group. We are proposing in hypothesis 9.3 that therapy groups, faced with the need to deal with a new member (the plant), who has taken and repeatedly reaffirmed a deviant position on salient issues with regard to which the group has previously reached relative consensus, will be provided by his presence with a basis for developing attitudinal similarity in the form of a shared perception of the new member's deviance and a common motivation for changing his behavior, removing him from the group, or otherwise ameliorating the now worsened quality of their group's interactions. In essence, to the extent that such intermember attitudinal similarity is produced, the group is provided with a basis for the growth of a more cohesive and mutually attractive group culture. Starting with their mutual identification against the deviate's position, and aided by their success in "bringing him around," a stronger foundation for intermember attraction may be possible.

It is relevant to note that not only may such a procedure increase attraction by increasing attitudinal similarity, but an increment to attraction may also follow from the participation of the members in attempting to "win over" or "bring around" the plant. Cognitive dissonance studies examined in connection with hypothesis 3.1 clearly demonstrate that the very act of publicly supporting a position to which one is not fully committed may in itself enhance the attractiveness of the group for the defending members. This would be the case if statements supporting the attractiveness of group membership were evoked from group members whose own attraction to the group was borderline or in flux, by the extremeness of the plant's position.

Other Planted Roles

Since the use of a plant or accomplice is clearly a marked departure from standard group psychotherapy procedures, it may be noted in passing that this technique of independent variable manipulation has been utilized successfully in numerous studies of diverse types (e.g., Heller et al., 1963; Goldstein & Rawn, 1957; Schachter et al., 1960). The potential of the procedure gains in importance when we note that research relevant to group psychotherapy may profitably attempt to make use of planted group members to play roles other than that of slider which may be cohesiveness-enhancing. This is particularly applicable to the many desirable group behaviors that are often more meaningful for group members when initiated by fellow patients rather than by the psychotherapist. For example, Bach's (1954) selection of new group members in terms of needed functional roles currently unfilled by any group member, suggests that temporary use of planted members may be appropriate for such role occupancy purposes. Gula's (1944) use of a subgroup of normal boys, as part of a larger therapy group consisting mostly of disturbed boys, for purposes of providing a "closely inspectable approximate model of more normal behavior" for the latter type of group member serves as anecdotal evidence of the value of this particular type of quasi-stooge subgroup. Similarly, it is not difficult to conceptualize the increase in group efficiency and, perhaps, group cohesiveness wrought by the temporary inclusion of a plant to play the role of catalyst, stimulator of certain discussion topics, or encourager of certain group activities. Such a temporary member could be useful in shifting the group focus from leader-oriented to group-oriented, could provide temporary but perhaps sufficient support for an isolate group member, could assist in mediating between or breaking up conflicting subgroups, and so forth. The possibilities and potential of this procedure are clearly considerable.

INCREASING ATTRACTION BY RESOLUTION
OF SUBGROUP DIFFERENCES

A frequently noted phenomenon in the development of the internal structure of psychotherapy groups has been variously termed subgrouping, clique formation, coalition development and bilateral transferences. In essence, these terms refer to the development of strong mutual attraction between two or more members of the therapy group, but not among the entire group membership. Both group psychotherapists and, as we discuss later, group dynamics researchers, have suggested that subgrouping is not a uniformly positive or negative feature of group life. The nature of the subgroup, its primary basis for formation and continuance, and its effects both on subgroup members and nonmembers are among the several classes of considerations determining whether the existence of a given subgroup should be supported and encouraged or, instead, negatively reinforced or discouraged. Bach (1954), for example, notes that subgrouping provides an important opportunity for confronting patients, "in action," as it were, with the nature of their repetitious and idiosyncratic interpersonal behavior. The patients can show each other, with a minimum of authoritative, interpretative contributions from the expert psychotherapist, how their interpersonal conflicts and inner tension-evocations are a function of what Bach has called neurotic set-up operations. He suggests, as further beneficial consequences of therapy subgrouping, that (1) participation in subgrouping activities provides the patient and the therapist with information regarding the group's status hierarchy and, more generally, the strength and locus of both friendly and hostile influences in the group, (2) subgrouping in the form of cotherapeutic alliances in which the subgroup members have a marked influence on one another's behavior can result in distinctly favorable psychological change in patients when the essential character and capacity of the subgroup is of this favorable type, and (3) there are circumstances under which "the therapy group substructures are extremely important to the stability and maintenance of the (total) group" (p. 361). As already noted, subgroup formation may also be a decidedly negative influence on group functioning. As Bach (1954) comments, ". . . subgroup formations represent, at times, a threat to the cohesiveness and unity of the total group" (p. 394). He provides the following as a concrete example of such a threat to group cohesiveness:

The development of preferential liking is a selective process, which means that one or two members in the group discover to their dismay that no one in the group likes them the best or prefers them as subgroup partners. The creation of one or two isolates or leftovers arouses tension in the group. The group is aware of this tension, and noticing that there is a tendency for a nuclear clique, a social elite, to differentiate itself from a peripheral group of less popular members, the group immediately senses a source of tension, even a danger to its existence and its purpose. As a matter of fact, the therapeutic process may be seriously impeded because one then actually deals with a disrupted group, incapable of forming consensuses (p. 382).

Wolf and Schwartz (1962) similarly caution that clique or subgroup formation may result in the creation of isolates whose very existence is a threat to central aspects of the group's functioning. In addition, they point out that there may form at times a "clique of elite patients who underline the analyst's values or manage to establish a homogeneous bias to which they demand the remaining members conform" (p. 75).

In an analogous manner researchers interested in the functioning of nonpsychotherapeutic small groups have suggested that the influence of subgroups within larger total groups is variably positive or negative depending on a series of other considerations both internal and external to the group itself. Cartwright and Zander (1960), for example, comment:

We suggest that splinter-group formation will disrupt the larger organization when the goals of the smaller group are incompatible with those of the larger. In contrast, they will strengthen the cohesiveness of the total when the goals of the smaller group are the same as, or supportive of, the larger body's goals (p. 88).

Bass (1960) similarly underscores the primacy of goal orientation as the basis for the favorableness-unfavorableness of the presence of subgroups. Stogdill (1959) extends this position somewhat by his observation that group integration will be high when subgroups are well integrated into the larger group structure, when subgroup norms support the major objectives of the larger group, and when the activities of the subgroups are well coordinated in relation to over-all group functioning. When these conditions do not obtain, he holds, the progress of the larger group toward its primary objectives is impeded. Carlson (1960) adds that "when subgroups differ in basic goals or in their 'perception of reality' the likelihood of intragroup conflict increases" (p. 327). Studies by Carlson (1960), French (1941), and Thibaut and Kelley (1959) have satisfactorily demonstrated these speculations to be operative in problem-solving and related small groups. Within-group cliques or subgroups, when oriented toward divergent goals, do indeed have a deleterious effect on the functioning of the larger group. Thus, whether for reasons of divergent goals, the creation of subgroup-excluded isolates, or other considerations mentioned above, when subgroups serve to impede efficient group functioning and reduce the over-all level of group cohesiveness their dissolution or re-orientation appears essential. The hypothesis which follows centers on these potentially negative effects of subgrouping on group cohesiveness and, further, proposes a specific basis for altering such a group structure by means of procedures utilized successfully in this regard with problem-solving groups.

HYPOTHESIS 9.4: **Therapy group cohesiveness may be increased by dissolving or re-orienting diverging subgroups. The creation of a series of groupwide tasks characterized by superordinate goals with inherent task appeal and demanding interdependent linking across all group members for task completion will result in such subgroup dissolution or re-orientation.**

Investigations of Subgroup Dissolution

Two investigations in the group dynamics research area represent the main evidence for hypothesis 9.4. It will be recalled that in our earlier discussion of intergroup competition as a means of increasing intragroup cohesiveness, we placed considerable emphasis on an investigation conducted by Sherif in a camp for boys. An investigation (Sherif & Sherif, 1953) by the same research group subsequent to the initial study sought both to replicate and extend the first study's findings. The main emphasis in this extension was an attempt to answer the question: "How can the two groups in conflict now be brought into harmony?" Obviously this is precisely the issue to which our present hypothesis is addressed. As their initial attempt at reduction or removal of intergroup hostility and overt conflict, the investigators instituted measures based on the assumption that "pleasant social contacts between members of conflicting groups would reduce friction between them" (p. 136). Thus members of both camper groups were brought together for a series of social events. As the investigators note, however, ". . . far from reducing conflict, these situations only served as opportunities for the rival groups to berate and attack each other" (p. 136). The failure of this attempt to reduce intergroup conflict suggests that, in the group therapy setting, similarly unsatisfactory results may be likely to follow attempts to reduce intersubgroup conflict by having recourse to greater use of postmeetings or alternate sessions, that is, essentially social meetings of the patients with the therapist not present. This is particularly the case to the extent that such alternate sessions are allowed to remain as primarily unplanned, unstructured patient get-togethers. Clearly, a better planned, deliberate manipulative approach is called for. This is essentially the step that Sherif and Sherif (1953) took next. They comment:

> Just as competition generates friction, working in a common endeavor should promote harmony. It seems to us . . . that where harmony between groups is established, the most decisive factor is the existence of superordinate goals which have a compelling appeal for both which neither could achieve without the other. To test this hypothesis experimentally, we created a series of urgent, and natural, situations which challenged the boys (p. 137).

Three such situations are reported. The first involved a contrived breakdown in the camp's water supply. The second involved obtaining funds for the rental of a movie, when neither group had sufficient funds to do so but when pooling of resources would be sufficient. The last attempt at creating conflict reduction, by joint task effort of the type described, occurred in the middle of a hike when the truck which was supposed to go to a nearby town for food for the campers "broke down." The investigators note, rather symbolically, that "The boys got a rope—the same rope they had used in their acrimonious tug-of-war—and all pulled together to start the truck" (p. 137). Results of this series of manipulations clearly point to a happy ending for this nonfictional series of camp adventures. As the investigators comment:

> These joint efforts did not immediately dispel hostility. At first the groups returned to the old bickering and name-calling as soon as the job in hand was finished. But gradually the series of cooperative acts reduced friction and conflict. The members of the two groups began to feel more friendly to each other (p. 137).

This observation by the investigators of reduced intergroup hostility rests on considerable and consistent behavioral evidence: for example, the boys spontaneously decided to hold a joint campfire; members of the two groups treated each other to refreshments; they requested that they be allowed to go home together on the same bus instead of separately as they had in coming to camp; and there were a considerable number of shifts in expressed friendship choices from within their respective groups to the other group. Thus Sherif and Sherif's study may be taken as important evidence suggesting the efficacy of the set of intergroup conflict-reducing procedures embodied in hypothesis 9.4.

An investigation by Thomas (1960) focused on the implications of varying degrees of member interdependence on the functioning of small groups. By way of introduction, he observes:

> The behavior of a group is strongly affected by the degree of interdependence existing among its members . . . . For example, when interdependence is high rather than low, members seem to be more attracted to the group, to strive harder to achieve their goals, and to be more responsible to their fellows (p. 449).

Thomas employed 160 subjects in groups of five members each. Subjects were required to participate in a miniature construction task for 30-minute periods. In some groups members were made interdependent either by a complex division of labor or by the institution of a common team goal. In the noninterdependent groups members either worked independently, with no division of labor, or worked toward individual goals. A comparison of these two classes of groups, interdependent versus noninterdependent, on an attraction-to-group questionnaire given after the group session, yielded a significant difference favoring the interdependent condition. Thus though no presession attraction measurement was made for base line comparison purposes, Thomas' results do provide some evidence of a positive influence of member interdependence on group cohesiveness. It may also be noted at this point that a study conducted by Berkowitz and Levy (1956), which we discuss in more detail in connection with our next hypothesis, yielded support for their contention that ". . . high group task motivation related to high pride in group performance results from a perception of interdependence among the group members with respect to the attainment of reward" (p. 306).

To restate, we have generally indicated, in both the group therapy and the group dynamics literature, that subgrouping is variously an aid or a hindrance to the development of group cohesiveness, depending on a variety of other group-relevant circumstances. When it is a hindrance, dissolution or re-orientation of the conflicting subgroups seems clearly in order. We have cited two investigations that suggest that procedures instituted for such alteration of the group's subgroup structure may be constructed most effectively in terms of a series of group-wide tasks or activities toward which all members will be strongly motivated, that involve goals superordinate to the goals of the conflicting subgroups, and that require interdependent member activity for successful goal attainment. Although we readily acknowledge that the procedure just proposed is a complex one, and one not easily operationalized in the group psychotherapy setting, its potential is such that research attention to it seems clearly appropriate. This is not to say, however, that there are no other clique-busting or subgroup-altering techniques which may be available. Group dynamics research findings do point to other means for altering or removing negative subgroup influences. For example, Hare (1962) and Homans (1950) have indicated that the tendency for groups to split into subgroups becomes increasingly marked as group size increases. Perhaps, therefore, one means of altering subgroup structure lies in decisions about the initial group size or reductions in current group size. Bass (1960) and Simon and Guetzkow (1955) point out that the less effective the communication is within a group, the more likely the development of cliques or subgroups. Procedures aimed at altering the group's communication network, such as a shift away from therapist-centeredness and toward group-centeredness, may offer the possibility of resolving subgroup-originated group malfunctioning. Closely related to the issue of communication patterns and group effectiveness is the matter of the seating arrangement of group members. Bass (1960) reports that when "classes are split for the first time into subgroups on a chance or arbitrary basis, there is a strong tendency for these subgroups to reform during subsequent class periods, even though members are free to reform in new compositions of groups" (p. 369). Whether subgroup persistence originates from this chance base, from mutual attraction, or from other sources, the possibility exists that deliberate therapist intervention in the seating of given members may serve at least to start a movement toward subgroup dissolution. Studies conducted by Hearn (1957), Maisonneuve, Palmade, and Fourment (1952), Sommer (1959, 1962), and Steinzor (1955) concretely suggest directions which may be followed in attempts to alter the directions and rate of member-to-member interactions via manipulation of the group's seating arrangement.

One final point bearing on subgrouping seems appropriate. Gerard (1957) has demonstrated that subgroups which were in the minority within larger experimental groups showed evidence of stronger pressure toward uniformity within the subgroup than was true of the majority subgroups. This difference should be taken into account in research attempts aimed at resolution of subgroup conflicts when the subgroups vary significantly in size. Thus, to the extent that the superordinate goals of the groupwide tasks employed in any implementation of hypothesis 9.4 must partially favor the needs of one subgroup over the other, it may be that the smaller subgroup should be the one so favored since its resistance to change, according to Gerard's finding, may be greater. Our suggestions about reducing group size, changing communication patterns, or altering the group's seating arrangement may also include consideration of between-sub-group differences in pressures of conformity.

INCREASING ATTRACTION BY VERBAL REINFORCEMENT TECHNIQUES

In Chapter 4 we examined a number of implications of verbal conditioning research for individual psychotherapy. In general terms, the techniques and findings associated with the basic verbal conditioning paradigm appear to offer considerable potential for improved understanding and control of the individual therapeutic interaction. At present we wish to re-enter this research area very briefly. The material that follows is aimed essentially at suggesting the relevance of verbal conditioning research for group psychotherapy in general, and for the cohesiveness of therapy groups in particular.

HYPOTHESIS 9.5:   Therapy group cohesiveness may be increased by differential reinforcement by the therapist of patient group-oriented verbalizations versus individual-oriented verbalizations.

Verbal Conditioning in Groups

A few investigations generally point to the meaningfulness of the verbal conditioning model in the group setting. A study reported by Oakes (1962), for example, yielded evidence that the response class "giving opinion," derived from Bales (1950) category system, was conditionable in the group context. Twenty-four groups of four subjects each met to discuss selected psychiatric case history material. Subjects were told that the aim of the investigation was to assess the degree of psychological insight of psychology students. During the actual discussion sessions subjects received reinforcements in the form of flashes of a signal light structured as "indicating that their statement exhibited psychological insight" for verbal responses falling into selected Bales' categories. A comparison of the mean "giving opinion" scores for groups reinforced for the category with groups not so reinforced yielded a significant difference favoring the reinforced groups. It is important to note that this finding is logically consistent with the subject's perception of the group task and also replicates an earlier, very closely related finding by Verplank (1955) regarding the conditionability of opinion-giving behavior. However, we must also note that the remaining Bales' categories proved resistant to the conditioning attempt. In all, therefore, Oakes' study may be viewed as providing evidence of the conditionability of a selected class of verbal responses in the group setting and further cautions that the response category whose conditioning is attempted must be carefully chosen in terms of relevance for the group's task and group member's orientation. Ullman, Krasner, and Collins (1961) report a second group therapy-relevant study. They had the psychological status of a series of group therapy patients rated by their therapists. All patients were then organized into three experimental groups. The three groups met separately for four sessions over a two-week period. Their task essentially involved storytelling. In the first group emotional words were followed by the verbal reinforcer "mm-hmm." In the second group emotional words were followed by an impersonal "clicker." Patients in the third group simply met and told stories without reinforcement for class of verbalization. Krasner (Strupp & Luborsky, 1962) comments:

> We predicted that the behavior of the patients receiving positive personal reinforcement would change in a desirable direction in the group because previous studies had shown a direct relationship between the use of emotional words and patient behavior in group psychotherapy. . . . Our results indicated that we could influence the group therapy behavior by the kind of reinforcement we have in the experimental situation. That is, the group that received the interpersonal reinforcement "mm-hmm," significantly improved in their rated behavior at the end of the two week period, as compared with the other two groups (p. 266).

When we note that this investigation was both very carefully conducted (two levels of controls, rater-blindness as to experimental condition of subjects, etc.) and successfully replicated, we may view it as a convincing contribution to our general proposition regarding the relevance of conditioning techniques and findings to group psychotherapy. It may also be noted that Bachrach, Candland, and Gibson (1960) report a series of verbal conditioning studies in a group setting which led them to conclude that "the findings indicate that verbal behavior in a small group situation is subject to the same laws of conditioning that have been found to hold for single individuals . . ." (p. 34).

Another series of investigations bears even more directly on hypothesis 9.5. Our hypothesis proposes, in essence, that therapy group patients receiving therapist approval, reward, or support for patient statements that have the group as a whole as their referent will evidence greater group cohesiveness or patient attraction to the group or "we-ness" than will therapy group patients whose verbalizations are not subjected to such selective therapist reinforcement. Two investigations reported by Dinoff and his colleagues (1960a, 1960b) are particularly relevant. In general, their aim was to demonstrate the occurrence and duration of verbal conditioning of schizophrenic patients in a quasi-group therapy setting by means of verbal eliciting and reinforcing techniques. Their subjects were ten male chronic schizophrenic inpatients. For purposes of determining baselines or initial response levels, the subjects first met for three group sessions of more or less free discussion. These initial sessions were observed and judged by two independent observers. The judgment task consisted of scoring the referent of each patient verbalization as personal (P), therapist, environmental, group (G), or ambiguous. The subjects were then divided into two matched groups of five subjects each. Each group met separately with the investigator for six 50-minute sessions. With one of the groups, the investigator elicited P responses by questions five times from each patient each hour and reinforced them by his approval. Any spontaneous P remarks were similarly reinforced. The other experimental group underwent the same procedures except G, and not P, verbalizations were elicited and reinforced. Following this series of meetings, the patients returned to the combined group situation, with the investigator not present, and were again asked to speak about whatever they wished. These last three 50-minute sessions were observed and judged by the same judges who had observed the initial free discussion sessions. The degree of interjudge agreement reported is clearly satisfactory. Four of the five subjects in the P groups increased in percentage of P responses, while four of the five subjects in the G-reinforced group decreased in P responses.

This, then, is their major finding of relevance to hypothesis 9.5. The result reported is far from unequivocally supportive of our prediction, but it certainly represents encouraging, suggestive evidence of the further potential of this line of research. Their second study takes us a good bit further in this direction. Dinoff et al. (1960a) note that in the first investigation the test of learning occurred when the Ss were reunited, creating a stimulus situation quite different from the group settings in which conditioning took place. Since the only test of learning occurred under these altered stimulus conditions, it could be argued that generalization rather than actual strength of learning was tested. The purpose of the second experiment (Dinoff et al., 1960b), therefore, was to employ a measure of learning during the conditioning process itself. Twelve schizophrenic patients participated in initial free discussion and experimental sessions in a manner directly analogous to the first study. In one group of six patients G referents were elicited and reinforced; in the other group, P referents were so treated. Rather than reorganize the members into a larger, 12-person group, the investigator left the room following each conditioning session, having instructed each six-patient group to continue its discussion for another 50 minutes. These sessions were observed and judged as before. Their results indicate a highly significant increase of G and P responses in the G and P groups, respectively, over the course of the experimental sessions. Thus we are provided with less suggestive, more clearcut evidence to the effect that verbal conditioning techniques may be used effectively in a group setting and, more specifically, that verbalizations of a group-reference nature are one class of reinforceable patient verbalization.

The potential usefulness of this conditioning procedure for enhancement of group cohesiveness is further suggested by a closely related series of studies, designed to examine member attraction to group and related group dimensions when group leader reward or approval is directed to the group as a whole, rather than to individual members. Berkowitz and Levy (1956) established 25 three-man groups of Air Force personnel and assigned them to work on a simulated air defense task. All groups received an initial trial, on the basis of which they supposedly were evaluated, a "break" period, and then a second trial. In all, there were five experimental conditions: two in which group performance on the initial trial was favorably evaluated, two in which this performance was evaluated unfavorably, and a nonevaluated control condition. One of the favorably evaluated and one of the unfavorably evaluated conditions called for group members to receive evaluations of the group as a whole, while members of groups under the other experimental conditions received evaluations as individual members. In each case, the evaluations were provided through ratings constructed in advance of the group meetings. The amount of task-oriented discussion during the "break" period served as a measure of task motivation. In support of their hypothesis, the investigators found that groups receiving favorable evaluations of their group as a whole had higher pride in group performance and greater concern with the assigned group task than did groups having either unfavorable group evaluations or evaluations, favorable or unfavorable, of the individual group members.

Similarly, in the study by Sherif and Sherif (1953) discussed earlier, note was made of the increment to the formation of ingroup solidarity when "all rewards given in this period were made on a group-unit basis, not to particular individuals" (p. 239).

Thus we have attempted to illustrate the potential of hypothesis 9.5 by citing evidence which suggests (a) the appropriateness of using verbal conditioning techniques in a group setting as a means of altering patient behavior, (b) that use of these techniques can bring about an increase in subject verbalizations which have the group as a unit, rather than a specific individual, as their referent, and (c) the more general, related point that reward oriented toward the group as a unit appears to provide a significantly greater increment in member attraction to group than reward oriented toward the individual members. From our perspective, these lines of research evidence provide ample encouragement for the further research examination of the hypothesis we have been considering. In addition, and in some ways perhaps more important, the evidence we have cited and the fuller body of verbal conditioning research findings clearly point to the value of more general application of verbal conditioning techniques in group psychotherapy research. Do these techniques offer a potential means of increasing the amount of member-therapist behavior on the part of selected patients, of increasing the absolute rate of interaction for more recalcitrant patients, of reinforcing patient verbalizations aimed at reducing subgroup conflict, and, more generally, of reinforcing other apparently desirable, improvement-mediating classes of patient behavior? These are but a handful of the relevant questions toward which verbal conditioning research in group psychotherapy may be profitably addressed.

REFERENCES

Alexander, S., & Drucker, E. H.   The effects of experimentally modified interpersonal perceptions on social behavior and adjustment. Group Effectiveness Research Laboratory, University of Illinois, 1960 (mimeo.).

Appel, V. H.   Client expectancies about counseling in a university counseling center. Presented at Western Psychol. Assoc., San Jose, Calif., April, 1960.

Allport, G. W.   *The nature of prejudice.* Cambridge, Mass.: Addison-Wesley, 1954.

Apfelbaum, B.   *Dimensions of transference in psychotherapy.* Berkeley: Univer. of California Press, 1958.

Asch, S. E. Forming impressions of personality. *J. abnorm. soc. Psychol.,* 1946, 41, 258–290.

Asch, S. E. *Social psychology.* New York: Prentice-Hall, 1952.

Bach, G. R. *Intensive group psychotherapy.* New York: Ronald Press, 1954.

Bachrach, A. J., Candland, D. K., & Gibson, J. T. Experiments in verbal behavior. 1. Group reinforcement of individual response. Contract Nonr. 474 (8), Group Psychology Branch, Office of Naval Research, April, 1960.

Back, K. W. Influence through social communication. *J. abnorm. soc. Psychol.,* 1951, 46, 9–23.

Bales, R. F. *Interaction process analysis: A method for the study of small groups.* Cambridge, Mass.: Addison-Wesley, 1950.

Bass, B. M. *Leadership, psychology and organization behavior.* New York: Harper, 1960.

Beilin, H. Effects of set upon impression formation. Paper presented at American Psychological Association, Chicago, September, 1960.

Berkowitz, L. Group standards, cohesiveness and productivity. *Hum. Relat.,* 1954, 7, 409–419.

Berkowitz, L., & Levy, B. Pride in group performance and group task motivation. *J. abnorm. soc. Psychol.,* 1956, 53, 300–306.

Bieri, J. J. Changes in interpersonal perception following social interaction. *J. abnorm. soc. Psychol.,* 1953, 48, 61–66.

Blake, R. R., & Brehm, J. W. The use of tape recording to simulate a group atmosphere. *J. abnorm. soc. Psychol.,* 1954, 49, 311–313.

Blake, R. R., & Mouton, J. S. Competition, communication and conformity. In I. A. Berg & B. M. Bass (Eds.), *Conformity and deviation.* New York: Harper, 1961. Pp. 199–229.

Byrne, D. Interpersonal attraction and attitude similarity. *J. abnorm. soc. Psychol.,* 1961, 62, 713–715.

Carlson, E. R. Clique structure and member satisfaction in groups. *Sociometry,* 1960, 23, 327–337.

Cartwright, D. Achieving change in people: some applications of group dynamics theory. *Hum. Relat.,* 1951, 4, 381–392.

Cartwright, D., & Zander, A. (Eds.). *Group dynamics.* Evanston, Ill.: Row, Peterson & Co., 1960.

Dinoff, M., Horner, R. F., Kurpiewski, B. S., & Timmons, E. O. Conditioning verbal behavior of schizophrenics in a group therapy-like situation. *J. clin. Psychol.,* 1960a, 16, 367–370.

Dinoff, M., Horner, R. F., Kurpiewski, B. S., Ricard, H. C., & Timmons, E. O. Conditioning verbal behavior of a psychiatric population in a group therapy-like situation. *J. clin. Psychol.,* 1960b, 16, 371–372.

Dittes, J. E. Attractiveness of group as function of self-esteem and acceptance by group. *J. abnorm. soc. Psychol.,* 1959, 59, 77–82.

DiVesta, F. J., & Bossart, P. The effects of sets induced by labeling on the modification of attitudes. *J. Pers.,* 1958, 26, 379–387.

Emerson, R. M. Deviation and rejection: an experimental replication. *Amer. soc. Rev.*, 1954, **19**, 688–693.

Festinger, L., Schachter, S., & Back, K. *Social pressures in informal groups.* New York: Harper, 1950.

Festinger, L., Gerard H., Hymovitch, B., Kelley, H., & Raven, B. The influence process in the presence of extreme deviates. *Hum. Relat.*, 1952, **5**, 327–346.

Frank, J. D. Some determinants, manifestations, and effects of cohesiveness in therapy groups. *Int. J. grp. Psychother.*, 1957, **7**, 53–63.

Frank, J. D. The dynamics of the psychotherapeutic relationship. *Psychiat.*, 1959, **22**, 17–39.

Frank, J. D., Gliedman, L. H., Imber, S. D., Stone, A. R., & Nash, E. H., Jr. Patient's expectancies and relearning as factors determining improvement in psychotherapy. *Amer. J. Psychiat.*, 1959, **115**, 961–968.

French, J. R. P., Jr. The disruption and cohesion of groups. *J. abnorm. soc. Psychol.*, 1941, **36**, 361–377.

Gerard, H. B. Some effects of status, role clarity, and group goal clarity upon the individual's relations to group processes. *J. Pers.*, 1957, **25**, 475–488.

Goldstein, A. P. Therapist and client expectation of personality change in psychotherapy. *J. counsel. Psychol.*, 1960, **7**, 180–184.

Goldstein, A. P. *Therapist-patient expectancies in psychotherapy.* New York: Pergamon Press, 1962.

Goldstein, A. P., & Heller, K. Role expectations, participant personality characteristics, and the client-counselor relationship. Unpublished manuscript. Syracuse University, August, 1960.

Goldstein, A. P., & Rawn, M. L. The validity of interpretive signs of aggression in the drawing of the human figure. *J. clin. Psychol.*, 1957, **13**, 169–171.

Goldstein, A. P., & Shipman, W. G. Patient expectancies, symptom reduction and aspects of the initial psychotherapeutic interview. *J. clin. Psychol.*, 1961, **17**, 129–133.

Golembiewski, R. T. *The small group.* Chicago: Univer. of Chicago Press, 1962.

Gross, N., & Martin, W. E. On group cohesiveness. *Amer. J. Sociol.*, 1952, **57**, 547.

Guetzkow, H. S. *Groups, leadership and men.* Pittsburgh: Carnegie Press, 1951.

Gula, M. Boy's House—the use of a group for observation and treatment. *Ment. Hyg.*, 1944, **28**, 430–437.

Hall, R. Social influence on the aircraft commander's role. *Amer. soc. Rev.*, 1955, **20**, 292–299.

Hare, A. P. *Handbook of small group research.* New York: The Free Press of Glencoe, 1962.

Hearn, G.   Leadership and the spatial factor in small groups. *J. abnorm. soc. Psychol.,* 1957, **54**, 269–272.

Heine, R. W., & Trosman, H.   Initial expectations of the doctor-patient interaction as a factor in continuance in psychotherapy. *Psychiat.,* 1960, **23**, 275–278.

Heller, K., & Goldstein, A. P.   Client dependency and therapist expectancy as relationship maintaining variables in psychotherapy. *J. consult. Psychol.,* 1961, **25**, 371–375.

Heller, K., Myers, R. A., & Kline, L. V.   Interviewer behavior as a function of standardized client roles. *J. consult. Psychol.,* 1963, **27**, 117–122.

Hoehn-Saric, R., Frank, J. D., Imber, S. D., Nash, E. H., Jr., Stone, A. R., & Battle, C. C.   Systematic preparation of patients for psychotherapy. I. Effects on therapy behavior and outcome. *J. psychiat. Res.,* 1964, **2**, 267–281.

Homans, G. C.   *The human group.* New York: Harcourt Brace, 1950.

Horowitz, M. W., Lyons, J., & Perlmutter, H. V.   Induction of forces in discussion groups. *Hum. Relat.,* 1951, **4**, 57–75.

Janis, I. L.   *Psychological stress.* New York: Wiley, 1958.

Jones, E. E., & Daugherty, B. N.   Political orientation and the perceptual effects of an anticipated interaction. *J. abnorm. soc. Psychol.,* 1959, **59**, 340–349.

Kelley, H. H.   The warm-cold variable in first impressions of persons. *J. Pers.,* 1950, **18**, 431–439.

Kelley, H. H., & Thibaut, J. W.   Experimental studies of group problem solving and process. In G. Lindzey (Ed.), *Handbook of social psychology.* Cambridge, Mass.: Addison-Wesley, 1954.

Lanzetta, J. T., Haefner, D., Langham, P., & Axelrod, H.   Some effects of situational threat on group behavior. *J. abnorm. soc. Psychol.,* 1954, **49**, 445–453.

Lennard, H. L., & Bernstein, A.   *The anatomy of psychotherapy.* New York: Columbia Univer. Press, 1960.

Maisonneuve, J., Palmade, G., & Fourment, C.   Selective choices and propinquity. *Sociometry,* 1952, **15**, 135–140.

McGrath, J. E.   The influence of positive interpersonal relations on adjustment and effectiveness in rifle teams. *J. abnorm. soc. Psychol.,* 1962, **65**, 365–375.

Mensh, I. N., & Wishner, J.   Asch on "forming impressions of personality": further evidence. *J. Pers.,* 1947, **16**, 188–191.

Moreno, J. L.   Psychodramatic frustration test. *Group psychother.,* 1954, **6**, 137–167.

Myers, A.   Team competition, success, and the adjustment of group members. *J. abnorm. soc. Psychol.,* 1962, **65**, 325–332.

Newcomb, T. M.   *The acquaintance process.* New York: Holt, Rinehart & Winston, 1961.

Oakes, W. F.   Reinforcement of Bales' categories in group discussion. *Psychol. Rep.*, 1962, 11, 427–435.

Pepitone, A., & Kleiner, R.   The effects of threat and frustration on group cohesiveness. *J. abnorm. soc. Psychol.*, 1957, 54, 192–199.

Raven, B. H., & Reitsema, J.   The effects of varied clarity of group goal and group path upon the individual and his relation to his group. *Hum. Relat.*, 1957, 10, 29–45.

Rosenbaum, M., & Blake, R. R.   Volunteering as a function of field structure. *J. abnorm. soc. Psychol.*, 1955, 50, 193–196.

Rosenthal, D., & Cofer, C. N.   The effect on group performance of an indifferent and neglectful attitude shown by one group member. *J. exp. Psychol.*, 1948, 38, 568–577.

Schachter, S.   Deviation, rejection and communication. *J. abnorm. soc. Psychol.*, 1951, 46, 190–207.

Schachter, S., Ellertson, N., McBride, D., & Gregory, D.   An experimental study of cohesiveness and productivity. In D. Cartwright and A. Zander (Eds.), *Group dynamics*. Evanston, Ill.: Row, Peterson & Co., 1960. Pp. 152–162.

Sherif, M., & Sherif, C. W.   *Groups in harmony and tension*. New York: Harper, 1953.

Simon, H. A., & Guetzkow, H.   Mechanisms involved in group pressures on deviate-members. *Brit. J. statist. Psychol.*, 1955, 8, 93–100.

Smith, E. E.   The effects of clear and unclear role expectations on group productivity and defensiveness. *J. abnorm. soc. Psychol.*, 1957, 55, 213–217.

Snyder, W. U.   Warmth in non-directive counseling. *J. abnorm. soc. Psychol.*, 1946, 41, 491–495.

Sommer, R.   Studies in personal space. *Sociometry*, 1959, 22, 247–260.

Sommer, R.   The distance for comfortable conversation: a further study. *Sociometry*, 1962, 25, 111–116.

Steinzor, B.   The spatial factor in face to face discussion groups. In A. P. Hare, E. F. Borgatta, & R. F. Bales (Eds.), *Small groups*. New York: Alfred A. Knopf, 1955. Pp. 348–353.

Stogdill, R. M.   *Individual behavior and group achievement*. New York: Oxford Univer. Press, 1959.

Strupp, H. H., & Luborsky, L. (Eds.).   *Research in psychotherapy*. Washington: Amer. Psychol. Assoc., 1962.

Thibaut, J. W.   An experimental study of the cohesiveness of underprivileged groups. *Hum. Relat.*, 1950, 3, 251–278.

Thibaut, J. W., & Kelley, H. H.   *The social psychology of groups*. New York: Wiley, 1959.

Thomas, E. J.   Facilitative role interdependence and group functioning. In D. Cartwright and A. Zander (Eds.), *Group dynamics*. Evanston, Ill.: Row, Peterson & Co., 1960. Pp. 449–471.

Truax, C. B.   The process of group psychotherapy. *Psychol. Monogr.,* 1961, **75,** Whole no. 511.

Ullmann, L. P., Krasner, L., & Collins, B. J.   Modification of behavior in group therapy associated with verbal conditioning. *J. abnorm. soc. Psychol.,* 1961, **62,** 128–132.

Van Bergen, A., & Koekebakker, J.   Group cohesiveness in laboratory experiments. *Acta Psychologica,* 1959, **16,** 81–98.

Verplank, W. S.   The control of the content of conversation: reinforcement of statements of opinion. *J. abnorm. soc. Psychol.,* 1955, **51,** 668–676.

Wilson, W., & Miller, N.   Shifts in evaluations of participants following intergroup competition. *J. abnorm. soc. Psychol.,* 1961, **63,** 428–431.

Wishner, J.   Reanalysis of "impressions of personality." *Psychol. Rev.,* 1960, **67,** 96–112.

Wolf, A., & Schwartz, E. K.   *Psychoanalysis in groups.* New York: Grune & Stratton, 1962.

Wright, B. A.   *Physical disability—a psychological approach.* New York: Harper, 1960.

10

FURTHER EXTRAPOLATIONS—
GROUP THERAPY

Therapy group composition, therapist orientation, and group cohesiveness have been considered at some length. In the present, concluding, discussion of issues related to group psychotherapy, we attempt briefly to examine a series of questions raised or hinted at in the preceding chapters.

MULTIVARIATE RESEARCH DESIGN

At several points in the development of our various hypotheses relevant to group psychotherapy, as well as in our discussion of research methodology, we have mentioned that research designs that focus on the simultaneous influence of two or more variables as they interact appear to correspond more realistically to the facts of group therapeutic life than do more simple, univariate designs. To reinforce this perspective on group psychotherapy research further, we wish at this point to illustrate in more detail the manner in which one such variable may function to potentiate, inhibit, or otherwise influence the effects of other variables which may be used as predictors. The variable we have chosen to examine in this manner is authoritarianism, typically operationalized in terms of the F scale (Adorno et al., 1950).

In our discussion of therapist orientation we hypothesized a variety of consequents of leader-centered and group-centered therapist styles. The hypotheses qualified the predictions to some extent by inclusion of stage-of-therapy considerations, but note how much more accurately we can predict patient reaction to these therapist styles if information regarding patient and therapist authoritarianism is available. Both Sanford (1950) and Medalia (1955) have demonstrated that high-authoritarian group members, in contrast to their more equalitarian counterparts, clearly prefer status-laden leadership, strong authority and direction "from the top" and that generally they are more accepting of leader-centered leadership and much more uncomfortable when operating in a group-centered setting. Sanford (1950) has also demonstrated that high-authoritarian group members are more openly hostile to nonassertive leaders and are more concerned with locomotion toward the group goal than with receiving interpersonal warmth from the leader. Goodrich (1954) reports that such group members tend to pull more assertive leadership behavior from the group leader, and Adorno, Frenkel-Brunswick, Levinson, and Sanford (1950) indicate that high authoritarians in groups (1) prefer a rigid set of rules, (2) tend to be uncritically submissive to powerful leaders, and (3) are quick to punish or reject deviates from the group's regulations. Block and Block (1952) and Kelman (1950) provide evidence that high authoritarians are more suggestible. Thibaut and Riecken (1955) found that such group members will accept a hostile high-status leader but reject a hostile low-status leader; and Siegel (1954) reports that authoritarianism is significantly associated with anxiety, intolerance of ambiguity, stereotyping behavior, and a need to differentiate ingroup and outgroup members.

Leader authoritarianism has also been identified as having important correlates. Haythorn, Couch, Haefner, Langham, and Carter (1956) found that high authoritarian leaders, regardless of the level of authoritarianism of group members, strive less for the approval of group members, are less equalitarian and more autocratic in their overt leadership behavior, and are less sensitive to the needs and wishes of group members than are low authoritarian group leaders. In a related study Carter et al. (1951) provide evidence that group members who emerge as group leaders are likely to be high authoritarians. This same group of researchers (Haythorn, Haefner, Langham, Couch, & Carter, 1956) have also reported that a change in the nature of group membership from high to low authoritarian persons results in less authoritarian behavior on the part of the leader, regardless of the level of his own authoritarianism. The studies of Lewin et al. (1939) noted earlier, as well as the several leadership orientation investigations which followed from them, similarly point to influences of leader authoritarian behavior on leader-follower relations. In two investigations of authoritarianism in differing communcation networks,

Shaw (1961) found that groups led by high authoritarian leaders performed best in centralized networks, whereas low authoritarian leadership resulted in maximal performance in decentralized nets. Shaw reflects our present theme when he notes that his findings "demonstrated once again that the effects of any given variable are likely to be modified by variations in other factors or conditions" (p. 144).

The implications of these several findings for the various group psychotherapy hypotheses we have presented are considerable indeed. Note that we have examined only a single "extenuating" variable. Thus it is clear that our predictions regarding the influence of therapist orientation on patient hostility and attraction to the group and to the therapist *must* reflect attention to both patient and therapist authoritarianism. Further, it appears most likely that the speed and ultimate success of techniques such as leadership defaulting may depend to a large extent on such patient and therapist characteristics. The same contingency relationship is probably also directly relevant to any research comparisons of leadership defaulting and successive structuring, and much the same point may be made for our hypothesized techniques for manipulating group cohesiveness. For example, the tendency of high authoritarian group members to reject quickly from the group those who deviate from the group rules or norms is clearly a factor of relevance to our recommendation for the use of deviant plants in therapy groups. It is also most likely that the success of verbal conditioning techniques aimed at increasing cohesiveness will reflect therapist-patient compatibility on the authoritarianism dimension, the relationship of authoritarianism and suggestibility being just one of several possible bases for this prediction. In an analogous manner, Siegel's (1954) demonstration of a strong relationship between authoritarianism and need to maintain ingroup-outgroup boundaries clearly suggests the need to take account of patient authoritarianism in attempts at resolving subgroup conflicts in therapy groups via the institution of super-ordinate goals and related procedures recommended in hypothesis 9.4.

Our focus on the many possible interactive effects of authoritarianism, and our frequent mention that many more such variables exist, may at first glance conjure up, as the reader's picture of the type of research we are proposing, an overly complicated quagmire involving a many-leveled, many-conditioned, multivariate design. Such a vision may be particularly salient for the budding researcher in the group psychotherapy area, where research at its best has characteristically been univariate in design. The gross inaccuracy of such a vision, however, is most readily made apparent by the very many and very varied successful uses of such a research approach in most fields of psychological interest and in many other broad areas of scientific investigation. The use of multivariate research techniques offers the potential for systematic clarification of a host of issues central to group psychotherapy, only a few of which are examined in the present book. The use of this approach for the increased understanding, teachability and effectiveness of group psychotherapy is, in short, long overdue.

Finally, it should be noted that although the foregoing discussion of multivariate research design was addressed to the researcher contemplating formal, as opposed to clinical, research in group psychotherapy, it is also, in a very special sense, addressed to the thoughtful, curious clinician or clinical researcher. The multivariate approach to clinical research may best be described in terms of an attitude on the part of the practicing group psychotherapist characterized by increased tolerance for ambiguity, recognition that much if not most conceptual closure on "facts" of group therapy practice is premature closure, and heightened respect for the likely interactive effects of many other variables that enter into relationships presently viewed in a univariate and, at times, unvarying manner.

OTHER BASES FOR EXTRAPOLATION

In order that the eleven hypotheses presented in the preceding three chapters might be developed in depth, as a means of most fully encouraging their eventual implementation and to provide comprehensive examples of the value of extrapolating from nonpsychotherapy research, we focused only on three broad areas of relevance to group psychotherapy. The discussion to follow, shifting away from this exploration-in-depth approach, very briefly presents a number of nonpsychotherapy research findings—particularly from group dynamics research—and the informal therapy-relevant hypotheses or exploratory questions to which they give rise. Hopefully this presentation will serve to illustrate the wide breadth of research materials potentially useful as predictive bases for group psychotherapy hypotheses.

Member-Therapists

One potentially significant phenomenon occurring in group psychotherapy, whose implications may be clarified by recourse to predictions based on group dynamics research, is therapist-like behavior on the part of patient-members of the group. Studies of leadership orientation in problem-solving groups, for example, suggest that the emergence of such "lieutenants," "doctor's helpers" or "member-therapists" is more likely to occur in a group-centered than a leader-centered group atmosphere. Crockett (1955), Heyns (1948), and Kahn and Katz (1953) provide evidence that when a designated leader fails to perform the leadership functions he is supposed to in the eyes of the group members, some of the members themselves step in and perform them in his stead. Indeed, this is the very basis of the "leadership by default" technique. Conversely, Haythorn (1952) reports that when one member of a group assumes considerable initiative for its leadership, other members demonstrate less leadership behavior than they have previously done in less actively led groups. Tannenbaum and Allport (1956) have indicated similar findings. Gorlow, Hoch, and Telschow (1952) investigated member-therapist behavior more directly, in a series of studies examining nondirective group psychotherapy. Under their experimental conditions, member-therapist behavior was both predictable from pretherapy personality measures and predictive of subsequent ratings of patient improvement. Group members who were initially low on anxiety and hostility measures utilized more positive and less negative member-therapist behavior than did more anxious or hostile group members. The former were also rated as profiting more from their therapeutic participation. Longitudinally, more positive and less negative member-therapist behavior emerged as the course of psychotherapy progressed. The quality (positive or negative) of such member-therapist behavior toward other patients was also clearly related to member-to-member attraction. The more favorable the feelings of a given patient toward another, the more likely was the member-therapist behavior directed toward this other patient to be accepting, supportive and permissive, and the less likely was it to be evaluative or critical. What do these group dynamic and group therapy findings suggest? As a whole, they strongly point to the likelihood that both the emergence and the quality and quantity of member-therapist behavior in group psychotherapy are influenced by and in turn may influence the group's composition and cohesiveness, and the therapist's orientation. Thus we may view therapist-like behavior on the part of group therapy patients as potentially related in important ways to the three broad areas of group psychotherapy our earlier sections have singled out as being central research domains for the advance of group psychotherapy.

Therapist Consistency

In Chapter 7 as we developed the concept of functional composition of therapy groups we examined a series of studies in which non-therapeutic groups were constituted and reconstituted from a discrete pool of individuals. These studies pointed to a moderately high degree of individual consistency across groups in terms of several types of group-relevant behavior, including leadership behavior. We suggest that analogous research may profitably be undertaken, this time directed at examining the consistency of the therapist's behavior across groups. In addition to the investigations of emergent leadership noted above, studies by Borgatta, Couch, and Bales (1955), aimed at investigating the "great man" theory of leadership, also clearly demonstrate a moderate, but reliable consistency in an individual's leadership behavior across groups. The potential of research of this general class is further underscored by findings from studies of individual psychotherapy. Fiedler (1950), for example, found that psychotherapists tend to have patients whose relationship scores remain relatively similar from patient to patient for a given therapist. Similarly, Chance (1959) reports a marked degree of consistency in therapists' anticipations of patient behavior. She notes that these expectations regarding in-therapy patient behavior "appear to be personal and characteristic for that clinician." It may be that in addition to the perhaps obvious need for eventual "therapist consistency" research aimed at therapeutic outcome across a given therapist's groups such research should also aim at the intermediate concerns of degree of consistency across groups in terms of leadership style, cohesiveness developed, types of patients emerging as member-therapists, dropout rates, duration of therapy course, role expectations, and so forth.

Observational Span

One further research area of direct relevance to therapist operations may be noted. Involved here is the question of group size as it affects the therapist's or observer's ability to note or to record significant events and interactions as they occur within his group. Hare (1962) reviews a series of studies in which subjects were required to estimate the number of dots in a visual field under short exposure time conditions. Up to six or seven dots, there were few errors and high subject confidence. Beyond this number, errors increased sharply, suggesting that an estimation procedure such as grouping was occurring. Hare comments, "Observers rating group members face a problem not unlike that of the dot estimators in the sense that they can pay attention to only a limited number of persons at a given time" (p. 228). It is interesting to note in this regard that Bass and Norton (1951) found that observers reach maximum agreement on assessments of leadership behavior when the groups observed consisted of six members, in contrast to groups with sizes of two, four, eight, or twelve members. As Hare suggests, the ability of the observing individual to perceive, keep track of, and judge each member separately in a group interaction situation may reach a maximum at about six or seven persons. If this is the case, we may anticipate that members of groups larger than that size frequently will tend to perceive and react to other members in terms of subgroups or classes, rather than as individuals.

In addition to the research possibilities involving this issue of observational span and both subgroup perception and group size, we wish to add that the therapist's observational capacity is equally relevant to research oriented toward the use of cotherapists and silent, nonparticipating observers. Further, observational capacity of the therapist, cotherapist, observer, or group member, as it is influenced by leadership orientation, functional composition of the group, and the more concrete matter of recording procedures, appear to be additional matters of research interest.

Alone versus Together

A great many studies have compared productivity of individuals working alone and working in groups. Kelley and Thibaut (1954), summarizing a number of such investigations, report that the group situation is associated with a greater individual productivity if the task calls for primarily physical output, less productivity on essentially intellectual tasks. The group setting, on a more qualitative basis, also tends to result in more moderate individual positions on judgmental tasks.

This assumption of less extreme positions when group rather than individual tasks are involved has been explained by Bos (1937) in terms of processes of leveling and sharpening. Other perception and group researchers have discussed this phenomenon in terms of restraints to communication effects of combining and weighting individual group member positions, internalization of group norms, and a process of "conversationalizing" that Allport (1955) explains as, "when working with others we respond in a measure as though we were reacting to them" (p. 274). On an individual versus group learning task, Perlmutter and Montmollin (1952) found sequence effects to be an important consideration. All subjects worked under both individual and group conditions. Results indicated that subjects working first in the group context had significantly higher total scores and a better rate of recall than did the individuals who worked separately first on the particular experimental task. Allport (1955) reports that although the speed of free association (in the classical, experimental—not psychoanalytic sense) is clearly enhanced by the presence of a coworking group, the nature of the task is a very strong determinant of which working context will prove superior. Such task or goal considerations, as well as issues of individual motivation, rivalry, and related considerations, make only the most qualified generalizations appropriate for characterizing the results of studies in this area.

The broad research question growing from these studies asks whether such "alone versus together" research is relevant to the continuing issue of individual versus group psychotherapy. Does the gross physical similarity of these two situations enhance their relatedness, or does the very diverse nature of the goals involved make the former irrelevant as a source of extrapolated hypotheses for the latter context? Clearly, these are questions answerable only by further investigation.

Open versus Closed Groups

A long-standing and yet-to-be-resolved issue relevant to the conduct of therapy groups is whether they should best be "open" or "closed." More precisely, under what conditions should terminating group members be replaced with new ones and under what conditions should the original membership be left intact, with no replacements? Partly because of the realities of dropout rates, most contemporary therapists lean toward the open group structure. Earlier we suggested that the level of cohesiveness in the therapy group influences its acceptance of and reaction to newcomers. Level of cohesiveness and the increasing similarity of membership we predicted would follow from continued use of the voting-in procedure are clearly pertinent to the issue of openness to new membership. The relevant group dynamics research, though perhaps pointing to concrete research directions, does not directly bring us much closer to an answer. Travers (1941), Wood (1948), Gordon (1951), and others have shown an increasing tendency for members to underestimate the discrepancy between their own position and the group consensus the longer a group is established. In reviewing these investigations, Kelley and Thibaut (1954) note, "These groups would presumably be characterized both by more

efficient communications and by closer adherence to group standards"
(p. 768). Also of possible relevance to the openness of therapy groups
to new members is research on group equilibrium conducted by Chapple (1942). He comments:

> The degree of stability has an important bearing on the ability of the
> individual or group to withstand disturbances of equilibrium; as a rule, the
> greater the stability, the stronger, and, at the same time, less elastic is the
> state of equilibrium. For example, a group with a high interaction rate and
> a long history of continued stability will maintain its equilibrium under the
> impact of powerful external forces, but an internal change, such as the loss
> of a member, will produce serious effects, and its adjustment to a new equi-
> librium after the loss will be a slow and difficult process, if such an adjustment
> can be made at all (pp. 56–57).

Chapple here points to a major negative consequence which may
follow from the unavoidable disruption of long-standing closed groups.
Studies by Rasmussen and Zander (1954) and Stotland et al. (1957)
demonstrate the extent to which a group standard may become a
personal level of aspiration, suggesting that under certain circumstances a patient joining a long-established therapy group may be aided
in largely circumventing or telescoping the negative consequents often
associated with early stages of group therapy via his identification
with or introjection of these existing group standards.

These investigations serve primarily to illustrate the more complex issues underlying the superficially simple open-group versus
closed-group dichotomy. Surely generalizations on the appropriateness
of one approach or the other are premature. More fitting, it seems,
are studies which view this problem from a more circumspect, detailed,
and manipulative perspective.

Postsessions

One final contemporary group therapy procedure may be noted.
Both Bach (1954) and Wolf and Schwartz (1962) are among the apparently increasing number of therapist making use of postsessions,
alternate sessions or, more generally, patient sessions regularly convened in the absence of the group psychotherapist. Although, like
much of the "evidence" supporting current group therapy practices,
the postsession technique appears to be associated with face validity
on a variety of clinical impressionistic bases, more rigorous examination of its usefulness is clearly in order. Just as with individual versus
group or closed versus open groups, research examining the value of
postsessions must aim at the specific conditions under which it is of

value. The Stotland et al. (1957) finding, in an industrial setting, that subordinates allowed to assemble for meetings in the absence of their supervisor reacted less favorably to him and rated him as less coopera- tive and reasonable than did employees for whom this was not per- mitted, serves to underscore the necessity for research examination of this supposed therapeutic innovation.

BALES INTERACTION PROCESS ANALYSIS

Before turning to the Bales system a general word or two seems in order regarding the applicability to group therapy of observational and measurement techniques developed in group dynamics and related contexts. Observational rating systems need detain us only very briefly. We have sketched a half dozen or so of the apparently more promising ones—in the sense of translatability to the therapy setting— in our earlier discussion of functional composition of therapy groups. We need add only the perhaps obvious comment that their usefulness as a means of assisting in the clarification of additional important group therapy dimensions may be considerable. To be sure, they are not equally comprehensive, reliable, or "extrapolatable," nor do we suspect that any may be used as means of rating and categorizing *therapy* group interactions without first undergoing carefully con- ceived modification. Nevertheless, their potential usefulness appears to be both real and substantial. Our oft-repeated appeal to further research appears equally appropriate in the present instance.

The same general points regarding apparent potential usefulness and the need for recourse to further research for more final determina- tion of usefulness may be made regarding measurement techniques and devices not heretofore used, or used quite rarely, in studies of group psychotherapy. Our recommendation list includes such group dynamics and related research devices as (1) sociometric and near- sociometric techniques (Jennings, 1943; Moreno and Jennings, 1944; Tagiuri, 1952), (2) the more widely used attraction-to-group question- naires (Lorr & McNair, in process; Schachter et al., 1960), (3) the revealed differences technique developed by Strodtbeck (1955), and (4) the interpersonal behavioral inventories developed primarily for individual psychotherapy research by Lorr & McNair (1963) and by Leary (1957).

Emphasizing once again that both the foregoing and what follows are offered not only as a means of encouraging use of specific proce- dures or measures, but also, and perhaps more importantly, to encourage a general philosophy or orientation toward the most appropriate sources for group psychotherapy research hypotheses, we may now turn to fuller examination of Bales' Interaction Process Analysis (IPA) (Bales, 1950).

The nature of the twelve IPA categories was generally introduced in our earlier look at group composition. More specifically, we now note that the system consists of the following categories:

1. *Shows solidarity,* raises status of others, gives help, reward.
2. *Shows tension release,* jokes, laughs, shows satisfaction.
3. *Shows agreement,* passive acceptance, understands, concurs, complies.
4. *Gives suggestion,* direction, implies autonomy for others.
5. *Gives opinion,* evaluation, analysis, expresses feeling, wish.
6. *Gives orientation,* information, repeats, clarifies, confirms.
7. *Asks for orientation,* information, repetition, confirmation.
8. *Asks for opinion,* evaluation, analysis, expression of feeling.
9. *Asks for suggestion,* direction, possible ways of action.
10. *Shows disagreement,* passive rejection, formality, withholds help.
11. *Shows tension,* asks for help, withdraws out of field.
12. *Shows antagonism,* deflates status of others, defends or asserts self.

The development of the Bales IPA category system clearly represents a careful and painstaking effort (Bales, 1950), associated reliabilities are impressive (Bales, 1950), and the number and nature of associated research findings involving use of this system are considerable. Two such findings, in particular, are worthy of note.

Phases and Equilibrium in Nontherapy Groups

Bales and Strodtbeck (1951) were interested in identifying the nature of the phases or stages through which problem-solving groups pass in their efforts at goal attainment. Their data consisted of complete protocols of 22 group problem-solving sessions. The investigators hypothesized that in sessions "in which groups work toward the goal of a group decision on a full-fledged problem" group members move in their interactions from initial emphasis on interactions characterized by *orientation* (IPA categories 6 and 7) to interactions of *evaluation* (IPA categories 5 and 8) and subsequently to interactions emphasizing *control* (IPA categories 4 and 9). It was also hypothesized that concurrent with these phase transitions the relative frequency of both positive (IPA categories 1, 2 and 3) and negative (IPA categories 10, 11 and 12) interactions would increase. The sequential interaction for each session was divided into thirds, so that each third contained an equal proportion of the total number of acts transpiring in the given session. The frequency of each IPA category's occurrence was then tallied for each one-third session. Clear confirmation of the phase hypothesis emerged: the orientation-evaluation-control phase movement and the increase in both positive and negative interactions across phases were consistently in evidence.

In addition to identification of phases and phase sequence in the operation of problem-solving groups, Bales (1955) has focused in some detail on what he terms the "equilibrium problem." Generally involved here is an attempt to identify regularities in the initiation-reaction sequences characterizing problem-solving group interactions. Sixteen meetings of five-member groups served as the source data for this study. The twelve IPA categories were grouped into four classes: questions (asks orientation, asks opinion, asks suggestion), attempted answers (gives orientation, gives opinion, gives suggestion), positive reactions (shows solidarity, shows tension release, shows agreement), and negative reactions (shows antagonism, shows tension, shows disagreement). Codification of the group protocols in this manner revealed a generally consistent pattern across group sessions:

. . . about one-half of all acts were Attempted Answers which moved the group towards its external goal—the solution of the problem. Such task-oriented attempts, in turn, tended to provoke Reactions—positive, negative or questions. About one-half of the observed Reactions were positive. The remaining one-half were distributed in a binary fashion: Half of them were negative, and the other half were equally divided between Questions and further Attempted Answers. Thus, an average profile has the following percentage distribution of acts:

Type of Act	Frequency (percent)
Attempted Answers (initial acts)	50
Positive reactions	25
Negative reactions	12
Questions	6
Attempted answers (reactions)	7
	————
	100

Phases and Equilibrium in Therapy Groups

Following the successful confirmation of the phase movement and equilibrium hypotheses, a large number of related findings concerning problem-solving group interaction have been forthcoming. Concurrent with this has been a spread in the use of the IPA system to studies directly or indirectly focused on group psychotherapy or closely related clinical concerns. Ruesch and Prestwood (1950) provided an early consideration of interaction process features possibly operating in the psychotherapeutic context; Roberts and Strodtbeck (1953) contrasted the interactions of paranoid schizophrenic and depressed patients in terms of IPA categories; Blake (1953) provided early emphasis on the potential value of the system for clarification of group psychotherapy in particular; Strupp (1955) demonstrated the value of this approach in an individual psychotherapy investigation exploring differences in therapist behavior as a function of their experience level, theoretical background, and professional affiliation; and a study by Oakes (1962), noted in an earlier discussion of verbal reinforcement in group psychotherapy, provides additional demonstration of the potential applicability of IPA to the group therapy context. Even more to the point, four investigations exist which aimed explicitly at determining the value of the Bales category system for capturing and clarifying the interaction of psychotherapy groups. Those by Munzer and Greenwald (1957) and Noble, Ohlsen, and Proff (1961) will not be considered in detail here. They are generally supportive of this approach, but do not touch issues central to our present discussion as do the other two studies. These, by Talland (1955) and Psathas (1960), examine in considerable detail many issues of direct relevance to the broad question of the appropriateness of extrapolating from group dynamics research as a means of framing hypotheses about group psychotherapy. As such, these two investigations are clearly among the most consequential of the many studies we have examined throughout this chapter.

Talland addressed himself to this problem at the outset, when he introduced his study:

Psychotherapy groups . . . differ from experimental problem-solving groups in several clearly marked respects. They meet in order to discover problems rather than to solve one nearly formulated for their attention; they neither have to reach a solution nor must they finally close a case unresolved at the end of a meeting. Insofar as the psychotherapeutic technique stresses spontaneity, the discussion is allowed a free course, whereas in the laboratory its trend is implicitly determined by the task even in the absence of directive chairmanship. Finally, discussing a hypothetical or didactic case and a transient acquaintance do not lead to deep emotional involvements that occur when patients grapple with their own and each other's personal problems, baring their inmost thoughts and experiences week after week in intimate fellowship. Consequently the process of interaction would be expected to differ in the two situations, and more particularly in such dynamic aspects of the model as the phase sequence of acts indicated by and the equilibrium properties of the interaction system inferred from observations made in laboratory debates (pp. 457–458).

Talland's experimental efforts, following this line of reasoning, were aimed at discerning whether these two phenomena—phase movement and equilibrium tendencies—did in fact characterize the interaction of psychotherapy groups. His experimental subjects were psychoneurotic outpatients in four psychotherapy groups of six to eight members each. The interactions within the groups during a total of 18 ninety-minute sessions taken from the first eight weeks of therapy were observed and categorized according to the Bales IPA. Therapist responses were not included, nor were nonverbal acts. In addition, because of the infrequency of occurrence (when nonverbal acts are excluded), Bales' categories 2 and 11 were omitted from the data analysis. Talland's results failed to confirm the occurrence of either phase movement or equilibrium tendencies in the interactions of his therapy groups. More specifically, individual group therapy sessions showed no consistent movement from orientation through evaluation to control and the problem-solving group equilibrium tendencies noted earlier also failed to appear with any degree of consistency. Thus on at least two apparently central group dynamic interactional dimensions Talland's results demonstrate a basic dissimilarity between problem-solving and psychotherapy groups. At first glance these findings represent initial evidence suggesting that in certain important respects group dynamics research material may be an inappropriate basis for forming predictions about the interactions within therapy groups. However, going beyond this first glance, Psathas (1960) reports an investigation which most clearly reaffirms the basic potential of the approach to group psychotherapy hypothesis development we have been encouraging throughout.

Psathas observes, and attempts to correct in his own study, a series of basic deficiencies in Talland's earlier, groundbreaking investigation. Specifically, in an effort to reflect more accurately the nature of group psychotherapy interaction, Psathas included acts initiated by the therapist and nonverbal behavior in his recording and included the IPA categories omitted by Talland, that is, showing tension and showing tension release. As will be seen in his findings, these experimental design improvements instituted by Psathas contribute to a considerably different experimental outcome than that characterizing Talland's study. Psathas' subjects were eight patients in two therapy groups of four members each which met twice-weekly for 90-minute sessions over a period of one year. The psychotherapist who led both groups was apparently somewhat more active (although still generally group-centered) than those in Talland's study. Nine sessions of each group were observed, an equal number of sessions chosen from early, middle, and late periods in therapy. This is in contrast to Talland's use of the first eight weeks of therapy, a contrast of direct relevance to efforts aimed at discerning phase movement. Agreeing with Talland that there was probably little likelihood of orientation to control closure within *single* therapy sessions, Psathas hypothesized the existence of phase movement more longitudinally, across the full course of therapy sessions. Comparison of early, middle, and late sessions clearly supported the prediction of movement from orientation to evaluation and ending in control type therapy group interactions. His findings regarding equilibrium tendencies are also congruent with those reported by Bales (1955), noted earlier, as consistently operating in problem-solving groups. Psathas notes that it is probably his inclusion of acts initiated by the psychotherapist that causes the marked contrast of his and Talland's equilibrium findings. His findings indicate major problem-solving group-therapy group similarity not only on phase movement and equilibrium dimensions but on other interactional dimensions as well. For example, consistent with frequently reported group dynamics research findings, Psathas' results indicate that ranking of group members in terms of the number of acts each originates is identical in order to ranking based on number of acts received. Similarly, ranking of members by acts initiated also corresponds to ranking by number of acts directed toward the group as a whole. Thus a series of findings leads the investigator to conclude, "These therapy groups show patterns of interaction which are similar to laboratory problem-solving groups in terms of the phase sequence of category acts, equilibrium tendencies and communication channels" (p. 190).

Taken together, the Talland and Psathas studies are a miniature model of the course of group research we strongly encourage. Talland made the initial extrapolatory effort in this specific area. His results were generally nonsupportive of an extrapolatory research orientation, yet at the same time provided the building blocks for others to stand on if they wished to look further into this issue. Psathas responded to the challenge inherent in Talland's findings, made several crucial improvements in experimental design, and came up with evidence clearly supportive of an extrapolatory approach, at least as far as interaction process analysis is concerned. Obviously these two investigations do not provide the last word on the appropriateness of IPA for study of therapy group interactions, let alone the more general issue of the soundness of extrapolating from the broader array of group dynamics research. That they combine to provide an important start in this direction cannot be denied. That further studies following their general direction are called for should be equally apparent.

REFERENCES

Adorno, T. W., Frenkel-Brunswick, E., Levinson, D., & Sanford, R. N. *The authoritarian personality*. New York: Harper, 1950.

Allport, F. H. The influence of the group upon association and thought. In A. P. Hare, E. F. Borgatta, & R. F. Bales (Eds.), *Small groups*. New York: Alfred A. Knopf, 1955. Pp. 31–34.

Bach, G. R. *Intensive group psychotherapy*. New York: Ronald Press, 1954.

Back, K. W. Influence through social communication. *J. abnorm. soc. Psychol.*, 1951, 46, 9–23.

Bales, R. F. *Interaction process analysis: a method for the study of small groups*. Cambridge, Mass.: Addison-Wesley, 1950.

Bales, R. F. The equilibrium problem in small groups. In A. P. Hare, E. F. Borgatta, & R. F. Bales (Eds.), *Small groups*. New York: Alfred A. Knopf, 1955. Pp. 424–456.

Bales, R. F., & Strodtbeck, P. L. Phases in group problem solving. *J. abnorm. soc. Psychol.*, 1951, 46, 485–495.

Bass, B. M., & Norton, F. M. Group size and leaderless discussion. *J. appl. Psychol.*, 1951, 35, 397–401.

Blake, R. R. The interaction-feeling hypothesis applied to psychotherapy groups. *Sociometry*, 1953, 16, 253–265.

Block, J., & Block, J. An interpersonal experiment on reactions to authority. *Hum. Relat.*, 1952, 5, 91–98.

Borgatta, E. F., Couch, A. S., & Bales, R. F. Some findings relevant to the great man theory of leadership. In A. P. Hare, E. F. Borgatta, & R. F. Bales (Eds.), *Small groups*. New York: Alfred A. Knopf, 1955. Pp. 568–574.

Bos, M. C. Experimental study of productive collaboration. *Acta Psychologica*, 1937, 3, 315–426.

Carter, L. F., Haythorn, W., Shriver, E., & Lanzetta, J. The behavior of leaders and other group members. *J. abnorm. soc. Psychol.*, 1951, 46, 589–595.

Chance, E. *Families in treatment*. New York: Basic Books, 1959.

Chapple, E. D.   The measurement of interpersonal behavior. *Trans. N. Y. Acad. Sci.*, 1942, 4, 222–233.

Crockett, W.   Emergent leadership in small decision-making groups. *J. abnorm. soc. Psychol.*, 1955, 51, 378–383.

Festinger, L., & Thibaut, J.   Interpersonal communication in small groups. In G. E. Swanson, T. M. Newcomb, & E. L. Hartley. *Readings in social psychology.* New York: Holt, 1952. Pp. 125–134.

Fiedler, F. E.   The concept of an ideal therapeutic relationship. *J. consult. Psychol.*, 1950, 14, 39–45.

Freedman, M. B., Leary, T. F., Ossorio, A. G., & Coffey, H. S.   The interpersonal dimension of personality. *J. Pers.*, 1951, 20, 143–161.

Goodrich, D. C.   Aggression in the projective tests and group behavior of authoritarian and equalitarian subjects. *American Psychologist,* 1954, 9, 380. (Abstract)

Gordon, T.   Group-centered leadership and administration. In C. R. Rogers, *Client-centered therapy.* Boston, Mass.: Houghton Mifflin, 1951. Pp. 320–383.

Gorlow, L., Hoch, E. L., & Telschow, E. F.   *Non-directive group psychotherapy.* New York: Teacher's College Studies in Education, Columbia University, 1952.

Hare, A. P.   *Handbook of small group research.* New York: The Free Press of Glencoe, 1962.

Haythorn, W.   The influence of individual group members in the behavior of co-workers and on the characteristics of groups. Uupublished doctoral dissertation, University of Rochester, 1952.

Haythorn, W., Couch, A., Haefner, D., Langham, P., & Carter, L. F.   The behavior of authoritarian and equalitarian personality groups. *Hum. Relat.,* 1956, 9, 57–75.

Haythorn, W., Haefner, D., Langham, P., Couch, A., & Carter, L.   The effects of varying combinations of authoritarian and equalitarian leaders and followers. *J. abnorm. soc. Psychol.,* 1956, 53, 210–219.

Heyns, R.   Effects of variation in leadership on participant behavior in discussion groups. Unpublished doctoral dissertation, University of Michigan, 1948.

Kahn, R. L., & Katz, D.   Leadership practices in relation to productivity and morale. In D. Cartwright & A. Zander (Eds.), *Group dynamics.* Evanston, Ill.: Row, Peterson & Co., 1953. Pp. 554–570.

Kelman, H. C.   Effects of success and failure on "suggestibility" in the autokinetic situation. *J. abnorm. soc. Psychol.*, 1950, 45, 267–285.

Kelley, H. H., & Thibaut, J. W.   Experimental studies of group problem solving and process. In G. Lindzey (Ed.), *Handbook of social psychology.* Cambridge, Mass.: Addison-Wesley, 1954.

Jennings, H. H.   *Leadership and isolation.* New York: Longmans, Green, 1943.

Leary, T. *Interpersonal diagnosis of personality.* New York: Ronald Press, 1957.

Lewin, K., Lippitt, R., & White, R. Patterns of aggressive behavior in experimentally created "social climates." *J. soc. Psychol.,* 1939, **10,** 271–299.

Lorr, M., & McNair, D. M. An interpersonal behavior circle. *J. abnorm. soc. Psychol.,* 1963, **67,** 68–75.

Lorr, M., & McNair, D. M. An exploratory study of the structure and function of therapy groups. In process.

Medalia, N. Z. Authoritarianism, leader acceptance, and group cohesion. *J. abnorm. soc. Psychol.,* 1955, **51,** 207–213.

Moreno, J. L., & Jennings, H. H. Sociometric methods of grouping and regrouping: with reference to authoritative and democratic methods of grouping. *Sociometry,* 1944, **7,** 397–414.

Munzer, J., & Greenwald, H. Interaction process analysis of a therapy group. *Int. J. grp. Psychother.,* 1957, **7,** 175–190.

Noble, F., Ohlsen, M., & Proff, F. A method for the quantification of psychotherapeutic interaction in counseling groups. *J. counsel. Psychol.,* 1961, **8,** 54–61.

Oakes, W. F. Reinforcement of Bales' categories in group discussion. *Psychol. Rep.,* 1962, **11,** 427–435.

Perlmutter, H. V., & Montmollin, G. Group learning of nonsense syllables. *J. abnorm. soc. Psychol.,* 1952, **47,** 762–769.

Psathas, G. Phase movement and equilibrium tendencies in interaction process in psychotherapy groups. *Sociometry,* 1960, **23,** 177–194.

Rasmussen, G., & Zander, A. Group membership and self-evaluation. *Hum. Relat.,* 1954, **7,** 239–251.

Roberts, B. H., & Strodtbeck, F. L. Interaction process differences between groups of paranoid schizophrenic and depressed patients. *Int. J. grp. Psychother.,* 1953, **3,** 29–41.

Ruesch, J., & Prestwood, A. R. Interaction processes and personal codification. *J. Pers.,* 1950, **18,** 391–430.

Sanford, F. H. *Authoritarianism and leadership.* Philadelphia: Inst. for Research in Human Relations, 1950.

Schachter, S., Ellertson, N., McBride, D., & Gregory, D. An experimental study of cohesiveness and productivity. In D. Cartwright & A. Zander (Eds.), *Group dynamics.* Evanston, Ill.: Row, Peterson & Co., 1960, 152–162.

Shaw, M. E. Group dynamics. In P. R. Farnsworth, C. McNemar, & Q. McNemar (Eds.), *Annual review of psychology.* Palo Alto, Calif.: Annual Reviews, Inc., 1961. Pp. 129–156.

Siegel, S. Certain determinants and correlates of authoritarianism. *Genet. psychol. Monogr.,* 1954, **49,** 187–229.

Stotland, E., Thorley, S., Thomas, E., Cohen, A., & Zander, A. The effects of group expectations and self-esteem upon self-evaluation. *J. abnorm. soc. Psychol.,* 1957, **54,** 55–63.

Strodtbeck, F. L.   Husband-wife interaction over revealed differences. In A. P. Hare, E. F. Borgatta, & R. F. Bales (Eds.), *Small groups.* New York: Alfred A. Knopf, 1955, 464–472.

Strupp, H. H.   An objective comparison of Rogerian and psychoanalytic techniques. *J. consult. Psychol.*, 1955, **19**, 1–7.

Tagiuri, R.   Relational analysis: An extension of sociometric method with emphasis upon social perception. *Sociometry*, 1952, **15**, 91–104.

Talland, C. A.   Task and interaction process: Some characteristics of therapeutic group discussion. In A. P. Hare, E. F. Borgatta, & R. F. Bales (Eds.), *Small groups.* New York: Alfred A. Knopf, 1955. Pp. 457–463.

Tannenbaum, A., & Allport, F. H.   Personality structure and group structure. *J. abnorm. soc. Psychol.*, 1956, **53**, 272–280.

Travers, R. M. W.   A study in judging the opinions of groups. *Arch. Psychol.*, 1941, No. 266.

Thibaut, J. W., & Riecken, H. W.   Authoritarianism, status, and the communication of aggression. *Hum. Relat.*, 1955, **8**, 95–120.

Wolf, A., & Schwartz, E. K.   *Psychoanalysis in groups.* New York: Grune & Stratton, 1962.

Wood, H. G.   An analysis of social sensitivity. Unpublished doctoral dissertation, Yale University, 1948.

APPENDIX

RESEARCH HYPOTHESES

In order to provide the reader with a brief review of this book's orientation, as well as a convenient page reference for its major proposals, the formal research hypotheses we have developed are presented with the inclusive pages on which each appears.

AUTHOR INDEX

SUBJECT INDEX